# Child and Adolescent Mental Health
## Theory and Practice

**Second Edition**

Margaret Thompson, Christine Hooper,
Cathy Laver-Bradbury, Christopher Gale

**CRC Press**
Taylor & Francis Group
Boca Raton  London  New York

CRC Press is an imprint of the
Taylor & Francis Group, an **informa** business

First published in Great Britain in 2005 by Hodder Arnold
This second edition published in 2012 by
Hodder Arnold, an imprint of Hodder Education, Hodder and Stoughton Ltd, a division of Hachette UK

338 Euston Road, London NW1 3BH

**http://www.hodderarnold.com**

Hachette UK's policy is to use papers that are natural, renewable and recyclable products and made from wood grown in sustainable forests. The logging and manufacturing processes are expected to conform to the environmental regulations of the country of origin.

Whilst the advice and information in this book are believed to be true and accurate at the date of going to press, neither the author[s] nor the publisher can accept any legal responsibility or liability for any errors or omissions that may be made. In particular (but without limiting the generality of the preceding disclaimer) every effort has been made to check drug dosages; however it is still possible that errors have been missed. Furthermore, dosage schedules are constantly being revised and new side-effects recognized. For these reasons the reader is strongly urged to consult the drug companies' printed instructions before administering any of the drugs recommended in this book.

*British Library Cataloguing in Publication Data*
A catalogue record for this book is available from the British Library

*Library of Congress Cataloging-in-Publication Data*
A catalog record for this book is available from the Library of Congress

ISBN-13    978 1 444 145 991

1 2 3 4 5 6 7 8 9 10

Commissioning Editor:      Caroline Makepeace
Project Editors:           Joanna Silman and Mischa Barrett
Production Controller:     Joanna Walker
Cover Designer:            Peter Banks

Cover image © Kristian Sekulic/istockphoto.com

Typeset in 9.5 on 12pt Rotis Semi Sans by Phoenix Photosetting, Chatham, Kent ME4 4TZ
Printed and bound in the UK by MPG Books, Bodmin, Cornwall

What do you think about this book? Or any other Hodder Arnold title?
Please visit our website: www.hodderarnold.com

# Contents

## Appendices

# Contributors

**Kirsteen Anderssen**, Family Nurse Partnership, Southampton, UK

**Shilpa Balakrishna**, Specialist Trainee, Child and Adolescent Psychiatry, Portsmouth, Southampton and Wessex Rotation, UK

**Joanna Barker**, Specialist Registrar, New Forest Child and Adolescent Mental Health Service, Ashurst Hospital, Southampton, UK

**Melissa Bracewell**, Community Paediatrician, Ashurst Education Centre, Southampton, UK

**Lee Bradley**, Modern Matron, Bluebird House, Calmore, Southampton, UK

**Anne Brewster**, Family Therapist, Dorchester CAMHS, The Children's Centre, Dorchester, UK

**Josie Brown**, Consultant Child and Adolescent Psychiatrist, Paediatric Department, Southampton General Hospital, Southampton, UK

**Claire Campbell**, Clinical Ward Manager, Bluebird House, Calmore, Southampton, UK

**Pamela Campbell**, Consultant Nurse, Homelessness and Health Inequalities, Homeless Healthcare Team, Southampton, UK

**Kim Cartwright**, PhD student Psychologist, Developmental Brain Behaviour Laboratory School of Psychology, University of Southampton, Southampton, UK

**Angela Caulfield**, Specialist Sleep Disorder nurse, Southampton Children's Sleep Disorder Service, Ashurst Education Centre, Southampton, UK

**Wai Chen**, Senior Lecturer/Consultant Child and Adolescent Psychiatrist, Child and Adolescent Psychiatry, Ashurst Hospital, Southampton, UK

**Georgia Chronaki**, Post-doctoral research fellow Psychology, Division of Clinical Neuroscience, Developmental Brain Behaviour Laboratory, School of Psychology, University of Southampton, Southampton, UK

**Christine Cornforth**, Senior research fellow Psychology, Developmental Brain Behaviour Laboratory, School of Psychology, University of Southampton, Southampton, UK

**Anthony Crabb**, Consultant Child and Adolescent Psychiatrist, University Hospital Southampton NHS Foundation Trust and Care Group – Child Health, Division of Women and Children, Paediatric Medicine MP44, Southampton General Hospital, Southampton, UK

**David Daley**, Professor of Psychological Intervention and Behaviour Change, Division of Psychiatry School of Community Health Science, University of Nottingham, Nottingham, UK

**Karen Davies**, Senior Practitioner – Governance and Quality Lead, Brookvale Youth Mental Health Service, Portswood, Southampton, UK

**Suyog Dhakras**, Consultant Child and Adolescent Psychiatrist, Solent Healthcare NHS Trust, Southampton, UK

**Susie Dutton**, Social Worker and Play Therapist, The Orchard Centre, Specialist Mental Health Team, Western Community Health Site, Southampton, UK

**Anan El Masry**, Specialist Trainee, Child and Adolscent Psychiatry, Portsmouth, Southampton and Wessex Rotation, UK

**Graeme Fairchild**, Lecturer in Clinical Psychology, School of Psychology, University of Southampton, Southampton, UK

**Matthew Fealey**, Specialist Trainee, Child and Adolescent Psychiatry, Portsmouth, Southampton and Wessex Rotation, UK

**Janet Féat**, Retired Service Manager, Hampshire County Council Children's Services Department, now working independently

**Val Forster**, Child Psychotherapist, Ashurst Hospital, Ashurst, Southampton, UK

**Christopher Gale**, Lecturer in Child and Adolescent Mental Health, Faculty of Health Sciences, University of Southampton, Southampton, UK

**Sarah Gale**, Outreach and Resettlement Support Worker, Street Homelessness Prevention Team, Southampton City Council, Southampton, UK

**Stuart Gemmell**, Strategic Lead, Solent West, Child and Adolescent Mental Health Services, Southampton, UK

**Ettore Guaia**, Consultant Child and Adolescent Psychiatrist, Learning Difficulties, The Orchard Centre, Specialist Mental Health Team, Western Community Health Site, Southampton, UK

**Chris Hardie**, Associate Specialist Community Paediatrician, Ashurst Child and Family Centre, Lyndhurst Road, Ashurst, Southampton SO4 7AR

**Erika Harris**, Consultant Child and Adolescent Psychiatrist, CAMHS Sussex Partnership, NHS Foundation Trust, Chichester, UK

**Helen Harris**, Senior Nurse Prescriber ADHD, The Orchard Centre, Specialist Mental Health Team, Western Community Hospital Site, Southampton, UK

**Clair Henry**, Specialist Trainee in Child and Adolescent Psychiatry, Wessex Rotation, UK

**Diane Henty**, Lead, Family Nurse Partnership, Southampton, UK

**Catherine M Hill**, Senior Lecturer in Child Health, Division of Clinical Experimental Sciences, University of Southampton

**Margaret Hobbs**, Senior Nurse Therapist, Ashurst Child and Family Centre, Ashurst, Southampton, UK

**Sarah Holden**, Therapeutic Social Worker and Play Therapist, Behaviour Resource Service, Southampton, UK

**Simone Holley**, Psychologist, Southampton General Hospital, Southampton, UK

**Chantal Homan**, Clinical Nurse Specialist (Learning Disability Mental Health), The Orchard Centre, Specialist Mental Health Team, Western Community Hospital Site, William MacLeod Way , Trebourba Way, Southampton SO16 4XE

**Christine M Hooper**, Retired Family and Marital Therapist

**Carlos Hoyos**, Consultant Child and Adolescent Psychiatrist, The Orchard Centre, Specialist Mental Health Team, Western Community Hospital Site, Southampton, UK

**Helena Hoyos**, Chartered and Educational Psychologist, Hampshire County Council, Local Education Office, Havant, UK

**Leanne Johnson**, Trainee Clinical Psychologist, Ashurst Child and Family Health Centre, Southampton, UK

**Margaret Josephs**, Art Therapist, Hampshire Specialist CAMHS – Fareham and Gosport, Fareham, UK

**Jacquie Kelly**, Community Therapist/Counsellor, *Brookvale Youth Mental Health Service*, South West Hampshire. UK

**Hanna Kovshoff**, Senior Research/teaching fellow in psychology, Development Brain Behaviour Laboratory, School of Psychology, University of Southampton, Southampton, UK

**Jana Kreppner**, Lecturer in Psychology, Development Brain Behaviour Laboratory, School of Psychology, University of Southampton, Southampton, UK

**Cathy Laver-Bradbury**, Consultant ADHD Nurse, The Orchard Centre, Specialist Mental Health Team, Western Community Hospital Site, Southampton, UK

**Rachel Leeke**, Clinical Psychologist, Ashurst Child and Family Centre, Southampton, UK

**Helen Mabey**, Chartered Educational Psychologist, Hampshire County Council, Winchester, UK

**Roxanne Magdalena**, Specialist Registrar, Hampshire Specialist CAMHS – Fareham and Gosport, Fareham, UK

**Liz McCaughey**, Community Paediatrician, Wordsworth House, Tremona Road, Southampton SO16 6HU

**Fiona McEwan**, Research fellow psychology, Developmental Brain Behaviour Laboratory, School of Psychology, University of Southampton, Southampton, UK

**Ravi Mehendra**, Specialist Trainee, Portsmouth, Southampton and Wessex Rotation, UK

**Mary Mitchell**, Consultant Child and Adolescent Psychiatrist, Southern Health NHS Foundation Trust, Leigh House Hospital, Winchester, UK

**Tania Morris**, Senior Lecturer in Mental Health Nursing, Mental Health Nursing, University of Northampton, Northampton, UK

**Andrew O'Toole**, Poole CAMHS/Children's Learning Disability Service, Poole, UK

**Miranda Passey**, Consultant Child and Adolescent Psychotherapist, The Orchard Centre, Specialist Mental Health Team, Western Community Health Site, Southampton, UK

**Julia Pelle**, Lecturer in Mental Health, University of Southampton, Faculty of Health Sciences, Southampton, UK

**Jason Phillips**, Child and Adolescent Psychiatrist/ Junior doctor, Royal County Hospital Winchester, Winchester, UK

**Claire Pollock**, Centre for Child Health, Dundee, UK

**Jonathan Prosser**, Consultant Child and Adolescent Psychiatrist, Hampshire Specialist CAMHS – Fareham and Gosport, Fareham, UK

**Charlotte Pyatt**, Senior Community Practitioner – Registered Mental Health Nurse, The Crisis Resolution and Home Treatment Team, Southern Health NHS Foundation Trust, UK

**Maggie Rance**, West Adoption Team, Hythe, UK

**Sue Ricketts**, Child Psychotherapist, Westwood Supportive Care Team, Southampton, UK

**Sarah Robotham**, Counselling Psychologist,

**Salvatore Rotondetto**, Associate Specialist in Child Health Community Paediatrician, Ashurst Child and Family Centre, Ashurst, Southampton, UK

**Liz Smith**, Research psychologist, Psychologist Developmental Brain Behaviour Laboratory, School of Psychology, University of Southampton, Southampton, UK

**Roy Smith**, Mental health worker, The Orchard Centre, Specialist Mental Health Team, Western Community Hospital Campus, Southampton, UK

**Ann Spooner**, Business Manager, Homeless Healthcare Team, Southampton, UK

**Janet Stevens**, Senior Speech Therapist, Speech and Language Therapy Department, Southampton, UK

**Kirsteen Stevenson**, Consultant Child and Adolescent Psychiatrist, Portsmouth CAMHS, Falcon House, St James Hospital, 151 Locksway Road, Portsmouth PO4 8LD

**Sandy Teal**, Independent ASC (Autistic Spectrum Condition) Consultant, New Forest Area, UK

**Catherine Thompson**, Research psychologist/ paediatrician

**Margaret Thompson**, Honorary Consultant/Reader in Child and Adolescent Psychiatry, Psychologist Developmental Brain Behaviour Laboratory, School of Psychology, University of Southampton, Southampton, UK

**Susan Thompson**, Commissioning Lead, Early Years and Sure Start, Southampton, UK

**Darko Turic**, Research Fellow, Department of Psychiatry, School of Medicine, University of Southampton, Southampton, UK

**Julie Waine**, Consultant Child and Adolescent Psychiatrist, Brookvale Youth Mental Health Service, Portswood, Southampton, UK

**James Walker**, Professor of Obstetrics and Gynaecology, Leeds Institute of Molecular Medicine, St James University Hospital, Leeds, UK

**Nischint Warikoo**, Specialist Trainee, Portsmouth, Southampton and Wessex Rotation, UK

**Sally Wicks**, Consultant Child and Adolescent Psychiatrist, Bursledon House, Southampton General Hospital, Southampton, UK

**Charlotte Young**, Community Mental Health Nurse, CAMHS Integrated 14–18 Team, Portswood, Southampton, UK

# Foreword

The need for a second edition of any work is usually a reflection of the success and usefulness of the first. This certainly is the case here, the first edition fulfilling its role in providing information and guidance for professionals in the child and adolescent health services as well as medical and nursing students and junior doctors and managers.

Advances in research and clinical practice call for regular updating. Our knowledge base is changing. The worlds of childhood and adolescence are on the move - consider such issues as obesity, school pressures, media influences, the impact of electronic devices and career uncertainties. So the scene calls for a fresh appraisal.

This is available to us in the new edition. Consideration is given to the place of genetics in clinical practice. Attention is drawn to the effects of early institutionalization on brain development. We are shown how CAMHS stands in relation to current government policy. Early intervention services are described. The role of schooling and related psychological services is, rightly, described in greater depth. The problems and needs of children with learning difficulties come into sharper focus - a pleasing development as, surprisingly, input in this field is often very effective and much appreciated by parents.

Recently, in the course of turning out some fifty year old paediatric and child health textbooks, I became aware how little attention was formerly given to mental health issues. Everyone in child health needs to know more about this. Once again, Margaret Thompson and her team have come to the rescue

**Leslie Bartlet**
Consultant Emeritus/Honorary Research Fellow
Child and Adolescent Psychiatry
Hampshire, UK

# Acknowledgements

To all the families and colleagues who have furthered our knowledge and understanding of child and adolescent mental health, to our contributors for their expertise and the time they have given to this project and to our own families for their patience.

# Towards comprehensive Child and Adolescent Mental Health Services (CAMHS)

## Margaret Thompson

---

### Key concepts

- Behaviour and emotional problems in children are an increasing concern to parents, schools and society.
- Research has indicated that problems of aggression, hyperactivity and extremes of temper do not go away. Children who present with this constellation at a young age are extremely likely to retain similar problems in middle childhood (Richman et al., 1982; Campbell and Ewing, 1990; Sonuga-Barke et al., 1997); adolescence (Farrington, 1995; Moffit et al., 1996, Moffit et al., 2007); or adulthood (Barkley et al., 1990).
- About one in ten children will have a serious mental health problem at any one time (Meltzer et al., 2000).
- Estimates of prevalence vary from just over 5 per cent in pre-school children (Egger and Angold, 2006) to 4–25 per cent of children seen in secondary schools (Kessler et al., 2001).
- Only the most severe problems are referred into specialized child mental health services (around 10–20 per cent of all problems).
- Most emotional and behaviour problems will present in primary care to health visitors, school nurses, teachers, general practitioners and community paediatricians.
- Many families would prefer to be offered advice by professionals they know.
- Behaviour problems must be assessed within the context of parenting style, parental mental illness and parental attention deficit disorder (Sonuga-Barke et al., 2005), temperament of the child, environment and the support available to the parents.
- Since these problems develop early and persist, it is sensible to build on services that are already working with young children and their families, so that by intervening early, problems can be assessed and treated. This would, hopefully, prevent the persistence of these problems into early and late childhood.
- Support could come from mental health professionals, in addition to other professionals.

---

## Introduction

It is becoming increasingly clear to government ministers, planners and the adult services, that child and adolescent mental health is everyone's business.

Intervening as early as early as possible in the presentation of problems would seem to be sensible. It is important, where possible, to use evidence-based practice.

It makes good sense to develop skills in staff who work with children all the time, to help them to assess and treat early.

From a period of growth of services with government funding in the late 1990s and early 2000s, the situation now seems to be in reverse. Services may need to change priorities and concentrate on the more serious mental health problems presenting, with less emphasis on prevention. This seems to be a retrograde step.

'In addition, mental illness accounts for more disability, adjusted, life years lost per year, than any other health condition in the UK. The figures for 2004 show that 20 per cent of the total burden of disease was attributable to mental illness (including suicide) compared with 16.2 per cent for cardiovascular diseases and 15.6 per cent for cancer. No other condition exceeded 10 per cent. Mental illness begins early with 50 per cent of lifetime mental illness present by the age of 14' (New Horizons: a shared vision for Mental Health, Department of Health, 2009).

These are worrying statistics and important not only because, as comprehensive Child and Adolescent Mental Health Services (CAMHS) professionals, we should be trying to be proactive at preventing the trajectory of illness for our young people, but because many of their parents will themselves have a mental illness or disability which may affect their parenting ability. With the move towards Care in the Community and cutting of services, many of our young people are carers to their sick parents (see Chapter 62, Young carers).

Because resources are tight, Specialist CAMHS must be used creatively. Children's mental health problems are increasingly becoming a focus of concern as it becomes clear that children and young people with problems of depression or other severe mental illness or behaviour problems are at risk of suicide and chronic illness, failure at school and within relationships and may continue to have problems into adult life. Several past and recent documents have highlighted the need to deliver services to this group of children and their families. All have emphasized that services should be creative, flexible and deliver assessment and treatment as near to the families as possible.

Children present with behaviour and emotional problems in primary care in schools and to primary care staff, GPs, health visitors and school nurses. Several documents have emphasized the importance of early intervention and that of supporting and developing the skills of staff working in primary care. The intention is to prevent problems becoming more serious and more difficult to treat.

Early intervention into psychosis and a reduction in the suicide rate are government targets. The prevention of anti-social behaviour, teenage pregnancy and alcohol abuse have all been highlighted. CAMHS services have a role to play in all these issues.

A comprehensive CAMHS should mean that children and their families will be able to seek help with behaviour and emotional problems as soon as they are concerned. Problems would be assessed

and treated before they become more serious. Problems that are more serious or chronic, could be referred into the appropriate agency and tracked to make sure that they are being monitored to prevent the problems escalating.

The challenge for all professionals is how to respond, so that families feel empowered and not de-skilled, but do not become dependent on professionals.

Early documents stress the importance of mental health in children (Kurtz, 1996; The Audit Commission, 1999; The BPA 1996; HAS documents, 1986, HAS documents, 1995); and lay out the idea of a comprehensive CAMHS, highlighting the tiers in which professionals work, e.g. the Health Advisory Document (1995).

For a useful review of government policy and how that has affected the development of CAMHS see Williams and Kerfoot (2005).

# Tier system: (HAS document (1995))

Four tiers were proposed:

**Tier 1** would provide a frontline service and consist of non-specialist primary care workers, e.g. school nurses, health visitors, general practitioners, teachers, social workers and educational welfare officers in addition to the volunteer services. Problems seen at this level would be the common problems of childhood: e.g. sleeping, feeding, temper tantrums, parent–child interaction, behaviour problems at home and at school, and bereavement.

**Tier 2** consists of specialized primary mental health workers (PMHWs) who, by working relatively independently from other services, would take referrals and provide support to primary care colleagues and, if appropriate, offer assessment and treatment on problems in primary care, e.g. family work, bereavement, drop-in groups for parents, i.e. parenting groups or groups addressing behaviour problems or anger management. Educational psychologists or clinical psychologists might operate at this level. The PMHW would also mediate between the primary care level and Tier 3.

**Tier 3** would consist of multidisciplinary teams, who work in child guidance clinics and other specialized units (Specialized Child Mental Health Services (SCAMHS). Problems seen here would be those too complex to be dealt with at Tier 2, e.g. assessment of developmental problems, autism, hyperactivity, depression, early psychosis and severe eating disorders. Joint work, family therapy and psychotherapy, might be offered.

**Tier 4** consists of specialized day and inpatient units, where patients with more severe mental illness can be assessed and treated (e.g. adolescent units, specialized social services therapeutic homes).

Most professionals would view the services as concentric rings of services (see **Figure 1.1**).

More recent documents have continued this theme, emphasizing the importance of joint working, in particular, in the arena of child abuse (Laming, 2009).

The National Service Framework (Appleby, 2004) outlined standards and milestones for CAMHS and the CAMHS grant guidance (2003/4) indicated how services might look with suggestions of the priorities to be tackled.

The Department of Health Priorities and Planning Framework (2002a) stated that a comprehensive CAMHS should be established in all areas by 2006, with services at each tier to address levels of seriousness of problems. There was an expectation that there would be an increase of capacity of 10 per cent across all services indicated by increased staffing, patient contact or investment.

The government awarded CAMHS grants (DOH, 2003a) to local authorities and to Primary Care Trusts (PCTs). Decisions were reached at local level about how these grants were to be used. However, the money was not always ring-fenced for CAMHS. CAMHS regional developmental workers were appointed, whose task was to work with local CAMHS and to help them seek funding to implement planning guidelines.

The green paper 'Every Child Matters and the Children's Bill' (DOH, 2003b) consolidated the importance of joint working and suggested that

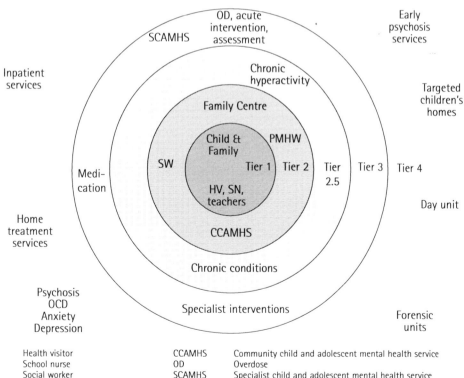

| | | | | |
|---|---|---|---|---|
| HV | Health visitor | CCAMHS | Community child and adolescent mental health service |
| SN | School nurse | OD | Overdose |
| SW | Social worker | SCAMHS | Specialist child and adolescent mental health service |
| PMHW | Primary health worker | OCD | Obsessive-compulsive disorder |

Figure 1.1 Tier system. Tier 2.5 is a new tier to hold chronic conditions.

children's services should be jointly planned at a strategic level in virtual or 'real' Children's Trusts to allow joint commissioning.

Hampshire brought in the first Children's Trust for CAMHS in the country (2004): other regions followed. They were moderately successful. One of the difficulties was that each service approached the concept of mental health from a different point of view and the success of a Trust depended on which agency was in the chair. Some other areas had 'virtual reality' trusts, where there is joint planning and sometimes, joint budgets, but the agencies are not under joint management at senior level (e.g. Southampton city). As CAMHS grants were tailored, this joint work is being curtailed.

More current reviews and documents have described how CAMHS should revisit their ways of working (Children and Young People in Mind: the Final report of the National CAMHS Review (DOH, 2008a); Keeping Children and Young People in Mind: The Governments Response to the independent review of CAMHS (DOH, 2012)).

The first Consultant Nurse role was developed in 1999 with the DOH giving guidance in 2000 that 'the role should consist of 50 per cent of the consultants' time working directly with patients ensuring faster, better and more convenient services. In line with the seniority of these posts, their contribution will be crucial to the development of professional practice, to research and evaluation, and to education, training and development' (DOH, 2000a). Many of these Consultant Nurses specialize in different areas and the role has proved very successful. Sadly, due to funding restrictions, new Consultant Nurses are no longer being appointed (see later in the chapter).

Other innovations have been the role of the prescribing nurse, particularly successful in the attention deficit hyperactivity disorder (ADHD) services (see Chapter 36, Attention deficit hyperactivity disorder) and the primary Health Nurse (see Chapter 4, Who does what in Child and Adolescent Mental Health Services?).

As funding is curtailed, services are melded and reduced with some services put out to tender, more innovative ways are being considered.

The document 'Building and Sustaining Specialist CAMHS' (York and Lamb, 2005) describes the capacity for CAMHS for a population, suggesting 40 cases to be the caseload for a whole time equivalent (WTE). The authors describe the differing roles of professionals at each tier.

# Choice and partnership approach

As it has become clear that CAMHS will have to change their way of working in order to improve capacity (and prevent 'burn out'), many services have adopted the Choice and Partnership approach (CAPA) (York and Kingsbury, 2009).

The book outlines The '7 Helpful Habits Assessment Tool' to assist teams to decide how best to target their skills and resources, and describes the CAPA approach of allowing families a choice of appointment times; an initial 'choice' appointment (a triage appointment) to allow an initial decision on the next step (one of which might be 'signposting' onto other services); and then a 'partnership' appointment, where a therapist completes the assessment and reaches a decision about the problem and the therapy required (if any).

This approach has worked well for many services, partly because the initial step in the process, after completing the '7 helpful habits', is to clear the waiting list before introducing CAPA. If it works well, it allows therapists not to be overburdened by cases.

Where it has not worked so well is when there are no community resources to 'pick up' families and where clinics are oversubscribed with patients with ADHD or patients with other chronic ongoing conditions.

# Outcomes

The CORC group led by Miranda Wolpert has been trying to steer CAMHS to adopt a core group of questionnaires to establish evaluation within CAMHS. Initially, the HoNOSCA questionnaire (Gowers et al., 1988) was recommended but generally the ones used by most services are the Strength and Difficulties Questionnaire (Goodman, 1997) and C-GAS (Shaffer, 1983, www.corc.uk.net).

To carry out regular evaluation, clinics need a system to collect the questionnaires at baseline and at regular intervals, for example, at six months or at closure.

This requires commitment by all clinicians, a good administrator and a database. If the capture rate is not at least 70 per cent, it becomes less meaningful. Many clinics collect satisfaction questionnaires from parents and patients. An administrator with the skills to audit the data regularly and to provide the statistics as required is essential.

If this information is collected regularly, it can be used for planning services, for appraisal and workforce management and for submission to commissioners (Wolpert et al., 2005).

CAMHS 'mapping' has helped in the planning of services and for commissioners to assess shortfalls (www.dur.ac.uk/camhs.mapping/).

# What else is important?

It is essential to understand why some children and families have more difficulties, to find ways to intervene and set the children's emotional development back on track.

Understanding the emotional nutrient and care that children need from their environment, their school, their friends and from society, will help professionals to work to improve the opportunities for them.

It is important for CAMHS teams to participate in research to develop connections within disorders and to develop new interventions.

The use of evidence-based practice is essential: a useful document on the CAMHS website (www.camhsnetwork.co.uk) summarizes NICE findings. Quick guide: Guidance from the National Institute for Health and Clinical Excellence (Workforce implications for child and adolescent mental health services, 2008).

# Summary

This book has been written as a practical, and we hope pragmatic, manual for professionals working with children and adolescents and their families in the field of mental health. It has been updated from the previous edition with current up-to-date practice. It outlines the roles of other services, both within and outside health, that work with young people with mental health problems.

We believe that good child and emotional health matters to everyone and we are encouraged to work closely with our colleagues, with the child and family as the focus.

## Key texts

Quick guide: Guidance from the National Institute for Health and Clinical Excellence Workforce implications for child and adolescent mental health services 2008 www.camhsnetwork.co.uk

Williams R, Kerfoot M. (2005) Setting the scene: perspectives on the history of and policy for child and adolescent mental health services in the UK, Chapter 1. In: Williams R, Kerfoot M (eds). *Child and Adolescent Mental Health Services: Strategy, Planning, Delivery, and Evaluation.* Oxford: Oxford Press.

Wolpert M, Thompson M, Tringay K (2005). Data collection, clinical audit, and measuring outcomes, Chapter 37. In: Williams R, Kerfoot M (eds). *Child and Adolescent Mental Health Services: Strategy, Planning, Delivery, and Evaluation.* Oxford: Oxford Press.

York A, Lamb C (eds). (2005) *Building and Sustaining Specialist CAMHS Workforce, Capacity and Functions of Tiers 2, 3 and 4 Specialist Child and Adolescent Mental Health Services across England, Ireland, Northern Ireland, Scotland and Wales,* Child and Adolescent Faculty, Royal College of Physicians.

York A, Kingsbury S (2009) *The Choice and Partnership Approach. A Guide To CAPA.* CAMHS Network.

## Web pages

www.dur.ac.uk/camhs.mapping/
www.camhsnetwork.co.uk
www.corc.uk.net/

# 2 Early intervention services

Margaret Thompson, Susan Thompson, Diane Henty and Kirsteen Anderssen

## The big society

The present Government has suggested that the place of the statutory services could be taken by the volunteer sector, in some areas.

There are many very successful services run by the volunteer sector, which are well-managed with an extremely skilled workforce, e.g. the NSPCC, who work in many geographical areas with abused children. They work especially with children who themselves abuse other children, a very important area.

Unfortunately in many towns the funding for these services, which comes in part from the Government or local councils, has been cut, services have been curtailed and skilled staff have had to leave. It is difficult to understand how the 'Big Society' will work in practice.

Other examples are services in the community for adolescents, e.g. 'the Safe House' described in the book, children's hospices and services for young carers, for all of which grants have been curtailed or stopped.

### Weblink

www.cabinetoffice.gov.uk/sites/default/files/resources/building-big-society_0.pdf

## Volunteer organizations: Home-Start

**Margaret Thompson**

Home-Start is a volunteer organization: volunteers with parenting experience work with parents in their own homes to support them with their own parenting. The volunteers see themselves as 'enablers', building on the parents' own strengths to enable change. They share their knowledge of children's problems and offer strategies.

Parents refer themselves to the organization for many different reasons, for example, their own mental health issues, children's behaviour problems, bereavement, chronic illness in the family or financial problems.

The volunteers offer time for parents to have some respite breaks and introduce them to other parents. They can steer them towards resources and help with applications to services. They will often accompany parents to hospital appointments with their children.

The quality of the work is maintained across the country with all Home-Start schemes working to national standards and training for the volunteers.

### Weblink

www.home-start.org.uk/about/what_we_do

## Statutory services

### Health visitors

A health visitor is a qualified and registered nurse or midwife who has undertaken further (post-registration) training at degree level to be able to work as a member of the primary healthcare team. The role of the health visitor is the promotion of health and wellbeing and the prevention of illness.

A health visitor will work alongside midwives to help women have a successful pregnancy and birth, while promoting a healthy lifestyle.

They support families in preparing for parenthood and with their young children; undergoing baby checks; immunization pro-grammes; developmental checks; and advice on child rearing, emotional and behaviour problems. They work with children and their parents from pregnancy to the child starting school.

They work closely with the rest of the primary care team, sometimes attached within GP surgeries and sometimes within area teams or Sure Start Centres.

They have a particular role in the field of child protection.

They work closely with other agencies, for example Sure Start, and will work with comprehensive Child and Adolescent Mental Health Service (CAMHS) under-five clinics.

Unfortunately, because of governmental decisions over the years, the numbers of health visitors have decreased and they now tend to work in teams with nursery nurses carrying out tasks under supervision. There are plans to increase their numbers again as the importance of early intervention becomes obvious.

## School nurses

School nurses work with children and their families at school. They will undertake the developmental checks when children start school and again at the start of secondary school. Many have developed a special expertise with the health and well-being of adolescents and run drop-in clinics in the schools.

## Education Welfare Officers

Education Welfare Officers are employed by education departments to work with a group of schools. Their concern is the welfare of students, in particular, around the causes of school non-attendance.

## Social workers

Social workers are employed by the Social Services Department (SSD). Their focus is the welfare of children and families. Because of the restriction of resources, their priorities are concentrated on child protection. In many local authorities, their role is that of a 'broker' assessing families and referring them on to suitable services.

# Sure Start Children's Centres giving every child the best start in life

**Susan Thompson**

> ## Key concepts
> - To improve children's life chances by better supporting their physical, social, emotional and mental development through improved and integrated services.
> - Core services were to include better access to high quality early education and play, health services for children and parents, family support and parenting advice.

Prior to the onset of Sure Start Local Programmes in 1999, early intervention and prevention in a child's early years were given limited priority and even more limited resources by policy-makers. Announced in July 1998 as part of the Labour Government's Comprehensive Spending Review, this initiative was important not only because of its generous funding, but as an example of 'joined-up government'; bringing policy together across government departments with the aim of linking services on the ground. The aim was to establish multidisciplinary teams with a range of early years practitioners, to better meet the needs of young children and their families. The plan was to develop 250 Sure Start Local Programmes in some of the country's areas of greatest need reaching up to 150 000 children, aged from under nine months to four years.

# Introduction

Sure Start Programmes were locally led and parental involvement in the ongoing provision and development of services was seen as a key element in building individual, family and community capacity.

In developing the programme, evidence from initiatives such as Head Start in the United States was used; it showed that a comprehensive early years' programme could make a difference to children's lives (Glass, 1999).

# Evaluation of Sure Start

## Margaret Thompson

In tandem, the Sure Start National Evaluation Strategy was established. The development of Sure Start provided a significant opportunity to contribute to our knowledge base of the impact of early intervention on young children and their families living in areas of disadvantage.

Sure Start Local Programmes' performance was closely monitored against a range of targets by the then Sure Start Unit.

The National Evaluation of Sure Start ((NESS, www.ness.bbk.ac.uk) led by Melhuish and Belsky), was set up to evaluate the impact of this new policy. Several reports have been written including the methodology, the costing, and the evaluation of the children at three years and, more recently, at five years. The evaluation was carefully set to evaluate all the 260 Sure Start Centres (SSC) with in-depth analysis of 26 of them.

The team looked at the management and coordination of each service; the access for families to Sure Start provision and services; how much local community involvement there was; how each SSC allocated their resources; the quantity of services provided by the programme; and the quality of services provided by the programme.

There were many difficulties in evaluating such a complicated set of resources, not least the fact that the government did not allow any randomization into allocation of SSC, so it was difficult to find areas to contrast and compare in a rigorous manner. Understandably, the team was evaluating services in a changing world, with free education vouchers introduced throughout England during the life of the evaluation, which would have an impact on all children's cognitive development.

The comparative group of children were chosen from the Millennium Birth Cohort Study. At three years, the children in Sure Start Local Programme (SSLP) areas had higher immunization rates and fewer accidental injuries than children in similar areas without an SSLP, but this could be because they used health services more effectively.

The latest evaluation of outcomes when the children were five years old (DFE-RB067, 2010) showed that the:

- children growing up in SSLP areas had lower body mass indexes (BMI) than children in non-SSLP areas. This was due to their being less likely to be overweight, with no difference for obesity (using WHO, 2008, criteria);
- children growing up in SSLP areas experienced better physical health than children in non-SSLP areas;
- the positive effects associated with SSLPs for maternal well-being and family functioning, in comparison with those in non-SSLP areas were that mothers residing in SSLP areas reported providing a more cognitively stimulating home learning environment for their children, a less chaotic home environment, greater life satisfaction and being engaged in less harsh discipline.

On the negative side, however, in comparison with those in non-SSLP areas:

- mothers in SSLP areas reported more depressive symptoms;
- parents in SSLP areas were less likely to visit their child's school for parent/teacher meetings or other arranged visits, although the overall incidence of such visits was low generally;
- there was no difference in emotional regulation in the two groups of children, although there had been at three years old;
- there was no difference in cognitive development.

# Expansion of Sure Start

## Susan Thompson

In March 2005, the Government announced its ambition for Sure Start children's centres in every community and increased the age range, from the original Sure Start programme, to support families with children from under nine months to five years old.

'Sure Start Children's Centres form a key part of the delivery of early years services by local authorities, increasingly as a major element in the planning and delivery of children's trusts arrangements. They '........'contribute to improving the child outcomes set out in *Every Child Matters*: being safe; healthy; enjoying and achieving; economic wellbeing; and making a positive contribution. The Government wants to see more co-located, multidisciplinary services that provide personalized support to children and their families. Children's centres are a key building block towards this goal.' (DfES, 2006).

By the target date of 31 March 2010, there were 3500 centres nationally; one in every neighbourhood. The service is universal at the point of delivery, i.e. any family with young children can use it, with more targeted services available for families who need them. Providing a universal service has ensured that there is no stigma attached to families who use the service and that no child is excluded from access to additional support when they need it. Sure Start children's centres in areas of higher deprivation receive more funding, as we know that young children and families in these areas need greater support to improve children's outcomes.

**Table 2.1** below shows the different level of services offered in children's centres according to area.

From April 2010 children's centres came under the inspection remit of Ofsted. The latest Evaluation Schedule for inspections can be found at www.ofsted.gov.uk.

# Southampton city

Southampton has 14 Sure Start children's centres, seven in 30 per cent areas of deprivation and seven in areas of more mixed economy. Three of those in the 30 per cent areas of deprivation were original Sure Start Local programmes.

Southampton's work in developing children's centres has been nationally recognized and, in 2010, was highly commended in the Best Achievement of

the Year in Children's Services category of the Municipal Journal Local Government Achievement Awards.

The key to success has been the development of partnership working with parents and agencies at both a strategic and operational level.

## Examples

Four case-loading midwifery teams in the children's centres serve communities within the 20 per cent most deprived areas in the country and are seen as national exemplars. Working collaboratively with other agencies, they deliver intensive ante-natal and post-natal support, contributing to improved outcomes and significant reductions in the equalities gap:

- Normal delivery rate in 2008/09 was 70.4 per cent within 20 per cent case-loading areas and 63.5 per cent citywide.
- Low birth weight rate was 7.0 per cent in 2006/07–08/09 within 20 per cent case-loading areas. The inequalities gap compared has narrowed, compared to the city average, by 1.9 per cent since 2003/04–05/06 to 0.4 per cent in 2006/07–08/09.
- Smoking rates at the time of midwifery booking were 26.5 per cent in 2008/09 within 20 per cent case-loading areas. The inequalities gap compared to city average has narrowed from 8.0 per cent in 2003/04 to 6.3 per cent in 2008/09.

Health visiting team boundaries were matched to those of children's centres, establishing a sound basis for local information sharing, planning and co-working.

A partnership with the Medical Research Council led to an innovative research programme to address healthy eating. This builds on the internationally renowned Southampton Women's Project and is based on findings about what influences mothers' choices in the food they buy.

The partnership between health and children's centres to implement the Family Nurse Partnership programme resulted in improvements in all key indicators for participating teenage parents and their children.

Southampton is one of 16 national Speech, Language and Communication Needs Commissioning Pathfinder projects focusing on children from birth to the end of Year R in school.

Work with the city's Parenting Commissioner has resulted in the provision of high quality evidence-based parenting programmes, such as the Incredible Years programme.

Close partnership working has facilitated the development of multi-agency 'teams around the child' in each children's centre, so that support can be offered as early as possible.

Each children's centre has an active parents' forum and there are bi-annual citywide workshops, which bring together parents and agencies to discuss and influence strategic and operational direction. This approach to parent and community involvement has been embodied in the strap line, taken from an African proverb, 'it takes a whole village to raise a child'.

Sure Start children's centres remain a relatively new and innovative early intervention programme. The coming years will see changes and developments in the configuration of services. It is to be hoped that longer-term research will lead to

an increasing body of evidence on how best to support positive outcomes in the health, emotional and mental wellbeing of young children at this key stage in their development.

# Southampton Sure Start children's centre

Every Child Matters Outcomes Framework
Safe from Harm, Economic Well Being, Be Healthy, Enjoy and Achieve, Economic Well Being
Golden Threads for Narrowing the Gap: essential features:

- Agencies working together through the Common Assessment Framework (CAF) system to identify support for the family.
- Sure Care Respite (respite childcare).
- Training and Employment officer providing long-term support building on employability skills, childcare and confidence with the goal of getting back to work.

Table 2.1 Level of services offered in children's centres according to area

| Children's Centres in 30 per cent most disadvantaged areas | Children's Centres in other areas |
| --- | --- |
| Sufficient early years education places for all three and four year olds | Sufficient early years education places for all three and four year olds |
| Family support and outreach services to identify/support those families in particular need | Outreach services to identify/support those families in particular need |
| Activity to help parents into work, including links with Jobcentre Plus | Links to Jobcentre Plus as appropriate |
| Information for parents about childcare and children's services and signposting to appropriate services | Information for parents about childcare and children's services |
| Support for childcare providers, including childminders | Support for childcare providers, including childminders |
| Access to ante-natal care and support and, on the birth of their child, a home visit from their midwife and health visitor | Access to ante-natal care and support and, on the birth of their child, a home visit from their midwife and health visitor |
| Links with schools | Drop-in sessions, e.g. parent and toddler groups, stay and play, adult education |
| Integrated child care and early learning for 0–5 year olds, open a minimum of 5 days a week, 48 weeks a year, 10 hours a day | Signposting to appropriate services |
| Child and family health services, including speech and language support | |
| Specialist support for children with special needs | |
| Parental involvement | |

# Case study

Sure Care respite childcare was requested as there were domestic violence issues within the family, behaviour issues with the children and some mental health worries and housing concerns. As part of the Sure Care agreement, pre-Children's Assessment Framework (CAF) assessments need to be completed to assess the needs of the family. Many issues presented at this initial meeting and a CAF was identified as the next step for the family. During the CAF meeting, the mother disclosed issues that raised concerns regarding her partner's abuse towards her. She was told that we had safeguarding procedures to follow should her partner return to the home. She made it clear that her partner was no longer welcome at the family home.

## What support could we offer?
- Provide Sure Care respite funding
- Signposting to Women's Aid
- Signposting to volunteer agencies, i.e. training and employment
- Family support when needed
- Support for help with housing

## What did we actually do?
- Sure Care respite funding
- Referral to Women's Aid
- Signposting to volunteer agencies, i.e. training and employment
- Family support worker referral
- Parenting Support Advisor
- Housing Support

## Outcomes
- Confidence building and better mental health outcomes for mother and older child
- Behaviour management at an early age for the younger child
- Better life opportunities for whole family
- Family support for whole family
- Safer housing for the family
- Long-term achievements for mother regarding training and employment opportunities

## What happened next?
- Partner is now in prison
- Mother is receiving Cognitive Behaviour Therapy for long-term abuse effects, receiving training and employment support and hopes to volunteer soon. She attends college and says that she is feeling much more confident
- Older child, aged 11, is receiving children's support from Women's Aid and school support for self-harm
- Younger child is receiving Sure Care to support socialization and development

## Identified issues
- Long-term issues still presenting regarding partner's release date from prison
- Safety of family
- Mental health of mother and older child
- Housing issues still ongoing

## What could we do differently?
Earlier intervention identified by working more closely with other agencies and sharing information.

*Key texts*

Glass N (1999) Sure Start: *The Development of an Early Intervention Programme for Young Children in the United Kingdom in Children and Society*, vol. 13. Wiley Online library: 257–64.
Department for Education and Skills (2006) Sure Start Children's Centres Planning and Performance Management Guidance. Crown copyright. This document can be downloaded from www.everychildmatters.org.uk. *Every Child Matters website*. Further information on the *Every Child Matters*. Change for Children programme and Sure Start children's centres can be accessed on the Every Child Matters website at the following address: www.everychildmatters.org.uk
Evaluation of Sure Start Centres http://www.ness.bbk.ac.uk

# The family nurse partnership: a Southampton model

## Diane Henty and Kirsteen Anderssen

---

### Key concepts

- The programme is underpinned by three basic theories; Human Ecology, Attachment and Self-efficacy.
- The programme goals are to improve the health, well-being and self-sufficiency of low-income first-time young parents and their children.
- The programme is delivered by highly skilled family nurses, from early pregnancy until the child is two years old.

---

## Introduction

The Family Nurse Partnership (FNP) has been running in Southampton since September 2008. The FNP is an evidence-based, licensed home-visiting programme that improves the health, well-being and self-sufficiency of low-income first-time young parents and their children. The FNP is strength-based, comprehensive and cost-effective (Isaacs, 2007). The FNP is underpinned by three main theories and these are thoroughly woven into practice.

Bronfenbrenner's *Theory of Human Ecology* looks at a child's development within the social contexts of his or her environment. It emphasizes the importance of the child's immediate family/community environment and their interactions with the larger environment, including cultural values, customs and laws (Bronfenbrenner, 1979). John Bowlby's *Theory of Attachment* holds that the earliest bonds formed by infants with their caregivers will have a lasting impact throughout their life. Attachment behaviours serve to keep the infant close to its mother, thereby promoting its chance of survival (Bowlby, 1988).

Self-efficacy theory is part of social cognitive theory and describes a person's belief in their own ability to succeed in specific situations. A person with high self-efficacy is someone who believes that they can perform well and who is more likely to view a difficult task as one that they can master, rather than avoid (Bandura, 1997).

Parents recruited onto the Family Nurse Partnership programme in Southampton are aged 19 or under and expecting their first baby. The majority are recruited at around 16 weeks of pregnancy and are visited by the family nurse (FN) every week for the first four weeks after recruitment, then every two weeks until the baby's birth. They are visited every week for six weeks following the birth and then every two weeks until the baby is 21 months old and then each month until the child is aged two. Family nurses follow a comprehensive programme that uses multiple intervention strategies to help mothers develop the knowledge, skills and self-efficacy to:

- improve pregnancy outcomes by engaging with antenatal care;
- improve diet and reduce use of cigarettes, alcohol and illegal drugs;

- improve child health and development by providing more responsible, competent and sensitive care for their child;
- improve economic self-sufficiency by developing a vision for the future, planning subsequent pregnancies, continuing in education and/or gaining employment.

## Case study 1: Julie

Julie was 16 years old when she was recruited onto the programme. She had a history of sexual abuse by her step-father, who was no longer living at home. At the time that she became pregnant she was living with her mother, who physically abused her. She was no longer in a relationship with the father of her baby, but she had a new partner with whom she frequently argued. Julie was a heavy smoker and drank alcohol at weekends.

### The programme

It was important for the family nurse to establish a trusting relationship with Julie and to establish an attachment relationship with her. It became apparent over time that Julie had an insecure avoidant attachment pattern, having learnt to be a 'grown up' and not show her feelings from an early age. She did not anticipate that other people would be able to respond to her needs. She 'acted out' this attachment pattern with her partner and they often argued. The family nurse observed that arguments between the two would become louder and louder as each competed for the other's support and understanding. Neither of them achieved their goal and the situation would escalate. The family nurse engaged in working with the couple to help them to understand each other better.

Using worksheets, role play and motivational interviewing techniques, the couple were able to explore and improve their communication. In being able to understand the needs and wants of the other more fully, a blueprint was created that could be transferred to their relationship with their unborn child. They were then able to consider the impact that their behaviour, i.e. arguing, smoking, drinking, might have on the baby, something they had been unable to do before. This helped create a healthier attachment with the baby once he was born.

Towards the end of her pregnancy, Julie's relationship with her mother broke down. She had wanted Julie to stop working with the family nurse. The family nurse had become aware that Julie was being physically abused at home. Social services were involved and Julie was moved into her own flat. The family nurse helped maintain the tenancy. When complaints were received about noise, drinking and smoking in the flat until the early hours of the morning, the nurse was able to reflect with Julie about the impact of her behaviour on her baby. In this way, Julie found the motivation to change her behaviour by prioritizing her son's need for a safe, stable home environment.

## Case study 2: Lisa

Lisa had been 'looked after' by the local authority since she was five years old, because of severe neglect and abuse. She was 15 when she was recruited to the FNP. She had been excluded from school due to several violent interactions with staff and students. Lisa had left school with no qualifications. Lisa had a 'difficult' relationship with her social worker and other healthcare professionals but demonstrated a high level of self-efficacy.

### The programme

Although Lisa was only 15, she wanted to live with the father of her baby. Historically, Lisa had always made her own choices, so the family nurse's challenge was to find a compromise that gave Lisa some of what she had decided upon, yet would protect her and her baby. The compromise suggested was that Lisa would stay in a mother and baby foster placement until her baby was six months old and if all went well, at that point, she would be supported to find accommodation for herself, her baby and her partner. Lisa reluctantly agreed. A placement was identified where Lisa and Jamie could live in an apartment in the garden of the foster parent. This suited Lisa well. She could have her independence but with the safety net and support of the foster parent. When Jamie was six months old, Lisa was supported to find and maintain a tenancy for her family.

Extensive work was undertaken around attachment and 'tuning in' to the baby's cues, as Lisa found it very difficult to interpret Jamie's behaviour, often thinking he was trying to manipulate her and be naughty, when he was only a few weeks old. Lisa and her partner were very responsive.

When it was time for Jamie to be weaned, Lisa found multiple reasons why she could not do it. She reported that Jamie refused to take solid food, choked on lumps and projectile vomited. At nine months of age, after being seen by the GP and by the local hospital where no physical problems were discovered, the family nurse decided to open up a discussion with Lisa about what it meant for her for her child to grow up and not be a baby any more. It became clear that for Lisa it was dangerous to grow up, because it was when she was a toddler that her abuse and neglect began. Subconsciously she was trying to keep Jamie as a baby, so that she could protect him from the experiences she had had. Once this was explored with Lisa and she understood the meaning of her misgivings about Jamie growing up, she was able to allow him to be weaned.

Lisa's high level of self-efficacy was used to encourage her to join a local project called Learning Links. She studied for a literacy and numeracy certificate, which helped her to gain a college place. It had been Lisa's 'heart's desire' to become an actress and she is currently enrolled at college on a performing arts course.

## Multiple choice questions

1. Attachment behaviours

   a. Apply only to the specific bond between a mother and her baby
   b. Are absent in premature babies
   c. Promote interaction between caregivers and their infants to promote survival
   d. Cannot be learnt
   e. Are only present in the first month after birth

2. The Family Nurse Partnership (FNP) programme

   a. Is designed for children with attachment problems
   b. Is a home visiting programme for families from birth until the child is five years old
   c. Consists of family nurses who work in the same way as social workers
   d. Works with vulnerable teenage parents to promote attachment and child development
   e. Consists of family nurses who prescribe medication and therapy to treat mental health disorders in young parents

### Key texts

Bandura J (1977) *Social Learning Theory.* Englewood Cliff, NJ: Prentice Hall.

Barnes J, Ball M, Meadows P, Belsky J (2011) *Nurse–Family Partnership Programme: Wave 1 Implementation in toddlerhood and a comparison between Waves 1 and 2a implementation in pregnancy and infancy.* London: DCSF.

Bowlby J (1988) *A Secure Base: Clinical Applications of Attachment Theory.* London: Routledge.

Bronfenbrenner U (1979) *The Ecology of Human Development.* Cambridge, MA: Harvard University Press.

Jewell D, Tacchi J, Donovan J (2000) Teenage pregnancy,

whose problem is it? *Family Practice,* **17**: 522–28.

Kitzman HJ, Olds DL, Cole RE et al. (2010) Enduring Effects of prenatal and infancy home visiting by nurses on children – follow up of a randomised trial among children at age 12. *Archives of Pediatric and Adolescent Medicine,* **164**: 412–24.

Macmillan HL, Wathen CN, Barlow J et al. (2009) Interventions to prevent child maltreatment and associated impairment. *Lancet,* **373**: 250–66.

Olds DL (2006) The Nurse–Family Partnership: an evidence-based preventative intervention. *Infant Mental Health Journal,* **27**: 5–25.

# 3 The role of the educational psychologist

Helena Hoyos

## Key concepts

- To apply psychological thinking and methodology to help children and young people to develop and learn to the best of their ability and in all areas of their lives.
- To help children develop emotional well-being and resilience, in addition to the more formal aspects of academic learning.
- Context is important and EPs work with parents and carers, in schools, with local authorities and other agencies concerned with social care and health.
- A key function is to carry out psychological assessments within the statutory framework for supporting children with Special Educational Needs (SEN). This is the framework within which decisions are taken about levels of educational need and the provision required to meet that need. A Statement of Special Educational Needs may be issued as a result of this process. (In March 2011 the Government published their Green Paper 'Support and aspiration: a new approach to special educational needs and disability'. This includes proposals for a change to the statutory assessment procedure, including the replacement by 2014 of the statutory assessment and statement with a new single assessment process and an 'Education, Health and Care Plan'. There is a four-month consultation period on the Green Paper and three of the consultation questions deal specifically with the role of the EP, which will inevitably change as the statutory assessment process changes. However, while the specifics of the role may alter, it is likely that the skills brought to it will remain similar.)

The role of the Educational Psychologist (EP) has developed and changed considerably since it was first established early in the twentieth century.

The work of EPs in England and Wales now focuses on children and young people from 0 to 19 years and in Scotland from 0 to 24 years. EPs remain mindful of the priorities established by the Children Act (2004) and the five outcomes of the government green paper entitled 'Every Child Matters – Change for Children' (DfES, 2004).

'Every Child Matters – Change for Children' (DfES, 2004) states that all children and young people have a right to:

- be healthy;
- stay safe;
- enjoy and achieve;
- make a positive contribution;
- achieve economic well-being.

In 2002 the Scottish Executive Education Department (SEED) published their 'Review of Provision of Educational Psychology Services in Scotland' (SEED, 2002). This defined the five core functions of the EP as:

1. Consultation
2. Assessment
3. Intervention
4. Training
5. Research.

These core functions are carried out at the levels of the:

- Child and Family
- School or Educational Setting
- Local Authority/Council/National.

While there are local and regional variations in how Educational Psychology Services are delivered, this remains a relevant summary of the overall role of the EP.

# How do educational psychologists carry out their core functions?

## Consultation

EPs offer consultation to a variety of clients, including early years settings, schools, parents, partner agencies and local authority staff. Consultation can take place through meetings within the educational placement, at alternative venues within the community or on the telephone. The focus of consultation is on joint, collaborative problem-solving, informed by the understanding of psychosocial processes which the EP brings.

## Assessment

EPs see assessment as a means of collecting information about a child or young person by a variety of methods and, ideally, over time. It may involve gathering information from a wide range of sources, including parents/carers, teaching staff, other professionals and from the child/young person. EPs are interested in the context in which the child/young person is developing and assessment will usually encompass cognitive, emotional and social factors.

EPs analyse what has been identified as the problem and form hypotheses about what underlying issues could be contributing to it. Assessment can be useful in testing out whether or not these hypotheses are valid and in helping to form alternatives, where appropriate. Assessment can take many forms, including talking to people who know the child/young person well, classroom observation, analysis of child/young person's work, reviewing success of existing interventions, questionnaires, curriculum-based assessment and the use of standardized assessment tools. Sometimes assessments carried out by EPs are used to help inform local authority statutory assessments

of children with SEN. Educational Psychology assessments are primarily used to help plan future interventions to help the child/young person.

## Intervention

EPs draw on their professional skills to develop carefully planned and evidence-based interventions.

EPs aim to help those living or working with the child/young person on a daily basis to develop their own capacity to support the child/young person. Interventions are usually developed in collaboration with these service users and may involve the EP delivering training and/or offering ongoing supervision. EPs collaborate with other professionals to help ensure that interventions are coordinated and do not overload the child/young person.

## Training

EPs are trained to understand the psychological processes behind the learning, behaviour and development of children and young people and how these may be affected by the environment and social context in which the child/young person is growing up. EPs have some training in organizational and systemic psychology, which informs their understanding of the local and national context. By offering training and support tailored to meet the needs of individual learners, EPs help others begin to link research and psychological theory with their everyday work with children and young people.

## Research

EPs are trained to carry out research in a range of settings and using a variety of experimental designs, from a local level to help review the effectiveness of particular interventions and inform future planning for individuals to the wider context of helping design educational practice and policy.

## Case study 1: Jane

Jane has cerebral palsy. She uses a wheelchair and has an electronic communication aid to help augment her limited speech and language. Due to the complexity of her needs, her Local Authority carried out a statutory assessment of Jane's SEN when she was three years old, to find out what she would need to support her at pre-school and when she started school. As part of the statutory assessment process, an educational psychologist visited Jane at home and in her pre-school setting. She talked to Jane's parents and her key worker and filled in a developmental chart with them. Through multi-agency meetings and by telephone, the educational psychologist liaised with Jane's paediatrician, physiotherapist, speech and language therapist, occupational therapist and specialist teacher. The educational psychologist observed Jane on two separate occasions in the different settings and played with her, using toys and some standardized assessment tools. Jane was given a Statement of SEN by her local authority.

A year later, Jane was ready for the mainstream school which her parents had chosen for her. The educational psychologist visited Jane again, carried out some more observations and completed the developmental chart, again with Jane's mother and key worker, to gauge Jane's progress over time. The educational psychologist attended the annual review of Jane's Statement of SEN, which was attended by the Special Educational Needs Co-ordinator (SENCo) from Jane's new school. At the annual review meeting, all those involved with Jane considered together about how best to support Jane in her move to school and the educational psychologist agreed to provide the school with some training on how best to work with her. The educational psychologist will see Jane when she starts school and will continue to monitor and review her progress regularly to ensure she is happy and successful in her new environment.

## Case study 2: John

John is in Year 4 at school and has literacy difficulties. A year ago, an educational psychologist visited John's school and offered staff training in how to carry out assessments with their children, including those for reading and spelling ages. John is eight years old, but his school has assessed his reading age as below six years. The SENCo asked the educational psychologist to talk to her and John's mother about John's results and how the school could support him to make better progress. John's mother, the educational psychologist and the SENCo looked together at John's results and analysed exactly where he was experiencing difficulty. The educational psychologist recommended some well-researched literacy programmes, which should help him. Together with John's mother, they identified some specific targets and the SENCo agreed to review his progress after two months following the programmes and to report back to the educational psychologist and John's mother at a review meeting.

John's mother was concerned that John was becoming very upset about his difficulty with reading and that sometimes he did not want to come to school. The educational psychology service had trained a member of school staff to work with children on their emotional literacy (see Chapter 13) and it was agreed that this member of staff would meet John for six sessions to help develop his self-esteem and feel more confident about his learning. The educational psychologist would supervise the work.

## Case study 3: Jack

Jack was taken into care eight years ago at the age of five. He lives with his fourth foster family and has been with them for a year. He seems very unhappy at school and is struggling to learn, despite having been assessed by the educational psychologist as being of high average intelligence. Jack finds it very hard to settle to work and he can be very rude and aggressive to his teachers. He has been involved in several fights at lunchtime and has been excluded from school for a total of 19 days this year. The school is worried that they may have to exclude him permanently if his behaviour does not improve. Jack is seen by the child and adolescent psychiatrist every six months and has been reported to have an Attachment Disorder (see Chapter 12).

With permission from Jack's foster parents and social care professionals, the educational psychology service provides key members of school staff with training on attachment at one of their staff training days. Advice on how to use appropriate strategies to help young people like Jack in the classroom is included. After the training day, evaluations show that staff empathy towards Jack has increased and they feel more confident in their ability to work positively with him. The educational psychologist who assessed Jack agrees to come in to school for termly meetings with the key members of staff supporting Jack to give them an opportunity to discuss their concerns and successes and to share and develop strategies for working with him.

## Multiple choice questions

1. Which statement about the role of the EP is correct?

   a. Educational Psychologists always work individually with children
   b. Educational Psychologists always carry out standardized assessments
   c. Educational Psychologists work with children, schools and families
   d. Educational Psychologists are primarily concerned with 'within child' factors

2. Which statement about the focus of EP work is correct?

   a. Educational Psychologists are only interested in children's academic learning
   b. Educational Psychologists are interested in all aspects of a child's development
   c. Educational Psychologists are only interested in children's behaviour
   d. Educational Psychologists are only interested in children's emotional well-being

3. Which of the following is a core function of the EP?

   a. Resiliency
   b. Economics
   c. Supervision
   d. Research

4. Which of the following is *not* an aspect of EP consultation?

   a. Collaborative problem-solving
   b. Variety of clients
   c. Psychological perspective
   d. Didactic approach

5. Which statement about EP assessment is correct?

   a. Educational Psychologists prefer to do a wide range of assessments over time
   b. Educational Psychologists only carry out cognitive assessments
   c. Educational Psychologists only take into account information given by the school
   d. Educational Psychologists are only involved in statutory assessments

### Key texts

Fallon K, Woods K, Rooney S (2010) A discussion of the developing role of educational psychologists within Children's Services. *Educational Psychology in Practice*, **26**: 1–23.

Hampshire Educational Psychology Service Statement (2008).

Scottish Executive Education Department (SEED) (2002) *Review of provision of educational psychology services in Scotland.* Edinburgh: SEED.

## 4 Who does what in Child and Adolescent Mental Health Services?

### Cathy Laver-Bradbury and Andrew O'Toole

---

### Key concepts

- Specialist CAMHS teams are made up of a variety of Health and Social Care professionals.
- There are many theories that can explain why a child/young person is behaving as they do.
- Team discussions, supervision and flexibility are needed when considering how to help.

---

Please note that the following is an example of the professionals that you may find working in a Child and Adolescent Mental Health Services (CAMHS) team. There are other professionals, who work within the team, e.g. counsellors, art therapists. It is important when working within a team that you learn about each others' theories and models; this is best done through good and regular communication. Other chapters in the book will cover some of these professionals' roles in more depth.

## Multidisciplinary working

The CAMHS Review called for specialist provision which is 'high quality, timely, responsive, appropriate and provides access to the full spectrum of treatments'. Specialist CAMHS should consist of a variety of professionals who work from differing theoretical bases to make sense of children's behaviour (National CAMHS Review, 2008). The richness of this way of working is that no theory should dominate, which allows for flexibility in thinking and working. The professionals within the CAMHS team come from a variety of backgrounds within the health and social science fields. They are often highly trained and encompass a variety of skills to help children and their families (DOH, 2012). Each team is unique so the following is a guideline to who may be within the CAMHS team.

## CAMHS management

The complexity of the workforce combined with the complexity of the children and families seen, means that careful management with a clear strategic vision is necessary in order for the CAMHS team to function successfully. Close working relationships between management and clinicians facilitate this. Ensuring that the vision of the organization in which the manager works is translated to the clinical team and in turn the clinical base, informs the vision for the organization. It is a 'which comes first chicken or egg' situation. Neither can function or exist without the other.

Managers have to work with the clinical team, but have also to hold the balance of what resources are available to meet those needs. CAMHS managers come from a variety of backgrounds. Often they have been clinicians who have trained in management techniques. They work hard to lead the services while ensuring the needs of the staff and organization are met.

Management is most effective when there is a strong management team made up of clinicians representing the CAMHS working alongside managers to understand the complexity of the services and where the teams see themselves as learning organizations (Birleson, 1988).

## Consultant child and adolescent psychiatrists

Consultant Psychiatrists are doctors who have completed their medical training and undertaken extensive specialist training in adult psychiatry and child and adolescent psychiatry. They have considerable expertise and knowledge about all childhood psychiatric disorders. Some will specialize in forensic psychiatry (see Chapter 34) and others in children with learning difficulties.

## Associate specialists, specialist registrars and staff grade doctors

These are doctors who have a special interest in child and adolescent psychiatry. They may be in training to become Consultants (i.e. Specialist Registrars) or have worked within the speciality for a number of years.

## CAMHS social workers

Specialist Social Workers were recently subject to a Care services improvement partnership (CSIP) review, published in 2005. It recommended that the role of the CAMHS social worker should include the following:

- Consultation and advice to CAMHS colleagues concerning:
  - Psychosocial explanations of mental health
  - Child protection thresholds and ACPC procedures, including advising the team on new arrangements under the Children Act and linking with the Safeguarding Board
  - Needs of Looked After Children and children on Child Protection Register
  - Coordination of work across complex systems and networks
  - Development of services accessible to marginalized groups
  - Mental health legislation and use of the Mental Health Act 1983/2007/Mental Health Capacity Act 2005.
- Clinical Practice:
  - Contribution to mental health assessments and provision of therapeutic interventions
  - Supervision of social workers employed elsewhere with specialist CAMHS roles.
- Interface with children's services:
  - Developing and enabling effective links between CAMHS and the children's services
  - Provision of consultation, advice and training to social care staff regarding mental health issues.

- Provision of Social Work perspective:
  - Promotion of client's own strengths, interests and rights
  - Mental health difficulties placed within wider social context
  - Oppressive and discriminatory processes actively challenged.

Social workers train in social work and then specialize in assessing and treating children and families with mental health difficulties. They may have additional training in other therapeutic approaches, such as family therapy.

## Specialist nurses (therapists)

Most nurses training now is moving towards an all-graduate nursing workforce with many universities restructuring the nurse training programme to meet the needs of the NHS. Nursing usually involves a three-year undergraduate training course in adult health, mental health, paediatrics or learning disability and then further training, depending on the specialist area in which they choose to work.

CAMHS nurses have specialized in the assessment and treatment of children and families with mental health problems. Within a CAMHS team they can be from a variety of backgrounds, including mental health, paediatric or learning disability nurses, health visitors and school nurses. They may have additional qualifications in cognitive behaviour therapy (CBT), parenting or family therapy for instance, in addition to using the nursing models and theories in the assessment and treatment of children with mental health difficulties and provide support both to the child and their family.

## Psychotherapists

Psychotherapists undergo extensive training in the emotional development of children and those traumatic events which may affect them. They offer individual work with the child and help explore the child's inner world and their understanding of the child's difficulties in relation to it. This is often through the medium of play. They train for a number of years and often offer supervision to the CAMHS staff.

# Clinical psychologists

Clinical psychologists have undertaken a first degree in psychology and then further training in applying psychological theories within a clinical setting. Clinical psychologists have a variety of skills. This often includes training in the assessment of children's abilities and they may work with cognitive behaviour therapy techniques to treat children presenting with a variety of difficulties. Such difficulties could include phobias and obsessive compulsive symptoms. They may use social stories techniques for children with neurodevelopmental disorders.

# Family therapists

## Andrew O'Toole

Family therapists have a professional background and undertake further training as family therapists. They train in family relationships and in how to change patterns of behaviour using a family or systems approach. There are different models of family therapy that can be applied to bring about change:

- Family therapists are an essential part of CAMHS teams. They focus on relationships and communication between people and how they are influenced by belief systems and meanings.
- They enable families to talk about difficult emotions, thoughts and behaviours.
- Family therapists work to understand the views and needs of all members of the family; and to identify the strengths and resources which will help them to make useful changes in their life.
- Family therapists work within a 'systemic' perspective, assessing difficulties in the different contexts that they occur, i.e. individual relationships, the web of family relationships and interactions with the cultural and social context.
- They are interested in what influences the development and maintenance of problems. They develop ideas or hypotheses relating to the assessment, which inform interventions with the family.

Family therapists work with families from a wide range of racial, cultural and religious backgrounds in a variety of family forms, including single parents, same-sex couples or families and extended families. They work with birth families, foster and adoptive families.

Family therapists provide consultation, supervision and training to other members of the multidisciplinary team, students and members of other agencies working with children and adolescents. In addition, they contribute to the overall development of the service and undertake audit and research activities.

# Occupational therapists

Occupational therapists are trained in helping children, especially those with developmental difficulties and motor coordination problems. They can assess children up to 18 years old who face challenges within their home, community or school to enable them to become more independent with activities of daily living. This can involve using formal assessments or even observing children within the nursery or school setting.

Some specialize in using play as a form of assessment to identify the child's areas of need and ability. Others may work with children with sensory defensive issues to help children overcome these difficulties.

# Play therapists

Play therapists work with children to allow the child to explore, at his own pace and with his or her own agenda, those issues past and current that are affecting the child's life in the present. The child's inner resources are enabled by the therapeutic alliance to bring about growth and change. Play therapy is child-centred, where play is the primary medium and speech is the secondary medium. This therapy is especially valuable with children too young to express their thoughts or feelings and those with difficulty in expressing them. Play therapists often belong to the British Association of Play Therapists (BAPT) and have undertaken training in play therapy: see Chapter 68, Child psychotherapy for further details of its origins.

# Consultant nurse role

## Cathy Laver-Bradbury

The first Consultant nurse role was developed in 1999 with the Department of Health (DOH) giving guidance in 2000 that 'the role should consist of 50 per cent of the consultants' time working directly with patients ensuring faster, better, and more convenient services. In line with the seniority of these posts, their contribution will be crucial to the development of professional practice, to research and evaluation, and to education, training and development' (DOH, 2000).

The Consultant Nurse role varies within CAMHS depending on their area of expertise. An 'evaluation of the impact of nurse, midwife and health visitor consultants' by Guest et al. (2004) demonstrated that out of 419 respondents (79 per cent of consultant nurses in post) 86 per cent were heavily engaged in leadership activities; 48 per cent in practice and service development, research and evaluation; 43 per cent in education, training and staff development; and 33 per cent in expert practice. Fifteen per cent reported that they were heavily engaged in all four functions while 11 per cent said they were not heavily engaged in any of them (Guest et al., 2004).

Over the last few years and with the financial constraints being placed on the NHS, some Consultant posts are not being replaced or there is a demand for the post to become managerial, something that was not outlined in the DOH recommendations. This leads to frustration in the lack of succession planning for their role and the lack of progression for experienced nurses looking to aspire to this role. Consultant Nurses are a valuable asset to the NHS, but because of their diversity, their value is often missed.

There are only two Consultant Nurses in the UK specializing in working with children with attention deficit hyperactivity disorder (ADHD). At present, both are involved in supporting nurses working in the field of ADHD on a national basis. They are also prescribing nurses. They hold their own clinical caseload, supervise junior nurses and provide training both within their respective trusts and in Higher Education. Both undertake regular audits of their practice. One is heavily involved in research. Each is fulfilling the initial recommendations of the Department of Health.

# Multidisciplinary working in practice

Given the wide variety of specialists and theories which can be drawn upon to make sense of a child's behaviour and the treatment options, it is unsurprising that this can be confusing to staff new to a CAMHS team and to the families. There must be careful explanation to families of the approaches available to them to address their child's presenting problems. It is important that consideration is given to the child and parents' wishes.

If a treatment approach does not appear to be working, there should be flexibility in changing approach. Discussions within the team allow for the change of direction to be documented and justified. This should enable children and families to realize that the CAMHS service is able to reassess the direction of treatment with them should a specific approach not be helpful. It is likely that, in very complex situations, several different approaches may be necessary.

There are sometimes occasions where the family are unhappy with the team's suggested therapy or they find it too difficult to carry through. The child or family may seek a different option. This can be a particular therapeutic challenge for clinicians, but it can be addressed through the use of team discussions and supervision. It may be possible for the parents to be encouraged to 'stay with this approach' for a while longer.

## Case study 1: Ben

Ben (aged eight) is a 'looked after child' having been placed with experienced foster parents two years ago. He had been in short-term foster care on several occasions in his early years but was finally received into the long-term foster care team when he was six. He had suffered physical abuse and extreme emotional abuse and was very frightened and anxious about his placement with the new family. Ben was assessed at the foster parents' request because he was 'different' from other children they had fostered in the past. He was reported to be impulsive, lack concentration and to experience extreme difficulties educationally.

At the first assessment the theory used to explain Ben's behaviour was based on attachment theory, because of Ben's very difficult early years history. Ben began individual psychotherapy and the foster parents were offered supportive therapy during this process.

Three months later, the psychotherapist working with Ben noticed that Ben's impulsivity and concentration were impeding his ability to use the therapy she was offering and she brought Ben's case to a team discussion.

As a result of this, a full ADHD and autism screening was undertaken using health models to explain Ben's behaviour. Ben met the criteria for ADHD and was subsequently treated with medication. His foster parents received help in understanding ADHD.

One month later, Ben restarted his psychotherapy and used the sessions appropriately, finding them extremely helpful in making sense of his inner world.

His foster mother now understood why Ben needed a different style of parenting, having learnt about ADHD and its implications for Ben. Liaison with his school about his difficulties in relation to his ADHD symptoms enabled his work to improve considerably and he was no longer at risk of exclusion.

This case study shows the importance of ongoing assessment during a specific treatment, careful supervision and good team working to ensure that other therapies are continually considered if, and when, necessary.

## Case study 2: Samantha

Samantha (aged 14) was referred to the specialist CAMHS team at her parents' request after missing ten months of school and being afraid of going out of the house. The initial assessment took place at home. Samantha was found to have a very low weight and an extreme anxiety about going outside, even into the garden. Her physical self-care was minimal. She had not had a bath or cleaned her teeth for months.

Several approaches were needed to manage Samantha's potentially life-threatening difficulties. A full medical was instigated to ensure there was no underlying physical problem that could account for her difficulties. This included a full blood screen, height, weight, blood pressure and pulse. A full psychiatric assessment was then undertaken including a risk assessment.

Admission to hospital was arranged and Samantha was treated as an inpatient for several months to help her to gain weight and become less physically compromised by her mental health difficulty. During this time Samantha's family was offered family therapy sessions to explore how her difficulties had arisen and to prepare for the time when Samantha came home and look at how the environment could support her recovery.

Samantha was offered individual therapy sessions once she was well enough to explore how her difficulties had arisen and to work on relapse prevention.

She continued with her education, which increased as her physical and mental health improved.

A very practical health approach was necessary initially to ensure Samantha's wellbeing. Afterwards a variety of approaches and theories were used to ensure her continued recovery.

## Summary

- Specialist CAMHS teams are made up of a variety of health and social care professionals.
- There are many theories to explain why a child/young person behaves as they do.
- Team discussions, supervision and flexibility are needed when deciding how best to intervene.

## Key texts

Birleson P (1998) Building a learning organisation in a child and adolescent mental health service. *Australian Health Review*, **21**: 223–40.

CSIP/NIMHE (2005) The social work contribution to mental health services: the future direction.

DOH (2008a) *Children and Young People in Mind: the Final Report of the National CAMHS Review*. London: Department of Health.

DOH (2012) *Keeping Children and Young People in Mind: The Governments Response to the independent review of CAMHS*. London: Department of Health.

DOH (2000). *Consultant Nurses*. London: Department of Health.

Guest et al. (2004) 'An evaluation of the impact of nurse, midwife and health visitor consultants'

## Web pages

www.bapt.info/British Association of play therapists

www.nmc-uk.org/Nursing and Midwifery council

www.gmc-uk.org/General Medical council

www.aft.org.uk/Association of Family Therapists

www.psychotherapy.org.uk/UK Council for Psychotherapy

www.bacp.co.uk/The British Association for Counselling and Psychotherapy

www.cot.co.uk/Homepage/British Association of Occupational Therapists

www.basw.co.uk/The College of Social Work

# 5 Nurse prescribing

Helen Harris

Although nurse prescribing was only introduced in America in 1969, historically nurses have been involved with their patients' medication in some form, mainly dispensing and administration (Ryan, 2010). In the UK, prescribing by certain groups of nurses began in 1986. The idea was thought up by the Cumberlege report (DOH, 1986). Health Visitors and District Nurses were initially permitted to prescribe from a limited formulary: further developments led to the introduction of independent extended prescribing and supplementary prescribing by all registered nurses, midwives and pharmacists in 2002 and 2003, respectively (Berry et al., 2006). Independent prescribers are fully autonomous and wholly accountable for the medications they prescribe, while supplementary prescribers only have the authority to prescribe agreed medications following collaboration with a medical practitioner (Creedon et al., 2009).

Some have expressed concerns about the nurse prescribing role, with reservations about nurses encroaching on medical territory and concern about their clinical skill base, and as Courtney and Carey's 2009 review of medical concerns outlines, fears that nurses may prescribe outside of their area of competence. The Nursing and Midwifery Council (NMC) has strict criteria governing conduct (Code of Professional Conduct, 2008) and have only received one case of inappropriate prescribing. The British Medical Journal (BMJ) recently reported nurse prescribers to be both effective and invaluable (Lomas, 2009).

The success of nurses/non-medical staff prescribing depends upon the contribution from all members of the prescribing team and their ability to work together effectively (Burns et al., 2002). Confidence is enhanced if doctors have an established relationship with a nurse prior to the adoption of prescribing and have experienced some of the tangible benefits of this role (Laver-Bradbury and Harris, 2008). Patients are confident about nurse prescribing: confidence being inspired by nurses' specialist knowledge and experience and a mutual trusting relationship (Bradley et al., 2005).

A key aim of modernizing the health service is to make it more accessible and responsive to patient needs (Latter, 2005). Changes to prescribing have helped to break down barriers across and within professions and enabled patients to gain faster and easier access to medicines (Bradbury et al., 2008).

It is vital that the best use is made of highly trained professionals, especially in the light of future resource availability. New ways of working are vital for service development, to enhance the patient experience and to allow better outcome measures.

Laver-Bradbury and Harris (2008) researched the efficacy of Advanced/Consultant Nurse Practitioner (prescribing) in Southampton Child and Adolescent Mental Health Services (CAMHS). Nurse prescribing for children with attention deficit hyperactivity disorder (ADHD) was a new initiative, with nurses assuming responsibility for diagnoses and prescribing. Prescribing for children with ADHD had historically been the responsibility of consultants and doctors working in CAMHS (Ryan, 2007). This change was in the context of the use of medication remaining a contentious issue, despite many years of use and NICE (2009) advocating the use of stimulants to treat ADHD. The research found nurse prescribing to be both successful and cost effective.

Both the long-term nature of ADHD and the costs of non-treatment have been recognized (Barkley et al., 1990), leading to the need to resource frequent medication reviews and support for both children and their parents.

Laver-Bradbury and Harris, 2008 noted that the advanced nurse practitioner (ANP)/consultant nurse found that being able to offer a holistic seamless service has been immensely satisfying in their clinical work and, importantly, beneficial to families. There is no evidence that nurse prescribing has marginalized the use of non-pharmacological interventions within CAMHS.

However, the prescribing initiative is being rolled out unevenly across teams, creating service inequities (Bradley et al., 2008) and the future challenge is to ensure that providers fully integrate non-medical prescribing into workforce planning and service delivery (Courtney, 2010).

## Case study 1: Sam (four years and two months)

### Pre-school

Sam was referred to CAMHS by the paediatrician. He displayed poor attachment to his mother and was constantly overactive, aggressive. Sam has poor social skills.

Pre-school report described Sam as having poor peer relationships, unable to stay on any task for more than a few moments and very immature behaviour when he does not manage to have things his own way. Hitting and biting has caused him to be sent home. At home, Sam's mother reports physical violence; Sam is unable to concentrate or sit still; always wriggling and disobedient. Sam's mother is really worried about his transition to school.

The ANP completed a full CAMHS assessment and two further 'play' assessments with Sam and his mother.

There are a range of tools and opportunities to use for assessment, including observation of patients in the waiting room: their appearance, parent/child interactions, how the child related to other children in the waiting room, how active Sam was and how both parent and child reacted when they were greeted by the nurse. See Chapter 19.

In the consultation, information was gathered using and observing verbal and non-verbal cues, as set out in Egan's (2002) model of helping. To help Sam articulate his main concerns, play opportunities were made available for him. Landreth (2002) believes that children often use play or drawings to inform adults of their worries or concerns.

Given the age group, the ANP has to consider normal developmental stages, including expected behaviours in this age group and attachment issues, before coming to a clinical decision. Children who may have ADHD can often elicit behaviours in their relationship with their main carer, i.e. 'chicken or egg' scenario (Johnston and Mash, 1989).

Although the ANP found evidence to make a diagnosis of ADHD for Sam, medication was not progressed. Daley et al. (2009) reported studies showing psychosocial intervention as a valuable treatment with magnitudes of the effects similar to those achieved using stimulant medication with older children. For Sam, it was felt that initially parent training was the first step in trying to distinguish which behaviours could be attributed to which difficulty.

In the past, Sam had witnessed domestic violence and his mother had experienced postnatal depression. These early years experiences for Sam could easily be one reason for his behaviour. It was important not to rush to diagnose or offer medication at this point in treatment.

If psycho-education, parent training and counselling for Sam's mother did not improve Sam's behaviour, the ANP might reluctantly consider medication. Ghuman et al. (2001) would support this unwillingness: their findings showed significant side effects for pre-school children. The only licensed medication for children of Sam's age is Dexamphetamine. It is licensed for children from three years old (The Joint Formulary Committee, 2010). More realistically, other psychosocial interventions would be considered, such as family or play therapy, combined with 1:1 individualized parent management.

## Case study 2: Matthew (eight)

### Primary school

Matthew was referred to CAMHS by the Educational Psychologist. Concern about levels of aggression, inability to stay on task, severe concentration difficulties, hyperactive, poor social skills, immature behaviours, sniffs other children, eccentric mannerisms and misinterpretation of language were reported. Matthew had been excluded many times from school.

Matthew's parents reported that Matthew was always 'different' and never socialized with friends. He was said to be always 'on the go', obsessed with numbers and to have poor attention skills, never focusing for more than a few moments. He had been violent towards his parents, on one occasion breaking his mother's nose.

The ANP undertook a school observation and completed a full CAMHS assessment with the family. There were two further individual assessments with Matthew. It became clear in the clinical formulation that Matthew had many co-morbid overlapping difficulties, including traits of ADHD, social communication problems, possible Asperger syndrome and elements of sensory processing difficulties.

A therapeutic plan was agreed, including further assessment for Autistic Spectrum diagnosis and sensory profile, support for school staff to continue to implement interventions 'as if' Matthew may have Asperger syndrome and to help them understand that he may have ADHD in addition to his other difficulties. This collaboration with the educational psychologist, school and home was a holistic response, in the best interests of Matthew and recognized as good practice (NICE, 2008 guidelines for ADHD).

Matthew was at serious risk of permanent exclusion from school, indicating a need for urgent action. Claude and Firestone (1995) believe it is vital to avoid the child's behaviour being associated with anti-social tendencies and school failure. The NICE (2008) guidelines state that, for school-age children and young people with severe ADHD, drug treatment should be offered as the first-line treatment.

Following appropriate individual and family screening, it was agreed to trial 10 mg Equasym (a slow release formulation of methylphenidate hydrochloride) for 2 weeks. Parent and child information and medication booklets were offered. It is important to optimize medication management. Ryan (2010) believes it is vital for the young person to be an active participant in prescribing decisions and to take 'on board' their viewpoint from the start.

The medication trial was complemented by psycho-education of ADHD/autistic spectrum disorders (ASD) for the parents to allow them to better understand their son; the medication was only one part of the treatment, but vital in the care pathway for Matthew and his family.

Parents should be offered an individual or group-based parent-training/education programme, e.g. The New Forest Parenting Programme (Sonuga-Barke et al., 2001). The therapeutic relationship is the key between the ANP, the child and the family. This enables the family to move through the varying stages of interventions and assessment. The relationship is often long term due to the nature of the complex difficulties and creating a 'window of opportunity', often via a medication trial, can be the one approach that makes the difference for the future.

Matthew's trial of medication was a success. His school reported better levels of engagement and less violence. Matthew seemed a much happier child.

His social communication difficulties seem to be improving, but this will be kept under review.

## Case study 3: Charlie (13)

### Secondary school

Charlie already has a diagnosis of ADHD and needed a formal review as his mother thought the medication was no longer working as well as it had done. He was currently being prescribed 36 mg Concerta XL at 8 am. Charlie was being increasingly punished with school detentions and there were reports of poor academic achievements in school. He was more angry and aggressive at home.

The ANP arranged a review meeting in school to ensure that both situations could be reviewed together. Before Charlie attended the meeting, the ANP consulted his mother and reviewed his symptoms against the diagnostic criteria for ADHD (ICD10) and checked that a full medical, family and developmental history had been previously taken. Using this, it was helpful to re-assess Charlie's levels of deficit to initiate the process of evidence gathering that informs the prescribing decision. The NPC (2003) believe medication reviews will improve the experience for the patient and ensure the safe prescribing of medications. Laver-Bradbury and Harris (2008) thought strongly that if schools are not consulted, it could be easy to make a misinformed decision about the reasons for deterioration. This could lead to an unnecessary or harmful change in medications or dosage. The NICE (2008) guidelines suggest that medication monitoring should be undertaken at least six-monthly. This meeting was two months since the last review.

Further evidence was obtained from school and home using clinical questionnaires. In Charlie's case, the Strengths and Difficulties (Goodman 1997) was used. This can help differentiate the extent of ADHD symptoms (hyperactivity, impulsivity and inattention) and their impact on academic achievements. The ANP was able to show the teacher and Charlie's mother that Charlie's levels of inattention and oppositional behaviour had increased since he was last seen.

Charlie's mother wanted an increase in medication due to falling school achievement. Even though her perceived solution may not have worked, it was vital that the ANP heard and understood her concerns. McKinnon (2004) believes that taking a good history is about 'how the world appears to the patient and suggests that evidence-based care plans are informed accordingly'. Understanding the mother's anxiety about the current situation and the related environmental factors was important in reaching and communicating sound clinical judgements, as described by Higgs and Jones (2000) model of clinical reasoning.

Charlie was clear that he did not want his medication changed! He became hostile towards his mother and eventually broke down in tears, saying that the medication made him feel 'weird', he was being bullied and that that no one understood him apart from his mate.

The need to 'fit in' is particularly important with this age group, as levels of maturity increase and there is a shift from the importance of their families value base to that of their peers. It is a time when emerging adult mental health symptoms can manifest themselves. Yet in Charlie's situation, it was more obvious that the bullying was the key to his behaviour change and not increased symptoms of ADHD.

Together, it was agreed to work out strategies to deal effectively with the bullying. Charlie's medication was in fact reduced to 27 mg ConcertaXL to trial reduction of gastrointestinal side effects (NICE, 2009). His mother was distraught, but at the end of the meeting felt she understood her son's behaviour better, planned to be more pro-active in listening to him and to try not to 'blame' his ADHD symptoms all the time! Charlie felt relieved about the outcome. It was agreed to review in 2 weeks by telephone contact to ascertain continued progress.

## Multiple choice questions

1. What is the recommended period for medication review?

   a. 1 month
   b. 2 months
   c. 6 months
   d. 12 months

2. What are the benefits of nurse prescribing in the ADHD field?

   a. Cheaper to administer
   b. Quicker access to services for patients
   c. Shorter-term interventions
   d. More specialized diagnostic decisions

3. What are the priorities for an ANP assessment?

   a. Identify most effective medication
   b. Identify cheapest medication
   c. Whether medication is appropriate at this stage
   d. Identify all alternatives to medication

4. Why is it important to talk directly to the child about their medication?

   a. To see if they like the taste
   b. To find out if they still want to take it
   c. To gain their cooperation in making decisions whether medication is appropriate at this stage
   d. In case the parent is not available

5. What are the options for a family before prescribing a medication for most cases?

   a. Individual therapy
   b. Psycho-education of a particular disorder
   c. Parent training
   d. All of the above

## Key texts

Bradbury E, Wain P, Nolan P (2008) Putting mental health prescribing into practice. *Nurse Prescribing*, 2008; **6**: 1.

Burns D, Bulley R, Curphey P (2002) Nurse prescribing: extended prescribing powers: three views. *Nursing Times*, **98**: 37–8.

Laver-Bradbury C, Harris H (2008) Advanced Nurse Practitioners for Attention Deficit Hyperactivity Disorder (ADHD). New Ways of Working: in child and adolescent mental health. Southampton City Primary Care Trust, *www.newwaysofworking.org.uk.*

National Prescribing Centre (2003) Maintaining Competencies in Prescribing. An Outline Framework to help nurse supplementary prescribers. Liverpool: NPC.

Ryan N (2007) Nurse prescribing in child and adolescent mental health services. *Mental Health Practice*, **10**: 35–7.

## Web page

www.nmc-uk.org/Nurses-and-midwives/The-code/The-code-in-full 2008 accessed 29/11/2009

# 6 Primary mental health in the community

## Margaret Thompson

It is known that about one in ten children and young people aged 5–16 years will have an emotional or behavioural problem at any one time that is serious enough to cause them or others concern for their functioning or well-being. Yet research suggests that still, at most, only one in five of those will be known to the Specialist Child and Adolescent Mental Health Services (Meltzer et al., 2000). This is no different from the results from the Isle of Wight survey (Rutter et al., 1970)!

Many children with such problems will be known to staff in schools, teachers, educational welfare officers or educational psychologists, school nurses or community paediatricians and other primary care staff, General Practitioners or health visitors. Following a relook at services, the authors of the NHS HAS report (Bridge over troubled waters, 1986) suggested that services for children and adolescents should be reconceptualized into a tier approach (see Chapter 1).

This accepted the fact that professionals in primary care were more numerous than those in Specialized Child and Adolescent Mental Health Services (SCAMHS) and were well placed to identify and hopefully intervene early when a child presented within their sphere of influence. This would mean that problems could be assessed and treated early or referred on as appropriate, to prevent problems from spiralling out of control.

Recent documents from the Department of Health (Health Advisory Service (HAS) NHS, 1986; Health Advisory Service (HAS) NHS, 1995; Kurtz, 1996; Audit Commission, 1999; National CAMHS Review, 2008; Keeping Children and Young People in Mind, 2010) confirmed the need to further develop the skills of primary care teams in the care of mental health. Better partnership between the primary care sector, education and social services, and with secondary care colleagues, i.e. paediatricians and child psychiatrists, was encouraged. Money was released from the

Department of Health to forward this work. Thus as suggested, health and education introduced more training and support for health visitors, school nurses and teachers.

Most specialist CAMHS began to work increasingly in the community, usually 'out-reaching' from their Tier 3 service, e.g. running workshops for health visitors on behavioural strategies for preschool problems (sleep, preschool attention deficit hyperactivity disorder (ADHD), maternal depression) (Hewit et al., 1990; Stevenson, 1990; Stallard, 1995; Thompson et al., 2003) and for GPs (Bernard et al., 1999). Staff began to work more closely with schools and voluntary adolescent support teams in the community.

The Consultation model was developed where professionals from CAMHS would meet, e.g. with GPs, health visitors or schools, to discuss clients that were of concern: names were only mentioned if the family had consented. This model is described by Appleton (2000), Thompson (2001), Thompson et al. (2003) and Thompson, 2003).

Some professionals began to work at Tier 2 and deliver services by training professionals, e.g. the Parent Advisor training (Davis et al., 1997; Davis and Spurr, 1998) and the Flintshire model (Appleton and Hammond Rowley, 2000). What began as an exciting way forward has become more difficult with the curtailing of health visitor and social work services and the changing role of the Educational Psychologist.

## A Primary Mental Health Worker

A Primary Mental Health Worker (PMHW) is a professional who works in the community, reasonably independently of other colleagues, and who works on a variety of tasks. It is a role well-developed by the Adult Services, usually by

Community Psychiatric Nurses. It has only recently been developed by CAMHS services following the introduction of the HAS Document, 1995. The aim is for the worker to operate at Tier 2.

In 1995, the Department of Health released money to improve CAMHS (DoH modernization funding, 1995a) and Primary Mental Health workers were appointed in many areas within a variety of models. Money was released to set up an MSc pathway for modular training for these new professionals.

A survey of PMHW was undertaken in 169 Mental Health Trusts in England, with a return rate of 59 per cent. This indicated that 22 specialist CAMHS had established this role and a further 42 were planning to develop it in the future (Lacey, 1999).

The PMHWs were spending about 35 per cent of their time in primary care offering consultation and training to primary health care workers, rather than in direct work with families and children. This situation could be a matter for debate. When Portsmouth district first developed PMHWs, following the closure of inpatient units, the nurses were offering mainly consultation and training, making no difference to the waiting list. The PMHWs had a separate management system and were not part of specialist CAMHS (Stevenson, personal communication). The service has subsequently changed to take referrals of families from their primary health colleagues and to have active caseloads. Management is now integrated into the specialist CAMHS. This has resulted in a reduced waiting list.

Most services would agree that the PMHW should be a senior mental health worker able to convey skills to professionals in the field and to determine which families can be dealt with in the community and which should be referred on into specialist services.

Through a series of surveys of primary care staff, Leicester CAMHS (Gale, 2001; Gale and Vostanis, 2003; Gale and Vostanis, 2005) have set up training programmes for primary care staff, social workers and other staff and now have an MSc course for primary health care staff to enable focused skills training for work with children and adolescents with behaviour problems. Their PMHW team is integrated with the Tier 3 specialist CAMHS.

There is a network for PMHWs – www.egroups.com/group/pmhw. There are 50 members and three conferences have been held (Network National Committee, Gale (2001)).

# Summary

## Research and practice issues from working in primary care

- Primary Mental Workers should be members of specialist CAMHS and managed from within the service.
- They should have dedicated time to work at Tier 2.
- Tier 2 workers should be skilled practitioners with extra training and with ongoing supervision from Tier 3 colleagues. They should work in both settings in order to improve skills, especially therapeutic skills.
- They should be locality based, e.g. to populations of 50 000 (10 000, 0–16 years).
- Consultation and training should be part of the task of PMHW, but so should 'hands on' work.
- The focus should be on high quality work with built-in outcomes.
- Packages with proven efficacy should be used, parenting (Webster-Stratton, 1985; Weeks et al., 1999; Sonuga-Barke et al., 2001; Thompson et al., 2007); behaviour work (Forehand and McMahon, 1981).
- If families need to be referred into Tier 2, the Tier 3 worker should 'culture carry' across to discourage parents from not attending at the next referral point.
- Work in schools can include drop-in clinics run by school nurses, jointly run parenting groups and nurturing groups with educational colleagues.
- Remember primary care staff want to develop their skills, but these strategies need to be tailored to their confidence level, time commitment (7 minutes for a GP, Bernard et al., 1999), classroom needs for teachers and caseloads for health visitors and school nurses.

### Key texts

Appleton P (2000) Tier 2 CAMHS and its interface with primary care. *Advances in Psychiatric Treatment*, **6**: 388–96.

Appleton P (1990) Interventions by health visitors. In: Stevenson J (ed.). Health visitor based services for pre-school children with behaviour problems. Occasional Papers No. 2. London: ACPP.

Appleton P, Hammond-Rowley S (2000) Addressing the population burden of child and adolescent mental health problems: a primary care model. *Child Psychology and Psychiatric Review*, **5**: 9–16.

Audit Commission (1999) Children in mind: child and adolescent mental health services. Portsmouth: Audit Commission.

Bernard P, Garralda E, Hughes T et al. (1999) Evaluation of a teaching package in adolescent psychiatry for general practitioner registrars. *Education for General Practice*, **10**: 21–8.

Children and Young People in Mind: the Final report of the National CAMHS Review (2008). London: HMSO.

Davis H, Spur P. (1998) Parent Counselling: an evaluation of a community child health mental service. *Journal of Child Psychology and Psychiatry*, **39**: 365–76.

Gale F, Vostanis P (2003) Developing the primary mental health worker role within child and adolescent mental health services. *Clinical Child Psychology and Psychiatry*, **8**: 227–40.

Gale F, Vostanis P (2005) Case Study the primary mental health team – Leicester, Leicestershire and Rutland CAMHS. In: Williams R, Kerfoot M (eds). *Child and Adolescent Mental Health Services: Strategy, Planning, Delivery, and Evaluation*. Oxford: Oxford Press, 439–44.

Health Advisory Document DoH (1995) *Together We Stand: A Thematic Review of Mental Health Services in England and Wales*. London: HMSO.

Kurtz Z (1996) Treating children well. A guide to using the evidence base in commissioning and managing services for the mental health of children and young people. London: The Mental Health Foundation.

Stevenson J (ed.) (1990) Health visitor based services for pre-school children with behaviour problems. Occasional Papers No 2. London: Association of Child Psychologists and Psychiatrists.

Thompson MJJ, Coll X, Wilkinson S, Utenbroek D (2003) The development of an effective mental health service for young children. *Child and Adolescent Mental Health Review*, **8**: 68–78.

Thompson M (2003) Working with Primary care. In: Garralda E, Hyde C (eds). *Managing Children with Psychiatric Problems*, 2nd edn. London. BMJ Publishing.

## Web page

Network National Committee PMHWs: www.egroups.com/group/pmhw

# 7 Primary mental health work within a specialist CAMHS team

## Roy Smith

I am a registered Social Worker who was employed for four years as a Primary Mental Health Worker (PMHW) alongside my colleagues within a 0–14 years specialist Child and Adolescent Mental Health Services (CAMHS) team in Hampshire, UK. In 2004, the National Committee for Primary Mental Health Workers defined the role as to 'act as an interface between universal first contact services for children and families (Tier 1) and Specialist CAMHS' (National Committee for Primary Mental Health Workers in CAMHS and National CAMHS Support Service, 2004).

Nationally, many PMHWs work within stand alone Tier 2 teams, but in 2007 we chose to provide an integrated Tier 2 comprehensive and Tier 3 specialist CAMHS service from within our Tier 3 team. An integrated model was important to allow our team to provide a coherent and effective service across the tiers for the local population. The model made efficient use of limited staffing resources, but importantly, it enabled practitioners access to regular specialist clinical supervision, assessments and interventions across the tiers within one team.

In addition to developing and reviewing the service, my specialism as a PMHW was to act as a prompt initial contact with families, providing clinical assessments and therapeutic interventions. Monthly group consultation with the local Tier 1 network was established and, as an integrated locality team, we provided circumscribed assessments and interventions for existing longer-term cases held by colleagues. In this way, families were able to quickly access specialist nursing, psychiatric, PMHW, occupational therapy (OT), therapist and clinical psychology specialisms during their time with us.

## Case study

### A representative example of work within the integrated model

I was initially the lead worker responsible for assessment and case management until we entered into more formal therapeutic sessions as part of the care plan. At this junction a colleague joined the system as a case holder, providing a link to the professional network, family and the rest of the team. This enabled us as a practitioner/family system to work in as clear a context as possible. The initial care plan included a referral for a formal Autistic Spectrum assessment and this expansion of the assessment process marked a transition into Tier 3 and enabled a coherent context for a change in roles.

Our family sessions considered family members understandings of each other, how to develop resilience in relation to external 'judgements' regarding the family and considered the significance for the family of a possible Autistic Spectrum disorder for the referred child, Oren. Issues of sexual identity and acceptance were relevant. The parents initially told us that family work would be a waste of time as Oren needed 'sorting out so that he could be more like us'.

The quality of relationships at the start of family therapy is illustrated in **Figure 7.1**. Oren was the focus for the problems and was on a long-term exclusion from school for an incident that had occurred some months previously. His brother, Pat, was seen as a successful and considerate youth and was particularly stressed in his relationship with Oren. Oren presented as a cheerful child with some idiosyncratic social skills, who appeared to want to be accepted and liked and was struggling with his position as a 'demonized' individual both locally and within his family. His parents were bemused, irritated and protective of their son and his behaviour.

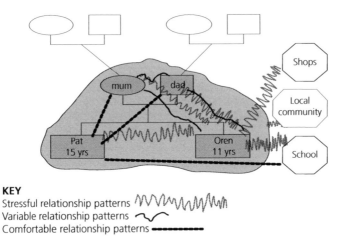

**KEY**
Stressful relationship patterns
Variable relationship patterns
Comfortable relationship patterns

Figure 7.1 A relational genogram illustrating patterns within the family's system.

I worked with the family to consider dominant problem-saturated stories in the context of the shy stories that they might relate to. My therapeutic framework was informed by my training in systemic psychotherapy and my experience of receiving psychodynamic supervision over a number of years. Flaskas and Perlesz (1996) note that 'Systemic therapy has as its central focus an interactional perspective and its theory has developed recursive ways of understanding patterns in relationships'.

Strong emotions permeated our sessions, and I used psychodynamic thinking to inform my thoughts and my questions; these were framed in systemic ways. Arundale and Bandler Bellman (2011), writing about analytical therapy, noted that 'emotional and mental events must be alive in the present moment, in exchanges between the patient and the analyst, in order for there to be psychic change'.

It was clear that Pat was particularly distressed by the relationship with his brother. We wondered what he hoped their relationship could be like and there were already examples within their lives. Pat's distress and frustration linked to his love, hope and fear for his brother and he was the first family member to articulate such insights.

Our initial hypotheses included the family's belief that attending the first session was a step to achieving an Autism diagnosis, this being the 'safe, certain' explanation for a range of difficulties involving Oren (Mason, 1993). Linked to this was a hypothesis that the family may hold cultural beliefs that, because our team is part of a wider medical system, we would be able to 'fix' Oren.

In the light of some reported behaviours, we wondered about sexuality and what hopes, fears and prejudices this might trigger for the family, myself and the wider system. We thought about how it was that the boys had 'good' and 'bad' polarized positions. Did this link with wider social values, to disappointment? What roles were they being placed into, how, why, who else in the family, past or present, has held such roles? What meanings were in those roles?

All the family were able to express and reflect on strong emotions and enrich their beliefs regarding the need for an Autism assessment. They were worried about their efficacy as parents: a diagnosis of Autism would bolster their belief in themselves. They needed to develop resilience to challenge the stories about them in the local community. Pride became an important emergent theme.

Oren listened carefully to what was said in the sessions and increasingly added considered reflections, including challenging other family members when he felt 'blamed'. He had a playful approach and was aware that this could cause him problems with other people who may perceive his staring as provocative or his frankness as rude.

We remarked that the parents began to challenge Pat when he berated his brother for 'not growing up'. Their challenges contained an increasingly robust position that Oren being 'different from them' was something they perceived as important for them to accommodate, rather than push for significant change in him.

Sexual identity emerged as an important theme in our sessions. We moved towards this topic via generalized conversations around unconditional support, highlighting this important value within the family. I asked if, in the future, either of the boys were to 'come out' as gay, how would he know they were supported? Oren immediately noted 'I'm gay' and laughed, saying he was 'only joking'.

Both boys heard that their parents would love them in all circumstances, the biggest drawback regarding homosexuality related to the possibility of a lack of grandchildren. It was apparent that this type of affirmative reflection had not previously taken place. Links with sexuality and the boys had been negative and blaming in relation to the family defending Oren's 'name' in wider contexts. We noted how all the family were already acting to support each other, especially in the face of local hostility.

More generally, we created a range of diagrams as we mapped similarities, differences and strengths of emotions in the sessions. This technique enabled Oren to actively participate in what could have been largely talk between 'the grownups'. I chose this approach because of my wider experience of working with children who might be on the Autistic spectrum and their general preference for visual aids in discussions.

Oren was able to return to school, itself a remarkable step given the potential for hostility he faced. Oren experienced his family articulating and 'enacting' acceptance, compassion and pride and Oren was able to show that he was happy with who he was.

**Figure 7.2** illustrates the patterns within the family's system at the time of our sixth and final session.

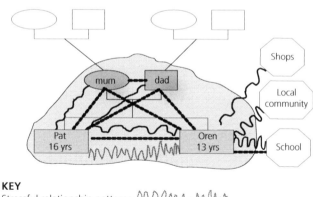

**KEY**
Stressful relationship patterns
Variable relationship patterns
Comfortable relationship patterns

Figure 7.2 A relational genogram illustrating patterns within the family's system at the time of our sixth and final session.

# Final thoughts

The PMHW role changed during our team's time with the family. I was initially the case holder and formulated a care plan that remained largely unchanged over the 18 months the family worked with us. An ASD assessment was completed and a diagnosis of Asperger syndrome made. I had left the process by this stage, the change from case holder role allowing me to begin work with a new family.

During my time with this family, my role developed to provide a therapeutic intervention in line with the care plan. It was appropriate for me to provide this role directly given the circumstances and my skill base. I would have recommended a different worker if I had become an active member of the professional network. The role change occurred prior to our team stepping into to the wider network.

Having worked for three years in separate Tier 2 and Tier 3 teams, I believe that locally an integrated approach provides a more coherent service for families. Importantly, the diversity that can be provided by the team is greater than when the tiers are separated. For practitioners, internal referrals for additional resources are, in my experience, significantly less stressful than the external referral process between different teams. Strong working relationships based on co-working developed and

this sense of respect was mirrored in our supportive and consultative roles within the wider professional network. I believe integrated working is worth considering as a way of delivering Primary Mental Health work in the UK.

## Key texts

Arundale J, Bandler Bellman D (eds) (2011) *Transference and Countertransference. A Unifying Focus of Psychoanalysis.* London, Karnac.

Flaskas C, Perlesz A (1996) *The Therapeutic Relationship in Systemic Therapy.* London: Karnac.

Mason B (1993) Towards positions of safe uncertainty. *Human Systems*, **4**: 189–200.

National Committee for Primary Mental Health Workers in CAMHS and National CAMHS Support Service (2004) The role of the child primary mental health worker, Department of Health, www.camhs.org.

# 8 *Aetiology and classification*
## Margaret Thompson

## Aetiology

It is important for those who are working with young people and their families to know about the incidence and aetiology of childhood mental and behavioural disorders, in order to aid assessment and come to the right strategy to help the child and family. This will hopefully decrease risk factors and increase protective factors, so that the best possible outcome for the young person and their family can be made more likely.

The aim here is to give an overview of the factors that have been shown to give better or worse outcomes for children.

When assessing any individual or family, it is helpful to consider what has brought this individual/family to this point at this stage in their lives and what is present to protect them from permanent difficulties or promote speedy recovery. It may be helpful to think of these aspects in the following way:

|  | Biological factors | Psychological factors | Social factors |
| --- | --- | --- | --- |
| Predisposing factors |  |  |  |
| Precipitating factors |  |  |  |
| Perpetuating factors |  |  |  |
| Protective factors |  |  |  |

In order for children to thrive, they need to have a variety of physical and emotional needs met. They need adequate nutrition for growth and development and a safe, warm place to live. They need the space and time to be able to play safely, in order to develop coordination, creativity, language and peer relationship skills.

They need affection and child-centred attention from their parents, which is predictable and continuous with appropriate rewards and sanctions. Parents who encourage play, language and problem-solving skills will encourage their children to separate and learn to cope on their own, as they develop their own problem-solving skills.

When dealing with children with emotional and behavioural disturbances, it is important to look at factors within the child, their family and the environment, as it is often the interplay between these factors that results in the difficulties with which the child is presenting (**Figure 8.1**).

For any conditions within Child and Adolescent Psychiatry, it is important to assess various features within a child which could contribute to the child's

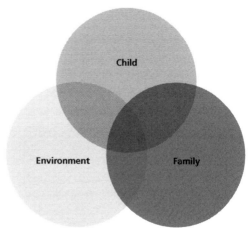

Figure 8.1 Child, family, environment.

presentation. This is outlined in the multiaxial framework below under Classification.

Further chapters will outline these factors in more depth:

- genetics;
- temperament;
- physical illness;
- learning difficulties;
- family background;
- environment.

Protective factors (these will be described in more depth in Chapter 13, Emotional well-being and literacy):

- female;
- positive self-image;
- adaptive temperament;
- secure attachments;
- supportive family.

# Classification

Rutter and his colleagues, who carried out a large epidemiological study on the Isle of Wight, defined psychiatric illness as an emotional disorder in a child that has been present for at least six months and has caused distress to the child and/or the family and/or the child's environment (Rutter et al., 1970).

There are three broad diagnostic groupings of disorders particularly relevant to child psychiatrists (see **Table 8.1**).

Classification is a means of ordering information in a language that can be understood by clinicians and researchers to describe specific disorders.

There are two main classifications currently in use, the International Classification of Diseases of the World Health Organization (ICD-10) (WHO, 1996) and the Diagnostic and Statistical Manual of the American Psychiatric Association (DSM-IV;

APA, 2000). These are both operationalized classification systems with fixed criteria that define 'caseness' resulting in many children with clear symptoms of a disorder not quite fulfilling the criteria and often falling into the sub-groups of 'not otherwise specified' labels.

This can sometimes make it difficult for parents if their child's symptoms do not fit into the clear category of, for example, attention deficit hyperactivity disorder (ADHD), when they consider that their child's behaviour or learning is impaired.

Both systems have research and clinical versions.

Current work will expand definitions within both systems, bringing them closer together. There was some debate as to whether the definition of impairment should be included to make it more useful for clinicians, but that has not been finally decided.

Often trying to settle on just one label to describe a child is equally limiting and it would be as important to record more than one diagnosis in different areas. For this reason, the multiaxial versions of DSM-IV and ICD-10 have been developed.

| ICD-10 | DSM-IV | Aspect of the child |
|---|---|---|
| 1 | I | Clinical psychiatric syndrome |
| 2 | I | Specific disorders of psychological development |
| 3 | II | Intellectual level |
| 4 | III | Medical conditions |
| 5 | IV | Associated abnormal psychosocial situations |
| 6 | V | Global assessment of psychosocial disability |

There are constant debates within clinical medicine and research as to whether a condition should be deemed as categorical or dimensional.

Table 8.1 Diagnostic groupings of disorders (Goodman and Scott, 1997)

| Emotional disorders (internalized) | Disruptive behaviour disorders (externalized) | Developmental disorders |
|---|---|---|
| • Anxiety disorders<br>• Phobias<br>• Depression<br>• Obsessive-compulsive disorder<br>• Somatization<br>• Schizophrenia | • Conduct disorder<br>• Oppositional defiant disorder<br>• Hyperactivity | • Speech/language delay<br>• Reading delay<br>• Autistic disorders<br>• Mental retardation<br>• Enuresis and encopresis |

Most conditions are dimensional, for example, blood pressure, and the level of clinical concern will depend on other factors to be considered, for example timing of blood pressure rise, familial factors, lifestyle etc. This is also true of psychiatric conditions, for example, depression or ADHD.

It is important therefore to consider all of the child's symptoms in the context of a careful clinical assessment (possibly using the multiaxial framework as above), but also including impairment across different domains and collecting information from more than one informant. Information gathering should always include the child or young person as their perspective on their symptoms may be different from their parents or school teachers. This is important, as unless the child understands his condition, he may not be fully committed to work on symptoms (see Chapter 21, Assessment of younger children and their families; individual interview of child).

Very rarely will any psychiatric condition present without co-morbidity and this must be weighed up when considering the primary condition. For example, within the ICD-10 classification system autism present in a child will 'trump' ADHD, however debilitating the ADHD symptoms may be. Yet both will need to be treated. Most clinicians will opt to mention both conditions.

It might seem 'over the top' to say to parents that their child has ADHD and oppositional defiant disorder (ODD), but parents are often searchers of the internet and if the ODD is omitted from the letter then the parents may feel the clinician has not been clear enough in his formulation. It may be that it is the ODD that causes the most concern to the parent or school. It will be important for the child's symptoms that both conditions are addressed with possible medication and behaviour work.

Guidelines have been written for many psychiatric conditions in order to give clinicians a framework to help diagnosis and treatment; e.g. for ADHD (NICE, 2008); the European Guidelines (Banaschewski et al., 2006; Taylor et al., 2004).

## Key texts

American Psychiatric Association (2000) Diagnostic and statistical manual of mental disorders (DSM-IV), 4th edn. Text revision. Washington, DC: American Psychiatric Association.

Banaschewski T, Coghill D, Santosh P et al. (2006) Long-acting medications for the hyperkinetic disorders. A systematic review and European treatment guideline. *European Child and Adolescent Psychiatry*, **15**: 476–95.

Goodman R, Scott S (eds) (1997) *Child Psychiatry*. Oxford: Blackwell Science.

National Institute for Health and Clinical Excellence (2008) Clinical guidance CG72. Attention deficit hyperactivity disorder: Diagnosis and management in ADHD in children, young people and adults. London: NICE, 2008. www.nice.org.uk/nicemedia/pdf/CG072NiceGuildelinesV2.pdf (last accessed 25/11/2010).

Rutter M, Tizzard J, Whitmore K (1970) *Education, Health and Behaviour*. London: Longmans.

Taylor E, Dopfner M, Sergeant J et al. (2004) European Guidelines for hyperkinetic disorder-first upgrade. *European Child and Adolescent Psychiatry*, **13**: 7–30.

Taylor E, Rutter M (2008) Classification. In: Rutter M, Bishop DVM, Pine DS et al. (eds). *Rutter's Child and Adolescent Psychiatry*, 5th edn. Oxford: Blackwell Publishing, 18–31.

World Health Organization (1996) *Multiaxial Classification of Child and Adolescent Psychiatric Disorders: the ICD-10 Classification of Mental and Behavioural Disorders in Children and Adolescents*. Cambridge, UK: Cambridge University Press.

# 9 Epidemiology of behaviour problems

## Christine Cornforth and Margaret Thompson

## Introduction

Epidemiology is defined as the study of patterns of health, illness and associated factors in a defined population. Epidemiological research of child emotional and behavioural problems is concerned with:

1. identifying the number of children in any given population who have clinically significant problems;
2. determining which predisposing or precipitating factors are associated with the distribution of problem behaviours.

Fewer than 100 studies have been published on the prevalence of mental health problems in childhood and adolescence (Barkmann, 2005) with fewer still focusing on the pre-school years. The most well-known international child mental health prevalence studies include: the Isle of Wight Study (Rutter et al., 1976); the Kauai Study (Werner, 1985); the Dunedin Study (Silva and Stanton, 1996); the Waltham Forest Study (Richman et al., 1982); the New Forest Development Project (Thompson et al., 1996); the National Health Interview Surveys (NHIS) Simpson et al., 2005); the Hamburg Health Survey (Barkmann and Schulte-Markwort, 2005); and the Puerto-Rico Study (Bird, 1996). Taken together, the findings from these suggest the prevalence of childhood emotional and behavioural problems varies widely between 5 and 24 per cent.

A major limitation of the majority of studies in this area is the lack of multiple informants. Structured interviews of the children themselves are beneficial but, in large epidemiological studies, not feasible. Previous studies have found that parents are better informants for externalizing disorders than for internalizing disorders (Fergusson et al., 1990; Ezpeleta et al., 1997), which means that the prevalence of internalizing disorders may have been underestimated in studies that have used parent report of child behaviour problems.

Furthermore, comparison between these studies should be made with caution as they are based in a number of different countries, have used varying sample sizes with children of different ages and have administered different behaviour rating scales and their relative cut-points to measure child psychopathology.

## Behaviour problems in pre-school children

Campbell (1995) suggested that the definition of a disorder in young children should include several components:

- the presence of a pattern or constellation of symptoms;
- a pattern of symptoms with at least short-term stability that went beyond a transient adjustment to stress or change, such as that subsequent to the birth of siblings or entry into child care;
- a cluster of symptoms evident in several settings and with people other than the parents;
- that it was relatively severe;
- that it interfered with the child's ability to negotiate developmental challenges, thereby reflecting some impairment in functioning. This should differentiate between normal age-appropriate behaviour, which might upset adults and behaviour which should be taken more seriously.

Therefore, a child may be considered to have significant emotional and behavioural problems when what are considered to be normal parameters are exceeded.

All behaviour problems in young children should be viewed within a developmental context. Although this definition applies to younger children, it is also relevant for older children.

The Waltham Forest Study (Richman et al., 1982) and the New Forest Development Project are the two main epidemiological studies from the UK that looked at pre-school children. Thompson et al. (1996; Thompson et al., 2001) looked at the 19-item Behaviour Check List (BCL) and showed the prevalence of a wide range of behavioural problems in three year olds (see **Table 9.1**).

Table 9.1 Behaviour problems and prevalence in preschool children (Thompson et al., 1996; Thompson et al., 2001)

| Behaviour | Percentage |
| --- | --- |
| **Feeding difficulties** | |
| Sometimes poor appetite | 31.8 |
| Nearly always poor appetite | 10.7 |
| Few fads | 57.2 |
| Very faddy | 12.5 |
| Significant food problems on both domains (poor appetite and faddy) | 14.7 |
| **Wetting and soiling** | |
| Wets the bed 1–2/week | 19.2 |
| Wets the bed 3+/week | 10.4 |
| Wets during the day 1–2/week | 12.4 |
| Wets during the day 3+/week | 3.0 |
| Soils 1–2/week | 7.1 |
| Soils 3+/week | 2.3 |
| **Sleep difficulties** | |
| Some difficulties settling | 23.9 |
| Takes over an hour to settle | 6.6 |
| Sometimes wakes at night | 43.9 |
| Frequently wakes throughout the night 3+/week | 10.1 |
| Occasionally sleeps with parents | 33 |
| Frequently sleeps with parents | 10.1 |
| Sleep problems in more than one domain | 22.5 |
| Significant sleep problems | 11.5 |
| **Activity and concentration difficulties** | |
| Very active | 8.4 |
| Concentration on play 5–15 minutes or variable | 44.2 |
| Hardly ever concentrates for more than 5 minutes | 5.7 |
| **Emotional behaviours** | |
| Upset if away from mother, but quickly recovers | 22.3 |
| Cannot be left with others (very 'clingy') | 2.0 |
| Seeks attention some of the time | 50.0 |
| Demands a lot of attention | 3.7 |
| Sometimes difficult to manage or control | 48.3 |
| Frequently difficult to manage or control | 7.4 |
| Occasional or short tantrums | 66.7 |
| Frequent or long tantrums | 6.3 |

| Behaviour | Percentage |
|---|---|
| Sometimes miserable or irritable | 11.5 |
| Frequently miserable or irritable | 1.6 |
| Sometimes worries for short periods | 29.7 |
| Many different worries | 3.5 |
| Has some fears | 33.7 |
| Very fearful | 0.9 |
| **Relationships** | |
| Some difficulties with siblings | 14.6 |
| Does not relate well with siblings | 0.3 |
| Some difficulties with other children | 16.3 |
| Finds it difficult to play with other children | 0.5 |

Studies elsewhere have found similar figures in pre-school children.

For example, Egger and Angold (2006) interviewed parents of children 2–5 years of age in a community sample, using a new instrument called the Pre-school Age Psychiatric Assessment (PAPA) in the USA. The authors found serious psychiatric disorders in 13 per cent of the children. (The PAPA algorithm gave a DSM-IV diagnosis.) The frequency of problems in pre-schoolers were: depressive symptoms 2 per cent, disruptive behaviour 8 per cent; attention deficit hyperactivity disorder 3 per cent.

Previous research has revealed that behavioural problems during childhood show considerable continuity. Richman et al. (1982) reported 61 per cent of children with problem behaviours at three years of age continued to have difficulties at age eight years. Sonuga-Barke et al. (1997) found that children at eight years of age, who continued to have problems from the age of three years, were those children who were more likely to present with overactive symptoms at three years.

Stallard, adding a Likert scale of parental concern, used the same questionnaire as Thompson et al. (2005) and Richman (1997) with three-year-old children, and found that 2 per cent of mothers reported serious concern with their child's overactive behaviour. Only 3 per cent of mothers, however, were concerned about night waking (Stallard, 1993).

Children may present with more than one problem. Parents may not always be concerned and might accept that the child will gradually grow out of it. This might be true of some problems, e.g. sleep, but less true of others, e.g. overactivity.

Campbell and Ewing (1990) showed that the children with less severe problems initially were found to improve, whereas those with more severe problems did not. Studies have examined the continuity of behavioural difficulties in the pre-school years in relation to psychopathology in adulthood. Researchers from the Dunedin Multidisciplinary Health and Development Study (DMHDS) reported that under-controlled and inhibited children at age three years were at greater risk of having a psychiatric disorder at age 21 years (Caspi et al., 1996).

A more thorough understanding of the origins, nature and developmental course of mental health problems throughout childhood is essential for both research and clinical purposes. Of particular importance are the mechanisms underlying the continuity of such problems during development. This is of particular importance as it is commonly accepted that the longer a child continues along a pathway which is considered to be maladaptive, the more difficult it becomes for him or her to return to a normal developmental trajectory.

# Behaviour problems in older children and adolescents

Two epidemiological studies carried out by Rutter et al. (1970) on the Isle of Wight focused on middle childhood and adolescence, but with specific age criteria. The Isle of Wight study showed an overall prevalence rate of 7 per cent in 10 and 11 year olds for behaviour problems, but what has been shown from subsequent studies is that the prevalence differs according to where the population is living, as shown by the Inner London Borough Study (Rutter et al., 1975), which showed higher incidences of a variety of disorders (11 per cent). The incidence will vary with different cultural populations being studied.

In a follow-up study, Graham and Rutter (1973) reported that 75 per cent of children aged between 10 and 11 years who received a diagnosis for conduct disorder and 46 per cent of children with an emotional disorder continued to have clinically significant problems up to four years later.

The study by Meltzer et al. (2000) examining the national prevalence of mental disorders in 5–15 year olds reported a wide variation in prevalence rates (see **Table 9.2**). The authors from this study supported findings from previous studies suggesting that children with mental health problems were more likely to be living with a lone parent or in a reconstituted family, where the interviewed parent had no qualifications and where the household income was less than £200 per week. These children were more likely to be living in social sector housing or in a terraced house.

Many children with psychiatric disorders meet the criteria for more than one disorder. For example, children who meet the criteria for ADHD often also meet the criteria for oppositional defiant disorder or conduct disorder. In fact, co-morbidity is the rule, rather than the exception, in childhood emotional and behavioural disorders.

The perception of problems is not the same in different cultures. For example, disruptive problems in children are less likely to be referred to clinical services in Thailand while emotional problems are more likely to be referred than similar problems in the USA. Parents and teachers in Hong Kong were more likely to be concerned about their children's hyperactive behaviour than those in the UK, though on objective measurement the rates were the same (Ho et al., 1996). There are behaviour scales that have different national norms (see Chapter 26, The use of questionnaires in the diagnosis of child mental health problems).

Several disorders tend to be more common among boys with others being more common among girls (see **Box 9.1**).

Table 9.2 The national prevalence of mental disorders in 5–15 year olds (Meltzer et al., 2000)

| Disorder | Percentage |
| --- | --- |
| Emotional disorders | 4.3 |
| Anxiety disorders | 3.8 |
| Separation anxiety | 0.8 |
| Specific phobia | 1.0 |
| Social phobia | 0.3 |
| Panic | 0.1 |
| Agoraphobia | 0.1 |
| PTSD | 0.2 |
| Obsessive–compulsive disorder | 0.2 |
| Depression | 0.9 |
| Conduct disorders | 5.3 |
| Oppositional defiant disorder | 2.9 |
| Hyperkinetic disorders | 1.4 |
| Pervasive developmental disorders | 0.3 |
| Tic disorders | 0.1 |
| Eating disorders | 0.1 |
| Any disorder | 9.5 |

Box 9.1 Prevalence of disorders in boys and girls

| Marked male excess | Male = Female | Marked female excess |
| --- | --- | --- |
| • Autistic disorders<br>• Hyperactivity disorders<br>• Conduct/oppositional disorders<br>• Completed suicide<br>• Tic disorders<br>• Nocturnal enuresis in older children<br>• Specific developmental disorders | • Pre-pubertal depression<br>• Selective mutism<br>• School refusal | • Specific phobias<br>• Diurnal enuresis<br>• Deliberate self-harm<br>• Post-pubertal depression<br>• Anorexia nervosa<br>• Bulimia nervosa |

Child Psychiatry (Goodman and Scott, 1997, reprinted with permission)

# Genes or environment in predicting the continuity of problems

The study of genetically related individuals is a powerful tool for unravelling the genetic and environmental architecture of individual differences in the development of behavioural and emotional problems. Family studies might give a first impression of familial aggregation, but they are limited, as they cannot distinguish between genetic and environmental effects. Similarities between family members may be created either by genetic relatedness or by sharing the same family environment. The twin design method allows the examination of this. Accordingly, the difference in relatedness between monozygotic (MZ) and dyzygotic (DZ) twin pairs gives information about the strength of the genetic and environmental influences on the trait under investigation. It further allows the separation of environmental influences into those of the environment shared by members of a family and those unique for each individual.

Rietveld et al. (2004) reported on the size of genetic and environmental effects on individual differences in attention problems at ages three, seven, ten and twelve years in twins. This study used the overactivity scale in the Child Behaviour Checklist (CBCL) for ages 2–3 years and the Attention Problem scale of the CBCL for ages 4–18 years. The results revealed less stability of overactivity at age three years to attention problems at age seven years, compared to the stability from attention problems at age seven and beyond. This study found that stability in overactivity and attention problems is accounted for by genetic influences and that children who do not display overactivity or attention problems at an early age are unlikely to develop these problems at a subsequent age.

A further study in this area reported that both genetic and shared environmental factors were most important for the stability of internalizing and externalizing problems between the ages of three and seven years, and that non-shared environmental factors were mainly age-specific. In particular, this study found that for the stability of internalizing problems, shared environment may become more important from early to middle childhood (Van der Valk et al., 2003).

In summary, extensive research has been conducted on the continuity of problem behaviours during childhood, with the majority of studies reporting that emotional and behavioural problems are relatively stable. Furthermore, children who have clinically significant problems at an early age are more likely to continue to experience such problems throughout development. The stability of problems is accounted for by both genetic and environmental influences.

## Key texts

Campbell SB (1995) Behaviour problems in preschool children: a review of recent research. *Journal of Child Psychology and Psychiatry*, **36**: 113–49.

Egger HL, Angold A (2006) Common emotional and behavioral disorders in preschool children: Presentation, nosology, and epidemiology. *Journal of Child Psychology and Psychiatry*, **47**: 313–37.

Meltzer H, Gatward R, Goodman R, Ford T (2000) *The Mental Health of Children and Adolescents in Great Britain.* London: The Stationery Office.

Richman N, Stevenson J, Graham P (1982) *Preschool to School: A Behaviour Study.* London: Academic Press.

Rutter M, Tizzard J, Whitmore K (1970) *Education, Health and Behaviour.* London: Longmans.

Thompson M, Stevenson J, Sonuga-Barke EJS et al. (1996) The mental health of preschool children and their mothers in a mixed urban/rural population 1. Prevalence and ecological factors. *British Journal of Psychiatry*, **168**: 16–20.

# 10 Genetics

Darko Turic and Wai Chen

## Key concepts

Genetic studies of psychiatric and behavioural phenotypes have consistently demonstrated for certain disorders that:
- genetic risk factors, when combined, are important aetiological components;
- genetic factors cannot completely account for observed risk, meaning these phenotypes are multifactorial traits, with important non-genetic (or environmental) contributing factors;
- the common disease-common variant (CD-CV) hypothesis predicts that common disease-causing alleles, or variants, will be found throughout the entire human population (i.e. people with and without the disorder). These genetic variants manifest a given disease when certain risk alleles (variants) of small effect size combine and interact to express a disorder state. Psychiatric and behavioural phenotypes are thus influenced by a large number of risk factors that are individually present within the range of normal human variation, but increase the disease risk when occurring in unique and specific combinations.

## Introduction

There have been intense research efforts to identify the epidemiological genetic and molecular genetic aetiological factors in psychiatry in the recent years. However, very few psychiatric disorders are the result of simple Mendelian patterns of inheritance. Most psychiatric disorders are complex in origin and are a complex interaction between genes and the environment. Disease traits are likely to have a continuous distribution in the population.

## Complex disorders

Family, adoption and twin studies are used in order to estimate the relative influence of genetic and environmental factors on a trait or disorder. Most readers are familiar with simple Mendelian patterns of inheritance, which concerns a single gene trait or disorder inherited by either a dominant or recessive mode of inheritance. The well-known examples include sickle cell disease, Huntington chorea, haemophilia and cystic fibrosis and so on. Single gene disorders are in fact rare, as the affected individuals are likely to express extreme severe phenotype, many of which affect long-term survival or reproductive fitness.

Most common disorders, including the majority of psychiatric disorders, are complex in origin. By 'complex', it is meant that such disorders are multifactorial in aetiology. A defining feature of complex disorders is that no single gene (variant) is either necessary or sufficient to produce a particular trait. Inheritance of such traits is governed by: (1) a combined effect of multiple genes, each of which is likely to have a small effect; and (2) these genetic risks are likely to manifest through the interaction with environmental factors. For these reasons, the disease trait is likely to have a continuous distribution in the population, where only the extreme end of the behaviour phenotype is regarded as 'diseased'.

## Behavioural epidemiological genetic studies

Family studies examine the recurrence rates among related individuals and the degree of familial clustering of a trait. If a disorder has a genetic contribution, the relatives of individuals with the condition are expected to have the disorder more frequently than individuals in the general population, and than the relatives of individuals without the disorder.

Because members of one family share both genetic and family environmental influences, adoption and twin studies are necessary to make a distinction between the relative contributions of genes and environment.

Adoption provides a natural experimental situation whereby environmental effects can be separated from the genetic effects. An adoptee is raised, often from an early age, by genetically unrelated individuals (the adoptive family). Any resemblance between the adoptee and his adopted relatives is thus likely attributable to the shared family environment. In contrast, any resemblance between the adoptee and his biological relatives is a result of shared genes, but not due to experiencing the same environmental influences (other than factors that influence mother and child during pregnancy).

The other major method used to disentangle genetic contributions from that of environment is twin studies. Monozygotic (MZ) or identical twins share an identical set of genes because they arise from the division of a single fertilized egg. Thus any phenotypic differences (the observable physical or biochemical characteristics of an organism, as determined by both genetic makeup and environmental differences) must be caused by differences in the environment. In contrast, dizygotic (DZ) or fraternal twins develop from separately fertilized eggs and, on average, share half of their genes. Phenotypic differences in DZ twins may be caused by differences in genes and/or environment. Twin studies utilize the differences between the phenotypic trait correlations (or disorder affection concordance rates) to compute 'heritability', which is a measure that quantifies the degree of phenotypic variance attributable to genetic causes. For example, the heritability of attention deficit hyperactivity disorder (ADHD) has been estimated by twin studies to be around 76 per cent (Biederman and Faraone, 2005), implying that about 76 per cent of the variance in the disease phenotype is attributable to genetic factors.

# Environment

Despite the strong evidence for the (high) heritability of many psychiatric disorders, the results of family, adoption and twin studies indicate that non-genetic or environmental factors (biological and psychosocial) are also important. Environmental influences can be partitioned into two different types: shared and non-shared environment. Shared environment are family, neighbourhood or schooling factors and are shared by siblings, making them more similar. In contrast, non-shared factors are those that uniquely affect a given individual, making that person different from his/her siblings. In some cases an individual evokes a certain response from the environment, thus making the response unique to that individual with an evoked genetic–environment response.

# Gene–environment interactions

Gene-environment interaction (GxE) has been a focus of behavioural genetic research. There are a very few cases in which a trait/disorder is almost entirely attributable to 'nature' (i.e. genes), or almost entirely to 'nurture' (i.e. environment). An example of the former is Huntington's disease in which individuals inherit a mutated gene (The Huntington's Disease Collaborative Research Group, 1993), and develop the disease in an almost entirely deterministic manner. In contrast, the latter can be illustrated by traits such as the learning of a native language. This is environmentally determined; and linguists have found that any child (if capable of learning a language at all) can learn any human language equally (Diesendruck, 2007).

In the case of complex disorders, however, genes and environment work in concert and the risk effect of specific gene variants is fully expressed if they are accompanied by exposure to a particular environmental risk factor. GxE interactions can be difficult to study. An environment can modulate the genetic risks in a positive (i.e. risk increment) or negative (i.e. risk reduction) manner. Genetic effects are better detected in the former case in exposed individuals; but better detected in the latter case in unexposed individuals. Environmental risks are best ascertained prospectively (i.e. prior to the development of the disease outcome) in order to minimize the effects of recall bias. Often large longitudinal samples are required to detect the effect of GxE interactions.

# Mapping genes for complex disorders

## Molecular genetic approaches

Family, adoption and twin studies are useful to establish a genetic component, yet such studies cannot identify which specific genes are associated with heritable diseases/traits. Molecular genetic studies, on the other hand, concern finding specific gene(s) in the neurobiological causal pathway of a condition. It identifies either a functional gene (which is contributory to the pathogenesis of the disease) or a marker gene (which is close to a functional gene, though the precise identity and location of the functional gene remains unknown). There are two common approaches used in molecular genetic studies: hypothesis based (candidate gene studies) and non-hypothesis based (genome-wide studies); candidate gene approach and genome-wide approach. The candidate gene approach is based on theoretical assumption of neurobiological pathways leading to specific hypotheses; and in contrast, the genome-wide approach is non-hypothesis driven and considers all genes as equally plausible candidates.

Candidate gene studies can detect whether the possession of a specific gene variant is associated with the disease. One easy way to understand this is to imagine the possession of such a gene is like an exposure to a disease risk factor. For instance, smoking is associated with an increased risk of developing lung cancer (Ezzati and Lopez, 2004); and as smoking precedes the development of the outcome, it can be regarded as an exposure to a pathogenic risk. Likewise, having the 7-repeat allele of the DRD4 gene is associated with an increased risk of having ADHD (Mick and Faraone, 2008). These cellular studies provide plausible biological mechanisms to account for this association, as this variant of the gene expresses DRD4 receptors which are less responsive to dopamine binding, thus reducing the functional effect of presynaptic

release of dopamine (van Tol et al., 1992; Asghari et al., 1995).

Candidate gene approach uses either case-control or family-based association designs. In case–control studies the frequency of candidate alleles or genotypes are compared in cases and controls. Family-based approaches examine patterns of genetic transmission (disequilibrium) across generations within affected families to examine whether the probability of transmission of an allele from parents to affected offspring differs from the expected Mendelian pattern of inheritance.

Genome-wide non-hypothesis-based approaches employ association and linkage designs models. In genome-wide linkage studies of related individuals, only siblings or those in extended pedigrees are studied in an attempt to capture chromosomal region(s), where genes influencing a trait are located by examining the familial co-segregation of the phenotype and genetic markers region.

Genome-wide association studies (GWAS) compare markers across a population rather than within families. Some GWAS designs compare a group with a disorder with a group without a disorder; whereas others compare markers across the range of a trait in the population. In the genome-wide approach, more in-depth studies are required to identify the functional genes involved by conducting fine-mapping of the chromosomal region localized by either a GWAS or linkage study.

Apart from identifying molecular genetic aetiology of a trait or condition, molecular genetics can also be used to conduct functional studies, thus elucidating how a polymorphism alters the function of a gene. The alternation may affect gene expression or protein structure, and thus biological mechanisms of a disorder.

# Genetics of childhood disorders

## Autism spectrum disorders

Several decades ago, autism was thought to be environmentally caused by unresponsive parenting (refrigerator mother theory) (Kanner, 1943, Kanner, 1949), prenatal viral infections (Desmond et al.,

1967; Chess, 1977), or neurotoxins such as heavy metals (Grandjean et al., 1997; Davidson et al., 1998). However, epidemiological genetic studies (Folstein and Rutter 1977; Ciaranello and Ciaranello, 1995; Ronald et al., 2006) have shown that genetic factors play a crucial role in autism, reporting heritability of around 90 per cent (that is, about 90 per cent of the autism phenotypic variance is attributable by genetic factors). In the case of autism, the likelihood that the sibling of an affected child also would be affected is between 2 and 8 per cent (Muhle et al., 2004). Although small, this rate is 100 times larger than the rate at which autism affects unrelated people in the population (Freitag, 2007).

The International Molecular Genetic Study of Autism Consortium (IMGSAC) was established to identify the genes involved in susceptibility to autism, and to understand the relationship of these genes to clinical outcome. A series of multiple independent whole genome scans have linked several candidate regions on chromosomes 2q, 7q, 16p and sex chromosomes with autism (IMGSAC, 1998, IMGSAC, 2001a, IMGSAC, 2001b; Lamb et al., 2005). More specifically, several studies have found links between autism and several genes with important cell functions: CDH9, CDH10 in nerve cell adhesion (Wang et al., 2009), SHANK3 in cell communication (Durand et al., 2007) and DOCK4 in the development of dendrites (Maestrini et al., 2010).

# ADHD and disruptive behaviour disorders (conduct disorder and oppositional defiant disorder)

Research has consistently shown that genetic factors are important in the aetiology of ADHD. Family studies have demonstrated ADHD as familial (Barkley, 1990; Roizen et al., 1996). The parents and siblings of ADHD children have higher risks of having ADHD or ADHD-like symptoms compared to relatives of controls (Biederman et al., 1990; Perrin and Last, 1996; Faraone and Doyle, 2001). Adoption studies reported higher rates of ADHD in biological parents of ADHD adoptees than in adoptive parents (Morrison and Stewart, 1973; Cantwell, 1975). Twin studies using different populations and measurement have consistently yielded similar

findings of high heritability of ADHD symptoms or disorder with the pooled estimate of ADHD heritability around 0.76–0.80 (Edelbrock et al., 1995; Eaves et al., 1997; Biederman and Faraone, 2005).

There have been several genome-wide linkage studies on ADHD with some inconsistencies (Fisher et al., 2002; Arcos-Burgos et al., 2004). A recent meta-analysis of seven ADHD linkage studies identified a specific genomic region on chromosome 16 – between 16q21 and 16q24 – as the most consistent linkage evidence across the studies (Zhou et al., 2008). Initial GWAS with hundreds of thousands of markers and thousands of patients have so far failed to identify a genome-wide significant association between ADHD and these markers (Lasky-Su et al., 2008; Neale et al., 2008). Based on the literature on other disorders, this is not unexpected, since the initial GWAS of 2000–3000 participants in general failed to reveal any associations that reached genome-wide levels of significance (Hirschhorn and Lettre, 2009). The strategy of combining samples to achieve increased power may lead to the documentation of association with genes.

The first candidate gene study of ADHD was reported in 1995 showing an association with the 10-repeat (480-bp) allele in the dopamine transporter gene (DAT1 gene) (Cook et al., 1995). Since then, numerous candidate gene studies have been conducted, mainly polymorphisms of dopamine, noradrenaline and serotonin neurotransmitter genes (Payton et al., 2001; Hawi et al., 2002; Turic et al., 2005). Several meta- and pooled analyses for single and multiple loci have been recently published (Maher et al., 2002; Faraone et al., 2005; Purper-Ouakil et al., 2005; Yang et al., 2007).

A recent meta-analysis (Gizer et al., 2009) showed significant associations for several candidate genes including DAT1, DRD4, DRD5, 5HTT, HTR1B and SNAP25. Furthermore, significant heterogeneity among different studies was observed for the associations between ADHD and DAT1, DRD4, DRD5, DBH, ADRA2A, 5HTT, TPH2, MAOA and SNAP25, suggesting that potential modulators (i.e. ADHD subtype diagnoses, gender, exposure to environmental risk factors) affect the associations between ADHD status and genotypes. Overall, candidate gene studies appear to confirm the aetiological roles of genes in the dopaminergic, serotonergic and noradrenergic pathways (Faraone et al., 2005).

Despite the common perception that oppositional defiant disorder (ODD) and conduct disorder (CD) are mainly caused by poor parenting, genetic studies have found that genetic factors play an important role in the development of these disorders. The data indicate that genetic input in ODD is different for boys and girls (38 and 21 per cent) while environmental rates are between 62 and 79 per cent (Hudziak et al., 2005). Heritability of ODD has been estimated to be around 0.60 (Eaves et al., 1997; Coolidge et al., 2000). Heritability rates for CD vary from 21 to 78 per cent (Eaves et al., 1997; Thapar et al., 2001; Gelhorn et al., 2005) with average at 40 per cent (Tacket et al., 2005). There is evidence that ADHD and CD/ODD share a common genetic aetiology (Thapar et al., 2001; Nadder et al., 1998), however family environment factors like mothers' psychiatric disorders or negative parenting practices could also be linked to the presence of co-morbid antisocial disorders (August et al., 1998).

Candidate gene studies in disruptive behaviours (CD and ODD) also mainly investigate neurotransmitter genes. Of these genes, the ones that code for the enzymes that influence the turnover of dopamine (DA) have received the most attention (COMT and MAO-A) (Pliszka et al., 1988; Haberstick et al., 2005; DeYoung et al., 2010). Recently, the first evidence from a genome-wide association study of a specific gene (C1QTNF7 – C1Q and tumour necrosis factor related protein 7) being associated with CD symptomatology has been reported (Dick et al., 2011).

## Mood disorders

For many decades family studies have shown that the recurrence risk for bipolar disorder, major depression, specific anxiety disorders (including panic and phobic disorders, obsessive-compulsive disorder, and generalized anxiety disorder) is higher in first degree relatives of affected probands compared to relatives of unaffected controls (Smoller and Finn, 2003; Merikangas and Low, 2004). Heritability rates are also substantial,

although they vary from 20 to 40 per cent for major depression (Wierzbicki, 1987), 40 per cent for anxiety disorders (Stein et al., 1999), and bipolar disorder from around 70 per cent (Edvardsen et al., 2008).

A large number of candidate genes have been examined in gene association mood disorder studies. One of the most extensively studied variants is a dinucleotide repeat in the promoter region of the serotonin transporter gene (5HTTLPR, short and long versions). The short allele of the 5HTTLPR, less functionally active, has been associated with anxiety-related traits (Lesch et al., 1996; Greenberg et al., 2000). Recently, genes like brain-derived neurotrophic factor (BDNF), Neuregulin 1 (NRG1), and DISC1 (Disrupted-in-Schizophrenia 1) have attracted a lot of interest, particularly in the field of bipolar disorder (Segurado et al., 2003; Serretti and Mandelli, 2008).

## Schizophrenia

Schizophrenia is a highly familial disorder, with increasing recurrence rates according to the degree of relatedness within families (O'Donovan et al., 2003). Those who have a third degree relative with schizophrenia are twice as likely to develop schizophrenia as those in the general population (1 per cent) (Gottesman and Shields, 1971; Shields and Gottesman, 1972). Those with a second degree relative have a several-fold higher incidence (2–6 per cent) of schizophrenia than the general population, while first degree relatives have an incidence of 6–17 per cent of schizophrenia (Shields and Slater, 1975). Heritability is high, estimated to be around 80 per cent by most studies (Cardno et al., 1999).

The current belief is that there are a number of genes (similarly to other complex disorders) that contribute to susceptibility or pathology of schizophrenia, with no major contribution of any particular gene variant (Bondy, 2011). The results from molecular genetic studies are mixed, the best supported variants are in genes disrupted in Schizophrenia 1 (DISC1) (Millar et al., 2000), zinc finger protein 804A (ZNF804A) (O'Donovan et al., 2008) and reelin (RELN) (Impagnatiello et al., 1998).

## Multiple choice questions

1. Which types of behavioural genetic studies are used to make distinction between the relative contributions of genes and environment?

   a. Family studies
   b. Family and adoption studies
   c. Family and twin studies
   d. Adoption and twin studies
   e. All of the above

2. Which statement about complex disorders is true?

   a. Huntington's disease is a complex disorder
   b. No single gene variant is either necessary or sufficient to produce a particular complex trait/disorder
   c. Complex disorders are entirely due to genetic causes
   d. Complex disorders follow simple Mendelian mode of inheritance
   e. Complex disorders are entirely due to environmental causes

3. Heritability of about 90 per cent is reported for:

   a. ADHD
   b. Autism
   c. Bipolar disorder
   d. Conduct disorder
   e. Depression

4. Genome-wide association studies (GWAS):

   a. Require very few participants
   b. Can estimate environmental influence
   c. Compare genetic markers within families
   d. Are the same as functional gene studies
   e. Are non-hypothesis driven

5. The common disease-common variant (CD-CV) hypothesis predicts that common disease-causing variants are:

   a. Found in people with and without the disorder
   b. Population (country) specific
   c. Found only in healthy people
   d. Found only in people with the disorder
   e. None of the above

### Key texts

Bondy B (2011) Genetics in psychiatry: are the promises met? *World Journal of Biological Psychiatry,* **12**: 81–8.

Cardno AG, Marshall EJ, Coid B et al. (1999) Heritability estimates for psychotic disorders. *Archives of General Psychiatry,* **56**: 162–8.

Folstein S, Rutter M (1977) Genetic influences and infantile autism. *Nature,* **265**: 726–8.

Mick E, Faraone S (2008) Genetics of attention deficit hyperactivity disorder. *Child and Adolescent Psychiatric Clinics of North America,* **17**: 261–84, vii–viii.

Muhle R, Trentacoste SV, Rapin I (2004) The genetics of autism. *Pediatrics,* **113**: 472–86.

Neale BM, Lasky-Su J, Anney R et al. (2008) Genome-wide association scan of attention deficit hyperactivity disorder. *American Journal of Medical Genetics. Part B. Neuropsychiatric Genetics,* **147B**: 1337–44.

# 11 Assessing paediatric and psychological development

Catherine Thompson
edited by Salvatore Rotondetto and David Daley

---

## Key concepts

- The neurocognitive processes required for normal development.
- The relevant anatomical, physiological and psychological elements of those areas.
- A comparison of these factors with the traditional task test/observational markers that are used, with validated tools, to screen for developmental delay.

---

In this chapter a framework is laid out, in order to study the development of children and so begin to understand when certain skills develop, in which order these are acquired and the neuro-anatomical, -physiological and -psychological reasons why development proceeds in this manner. The neurocognitive processes have been explained in terms of the developing brain and the physiological and anatomical methods by which cognitive abilities evolve. Understanding them in this way will then feel more valid in the context of the general assessment of a child.

This will help in understanding why many psychiatric problems present the way they do.

Fascinatingly, this pattern of development occurs not only in all children in Britain but, given adequate opportunities and circumstances, in all humans across the planet, with only small cultural variations, demonstrating that cognitive maturation cannot (in the mind of most modern scientists) be purely a learnt, behavioural phenomenon.

The developmental milestones will be listed in table format with explanations tying the cognitive processes that work in parallel to allow success in the undertaken task (**Table 11.1**).

## Cognitive functions: anatomical, physiological and psychological evolution in the first five years of life – general points with regard to child development

The relative size of different parts of a newborn baby or infant's brain is different from those of the older, more cognitively aware, child (8, 9 or 10 years of age). The brain continues to evolve beyond infancy, mainly in executive functioning, emotion and other empathic/relationship-based abilities. Different sub-divisions of the cerebral cortex and brainstem are relatively more developed than others at birth. The cerebellum, medulla and pons (brainstem areas) are roughly equivalent in volume to what they will be in the older child.

The majority of the higher cortical areas, however, are less well developed. Additionally, although these areas undergo a relatively large degree of functional maturation and specialization after birth, the number of neurones we are born with is, for the most part, all we will have and need.

Functional ability and diversity is achieved via several mechanisms. The addition of new synapses between neurones is the first stage of maturation.

Table 11.1 Motor assessment

| Age | Motor assessment |
| --- | --- |
| 6 weeks | Ventral suspension: Head level with body |
| 3 months | Ventral suspension: Head at 90°<br>Prone: Rests on forearms<br>Standing: Sags at knees |
| 6 months | Prone: On straight forearms<br>Standing: Takes weight on legs<br>Sitting: With support<br>Extras: Can roll |
| 9 months | Prone: Crawls<br>Sitting: Steadily for 10 min without support<br>Standing: Held standing bounces or stomps |
| 12 months | Stands: Pulls to stand and stands alone for a few seconds<br>Walking: Cruises |
| 15 months | Walking: Walks well |
| 18 months | Walking: Picks up toy and carries it while walking |
| 2 years | Walking: Runs<br>Stairs: Goes upstairs using two feet per step<br>Ball play: Kicks ball<br>Extras: Climbs furniture |
| 2½ years | No gross motor milestones |
| 3 years | Walking (1): Stands briefly on one foot<br>Walking (2): Pedals<br>Walking (3): Jumps<br>Stairs: Goes upstairs using one foot per step<br>Ball play: Throws a ball over arm |
| 4 years | Walking (1): Hops<br>Walking (2): Stands on foot for four seconds<br>Stairs: Goes upstairs AND downstairs using one foot per step |
| 5 years | Walking (1): Stands on one foot with his arms crossed<br>Walking (2): Tip toe walks well<br>Walking (3): Skips<br>Ball play: Bounces and catches ball |

Creation of synaptic linking of different neuronal pathways by bridging/inter-neurones allows regulation, coordination and feedback of information, e.g. with the retina of the eye, amacrine and horizontal cells collate information from several cone/rod cells and interact with bipolar and retinal ganglia cells.

Myelination of neurones improves conduction velocity, allowing the flow of information in both afferent neurones (sensory or receptor neurones which carry nerve impulses from the periphery towards the central nervous system, for example a painful stimulus carries the signal to the brain and so pain is felt) and efferent neurones (motor or effector neurones which carry messages away from the central nervous system to effectors (organs) such as glands or muscles) to be as efficient as they need to be for the higher functioning of independent adulthood.

Pruning of unwanted and redundant neural cells occurs throughout ongoing cognitive maturation. If areas of the brain are damaged due to any cause, the supporting cells of the central nervous system, variants of the glial cells from which neurones have specialized, can re-differentiate and aid the recovery of some or all of the functions rendered deficient following the insult. This is called 'plasticity' of the brain and, although far more effective and dramatic if an injury occurs in infancy or early childhood, it is thought to be responsible for recovery after acute brain injury occurring in the later years of one's life as well.

The parts of the central nervous system mentioned above, the cerebellum, medulla and pons, all contain areas with a high concentration of neural cell bodies, or nuclei, which constitute the basic relay systems required for baseline functioning, awareness and the innate reflex responses which aid the survival of the newborn child. These basic functions include such things as sleeping and waking mechanisms, eye movements, startle responses, sucking and rooting, along with swallowing, breathing and prevention of aspiration. Development post-partum during the neonatal period and early infancy is predominantly noticeable in the motor and sensory systems. Fine and gross motor development occurs in a cephalic (head) to caudal (spine/tail) direction and with the proximal musculature before the distal.

# Motor system

Development of the motor system occurs initially in the head and neck muscles followed by those in the trunk. Distinct collections of neurones are involved in carrying information from the cerebral cortex, the cerebellum and the brain stem to the different muscle groups in the peripheries. The origins, routes and resulting effects produced by the neurones in these fibre tracts tend to be relatively specific and well circumscribed. The majority of motor efferent pathways are not involved in facilitating voluntary muscle movements, but instead are involved using sensory information from the visual array, the auditory system and proprioceptive information from muscle spindles, to maintain anti-gravity movements and posture. These pathways exert reflex, instinctive and subcortical responses to stimuli and coordinate synergistic muscle groups and organ systems preventing unnecessary excess energy use.

Initially head and neck movements, followed by the axial musculature, strengthen, presumably due to their importance and regular use in the goal-directed behaviours of early infancy. Increase in muscle bulk and improved coordination of synergistic groups acting together (via spinal cord sensory and motor feedback loops) facilitates improved head, neck and truncal control.

Development of other cognitive areas (coordination, procedural memory, visuospatial awareness, executive function, emotion and reward) is required and gradually, with adequate support, exposure, play and experimentation, the fine muscles of the hands and fingers come under coordinated, strong, conscious control over the first 3–4 years of life (see **Table 11.1**).

# The basal ganglia

This is a collective term for a group of grey matter areas located inferior to the lateral ventricles and occupying the deep cortical areas around the internal capsule and the third ventricle. The basal ganglia can be split functionally into the thalamus, the striatum (caudate nucleus and the putamen), the·lateral segment of the globus pallidus and the substantia nigra together with, and lastly, the medial segment of the globus pallidus.

The basal ganglia nuclei are essential partners of the motor system. As a unit they are responsible both for preventing unwanted movements from being instigated, along with allowing the current constellation of motor signals, already occurring between the cortex and the spine, to continue to be relayed, unimpeded. The indirect pathway is

responsible for the former, the direct pathway, the latter.

The neurones that interconnect the nuclei are either excitatory (glutaminergic) or inhibitory (gabaergic) in nature and signals are facilitated by different neurotransmitters, as indicated in the parentheses. A third set of neurones, thought to have both excitatory and inhibitory function, depending on circumstances, originate in the substantia nigra and utilize dopamine as a chemical messenger. It is these neurones that degrade in Parkinson's disease and lead to the gradual onset of paucity of movement seen in these patients. L-DOPA, one of the drugs used to treat Parkinson's, is one of the breakdown products of dopamine that is metabolically active, i.e. binds to the receptors on the postsynaptic membrane of dopaminergic synapses and so exerts the same effects as dopamine itself.

The basal ganglia are also involved in some common paediatric psychiatric conditions, e.g. anxiety, depression, attention deficit hyperactivity disorder (ADHD) and dyspraxia.

# Cerebellum

The cerebellum is relatively well developed at birth when compared to the higher cerebral cortex. It receives information from various sensory organs and cognitive areas: the auditory system (vestibular nuclei and the superior olivary nucleus), the optic pathway (inferior olivary nucleus), proprioceptive feedback (spinocerebellar tract), basic autonomic information (from cranial nerve and brainstem nuclei) and higher cortical information (the planning, execution, adjustment in approach and emotional reactions to, ongoing tasks). The cerebellum, in turn, sends efferents back to all those aforementioned areas, creating essential feedback loops. This allows instigation, coordination and regulation of both reflex-based movements and higher motor pathways and combines these functions with information from vital sensory systems.

Three 'cerebellar syndromes' are regularly described and can be correlated with the lesion/damage site: Unilateral cerebellar damage (i.e. ipsilateral ataxia, dysmetria (inability to judge distance or scale), dysdiadochokinesia (inability to produce rapid alternating movements), past pointing, intention tremor and hypotonia); Medial cerebellar damage: truncal ataxia (broad uncoordinated gait but associated with intact limb coordination); The posterior cerebellar syndrome; nystagmus which is greatest when the subject is looking in the direction of the lesion. This occurs along with symptoms of brainstem compression; headaches, nausea and vomiting and dizziness, but with absence of raised intracranial pressure with papilledema.

The cerebellum is thought to be important in dysmetria, dyscalculia, dyspraxia and poor time perception, all of which are seen with more frequency in children with ADHD as well as occurring in other isolated conditions.

# The visual system

The visual system can be split into three sections: the anterior visual system, the primary visual cortex and the associative visual processing streams (the ventral/parietal and the dorsal/temporal streams).

The anterior visual system incorporates the optic globe, the retina and its histological components (rod and cone receptor cells, amacrine and horizontal cells, bipolar cells and the retinal glial cells) and up to the formation of the optic nerve.

Systemic conditions with a psychological component often have associated eye signs which can be observed with a hand-held ophthalmoscope: Kayser–Fleischer rings in Wilson's disease and retinal harmatomas in tuberous sclerosis (TS) are two examples. Both these disorders have insidious onsets and early discovery can either allow treatment to be instigated early, preventing further severe morbidity (in the case of Wilson's), or allow screening of other family members who may in time display a more severe phenotype than the index case thus identified (TS).

In the initial period of visual development the brain develops by utilizing synaptogenesis (formation of synapses), the creation of interneurones (connector neurones), and myelination resulting in the coordination of eye movements. This is synchronized via the cerebellum, using information from both gravity and head position and this finally ensures that the basic visual

information streamed to the primary visual cortex is organized in such a way that the visual array can be reproduced accurately to perceive a single image.

Information from the temporal portion of the visual field of each eye, which is projected onto the medial aspect of the retina, decussates at the optic chiasm; whereas the nasal field input remains ipsilateral when it projects to the occipital lobe. The information of the right visual field (from centre of the nose to the extremes of the right temporal field) is therefore projected to, and ultimately represented as, an inverted, spatially accurate map in the left occipital lobe. The anatomy of this is important so that if a detected developmental delay can be explained exclusively by, or is found to be associated with, defects in the visual fields, this will allow the anatomical location of a potential unifying lesion or disease process to be identified.

Finally, two long-fibre cortical pathways link the primary visual areas of the occipital lobe with the parietal and the temporal lobes. The former evaluates the visual information with regards to the spatial organization of objects. These cells do not receive information pertaining to certain aspects of the visual array, colour vision for example, or information from the fovea, as this information is obsolete with regards to their task. The cells instead are able to undertake the following: utilize binocular information and thus judge perspective and depth; evaluate the speed at which an object is moving; assess the relative relationship of separate parts of an object to the object as a whole; and analyse the interaction of multiple objects within the visual array, allowing them to be separated and their semantic category to be identified.

The temporal lobe is thought to be involved in this process of identifying objects in relation to semantic class (meaning of the word) and the young child's developing language lexicon (the internal filing system, allowing quick recall of an object's identity and vague function, incorporating this with declarative memory (explicit or factual memory) and emotional responses associated with previous encounters with such objects or situations). This facilitates further development/learning of language and other higher cerebral functions and allows quick, reflex responses to visual stimuli that might be, for example, associated with danger.

# The auditory system

The auditory system can be split into three components; the external auditory apparatus, the primary auditory cortices (I and II) and the higher cortical projections.

The fibres carrying information on tone, pitch and frequency of incoming sound waves, detected by the ear, once coded, make up the cochlear nerve. Hair cells (the histological sensory unit) are located within the central core of the cochlear apparatus, a coiled structure located in the inner ear. The direction and degree of distortion of fluid surrounding the hair cells is dependent on the frequency and intensity of the incoming sound wave, which causes the hair cells to fluctuate. This produces a responsive action potential.

Receptive hair cells located in the centre of the coiled cochlear apparatus are sensitive to sounds of low-frequency, whereas the proximal hair cells detect sounds of higher frequencies. This information is relayed to the two primary cortical areas responsible for analysis of basic sound information, auditory I and II, via the inferior colliculus and the medial geniculate nucleus of thalamus. Cells within both the thalamus and the cortical areas associated with hearing organize these inputs in such a way that they have an accurate spatial representation of the location at which the sound originated.

The vestibular nerve (the other portion of the eighth cranial nerve) carries information on gravitational movement, vibration and linear/angular acceleration of the head relative to gravity. Sensory information is again detected by a hair cell apparatus activated by fluid shifts. These shifts occur within various subdivisions of three contiguous, semicircular canals, which are located in the inner ear, superior to the cochlear apparatus. Each of these canals is orientated in a different three-dimensional plane, allowing a complete evaluation of relative orientation of the head and body.

This basic phonological information is projected to three main areas within the brainstem, to either the inferior colliculus (fibres of the cochlear portion of CN VIII) or one of the four vestibular nuclei (information for the vestibular apparatus); to the cerebellum; or to the auditory cortex via the thalamus.

Higher cortical areas receive this information for further processing via two large trans-cortical bundles; the superior longitudinal fasciculus (linking receptive and productive speech areas) and the left uncinate fasciculus (which is thought to facilitate auditory verbal memory specifically of the declarative type).

# The reticular activating system

The reticular activating system is the underlying constellation of basic cortical nuclei and a series of diffuse fibre networks that link these nuclei with key midline subcortical structures and the whole of the higher cortex. The neuronal processes involved with keeping a subject awake and alert utilize, in general, the neurotransmitter noradrenaline. Its counterpart, which is inhibitory in nature and sleep-inducing, is the anticholinergic pathway. Other associative neurotransmitter pathways exist and are further involved in this sleep–wake balance.

These pathways vary in degrees of activation and inhibition during rapid eye movement (REM) sleep versus non-REM sleep. The hypothalamus and the pineal gland are involved in further regulating the sleep–wake cycle and this involves the release of cortisol and melatonin in diurnal patterns.

The sleep–wake cycle of adults is actually 25 hours long. This adult pattern of sleep is not fully established until the age of 5–7 years and involves the cyclical variation of cortisol levels throughout the day. It is the lack of this diurnal variation in cortisol levels that results in an infant both sleeping for a much larger proportion of the day than adults and waking roughly every 4 hours requiring feeding. This is because the blood cortisol levels regulate the conversion of glucose into glycogen via the release of insulin and its breakdown, facilitated by glucagon. If an infant, prior to transition towards a more mature diurnal rhythm, is not regularly fed, hypoglycaemia can ensue.

This can occur in infants even if they do not have an underlying metabolic disorder if it is associated with other stressors on the metabolic system (illness or failure to effectively establish feeding for whatever reason). Practically, a sleep–wake cycle 25 hours in length would not lead to good sleep hygiene. The sleep wake cycle is regulated to the 24-hour mark due to the sensitivity of cortisol release to daylight and hours of darkness.

More recent examination of the diffuse cortical pathways involved in the reticular activating system has led to a distinction between fibres that project directly from the brainstem nuclei to the cortex and the fibres previously mentioned that project to the cerebral cortex via the thalamus. It appears that, although these two pathways operate separately, malfunctioning of either one of them renders the function of the other impossible.

# Gross motor development

Table 11.1 shows the age at which the majority of children, with no known disability, will achieve a task/developmental stage.

The first muscles to develop in the newborn are the muscles of the face, as they are needed for survival, followed by the muscles of the neck and shoulders.

The spinal pathways assist in the coordination of these with feedback loops and the mylination of the nerve sheaths. The muscles then become strong.

The proximal muscles in the limbs develop earlier than the distal muscles. This is probably due to the effect of gravity and postural actions and because there is a larger muscle bulk proximally.

The ability to carry out more complex tasks, such as throwing a ball or riding a tricycle, is limited by both motor factors such as coordination and voluntary control, and by other areas: the ability to see an object effectively so it can be identified; deciding why and how a particular object is to be used and in what context it should be used; the ability to track an object visually at long distances and to establish, in the visuospatial context, what the relationship of that object is to the person (the depth, location and orientation).

This has all to be assimilated before executing the motor functions that are required. These motor functions are constantly evaluated and adjusted following feedback, if necessary. This requires working memory, selective attention and procedural memory, to name but a few skills, and is therefore only seen in children beyond the age of three years or so.

The child has to be motivated to go through trial and error to try out different movements to improve and develop further skills. This will result in improvement and progressive development in the ability to carry out more than one task both simultaneously and in series. This is complex and will occur in the later pre-school years.

# Fine motor and vision

Initially, this area of development is limited before the development of binocular vision and the ability to focus on objects. From there, spatial skills, such as depth perception, can begin to be established, with the maturation of parietal cells which process basic information from the visual array (the angle of lines, intersecting lines, shadows and overlapping objects, rotation of objects) and of temporal cells (mapping: identifying objects within the visual array and linking these with nominal information being heard verbally).

The techniques used to develop visual spatial information processing, along with the coordination and use of the fine muscles of the hands, will depend on the infant's ability to see and follow objects and the development of type and strength of grip.

The ability to draw a vertical line can only occur once an infant has developed a strong and reliable pincer grip with which he can exert continuous pressure downwards onto the drawing paper. Due to the infant's ability to follow objects at first only through 90°, an infant can vertically scribble before he can produce a horizontal line.

The coordination and visuospatial ability of a toddler (eight months onwards) limits the ability of that child to copy shapes on paper. However, shape matching requires less mechanical skill and, due to the option of trial and error, less visuospatial prowess. The complexity of the shape becomes the rate limiting factor. With the development of links between the cells involved in visual spatial processing, the young child can learn to differentiate between the angles of lines and shapes. As a result, a circle can be matched before a square, which can in turn be matched before a triangle. As the strength and precise nature of the pincer grip is developed, a child can learn to draw these objects in the same consecutive sequence (circle, square then triangle).

Blocks are used initially in the assessment of fine motor ability (with coordination and basic problem-solving) in the infant/young child. Again, once a child is able to identify and orientate shapes within the visual array, he can use this and his improving cognition to build various shapes out of the blocks that are demonstrated to him by the examiner. These tests can increase in complexity depending on the age of the child.

A useful assessment tool in an older child is the 'Draw a man' test (see **Table 11.2**).

Table 11.2 Fine motor and vision

| Age | Fine motor + vision |
| --- | --- |
| 6 weeks | Fixation: Fixates on a brightly coloured object through 90° (i.e. does not cross the midline) |
| 3 months | Fixation: Fixates on a brightly coloured object through 180° (i.e. can follow the object from one extremity of lateral vision to the other across the midline) <br> Grip: Has a palmer grip of a large object, e.g. a rattle |
| 6 months | Grip (1): Palmar grasp <br> Grip (2): Puts to mouth <br> Grip (3): Transfers <br> Vision: Watches rolling ball two metres away if the object is in same horizontal plane of vision (i.e. when baby is on the floor and ball is rolled away from him) |
| 9 months | Grip: Elementary pincer grip <br> Vision: Looks for dropped toys (object permanence) <br> Blocks: Bangs two blocks together |
| 12 months | Vision: Casting <br> Blocks: Puts a block in a cup |
| 15 months | Grip: Perfected pincer grip |
| 18 months | Grip/drawing: Scribbles <br> Blocks: Tower 3–4 <br> Shape matching: Shape matches a circle <br> Extras: Turns pages of a book, given the book has thick, cardboard pages |
| 2 years | Grip/drawing (1): Copies a vertical line <br> Grip/drawing (2): Circular scribble <br> Blocks: Builds a tower of 6–7 blocks once the principle is introduced <br> Shape matching: Shape matches a circle and a square <br> Extras: Can thread large beads (normally sewing thread stools) onto string |
| 2½ years | Grip/drawing: Copies a horizontal line <br> Blocks: Copies a 'train' model using blocks after it is demonstrated |
| 3 years | Grip/drawing: Copies a circle <br> Blocks: Builds a tower of eight blocks once the principle is introduced <br> Shape matching: Shape matches a circle, square and a triangle <br> Colour matching: Matches two colours (this can be done using a specific colour matching board as with shape matching or combined with language assessment by identifying, n.b. NOT naming as will be explained later, colours from a book or using the blocks available) <br> Extras: Able to use scissors independently |
| 4 years | Grip/drawing (1): Copies a cross <br> Grip/drawing (2): Draws a man with three distinct parts <br> Blocks: Copies a 'gate' model using blocks after it is demonstrated |
| 5 years | Grip/drawing (1): Copies a square <br> Grip/drawing (1): Copies a triangle <br> Grip/drawing (2): Draws a man with six distinct parts <br> Grip/drawing (1): Writes his name on request <br> Blocks: Copies a 'three tiered step' model using blocks after it is demonstrated <br> Extras: Can thread tiny beads onto cotton thread |

# Speech and language

Language acquisition can be functionally separated into receptive and declarative language and that received via the auditory route versus the written word. There are two main schools of thought with regard to how children develop language and, from there, how the 'language explosion' (the transition from knowledge of only a few words of an 18-month-old toddler into the language ability expressed by the first-day pre-schooler on the classroom steps) occurs.

Protagonists of the empirical train of thought, such as Locke, Hume and, to a degree Piaget and Inhelder (1962), based their theories on the principle that children gain language purely by behaviourist techniques, i.e. reward-based with external stimulation. This view was radically challenged in the sixties by Chomsky's extensive publications on language theory (Chomsky, 1957). He reframed the idea of language acquisition and presented the empirical evidence found up to that point in support of his theory. This was based on the principle that an innate framework is present at birth with regard to the phonetics (sounds of human speech), semantics (study of meaning) and syntactics (principles and rules of language) of language.

This work was further expanded and discussed by others pertaining to this rationalistic view (Skinner, 1969; Pinker, 1994).

There is a pattern to developing language in the first few years, independent of the precise theory by which a child might learn language. Prior to the onset of babbling, during the first 1–4 months of life, an infant develops phonological distinctions, attempting to extract specific components of language from the overall cacophony of noise that he can hear.

There are various techniques that appear to aid a child's acquisition of language and these are universally found in all infants no matter what their language of origin. Examples of these techniques include: location of syntactic boundaries (rules of grammar), 'bootstrapping' (which involves isolating words according to their common first stem, so allowing even more words to be identified from the background noise), clustering, i.e. screening for phonological sounds that tend to occur together in different words and development of sensitivity to the prosody of language (the rhythm, intonation and related attributes of speech).

This wealth of knowledge with regard to the auditory structure of words is followed by the onset of babbling. It has not been established whether babbling plays a vital role in developing speech and therefore whether the structure of babbling should be more carefully examined.

Evidence for the role of babbling in language development comes from the observation that babbling is seen in deaf children who have been exposed to sign language in infancy. However, supporters of the view that babbling is essential would agree that, for this theory to be fully substantiated, babbling should include all the common phonological stems that are required for an infant to develop language in any culture. This has not been found to be the case. Other reasons for a child babbling may be to improve motor coordination of the fine muscles in the face, larynx and pharynx or to help develop the prosody of language.

After a period of babbling and then a possible, depending on differing theories, time with paucity of sound, the infant begins to use other new sounds and then begins by trial and error to form words.

During this production of early speech, infants and toddlers seem to make errors and these errors can be seen to occur in regular predictable formats, both within a single child's speech development and between subjects. A further issue at this time is the semantic development of language. This has been extensively investigated and the methods by which the young child links the sound of the word to its underlying meaning, shape and use are generally grouped under 'mapping'.

A child will use different techniques to overcome the mapping problem: a mixture of using the grammatical (in the linguistic sense, not in the educational sense) rules of language, grouping objects according to different factors, as well as using non-verbal social cues to understand how his carer is using language in an interaction in order for him to learn to assign meaning. Once the rules of semantic association (how a child builds a cognitive template with which he can combine his limited knowledge of language into a limitless productive method of communication and description) has been overcome, there follows the 'language explosion', which occurs at around two years of age.

The next stage of language development is syntactic development (the rules of language) and this depends on the following factors: a child's underlying cognitive ability and exposure to language; a child's emotional development and the development of theory of mind (the understanding that others exist independently of oneself and that actions have consequences on others' emotions and actions) and the ability to problem solve and executively function (see **Table 11.3**).

# Emotion

Emotion is a complex phenomenon to both try to visualize and to investigate. This makes it difficult to create a mechanism in one's head by which emotion may be organized anatomically and work in a functional manner. How emotion may then be altered by disease processes (those both frankly organic and those with more diffuse features, as in psychiatric/psychological origin) is a problem and this is true for all cerebral functions that are deemed 'higher' in origin. This is further exacerbated by the need to understand what a child's innate emotional functioning might be, especially in the context of the rapid development in the first few years and how this might be affected by outside influences.

There are several cognitive processes that need to be developed during the early years before an identifiable, organized and consistent emotional self-profile can be established. Such processes are: long-term declarative (mainly episodic) memory; an understanding that one is a separate being from others, and that one's actions have consequences on the other ('theory of mind'); key executive function abilities, along with selective attention and inhibition, allowing a child to make informed consistent judgements; and a development of the autonomic system to produce physiological response to emotional states.

We know that damage to the limbic system (head of the caudate nucleus, anterior cingulate gyrus, the amygdala, and ventral and dorsolateral aspects of the frontal lobe) and also to some long-fibre bundles linking areas of basic and higher cognitive functions, can result in symptoms such as hallucinations, hypersexuality and general dysinhibition.

Depending on the exact location of damage to the limbic or other midline subcortical regions, emotional disturbance can take the form of two opposite syndromes of abnormal emotional

Table 11.3 Speech and language

| Age | Speech and language |
|---|---|
| 6 weeks | Response to sound: Stills to sound |
| 3 months | Response to sound: Turns if on level with ear |
| 6 months | Response to sound: Looks to parents' voice<br>Vocalization: Babbles (consonants) |
| 9 months | Response to sound: Distraction test<br>Language use: Two syllable babble<br>Language comprehension: 'No' |
| 12 months | Words: Has 1–2 words<br>Extras: Object recognition – use brush to brush |
| 15 months | Words (1): Has several words<br>Language use (1): Jabbering<br>Language use (2): Echolalia |
| 18 months | Words (1): Has 10–20 words<br>Words (2): Understands up to 50 words<br>Words (3): Picture card: IDs one (where is the...)<br>Body parts: Two body parts<br>Commands: 1 step command |
| 2 years | Words (1): Understands up to 50 words<br>Words (2): Picture card: IDs 5 (where is the)<br>Words (3): Names 3 (what is this)<br>Language use (1): Two word sentences<br>Language use (2): Understands fx of verbs<br>Body parts: 5–6 body parts<br>Commands: 2 step command |
| 2½ years | Words (1): Picture card: IDs 7 (where is the)<br>Words (2): Names 5 (what is this) |
| 3 years | Words: Names 8 (what is this)<br>Language use (1): Talks in sentences 3–4 words<br>Language use (2): Name, age, sex on request<br>Language use (3): Pronouns and plurals<br>Colours: Knows some colours |
| 4 years | Language use (1): Counts to 10<br>Language use (2): Tells stories<br>Language use (3): Past tense<br>Colours: IDs several colours |
| 5 years | Language use (1): Prepositions<br>Language use (2): Opposites<br>Language use (3): Definitions e.g. banana<br>Language use (4): Size adjectives<br>Commands: 3 Step command<br>Language comprehension: What do you do if cold, hungry, thirsty |

response. First, a syndrome of complete absence of emotion and second, a higher autonomic and higher emotional responses in certain situations than would be expected. This latter overstimulated emotional system, seemingly without awareness of the consequences, is seen in some congenital disorders and the underlying pathology is presumably similar in some psychiatric diseases in which patients show similar extremes of positive emotional behaviour. Examples include William's syndrome, Noonan syndrome, TS, early childhood autism (before more diagnostic features, such as failure to acquire language become apparent), storage diseases such as abnormal glycogen metabolism or heavy metal poisoning, temporal or frontal lobe epilepsy, mood disorders, ADHD, fetal alcohol syndrome, post-radiotherapy effects and substance abuse.

The alternate mood state that can be induced by acquired or inherited disease is a flat, unresponsive, unemotive affect. This can occur in Beckwith–Wiedemann syndrome, hypothyroidism or severe depression from primary or secondary causes.

# Memory

Memory, learning and attention, along with executive functioning, are functions that are heavily dependent on each other.

In order to lay down information in the brain ('encode' information), organize it into a format ('storage') which allows for retrieval of that content at a later date in the appropriate situation and in an efficient, timely manner, some sort of rehearsal process is thought to be required. This allows processing of the relevant information including the frank identification of what a person is experiencing along with relevant contextual information that will give markers as to when that information may be needed in situations to come. Various theories into how a 'working memory' system may be structured have been postulated. The most prominent of these involves an internal 'auditory loop', whereby one repeats the sounding of the things to be remembered continuously in their head until it is fully processed. This is part of the Baddeley and Hitch model of working memory (Baddeley and Hitch, 1974). These authors have more recently added an additional arm to their theory explaining a method by which information

presented in the visual array, the 'visuo-spatial sketch pad', may be kept active. Once fully processed and identified, this information, of whatever type or source, needs to be held in some sort of temporary store until the information can be adapted and organized to allow it to be incorporated into events in the future.

The function and neuropsychological testing of memory hypotheses are two-fold: is memory capacity finite or non-finite and is it domain or non-domain specific (procedural versus declarative memory for example)? This is often investigated in normal subjects or those who can all be said to have memory deficits of a similar nature. Dual task methods are often the experimental set-up of choice. This involves the presentation of auditory or visual stimuli to one side of the brain or other in isolation, often using either the left or the right visual or auditory systems. Distracter stimuli of different modalities are added to limit the capacity of primary/short/working memory or long-term memory depending on which aspect is being explored. Work has also been undertaken in patients with split brain syndromes (a surgical technique that was used as a treatment for intractable epilepsy in the past) and those with certain anatomical abnormalities in areas considered to be fundamental to normal memory function.

Long-term memory is thought to be more a diffuse function that has been covered within the relevant sections: language, emotion, attention and executive functioning. The anatomical structures involved in memory tend to be located in the midline of the brain; these include the hippocampus and the amygdala which are located below the level of the lateral horns of the main brain ventricles and are associated with the caudate nucleus, a semi-circular structure following the contours of those fluid spaces. Damage to these structures, to adjacent fibre networks or long-term changes in the synaptic links between neurones in these brain areas are thought to cause functional impairment to both memory and associated functions such as learning and emotional response.

# Executive functioning

Executive functioning has been studied extensively and was one of the first interests of neurologists, anatomists, surgeons and psychiatrists. Early work was mainly based on patients with acquired anatomical lesions secondary to injury and the resultant symptoms and disability that were found.

As a result of this research, many of the functions that were initially believed to be controlled by the frontal lobe, including problem-solving, planning and organization, selective attention, working memory, ability to set shift, are now thought to be better described as being the product of assimilation and organization of projected information to the

frontal lobe from associated centres of cognitive function. However, it is likely that the frontal lobe does play a significant role in facilitating these so-called higher cognitive functions.

## Attention

The flowchart below outlines the main points of investigations and debate within the field of attention and related cortical processes.

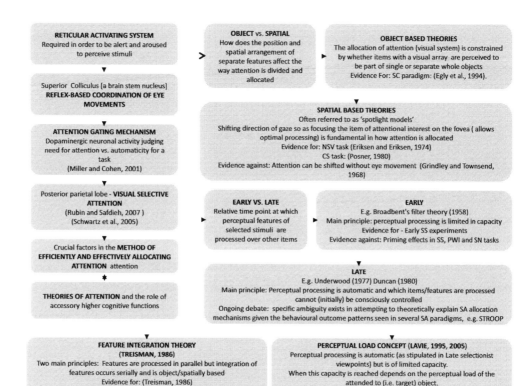

SC, Spatial Cuing Paradigm; SS, Selective Shadowing Tasks; NSV, Non-search (visual) tasks; CS, Choice Spatial Task; VS, Visual Search Paradigms; RCP, Response Competition Paradigm.

### Key texts

Baddeley A, Hitch G (1974) Working memory. In: Bower GA (ed.) *Recent advances in learning and motivation*, vol. 8. New York: Academic Press, 47–60.

Beattie M (2006) *Essential Revision Notes in Paediatrics for the MRCPCH*, 2nd edn. Cheshire: PASTEST Ltd.

Bee HL (1994) *Lifespan Development*. New York, NY, US: HarperCollins College Publishers.

Chomsky N (1957) *Syntactic Structures*. The Hague: Mouton.

Gazzaniga MS, Ivry RB, Magnum GR (1998) *Cognitive Neuroscience: The Biology of the Mind*. New York: W.W. Norton, 1998.

Harley T (2001) *The Psychology of Language: From Data to Theory*. Taylor and Francis Group.

Piaget J, Inhelder B (1962) *The Psychology of the Child*. New York: Basic Books.

# 12 Emotional development and attachment
### Carlos Hoyos and Christopher Gale

## Key concepts

- Three key theoretical approaches to understanding emotions are psychodynamic, attachment and emotional literacy.
- Central to the psychoanalytic approach to understanding emotions are the concepts of transference and counter-transference.
- Central to attachment theory is the concept of the 'secure base' provided for a child by their primary caregiver (usually the mother). This enables a child to explore the world with confidence, but know that he can seek comfort and safety in times of perceived danger or anxiety.
- There are four broad patterns of attachment in infants and children: secure, insecure/avoidant, insecure ambivalent and disorganized/disorientated. They broadly correspond to attachment representations in adolescence and adulthood. Only disorganized attachment predicts mental health problems. Insecure attachment does not. This is a common misconception that we should not propagate further.
- Emotional literacy is a concept used by education professionals to describe the ability to perceive, interpret, label and communicate appropriately an individual's emotions.

## Introduction

The term 'emotion' is generally used to describe mental states that involve feelings, the psychological and physiological changes that these produce, and sometimes the behaviour that accompanies them. Despite large amounts of empirical research, it is difficult to add to this definition without stepping into controversy. Emotional experiences have also been described as 'agitations' or 'disturbances' of the mind, and as cognitive states that arise by association of stimulus, without the participation of rational thought. Indeed, the expression 'absence of rational thought', is used sometimes as a shortcut for emotions. While it takes months for a rational mind to be recognizable in infants, and many years for it to develop fully, it is clear that emotions are a very substantial part of babies, infants and children's mental experience from the moment of birth. It could be argued that rational thought is only possible once the child is able to have some mastery over emotional responses.

## Theories of emotion

There is no unified theory of emotional development; however, this chapter will introduce some concepts and insights produced by three theoretical approaches that have contributed to how current clinicians understand emotions: psychodynamic, attachment theory and emotional literacy. Before exploring these three theories, it is important to mention some other approaches that have laid the foundations and contributed to the establishment of those three approaches.

1. *Eysenck's concepts of 'extraversion' (E) and 'neuroticism' (N)*, originally developed as personality constructs, have been used to explain differences in individuals' emotional make-up. The reason why some infants would show markedly increased expression of negative emotions would be explained in terms of them having a different N score, i.e. a personality difference and therefore, constitutional (see Eysenck and Sybil, 1964).
2. *Learning theory and classic conditioning*

has also contributed to the understanding of emotions. It is possible to classically condition fear responses, and this offers some insight into the nature of fear. However, classic conditioning has proved to be an inadequate model to explain general fear acquisition, not to mention other emotional responses (see Anderson, 2000).

3. *Seligman's construct of 'learned helplessness'* provided some understanding on how a 'cognitive set', engendered by an individual's lack of control over trauma, mediated its emotional response; somehow anticipating the concept of 'internal working model' later developed by Bowlby (1969). Other authors studying cognitive processes emphasized the influence that these have on emotions, often linking emotional developmental milestones to the acquisition of cognitive abilities. Two examples of this are Piaget's understanding of 'primary decentralization' and Kagan's description of the change in an infant's fear of strangers as an 'unassimilated discrepant event' (see Abramson et al., 1978).

# Psychoanalytic theories

Psychoanalytical theory has explicitly made emotions its main concern. It has provided a series of conceptual frameworks and descriptions of emotional processes that have permeated into many other areas of psychology, clinical work and even popular culture. Most of these concepts have proved difficult to verify in empirical research and often are clearly incompatible with neurobiological findings. Nonetheless, they now form part of the vocabulary of most child mental health professionals and their role in shaping other theories, such as attachment, is evident.

Freud is considered to be the father of psychoanalysis. Central to his understanding of emotions was the idea that emotions derive from the mental energy produced by the interactions between conflicting wishes arising from the instinctual search for pleasure ('drive theory'), and that this energy can transform and manifest itself in many emotional and behavioural guises, including somatic symptoms ('hydraulic model'). Although this concept is contrary to current neuroscience

(that does not entertain the idea of any mental energy other than action potentials), many useful terms that are used to refer to emotional experiences derive from it. Familiar expressions such as 'emotional conflict' or 'somatic conversion' are examples of how the hydraulic model of emotions underpins everyday language about emotions.

Arguably, the most important contribution of Freud to our current understanding of emotions, are the ideas of transference and counter-transference:

- *Transference* – intense emotions expressed during a consultation and perceived by the patient as being inspired by the clinician were pre-existing emotional experiences directed, or caused by, other characters in the patient's life that had subconsciously been attributed to the clinician.
- *Counter-transference* – the redirection of the clinician's feelings towards the patient, or possibly their emotional entanglement with the patient.

Freud later made transference and counter-transference the cornerstone of his psychoanalytic technique and they became a crucial part of many derived therapeutic approaches popular in child mental health, such as art therapy and play therapy. Transference and counter-transference is discussed further in Chapter 68, Child psychotherapy.

One of the applications of the concepts of transference and counter-transference is its use in the close observation of mothers and babies. If the premise that all communication between mothers and babies of this kind is accepted, it follows that the emotional states of mothers, in close and intimate relation with their babies, are partly the result of the baby's own emotional states. This concept has been very useful to the development of attachment theory.

# Attachment theories

*We are, all of us, moulded and remoulded by those who have loved us, and though that love may pass, we remain nonetheless their work – a work that very likely they do not recognize, and which is never exactly what they intended.*

**(Francois Mauriac, 1952)**

Attachment theories refer to a constellation of ideas about emotional development that emphasize the importance of the mother–infant relationship. This theoretical framework, unlike the previous, has proved susceptible to empirical experimentation, and this has permitted its development within mainstream scientific parameters. It has illuminated several aspects of early emotional development namely, how emotions are socialized, how they are expressed and how communication of emotions is made acceptable.

The main premise of attachment theory is that the bond between mother and infant is biologically determined and forms the psychological umbilical cord by which children develop, both physically and psychologically. It proposes that the quality of this relationship and its subsequent influence on the social and emotional development of the child is determined by:

- temperamental factors in the child;
- the mother/primary caregiver's own experience of attachment;
- the circumstances in which it develops.

John Bowlby is generally credited as the father of attachment theory. His work during the 1950s and 1960s (Bowlby, 1969), and his collaborations with Mary Ainsworth and other authors, form the founding premises of what has come to be known as attachment theory. However, his ideas build on some fundamental insights provided by experimental observations carried out before him (Harlow and Zimmermann, 1959; Lorenz, 1979).

## Harlow's monkeys

One such experiment was performed by Harry Harlow in Wisconsin (Harlow and Zimmermann, 1959). Harlow set out to disprove that infant behaviour was the product of learning. He isolated infant monkeys from their mothers at 6–12 hours after birth, and placed them with substitute or 'surrogate' mothers, made either of heavy wire or of wood covered with soft terry cloth. In the most famous experiment, both types of surrogates were present in the cage, but only one was equipped with a nipple from which the infant could feed. Even when the wire mother was the source of nourishment, the infant monkeys spent a greater amount of time clinging to the cloth surrogate, therefore proving that infant behaviour is instinctive. The most interesting finding, however, was to happen a few years later, when surrogate-raised monkeys became bizarre later in life. They engaged in stereotyped behaviour patterns, such as clutching themselves and rocking constantly back and forth; they exhibited excessive and misdirected aggression and were incapable of caring for their own infants. Thus showing that maternal behaviour is not instinctive, but learned in early infancy.

## Lorenz's filial geese

The second of these experiments was Konrad Lorenz's demonstrations of filial imprinting in geese at the turn of the century (Lorenz, 1979). He demonstrated that there was a short period (35 hours) after hatching when chick geese bred in an incubator would select an object and follow it around. The importance of this experiment for Bowlby was that it emphasized the idea of critical periods in development and a biologically determined proximity-seeking behaviour.

Bowlby then proceeded to describe the stages of separation: protest, despair and denial, and set the ground for Mary Ainsworth's experiments in the strange situation (Ainsworth et al., 1978). It produced the empirical foundation for one of attachment's most powerful concepts: secure and insecure attachment.

## The strange situation and categories of infant attachment

Mary Ainsworth and colleagues (Ainsworth et al., 1978) described three main patterns of attachment

> ## Key concepts from Bowlby's attachment theory
>
> - *Attachment behaviour*: any behaviour by the infant that had the effect of increasing the proximity to his/her carer.
> - *The attachment behaviour system*: the repertoire of attachment behaviours and the decision-making process which identified what behaviour was more effective in different circumstances. This decision-making process involves some level of cognition and some degree of representation of the external world and he named this the 'internal working model'.
> - *The emotional bond*: entails a representation in the internal organization of the individual that is persistent, specific, significant and where there is distress and a wish for contact when separated.
> - *The attachment bond*: as the emotional bond that is activated when the infant is in distress or under threat. A child's attachment figure is that person to whom he/she runs, when under threat.

in their observations of infant children in the 'strange situation test'. They were:

- Secure attachment: When a child is securely attached, the mother provides a safe base from which the child is able to explore and the child is readily comforted, if distressed. When reunited with his mother, the distressed child will immediately seek and maintain comfort.
- Insecure/avoidant attachment: A child with this pattern of attachment has no confidence that his caregiver will respond helpfully and, in fact, expects to be rebuffed. He will happily explore away from his mother and is unduly friendly with strangers. When reunited with his mother, the child will ignore or avoid her.
- Insecure/resistant attachment: The child who shows this pattern of attachment is unsure

whether his mother's response will be available or helpful and he is therefore uncertain about exploring and wary of new situations and people. He will be prone to separation anxiety and appear clingy. When reunited after separation he may be aggressive, angry and refuse to be comforted.

A further pattern has subsequently been recognized (Bretherton,1985):

- Disorganized/disorientated attachment: These children seem confused and show stereotypes and, when reunited with their mothers, seem to show conflicting feelings of fear, anger and a wish to be with her. Children in this category may also display behaviours that would fit within the other two categories of disordered attachment (avoidant and resistant).

## Attachment disorders

The ICD-10 (WHO, 1992) outlines the diagnostic criteria for only two specific disorders of attachment:

| Reactive attachment disorders with inhibition of attachment behaviour (F94.1) | Reactive attachment disorders with disinhibition of attachment (F94.2) |
|---|---|
| The capacity of these children to attach with adults is described as very inhibited | Children show a diffuse, non-selectively focused attachment behaviour: attention-seeking and indiscriminately friendly behaviour; poorly modulated peer interactions; depending on circumstances there may also be emotional or behavioural disturbance |
| They react with ambivalence and fear to the attachment figure | Children with a disinhibited propensity seek contact without boundaries with the most varied caregivers |
| They exhibit an emotional disorder with withdrawal, over-caution, and impairment in their capacity for social play | |

Brisch (2002) describes other types of attachment disorders that supplement those described in the diagnostic manuals. They are:

Type I: Little or no overt attachment – no protest on separation, even in very threatening situations.

Type IIa: Undifferentiated – similar to F94.2 – lack of preference for a particular attachment figure.

Type IIb: Risky behaviour – seeks out dangerous situations to force others into care-giving behaviours.

Type III: Excessive clinging – fear of separation or loss of attachment figure is generalized, with a constant need for closeness and physical contact.

Type IV: Inhibited attachment behaviour – similar to F94.1 – manifests in over-conforming behaviour, frequently as a result of domestic violence. Children more fearful of exploring their surroundings.

Type V: Aggressive form of attachment behaviour – aggression a result of frequent rejection by attachment figure.

Type VI: Role reversal – child serves as a secure emotional base for their parents, so gets little or no useful help in threatening situations.

Type VII: Attachment disorder with psychosomatic symptoms – i.e. bed-wetting, eating problems or sleep disorder.

# Attachment in children with learning disabilities or high on the autistic spectrum

Attachments fail to form in young autistic children, but the presentation is different to the failed attachment shown in otherwise normal children. Autistic children show no interest in other people and will often show an apparent attachment to an inanimate (usually non-cuddly) object or collection. A similar picture may present in children with severe learning difficulties.

# Attachment representations in older adolescence and adulthood

The last important research tool that needs to be mentioned in any attachment primer is the Adult Attachment Interview (AAI – Main et al., 2002). This tool asks adults to make a list of characteristics of important figures in their childhood, and examines their capacity to construct a narrative around the details that are given. The adult attachment status elicited from the AAI can be useful when working with older adolescents and the categories respond to those identified by the Strange Situation test:

*Autonomous (secure)* – the narrative is coherent and collaborative. The individual is neither derogatory nor angry towards parents, understanding the value of attachment relationships in the past and their influence on present relationships. Within close relationships they experience relative ease in becoming close to others and being dependent and depended upon. They are less worried about abandonment or someone becoming too emotionally close to them.

*Dismissive (anxious/avoidant)* – there are minimal explanations and no narrative is constructed. These individuals will most likely have been emotionally and/or physically rejected and/or neglected during childhood, but work hard to present an idealized view of parents/carers. They dismiss value of childhood attachment relationships and avoid discussion on a range of strong emotions (fear, anger, disappointment, hurt and loneliness). They will minimize the importance of any current difficulties and present as invulnerable. Within relationships they are uncomfortable being close to others and being interdependent; partners will often want them to be more intimate.

*Preoccupied (anxious/ambivalent)* – driven by the memories. The individual is often angry and confused about their childhood relationships with parents/carers. They value the importance of attachments, but narrating the past can be painful and involving. Anger within close relationships is seen as the least painful, most self-protective way to cope. However, they often want to emotionally merge with others completely, but find that others are reluctant to become as close as they would like and will sometimes be scared away. The preoccupied adolescent/adult will often worry that their partner does not love them or will not want to stay with them.

*Unresolved (disorganized/disorientated)* – grieving loss or trauma of childhood – not yet 'in the past'. Those who have been subjected to significant levels of abuse and/or neglect at the hands of parents/carers will often feel unreasonably responsible in some way for the loss or trauma they have experienced. For the unresolved individual there is no consistent pattern for dealing with stress, arising from a failure to integrate thoughts and feelings – essentially they have no internal working model. As a result they can possibly become violent and aggressive within any close relationships they manage to form, being extremely sensitive to criticism or implied humiliation, but insensitive to others' feelings. Having no trust or respect for the feelings of others and systems of authority, the unresolved individual is likely to become involved in the criminal justice system.

Status in the AAI and strange situation gives an indication of the nature of the person's 'internal working model'. This is very important when considering the risk and resilience around the development of mental health problems in later life.

- Secure/autonomous attachments indicate a perception of the main carer and later close others as responsive and assume that expressing emotions brings on a helpful response.
- Anxious avoidant and ambivalent indicates a perception of the main carer as unresponsive and an assumption that expressing emotions does not necessarily bring comfort or help. Therefore emotions are best dealt with internally, which may increase the risk of internalizing mental health issues, such as depression, anxiety, deliberate self-harm and eating disorders.
- Unresolved indicates an absence of an internal working model, as the main carer did not give a consistent response. As there can be no underlying assumption as to how expressed emotions will be responded to, there is no consistent way to deal with emotions. This may increase the risk of the development of anxiety, substance misuse and emerging personality disorders.

It is important to highlight that while attachment representations may increase or decrease the risk of developing mental health problems, it is by no means the only contributory factor, and therefore should not be the sole basis for diagnosis of mental disorder.

# Intergenerational transmission of attachment

The research literature around the transmission of attachment representations appears to indicate that if there is at least one autonomous parent/carer in the family unit, they will nurture securely attached children. However, with insecurely attached adults the transmissional pattern can be more complex and not necessarily corresponding (Crittenden, 2008; Shah et al., 2010). A dismissing parent/carer may evoke an intense ambivalent response in the child in order to increase the probability of caregiver response or reduce caregiver control. Conversely, a preoccupied parent/carer may employ angry or helpless demands, so the child may employ a strategy of caring for or complying with the caregiver (avoidant).

# Summary of attachment

Attachment theory has contributed greatly to our understanding of emotional development, providing important conceptual tools that have, and hopefully will continue to, make the study of emotional phenomena accessible to empirical research. It has also placed the understanding of emotions by themselves on the research agenda.

# Emotional literacy

Emotional literacy is the ability to recognize, understand, handle and appropriately express emotions. It is neither a theory nor a body of research that has contributed to our knowledge of emotions. It is essentially a code word that defines emotional development in educational terms. In doing so, the development of the ability to perceive, interpret, label and communicate appropriately an individual's emotions places emotions away from a biological and sociological arena and into a social and educational context. The educational system has significant potential to help children in this respect and it is crucial that health professionals work with colleagues in education services. (Emotional literacy is reviewed in greater depth in Chapter 13, Emotional well-being and literacy).

# Summary

Emotions are complex psychological phenomena that form a very important part of children and young people's mental experience. Although in the past emotions were seen mainly as secondary phenomena, only worthy of study when they interfered with other aspects of life, or when it was necessary to control negative ones, the interest started by psychoanalysis and the advances made by attachment theory have made their study an important subject. The understanding of emotions in children will always need to take a developmental perspective, but the involvement of educationalists holds great promise.

## Case study: Michael

Michael is a 16 year old referred to the comprehensive Child and Adolescent Mental Health Service (CAMHS) by his Youth Offending Team (YOT) worker (drug-related offences) because of acute episodes of anxiety and hearing voices.

Michael attended the assessment with his YOT worker. He reported a history of physical abuse and neglect under the care of his mother, who had recently asked him to leave home. Michael is the eldest of four siblings and considered them to have been treated better than him.

Michael reported a history of difficulties with his peer group and had no close friends, which he attributed to outbursts of anger. His education history was sporadic, with a number of exclusions from secondary school and attendance at a Pupil Referral Unit.

Michael's 'voices' were attributed to his acute anxiety about being out of the house, fearing that he would be assaulted by other young people. He moved about, staying on floors in 'safe' places, which included wider family members and casual friends.

At the assessment Michael presented as hostile and demanding, stating that medication would be the only way he could be helped. He was mistrusting of those conducting the assessment, asking why they were asking the questions they were and who would the information be shared with.

### Formulation

From an attachment perspective Michael would appear to fit within the unresolved (disorganized/ disorientated) category of adult attachment representation (with some evidence of ambivalent/ preoccupied representation), for the following reasons:
- reported physical abuse and neglect by his mother;
- history of difficulties within peer relationships, due to anger/aggression;
- poor engagement in education;
- involvement in the criminal justice system;
- mistrustful, hostile and demanding in the assessment session.

Michael desires to 'feel safe', which would be afforded him within a close and trusting relationship, but his behaviour resulting from an inability to form an internal working model means that he often alienates others.

From a transference/counter-transference perspective Michael may display his intense anger/ hostility with the CAMHS clinicians (and others before) as a way of projecting the anger/distress he has experienced at the hands of adults throughout his life. For any CAMHS clinician it may be very hard to 'like' Michael when he is presenting in this hostile and demanding way; the counter-transference that takes place here would be important to recognize, as it will give the clinician an insight into how others respond to Michael and how he feels about himself.

## Working with Michael

When trying to engage therapeutically with a young person such as Michael, the following would be important to consider:

- It may take a long time to properly engage with the young person before any formal therapeutic work could take place. Michael will most likely anticipate, consciously or not, that the clinician/therapist will abandon and/or reject him at some stage. Therefore, his own behaviours may be very hostile and dismissive regarding the work being done within sessions (and the clinician's competence).
- Michael's basic needs will have to be met first in order to increase his sense of safety, i.e. securing permanent accommodation.
- As such, it is important from the beginning to set the boundaries around where, when and how often sessions would take place, in order to provide a sense of containment within the relationship.
- Any future sessions missed through clinician annual leave or training would need to be discussed well in advance, so that Michael is able to grasp that this is not abandonment or rejection.
- If any sessions are cancelled by the clinician due to unforeseen circumstances, he should expect a level of hostility or lack of engagement by Michael in response (punishment).
- As Michael's contact with the YOT is likely to be time limited if he does not commit any further petty crime, the clinician may become the 'secure base' for Michael. As long as professional boundaries are maintained, this can be healthy within the therapeutic relationship, as in the longer term it would be the launch pad from which Michael could test out alternative, more positive approaches within his social relationships.
- The ending of any work with Michael should be planned well in advance, for the reasons already cited here.

## Multiple choice questions

1. What is transference from the psychoanalytical perspective?

   a. Intense emotions expressed during a session and perceived by the patient as inspired by the clinician, but actually are pre-existing emotional experiences directed, or caused by, other characters in the patient's life.
   b. Intense emotions expressed during a consultation and perceived by the patient as inspired by the clinician, who is projecting his own experiences of working with similar patients in the past.
   c. A deliberate approach adopted by the clinician to elicit intense emotions in the patient during a session, in order to understand where the underlying feels originated.
   d. The redirection of the clinician's feelings towards the patient, or possibly their emotional entanglement with the patient.

2. Which of the following is *not* an attachment pattern/representation?

   a. Secure/autonomous
   b. Insecure avoidant/dismissive
   c. Role reversal/rescuer
   d. Disorganized/unresolved

### Key texts

Allen JP, Land D (1999) Attachment in adolescence. In: Cassidy J, Shaver PR (eds). *Handbook of Attachment: Theory, Research, and Clinical Applications.* New York and London: Guilford Press, 319–35.

Crittenden P (2008) *Raising Parents: Attachment, Parenting and Child Safety.* Cullompton, UK: Willan Publishing.

Gerhardt S (2004) *Why Love Matters: How affection shapes a baby's brain.* London and New York: Routledge.

# *Emotional wellbeing and literacy*

**Tania Morris and Helena Hoyos**

# *Developing a child's emotional wellbeing and emotional competence*

## Tania Morris

Studies suggest that the development of emotional wellbeing has many benefits, in that it can improve a child's life chances by positively impacting on his or her learning abilities, therefore improving his or her educational and career success (Weare and Gray, 2003). In addition, it can positively influence a child's motivation, behaviour and self-esteem (Coughlan, 2010). Studies suggest that the development of emotional wellbeing can reduce the potential for mental health problems such as anxiety, eating disorders, self-harming behaviours and depression (Weare and Gray, 2003).

---

### Key concepts

- *Emotional competence*: described as the essential social skill to recognize, interpret and respond constructively to emotions in yourself and others.
- *Emotional regulation*: so far there is no one agreed upon definition of the term 'emotion regulation'. Many researchers define emotion regulation as the ability to enhance or reduce emotions as needed.
- *Emotional resilience*: the positive capacity of people to cope with stress and adversity. This coping may result in the individual 'bouncing back' to a previous state of normal functioning despite adversity or difficulty.
- *Emotional intelligence*: a self-perceived ability to identify, assess and control the emotions of oneself, of others and of groups.

---

How to promote emotional wellbeing is especially important when the numbers of children presenting with mental health difficulties continues to rise (Unicef, 2007). Strong evidence such as this is why modern-day policy, such as *Every Child Matters and National Healthy Schools Status*, emphasizes the importance of all agencies involved in working with children play their part in promoting a child's emotional wellbeing. Terms such as, *emotional intelligence, emotional resilience, emotional regulation* and *emotional literacy* are now common terminology used by a wide array of professionals working in fields such as child health care and education and all relate to aspects of *emotional competence*.

It is important to understand that the terms cannot be used interchangeably: they have their own meanings and emphasis and by better understanding the concepts and theory that underpin these terms, the helping professionals can glean important knowledge that can aid them to help a child develop his or her emotional wellbeing and competence.

Emotions are complex subjective phenomena; a state of mind that involves complex feelings. Emotions motivate our behaviour and are often evoked or stimulated by a combination of factors; what is going on externally to the person (in their environment) and what it going on internally inside their body and the biochemical influences on the brain. Emotions are commonly associated with mood, temperament and personality disposition.

Understanding and exploring the phenomena of emotion is complex and many theories related to emotion exist from neurological emotional theories, based on the discoveries made through neural mapping to the emotional centre of the brain, the limbic system.

Understanding and exploring the phenomena of emotion is complex and many theories related to emotion exist from neurological emotional theories, based on the discoveries made through neural mapping to the emotional centre of the brain and the limbic system, to cognitive emotional theories, examples of which are the Cannon-Bard theory, which suggests that emotions lead to physiological changes and the James Lange theory, which is a somatic emotional theory, which argues the opposite, that physiological changes lead to emotion. It is not within the scope of this chapter to write about all the emotional theories.

However, what will be summarized are two theories that are closely linked with the promotion of emotional wellbeing and competence, namely emotional intelligence and emotional resilience.

Notably these theories underpin the interventions our schools commonly use to promote pupil emotional wellbeing in our schools, interventions such as restorative Justice Programmes, Social, Emotional, Aspects of Learning (SEAL) programmes, and nurture groups in primary schools.

# Emotional intelligence theory and Goleman's four-quadrant model

The majority of us are familiar with the term intellectual intelligence or IQ which can be defined as cognitive skills of perception, analysis, synthesis, reasoning, intuition, imagination, judgement and decision making, but are less familiar with the concept of emotional intelligence (EI). Notably it is a relatively new area of psychological research and is derived from the notion that was proposed by Howard Gardner back in the 1970s; that there are multiple intelligences. Gardner identified seven intelligences: linguistic, logical-mathematical, musical, bodily-kinesthetic, spatial, interpersonal intelligence and intrapersonal intelligence. It was not until the 1990s that the concept of emotional intelligence was brought to the forefront, when Mayer and Salovey published their seminal paper on *Emotional Intelligence* defining it as 'the ability to monitor one's own and other's feelings and emotions and to use this information to guide one's thinking and action' (Mayer and Salovey, 1997). They broke down emotional intelligence into four parts: identifying emotions, understanding emotions, using emotions and managing emotions.

In 1995, Daniel Goleman published a book entitled 'emotional intelligence' which highlighted research suggesting that emotional intelligence determines more than 80 per cent of an individual's success and is an ability to recognize and regulate emotions in the self and others (Goleman, 1995). It is a direct derivative of emotional wellbeing and emotional competence and what is important is that it is a learned capability. Goleman suggested that emotional competence is one's self-knowledge, self-awareness, social sensitivity, empathy, self-confidence, self-control and ability to listen successfully. It is a sense of timing and social appropriateness, with the possession of positive attitude. It is having the courage to acknowledge weaknesses and express and respect differences. Goleman proposed the four-quadrant model (see **Figure 13.1**).

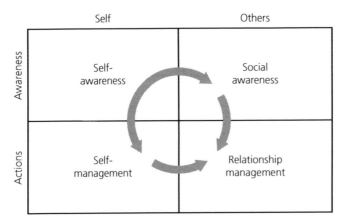

Figure 13.1 Daniel Goleman uses the following four-quadrant model to define the skills and behaviours needed for the development of emotional intelligence; this model suggests that one's emotion intelligence stems from a good self-awareness, a social sensitivity and self-confidence, and an ability to regulate and control one's emotions in order to display a social appropriateness, and a positive attitude which in turn leads to the individual being more able to positively manage relationships with others.

## Case study: Jack

Jack is eight. He helps his father care for his mother, Cynthia, who has multiple sclerosis. Cynthia's condition has deteriorated over the last couple of years. She is now wheelchair-bound and relies very heavily on her husband to care for her. When her husband is out at work, Jack has much of the responsibility. Jack's teachers have noticed that he is the first child to react to another child's distress, he picks up on other children's distressed emotional cues, offers consoling words, listens and is generally a very caring, gentle and kind child. However, he is not so good at talking about his own emotions and feelings. Teachers sometimes notice him becoming very anxious about starting or finishing his work on time and when carrying out group classroom activities. He is very anxious when his classmates are not doing what they should be doing.

Jack is clearly very emotionally intelligent when it comes to social relationships and social awareness, but his emotional intelligence is lacking in other areas, self-awareness and self-management. Jack is perhaps unaware of the stress he is feeling. Nor is he able to manage this distress. This case study demonstrates Goleman's four-quadrant model in action and how you may be good in two of the four aspects, but weak in other areas.

## Emotional resilience theory

Resilience can be referred to as an 'individual's capacity to successfully adapt to change and stressful events in healthy and constructive ways' (Catalano et al., 2002). Resilience has been defined in simpler terms as: 'the ability to take hard knocks, to weather the storm and to continue to value oneself whatever happens'.

Emma Werner was one of the first scientists to use the term 'resilience', way back in the 1970s. She studied a cohort of children with alcoholic parents: many of the parents were out of work. Werner noted that two-thirds of the children exhibited destructive behaviours in their teenage years; however, the other third of youngsters did not exhibit any destructive behaviour. Werner called this group of youngsters resilient and noticed that they had traits different from the other group of children (Werner, 1971). Researchers have since been devoted to discovering the protective factors that explain children's adaptation to adverse conditions for example, to disaster, war, maltreatment and poverty.

The table below outlines what researchers exploring the concept of resilience have identified as factors that can protect a child from psychological distress.

| Resilient factors in the child | Resilient factors in the family | Resilient factors in the community |
|---|---|---|
| • Secure early relationships<br>• Being female<br>• Higher intelligence<br>• Easy temperament when an infant<br>• Positive attitude<br>• Problem-solving approach<br>• Good communication skills<br>• Planner and a belief in control<br>• Humour<br>• Religious faith<br>• Capacity to reflect | • At least one good parent–child relationship<br>• An ability to demonstrate affection<br>• Clear firm and consistent discipline<br>• Support for education<br>• Supportive long-term relationship and absence of severe discord | • Wider supportive network<br>• Good housing<br>• High standard of living<br>• High moral school with positive policies for behaviour, attitudes and anti-bullying philosophy<br>• Schools with strong academic and non-academic opportunities<br>• Range of positive sport/leisure activities |

Like emotional intelligence, resilience can be developed. Many authors have highlighted that it is likely to grow and be sustained through developing valued skills in real life situations, through praise, positive affirmation, a sense of mastery and taking a pride in one's efforts. Resilience, if promoted, has the potential to protect the child.

Promoting resilience is a three-pronged approach in that the child/young person needs to think positively (cognitive resilience), be able to assert control over their behaviour, for example, deal with anger or frustration and work through his or her problems in a systematic way (behavioural resilience). The third form of resilience is emotional resilience and focuses on the importance of the child/young person receiving emotional support in the form of good parenting, supportive friendships or happy school environments.

## Case study: Kenny

Kenny is 15 years of age; he has recently commenced a new school in a new town. He lives with his mother and older brother. He has always had a close relationship with his mother, despite her severe mental illness (bipolar affective disorder). Kenny is presently worried about his older brother who has become involved in drug crime, does not work and is rarely at home. Kenny has a diagnosis of Attention Deficit Disorder and has always found concentrating in class difficult. He sometimes becomes distracted and disrupts class activities with his silly behaviour. Kenny has recently approached his school pastoral counsellor because he feels the need to speak to somebody about his problems and his inability to concentrate in class. Kenny is aware that he needs to obtain GCSE passes in Maths and English in order to secure a place in the Royal Marines.

By speaking to his school counsellor, Kenny was able to identify his own strengths, as well as the challenges he faces in his life and explore his life goals, aspirations and solutions to some of his problems. As the school year progressed, Kenny began to sort out his emotional and behavioural difficulties, leading to an improved focus and increased self-esteem, and more importantly hope for the future.

This case example demonstrates some of the inherent factors that promote Kenny's resilience and how his resilience was promoted.

Kenny is resilient because, despite his mother's obvious problems, he has always had a parent who cares. Children do not need their parent to be 'perfect'. They do, however, need them to be there, and Kenny's mother was a constant fixture for him (family resilience).

He had other adults, most notably his teachers and counsellor, who believed in him and supported him. These individuals made an impact even though they did not become part of Kenny's life until he was 15 years old (community resilience).

Kenny's willingness to seek out the help of his school pastoral counsellor suggested that he had the insight to know his future was in his own hands. This personal strength was encouraged and supported by a counsellor who fuelled his belief and faith in himself, thus giving him hope. When working with a client to build hope, just believing in the client can be very powerful (individual resilience).

## Summary

By promoting emotional resilience and intelligence, emotional competence and emotional wellbeing is promoted, in that the following is shared:

- helping the child to recognize and process their emotions in order that they can better manage them;
- helping the child to consider and care for others;
- helping the child to make responsible decisions;
- helping the child to establish positive relationships;
- helping the child to handle conflict or cope when faced with a challenging situation.

## Multiple choice questions

1. Emotional intelligence is not:

    a. Self-awareness
    b. An ability to think mathematically
    c. An ability to pick up on emotional cues
    d. An ability to manage oneself

2. A child's resilience will not be promoted if:

    a. They live in poverty
    b. They are female
    c. They have a positive attitude
    d. They have a religious faith

# What is emotional literacy: how is it implemented in schools?

## Helena Hoyos

*We have gone too far in emphasising the value and import of the purely rational – what IQ measures – Intelligence can come to nothing when emotions hold sway.*

**(Daniel Goleman)**

### Key concepts

- Emotional health and wellbeing is now recognized as being of primary importance within schools and in the wider community.
- Indeed, when visiting schools, OFSTED takes into account 'the extent to which pupils know and understand factors which impact on their physical, mental and emotional health'.
- Emotional literacy is the descriptive term used in schools and is actively promoted.

When Goleman wrote about emotional intelligence in 1996, he was one of the first to publicly champion the importance of meeting children's emotional needs in order to enable them to learn effectively.

Although the work of Goleman and his predecessors, such as Howard Gardner, Peter Salovey and Jack Mayer, uses the term 'emotional intelligence', the term 'emotional literacy', first introduced by Claude Steiner (1984), has now been adopted by schools and is widely used by them. It is likely that one reason for this is to present a challenge to the idea of a fixed and unchanging state usually associated with the concept of 'Intelligence', while we are familiar with the idea that 'literacy' can be taught and learned.

The following definition of emotional literacy was first applied to emotional intelligence by Mayer and Salovey in 1997:

- the ability to perceive accurately, appraise and express emotion;
- the ability to access and/or generate feelings which facilitate thought;
- the ability to understand emotion and emotional knowledge;
- the ability to regulate emotions to promote emotional and intellectual growth (Mayer and Salovey, 1997).

In other words, emotional literacy is about learning to understand and talk about how we feel, to reflect on our emotions and how they are affecting our thinking and behaviour, and to manage our emotions and those of other people in a productive way.

Emotional literacy is now actively promoted in many schools. This can take the form of a whole school curriculum aimed at enabling staff and pupils to become more emotionally literate, for example, through the use of the Government's SEAL materials. It can involve training specific individuals among the staff to work with children who are experiencing difficulty in recognizing and managing their emotions. These staff members are often trained and supervised by Educational Psychologists.

# Why focus on emotional literacy?

The field of psychology has contributed greatly to our understanding of why emotional literacy is important. As early as 1943, Abraham Maslow was beginning to develop his theory of a hierarchy of basic needs, which motivate us as human beings (Maslow, 1943).

# Maslow's hierachy of needs

In the original version of his theory, Maslow suggests that there are five levels of need which must be met in order for an individual to be able to thrive, learn and fully develop as a well-rounded and fulfilled person. The needs he proposes are:

- Physiological – the need for food, water, air, sex, sleep, homeostasis.
- Safety – the need for physical, emotional and moral safety.
- Belonging and love – the need to belong to a group or tribe, including family, friends and intimacy.
- Self-esteem – the need for a sense of self-worth, confidence, respect from self and others.
- Self-actualisation – the need to grow and develop as an individual, in order to fully recognise our potential.

These levels of need are usually represented as a hierarchy with the most basic needs comprising the first level, moving through in a linear sequence to self-actualisation. They are often represented diagrammatically as a pyramid, with the suggestion that each level of need must be met in turn before the next level may be achieved. In recent years there has been a move towards suggesting that, whilst the different levels remain valid, there is more fluid movement between them. However, Maslow's suggestion that all human beings must have the four lower levels of need met before they are able to focus on the personal growth, development and learning characterised by the higher layer remains relevant today. Sadly, many of the children in our schools are struggling to have their basic needs met and are not therefore, emotionally open to the learning opportunities which schools present. By introducing emotional literacy into schools, adults are helped to recognize these needs in children and to respond appropriately.

For example, a child who feels unsafe or unheard due to an unstable home environment or bullying in the playground can be helped at school by the creation of a calm, ordered learning environment, with access to adults who listen and respond effectively. A child who feels unwanted at home and isolated at school can be helped to develop by interventions at school that foster a sense of belonging and being valued. Once this sense of belonging and being accepted is in place, increased self-esteem can follow and then the child will be ready to learn.

Howard Gardner's theory has already been outlined in the previous section (seven intelligences: linguistic, logical-mathematical, musical, bodily-kinesthetic, spatial, interpersonal intelligence and intrapersonal intelligence) (Gardner, 1983) and the concept of emotional literacy draws strongly on his idea of intrapersonal intelligence – the ability to understand oneself; and interpersonal intelligence – the ability to understand and interact effectively with other people.

Goleman (1998) highlighted these two areas which he characterized as personal and social competence. Goleman suggested that if people could be helped to develop their ability to manage themselves and their interactions with other people, they would become much more successful in all areas of their lives.

# What does emotional literacy include?

Emotionally literate people are able to understand and talk about their feelings and manage those feelings effectively, so that they do not overwhelm their capacity to think. They tune in to the feelings of other people and work cooperatively and sensitively with them. There are several components to emotional literacy which make this possible.

## Conscious awareness and communication skills

We all need to learn to be aware of how we are feeling and to develop a vocabulary which allows us to reflect on these feelings and communicate them appropriately to other people. This is often the first step for those working with children to help them develop their emotional literacy.

## Case study: Mary

Mary usually feels very strong emotions which she labels as 'good' or 'bad'. She does not yet have the understanding or vocabulary to break these categories down into smaller categories such as happy/excited or angry/sad. She tends to show the same 'good' or 'bad' behaviour in response to her feelings. One day, Mary refuses to do what her teacher asks her in class. She is rude to the teacher and is sent out of class. That morning, Mary's mother was ill and Mary feels worried about her, but because she is unable to recognize or talk about that feeling she is only able to show that she feels 'bad' by misbehaving. Her teacher reacts to the behaviour, not knowing the reason behind it, and so the situation worsens for Mary.

## Understanding thoughts, feelings and actions

We need to understand thoughts, feelings and actions so that our behaviour is guided by informed choices, rather than being based on impulse.

## Case study: Daniel

Daniel hits his friend when he asks to borrow Daniel's pen. Earlier in the day, Daniel's teacher told him off and Daniel feels angry because he thinks this was unfair. However, instead of understanding that he feels angry with his teacher, Daniel just feels generally angry and takes this out on his friend. As a result Daniel falls into more trouble, has difficulty with his friendship and feels increasingly angry. However, had he been helped to understand the source of his anger he might have been able to control his response to his friend and the following difficulties would have been avoided.

## Managing feelings

We need to manage feelings so that we are able to control our responses and have our needs met, without our feelings overwhelming us and standing in the way.

> ### Case study: Susan
>
> Susan is often in trouble at school because she shouts out answers to questions, rather than putting up her hand and waiting her turn. Following some emotional literacy work, Susan becomes more able to manage her feelings of frustration and anxiety and is able to wait her turn. She begins to receive praise from her teacher and to feel much happier at school and better about herself. Learning to manage her feelings has also promoted her self-esteem.

## Managing conflict

With increasing emotional awareness we are more able to manage conflict effectively. We begin to recognize the triggers that make us angry and the signs that our anger is building, which are often felt in the body's reactions. This increased awareness gives us the choice to avoid the conflict before it escalates beyond our control. The benefits for all of us will be obvious and will have particular relevance for those working with children and young people at school.

## Understanding groups

As we become more aware of our own feelings and reactions and those of other people, we become more able to share attention and recognize the strengths and needs that we and others bring to any situation. This helps us cooperate and communicate much more effectively in groups.

# So why is emotional literacy important?

As a responsible society, we have a duty to help children develop and reach their potential as well-rounded, emotionally healthy individuals who can play a full and active part in the society of their future. The development of emotional literacy is at the heart of how we can do this, in our homes, schools and all aspects of our lives.

## Multiple choice questions

1. Which of the following statements is correct?

    a. Emotional literacy is about reading and writing
    b. Emotional literacy is a fixed and unchanging state
    c. Emotional literacy helps children's development
    d. Emotional literacy is not taught in schools

2. Which of the following is not one of the seven intelligences proposed by Gardner?

    a. Visual/spatial
    b. Emotional/feelings
    c. Logical/mathematical
    d. Verbal/linguistic

3. Which of the following is not a feature of Maslow's Hierarchy of Needs?

    a. All people need to have their physical needs met
    b. All people need to feel a sense of belonging
    c. All people need to feel safe
    d. All people need to be formally educated

4. Which of the following is not a key component of emotional literacy?

    a. The ability to communicate feelings effectively

    b. The ability to share attention with other people in groups

    c. The ability to explain the principles of emotional literacy

    d. The ability to understand links between feelings, thoughts and actions

5. Which of the following people have been important in developing the theory of emotional literacy?

    a. Goleman, Steiner and Marlow

    b. Gardman, Steinbeck and Mayer

    c. Salovey, Mayer and Goleman

    d. Saloman, Mayer and Gardner

# Acknowledgements

To Lucy Manger, Educational Psychologist, for additional materials and comments.

## Key texts

Coughlan BJ (2010) Critical Issues in the Emotional Wellbeing of Students with Special Educational Needs. [Online at https://www.ssatrust.org.uk/pedagogy/networks/specialschools/CLDD/Pages/ThinkPiece6.aspx].

Department for Education and Skills/Department of Health (2005). National Healthy Schools Status: A guide for schools. London: DH Publications.

Goleman D (1998) *Working with Emotional Intelligence.* New York: Bantam Books.

Weare K, Gray G (2003) What works in developing children's emotional and social competence and wellbeing? London, UK, Department for Education and Skills.

# 14 Current legal framework and relevant legislation

Janet Féat

## Introduction

This chapter will track the law and social policy relevant to children today, beginning with the Children Act 1989 (implemented 1991) and continuing through the Children Act 2004, the Children and Young Persons Act 2008 and related policy and guidance up to 2010. In the intervening 21 years, the focus has broadened from the recognition of the paramount importance of the welfare of the child, the rights of children to express their wishes and feelings, and the duties of local authorities, towards the recognition that all agencies, whether education, health, social care or any other agency offering services to children and families, need to work together to address the needs of all children, at an early stage, to listen to their views and to identify those who are the most vulnerable.

The legislation covered in this section is not comprehensive in that it focuses on the welfare of children generally and does not cover the Education Acts, the Criminal Justice legislation with respect to children, or adoption law and policy. It is subject to a caveat: legislation and policy may change, especially when we have a new government, so a check for continuing relevance is advised.

## The welfare of the child

The Children Act 1989 (referred to hereafter as 'the 1989 Act') was described by the Lord Chancellor in 1988 as 'the most comprehensive and far reaching reform of child care law which has come before Parliament in living memory'. It introduced new concepts along with new terms, for example: 'residence' rather than custody, 'contact' for access and 'parental responsibility' rather than parental rights and duties. These new terms reflect the centrality of the child, rather than the parent, in the legislation. Equally, 'significant harm', the threshold

for Care or Supervision Orders, refers to the effect on the child rather than specifying the actions of others.

Other important concepts of the 1989 Act are the avoidance of delay in court proceedings: that is, there is a statutory presumption that delay in determining by whom a child shall be brought up is prejudicial to the child's welfare, and the 'no order principle': that is, that for an order to be made, it must be shown that it is better for the child than making no order.

The welfare of the child as paramount is a key concept of the 1989 Act. The 'welfare checklist' explains how it is to be interpreted.

## The welfare checklist

The court must have regard in particular to:

- the ascertainable wishes and feelings of the child concerned (considered in the light of his age and understanding);
- his physical, emotional and educational needs;
- the likely effect on him of any change in his circumstances;
- his age, sex, background and any characteristics of his that the court considers relevant;
- any harm which he has suffered or is at risk of suffering;
- how capable each of his parents, and any other person in relation to whom the court considers the question to be relevant, is of meeting his needs;
- the range of powers available to the court under this Act in the proceedings in question.

The welfare checklist applies in all public proceedings under Part IV of the 1989 Act, i.e. Care and Supervision Orders, whether contested or not, but in private proceedings under Part II of the Act, i.e. Section 8 orders, only when they are contested. It does not apply to short term orders, e.g.

Emergency Protection Orders. The welfare checklist is a tool for the use of the court in family proceedings, but it provides a good framework for deciding what, and if, action is needed, in *any* circumstances.

# Every child matters

The words 'wellbeing' and 'welfare' are used in both the Children Act 2004 (referred to hereafter as 'the 2004 Act') and the Children and Young Persons Act 2008 (referred to hereafter as 'the 2008 Act') as the looked-for outcome of services offered to children by all agencies, not just local authorities.

Wellbeing is defined in terms of the outcomes set out in *Every Child Matters*, the Green Paper published in 2003, following the publication of the Joint Chief Inspectors' Report *Safeguarding Children*, in October 2002 and in February 2003 of Lord Laming's Report on the death of Victoria Climbié. Consultation with children and young people had produced five desirable outcomes: to be healthy, to stay safe, to enjoy and achieve, to make a positive contribution and to achieve economic wellbeing.

These are set out in Section 10 (2) a) to e) of the 2004 Act as:

- physical and mental health and emotional wellbeing;
- protection from harm and neglect;
- education, training and recreation;
- the contribution made by them to society;
- social and economic wellbeing.

Section 7 (1) of the 2008 Act makes it the general duty of the Secretary of State to promote the wellbeing of children and Section 7 (5) refers to the aspects of wellbeing found in the 2004 Act above.

The 1989 Act gives both general and specific duties to local authorities in respect of all children, children in need and children in need of protection. Its primary focus is on children in need, but the local authority is nonetheless given additional duties to provide preventative services.

# Local authority duties: all children

- Reduce the need to bring proceedings (care/criminal)
- Reduce the need to use secure accommodation

- Provide services to prevent children suffering ill-treatment or neglect
- Provide family centres, as appropriate
- Provide information about services
- Ensure that people who may need them know about services

**(Children Act 1989: Schedule 2, Part I)**

The Children Act 2004 became law in November 2004, embedding in legislation the five outcomes for children and young people quoted above, as the purpose of partnership working, proposing a Children's Commissioner for England to represent the views and interests of children, reporting to Parliament through the Secretary of State on progress against those outcomes. In December 2010, however, the coalition Government established earlier in the year welcomed an independent review of the role of Children's Commissioner, which recommended increased independence from government for the role, as well as the merging of the Office of the Children's Rights Director in Ofsted to create a new Office of the Children's Commissioner for England. As well as reporting directly to Parliament, the Commissioner would report to the UN Committee on the Rights of the Child.

A major change in the 2004 Act from previous legislation was the provision for pooled funding of children's services, to facilitate the development of Children's Trusts, commissioning bodies with representation from Children's Services (education and children's social care), Health and relevant voluntary organizations. The aim was to increase the joint commissioning ability to have a significant impact on what is provided, not just universally but, in particular, for vulnerable children and families before they meet the criteria for children in need. To support this, the Act provided for a joint inspection framework, led by the Chief Inspector of Schools, with performance measures focusing on how services are jointly delivered. While Children's Trusts do not feature in the policy of the coalition government formed in May 2010, the ability to commission jointly may well continue.

# Children in need

Under the 1989 Act, a child is considered to be in need if:

- he is unlikely to achieve or maintain, or have the opportunity of achieving or maintaining, a reasonable standard of health or development without appropriate provision for him of services by a local authority;
- his health or development is likely to be significantly impaired, or further impaired, without the provision for him of such services;
- he is disabled.

**(Children Act 1989: Part III Section 17(10))**

'Family', in relation to such a child, includes anyone who has parental responsibility for the child and any other person with whom he has been living. 'Development' is further defined as meaning physical, intellectual, emotional, social or behavioural development and 'health', both physical and mental health.

The 2004 Act extended the duty to safeguard and promote welfare to all key agencies working with children, and Sections 18 and 19 required local authorities to put in place a Director of Children's Services and a Lead Member to be responsible for, as a minimum, education and children's social care functions. This has happened in the majority of local authorities in England.

## Local authority duties: children in need

### General

- Safeguard and promote welfare: extended to all agencies offering services to children by S 11 (1) and (2) Children Act 2004
- Promote the upbringing of the child within the family by providing a range and level of services appropriate to their needs

### Specific

- Identify numbers of children in need in their area
- Provide day care, as appropriate
- Have regard to ethnicity
- Provide accommodation where there is no parent, or parent cannot provide care
- Facilitate provision of services by others, e.g. voluntary organizations

- Provide, for children in their families: advice, guidance, counselling; occupational, cultural, social, recreational activities; home help; facilities so they can make use of services; assistance with holidays
- For children living away from home but not 'looked after': take steps to enable them to live with their families, or promote contact with families

**(Children Act 1989: Part III and Schedule 2, Part I)**

The 2008 Act extends the local authority's power, (conferred by the 1989 Act Section 17(6)) to make cash payments to children in need and their families in exceptional circumstances, to do this in circumstances which are *not* exceptional.

## Aiming high for disabled children

Under the 1989 Act, disabled children are automatically seen as children in need (see above). As a result of lobbying by parents and voluntary organizations as well as a comprehensive review of services, it was apparent that, as an integral part of the *Every Child Matters* agenda, there was a general need to provide better services for disabled children and their families which offered not only positive and enjoyable activities for the children, but a break from caring for the parents and carers.

The central government programme *Aiming High for Disabled Children*, launched in May 2007, marked the culmination of the Disabled Children's Review and aimed to transform services for disabled children and their families in the following areas with guidance, funding and resources:

- empowerment: offering parents and their disabled children choice and the power to take decisions about their own care and influence local priorities, to improve service quality and responsiveness;
- responsiveness: prioritizing disabled children at a local and national level, with early interventions, coordinated and timely support, to bring up standards of provision across the country, make it easier for families to access holistic support, and prevent conditions deteriorating;

- service quality and capacity: boosting provision of services which are vital
- for improving outcomes for disabled children and their families, focusing mainly on specialist services such as short breaks (for children as well as carers and not confined to respite, but to include activities chosen by children themselves), equipment and therapists, and tackling barriers to accessing universal services such as childcare.

The importance of breaks for carers is recognized in legislation: Section 25 of the 2008 Act adds to the 1989 Act (Schedule 2 Section 6) the local authority's duty to provide breaks in caring for those who care for disabled children.

The *Aiming High for Disabled Children* programme includes guidance on early intervention and support, transition to adulthood, and palliative care for children with life-limiting disabilities.

# Children in need of protection/safeguarding

The concept of 'significant harm' is central to the 1989 Act. 'Harm' is defined in Section 31 (9) as 'ill-treatment or the impairment of health or development' (using the same definitions of health and development as in Part III): ill-treatment is defined as including 'sexual abuse and forms of ill-treatment which are not physical'. The term 'significant' is interpreted in Section 31 (10) thus: 'Where the question of whether harm suffered by a child is significant turns on the child's health or development, his health or development shall be compared with that which could reasonably be expected of a similar child'.

## Local authority duties: children in need of protection

Duty to make enquiries where:
- a child is subject to Emergency Protection Order or Police Protection (S47, S46);
- there is reasonable cause to suspect a child is suffering, or likely to suffer, significant harm in order to decide whether to take action to promote or safeguard a child's welfare (S47);
- in family proceedings in which a question

arises as to the child's welfare, the court directs (S37);
- on discharging an education supervision order, the court directs (Schedule 3);
- there is persistent failure to comply with an education supervision order (Schedule 3).

Following the implementation of the 1989 Act, *Working Together to Protect Children*, a guide to inter-agency working in child protection cases, was published in 1991. Child deaths in the 1970s and 1980s (beginning with the case of Maria Colwell in 1974) had influenced the child protection system and the setting up of Child Protection Registers in each Social Services authority. Area Child Protection committees had been set up as a forum for health, education, social services and probation agencies to work together to protect children. The necessity for working together had been stressed again and again whenever a child abuse tragedy had resulted in a death. The Cleveland Inquiry (1988) brought the subject of sexual abuse of children within families to both professional and public awareness.

The Department of Health commissioned research studies to address the working of the child protection system post the 1989 Act, responding to questions which had been raised by some inquiries about the emphasis on child protection (Section 47) investigation to the detriment of providing supportive services to children and families (Section 17). An overview of research at the time, *Child Protection Messages from Research* (Department of Health, 1995b), summarized the principal messages, addressing in particular the balance between child protection and family support services envisaged by the 1989 Act. The conclusions were that 'for the majority of cases, the need of the child and family is more important than the abuse or, put another way, the general family context is more important than any abusive incident within it.'

From 1999, editions of the government guidance changed the title to *Working Together to Safeguard Children*. The word 'safeguard', taken from the 1989 Act, is reflected in legislation and policy from this time. The 2004 Act Section 13 required each children's services authority in England (that is, an authority with education and children's social care functions) to establish a Local Safeguarding Children Board (LSCB), replacing the non-statutory Area Child Protection Committees. The LSCB is the key statutory mechanism for agreeing how the relevant organizations working with children in each local area will cooperate to safeguard and promote the welfare of those children and for ensuring their effectiveness. The 2004 Act sets out the agencies which should comprise the LSCB (Section 14) and how the Boards should be funded.

The 2006 edition of *Working Together* reflected the wish of government to dispose of the duty to provide for a Child Protection Register as a separate database, on the basis that clear records should be available electronically of all children with a child protection plan (as decided by a Child Protection Conference). The 2010 edition of *Working Together* defines safeguarding and promoting the welfare of children as (Department for Children, Schools and Families, 2010c):

- protecting children from maltreatment;
- preventing impairment of children's health or development;
- ensuring that children are growing up in circumstances consistent with the provision of safe and effective care.

The last point is evidence of the increasing awareness of the broad context of children's lives beyond incidents of abuse and neglect, and the duty to all children in the LSCB area.

# Care matters: duties to children looked after

A child 'looked after' by a local authority refers to any child either placed under a Care Order by a court, whereby the local authority shares parental responsibility with the parent, or accommodated by the local authority at the request of a parent, whereby the parent retains exclusive parental responsibility. Before making any decision with respect to a child whom they are looking after, or proposing to look after, however, the Act requires a local authority 'as far as is reasonably practicable' to ascertain the wishes and feelings of the child, his parents, any person who is not a parent but who has parental responsibility and any other person whose wishes and feelings the authority considers to be relevant. It should be noted that the need for local authorities to safeguard and promote welfare in the Act goes beyond the need for protection and

applies equally to children in need living with their families and to children looked after.

## Local authority duties: children looked after

- Safeguard and promote welfare (S22)
- Make use of services available to children cared for by their own parents (S22)
- Give due consideration to the wishes and feelings of the child, having regard to his age and understanding, and to those of any other relevant people (S22)
- Give due consideration to the child's religious persuasion, racial origin and cultural and linguistic background
- Provide the child with accommodation and maintain him in other respects (S22A and S22B)
- Secure that the accommodation is near to his home (S22C)
- Secure that siblings are accommodated together (S22C)
- Where a child is disabled, secure that the accommodation is not unsuitable to his particular needs (S22C)
- Advise, assist and befriend the child with a view to promoting his welfare when he ceases to be looked after (S24)

Key research studies carried out both before and after the implementation of the Children Act 1989 influenced social policy for both children looked after and those in need of other services, i.e. family support and child protection. For children looked after, weaknesses in the system for providing their care had been identified in the two decades prior to the 1989 Act, with increased attention being paid to the isolation of children in care, political concerns about accountability, and the lack of evidence about the long-term effects of care.

This research, in addition to the duty of local authorities to provide a standard of care similar to that which one would expect of a reasonable parent (outlined in the 1989 Act), has influenced succeeding systems for planning for and review of looked after children's cases and is intended to strengthen working partnerships between key people in a child's life and help all those concerned to listen attentively to a child or young person's views and wishes. In particular, the publication of the government White Paper *Care Matters: Time for Change* (Government White Paper, 2007), recognizing that 'despite high ambitions and a shared commitment for change, outcomes for children in care have not sufficiently improved', set out plans to further improve outcomes for looked after children and care leavers in terms of their health, education and general wellbeing. The executive summary of the White Paper stated: 'Children and young people in care tell us that they want to lead normal lives. They want to succeed in education, enjoy a wide range of positive activities and make a successful transition to adult life'.

The purpose of the 2008 Act (which received Royal Assent in November 2008) was to reform the statutory framework of the care system in England and Wales, forming part of the government programme to ensure children receive high quality care and support. It implements many of the changes required in *Care Matters* and puts them on a statutory basis:

- S8 of the 2008 Act replaces S23 of the 1989 Act with Sections 22A-F (see above);
- S9 inserts into the 1989 Act a further general duty for the local authority to secure sufficient accommodation for looked after children (S22G);
- S1 empowers local authorities to enter into arrangements with other bodies in the discharge of their care functions;
- S10 sets out the duties in respect of Independent Reviewing Officers (IROs) and their functions which are inserted into the 1989 Act (S25A and S25B), the main change being that IROs should monitor the performance of a local authority not just in relation to a child's review, but in relation to the child's case;
- S20 sets out the duty of a maintained school to appoint a designated teacher to have responsibility for promoting the educational achievement of pupils who are looked after.

The 2008 Act was followed by a raft of new regulations and guidance relating to care planning, placement and case review for looked after children; promotion of their health and education (including designated teachers and the obligation to provide a bursary for any child who had been looked after entering higher education); national minimum standards for fostering and children's homes, and regulations making it easier for family and friends to provide placements. The aim was to provide a streamlined set of guidance documents which mirrored a child's journey through the care system, including after they left care, and made provision for vulnerable children not looked after, such as short breaks for carers of disabled children, provisions in relation to private fostering, and notification of child deaths to LSCBs and appropriate national authorities. The guidance and regulations are all to be implemented by April 2011.

# Children's guardians

The children's guardian service was set up in 1984, when they were known as guardians *ad litem*. The Children Act 1989 extended the number of situations in which a guardian *ad litem* should be appointed by the court to ensure that the child's interests would be represented by a social worker independent of the local authority, who would be able to instruct a solicitor (Sections 41 and 42).

The Criminal Justice and Court Services Act 2000 set up the Children and Family Court Advisory and Support Service (CAFCASS) to include children's guardians ('*ad litem*' is no longer used), the Court Welfare Service and the functions of the Official Solicitor in respect of children.

The purpose of CAFCASS is 'to ensure children and young people are put first in family proceedings; that their voices are properly heard; that the decisions made about them by courts are in their best interests; and that they and their families are supported throughout the process' (*Putting Children and Young People First*, CAFCASS Corporate Plan 2003/06). The function of CAFCASS set out in the 2009–2011 Business Plan is, in respect of family proceedings where the welfare of children is or may be in question, to:

- safeguard and promote the welfare of children;
- give advice to any court about any application made to it in such proceedings;
- make provision for the children to be represented in such proceedings;
- provide information, advice and other support for the children and their families.

Guardians are appointed by the court whenever decisions are to be made about children in vulnerable situations and to report to the court on their findings in the interests of the child. The role of the guardian is to interview children (age-appropriately), parents, the local authority social worker and anyone else relevant, ascertain the background to the case and look at the records. Children have the opportunity to participate directly in their guardian's assessment through *How it looks to me*, a child impact tool.

In addition, there is now a statutory requirement, set out in S16a of the Children and Adoption Act 2006, for guardians to complete a risk assessment, in some circumstances reporting through a separate risk assessment tool.

# The framework for the assessment of children in need and their families

Good assessment has always been at the heart of good practice in delivering children's services. The increasing need for a consistent and systematic process for assessment was taken forward by the publication of the *Framework for the Assessment of Children in Need and their Families* (Department of Health, Home Office, Department of Education and Employment, 2000) in terms of initial and core (more detailed) assessments and timescales. It complemented the updated inter-agency child protection guidelines *Working Together to Safeguard Children* 1999. The emphasis on the Children Act terms 'safeguarding' and 'promoting the welfare' of children indicate the move from the focus on abusive incidents to the broader context of the child's needs and life experience.

The framework for assessment (see Appendix) is visually expressed as a triangle with the child literally and symbolically at the centre and three domains along the sides: the child's developmental needs, the capacity of the parent/s or carers to meet those needs and the family and environmental factors which impact on both. Each domain has a number of dimensions to be assessed and the *Framework for Assessment* states what is to be covered in each of the dimensions. It emphasizes that 'a key principle of the Assessment Framework is that children's needs and their families' circumstances will require inter-agency

collaboration to ensure full understanding of what is happening and to ensure an effective service response' (para 5.1).

# Assessment of risk

The Assessment Framework covers the basis for the assessment of risk, indicating whether or not children's needs were being met within an assessment of parenting capacity, or whether there were real deficits in the parents ability to meet these needs, and the family and environmental factors which might militate against the successful addressing of these deficits. The Framework emphasizes that assessment should look at strengths, positives and protective factors in the family, which would promote resilience in the child. It requires that strengths are recorded alongside deficits, important to an assessment of risk.

However, where the possibility exists that significant harm, or failure to prevent harm, has occurred, the Assessment Framework has always needed to be used alongside the succeeding editions of *Working Together to Safeguard Children* (from 1999 to 2010) with its definitions of physical, emotional, sexual abuse and neglect and their impact on the child, and further guidance on the concept of significant harm.

This guidance has changed little over the years and is useful to an assessment of risk within the context of the child's wider welfare needs:

*There are no absolute criteria on which to rely when judging what constitutes significant harm. Consideration of the severity of ill-treatment may include the degree and the extent of physical harm, the duration and frequency of abuse and neglect, and the extent of premeditation, degree of threat and coercion, sadism and bizarre or unusual elements. Each of these elements has been associated with more severe effects on the child, and/or relatively greater difficulty in helping the child overcome the adverse impact of the ill-treatment. Sometimes, a single traumatic event may constitute significant harm, e.g. a violent assault, suffocation or poisoning. More often, significant harm is a compilation of significant events, both acute and long-standing, which interrupt, change or damage the child's physical or psychological development. Some children live in family and social circumstances where their health and development are neglected. For them, it is the corrosiveness of long-term emotional, physical or sexual abuse that causes impairment to the extent of constituting significant harm. In each case, it is necessary to consider any ill-treatment alongside the child's own assessment of his or her safety and welfare, the family's strengths and supports, as well as an assessment of the likelihood and capacity for change and improvements in parenting and the care of children and young people.*

**(Working Together to Safeguard Children (2010) para. 1.28)**

The Framework for Assessment is the means within which to build a careful picture of developmental risk factors for the child, with any risks arising from parental capacity and environmental factors and weigh these relative to one another, assessing the likelihood and capacity for change, *within a timescale relevant to the child.* The services that can be made available to the child and the family, the child or family's ability to use them, and their likely impact on the child's health and development in the future, have to be taken into account.

Further, more detailed specialist assessments may be needed in order to make an accurate assessment of the possibilities for the child, e.g. if a child is traumatized or very disturbed, or a parent has mental health or substance misuse problems, or learning disabilities. For the parent who is a sex offender, the Sex Offenders Act 1997 requires those convicted of specified sexual offences to register with the police, and an assessment of their potential to re-offend to be made. Assessment and treatment of sexual abuse perpetrators who have not been convicted, perhaps because there is insufficient evidence, or the child involved has been unable to give evidence, is less straightforward. Specialist training is required to handle the denial, justification or minimization and cognitive distortions that characterize many abusers. For children and young people who sexually abuse, the necessity to understand the reason for and context of the

abusive behaviour, particularly if the abuser has been a victim him/herself, the parental capacity to accept the need for care, supervision and monitoring, and the need to address community safety and the supports needed by parents to do this, will be part of a specialist assessment.

# Parenting orders

Section 8 of the Crime and Disorder Act 1998 provides for a parenting order to be made in a number of court settings, both civil and criminal, along with a range of other orders. A parenting order is intended to help and support parents to address and deal with a child's non-attendance at school, anti-social or offending behaviour, by requiring the parents to attend counselling or guidance sessions once a week for up to 12 weeks. Other requirements may relate to controlling specific aspects of the child's behaviour and can last for up to 12 months. These requirements are intended to support parents. However, the sanctions for non-compliance can be a fine or probation order, which would add to the problems experienced by parents and would not be perceived as supportive. For the court to make a parenting order, the resources of guidance and counselling for parents have to be available.

# Human Rights Act

The specific rights of children are contained in the United Nations Convention on the Rights of the Child which was ratified by the United Kingdom in 1989, but although influential, it is not part of UK domestic law, so direct challenge in the courts is not possible. However, the Human Rights Act 1998, which came into force in October 2000, established a statutory framework for applying the rights contained in the European Convention on Human Rights to domestic law. This means that United Kingdom law has to be interpreted, and public authorities have to act, in a way which is compatible with the Convention.

The Human Rights Act has not been in force long enough for an extensive body of case law to have built up, and what follows is a summary derived from more potential than actual cases.

Article 2: *The right to life*: child deaths which show that public authorities were aware of a real and immediate risk to a child, and failed to act, could be claimed to be a breach of this article. It remains to be seen, in addition, whether the duties of local authorities with respect to child protection (Children Act 1989, Part V) amount to the protection of life by law required by Article 2.

Article 3: *The right not to be subjected to torture or to inhuman or degrading treatment or punishment*: this is an absolute right which means that if a violation is found, it must be unlawful. Any enforced treatment, including drugging or feeding, behavioural regimes and discipline, could breach this article if medical necessity cannot be proved, and issues may be raised over the growing use of Ritalin and similar drugs to control behaviour, where there is no informed consent by the child. However, a minimum level of severity must be reached for this article to be relevant. Violations of Article 3 have been found by the European Commission in the case of children whose local authority failed to protect them from five years of severe neglect and ill-treatment and in the case of a young boy beaten by his stepfather, which was considered 'reasonable chastisement' by the domestic court. (The current law is under review but so far limitation, rather than removal of 'reasonable chastisement' seems likely.)

Article 6: *The right to a fair trial*: in the first case before the European Commission cited above, a breach of Article 6 was found, because the immunity of the local authority prevented a fair and public hearing of the applicant's civil rights and obligations.

Article 8: *The right to respect for private and family life*: this right should be considered in relation to a potential violation of Article 3, because it protects individuals from less extreme forms of inhuman and degrading treatment which would not meet the minimum severity needed by Article 3. The right in Article 8 is a qualified right whereby interference in family life is sanctioned if it is lawful, serves a legitimate purpose, is necessary in a democratic society and is not discriminatory.

Article 14: *Prohibition of discrimination*: this overarching principle should be read in conjunction with one or more of the Convention rights, and could be applied to the discrimination against children of unmarried parents, or the right to education (first protocol to Article 2) of looked after children, if, for example, local authorities do not appeal against exclusion or admission practices of schools.

The Human Rights Act can have a significant impact not just on law but on the roles and responsibilities of public authorities in health and social care in the future.

## Conclusions

While the 1989 Act as amended by later Acts of Parliament remains the basis for much of the legislation in respect of children that followed, the brief accounts of the provisions of the 2004 and 2008 Acts above confirm the broadening perspective referred to in the introduction. Support for parents and carers is seen by government as the main aim for improving children's long-term wellbeing, especially if it is available at an early stage in the lives of children, the premise being that joint planning of non-stigmatizing services by the statutory agencies in partnership with voluntary and community organizations and with children and families themselves, is likely to prevent some children from becoming children in need.

The research carried out following the Children Act 1989 and the White Papers *Every Child Matters* in 2003 and *Care Matters: Time for Change* in 2007, after consultation with children themselves, pointed the way to a focus not just on local authorities looking after and keeping children safe, but extending duties to all agencies to take account of all the different aspects of children's lives to promote their wellbeing (Government White Paper, 2003; Government White Paper, 2007). Subsequent social policy and legislation has sought to ensure work with children and families which, while keeping the child at the centre, focuses on the broader context of family, education, health and community, with the objective of improved outcomes for any child at risk of social exclusion.

## Case example: Jenny and David

Jenny (6) and David (3) have been living with their mother, who has mental health problems. Their father's whereabouts are currently unknown. When he left their mother, he was known to be misusing drugs and to be violent on occasions. The parents are not married. A situation recently arose where the children's mother threatened her own life and theirs, and an Emergency Protection Order was made in respect of Jenny and David, who were placed with foster carers. Since then, the paternal grandparents have come forward to say that they would like to care for both children.

The local authority needs to consider how best to safeguard and promote Jenny's and David's long-term safety and welfare.

There are several possible scenarios, of which five are outlined below:

1. The children become the subject of care proceedings, with the care plan being, if a Care Order is made, to place them permanently, eventually, with adopters.
2. The children become the subject of care proceedings, with the care plan being, if a Care Order is made, for them to be looked after either by local authority foster carers or by their paternal grandparents, who have been approved as foster parents for them, with or without the possibility of returning to their mother's care, if appropriate.
3. The children become the subject of care proceedings with either of the above care plans, which are contested by the grandparents, but actually the court decides to make a Residence Order to the grandparents with a Supervision Order to the local authority.
4. The children move to live with paternal grandparents on the expiry of the Emergency Protection Order and the grandparents apply for a Residence Order or a Special Guardianship Order.
5. The children move to live with paternal grandparents on the expiry of the Emergency Protection Order, returning to live with their mother as soon she is assessed as able to care for them.

### Analysis

1. A Care Order means that parental responsibility is shared between the local authority and the children's mother, though the local authority can decide the extent to which the mother can exercise that responsibility, while the Care Order is in place. An Adoption Order means that the mother loses parental responsibility, and her consent to Jenny's and David's adoption would normally be needed. For the local authority to consider adoption and not to take up the offer made by Jenny and David's paternal grandparents, they would need evidence that, all other possibilities having been thoroughly investigated, only this care plan would meet both the children's need for safety and their welfare needs.
2. Parental responsibility would be with the local authority and the mother as above. Again, the local authority would need evidence for why the paternal grandparents could not meet Jenny's and David's needs, or, if they could, why a Care Order was needed in addition. (The Court would be applying the 'no order' principle, in addition to the welfare checklist.)
3. This would mean that parental responsibility would be with the grandparents, as well as the mother, and that the local authority had not been able to provide sufficient evidence that a Care Order was needed in order to safeguard and promote the children's welfare. A Supervision Order would mean that the local authority, however, would continue to 'advise, assist and befriend' the children for 1–3 years and possibly supervise parental contact.
4. Parental responsibility with mother and grandparents as above: this would mean that the local authority have assessed the grandparents and their situation as likely to safeguard and

promote Jenny's and David's welfare and that the local authority support their application for a Residence Order or Special Guardianship Order to secure the children's future in the long term. The advantage of a Special Guardianship Order would be that if there should be conflict between the parent and the special guardian(s) over decisions about the children, then the special guardian's opinion would prevail.

5. Parental responsibility remains with mother: this would mean that the local authority were satisfied that the mother had agreed to Jenny and David staying with paternal grandparents until she was able to resume their care, and that her mental health would stabilize within a timescale appropriate to the children.

The above analysis has emphasized parental responsibility status to draw attention to who can make decisions about the children in each possible scenario. Clearly, the amount of local authority intervention in each scenario covers a continuum between maximum and minimum. It is equally clear that the results of assessment of the children's developmental needs; their mother's and grandparents' capacity to meet those needs, both currently and in the future; the future role, if any, of their father; and whether the family relationships are likely to encourage or impede the promotion of the children's welfare, will be central to effective decision-making. These assessments would involve early years and school staff (Jenny attends school and David a nursery), health, adult mental health and any other agency involved with the adults or children in this case, as well as Adults and Children's social care services.

## Multiple choice questions

1. Which Act of Parliament embeds the five desired outcomes for children set out in Every Child Matters?

   a. 1989 Children Act
   b. 2004 Children Act
   c. 2008 Children and Young Person's Act

2. A disabled child is a child in need according to which legislation?

   a. 1989 Children Act
   b. 2004 Children Act
   c. 2008 Children and Young Person's Act

3. Was Care Matters: Time for Change published in

   a. 2003
   b. 2005
   c. 2007

## Key texts

Children Act (1989) *Regulations and Guidance* (updated).

Department for Children, Schools and Families (2010a) *IRO Handbook: statutory guidance for Independent Reviewing Officers and local authorities on their functions in relation to case management and review for looked after children.* London: The Stationery Office.

Department for Children, Schools and Families (2010b) *Short Breaks: statutory guidance on how to safeguard and promote the welfare of disabled children using short breaks.* London: The Stationery Office.

Department for Children, Schools and Families (2010c) *Working Together to Safeguard Children – A guide to inter-agency working to safeguard and promote the welfare of children.* London: The Stationery Office.

Department for Children, Schools and Families, Department of Health (2009) *Aiming High for Disabled Children; Best Practice to Common Practice.* London: The Stationery Office.

Department for Children, Schools and Families, Department of Health, NHS (2008) *Aiming High for Disabled Children: Transforming Services for disabled children and their families.* London: The Stationery Office.

Department for Children, Schools and Families (2007) *Vol 1: Court Orders.* London: The Stationery Office.

Department for Education (2010a) *Vol 2: Care Planning, Placement and Case Review.*

Department for Education (2010b) *Vol 3: Planning Transition to Adulthood for looked after children.*

Department of Health (1995b) *Child Protection Messages from Research.* London: HMSO.

Department of Health, Home Office, Department for Education and Employment (2000) *Framework for the Assessment of Children in Need and their Families.* London: The Stationery Office.

Government White Paper (2007) *Care Matters: Time for Change* Cm 7137.

Government White Paper (2003) *Every Child Matters* Cm 5860.

HM Treasury and Department for Education and Skills (2007) *Aiming High for Disabled Children: better support for families.*

# 15 Making treatment decisions with young people

Suyog Dhakras

---

## Key concepts

- The development of Human Rights Law has contributed to the increasing recognition that greater weight should be given to the views of children and young people.
- This would involve taking into account the developing understanding and ability of children and young people to make decisions for themselves.
- Decision-making with regards to treatment of children and young people with mental disorders occurs within a legal framework which includes Statute Law, i.e. laws passed in Parliament, as well as Case law or Common law, i.e. precedents created through judgments in specific cases.
- In addition to Statute and Common law, every child and young person, up to the age of 18 years, is subject to the Inherent Jurisdiction of the Court, which can supersede parental authority.

---

The treatment of children and young people with mental disorders and mental health problems involves balancing on the one hand the need to give due weight to the views of children and young people themselves; and on the other hand to ensure that the treatment decisions achieved are safe and in their best interests. The process of achieving treatment decisions needs to take into account the views of the parents/carers/persons with parental responsibility.

## UN convention on the rights of the child 1989 (UNCRC)

The UN convention on the rights of the child (UNCRC) sets out a range of civil and political, socioeconomic and cultural rights that apply to all persons up to the age of 18 years. Although this charter is not a part of UK law, the Government of the UK, by ratifying the charter, has agreed to take all the steps it can to implement it. Courts in the UK as well as the European Court may take into consideration the UNCRC charter when making decisions about the rights of a child.

The UNCRC guiding principles are:
- Article 2: All of the rights in the convention apply equally to all children.

- Article 3: The best interests of the child shall be a primary consideration in all actions considering the child.
- Article 5: States should respect the responsibilities, rights and duties of parents to make decisions in relation to their children 'in a manner consistent with the evolving capacities of the child'.
- Article 6: Every child has a basic and unequivocal right to life and to survival and development.
- Article 12: All children have the right to express their views and have their views given due weight in all matters that affect them.

## Human Rights Act 1998 (HRA'98)

The Human Rights Act 1998 (HRA'98) incorporates the rights set out in the European Charter of Human Rights (ECHR) into UK domestic law. The HRA'98 places an obligation on public bodies to work in accordance with the rights set out in the ECHR:
- Article 3: Freedom from torture and inhuman or degrading treatment
- Article 5: The right to liberty

- Article 6: The right to a fair hearing
- Article 8: The right to private and family life
- Article 10: Freedom of expression
- Article 14: Freedom from discrimination.

Following the implementation of the Human Rights Act 1998 in the UK, individuals working for statutory and public authorities, whether in the delivery of services or in making policy, must ensure that decisions taken do not contravene the articles of the Human Rights Act.

The developments on human rights law are now recognized in relation to the admission to hospital and treatment of mental disorder in young people, for example through the amendments to the Mental Health Act 1983.

In spite of the increased recognition of the rights of young people to make decisions regarding their treatment, the role of persons with parental responsibility, usually the parents, or the Local Authority if the minor is under a Care Order, is still an important one. The Children Act 1989 is useful in determining who, individual or agency, has parental responsibility with regards to a particular minor.

# Consent

Consent is defined as the act of saying that one is willing to do something or allow what somebody else wishes, i.e. giving permission or agreement.

In the medical sense, consent to treatment is defined as acquiescence to treatment.

Consent can be implied in certain circumstances and does not always have to be in the written form. For example, a patient who consults a doctor about a sore throat and then opens his mouth for examination will be considered to have given his consent for the examination. In this case, consent is implied and the patient could not then complain if the doctor puts a spatula in his mouth.

In the absence of consent, the intervention may be liable to be considered as an assault on the patient.

In order for a patient's consent to be valid, the following are required:
- capacity to make the decision;
- sufficient information to make a decision;
- the decision should be made of his/her own free will and be free from pressure from others.

# Zone of parental control

In certain situations, persons with parental responsibility may consent on behalf of a child under the age of 16 or young people, 16 or 17 years of age, who may not be able to consent due to lack of capacity. In these circumstances, mental health professionals can rely on such consent only if it is within 'the zone of parental consent (ZPC)'. The concept of the ZPC derives largely from case law from the European Court of Human Rights in Strasbourg. The Code of Practice for the Mental Health Act 2007 gives some guidelines but it is difficult to have clear rules. Whenever there is doubt, legal advice should be sought.

To assess whether a decision falls within the ZPC, two key questions must be answered:
1. Is the decision one that a parent would be expected to make, having regard both to what is considered to be normal practice in our society and to any relevant human rights decisions made by the courts?
2. Are there no indications that the parent might not act in the best interests of the young person?

The more likely the answer to the two questions is 'yes' the more likely is it that the decision is in the ZPC. The parameters of the ZPC will vary from case to case. Mental health professionals might find it helpful to consider the following factors:
- The nature and invasiveness of what is to be done and the extent to which the liberty of the patient is to be curtailed; the more extreme the intervention, the more likely it is to fall outside the zone.
- Whether the patient resists; treating a child or young person who is consistently resisting treatment needs more justification.
- General social standards in force at the time concerning the sorts of decisions it is acceptable for parents to make; anything beyond the kind of decisions parents routinely make will need scrutiny.
- The age, maturity and understanding of the child or young person; the greater these are, the more likely it will be that it should be the child or young person who takes the decision.
- The extent to which a parent's interests may conflict with those of the child or young person; this may suggest that the parent may

not act in the child or young person's best interests.

Where the decision cannot be made on the basis of falling within the ZPC, consideration should be given to alternative methods of treatment.

It is helpful to consider the issues of consent, capacity; decision-making including treatment in hospital, with regard to mental disorders for young people aged 16–17 and those children and young people under the age of 16.

# Decision-making with young people aged 16–17 years of age

This age group is considered separately due to the significant changes to the legal frameworks in healthcare decision-making for 16–17 year olds.

# Family Law Reform Act 1969

Section 8 of the Family Law Reform Act (FLRA): 'The consent of a minor, who has attained the age of sixteen years, to any surgical, medical or dental treatment which in the absence of consent would constitute a trespass to the person, shall be as effective as it would be if he were of full age. And where the minor has by virtue of this section given effective consent, it shall not be necessary to obtain any consent for it from his parent or guardian'.

Thus capacity to give consent without the need for consent from persons with parental responsibility was made available to young people aged 16 years and over.

# Mental Capacity Act 2005

Capacity is a legal term denoting a patient's ability to consent to an intervention. Capacity is a statutory concept following the enactment of the Mental Capacity Act (MCA) (Department of Constitutional Affairs, 2007). The MCA applies to all persons aged 16 and over. Within the meaning of the Act, all persons aged 16 and over are presumed to have the capacity to make decisions about their health care, including treatment for mental

disorder, unless proven otherwise.

The assessment of capacity is a two stage test:
1. Does the person have an impairment of or disturbance in the functioning of the mind or brain?
2. Does the impairment/disturbance mean that the person is unable to make a specific decision when they need to? This means they cannot:
   a. understand and retain the information in their mind
   b. use or weigh that information in the balance as a part of the decision-making process
   c. communicate the decision.

# Mental Health Act 1983: amended in 2007

The amendments to the MHA in 2007 built upon the rights given to young people regarding consent to treatment through the FLRA, as well as through the MCA.

Section 131 of the MHA, i.e. regarding informal treatment of mental disorder, provides that:
- A 16–17 year old with capacity, according to the MCA, can consent to treatment or refuse treatment.
- Their consent or refusal cannot be overridden by a person with parental responsibility.

In a case of refusal, if treatment is thought to be necessary, the options are:
- Consider whether the young person would satisfy the conditions of the MHA for treatment under compulsion or
- If MHA conditions are not satisfied, and treatment is needed, then it may be necessary to seek authorization from the Court.

## 16–17 year old without capacity

If the young person does not have capacity, treatment may still be given using the following legal frameworks:
- Section 131 of the MHA will not apply.
- Treatment may be given under the MCA, in the best interests of the patient, using the best interests checklist provided in the MCA Code of Practice, as long as there is no deprivation of liberty.

- If there is deprivation of liberty, then common law principles may apply, allowing a person with parental responsibility to consent if the matter is within the ZPC.
- If the matter is outside the ZPC, consideration

should be given to whether the criteria for the MHA are met.
- If the MHA is not applicable, it may be necessary to seek authorization from the Court.

## Case study: Lily

Lily is a 16-year-old girl with anorexia nervosa and depression who was referred to the Community Specialist CAMHS clinic. In spite of assertive outreach treatment, her weight and physical state deteriorated along with a worsening of the symptoms of depression. Lily lived with her mother who was not closely involved in her treatment due to the pressure of her job. The mother had had an acrimonious divorce from Lily's father and the parents disagreed about the treatment options. Lily was admitted to the paediatric ward in the General Hospital. She needed naso-gastric tube feeding due to the physical problems. Lily resisted tube feeding and threatened to call her solicitors.

### Capacity

The paediatricians and the mental health professionals assessed Lily's capacity to consent to treatment. Their opinion was that Lily did not have capacity to consent due to the severity of the mental disorder.

### Parental consent and ZPC

Due to the strained relationship between Lily and her mother, the parents' acrimonious relationship, the invasive nature of the treatment (tube feeding) and Lily's consistent strong resistance, it was not considered treatment falling within the ZPC.

### Mental Health Act

Consideration was given to the MHA. Given the severity of the anorexia nervosa, the presence of a co-morbid depressive illness and the risk to her mental and physical health and wellbeing, Lily was considered to satisfy criteria for compulsory treatment under the MHA and treated accordingly under Section 3 MHA.

## Case study: Jordan

Jordan, a 17-year-old young man who had been in care until age 16, was referred to the CAMHS clinic for repeated self-harm in the form of self-cutting and repeated overdoses. He presented to accident and emergency having taken an overdose of a large number of paracetamol tablets several hours earlier. The paediatricians were concerned regarding the risk of serious, potentially fatal, damage to Jordan's liver. Jordan refused to have any blood tests or any treatment. Professionals in accident and emergency were concerned that on assessment, Jordan seemed to understand the need for treatment as well as the risks if he did not receive treatment. In the past, Jordan had accepted treatment for his self-harm. Due to the time elapsed since the overdose, accident and emergency doctors were extremely worried. They wondered whether they would need to treat Jordan under the MHA, but were concerned that arranging this would take up valuable time.

### Code of Practice (MHA)

The Code of Practice clearly states that in life-threatening emergency situations where any patient under the age of 18 capable of consenting to treatment refuses to do so or the person with parental responsibility refuses consent or there is no time to seek consent and there is no time to seek authority from the Court, the courts have stated that doubt should be resolved in favour of providing the necessary treatment to preserve life or prevent irreversible serious deterioration.

# Decision-making with children below 16 years of age

In the case of children below 16 years, the FLRA and MCA would not apply. The legal concept of capacity is not used. Instead the concept of 'Gillick Competence' is used to reflect the child's increasing development to maturity.

## Gillick competence

In the case of Gillick, the court held that children, who have sufficient understanding and intelligence to enable them to fully understand what is involved in a proposed intervention, will have the competence to consent to that intervention. This is referred to as the child being 'Gillick competent'. A child may be Gillick competent to consent to admission to hospital, medical treatment, research or any other activity that requires their consent.

If a child is Gillick competent and gives consent to a particular treatment, it is not necessary to gain consent from parent/person with parental responsibility. However, it is good practice to involve parents/carers in the decision-making process, if the child consents to information being shared.

If a child who is Gillick competent refuses admission or treatment, in the past courts have held that a person with parental responsibility can overrule the refusal. There is no post-Human Rights Act decision on this. The Code of Practice for the MHA states that the trend in recent cases is to reflect greater autonomy for competent children. It would be unwise to rely on the consent of a person with parental responsibility.

- In such cases, consider whether the child would meet the criteria for compulsory treatment under the MHA.
- If not suitable to use the MHA, it would be appropriate to seek authority from the Court.

If the child is not Gillick competent:

- It would be appropriate to gain consent from a person with parental responsibility, if the matter falls within the ZPC.
- If the matter falls outside the parameters of the ZPC, consider whether criteria are met for the MHA.

- If not, it would be appropriate to seek authority from the court.

# Emergency treatment

If in an emergency life-threatening situation, a competent child refuses treatment, the same rule applies as described in the section on treatment of 16–17-year-old young people.

# Legal frameworks

The legal frameworks within which decisions about the treatment of children are made include statute law, i.e. laws passed by parliament and case law/common law.

## Common law

Common law is not legislation, but a body of law based on custom and law court decisions. In healthcare, this defines the rights and duties of patients and healthcare professionals in areas untouched by legislation.

## Guiding principles

- There must be a degree of urgency together with safety/protection issues
- The intervention must end immediately when the emergency situation is resolved
- The rights of the patient must be protected at all times

## The Children Act 1989

The guiding concepts of the Act are:

- welfare of the child is paramount;
- participation of the child;
- partnership with parents or people with parental responsibility;
- race, culture, religion, language issues;
- only positive intervention.

An important aspect of the Children Act and requiring consideration when making decisions about children is the Welfare Checklist.

An important feature of this list is that the wishes and feelings of the child need to be taken into consideration in accordance with the child's age and understanding.

## Parental responsibility

Parental responsibility is defined under the Children Act as 'all the rights, duties, powers, responsibilities and authority which by law a parent of the child has in relation to the child and his or her property'.

Those who may hold parental responsibility include:

- the child's mother;
- both parents if they are married to each other at the time of the child's birth;
- both parents if married to each other at any time since the child's conception;
- mother only, if parents are not married to each other. Unmarried fathers can acquire parental responsibility by making a formal agreement with the mother or via a court order. The Adoption and Children Act 2002 provides that an unmarried father acquires parental responsibility where he and the child's mother register the birth of their child together.
- anyone holding a residence order;
- guardian of a child;
- adoptive parents;
- the Local Authority, if the child is subject to a Care Order or Emergency Protection Order;
- any person granted an Emergency Protection Order, for example the police, medical teams.

More than one person can have parental responsibility for the same child and in these cases, parental responsibility is shared with the mother who cannot lose parental responsibility, except in the case of adoption.

In cases where treatment is to be given under parental consent and parental responsibility is shared, the consent of only one person/agency with parental responsibility is required. This will still be the case even when parties do not agree. Of course, it is good practice to try to achieve an agreement between parties. In case of disagreements between persons holding parental responsibility, it may become necessary to seek legal advice and authority from the Court.

## Secure accommodation

Where a child or young person with a mental disorder needs to be detained, but the primary purpose is not to provide medical treatment for mental disorder, for example if the young person is behaviourally disturbed and there is no need for them to be hospitalized, their needs might be more appropriately met within secure accommodation under the Children Act 1989, Section 25 Secure Order. The Secure Order does not authorize medical treatment.

This option is used when the primary aim of the intervention is to achieve a measure of safety and protection for the young person rather than to provide medical treatment for mental disorder.

## Case study: Asha

Asha, a 16-year-old girl in the care of the Local Authority, was placed in foster accommodation in a neighbouring city. She was extremely distressed and angry at being moved away from her home town. She began repeatedly self-harming by cutting herself. She would abscond frequently from the foster placement. Asha was known to associate with older males and she was being exploited. She was admitted to the Paediatric ward of the local General Hospital after being found unconscious in a park, having been severely beaten up and having cut herself deeply. During assessment, Asha expressed her anger and distress at her current placement and repeatedly stated her intention to self-harm and to abscond if sent back to the foster placement. The social workers wondered whether Asha needed to be admitted to an adolescent psychiatric unit in view of the self-harm.

### Outcome

Following a planning meeting, it was agreed that in view of the repeated and frequent absconding and the risk of significant harm to Asha when she ran away, and the repeated and frequent self-harm, Asha needed the protection and safety offered by Secure Accommodation. Sec 25 was applied for and Asha was placed in a welfare bed in the local Secure Unit for 6 weeks. The self-harm stopped. On discharge, Asha was moved into a specialist supported accommodation where she has managed to significantly reduce the self-harm and has not absconded.

# Mental Health Act 1983 (2007 amendments) MHA 2007

The Mental Health Act provides for compulsory admission, detention and treatment of a patient deemed to have a mental disorder. In the past, the mental disorders were specified as mental illness, commonly diagnosed using ICD-10 criteria, psychopathic disorder, i.e. treatable personality disorder, mental impairment, i.e. learning disability or severe mental impairment in the terms of the 1983 Act.

According to MHA 2007, the definition of mental disorder has been broadened to 'any disorder of the mind'. The above sub-categories have been removed.

It is important to remember that sections of the MHA can be applied to all ages, except under guardianship, which only applies to those older than 16 years of age.

The MHA 2007 Code of Practice highlights issues specific to the care and treatment of children and young people:

- The best interests of the child or young person must always be a significant consideration.
- Children and young people must be kept as fully informed as possible, just as an adult would, and should receive clear and detailed information about their care and treatment in a format appropriate to their age and development.
- The views of the child or young person and their wishes and feelings should always be considered.
- The intervention for the treatment of the mental disorder should be the least restrictive, least stigmatizing, consistent with effective care and treatment, resulting in the least possible separation from family and friends and with least possible interruption of their education.
- All children and young people should receive the same access to education as their peers.
- Children and young people have as much right to expect their dignity to be respected as anyone else.
- Children and young people have as much right to privacy and confidentiality regarding information pertaining to them as anyone else.

The MHA 2007 has introduced the duty on hospital managers to provide age-appropriate hospital environment for the admission and treatment of children and young people.

In all MHA Section assessments it is important to consult with the patient's nearest relative, i.e. spouse, oldest parent, next of kin or legally appointed nearest relative, although only Section 3 requires permission from the nearest relative.

# Common applications of the MHA (1983) in children

| Purpose | Section | Requirements in addition to mental disorder | Powers |
|---------|---------|---------------------------------------------|--------|
| Assessment | 2 | Admission necessary for patient's own health and safety or the protection of others. Two doctors, one with Section 12 Approval and an approved social worker needed to make the assessment | Up to 28 days admission for assessment, or assessment followed by medical treatment. Not renewable. Patient may appeal against the Section within 14 days |
| Emergency order for assessment | 4 | As for Section 2: used when only one doctor is available | Up to 72 hours admission for assessment. Not renewable |
| Emergency detention of a voluntary inpatient | 5.4 | This is a nurse's holding power and can be used if necessary for the patient's own health and safety or the protection of others and no doctor or social worker is available. Patient must have been a voluntary inpatient who is no longer willing to stay | Up to 6 hours admission. Not renewable and must be reviewed by a doctor |

| Purpose | Section | Requirements in addition to mental disorder | Powers |
|---------|---------|---------------------------------------------|--------|
| Emergency detention of a voluntary inpatient | 5.2 | Necessary for patient's own health and safety or the protection of others. Only one doctor needed. Patient must be a voluntary inpatient for this to be applied | Up to 72 hours. Not renewable |
| Treatment | 3 | Inpatient treatment is appropriate and admission is necessary for patient's own health and safety or for protection of others. It is important that compulsory admission and treatment is considered to alleviate the mental disorder or prevent further deterioration. The patient's nearest relative must give consent for the Section to be applied. | Up to six months admission and is renewable. Treatment may be enforced for the first three months, but the patient would need to consent after this. If the patient does not consent, a second opinion is required from a doctor recommended by the MHA commission. Patient has the right to appeal against the Section after three months. |

# Supervised community treatment/community treatment order (SCT/CTO)

The MHA 2007 has introduced the supervised community treatment/community treatment order (SCT/CTO), which provides a framework for the management of suitable patients allowing them to be safely treated in the community. This treatment occurs in the context of the ability of the Responsible Clinician having the power of recalling the patient to hospital for treatment if necessary.

Only patients who have been treated in hospital under Section 3 MHA can be considered for SCT/CTO.

The SCT/CTO has several conditions that the patient must comply with in the community. The Responsible Clinician holds the power to recall the patient to hospital if he considers that the patient

can no longer be treated safely in the community. The SCT/CTO may be successful in providing the least restrictive alternative for suitable patients promoting recovery and participation in age-appropriate activities.

LILY: Lily was treated successfully in hospital under Section 3 MHA. After she had made a good recovery, she was given increasing periods of leave. She was then put on SCT/CTO. The conditions were that she would have weekly physical monitoring, take medication and meet members of the community team as required.

Lily complied with the conditions and was able to successfully sit for her GCSE exams and go on to college. After five months, she was discharged off the SCT/CTO.

The MHA 2007 also gives time scales at which Tribunal reviews of detention and compulsory treatment of children and young people would be carried out.

## Multiple choice questions

1. For a patient's consent to treatment to be valid they must have:

   a. sufficient information to make the decision
   b. an IQ of 100 or more
   c. agreement of their next of kin
   d. the capacity to make the decision

2. Which legislation introduced a statutory concept of 'capacity' for young people and adults over age 16?

   a. The 1989 Children Act
   b. The Human Rights Act
   c. The Mental Capacity Act (2005)
   d. Gillick competence

3. Under the Mental Health Act (1983), how long can a voluntary inpatient be detained in hospital in an emergency where they are considered to be at risk to themselves or others?

   a. Seven days
   b. 28 days
   c. 24 hours
   d. 72 hours
   e. 6 hours

## Key texts

Department of Constitutional Affairs (2007) *Mental Capacity Act 2005 Code of Practice*. London: TSO.

Department of Health (2008b) *Mental Health Act 1983 Code of Practice*. London: TSO.

National Institute for Mental Health in England (2009) *The Legal Aspects of the Care and Treatment of Children and Young People with Mental Disorder: A Guide for Professionals*. Department of Health Publication, Gateway ref: 10944.

# 16 *Fostering and adoption*
## Maggie Rance and Janet Féat

## Introduction

All Local Authorities, through their Social Services departments, have a statutory responsibility to all children under 18 years of age, who are considered to be vulnerable or at risk, and for any disabled children and young people up to age 25.

Although amended by later Acts of Parliament (see Chapter 15, Making treatment decisions with young people and below) the underpinning legislation remains the Children Act 1989.

This Act introduced the 'paramountcy principle', in that the needs of the child are paramount and all action must be based on the premise that, in an agent taking action, the child's needs could not be served in any other way.

## Looked after children

Fostering and adoption is a means of providing substitute family care for children, when remaining within their birth family is considered to be impracticable, poses an unacceptable level of risk or the options for reunification are untenable. Ideally, fostering is to be considered as a short-term measure to allow work to be undertaken which will explore solutions and determine safeguards to allow a child to live safely within their family network. However, there are some children and young people whose experiences, and life within their families, have had such a negative impact that long-term substitute family care is the only reasonable course of action. The challenging behaviour of some older children in particular can undermine all attempts to support them.

The difficulties in offering a supportive home environment to a Looked After child whose experience of family life has been unhappy can be overwhelming. It is hard for a child or young person to integrate into an unfamiliar setting at a time of high emotional turmoil. That setting may have a vastly different family culture, expectations and values: this will be especially difficult for the child if there have been traumatic events prior to his or her removal from home. Both the foster family and the child need to manage integration, while maintaining links with birth parents and complying with sanctions imposed either by the parents or the local authority. Adherence to other obligations must be considered: school attendance, social contacts, extended family and participation in the planning process.

It has always been difficult to match the numbers of adoption and fostering placements to the numbers of children requiring substitute family care. Most children in this situation wish to remain with familiar people, so that the process of integration is significantly less of a problem for children and carers. Kinship care and placements with friends and family are used when available and appropriate, sometimes supported by the local authority. Options other than fostering and adoption have increased with the introduction of the Special Guardianship Order in the Adoption and Children Act 2002 (Section 115). Section 38 of the Children and Young Persons Act 2008 further extends the list of those who can apply to be a Special Guardian to those who have cared for the child continuously for one year. Section 14A of the Children Act 1989 is inserted and amended by this subsequent legislation.

A Special Guardian is someone who has been appointed by the court in adoption proceedings or in any family proceedings where a question arises with respect to the welfare of the child or where there has been an application for special guardianship. The Special Guardian acquires parental responsibility for the child and can usually exercise parental responsibility to the exclusion of any other person with parental responsibility (apart from another Special Guardian). This allows children for whom adoption is not a suitable option, but who cannot return to their birth parents, to remain with a relative or other person who has been looking after them in a manner assessed as consistent with their best interests and welfare.

Foster carers are not employees of the local authority for which they provide a service and the allowances paid have often been considered inadequate as a reflection of the cost of meeting a Looked After child's needs. However, this situation could be improved: Section 49 of the Children Act 2004 amends the 1989 Act enabling secondary legislation to bring in a national minimum fostering allowance.

Rigorous investigations are made of families wishing to offer a foster placement to a Looked After child and training courses are mandatory prior to the approval of a placement. Despite the best preparation, the reality of a hostile or violent foster child who is rejecting the placement can frustrate the intention to support that child. Altruism is not enough; skills and strategies are essential to managing the feelings on both sides.

Henry (1974) describes two levels of deprivation: the first is inflicted by external circumstances out of the child's control and the second derived from internal sources as the child develops crippling defences, which inhibit the use of the support offered by foster carers or therapists. Britton (1981) described 'the profoundly disturbing primitive mechanisms and defences against anxiety' which, used by children and families, become re-enacted in the system by care professionals who may be the recipients of powerful projections.

This pattern of behaviour is often reflected in children who have been in the Looked After system for several years, have experienced many placements and for whom the process has replicated the original neglect by allowing them to 'fall through the net'. They are often not in education, not in receipt of clinical services, noted as non-compliant, have been involved in substance misuse, low level criminal activity and viewed as problematic. This form of re-enactment, combined with the double deprivation, can result in the 'triple deprivation' for children who are looked after by a local authority.

Much is invested in multiple placements, support of carers, inclusion of family networks, recruitment of clinical services and exploration of educational opportunities. It is apparent however, that despite this considerable input initially, if a Looked After child is not outwardly compliant, services can rapidly become less effective. This may confirm the child's view of their own worth and reduce the likelihood of future success for professionals and carers in engaging and sustaining them within a placement. Services withdraw, more reliance is placed on local housing and hostel provision and the problematic care leaver sadly may become someone likely to engage in offending behaviour and who may not access further education, employment or training.

Foster carers and adopters will have invested heavily in the concept that emotional rewards will compensate for the adjustments that have to be made within their family home. Disrupted placements will have a significant impact on their self-esteem, family life and confidence.

## Case study: Tom

All personal information in respect of the case study has been changed to preserve confidentiality and the permission of both the carer and the subject has been sought.

Tom is 13 years of age; he has three older brothers. Tom's father is a life prisoner; his eldest brother is serving a four-year sentence for aggravated assault and burglary. His two siblings are both 'looked after' by the local authority, one in a children's home following multiple placements, one serving an eight-month sentence in a young offenders institution. Tom's natural mother is tagged and under an Anti-Social Behaviour order, following shoplifting, handling stolen goods and assault charges.

Tom and his siblings were subject to a care order made by the local authority some six years ago, following the children's placement on the Child Protection Register for neglect, emotional and physical abuse.

Since being 'accommodated' Tom has experienced over 20 placements within family homes.

He is articulate, good-humoured and easy to engage. Initially, foster carers describe him as helpful, considerate and loving. He is readily welcomed into family systems. Plans are beginning to be put into place for his future, to which he usually responds in a positive and enthusiastic manner, thanking carers for giving him a chance to go back to school and live with a great family.

However, within each placement, at the point of breakdown, he has absconded, broken furniture, used abusive language, stolen items, threatened self-harm, harm to carers and others within the household.

At this time, he is described by carers as mentally ill, dangerous and not deserving of their affection, time or care.

Tom is able to re-enact this pattern so effectively that, despite foster carers' preparation and knowledge that others have preceded them, they are drawn to 'making a difference' by attempting to compensate for factors they feel have been missing in his early years.

In therapeutic sessions and discussions with social workers, Tom is able to acknowledge that he 'tests' carers and talks about his wish that he could act differently. He considers sanctions that will prohibit him from continually moving from placement to placement and, at his latest breakdown, requested that he was placed in a secure unit.

# Adoption

Adoptive parents face lengthy and invasive examination by the social services department. Their motivation, ability and suitability to parent a child are meticulously examined.

In the main, prospective parents want a baby. However, increasingly, the children available for adoption are older or have a disability. There are enormous moral and ethical considerations to address in placing any child, especially those children with a disability. It is important to be clear that the standards should be as rigorous as those standards set for adopting a non-disabled child.

The matching process can be difficult to achieve when in Hampshire, for instance, only up to half or slightly more of the potentially approved parents needed are available for the number of children requiring adoption.

For those parents who do adopt, there is a significant issue to consider; the child has a statutory right to know that their birth parents are different from their adoptive parents. Many adoptive parents have struggled with 'the right time' to tell their child about their birth family and have experienced huge anxieties regarding how the subject might be introduced, how it will impact on their family unit and how they might have to absorb another individual into the life of their child.

Adoptive parents think about which traits their child might have inherited from their genetic parents. They have to consider what they can influence and what they cannot, especially if they know the background of the birth parents of their child. The nature–nurture debate can sometimes be a contentious and fearful matter within adoptive households.

The rules that determine the payment of adoption allowances are to be found in The Adoption Support Services (Local Authorities) (England) Regulations 2003 and The Adoption Support Service Regulations 2005. If agreed, any adoption allowances would depend on an assessment considering the age of the child, the child's needs, the circumstances of the placement and/or the financial circumstances of the adoptive parents.

Adoptive parents are frequently anxious regarding their abilities, how they understand norms of child development and how they should use sanctions.

Children and parents who make the journey positively describe it as immensely rewarding. They view themselves as a family chosen and created, earned and tested and as strong, loving and supportive. In this journey, they have integrated the child's background and managed the countless issues that arise from participation in that process.

## Multiple choice questions

1. What is the 'paramountcy principle'?

    a. Children's wishes must be given priority
    b. A child's parent or carer has the final say
    c. The needs of the child are paramount
    d. A social worker decides what should happen

2. Special guardians

    a. Have looked after the child for six months
    b. Are blood-related to the child
    c. Are employed by the Local Authority
    d. Appointed by a court

### Key texts

Box S, Copley B, Magagna J, Moustaki E (eds) (1981) *Psychotherapy with Families: An Analytic Approach.* London: Routledge and Kegan Paul.

Britton R (1981) Re-enactment as an unwitting professional response to family dynamics. In: Box S, Copley B, Magagna J, Moustaki E (eds) *Psychotherapy with Families.* London: Routledge and Kegan Paul.

Department of Health (2001a) *The Children Act Now Messages from Research.* London: The Stationery Office.

Henry G (1974) Doubly deprived. *Journal of Child Psychotherapy,* **3**: 15–28.

# 17 The effect of early institutional deprivation on the brain: findings from the English and Romanian adoptees study

Jana Kreppner

## Key concepts

- Brain development is particularly sensitive to early experience.
- Prolonged institutional deprivation is associated with a pervasive deprivation specific pattern (DSP) of behaviour with deficits involving either quasi-autistic tendencies and/or disinhibited attachment with or without cognitive impairment and inattention/overactivity.
- Prolonged institutional deprivation in children may result in changes to the brain structure and function.
- Preliminary findings from the study sample suggest reduced brain size, altered amygdala volume and atypical responsivity to reward anticipation in the ventral striatal region.
- Heterogeneity in outcome may be explained, in part, by genetic variations in susceptibility to early experience. Findings from the English and Romanian Adoptees (ERA) study sample suggest that important alleic variations in specific genes moderate the effects of early deprivation. These involve the serotonin transporter gene 5HTT in moderating outcome in emotional problems and the dopamine transporter gene DAT1 in moderating the effects on attention deficit hyperactivity disorder (ADHD) symptoms.
- Putting together the findings from this study on affected brain regions and genetic variations suggests important candidate systems, which appear to be sensitive to early deprivation. These include the limbic system emotion regulation circuitry modulated by the activity in the neurotransmitter 5HT and the ventral striatal reward processing circuitry, extensively modulated by dopamine activity.
- Further research to corroborate these findings is imperative in this important area.

The findings from the ERA study (Rutter et al., 1998; Rutter et al., 2007; Rutter et al., 2010) provide important pointers as to how the developing brain might be affected by profound early institutional deprivation. This chapter will first provide a brief background of the study and summarize its key findings. Second, potential risk mechanisms associated with early deprivation, and which are implicated in brain development, will be discussed. Third, findings from the ERA study, which provide preliminary results on important structural and functional changes in the developing brains of children who experienced early institutional deprivation, will be summarized. Finally, the major

themes emerging from ERA's findings will be put forward. These should provide powerful leads for future investigations.

A cautionary note is necessary. The findings of the ERA sample are based on an extremely profound deprivation experience. Whether these findings can be generalized to other samples of institution-reared children who have not been exposed to the same degree of profound and pervasive deprivation or to samples of children who experienced early neglect and abuse of the sort that is typically encountered by professionals involved in child protection, remains to be established. Nevertheless, the data from the ERA sample provide important leads regarding the biological mechanisms that might be involved in altering brain structure and function in response to early experience.

# Background to the ERA study

The ERA study was set up in response to the many children adopted into the UK out of Romanian institutions following the fall of the Ceauşescu regime in 1989. The conditions in the Romanian institutions at the time were described as profoundly depriving in all respects (physical, psychological, social) (Reich, 1990; Children's Health Care Collaborative Study Group, 1992; Castle et al., 1999). The children were adopted into generally above average rearing environments in the UK. As such, these circumstances constituted an invaluable 'natural experiment' (Rutter, 2007; Rutter, in press).

The situation was rather unusual for several reasons (see Rutter et al., 2007; Rutter et al., 2010). First, families who adopted children from Romania did not always do so for reasons of infertility, but for altruistic reasons. Second, nearly all children were placed in the institutions in early infancy and hence it was unlikely that, at that time, any possible handicaps were apparent and were the reason for their placement in institutions. Third, as far as is known, prior to 1989, no children were adopted from institutions or returned to their biological families. This meant that the children who were placed in institutions most likely did not represent a selective sample, as is often the case with other samples of institutionalized children.

The ERA study was set up to address both policy and practice questions, and fundamental theoretical questions regarding the role of early experience on child development. Would such extremely depriving conditions have an enduring effect or would recovery be possible? Which mechanisms could offer explanations if enduring effects of early deprivation occurred?

## Summary of findings

The findings from the last follow-up of the ERA sample at age 15 years are summarized in Rutter et al. (2010). In brief, a substantial minority of the institution-reared children showed a specific pattern of deficits involving either quasi-autistic tendencies and/or disinhibited attachment with or without cognitive impairment and inattention/overactivity. We concluded that these patterns probably constituted a DSP. The pattern was present at age six and persisted through to our assessment at age 15. Importantly, DSP was associated with prolonged institutional deprivation beyond six months of age and the strength of this association was as strong at age 15 years as it was at 6 and 11 years. The persistence of difficulties resulting from the early institutional deprivation experience (Kumsta et al., 2010a; Kreppner et al., 2010) in the ERA sample, despite the change in environment following adoption, suggested that they involved fundamental alterations of brain structures and circuitry implicated in cognitive and social-emotional behavioural regulation.

# Early Environmental Influences on the brain in the era study: multiple risks, individual differences and possible explanatory mechanisms

Before looking at the specific findings from our ERA study with regard to alterations in brain structure and function, different types of putative risks associated with profound early deprivation experiences must be considered, together with a set of possible mechanisms through which deprivation-related early adversity might operate to produce such long-lasting effects (see Rutter and O'Connor, 2004; Kumsta et al., 2010b; Sonuga-Barke et al., 2010).

## Multiple risks

In the case of the ERA sample, a number of putative risks need to be considered that could have impacted on the developing brain:

- Nutritional deprivation may have impacted brain growth (Stoch et al., 1982; Golden, 1994), which in turn is associated with cognitive delay and behavioural difficulties (Liu et al., 2003; Liu et al., 2004).

- Psychosocial and cognitive deprivation have been shown to affect brain growth, structure and function in both animal and human studies (e.g. Teicher et al., 2003; de Kloet et al., 2005).
- The adverse effects of psychosocial deprivation might possibly operate through early insult on neurobiological regulation, perhaps resulting from harmful exposure to stress hormones (Gunnar, 1998; Leon-Carrion et al., 2009).
- Developmental programming effects involving experience-expectant and experience-adaptive programming of the brain during sensitive periods (Rutter and O'Connor, 2004) might have occurred.

## Individual differences

A large degree of heterogeneity in outcome was observed within the ERA sample (Rutter et al., 2001; Rutter et al., 2007; Rutter et al., 2010). For example, deficits in cognitive ability were more likely in the institution-reared children who suffered prolonged deprivation, but within this group a considerable number showed remarkable resilience. Some children had IQ scores well within the normal range despite prolonged institutional deprivation. What might account for such individual differences in response?

It might be, for reasons impossible for us to determine, that some children received differential treatment in the orphanages. Unfortunately, our data set does not allow us to test for this possibility. Post-adoption experience may offer another explanation. Our data, however, suggest that there was very little variation across our sample of adoptive families; almost all provided good quality care. There was no significant association with any of our outcome measures and post-adoption environment measures (see Castle et al., 2010). This does not mean, however, that the post-adoption environment did not play a crucial role in the remarkable improvement in functioning observed in this sample as a whole.

## Genetic variations in susceptibility

Findings from our study suggest a potential role for alleic variations in specific genes to moderate the effects of early deprivation. These involve the serotonin transporter gene 5HTT in moderating outcome in emotional problems (Kumsta et al., 2010c) and the dopamine transporter gene DAT1 moderating the effects on ADHD symptoms (Stevens et al., 2009). Because our ERA data set only provides a relatively small number for testing for genetic moderation (usually much larger numbers are required for statistical power), the findings can only be interpreted as preliminary. More research based on larger numbers corroborating our findings is needed.

In summary, the interplay between genes and environment in shaping brain architecture and function needs to be considered. Such an approach must consider the potential role of sensitive periods during which brain development is particularly susceptible to experience (see Knudsen, 2004).

## Possible explanatory mechanisms

Human brain development is driven by a dynamic and adaptive process involving input from both genes and environment to produce the brain's complex and highly differentiated structures and functions (Stiles and Jernigan, 2010). Huttenlocher's (e.g. Huttenlocher and Dabholkar, 1997) and Rakic's (Granger et al., 1995) work illustrated the processes of synaptic 'blooming' and 'pruning' during the post-natal period and showed that different brain regions mature at different times during development, with those regions associated with higher cognitive function developing later (Huttenlocher and Dabholkar 1997). The implication is that during these early months the brain may be particularly sensitive to experiences.

The view that sensitive periods may exist in brain development has recently attracted renewed interest. A growing body of evidence from both animal and human studies suggests that seriously adverse early experiences during sensitive periods can have enduring effects on the brain's structure and function, even when such experience is not maintained (Greenough and Black, 1992; Gunnar et al., 2001; McEwen and Lasley, 2002; Rutter and O'Connor, 2004; Weaver et al., 2004; Hubel and Wiesel, 2005; Meaney and Szyf, 2005; Parker et al., 2005; Wismer Fries et al., 2005). Specifically, such enduring effects may be either the result of damage to neural structures or two types of biological programming, including experience-expectant and experience-adaptive programming (Rutter and O'Connor, 2004).

Experience-expectant developmental programming requires specific experience for normal brain development to occur. In the absence of such experience, brain development will not follow its 'expected' path with associated enduring deficits or abnormalities in structure and function. Hubel and Wiesel's (1965) classic study showing that visual input is necessary for the development of the visual cortex in cats is one example for the existence of experience-expectant processes. Le Grand and colleagues (2001) demonstrated experience-expectant programming in human brain development. Their data show that deprivation of patterned visual input during the first months of life resulted in permanent deficits in configural processing of faces.

Experience-adaptive developmental programming occurs when the brain's structure and function are adapted to specific circumstances encountered at a specific stage of development. An example of experience-adaptive development is provided by studies on phonetic discrimination. Initially, young infants around the world discriminate phonetic contrasts from a 'universal' set of sounds, but with increasing age and exposure to their native language successful phonological discrimination becomes increasingly specialized to the sounds to which the infants have been exposed (Werker and Desjardins, 1995; Werker and Tees, 2005). Native speakers of several European languages can discriminate with ease between 'r' and 'l', a phonological contrast with which Japanese native speakers often have great difficulty. Accordingly, brain development following experience-adaptive processes is a function of the specific circumstances that operate during a sensitive period.

# Brain development following early institutional deprivation

Specific areas of the brain including the hippocampus, amygdala and corpus callosum have been identified to be sensitive to the impact of early adverse and stressful experiences in both animal and human studies (Suomi, 1997; Sanchez et al., 1998; Teicher et al., 2003). These areas of the brain have been associated with higher cognitive function, social behaviour and emotional processes (Teicher et al., 2003), exactly the sorts of behaviours that have been shown to be affected by early institutional deprivation in the ERA sample (Rutter et al., 2007; Rutter et al., 2010).

Three relevant reports suggesting important influences of early experience for brain development have been published thus far from the ERA study (Sonuga-Barke et al., 2008; Mehta et al., 2009a; Mehta et al., 2009b). The first key finding from these studies is that brain volume is reduced as a result of the effects of early deprivation (Sonuga-Barke et al., 2008; Mehta et al. 2009a). Importantly, psychosocial deprivation was found to have an effect on brain growth as measured by head circumference, even in the absence of sub-nutrition (Sonuga-Barke et al., 2008). This finding highlights the crucial role of psychological deprivation in impacting brain development (Sonuga-Barke et al., 2008). Our rather crude index of overall brain growth stunting had a relatively small but partially mediating effect on deprivation-specific disorders, providing the first direct evidence that brain size played a partial mediating role in psychological sequelae following early institutional deprivation (Sonuga-Barke et al., 2010). Even so, this effect was small, highlighting the need to focus on more subtle alterations in brain development.

There is evidence that the hippocampus, amygdala and corpus callosum undergo rapid growth during the time that the children in the ERA sample were exposed to institutional deprivation, namely the first three and a half years of life (Nishida et al., 2006). Using magnetic resonance imaging (MRI), in a pilot study of a sub-group of the ERA sample, total grey and white matter volumes were significantly smaller in the Romanian adoptees compared with a group of non-deprived, non-adopted controls. In addition, there was evidence that the institution-reared group had greater amygdala volume, especially on the right, after correcting for difference in brain size, than the control group (Mehta et al., 2009a). Within the institution-reared sample, left amygdala volume was significantly negatively related to time spent in institutions, with those spending longer time in institutions showing smaller left amygdala volume. Neither hippocampal volume nor corpus callosum mid-saggittal area was different between the groups after brain size was corrected. The authors argue that changes in amygdala volume may be implicated in disruptive emotional processing and social behaviour. Moreover, in this study, only changes in amygdala volume, but not corpus callosum or hippocampus, were observed suggesting that the amygdala may be particularly sensitive to early deprivation.

Although these findings are based on a small sample, amygdala abnormalities have also been reported in other studies of Romanian adoptees (Chugani et al., 2001; Eluvathingal et al., 2006). Importantly, in a larger study of previously institutionalized (PI) children, Tottenham and colleagues (2010) found larger amygdala volume in the PI group compared to never-institutionalized control group. In a subsequent study, heightened amygdala activity mediated the association between rearing environment and deficits in social behaviour (i.e. reduced eye contact; Tottenham et al., 2011). Taking all of the above together, it is clear that studying structural and functional changes in the amygdala in samples of post-institution-reared children must be a focus of future research.

A second pilot study of ERA participants examined the functional integrity of brain regions previously shown to be implicated in processes implicated in self-regulation (Mehta et al., 2009b). Abnormal (e.g. hypo) responsivity in ventral striatal regions in response to reward anticipation was found to be associated with a history of early institutional deprivation. Specifically, no reward-related activation was found in Romanian adoptees compared with the never-institutionalized controls. The findings are similar, albeit more marked, than those reported in studies of ADHD adolescents (Scheres et al., 2007). The authors argue that two behavioural responses are possible as a result of the hyporesponsivity present to reward anticipation. Either anhedonic or apathetic behaviour may result, or compensatory reward seeking. This means that post-institutionalized children may be at increased risk for substance abuse or other risk-taking behaviours associated with poor decision-making (Ernst and Fudge, 2009), although this remains to be established in future research.

In summary, findings from the ERA study together with those of other related samples (Chugani et al. 2001; Eluvathingal et al., 2006; Tottenham et al., 2010; Tottenham et al., 2011) suggest that important changes in brain structure and function result from early institutional deprivation. Specifically, the findings from the ERA study suggest overall reduced brain size, altered amygdala volume and atypical responsivity to reward anitcipation in the ventral striatal region in children who experienced prolonged institutional deprivation as compared to never-institutionalized children.

The findings reported by Mehta et al. (2009a, Mehta et al., 2009b) are based on a small sub-sample and will need to be replicated in future research. Nevertheless, together the findings suggest important candidate systems, which appear to be sensitive to early deprivation. These include the limbic system emotion regulation circuitry modulated by the activity in the neurotransmitter 5HT and the ventral striatal reward processing circuitry extensively modulated by dopamine activity.

Further examination of the effects of deprivation on these brain regions should be the focus of future research. The present review highlights the need for a multidisciplinary approach in future research in order to elucidate the changes in neuropsychological mechanisms which result from early institutional deprivation.

## Case study 1: Max

### Val Forster

Max was five years old when he began three times weekly individual psychotherapy that lasted for two years. He had been adopted when he was two and a half by a childless couple, who subsequently adopted his younger full sibling. Max was referred to the clinic because of extreme temper tantrums, which included violence to others and to himself and, at other times, withdrawal into a world of his own. His nursery school had been unable to manage him and in the reception class at his local school he was very quickly given a Statement of Special Educational Need and transferred to a small special unit attached to a mainstream school.

Max's birth parents were both heroin addicts with mental health problems. He spent the first 11 months of his life in their care. He was physically and emotionally neglected and lived in a household that was chaotic and domestically violent, until he was removed and placed in foster care. For the next 15 months, he had three foster placements plus numerous respite carers due to his difficult and demanding temperament.

Clearly, Max's first two years of life did not provide an experience of reliable, attuned caregiving but rather one of deprivation, trauma and numerous caregivers. He could not explain his distress but could only externalize it. His solution to the feelings of intolerable vulnerability was to be very tough, fighting and destroying things.

When therapy began, Max's adoptive parents felt that they could no longer continue and he was at risk of returning to the care system. What Max was unable to process consciously, let alone internalize, was gradually revealed in his therapy and his relationship with his therapist. His need for emotional containment and his struggle to make sense of relationships dominated the therapy. He was domineering and cruel in his play with no regard for the therapist who was bullied, alone and utterly helpless in the face of a powerful and uncaring tyrant. Therapy allowed him to express his terror of abandonment, helplessness and fear of his own destructiveness, through play. Over time it was possible to see a gradual shift in the themes enacted so that Max was more securely attached to his therapist and new themes of cooperation and caring evolved. During the course of two years of therapy, Max made a successful transition to mainstream school where he was happy and popular. His parents could barely recognize the damaged boy they had adopted. They felt they had a son at last.

## Case study 2: Stephen

Stephen was 12 when he began once weekly psychotherapy. He was six when he was received into care along with his three younger siblings. Following a period in foster care, his sisters and brother were placed for adoption while Stephen was felt to be 'un-adoptable' due to the level of damage and distress he displayed. He moved to an experienced foster family where he remained despite his severe developmental difficulties.

Stephen's birth mother had learning difficulties and abused alcohol. All the children were severely neglected by her. Stephen cared for his younger siblings as best he could. He had witnessed domestic violence, cruelty to animals and was exposed to pornographic material. There was often no food in the house and the children, like the animals, drank from the toilet. Stephen was ill treated and physically abused by one of his mother's partners resulting in his admission to hospital and the removal of all the children into care. His stepfather was imprisoned for his assaults on Stephen.

Stephen was diagnosed with ADHD when he was nine and responded to medication. This stabilized his behaviour at school and, in turn, this took some of the pressure off his foster parents. His foster mother was especially devoted to him and genuinely committed to making sure that he was given the best opportunity to try to overcome his severe early deprivation.

When Stephen began therapy he was impulsive and hyperactive. The transition to secondary school and the onset of puberty had been deeply unsettling. He was inattentive and attention seeking. He bullied other more vulnerable children and was in turn bullied by older boys, whom he baited. He stole food and money from home, which he used to buy friendship from peers. Stephen had sleep difficulties and wet the bed every night. His relationship with his foster parents deteriorated and Stephen was convinced that they would 'send him back'.

At first, Stephen was very physically active in the sessions. The therapy room was treated more like an adventure playground and there was a feeling that it was dangerous to stay still in one place for too long. Any attempt by the therapist to talk about how this may relate to Stephen's internal world was dismissed with distain or anger. Over time he became more used to the therapeutic space as a reliable and benign experience. Stephen began to express his thoughts that he would be like his stepfather, bad and cruel. He believed that the care and love he found with his foster parents was misplaced because he would turn out bad in the end. Any misdemeanor at school or any argument at home confirmed his view that he would become the terrifying figure from his childhood.

Stephen's individual therapy lasted for four years. In this time he stopped taking his medication and developed into a thoughtful and well-attuned young man. He gave up his identification with a cruel parental figure, which allowed him to look forward to a different future and to be nurtured by his foster parents. He became a school prefect and played in the cricket team, as well as becoming an air cadet. He achieved well in his GCSEs and was attending college before applying to join the armed forces.

## Multiple choice questions

1. According to findings from the ERA study, which brain structure appears affected by early institutional deprivation?

   a. Hippocampus
   b. Frontal lobe
   c. Amygdala
   d. Corpus callosum

2. The ERA study reported reduced brain size as a result of the effects of early deprivation. Importantly, _____ was found to have an effect on brain growth even in the absence of _____

   a. Psychosocial deprivation – nutritional deprivation
   b. Psychological stimulation – extra nutrition
   c. Physical deprivation – psychological deprivation
   d. Nutritional deprivation – social deprivation

## Key texts

Kreppner J, Kumsta R, Rutter M et al. (2010) Developmental course of deprivation-specific patterns: early manifestations, persistence to age 15 and clinical features. *Monographs of the Society for Research in Child Development*, **75**: 79–101.

Mehta MA, Golembo NI, Nosarti C et al. (2009a) Amygdala, hippocampal and corpus callosum size following severe early institutional deprivation: The English and Romanian Adoptees study. *Journal of Child Psychology and Psychiatry*, **50**: 943–51.

Sonuga-Barke EJ, Beckett C, Kreppner J et al. (2008) Is subnutrition necessary for a poor outcome following early institutional deprivation? *Developmental Medicine and Child Neurology*, **50**: 664–71.

# Introduction to assessment
## Cathy Laver–Bradbury

The importance of assessment in CAMHS work can never be underestimated. The skill of the assessment is to understand from the parent and child's perspective what the difficulties are and how these have occurred. The assessment process uses a variety of approaches in order to make sense of the child's behaviour.

Assessment should not be seen as something that is only done at the beginning of treatment but as a continuous process that happens each time you meet with the family, child or young person. The assessment builds up over time as trust is built. As the assessment proceeds, it may be that the original presenting problem becomes less significant and other problems assume priority for treatment.

The skill of the assessor is paramount, exploration of the surrounding systems is essential and none should be seen in isolation. This is an enormous task and the skills of working with families to bring about change is often under-recognized, either by the system in which the health and social care professions work or by the time restraints often in place. Chapter 18, Engagement and motivation, recognizes the skills required and gives an overview of how to interview using motivational techniques to bring about change and provides an underpinning of knowledge to apply to the various assessment techniques.

The subsequent chapters offer an outline of the approaches to assessment within CAMHS, using different therapeutic models and the questionnaires chapter discusses further ways to elicit information.

Assessments are often a treatment in their own right, raising awareness in the family about the issues they want help with and why these might have occurred can often in itself bring about a significant change. The importance of 'holding' the family through this process is paramount if the family is to feel safe in exploring their difficulties.

# 18  *Engagement and motivation*
## Margaret Thompson

## Key concepts

- Parental motivation will make a difference to outcome and engagement.
- It is helpful to assess where the parent is on the wheel of change on initial engagement.
- Therapeutic alliance is composed of personal alliance and task alliance.
- Motivational interviewing is a useful technique.
- Barriers to taking up programmes should be addressed.

## Introduction

This paper has been written to discuss the principles of motivation, and techniques that therapists might need to incorporate into their interviews to hold parents or patients in therapy. We have used these concepts in our work with parents in our parenting programmes. Therefore it is written from this viewpoint but would apply to any other therapeutic work.

This has been adapted from A practical guide to motivational interviewing in anorexia (Treasure and Ward, 1997) and other references, see end of chapter.

*Motivation* involves a need to do something or change something.

*Intrinsic motivation*: the client wants to change things for the sake of personal gain, or to change something in self.

*Extrinsic motivation* would be where the client comes into therapy because of concern for external controls or consequences. For example, if clients do not, their child may not get to stay in a nursery or professionals persuade them to come into a parenting programme, otherwise social services would consider child protection issues.

*Therapeutic alliance* is an umbrella term for a variety of therapist–client interactional and relational factors operating in the delivery of treatment.

This will include how the patient experiences the relationship with the therapist. Does she feel that the therapist is 'empathetic'; does she think that the therapist understands the problem, does the therapist give her space to work, and does the patient perceive that the task is mutual?

Hougaard (1994) discusses that both clinician and patient will contribute to this alliance with a 'personal alliance' which will be based on their relationship, and a 'task-related alliance' which will be based on the understanding of shared goals and shared acceptance of tasks. The motivation of the patient and her expectations before they start are important.

McCurdy et al. (2006) researched why some parents took up a home visiting service and others did not. Those that did were those that:

- perceived a need for the service for themselves or their child;
- perceived the costs from taking part outweighed the costs of not;
- expressed a readiness to change their parenting style;
- liked the therapist style of delivery;
- had good network support.

Those less likely to:

- were those who were not comfortable with someone in the house;
- first time mothers.

Routh et al. (1995) found that parents who found their parenting programme less useful were those that had a poor experience in childhood themselves, suggesting that their capacity for making relationships might be impaired, so they found it less easy to work within a therapeutic relationship to bring about change.

## Engagement

One of the aspects of engagement to be considered is how you encourage the parents on to your side. The process should be one of joint working, of facilitating, and empowering. The plan should be to make the parent a partner in the enterprise, so that she will own the problem also.

It is important to allow the parent to outline the problems she perceives with her child, taking a clear and full history so as to elicit any co-morbid problems like language delay, emotionality, motor problems.

## Process of change

This is important to address.

## Confrontation

This is not usually helpful. It can lead to resistance (which is not always easy to spot). If parents are confronted they can become passively aggressive (not overtly aggressive) and this can lead to therapist burn out. Confrontation may also lead to relapse of treatment.

The treatment approach should acknowledge the parent's ambivalence, if present, and this may lead to a healthier solution.

### Motivational interviewing

Looks at the interpersonal process (rather than internal to the client). Motivational enhancement therapy includes psychological and behaviour change.

## 12 step process (MATCH research group) (used in alcohol research)

FRAMES acronym: Objective *feedback*; Acceptance of personal *responsibility*; Direct *advice*; Provision of a *menu* of alternative treatment strategies; Rogerian *empathy* and *self-efficacy*.

Motivational interviewing should be collaborative work. The work will require the therapist to negotiate with the parent.

The parent will want benefits from therapy and will calculate the benefits and the costs, but that is not the therapist's agenda.

There are five stages of change:

1. *Pre-contemplation*: The parent will not want to consider change, and may fail to acknowledge he/she has a problem. The parent in the stage will cope with receiving information, better than being given advice.
2. *Contemplation*: Parent may be willing to consider examining the problem and might consider implications for change, but unlikely to take action. Therefore the therapist needs to address ambivalence for change, and to work with the parent to try to identify the positive and negative benefits of the present behaviour and the parent's willingness to change.
3. *Preparation/determination:* When the parent is at this stage there is an apparent readiness for change, but the parent does not know how to go about it.
4. *Action*: At this stage the parent may have begun to change her behaviour, but will need support to continue.
5. *Maintenance*: During this stage the parent will require topping up of support and therapy.

You have to establish parents (patients) place on the *wheel of change*. *Process* describes the activities brought into play to achieve change. The parental cognitions at first need to be addressed to identify *why* she might want to change and *why not*.

- The therapist will act as a facilitator, and needs to express confidence for change.
- The use of *reflective listening* in conjunction with affirmation will lead to confidence and the ability to change.
- The therapist needs to take a good history and listen to the problems.
- The parent should be encouraged to identify her own difficulties.
- The therapist needs to assess readiness for change.

- She/he should use reflective listening, and summarize and feedback, during the session.
- The therapist needs to undertake a cognitive re-evaluation of the problem.
- There needs to be a shift in balance of having the problem so that the parent owns it and it becomes shared.
- One of the most important tasks is to increase the self-efficacy of the parent.

*Level*: Describes the level in which change occurs.

*Therapeutic alliance*: There are two aspects to consider and work within in order to form a therapeutic relationship (Green, 2006; Kazdin et al., 2006).

## Personal alliance

- Parents have anxieties about not being in control.
- They want expertise they can trust.
- Quality of relationship is important: respect and 'attachment'.

If the experience is negative:
- parent further frightened;
- lacks trust;
- coping resources further reduced.

Therefore, parents need support:
- so need to 'scaffold', prompt and model;
- work on the transference for promoting

psychological change, but note that the client changes, not the therapist.

Parents' previous ability to make friendships and attachments is often indicative of their ability to make a positive personal alliance in the therapy (Routh et al., 1995).

## Task alliance

- The parent wants to understand goals and contracts.
- The process should be parent-orientated with focused goals.
- This, in turn, will lead to better parent engagement and planning.
- The therapist needs to remember to remind the parent that the child's behaviour may get worse at first.

The parents need to own the process in order to be able to be in control of the relationship, and thus begin to repair relationship difficulties which may stem from personal issues in own background.

The structure of the programme is important and the parent needs to understand what it is about so that she has faith in it. She should perceive that the therapist is well organized and enthusiastic.

Thus the training of the therapist, the quality of supervision and the treatment integrity and fidelity are important. This leads to fewer dropouts in treatment programmes.

# Guidelines of motivational interviewing

## General principles

1. The goal is to improve intrinsic motivation to change
2. Develop discrepancy between present behaviour and broader goals, between self-concept and behaviour
3. Express empathy and acceptance by selective, reflective listening
4. Support self-efficacy, hope or optimism
5. Improve self-esteem

Do:
1. Let parent present argument for change
2. Start with the parent's not the therapist's concern
3. Focus on eliciting parent's concerns
4. Empathizes personal choice and responsibility for deciding future behaviour, negotiate goals and strategies
5. Explore and reflect parent's perceptions

6. Use empathetic reflection selectively
7. Reflect feelings, concerns and self-motivational statements
8. Reflect by paraphrasing and summarizing
9. Reflect with statements rather than questions
10. Make a short summary of sessions at the beginning and end of each session
11. Offer advice and feedback where appropriate
12. Use affirmation and positive restructuring of the parent's statements to improve self-esteem and -efficacy

Don't:

1. Argue, lecture or persuade with logic
2. Assume an authoritarian or expert role
3. Give expert advice at the beginning
4. Order, direct, warn or threaten
5. Do most of the talking
6. Get into debates or struggles over diagnostic labelling
7. Make moral statements, criticize, preach or judge
8. Ask questions to which patients give short answers
9. Respond to patients' response to an open-ended question with another question
10. Ask a series of (three) questions in a row
11. Tell the patient she has a problem

**(Treasure and Ward, 1997)**

Barriers to taking up parenting programmes (Kazdin et al., 1997): Parents say that what makes it harder to attend programmes is finding the time with work pressures; loss of money if they miss work: embarrassment that the family or the young person has not done 'his homework'; child care for other members of the family; the relationship between parents and therapist; and how to agree way forward.

## Multiple choice questions

1. When using motivational interviewing what should be considered?

    a. Using arguments to tell the parents what they should do
    b. Make a short summary of what has been considered at the beginning and end of each session
    c. Give expert advice at the beginning

2. What are the five stages of change?

    a. Think about change, then do it.
    b. Contemplation, Action Process and Change
    c. Pre-contemplation, Contemplation, Preparation, Action, Maintenance

3. Therapeutic alliance is:

    a. Where the therapist sits in alignment with the parent
    b. Where you focus on the task in hand
    c. Is an umbrella term for a variety of therapist–client interactional and relational factors operating in the delivery of treatment.

## Key texts

Green J (2006) Annotation: The therapeutic alliance – a significant but neglected variable in child mental health treatment studies. *Journal of Child Psychology and Psychiatry*, **47**: 425–35.

Hougaard E (1994) The therapeutic alliance: A conceptual analysis. *Scandinavian Journal of Psychology*, **35**: 67–85.

Treasure J, Ward A (1997) A practical guide to motivational interviewing in anorexia. *European Eating Disorder Review*, **5**: 102–14.

# Structured assessment of preschool children: observation of parent–child relationship

Margaret Thompson, Margaret Hobbs, Fiona McEwan and Christine Cornforth

## Key concepts

- When assessing pre-school children it is important to take a careful history of the child's development, their environment and the parents' mental health.
- Early identification and treatment in the pre-school years prevents the problem becoming entrenched.
- Assessments should include observation of the child.

## An assessment schema: a young child example

### Case example: Nathan

#### Presenting behaviour – parent interview
It is always important to listen to a description from the parents regarding their child's behaviour. This should be in their own words giving a clear outline of such behaviour, including: the type of behaviour exhibited, the triggers to this particular behaviour, the outcome, the consequences and severity. Talk to the parents about why and in what situations such behaviour(s) usually happen and the effects on the child, the parents and siblings. Find out what the parents usually do about such behaviours and where there are two parents, is there agreement on what the solution to such behaviours might be. Finally, it is critical to determine whether parents are able and willing to work together on the problem.

Nathan is three years and eight months old. He is the middle of three boys and is very active; struggling to settle to play even with an adult to help him. Nathan can be very stubborn, refusing to do what others ask him, and going into a temper if he does not get his own way; shouting, crying and stamping. He will hit others.

At playgroup Nathan does not settle into activities but rushes about. He often comes into conflict with other children, refusing to share and unable to play nicely with his peers.

#### Perinatal history
Ask about:
- *Pregnancy*: health, illness and use of medication; history of alcohol, smoking and substance use;
- *Birth*: gestation, birth weight, labour complications, Apgar score and mode of delivery;
- *Neonate (up to 4 weeks)*: health of baby, admission to SCBU/NICU, maternal post-natal health; and mother's feelings after the birth.
- *Infancy (1–12 months)*: maternal and infant health, infant developmental milestones, infant temperament, infant sleeping and eating history (including breastfeeding), maternal social support and mental state.

Nathan weighed 6lb 6oz and was born by emergency Caesarean section at 42 weeks, following a difficult pregnancy. Nathan was sick for the first few days and was described as 'flat' at birth, having had the umbilical cord around his neck. Nathan is described as being a quiet baby who slept well and was bottle fed after difficulties with breastfeeding. Nathan's mother had a good pregnancy, she did not smoke, take other drugs or medication, and did not drink; she reports being tired after the birth but she did not have post-natal depression.

## Child's development
Ask about:
- physical development including height, weight;
- speech and language, including does the child ask questions, follow instructions, name items and general clarity of speech;
- temperament development, including shyness, fussing and crying and intensity of reactions when the child is upset;
- rituals or obsessional behaviours;
- how does s/he like to play?

Developmentally, Nathan is said to have been delayed across most areas; he crawled at 18 months, and his speech was delayed so that he had speech and language therapy. Parents report that he has had temper tantrums from about 18 months old and can be aggressive to his parents, brothers and other children.

His mother also reports that he tends to be emotional, becomes upset easily and has a strong reaction when he is upset. Nathan's height and weight are within the range that would be expected for a child of his age.

## Child's medical history
Ask about:
- general illnesses such as viruses and infections;
- conditions such as fits, heart problems, hearing or vision problems; and
- accidental injuries, such as broken limbs or unconsciousness.

Apart from being diagnosed with asthma (onset infancy) and eczema (onset 2.5 years), Nathan has been a healthy child. Nathan has had no accidental injuries which required medical attention.

## Preschool and school history
Ask about:
- separation difficulties;
- peer relationships;
- language skills;
- behaviour – different from at home?; and
- play – different from at home?

Nathan is described as being difficult in his interactions with others including his peers, and often ends up in a fight. He sometimes becomes upset when leaving his mother but usually recovers fairly quickly.

## Family history
Ask about:
- parental mental and physical health;
- parents' childhood and whether this was a positive experience for them (can be an indicator of the kind of parenting the parent had and would contribute to self-esteem and parenting skills);
- siblings' mental and physical health;
- family life events in the past and present; and
- is child like someone else in the family?

Nathan's mother's last paid job was as a chambermaid at a local hotel, however she is currently at home with the children, Nathan's father is currently unemployed and on sickness benefit. Both parents had good childhoods and Nathan's brothers are in good health mentally and physically.

## Observation

The child should be observed playing in the assessment room and interacting with their parent(s). It is useful to have a schema for this part of the assessment which you would administer in the same sequence, so that you cover all areas. This can however be varied if the child has oppositional difficulties and compromise is called for, or if it is a much younger child.

A useful schema for an observational assessment of a preschool child is shown in **Box 19.1**.

Box 19.1 Schema for an observational assessment of a preschool child

Aspects to consider:
- The child's culture, and
- The child's age and relevant milestones for their age.

Begin the assessment in a gentle playful manner – this is also a good way of settling the child at the beginning of the assessment.
- Coloured building bricks (this will test the child's ability to recognize and name colours, fine motor skills and coordination as they build a tower and bridge).
- Matching pairs – card sorting game (turn taking, impulsivity, colour and picture recognition, memory, language, social rules).
- Lego with figures (also assesses fine motor control and imagination).
- Tea set (engages the child's imagination as they prepare tea, coffee and cake for themselves, their parents and others in the room).
- Drawing different shapes and a figure of a person (this assesses fine motor skills, motor control, understanding of shapes in particular developmental level with the drawing a figure task).
- Large floor jigsaw (assesses the child's ability to have fun, to persevere with the demands of the task, understand shapes, colours and name objects). Observe parental scaffolding of this task, and general interaction with the parent.

Throughout all of these tasks observe the following and check that behaviour is appropriate to age and culture:
- Level of play (include imaginative play, initiated by both the child and the observer).
- Child's language (both expressive and receptive language ability).
- Child's interaction with observer and parent(s).
- Child's eye contact.
- Child's ability to concentrate.
- Child's attention span.
- Is the child distractible? Can s/he be brought back to task easily?
- Is the child defiant? and
- If the child refuses to do something, can s/he be helped to complete engage?

## Parent–child relationship

It is important to observe and think about the parent–child relationship as several theories recognize the importance of this relationship for the child's well-being and development; for behavioural and emotional regulation, and other social interactions.

Attachment theory recognizes that sensitive, responsive parenting during infancy and toddlerhood leads to the development of a cognitive-affective working model, allowing the child to develop a secure working model of themselves in relation to others, and more effective emotional regulation (Ainsworth et al., 1978).

Social Learning theory suggests that behaviour problems in children are established or maintained through dysfunctional parent-child interactions, with both the child and parent producing reinforcing behaviours in response to the other. Furthermore, parents of children exhibiting externalizing behaviours have often been found to be both power-assertive and lax in their discipline, with such inconsistency strengthening the child's behaviour pattern (Sansbury and Wahler, 1992).

Thinking together with a parent about factors that may have affected them and/or their relationship with the child can prove a powerful way of effecting change in the relationship and in the child's behaviour.

A useful schema for the assessment of a parent–child relationship is presented in **Box 19.2**.

Both parents related warmly to Nathan, giving reassurance, praise and comfort when appropriate. However, there seemed to be some disconnection between Nathan and his parents; he appeared to have his own agenda and could not be persuaded otherwise by his parents. During the observation Nathan's mother found it difficult to scaffold him and tended towards a negative response when he could not manage something.

# Physical development

Observe the following:

- fine motor skills including hand–eye coordination;
- is s/he right or left handed;
- gross motor skills (hop, jump, run, skip, go up and down stairs, walk on tip toe etc.).

# Physical examination

Some clinics prefer to make a physical examination. This is particularly important before starting a child on medication for attention deficit hyperactivity disorder (ADHD) (e.g. taking blood pressure, pulse rate, height and weight). This is often not required for this reason in preschoolers as this age group is rarely prescribed medication, however, in cases where this is necessary, a physical examination is important.

## Multiple choice questions

1. When assessing preschool children with behaviour difficulties you should:

   a. Ask the child to tell you their problems
   b. Wait until they are at least five years of age before you assess them
   c. Tell the parents not to worry, he will grow out of it
   d. Take a careful history to include pregnancy, development, parent–child relationship and observation

2. When observing a child you should?

   a. Provide them with toys which require a range of skills, e.g. jigsaws, lego, building blocks
   b. Ask them to stand in front of you
   c. Do not observe them as it is not needed
   d. Wait until they are asleep

3. When assessing the parent–child relationship you should consider:

   a. The level of hostility expressed about the child
   b. The level of warmth shown towards the child
   c. The parents understanding of normal development
   d. All of the above

Box 19.2 Schema for the assessment of a parent–child relationship

Aspects to consider – the parent:
- Their confidence in their own parenting skills
- Their ability to set limits
- Their consistency of approach and attitude
- Their perspective and background

The general attitude of the parent, including:
- Is s/he warm to the child or hostile?
- Does the parent cue the child?
- Does the parent praise the child or are they critical?
- Is the parent child-centred (i.e. aware of the child)
- How does the parent gain cooperation? (e.g. is s/he coercive?)
- Do the parents relate warmly to the child, in an age-appropriate manner (e.g. do they use language appropriate to the child and are their expectations of the child's behaviour within normal limits?)
- How would you describe the parent's emotional health and affect?

The child:
- Is s/he physically well (appropriate height/weight? Happy or sad?
- What kind of temperament does the child have? Active/passive? Emotionally labile or easy?
- What is the child's concentration level? Attention? Speech and language? Comprehension? Use of gesture? Vocabulary? Pronunciation?
- Can the child cope with frustration?
- Can s/he distinguish reality from fantasy?
- Assess the child's motor movement (is s/he clumsy? Does s/he fall over or bump into objects?)
- Whether the child relates easily to the parents

Assess:
- Fine motor control play skills
- Ability to engage in symbolic, creative, constructional or physical play
- Is play at the appropriate developmental level?
- Can the child extend play?
- Type of interaction by child with parents
- Ability to follow rules
- Ability to wait
- Ability to take turns
- Accepting losing
- Can the child accept criticism and praise?
- Can the child listen to and follow instructions?
- Is there eye contact child to parent? Parent to child? and
- Does the child have the skills to negotiate with the parent? Does it work?

## Key texts

Ainsworth M, Blehar M, Waters E, Wall S (1978) *Patterns of Attachment*. Hillsdale, NJ: Erlbaum.

Sansbury L, Wahler R (1992) Pathways to maladaptive parenting with mothers and their conduct disordered. *Behaviour Modification*, **16**: 574–92.

# 20

# *Parenting style*

## Christine Hooper

Each family is unique in its unwritten rules, myths and anecdotes. Families have been compared to systems in that each part is dependent on, and influences, every other part. Adult family members have all been 'programmed' to some extent, by their own experiences in childhood and by their later life experience.

Rather than be judgemental, we should assume that parents usually believe that they are acting in their child's best interests, even when their parenting style seems harsh and unhelpful.

Parenting styles vary. They can be loosely categorized as:

- authoritative;
- coercive;
- ambivalent/inconsistent;
- abusive.

# Authoritative

Authoritative parenting is confident, kind and consistent both over time and between a child's carers. Parental figures can be mother, father, grandparents, older siblings or mother's partner; indeed, anyone with responsibility for and care of the child. Ideally, the adults in charge should discuss and agree rewards and sanctions in response to the child's behaviour. Such discussions should take place privately, not in the child's hearing.

Children are troubled when they hear their parents argue. They prefer clear and reasonable expectations and praise when they comply with them. They learn to please their parents, build up their self-esteem and experience warmth and acceptance. Authoritative parenting is child-centred and child-sensitive. It is not easy to achieve or maintain and everyone falls short of the ideal at times.

# Coercive

Coercive parenting is over-strict and intrusive. These parents seem over-anxious to control their children's behaviour in case it becomes unmanageable. They may be worried about how others will judge both their children and themselves as parents. Some parents have experienced an over-strict upbringing and may believe and say, 'it never did me any harm'. They may be unable to or chose not to, recall how painful and isolated they felt as children or that they were in awe and frightened of their parents.

Coercive parenting is marked by punishments for misdemeanours being the preferred method of discipline. Punishments are often out of proportion to the offence, for example no TV for a month for a child who refuses to eat a meal. Sometimes the punishment is not carried through because the parent later realizes it is disproportionate, or further punishments may be imposed as the parent becomes increasingly afraid of losing control. Inconsistency means that the parents lose their children's respect.

It is important to explore with parents how they decided on this particular style and how effective they find it in shaping their children's behaviour. Positive strategies can be introduced; diaries and consistent reward programmes for compliant behaviour. Parents feel prouder of themselves when they are more relaxed around their children and confident that their children's behaviour will be acceptable, at home, at school and in the community.

## Ambivalent/inconsistent

Parents are distracted by worries and anxieties, for example bereavement, finances, chronic illness, marriage problems or redundancy, and it can be very difficult for even the best-intentioned parents to keep to consistent rules. Children often do not know from one day to the next which behaviour will be punished and which accepted. Nor can they be sure which punishments may be imposed for what. Life is unpredictable and the children feel insecure.

Parents have obviously usually come from differing backgrounds with different ideas and expectations of children's behaviour. Children soon learn to 'fit in' with whoever is in charge at the time and parents experience them as 'playing one off against the other'. When parents disagree, children will try to achieve the 'best deal' for themselves.

The therapeutic task here is to bring the inconsistencies to the parents' attention and work towards strategies that both parents can 'sign up to'. Underlying issues hindering the parents wish to be successful, for example post-natal depression, should be addressed.

## Abusive

It is human nature to love our children and only want the best for them. Only a minority of parents are deliberately abusive towards their children. Abuse can be physical, sexual or psychological. Children can be neglected physically and emotionally. A minority of children are abused in more ways than one. For instance, a child being sexually abused within the home may be physically intimidated to make them too fearful to disclose what is going on.

Abusive parents are the most difficult client group to work with. Abuse is usually secret. Fear and shame prevent other family members from asking for help and maintain the secrecy. It is often difficult and sometimes dangerous to work with families where abuse is ongoing. In these circumstances, it is imperative that colleagues in different agencies collaborate and support one another in a unified response.

# 21

# Assessment of younger children and families: individual interview of child

Cathy Laver-Bradbury

---

## Key concepts

- Early intervention is important. It can significantly help the parent and the young child
- Listening is a crucial part of the engagement process. Parents should be given the opportunity to tell their story and express their concerns freely without judgement.
- Observation skills are important; have a method of doing this

---

Early intervention is key in helping parents and children before problems become too difficult to change or that the child is suffering emotionally.

## What needs to be included in an assessment of a young child presenting with difficulties?

The child's *Presenting Behaviour*: it is always important to hear a description from the parents of their child's behaviour, in their own words, with a precise outline of this behaviour; type, triggers, outcome, consequences and severity.

The discussion with the parents should include why (and when) they think the behaviour happens, how does it affect their child and them, what do they do about it and do they agree about what the solution might be. Are they both able and willing to work together on the problem?

---

## Case study outlining assessment process

Matthew is an only child. He is a very quiet boy who has problems settling to sleep at night and whose parents often find him in their bed in the morning. They are unaware of when he gets in their bed. He wakes up early in the morning and likes his parents to play with him; he will play for hours enjoying many different types of games. Matthews's main difficulty is he finds it difficult to leave his parents when going to school. He can be stubborn at times but particularly when it involves doing something without his parents, for example if he is asked to get his bag ready to take to school he will get upset and cry saying he hates school. His mother is at a loss to know how to reassure him. His outbursts can go on all the way to school. Sometimes he is better if his father takes him, but not always. At the school gates his teacher has to take him from his mother to get him into the school. Eventually he calms down but it usually takes him about half an hour, which is putting an increasing burden on the school.

At school Matthew sits quietly, rarely interacting with his peer group, although he does have one quiet girl who he will play with. He has problems with his writing and says he cannot do tasks when asked but with encouragement he usually can succeed. At home he does his homework with help from his parents but he does find it difficult at times.

Assessment should include asking about:

- The pregnancy history: whether this was a planned pregnancy or not; the parent's health, any illness and use of medication; history of alcohol, smoking and other substance abuse.
- The birth history: gestation; labour (natural or induced); length; delivery type; Apgar scores (i.e. a measurement of the wellbeing of the baby at birth).
- The child's neonatal history: health as a baby, whether the child required extra care in a neonatal unit or not; and importantly the mother's feelings after the birth.
- A description of the first year: health of baby and mother, including mother's mental state and how she feels she coped. Take a feeding and sleeping history.

Matthew was born after a long pregnancy and delivery. He was okay after the birth but did have problems feeding and was fretful. His mother was delighted with her new baby but did suffer from post-natal depression for several months. She felt this was because she was so tired all the time. He was a poor settler and sleeper and fussy over feeding. He weaned with difficulty. The first year was difficult due to this, his mother had some support but her husband had taken a demanding but well-paid job to earn more so she could stay at home and so was less available to help. Her parents did help but lived 2 hours drive away, so this was sporadic.

- Child's development: include physical progress and speech development.

Matthews' development was normal and he talked and walked at the right time but speaking mainly to family and saying very little if strangers spoke to him.

He is a very cuddly child. He can say 'sorry' when he does something his parents do not like but gets very upset if told off. He is very sensitive to his parents' moods, for example, if his mother is upset he will cry too.

- Child's medical history: include history of fits, heart problems, hearing difficulties and accident history.

Apart from having the usual coughs and colds, Matthew has been a fit child with no illness. He has never had an accident.

- Preschool and school history: separation skills; include behaviour and peer relationships; language and negotiating skills.

At playgroup, when he was left Matthew cried continuously and so his mother stopped taking him.

- Family history: include physical and mental health; important family life events past, present and future. Ask about the parents' own childhood and whether, in their opinion, it had been positive for them. This is an indication as to the kind of parenting the parent himself/herself had. This would contribute to self-esteem and parenting skills. Ask about how the parents themselves fared at school.

Only father works outside of the home; he is an electrician. Mother would like to go back to work but feels it would distress Matthew more.

They both had good childhoods. Mother was the middle one of three children. Father was the eldest of four. Both sets of grandparents are helpful.

Mother was very shy as a child and still really only mixes with very close friends and family. One of her nephews has been diagnosed with ASD. There is no other medical or psychiatry history of note.

- Observation: The child should be observed playing in the room and interacting with his parents: observe the level of interaction, does the child relate easily to the parents or is there some hesitation? Do the mother and father relate warmly to the child, appropriate for age and circumstance (novelty situation, strangers present, tiredness and hunger level and so on), for example, do they use language appropriate to the child and are their expectations of his behaviour within normal limits?

It is useful to have a schema for playing with the children which you use in the same sequence, so as to cover all the domains. If necessary, this can be varied if a child is very oppositional and compromise is called for. Language can be tested throughout, checking comprehension for vocabulary, level of sentence complexity, ability to follow commands and so on.

For example, begin with bricks (colours, coordination); lego with figures (fine motor control, imagination); cup saucer, spoon, plate and figures (imagination and can involve mother and father in tea party); drawing (fine motor control, shapes, draw a man) (developmental level); floor jigsaw (fun, perseverance, shapes, colours, name objects, etc.).

For older children, drawing materials, jigsaws and lego should be available.

Observe the following and check that behaviour is appropriate to age and culture:

- Behaviour
- Level of play (include imaginative play, both initiated by child and also by observer)
- Language (both use of language and comprehension)
- Interaction with observer and with parents
- Eye contact
- Concentration
- Attention
- Is he distractible, can he be brought back to task?
- Is he a defiant child?
- If he does not want to do something, can he be helped to do it or not?
- Physical development: what is his hand coordination like, is he right or left-handed? Does he have good motor control (can he hop, go up and down stairs, walk on tip toe, etc)?
- Physical examination: some clinics may want to make a physical examination. This would be particularly important before starting child on medication for ADHD (blood pressure, pulse rate, height and weight).

Both parents related warmly to Matthew, giving reassurance and cuddles when appropriate. When Matthew was asked about school he became upset with the observer, who was trying to play with him.

Matthew was not good talking to the observer, he had poor eye contact (mainly turning into his mother when asked a question although he could be encouraged to look, if distracted). He found it hard to leave his mother's side even though there were toys he wanted to play with nearby; they had to be brought to him. If encouraged by his father his language skills were good. He easily finished the jigsaw when it was moved next to him. He was imaginative in his play.

## Initial formulation

Matthew is a young child presenting with separation anxiety and extreme shyness which is impacting on his education and in his relationships with his peer group. In the post-natal period his mother suffered from significant post-natal depression and had limited support; she also is very shy. Matthew had very little experience of playschool due to separation issues. There is a family history of ASD symptoms. On observation he can respond to distraction and motivational techniques and he does have some imaginative play though he is extremely anxious about leaving his mother.

## Treatment

Further assessment of Matthew's social communication skills and a closer look at his educational achievements may indicate a cognitive assessment is needed, with further exploration with his mother about the early attachment history and how she felt it has impacted on her relationship with Matthew. Psycho-education regarding separation anxiety to parents and behaviour strategies to help with these. CBT may be indicated for Matthew if his difficulties persist.

## Multiple choice questions

1. Where would you position toys to encourage them to play when assessing a shy young child?

    a. Nowhere, just leave them while you chat to their parents
    b. Have a range of toys within easy reach of him and next to his parents
    c. In the playroom, he has to learn to play on his own
    d. Any of the above

2. Listening is a crucial part of the assessment process. How do you demonstrate this to parents?

    a. By explaining that you will be asking questions to hear about their story
    b. By giving good eye contact and using running summaries to check you have understood what they have told you
    c. By giving them time to think about their answers before moving on to the next question
    d. All of the above

### Key texts

DeYoung A, Kenardy J, Cobham V (2011) Trauma in early childhood: A neglected population. *Clinical Child and Family Psychology Review*, **14**: 23–50.

Shouldice A, Stevenson-Hinde J (1992) Coping with Security Distress: the Separation Anxiety Test and Attachment Classification at 4.5 years. *Journal of Child Psychology and Psychiatry*, **33**: 331–48.

# 22

# Assessment of older children, young people and their families

Christopher Gale

## Key concepts

- A comprehensive assessment should be the basis underpinning interventions with young people who come into CAMHS.
- Assessment can be crucial in engaging the child, young person and family and beginning to form a therapeutic relationship.
- Assessments can vary in length and the process must consider the needs of the child/young person and family.

It is not uncommon for assessments to be incomplete after the initial contact. Several sessions may take place before a formulation can be made. As treatment progresses new issues may emerge that require reassessment and reformulation.

Consideration should be given to interviewing the child separately from the parents/carers, especially in adolescence where teenagers are encouraged to assume greater responsibility and autonomy in meeting their mental health needs. Separate interviews can be useful where there is a high level of hostility or blame between the young person and other family members.

## Specific assessment tools

Assessment tools will vary from one clinical setting to another, depending on the age of the child or young person, what is being assessed and the skills and experience of clinicians in using formal measures. Some may assess the global functioning of the young person (Children's Global Assessment Scale (CGAS) (Shaffer et al., 1983); Global Assessment of Functioning Scale (GAF) (American Psychiatric Association, 2000)). Though useful and usually easy to use, these should complement, rather than supplant, frameworks designed to assess specific symptoms and dimensions (Shaffer et al., 1983).

Alongside global measures of functioning, other measures may be used to screen for the identification of psychiatric disorders in youth – please see Chapter 26, The use of questionnaires in the diagnosis of child mental health problems. Others may be designed to identify specific mental disorders (i.e. Eating Disorder Examination Questionnaire (EDE) (Fairburn and Beglin, 1994) or the Beck Depression Inventory (BDI) (Beck et al., 1961)). Once individual work has begun, specific target measures may be used to assess the outcome of an experiment or activity set outside the clinical environment (i.e. food diaries, belief rating scales or frequency of panic attacks).

## The common assessment framework and care programme approach

There are several broad areas of enquiry which need to be covered by the assessing clinician(s) in the assessment interview. These often reflect the domains set out in the Common Assessment Framework (CAF) (Children's Workforce Development Council, 2009), focusing on the individual young person, observation of the parent-child relationship, family and environmental factors. Clearly the child/young person's developmental stage, as well as any protective factors present in their life, should be taken into account by the assessing clinician.

Example questions posed in these domains are:

- Development of the child or young person
  - Child/young person's developmental history (physical, speech/language, behavioural and medical)
  - What is the child/young person's view of the problem?
  - What is the impact of the problem/issue on daily functioning, including questions about sleep and appetite?
  - How does the child or young person cope at school/college/work with respect to academic success/problems, teachers and peers?
  - What is the child or young person's perception of the quality of their relationships with significant others (parents/carers, grandparents, siblings, wider family, friends)?
  - Description of the child/young person's mood. The clinician may choose to use a 0–10 rating scale to describe the current and historical mood
  - Does the young person use substances (tobacco, alcohol, illegal drugs)?
  - Is there motivation for things to change and for engagement in further work? The young person may be asked about aspirations and expectations they have for the future.
- Parent–child relationship
  - What is the quality of the attachment between child and parent/carer?
  - What is the general attitude of the parent/carer (i.e. warm, child-centred, cooperative or coercive, understanding of child/young person's developmental stage)?
  - What guidance and boundaries are put in place by parents/carers?
  - What is the parent/carers mental and physical health? How does this impact on the child/young person?
  - Is child or young person able to separate from parent/carer appropriately for their developmental stage?
- Family and environmental factors
  - What are the current challenges being experienced by the family (i.e. divorce, financial stress, abuse, home moves)?
  - What is the nature of individual relationships between family members?
  - What are the roles and expectations observed within the family? (i.e. is the child seen as 'the rebel' or 'the emotional one' and so on)?
  - What are the conscious and unconscious rules that govern how the family operates, especially in dealing with difficult issues? (Are these ignored or dealt with in a collaborative way?)
  - What are the strengths observed within the family (i.e. shared activities and interests)?
  - What are the wider systemic factors, such as social and community support, relevant for this young person and their family?
- Protective factors
  - Temperament/resilience/self-esteem of the young person
  - Strong sense of autonomy perceived by the young person
  - 'Good enough' parenting: warmth, responsive to child's needs, absence of parental discord?
  - Environment and wider support systems: good neighbourhood, schools, peer group.

The above domains of assessment are not exhaustive, but give an overview of the key questions/areas covered.

Use of the Care Programme Approach (CPA), widely adopted within adult mental health services since the 1990s, has recently been reviewed and its use encouraged within CAMHS (DoH, 2008c), especially in areas where the CAF is not being used formally. Both approaches require statutory and voluntary agencies involved with the young person and family to take a 'whole systems approach' to avoid duplication of assessment and intervention. At the heart of both approaches should be the young person (and their family), looking at their own perspectives on the issues faced and the goals achieved by any interventions. The use of CPA within mental health services should only apply to those complex cases which require multiple interventions from a number of agencies (e.g. a young person 'looked-after' by the local authority). In order to manage this complexity, a lead professional is identified to coordinate the network of support for the young person and family.

For further information on the use of CPA within CAMHS, see: Refocusing the Care Programme Approach: Policy and Positive Practice Guidelines (DoH, 2008c).

## Multiple choice questions

1. What does the term 'protective factors' mean when assessing a young person?

    a. Whether the young person is adequately dressed
    b. Do they use protection if engaged in sexual relationships
    c. They can hold their own in a fight
    d. They have an easy temperament, caring parents, a strong sense of autonomy, and a supportive wider environment

2. Why would you want to know about protective factors?

    a. To ascertain if they are likely to respond to treatment
    b. To ascertain what treatments may be effective before recommending one
    c. To help to assess the level of risk
    d. All of the above

3. What would you need to be mindful of if you are assessing a young person with their parents present?

    a. They may not want to discuss personal issues in front of them
    b. Answers a, c and d
    c. That the parents could react in a negative way towards the young person if they say something they don't like during the assessment
    d. They may not want their parents present

### Key texts

Children's Workforce Development Council (2009) *The Common Assessment Framework for Children and Young People: A Guide for Practitioners.* London: CDWC.

Department of Health (2008c) *Refocusing the Care Programme Approach: Policy and Positive Practice Guidance.* London: Department of Health.

Fairburn CG, Beglin SJ (1994) Assessment of eating disorders: interview or self-report questionnaire? *International Journal of Eating Disorders,* **16**: 363–70.

# 23

# *Family assessment*
### Andrew O'Toole and Anne Brewster

## Key concepts

- How does this family work? Using a genogram to look at aspects of closeness and conflicts (see Chapter 24, Genograms). Demographics over three generations looking at life cycle transitions, family strengths and vulnerabilities and patterns, e.g. dyadic and triadic. What are the family stories, myths, rituals, rules for living. How does the sibling subsystem relate to parent subsystem?
- How does the problem or issue that has brought the family to therapy relate to the way the family is? How has the family affected the problem or issue? How has the problem or issue affected the family?
- What relationship changes are needed to improve the problem or issue?
- What resources does the family have to make these changes happen? (from Rivett and Street, 2009)

## Introduction

For family therapists, there is an overlap between assessment and intervention. 'The therapist's joining changes things in the family' (Minuchin and Fishman, 1981). As part of the assessment session, the therapist introduces families to the service and talks about their hopes and expectations for attendance. It takes enormous courage to attend and this might be the only time the family comes to an appointment. Blocks may include shame, the fear of being judged or of being seen as 'damaged' or 'ill', especially for people from minority groups.

Beginnings that stimulate interaction are desirable (Burnham, 1986). Burnham suggests looking at everyone and at no one. Using an open, friendly approach, family therapists are curious about how people introduce themselves, who sits where, who takes charge, who does not speak. In 'warming the context', they might first engage the family in non-threatening areas of conversation within an atmosphere of purposeful interest. Haley (1976) describes this as the social stage.

Developing a secure base and building an effective working alliance are essential ingredients for assessment. The family therapist aims to establish a collaborative partnership with shared, but different, expertise. The family members are experts on their history and the family therapist is an expert on what has worked with other families and the up-to-date evidence base for difficulties.

What qualities do family therapists possess? Transparency, a respectful curiosity, sincerity and straightforwardness. Children and adolescents are the first to notice when there is a mismatch between what is said and the body language.

Each family member is invited to give their opinion on the presenting problem: its nature, frequency, intensity and successful or unsuccessful solutions. Family therapists track and follow the family's narratives and always act from an ethical standpoint.

In working with families we need to pay attention to issues of power, authority and difference. A useful framework for working with difference is the Social Grraacceess (Burnham, 1992, cited in Singh and Dutta, 2010). This acronym stands for Gender, Race, Religion, Age, Ability, Class, Culture, Ethnicity, Education, Sexuality and Spirituality. These are frameworks within which we identify ourselves and are identified by others.

There are three standard assessment formats in family therapy. These are:

1. The Circumplex model (Olsen, 2000) which assesses the dimensions of the family's adaptability and cohesion.
2. The McMaster model (Ryan et al., 2005) which assesses communication.
3. The Bentovim model (Bentovim, 2003) which assesses problem solving, behaviour control and affective responsiveness.

The aim is to focus intervention on whichever dimension will be most helpful. Byng-Hall (1995) describes the framing of a family's history as a 'script' that may be acted out repeatedly, improvised or re-written. New situations need new scripts from the tried and tested responses of the past. Parents generally 'replicate the scripts' of their own childhood, if it was happy and try a 'corrective' script, if it was miserable. Corrective scripts are less easy to devise. There is no blueprint to work from.

The quality of the parental relationship influences the security of the child's attachment. Children observe their parents' relationship as if they are the 'audience' and their parents the 'actors' on stage. This is how they learn the way to respond to their family environment. According to Byng-Hall, a secure family base is 'a family that provides a reliable network of attachment relationships which enables all family members.... to feel sufficiently secure to explore relationships with each other and with others outside the family'. He believed that the therapy situation could itself be a 'secure base' within which the family could explore new scripts.

A family assessment can carefully uncover the scripts that the family are working with, the better to understand their responses to the difficulties.

## Case study 1: Anna and Katie

Anna and Katie are a same-sex couple who have adopted a two-year-old boy, Oliver. Both women come from conventional middle-class families where heterosexuality was the norm. Katie's father died when she was young, her mother re-married and has now moved abroad. Anna's parents live locally and, initially, expressed dismay at their daughter's sexuality and disapproval of the couple's decision to adopt. Anna's family script is of two parents of different genders and the belief that a child needs a mother and a father to thrive. Katie's script is of abandonment by her parents, her father 'left' her early in her life and as soon as she could, her mother left Katie in England and made a new life for herself abroad.

Anna and Katie have had to adapt towards a different script for their family. They have decided that Anna will be 'Mummy' and Katie will be 'Katie', thereby improvising the script to 'fit' their circumstances. In other respects, their parenting style, of gentle correction and consistent rules, is similar to the one Anna observed as a child. Katie appreciates the certainties of Anna's approach to parenting. Her own experience of childhood was more chaotic. In a way, Anna is re-scripting Katie's experience.

Anna's parents have gradually been 'won over' to an acceptance of the situation, largely because Oliver is their first grandchild and is clearly contented. In addition, they and Anna's brother have attended two family therapy sessions to allow them (from that secure base) to explore their own pre-conceptions of what constitutes a normal family.

## Case study 2: Daniel and Chloe

Re-constituted families are less and less unusual in contemporary Britain. It is estimated that one in five young adult men are bringing up children to whom they are not a natural parent. Step-parenting does not have a recognized script. It does not have legal status, unless the step-parent formally adopts the children of their new partner.

Daniel (10) is Jane's only child. She is a single mother. Chloe (14) is Edward's daughter from his first marriage. Chloe has a brother, William (16). Both children chose to stay with their mother after the divorce, but Chloe has fallen out with her mother and come to live with her father. Daniel and Chloe are often at loggerheads and the fledgling relationship between Jane and Edward feels threatened.

This family must invent a new script from those they have used before. Jane never lived with Daniel's father and is unused to compromising on parenting issues. She was an only child and her parents often argued about how to manage her behaviour. She had found being a sole parent and in charge of discipline calmer than her experience of being a child herself. Daniel's father abandoned Jane once she was pregnant. It was several years before Jane felt able to abandon that 'script' and trust herself to live with a man again. Edward and his first wife had a conflicted relationship which upset their two children and means that Chloe is wary around Edward and Jane in case an argument breaks out and her own 'secure base' here is rendered unsafe.

Edward and Jane need to discuss thoroughly, out of earshot of Daniel and Chloe, which rules, rewards and punishments they can agree on. It is especially important that they do not quarrel in front of the children. Daniel has to learn to listen to Edward and not to seek to recruit his mother onto his side. Jane has to support Edward there. Chloe needs to experience a more harmonious parental relationship to restore her security. Jane and Edward must accommodate frequent weekend visits from William, who brings with him the different rules that operate at his mother's. Chloe would like to re-establish a relationship with her mother and to encourage that, Jane has to 'let go' of her feelings about Chloe's sudden arrival into the family and about Edward's first wife, whom she blames for the breakdown of his marriage.

An exploration of what everyone expects from family life would be the core of the family assessment here.

## Multiple choice questions

1. How many generations should a genogram attempt to illustrate?

   a. Only the family of the individual with the presenting symptoms
   b. Four generations, at least
   c. A comprehensive historical family history covering the last century should be asked for?
   d. Three generations

2. What is meant by 'joining with the family'?

   a. Sitting next to the oldest member of the family
   b. Making everyone a cup of tea
   c. Asking everyone the same question
   d. Making a home visit

3. What does the McMaster Model assess?

   a. How well the family communicate together
   b. The severity of the problem
   c. The quality of parenting
   d. How well the children behave in the session
   e. What has already been tried

4. Who wrote about 'family scripts'?

   a. John Burnham
   b. Minuchin and Fishman
   c. Bentovim
   d. John Byng-Hall
   e. Rivett and Street

## Key texts

Burnham J (1986) *Family Therapy: First Steps Towards a Systemic Approach.* London: Routledge.

Haley J (1973) *Uncommon Therapy: Psychiatric Techniques of Milton H Erickson, MD.* New York: W.W. Norton.

Minuchin S, Fishman HC (1981) *Family Therapy Techniques.* Cambridge, MA: Harvard University Press, 149.

# 24

# *Genograms*
## Christine Hooper

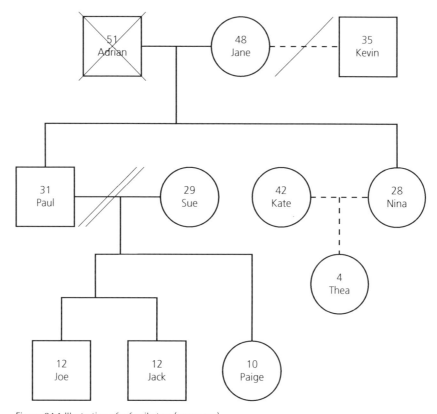

Figure 24.1 Illustration of a family tree (genogram).

What can we learn from this family tree?

- Family trees should, whenever possible, illustrate at least three generations of the family. Children often enjoy helping out with drawing up the family tree and sometimes like to add in their friends and pets!
- We see here that Adrian and Jane were married and had two children, Paul (now 31) and Nina (now 28). Paul was married to Sue, but they are now divorced. They have three children, twin boys Joe and Jack (12) and a daughter, Paige (10).
- Nina is in a same-sex relationship with Kate, who at 42 is several years older than she is. They have a daughter, Thea (4).
- Adrian died young, aged only 51. Jane has since had a relationship with Kevin, a younger man, but he is no longer living with her.
- There is a pattern of early parenthood in this family.

## Presenting problem

Paul and Sue's three children have lived with their mother since their parents' divorce. Joe's behaviour has recently been out of control at school and he has been aggressive at home towards his mother and his younger sister. The family GP has referred the family to the CAMHS service. Sue has come with the three children. Paul has told her he will come another time if he is asked to.

## Possible assessment questions

- When did Joe's behaviour first begin to be so difficult to manage? What has been tried so far? Who has been helpful: family, friends, neighbours or professionals?
- How much did the children know about the potential for their parents to divorce? Was it a complete shock? What do they think went wrong? Have they taken 'sides'? How would they describe the relationship between their parents – friendly, civil or hostile?
- How often do Joe, Jack and Paige see their father since the divorce? How consistent is he about contact?
- How prepared were the children for the death of their grandfather? Was that a surprise, and sudden, or had he been ill for some time? What would grandfather be saying to Joe if he were still alive?
- Had Adrian and Jane been involved in child care when Sue was at work? What part did

Kevin play in their lives? How long was he around? How did Jane manage her life after Adrian died?
- How much contact is there with Nina, Kate and Thea? What was the family's reaction generally towards their same-sex relationship?
- What is Joe's attitude towards his behaviour – regret, remorse, defiance?
- How much support has Sue's family been able to offer? (the maternal extended family can be added in to the diagram).

NB Other questions will occur to the therapist as they react to the family's responses.

## Outcome

Looked at in this family context, it is obvious that Joe and his siblings have suffered several disruptions in their life, losing their grandfather, their father's day-to-day presence and for Joe and Jack, their primary school. It seems that their grandmother was depressed after Adrian's death, which was very sudden, and withdrew her usual child care support. Sue still had to work and the children were left under-supervised after school and in the holidays.

Joe has felt lost and abandoned. Sue has two brothers who have offered to take more interest in Joe and Jack, to be male role models for them. Paul has agreed to come to the next appointment, an important message for Joe.

# 25

# Narrative therapy

Andrew O'Toole and Anne Brewster

## Key concepts

- Narrative theory is based on the supposition that in large measure people are the stories they tell themselves and that are told about them.
- Stories shape our lives rather than reflect them back to us.
- According to this position, the process of therapeutic 're-authoring' of personal narratives, changes lives, problems and identities, because personal narratives are constitutive of identity (Carr, 1998).
- The foundation of clinical practice is based on collaborative understanding and re-authoring of meanings.
- One of the tasks is to help people make sense of their lives, which is a far different project from explaining or diagnosing their behaviour.
- An important difference of the narrative approach is shifting the attention from what *the therapist thinks* about what the clients are saying, to trying to understand what *the clients think* about what they are saying.
- Seeing oneself *in relation* to a problem, instead of *having* or *being* a problem, creates the possibility of imagining oneself in a different relationship to the problem.

*There are those who think a story is told only to reveal what is known in this world. But a good story also reveals the unknown.*
**(Griffin 1992, cited in Weingarten 1998)**

## What is narrative therapy?

Narratives can occur at different levels of social functioning. There are social and cultural narratives, interpersonal narratives and intrapersonal narratives. The narrative approach rests on the assumption that narratives are not representations of reflections of identities, lives and problems. Rather narratives constitute identities, lives and problems. Our stories are embedded in, and influenced by, a wider social and cultural context.

One of the central ideas of narrative theory is the idea of discourse. Discourse relates to the idea of concepts that have negotiated and accepted meanings. A possible discourse might be 'fatherhood'. When a man becomes a father, the story he will tell about being a father will be influenced by the wider accepted meaning and language about fatherhood present in his contemporary society and culture. It will be influenced by personal experiences of fatherhood or its absence, interpersonal relationships and internalized models of those relationships. The discourse on fatherhood does not exist discretely, but is influenced by other discourses, patriarchy, motherhood, sexuality, power and so on. Whether we are aware of a discourse or not, it can powerfully influence the stories we can tell and the stories we can hear.

A discourse can be described in terms of:

*Historically, socially, and institutionally-specific structures of statements, terms, categories and beliefs that are embedded in institutions, social relationships and texts.*
**(Carr, 1998)**

# Narrative assessment

- The goal of assessment is to encourage the development of a narrative, a telling and re-telling of events in a way that allows new understanding and meaning to emerge.
- What traditionally may have been regarded as information leading to a diagnosis and intervention by an expert is instead used to facilitate the child and family in a conversation of understanding.
- The object is not to explain but to understand, giving meaning to the child's presenting problem.
- To assess a child is simply to have a desire to hear his or her story, while the therapy is about encouraging this desire in all family members.

# Key narrative strategies

## Re-authoring

- Focuses on the person's lived experience
- Adopts a collaborative co-authoring position
- Encourages a perception of a changing world through the plotting or linking of lived experience, over time
- Helps clients view themselves as separate from their problems by externalizing the problem
- Helps clients pinpoint times in their lives when they were *not* oppressed by their problems, by finding 'unique outcomes'
- Helps clients develop new stories based on the unique outcomes
- Links unique outcomes to other events in the past and extends the story into the future, to form an alternative and preferred self-narrative, in which the self is viewed as more powerful than the problem

- Invites significant members of the person's social network to witness this new self-narrative
- Documents new knowledge and practices, which support the new self-narrative using literary means
- Allows others, who are trapped by similar oppressive narratives, to benefit from their new knowledge.

'Externalizing' is a concept developed by White and Epston (1990). Externalizing conversations separate persons from problems and block the fusing of the person with the problem. Seeing oneself *in relation* to a problem instead of *having* or *being* a problem creates the possibility of imagining oneself in a different relationship to the problem.

## Externalizing the problem

- Decreases unproductive conflict between individuals, including those disputes over who is responsible for the problem
- Undermines the sense of failure that has developed for many individuals because of the continuing existence of the problem, despite their attempts to resolve it
- Paves the way for people to cooperate with each other, to unite in a struggle against the problem
- Opens up new possibilities for them to take action to retrieve their lives and relationships from the problem and its influence
- Frees individuals to take a lighter, more effective, and less stressed approach to the 'deadly' serious
- Presents options for dialogue, rather than monologue, about the problem.

## Case study: Nick

White and Epson (1990) describe the case of Nick, a six year old brought by his parents. He had a very long history of encopresis. They describe how Nick made the 'poo' his playmate, smearing and streaking it, rolling it into ball and flicking it behind cupboards and wardrobes. The family was asked how the 'poo' was influencing their lives; what was its sphere of influence? They outlined a number of ways. For Nick, it isolated him from his peers and prevented him from being seen for who he was. For his mother, the 'poo' was creating misery, forcing her to doubt her capacity to be a good parent. She felt overwhelmed by it. Nick's father was deeply embarrassed by the 'poo' and felt that it isolated him and the family.

White and Epston develop the assessment like this. It is made clear that the 'poo' is a 'Sneaky Poo', because it claims to be Nick's friend, but it causes so many problems. So the encopresis becomes externalized as 'Sneaky Poo'. They begin to look for 'unique outcomes', times when the 'Sneaky Poo' was not allowed to have a negative effect. Battle is waged against 'Sneaky Poo' until its sphere of influence is reduced. Each member of the family can reclaim their lives through the telling of new stories about how they live in a world controlled by them and not by 'Sneaky Poo'.

## Exceptions

There are always alternative stories to the ones currently dominant in a person's life. It is helpful for both the storyteller and the listener to be mindful that this is only one version of the story, the current version.

## Unique outcomes

One strategy for generating alternative stories is the identification of unique outcomes. A unique outcome is when something happens that disconfirms the current story and allows alternatives (new meanings) to emerge. These unique outcomes might be historic, current or potential (future).

## 'Not knowing' or 'suspended knowing'

One of the difficulties of the narrative approach is how the professional might be able to contribute expertise, without disempowering the client narrative. Empowerment, from a narrative perspective, is related to one person experiencing another person as accepting and elaborating what they have to say, without challenging its basic integrity. A response to this dilemma is the 'not knowing' or 'suspending knowing' stance. The professional keeps professional knowledge in the background, in order to 'privilege' the client's story. Once the story has unfolded, an exchange of meaning and ideas can take place.

## Re-positioning

A further key idea in narrative theory is the notion of 're-positioning', i.e. taking up a different position in relation to the young person and/or the problem. Both 'externalizing' and 'suspending knowing' are examples of re-positioning.

## Noting the characteristics of the story

The narrative task is to help people tell those stories whose effects on their lives are preferable to the stories they are currently telling. In doing this, paying attention to the characteristics of the story is important. Weingarten (1998) identifies three important features of the story:

1. Narrative coherence: Narratives can be more, or less, coherent. Coherence is established by the inter-relationships between plot, characters' roles and themes. In attachment narratives, the degree of the coherence of the narrative is a predictor of secure attachment. Coherence has been linked to wellbeing ('salutogenisis').
2. Narrative closure: Occurs when a story is told that seems to have only one way to understand it.
3. Narrative interdependence: Refers to the relationship of one person's narrative to another's. The stories we tell ourselves almost always create 'positions' for those we speak about, some of which are more desirable than others.

Crossley (2000) offers further strategies for exploring the story:

- Narrative tone: A pervasive feature of a personal narrative conveyed both in the content and the manner in which the story is told. The tone might be, for example, predominately optimistic or pessimistic.
- Imagery: Look out for the unique way in which imagery is employed in the story. It might be helpful to look at the origin of such imagery. Is it embedded in early experience or in the wider dominant discourses of the society the storyteller lives in?

- Themes: What are the dominant themes or patterns of the story as it unfolds? What are the motivational themes behind the story? Love and power have been suggested as common themes in human stories. Power is seen both in terms of a sense of agency, self-efficacy and love and in terms of the desire for connection and dependence.

# Conclusion

It is unlikely that many practitioners will use a purely narrative approach. However, narrative offers an interesting dimension to the process of assessment and treatment. Perhaps the most significant element is the 'privileging' of the client story over other forms of knowing about and describing the problems the family have. Such a strategy is likely to enhance trust, respect and engagement. Some narrative strategies, e.g. 'externalizing', could be used very effectively, alongside other therapeutic approaches.

## Key texts

Carr A (1998) Michael White's narrative therapy. *Contemporary Family Therapy*, **20**: 485–503.

Crossley ML (2000) *Introducing Narrative Psychology: Self, Trauma and the Construction of Meaning.* Buckingham: Open University Press.

Weingarten K (1998) The small and the ordinary: the daily practice of a post-modern narrative therapy. *Family Process*, **37**: 3–15.

White M, Epston D (1990) *Narrative Means to Therapeutic Ends.* London, New York: WW Norton and Company.

# 26 The use of questionnaires in the diagnosis of child mental health problems

Christine Cornforth, Kim Cartwright and Margaret Thompson

## Introduction

Rating Scales and standardized behaviour checklists are generally inexpensive and used widely to assist in the diagnosis of many childhood disorders. This form of clinical assessment has been developed over the past 30 years and offers a number of advantages which have led to widespread use in clinical settings.

- They can be used to assess a child's emotional state and behaviour in a number of situational contexts, for example at home and at school.
- They are convenient and easy to administer at home, school, or in a clinical setting.
- They draw information from multiple informants, such as parents, teachers and swimming/football coaches.
- They collect information which is collapsed across long time intervals.
- They can be used to provide baseline and treatment/intervention effects.
- Many provide normative references which can be used to compare scores.

A common list of such questionnaires is given in **Table 26.1**.

## Are scales age appropriate?

The clinical significance of a child's behaviour must take into account the child's developmental age as behaviour problems can be considered normal when they occur at a specific age (for example, most preschool children experience inattention and separation anxiety). It is therefore crucial that rating scales provide comparative data with normative samples of children of the same age and sex for evaluating behaviours. Rating scales that provide the same scale for different age groups, but also have age standardized norms, can be useful, as scores obtained for children at one age can be compared directly with scores obtained for the same children at a later age. This enables the clinician to compare the behaviour of the same child at different developmental stages.

## Informants

Given that child behaviour problems can be situation specific, when making an accurate assessment of a child's behaviour it is important to obtain information from multiple informants assessing behaviour in a number of settings (Verhulst and Van der Ende, 2005).

Clinicians have long understood that information from both parents and teachers is vital for making correct diagnoses of school-aged children. The importance of teacher information for the diagnosis of Attention Deficit Hyperactivity Disorder (ADHD) was first formalized by DSM-III (APA, 2000) which noted that when reports of teachers and parents conflict, primary consideration should be given to the teacher reports because of their greater familiarity with age-appropriate norms. However, in order for clinicians to determine the degree of agreement between parent and teacher reports of a child's behaviour, they must first account for any differences in the questionnaires used. It is likely that variations may reflect the differences in response bias between parents and teachers rather than real differences in the child's behaviour (Verhulst and Van der Ende, 2005).

## Child behaviour as a dimension

Behaviour rating scales are generally developed using psychometric principles, and therefore assume that problem behaviours constitute quantitative variations rather than clear-cut 'normal' or 'abnormal' categories. In order to obtain quantitative measurements, multiple items are rated by a respondent and then such items usually form subscales, such as depression or impulsivity. In order to quantify a child's behaviour, some scales (for example, the Conners' Rating Scale – Revised) assess the degree to which a child's behaviour differs from that of comparable children of the same age and sex in normative samples. Such scales are as good as the normative samples on which they are based, and the quality of normative samples can vary. Some scales, such as the Conners' Rating Scale – Revised, use large samples from the general population, while others such as the Strengths and Difficulties Questionnaire (SDQ) have used convenience samples.

## Item content and response scaling

Item content refers to what the rating scale has been designed to measure. Generic rating scales are designed to measure a range of psychopathology. They use items that are applicable to a variety of child psychopathologies. For scales such as the Child Behaviour checklist (CBCL, Achenbach, 1983) that have been developed over a number of years, information from studies is used to re-examine the items in the questionnaire and thus the questionnaire is improved over time and incorporated in newer versions. A further example is the Conners' Rating Scale – Revised which now includes DSM-IV based items relevant to a diagnosis of ADHD.

Most scales incorporate a 3-point (Likert) scoring system and some use a 4-point scale. Few behaviour rating scales use a 2-point 'true/false' scale.

## The development of scales

There are two main approaches which are adopted when designing rating scales – the 'empirical' and the 'a priori' approaches. Empirical approaches use statistical techniques to identify clusters of items (symptoms) which ultimately form subscales. This approach begins with the data which have been empirically derived from informants with no assumptions made about whether the syndrome

reflects predetermined diagnostic categories. The 'a priori' approach uses diagnostic categories of international classification systems as the basis for the disorders measured. It is therefore possible to score symptoms as present or absent by using cut-off points that are based on DSM-IV or ICD criteria.

The samples required to create rating scales can be a topic of debate. Some support the use of clinic samples as they yield items with frequencies high enough to be retained in reliable factor analyses. However, others suggest that scales should be based on the general population, as they believe the factor structure should reflect the underlying structure of problems in the samples studied. In general, it is accepted that both approaches are important as they capture different information which together may contribute in increasing our knowledge in this area (Verhulst and Van der Ende, 2005).

Many suggest that, although the two approaches are similar, they are not so similar that one can easily replace the other (Edelbrock and Costello, 1988). It is therefore recommended that both approaches be used together. For example, the CBCL makes it possible to score items on the two sets of scales.

## Scoring

Various subscales of the same instrument have different mean scores in normative samples because of the difference in items for each scale. One approach is the use of percentiles – this is the percentage of individuals who score below a certain value. Percentiles can also be computed on the basis of questionnaire scores for a representative normative sample of children whose scores are ranked from the highest to the lowest. The main advantage of percentiles is that they are easy to interpret. For example, if a child receives a score on an anxiety scale corresponding with the 95th percentile, this means that only 5 per cent of normally developing children of the same age would obtain higher anxiety scores.

Another approach would be to transform scores so that they can be compared across scales with different types of measurements. This can be achieved using $T$-scores, which are scores that have a mean of 50 and a standard deviation of 10. A *T*-score of 50 will correspond with the 50th percentile. The advantage of both percentiles and *T*-scores is that they allow the clinician to determine where an individual's score stands in relation to scores of individuals of the same sex and age. The usefulness of these scores depends on the size and representativeness of the reference samples.

The scoring procedures and interpretation of the results of a rating scale should be easy to follow and understandable. Most rating scales have scoring profiles and easy to follow graphic displays that clearly represent an individual's scores relative to the norms.

# Short versus long scales

Most scales take between 5 and 20 minutes to complete. The majority of rating scales in their standard format are relatively brief.

There are few studies that compare short with long formats of rating scales. One such study has compared the short SDQ with the much longer CBCL (Goodman and Scott, 1999). Scores from the SDQ and CBCL were equally able to discriminate children with psychiatric illness from those without. Compared with a semi-structured interview, the SDQ was better than the CBCL at detecting inattention and hyperactivity and did equally well detecting internalizing and externalizing problems.

Table 26.1 Summary of popular questionnaires available for the assessment of a child/young person's behaviour

| Scale | Author(s) | Description/properties | Additional details |
|---|---|---|---|
| **A. Behaviour Rating Scales** | | | |
| Strengths and Difficulties Questionnaire (SDQ) | Goodman, 1997 | Screen for emotional and behavioural problems including, peer problems, attention-deficit/hyperactivity disorder, emotional problems, conduct problems, and pro-social behaviour | 4–18 years <br> Parent and teacher report <br> Self-report – 11 years and older <br> Time Frame: last six months <br> *Norms available* <br> Available for free at www.sdqinfo.com |
| Child Behaviour Checklist (CBCL) | Achenbach and Edelbrock, 1983; Achenbach, 1991a; Achenbach, 1991b; Achenbach, 1992 | Screen for all child psychiatric disorders | 4–18 years <br> Parent and teacher report <br> Self-report – 11 years and older <br> Preschool (2/3 years) version also available <br> Time Frame: last six months <br> *Norms available* <br> Available from author |
| Conners Comprehensive Behaviour Rating Scale (Conners CBRS) | Conners, 2008 | Screen for a range of social, behavioural, emotional and academic problems | 6–18 years <br> Parent and teacher report <br> Self-report – 8–18 years <br> Time Frame: last six months <br> *Norms available* <br> Paid for content |
| Behaviour Rating Profile (BRP-2) | Brown and Hamill, 1990 | Screen for assessing a child's general behaviour at home and at school | 6–18 years <br> Parent and teacher report <br> Self-report – 11 years and older <br> Peer report <br> Time Frame: last six months <br> *Norms available* <br> Paid for content |

| Scale | Author(s) | Description/properties | Additional details |
|---|---|---|---|
| Eyberg Child Behaviour Inventory (ECBI) and Sutter-Eyberg Student Behaviour Inventory – Revised (SESBI-R) | Eyberg and Pincus, 1999; Sutter and Eyberg, 1984 | Assess conduct problems in home and school settings. Both parent and teacher reports have identical format; each assesses behaviour on two scales: Intensity (how often behaviours occur) and Problem Scale (identifies specific behaviours that are currently a problem) | 2–16 years<br><br>Parent and teacher report<br><br>Time Frame: current<br><br>*Norms available*<br><br>Available from author and online |
| **B. Developmental Disorders** | | | |
| Pervasive Developmental Disorder Behavior-Inventory (PDDBI) | Cohen and Sudhalter, 2003 | Assessment of problem behaviours and social communication skills (e.g. communication, reciprocal social interaction, ritualistic activities, and learning skills) for children with pervasive developmental disorders (PDD) (autistic disorder, Asperger's disorder, PDD-NOS, Rett's disorder or childhood disintegrative disorder) | 1.5–12.5 years<br><br>Parent and teacher report (short and long versions available)<br><br>Time Frame: not specified<br><br>*Norms available*<br><br>Paid for content |
| Behavioural Summarized Evaluation – Revised (BSE-R) | Barthelemy et al., 1990; Barthelemy et al., 1997 | Screen for autistic behaviours | Completed by two raters who have observed the child during a 5-day period<br><br>Available from author |
| Checklist for Autism in Toddlers (CHAT) | Baron Cohen et al., 1992; Baron Cohen et al., 2000 | For early identification of autism in children aged 18 months which focuses on two behaviours: (1) joint attention and (2) pretend play. If children are lacking these behaviours they are considered at risk for a social-communication disorder | 18 months<br><br>Parent report and report by primary health care workers (e.g. GPs and health visitors)<br><br>Time Frame: not specified<br><br>*Norms not available*<br><br>Available for free at www.paains.org.uk/Autism/chat.htm or www.autismresearchcentre.com/tests/chat_test.asp |
| Modified Checklist for Autism in Toddlers (M-CHAT) | Robins et al., 2001 | Screen for autism which includes nine parent report items from the Checklist for Autism in Toddlers (CHAT; Baron Cohen et al., 1992). It also includes items pertaining to autism in very young children | 18–30 months<br><br>Both parents and primary health care workers<br><br>Time Frame: not specified<br><br>*Norms not available*<br><br>Available for free at www.firstsigns.org |
| Social Communication Questionnaire (SCQ) | Lord et al., 2003a | Screen for the Autistic Diagnostic Interview-Revised (ADI-R; Lord et al., 1989). Items were selected to match the content of this instrument, but the SCQ is much briefer | 4–40 years<br><br>Parent report<br><br>Time Frame: lifetime or current – last three months<br><br>*Norms available*<br><br>Paid for content |

| Scale | Author(s) | Description/properties | Additional details |
|-------|-----------|------------------------|---------------------|
| Social Responsiveness Scale (SRS) | Constantino and Gruber, 2005 | Screening and diagnostic instrument for the assessment of autistic spectrum disorders. Subscales include: social awareness, social cognition, social communication, social motivation and autistic mannerisms. It also includes scales for treatment | 4–18 years<br>One form that can be completed by parent or teachers<br>Time Frame: last six months<br>*Norms available*<br>Paid for content |

## Multiple choice questions

1. What does item content refer to?

   a. The number of items included on the questionnaire
   b. What the rating scale has been designed to measure
   c. The item profile for each child
   d. The scoring for each item
   e. Reversed scoring

2. What are the two main approaches adopted when designing rating scales?

   a. *'A priori'* and empirical
   b. Empirical and nosological
   c. Categorical and continuous
   d. Dimensional and categorical
   e. Clinical and population based

3. A percentile is

   a. A mean of 50 and a SD of 10
   b. The summed total of raw scores
   c. The percentage of individuals who score higher than the norm
   d. The percentage of individuals who score below a certain value
   e. Total score out of 100

4. Behaviour rating scales are important to clinicians as

   a. They provide a clear diagnosis for each child
   b. They let you know which treatment you should use
   c. They are free of charge
   d. They can be scored by the informant
   e. They draw information from multiple informants

5. It is important that rating scales provide

   a. A clear diagnosis
   b. Scoring sheets
   c. Comparative data from normative samples
   d. A self-report version
   e. Reverse scoring

### Key texts

Edelbrock C, Costello AJ (1988) Structured psychiatric interviews for children. In: Rutter M, Tuma AH, Lann IS (eds). *Assessment and Diagnosis in Child Psychopathology.* New York, London: The Guilford Press, 87–112.

Goodman R, Scott S (1999) Comparing the strengths and difficulties questionnaire and the child behavior checklist: Is small beautiful? *Journal of Abnormal Child Psychology,* **27**: 17–24.

Verhulst F, Van der Ende J (2005) Rating Scales. In: Rutter M, Taylor E (eds). *Child and Adolescent Psychiatry,* 4th edn. Oxford: Blackwell Publishing.

# Cognitive assessment in children and young people

Rachel Leeke

## Key concepts

- For some young people referred to mental health services, cognitive difficulties are the primary problem, underlying the emotional and/or behavioural difficulties they present with.
- Cognitive assessments can measure a range of cognitive abilities including general ability (IQ), verbal and non-verbal skills, memory, attention and educational attainment.
- Findings from cognitive assessments can contribute to information obtained from other sources to produce a comprehensive assessment of young people's difficulties.
- Understanding where a young person's primary difficulties lie can help with diagnosis and with focusing support appropriately.
- Information obtained from cognitive assessments can help tailor intervention and treatment strategies in a way that means that young people are most likely to benefit from them.

## Introduction

Cognitive skills are the basic mental abilities we use to think, study and learn. For many young people, emotional and/or behavioural difficulties can impact upon their cognitive abilities, for example by making it harder to concentrate or to process what is being said. However, for other young people, cognitive difficulties in the form of a learning disability or some more specific form of developmental delay can lead to emotional and behavioural problems (e.g. anxiety, low mood, not concentrating and misbehaving, frustration and anger outbursts). In these cases cognitive difficulties may be the primary problem that underlies, and has led to, the emotional and behavioural difficulties that the young person presents with. Understanding young people's primary difficulties and whether any cognitive difficulties are underlying or exacerbating their emotional and/or behavioural difficulties, can be extremely useful in terms of understanding what is going on for them and knowing where to focus support.

## How can cognitive assessments help?

Cognitive difficulties can be subtle, not easily recognizable, or difficult to pin down and quantify in face-to-face conversations alone. However, cognitive assessments are a way of measuring them. They provide information about a young person's abilities in a range of areas, including verbal and non-verbal skills, memory and processing speed (Wechsler 2002, Wechsler, 2003). They can be used to gain an estimation of a young person's general abilities (an intelligence quotient or IQ) as well as a profile of his strengths and weaknesses. Additional measures (such as those looking at educational attainment or specific cognitive domains such as memory, attention or executive function) can be administered if this is clinically indicated.

Combined with information from other sources, cognitive assessments can add to our understanding of why young people think, feel and behave as they do. In turn, this information can then be used to help inform decision-making, educational planning and clinical intervention. Understanding what is the stage of development of a young person's ability to attend to, comprehend and reason, can help ensure that interventions are pitched at an appropriate level.

# Who can carry out cognitive assessments?

Cognitive assessments can only be carried out by psychologists (including Clinical Psychologists, Educational Psychologists and Assistant or Trainee Psychologists under supervision).

# When to consider a cognitive assessment

Completing assessments can, on occasion, be anxiety provoking or stressful for young people, and the process of administering, scoring, interpreting and writing these up can be a lengthy and time-consuming one. The value added in terms of understanding the young person's difficulties and planning interventions and support therefore needs careful consideration.

Other indicators of cognitive ability may be available from different sources and provide equally useful information about a young person's abilities; one example of this would be the cognitive attainment tests (CATs) that are carried out in school.

# Points to consider in relation to cognitive assessments

When a young person completes a cognitive assessment, how they behave during the assessment is crucial in terms of deciding how valid are the data obtained. The data obtained from cognitive assessments need to be considered alongside information obtained from other sources including discussions with parents/carers, and school reports (Flanagan and Kaufman, 2009). In this way a comprehensive picture can be formed about a young person's cognitive abilities and how these relate to his day-to-day functioning and presenting problems.

Cognitive assessment is a highly individualized process and the purpose of the assessment therefore needs to be clear. When considering whether a young person might benefit from a cognitive assessment, it is important to identify what question this might help answer. Examples of such questions include 'could this young person's anxiety be because he has a developmental delay and is struggling to meet other people's expectations of him?' Or 'could this young person's behavioural difficulties be due to him not understanding what is being said to him?' Specifying the specific reasons for referring a young person for a cognitive assessment can help the psychologist tailor the assessment and focus on particular areas of concern.

It should be noted that cognitive ability follows developmental trajectories and a young person's general ability compared to his peers (e.g. his IQ) is not expected to change dramatically over time. Exceptions to this would include where a young person has had a brain injury. When making a referral for a cognitive assessment it is therefore advisable to check whether or not an assessment has been carried out previously.

## Case study

### Referral

Jamie (aged 9) was referred to CAMHS due to destructive temper outbursts and self-injurious behaviour (repeatedly banging his head against the wall when distressed). Initial assessment revealed that Jamie was having a daily 'outburst' during which he would shout, throw things, hit and kick. Self-injurious behaviour followed these. He was noted to have difficulties with attention and concentration, but not hyperactivity, and to have difficulties retaining information. Developmentally he was thought to have met his milestones within the time frame expected, but was found to be struggling with some aspects of language when he started school; he received a short programme of speech and language therapy to rectify this. A referral for a cognitive assessment was made in order to ascertain whether any cognitive difficulties could be underlying or exacerbating his frustration, distress and behavioural outbursts.

### Cognitive assessment findings

Cognitive assessment revealed that Jamie was of average cognitive ability but had significant difficulties in terms of his verbal skills. These were considerably weaker than expected, and at a level more typical of a six year old than a nine year old.

### Contribution to overall assessment and treatment plan

Jamie's many strengths in other areas meant that his verbal difficulties were not always apparent to those talking to him. He was often able to comply with instructions by copying those around him and his 'cheeky', 'endearing' manner meant that he was generally able to cope socially even if he did not understand what was being talked about. However, the fact that he was so much weaker in one area than in all others was a source of considerable frustration for him. It also meant that he struggled academically and got things wrong due to misunderstanding. This was a significant contributing factor to his outbursts and self-injurious behaviour. His verbal difficulties were also a significant factor in terms of his attention difficulties as he 'switched off' when he did not understand what was being said.

Intervention was needed to include those around Jamie pitching their language at the right level for him to understand. Supporting verbally presented information with non-verbal information (e.g. pictures, diagrams, etc.) would also help him understand what was being asked of him, thereby reducing frustration and anxiety.

## Multiple choice questions

1. Which of these statements is not true? Cognitive difficulties can

    a. Always be recognized easily
    b. Be exacerbated by emotional and/or behavioural difficulties
    c. Lead to emotional and/or behavioural difficulties
    d. Be subtle and difficult to pin down and quantify

2. Which of these statements about cognitive assessments is correct?

    a. Cognitive assessments are quick and easy to undertake
    b. Data from cognitive assessments can be used in isolation to draw conclusions about young people
    c. Cognitive assessments simply measure IQ
    d. Cognitive assessments can only be carried out by psychologists

3. Which of these abilities do cognitive assessments not measure?

    a. Processing speed
    b. Non-verbal skills
    c. Sensory abilities
    d. Working memory

4. Which of the following is not true?

    a. Findings from cognitive assessments can help with knowing how a young person's difficulties started
    b. Findings from cognitive assessments can help with knowing where to focus support for a young person
    c. Findings from cognitive assessments can help with knowing what level a young person is functioning at
    d. Findings from cognitive assessments can help with knowing what level to pitch interventions at

5. The following should be considered when deciding whether or not a cognitive assessment might be useful?

   a. What questions it could help to answer
   b. Whether information about the young person's cognitive abilities is available from any other sources
   c. Whether a cognitive assessment has been completed in the past
   d. All of the above

## Key texts

Flanagan DP, Kaufman AS (2009) *Essentials of WISC-IV Assessment.* Hoboken, NJ: Wiley and Son.

Wechsler D (2003) *The Wechsler Intelligence Scales for Children,* 4th edn (WISC-IV UK). Harlow, UK: Pearson Assessment.

Wechsler D (2002) *The Wechsler Preschool and Primary Scales of Intelligence,* 3rd edn (WPPSI-III UK). Harlow, UK: Pearson Assessment.

# 28 *Speech and language assessment*

Janet Stevens

## Key concepts

- Communication is an interactive process.
- Speech and language development is affected by several factors: medical, sensory, environmental, social, behavioural and/or emotional.
- Speech and language development follows a chronology across six domains: attention and listening, play, understanding, spoken language, speech sounds, pragmatics.
- Speech and language development can be delayed or disordered.
- Research indicates a high level of co-occurrence of speech and language difficulties with emotional and behaviour problems in children.
- Language disorder is a predictor of later psychiatric or mental health problems.

## Introduction

Language is not learned in a vacuum. It evolves through an interactive process incorporating significant adults and a responsive environment. Speech and language concerns in children may be manifested through:

- emotional and behavioural difficulties;
- dysfluency;
- selective mutism;
- pragmatic language disorders;
- poor receptive and expressive language skills.

Research indicates that the neonate is motivated to communicate and is indeed born 'hard-wired' to do so. Noam Chomsky, an American linguist, identified what he called a 'Language Acquisition Device', which he defined as an innate capacity to learn language, often despite adverse environmental, medical and social factors.

Language acquisition takes place within the context of securely attached relationships, usually with one or two primary caregivers in the first instance. These adults will support, imitate and reciprocate the baby's early movements and vocalizations, to enable the child to move from pre-intentional communication at birth to intentional interaction within a few months of birth; at just 17 minutes old a child is able to imitate his father poking his tongue out (Social Baby DVD).

Recent progress in brain-imaging and scanning techniques have enabled us to observe the damaging effect of a lack of attachment on the size and capacity of the developing infant brain. Secure relationships help to promote the intentionality of communication, which means that it is vital for parents and care-givers to be made aware of the importance of talking with babies, even if the perception is that 'babies don't talk back'. There are thought to be several 'windows of opportunity' for speech and language development during the child's early years, but by three years of age, the critical window for speech development begins to close.

It is known that the time spent in carer–child joint attention predicts subsequent vocabulary growth; research indicates that children from high-talking families have, at three years of age, at least three times more receptive vocabulary, i.e. words understood, than peers from low-talking families and consequently at least twice as many words in their own spoken vocabulary (Hart and Risley, 1995). So from the beginning 'communication, language and thinking are rooted in relationship' (EYFS, 2007).

Communication is fundamentally interactive, in that it requires reciprocity by both communication partners. Communication does not happen when a child is playing a computer game or spends hours watching television programmes or DVDs alone. It involves the passing of verbal and non-verbal messages; in fact, it is believed that approximately 80 per cent of human communication is non-verbal. Speech and language skills develop within this broader context of communication; the symbolic system known as *language* comprises six specific components that combine to represent meaning within a culture.

These elements are:
1. phonology (sound system)
2. prosody (rhythm and intonation)
3. syntax (grammatical structures)
4. morphology (grammar)
5. semantics (meaning of words)
6. pragmatics (language in social context).

Bloom and Lahey (1978) devised a model to illustrate the relationship between the component parts of communication in children who are developing their language skills normally (**Figure 28.1**).

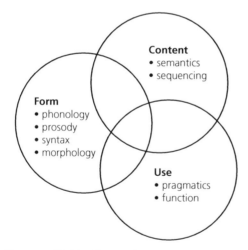

Figure 28.1 Model to illustrate the relationship between the component parts of communication in children who are developing their language skills normally.

Language learning is a unique and individualized process. It follows a chronology from birth to approximately seven years of age but there is a wide range of what would be considered 'normal' development (I Can DVD).

Significant language problems will be identified for approximately 7–10 per cent of the preschool population in England and Wales. Research has indicated several significant factors, which may potentially affect a child's language development (Law, 1992).

# Medical factors

- Prematurity
- Birth trauma, e.g. cerebral palsy
- Epilepsy
- Chromosomal disorders e.g. Down's syndrome
- Impaired sensory input should be considered: visual impairment; hearing impairment, from fluctuating or intermittent glue ear, to a more permanent sensory-neural loss.

# Environmental and social factors

- Mother/carer–child interaction
- Parenting style
- Home environment and socioeconomic status
- Mother's level of education and her access to a support network.

# Familial factors

- Gender (boys are twice as likely to have speech and language problems as girls)
- Position within the family
- Family history of speech and language difficulties.

# Behavioural factors

- Attachment difficulties
- ADHD-type presentations.

# Cultural factors

- Learning language as a bi- or multilingual speaker
- Cultural-specific attitudes to 'play'.

Language skills are assessed and monitored across six domains and difficulties in one or more of these areas may result in a diagnosis of speech and/or language delay or disorder. Speech and language development is described as 'delayed' if the child's level of skill is below that expected for their chronological age, but following the normal developmental pattern.

Speech and language development is described as 'disordered' if the normal developmental pattern is not followed and an uneven profile of strengths and deficits is identified.

The six domains considered are:

1. attention and listening
2. play skills
3. understanding (receptive language)
4. spoken language (expressive language)
5. speech sounds
6. social use of language (pragmatic language).

Skills develop between birth and seven years of age, following a recognized chronology and pattern, in each of these areas.

A growing body of research evidence has linked language difficulties with a variety of emotional and behavioural problems.

Poor receptive and expressive language skills frequently present in the populations of excluded school children and among young offenders. There is a growing awareness of the occurrence of undetected communication difficulties among children with behavioural, emotional and social difficulties (BESD). Studies suggest the incidence of communication difficulties in this group to be between 55 and 100 per cent (Giddan et al., 1996). Several longitudinal studies show that in the absence of appropriate support, these children are more likely to develop associated behavioural difficulties than their peers.

A recent report by Stringer et al. (2003) indicates that the rates of behaviour difficulties reported in children with speech and language disorders are around 50 per cent, compared with 10 per cent in the 'normally developing' population. As they grow older, these children are more at risk of poor emotional health and have a stronger likelihood of mental health problems in adulthood (Clegg et al., 1999). These young people may have difficulties understanding complex instructions and expressing their emotions and feelings verbally. Intervention may focus on improving listening skills and on

building self-esteem. In mainstream schools, the Speech and Language Therapist may contribute to the behaviour programme delivered by the Emotional Literacy Support Assistants (ELSA).

All research indicates that language disorders are more closely associated with behaviour difficulties than speech disorders. Indeed, language disorder has been shown as a predictor of later psychiatric problems (Davison and Howlin, 1997).

How do emotional and behavioural difficulties manifest themselves in speech and language problems assessed at community clinics and in schools?

Dysfluency or stammering has a multi-factorial basis, which considers environmental, linguistic, medical and psychological factors and examines how difficulties in some, or indeed all of these areas, may trigger a stammer in particular individuals. It is a disorder principally of childhood; approximately 5 per cent of the population of three year olds at any time are likely to develop a stammer; of these, 2 per cent will recover spontaneously, 2 per cent will either recover or develop sufficient compensatory strategies to manage the stammer well and 1 per cent will stammer into adulthood.

Therapeutic intervention will initially consider parent–child interaction strategies, often through the medium of video-footage and subsequent discussion between the parents and the Speech and Language Therapist. The outcome of these discussions may lead to modifications to family routines or expectations, which remove or reduce the environmental or psychological triggers to stammering. Other interventions will be designed to devise ways to enable the child to better balance emotional or linguistic demands, with his current capacity and skill level.

Selective mutism is defined in the DSM 1V (revised 1994) as 'a persistent failure to speak in specific social situations, despite being able to speak in other more familiar situations'. Intervention may consider a behavioural approach to reducing the child's anxiety, comprising a systematic, stepped progression, changing one variable at a time, simultaneously maintaining a consistent approach within the environment where the child is not talking and gradually enabling the child to become an active partner in the treatment process (Johnson and Wintgens, 2001).

Pragmatic language disorder may co-occur with

symptoms of Autistic Spectrum Disorder (ASD) or may present as discrete specific language impairment. Difficulties include problems with verbal reasoning, understanding and using higher level language skills, such as inference, for example the picture of a boy sitting in a bath wearing his clothes and the question 'Why is this funny?' and responding appropriately, rather than literally, to idiomatic language, for example 'Pull your socks up'. Therapeutic intervention may work on social skills training, for example 'Talkabout', the use of visual prompts and timetables, to reinforce spoken instructions and reduce anxiety about routines and developing 'social stories' (see Chapter 73, Social stories) to prepare the child for change and transition or to modify a socially unacceptable behaviour.

A recent Education and Skills Committee report (2005–06) noted a high correlation between children with Special Educational Needs and youth crime: in a recent study 25 per cent of young offenders had been identified as having special educational needs. More specifically, between 50 and 60 per cent of the UK prison population has been identified as having literacy difficulties, compared with 17 per cent of the general population. At least half of these offenders have speaking and listening skills at a basic level, but appropriate training and support to develop their oral communication skills has been shown to help reduce recidivism. Recent research indicates that approximately 40 per cent of young offenders are likely to have difficulty with mediation involving spoken language (Bryan, 2004).

## Multiple choice questions

1. What are the optimal conditions for a baby to begin to develop his communication skills?
   a. Spending time in a room with noisy adults with the television on
   b. Spending time with parents who make efforts to include their baby in all social interactions and talk to their baby about everyday events and routines
   c. Spending time with a series of different adult carers who have no relationship with the baby
   d. Mother has Post-Natal Depression and has struggled to bond with her child
   e. Spending hours in front of the television with no adult support

2. What is meant by 'interactive' when describing communication?
   a. It just happens like all other aspects of development
   b. If you leave the child alone, he'll learn by himself
   c. There's no point talking to a baby as he can't talk back
   d. Both communication partners are engaged in the conversation
   e. A baby will learn by watching television
   f. He'll learn to talk at nursery

3. What factors should we consider when speech and language development goes wrong?
   a. Prematurity, family history and glue ear
   b. Parents cannot read or write well
   c. Family has not engaged with any support services
   d. He's lazy
   e. Father has a strong Scottish accent

4. What presentations might you see in a child with 'pragmatic language disorder?'
   a. Unable to say words beginning with 's'
   b. Engages in long conversations with familiar adults
   c. Responding appropriately to questions
   d. Chooses not to speak at school
   e. Stammers on the first word in the sentence
   f. When told by his teacher to 'pull your socks up' with reference to working harder for his exams, he interprets this literally and does what he has been asked to do

5.  Which would be a valid therapeutic intervention for preschool dysfluency?

   a.  Practise saying words beginning with 't' daily
   b.  Take calpol three times a day
   c.  Apply for the X-Factor
   d.  Parent–child interactions filmed then discussed to change environmental behaviours at home
   e.  Wait for the child to 'grow out of it'

## Key texts

Bryan K (2004) Preliminary study of the prevalence of speech and language difficulties in young offenders. *International Journal of Communication and Language Disorders*, **39**: 391–400.

Davison F, Howlin P (1997) A follow-up study of children attending a primary age language unit. *European Journal of Disorders of Communication*, **32**: 19–36.

Law J (ed.) (1992) *The Early Identification of Language Impairment in Children*. London: Chapman and Hall.

# 29 Occupational therapy assessment
## Claire Pollock

## Introduction

The College of Occupational Therapists (COT) defines Occupational Therapy (OT) as 'the treatment of people with physical or psychiatric illness through specific selected occupation for the purpose of enabling individuals to reach their maximum level of function and independence in all aspects of life'.

The OT aims for a holistic approach in assessing the psychological, physical and social functions of the individual, identifying areas of dysfunction. The OT will then involve the individual in determining joint goals towards a structured programme, with environmental adaptations and/or equipment considered where appropriate, to overcome dysfunction. The activities selected are set in context of the client's personal, social, cultural and economic needs and reflect the environmental factors which govern their lives.

Occupational Therapy is based on a unique conceptual framework and set of core skills, to promote and restore health and wellbeing, through using purposeful occupation as the process or ultimate goal. For children and young people, occupation is the meaningful use of activities, occupations, skills and life roles, which enables children and their families to function purposefully in their daily lives.

The broad undergraduate training of occupational therapists, which includes mental health modules, gives them:

- an understanding of psychologically based approaches and an ability to translate them into practical strategies
- an ability to analyse a child and family's function or dysfunction in areas of daily living e.g. emotional or physical development, interaction, social skills and organisational skills
- the skills to devise therapeutic activity for children, parents and families, bearing in mind their needs and their roles in different contexts e.g. family, school, social
- skills in group work, offered in community, out-patient, day-patient or in-patient settings
- the ability to analyse, select and apply occupations as specific therapeutic media

## Core skills for practice

- Use of purposeful activity and meaningful occupation as therapeutic tools in the promotion of health and wellbeing
- Activity analysis: ability to change, adapt and modify intervention according to need
- Enabling child and family to achieve meaningful lifestyle by the preparation for or return to their occupational role, for example school, leisure time, etc.
- Practical advice/support for young person, carers and their family
- Professional advocacy for the young person/family
- Promotion of competence in the young person or family so that they are able to function to a level that they find both acceptable and achievable
- Work with individuals, families or groups, or alongside parents in exploring and developing their parental management styles and the parent–child relationship.

## COMMON PRESENTING PROBLEMS IN CHILDREN & YOUNG PEOPLE

- aggression, destructiveness, temper tantrums and anti-social behaviour
- restlessness, poor concentration and distractibility
- poor peer relationships
- abnormal mood, depression, attempted suicide
- fearfulness, anxiety, school refusal, specific phobias
- disturbed eating/feeding problems
- bizarre and inappropriate social behaviour
- abuse: physical, sexual and/or emotional
- sensory integrative dysfunction ( sensory modulation)
- developmental co-ordination disorder
- developmental delay
- stressful life events, which are *unscheduled* e.g. bereavement, fostering or trauma
- psychological effects of chronic illness or disability
- self-esteem and self-confidence problems

Occupational Therapy assessment can provide much information which can contribute to the formation of a diagnosis, but more importantly provide a greater understanding of the problem for the young person, family and team, and identify additional needs (see **Figure 29.1**).

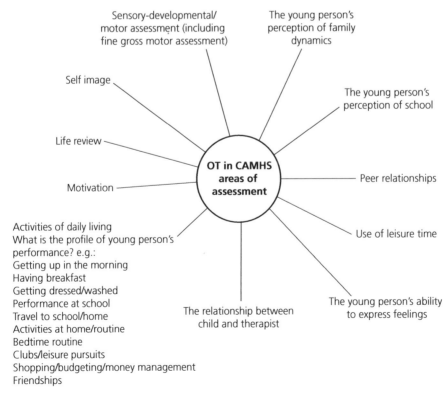

Figure 29.1 Areas of assessment.

The Occupational Therapist:
- will use their specially trained skill of activity analysis to select age-appropriate, creative and structured activities, for example play, art, dance, puppetry, drama, games or cookery to assess and treat clients;
- will be familiar with a range of theoretical models, e.g. psychodynamic, humanistic, behavioural, cognitive-behavioural, systemic, sensory integration and developmental;
- models of practice will be influenced by the team ethos and the individual OTs theoretical stance, for example life skills training, parent training, creative therapies (art, drama and dance), group therapy, individual psychodynamic therapies, play therapy, sensory integration (alert programme, therapeutic listening), family work, social skills training, problem-solving skills training, play/structured activity, brief solution focused therapy, cognitive therapies, behaviour treatments.

# Acknowledgements

With thanks to the Occupational Therapy team at the Centre for Child Health, Dundee and Sue Evans.

## Multiple choice questions

1. What would be considered within 'Occupational Roles' for a child or young person?

2. Provide an explanation of 'Activity Analysis'.

3. What would constitute fine and gross motor skills required in the classroom?

4. What is meant by working holistically?

5. In which settings might an OT assess a child?

## Key texts

DfES (2003) Every Child Matters Cm 5860.
Kranowitz CS (1998) The Out-of-Sync Child: *Recognising and Coping with Sensory Integration Difficulties.* New York: Perigree Books.

Lougher L (2000) Occupational Therapy in Child and Adolescent Mental Health
College of Occupational Therapists www.cot.co.uk

# Introduction

## Margaret Thompson

The aetiology of problems in children and adolescents is multi-factorial.

This is especially true when the problems present as externalizing disorders, particularly affecting those around the child, although by definition, affecting the young person, because of the 'fallout'.

Many difficulties will have a genetic component, for example, conduct disorder, but the behaviour of the child will be influenced by the parenting he receives and the attitude of the rest of his family, his teachers and his peers.

The child's innate temperament, resilience and intelligence will all affect the outcome.

These observations will also hold true for the neurodevelopmental disorders.

All behavioural problems are a worry to children, young people and their parents, but children who present with severe externalizing problems present a major emotional cost to families and a financial burden both to their families and the state.

Intelligent early intervention is of the essence.

# 30 *Temperament*
## Christine Cornforth and Margaret Thompson

*Temperament is a child's nature, his/her make up, the way he/she responds in different situations.*
**(Thomas et al., 1968)**

## Key concepts

- The word 'temperament' is used to describe a child's nature, make-up and the way s/he responds in different situations.
- Temperament qualities in infanthood (such as activity, regularity, initial reaction, adaptability, intensity, mood, distractibility, persistence and attention span and sensitivity) are thought to influence adjustment throughout life (Thomas et al., 1968).
- Temperament characteristics affect how well a child will fit in at school (e.g. forging good relationships with their teachers and peers) and at home (e.g. having good relationships with parents, siblings and other family members).
- The behaviours associated with these characteristics are thought to be on a continuum with problems occurring for those children who fall at the high or low end of the scale.
- In the longer term, there is strong evidence that children's early-emerging temperament/behavioural styles can predict their characteristic behaviours, thoughts and feelings as adults (Caspi et al., 2003).

Buss and Plomin (1984) developed the EASI Scale (Emotionality, Activity, Shyness and Impulsivity Scale) in an attempt to measure reactivity and regulation in childhood. This scale was completed by parents of a community-based birth cohort of three-year-old children. One per cent were children who were said by their parents to be at the extreme end of the spectrum of 'fuss and cry' a lot (5/5) and were very irritable. Eight per cent had a score of 4 and 4 per cent a score of 4.5% (Thompson, 2001).

The following chapter will present a review of the factors found to contribute to temperamental differences in individuals together with how a difficult temperament in childhood (e.g. emotionality, impulsivity) has been found to be predictive of both internalizing and externalizing problems (Lavigne et al., 1998).

# The theory behind temperament and self-regulation

## Bio-behavioural approach

Nigg (2006) suggests a direct pathway from temperament to personality, with both temperament and personality sharing common characteristics. It is possible that encouraging and directive behaviours, such as positive parenting, may positively influence and enable a child's ability to self-regulate and consequently alter their personality. This type of approach is referred to as a bio-behavioural approach and is believed to alter neural networks.

## Genetics

The genetic influence on temperament is distributed continuously in the general population, showing substantial environmental influence in addition to genetic influence and is likely to be influenced by many genes, each of varying effect (Saudino, 2005; Plomin et al., 1994). Genes of small and varying effect size, which contribute to quantitative traits, are referred to as quantitative trait loci (QTLs).

There is evidence from twin studies that emotional lability can be accounted for by 20–60 per cent of the variance in monozygotic twins compared to dizygotic twins (Stevenson and Fielding, 1985; Saudino, 2005).

The influence of genetics on temperament increases with the age of the child. The resulting temperament is thought to depend on the inter-action between genes and the shared environment (family environment) and the non-shared environment (the relationship between the child and their parents, siblings, peers, teachers) and the effect of other factors such as accidents or illness.

In adult studies, personality stability has been found to be accounted for by genetic influences. However, personality change has been found to be associated with the non-shared environment (Emde and Hewitt, 2001; Saudino et al., 1996).

## The role of serotonin-modulating genes

Ebstein and colleagues (1998) studied a relatively large group ($n = 81$) of neonates aged 2 weeks and examined the behavioural effects of two common polymorphisms linked respectively in some, but not all, studies to novelty seeking (dopamine D4 receptor (DRD4)), neuroticism and harm-avoidance (serotonin transporter promoter region (STPR)). Neonatal temperament was assessed using the Brazelton Neonatal Assessment Scale (BNAS). The results of this study revealed a significant association of DRD4 across four behavioural clusters pertinent to temperament, including orientation, motor organization, together with both range and regulation of state. A significant multivariate interaction was observed between DRD4 and STPR. This suggests that temperamental behaviours, even in neonates, may be influenced by the expression of genes.

## Children's temperament will be influenced at different levels

- Behavioural level: The non-shared and shared environment will be important, with unfamiliar contexts influencing behavioural inhibition. This manifestation of the child's behaviour will depend on the child's ability to self-regulate.
- Psychological level: Should the child also be prone to anxiety, then this will influence the control of behaviour. The child's ability to cope with change might influence their reaction to situations.
- Neural level activity: the activation of the limbic system is an important factor in the control of self-regulation.
- Physiological level: autonomic arousal; the stress diathesis (with effortful control and reactive control). The role of cortisol levels will be important here both before and after birth.

# Brain pathways and the importance of the amydala in the regulation of emotions

A possible schema is shown in **Figure 30.1**.

The amygdala is considered to be one of the most important areas in the brain for emotional regulation (see Chapter 17, The effect of early institutional deprivation on the brain: findings from the English and Romanian adoptees study). It is located in the central nervous system in the frontal limbic neural network, an area thought to be the control centre of cognitive control (Nigg, 2006).

The amygdala is involved in many processes including those involved with facial discrimination, emotional responses and, consequently, social behaviours. The amygdala is thought to be involved in attaching emotional significance to visual configuration and is the route to the brainstem, which triggers emotional arousal. This task may be more difficult for children with attentional and concentration problems: they may be unable to recognize signals, such as disapproval. Consequently, it is possible that such children are less likely to use this information in order to learn to self-regulate.

Functional magnetic resonance imagining (fMRI) techniques have been used to demonstrate the role of the amygdala in emotional processing. For example, the ventral amygdala is involved in recognizing fearful faces (withdrawal), while the nucleus accumbens is involved with happy faces (approach).

## Emotional lability

Emotionality lability refers to the regular inability to control expressions of emotion and is often found in children with disorders such as attention deficit hyperactivity disorder (ADHD), oppositional defiant disorder, anxiety and depression. Moreover, it is associated with more severe symptoms of ADHD (Sobanski et al., 2010).

## Irritability

Irritability in young children is very commonly observed in child psychiatry and in recent years has been studied in older children.

Results from a longitudinal follow-up study revealed that irritability in adolescence (age 13 years) predicted major depressive disorder, generalized anxiety disorder and dysthymia, but not bipolar disorder, in later young adulthood (Stringaris et al., 2009).

A distinction between episodic and chronic irritability has been made, with these subtypes being found to differ in their associations with age. More stability over time has been found with the chronic irritability type than between types. Chronic irritability at time 1 (mean age $13.8 \pm 2.6$ years) predicted attention deficit/hyperactivity disorder at time 2 (mean age $16.2 \pm 2.8$ years) and major depression at time 3 (mean age $22.1 \pm 2.7$ years). Episodic irritability at time 1 predicted simple phobia and mania at time 2 (Leibenluft et al., 2006).

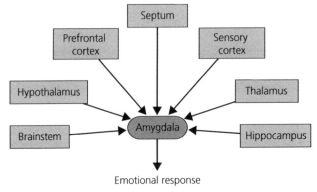

Figure 30.1 A possible schema.

# Presenting features of temperamentally difficult children

Children who are considered slow or even difficult 'to warm up', who fuss, cry excessively and have high emotionality are sometimes referred to as 'temperamentally fragile'. Such children often exhibit the following behaviours:

- may have been a difficult baby to take care of (e.g. difficult to soothe);
- may not have a regular rhythm and be a poor sleeper;
- may be easily upset and react very strongly when upset;
- become upset about minor things;
- dislike change and take time to become used to new situations;
- can be fussy and difficult feeders;
- may be very demanding;
- have low self-esteem.

Such children often manage to have their own way. Parents will understandably 'give in' for a quiet life; whining and crying are exhausting to live with. This can ultimately result in an unhappy parent–child relationship, where the parent does not feel fully in control. Furthermore, it is likely that the child will not be very happy, as children can feel very unsafe about having too much control.

Whatever parents do for such children is never enough. Temperamentally fragile children will often moan at the end of treats and always want to stay longer or 'have another one'. These children are very hard work for parents, who inevitably become impatient and critical.

## Management strategies

- Suggest that the parents do not take the child's behaviour personally.
- It is important to help the parents to accept the child they have. The child's temperament is the way it is and by adjusting their parenting style, life can become more pleasant for the whole family.
- Routines and structure are very helpful for these children. They also need some space and 'quiet time' in their day.
- Clear boundaries are very important.
- Work out with the parents those family rules that are important and those that are less so and encourage the parents to be consistent in what to expect. For example, safety rules are important but it may not be worth having battles over what the child wears or whether they have left a toy on the floor.
- Avoid confrontation as much as possible. Use distraction and try to identify and diffuse situations early.
- Improve listening skills. Keep instructions short and clear. Maintain eye contact by gently holding the child's head, if necessary.
- Often these children cannot cope with too many choices and cannot make up their mind; therefore suggest two choices, for example, what you want to achieve and something less exciting.
- Children who are sensitive hate being confronted. They usually say 'no'. This is because (a) they do not know how to do something or (b) they are often afraid of failure.
- An indirect approach often succeeds where a direct one does not. Try to enable the child to say 'I don't know how, please help me', rather than putting them in the position where 'no' is the inevitable response.
- Improve the child's self-esteem by using praise as much as possible. Warm touches can be helpful, a stroke or a pat as the parent walks past can be very affirming.
- Cuddles and loving touches, even massage, are helpful to soothe this kind of child.
- Always end the day on a positive note.

## Temper tantrums

Much of the advice given to adults about coping with temper tantrums suggests that the child should be gently held until they calm down. In some children this can cause the tantrum to worsen, rather than calm the child. It is important that parents/adults work out what is best for their child. If the child hates being held, then do not touch, hold or man-handle them, especially when they are temporarily out of control. Furthermore, 'time-out' does not work in children who are sensitive, as it can feel like rejection. In such situations, you can recommend the following to the parent/s:

- Suggest to the parent/s that they use the 'we' word rather than 'you'. For example 'we need some quiet time' or 'when we are both calm we can be friends again'.
- Make sure the child knows what the pattern of the day is to be; some of these children hate change and need to be prepared for it.
- Advise the parent that she should always try to remain calm and in control. She should talk calmly to the child and say that as soon as s/he is calm, they will talk about the situation without shouting or blaming.
- Safety issues have to take precedence. Some children have incredible strength when very upset and adults trying to cope with the child could be injured if they try to physically restrain them.
- The focus is the positive behaviour. Many of these children have a very poor self-image and negative comments reinforce this.

- Social and emotional maturity may be only two-thirds that of other children of their own age.
- Using a daily communication book, rather than a good/bad diary (as s/he will lose or destroy the latter in order to protect his sensitive personality) between home and playgroup is helpful if someone else is picking the child up. If the child has a bad day, it is preferable to ask the school to contact you.
- It is helpful for parents to consider whether they are able to express to their child how they feel. Expressing feelings about being sad or happy is useful to the child as the parent can show the child how to use words to describe how they are feeling. This will encourage the child's social skills.
- If a child feels valued, worthwhile and approved of, s/he will feel loved and respected.

## Case study: Esmeralda

Esmeralda was born on time with normal birthweight. She was a planned first child of two parents, who were both looking forward to her birth. Her mother was a primary school teacher and was planning to stay at home with Esmeralda until she started school (age 4 years). Esmeralda's father worked full time as a sales manager.

From when Esmeralda was a baby she cried continuously, suffered from colic from an early age and was very difficult to put onto a schedule. As she grew older, she was difficult to soothe when distressed and was never satisfied with hugs, toys or trips out; she always seemed to want more; she continually believed that she was given less than the next child. When she was three years old, her brother, Christopher, seemed laid back in comparison and he found his sister rather puzzling. At that point Esmeralda's mother asked her health visitor for help.

After listening carefully to the problems, the health visitor explained that Esmeralda was a temperamentally fragile child, who found life confusing and had difficulties navigating around it. She was sure that life was 'against her'. She was the kind of child who said 'no' to most requests automatically and her health visitor said that it was really important that Esmeralda's mother tried to avoid confrontations with her. If she did not, there was the danger that she would find herself in a very negative cycle, with the possibility of Esmeralda becoming an oppositional child with deteriorating behaviour.

The health visitor gave Esmeralda's mother an information leaflet, explained about the temperament of her child and offered ideas about how to handle her.

Gradually, Esmeralda's parents learned how to work around her, and help her to learn to regulate her behaviour. Esmeralda was happier and gradually settled into school and made friends.

## Multiple choice question

1. Which is not correct?

    a. There is a genetic component to temperament
    b. Children with an easy temperament do better in life
    c. Irritabilty in childhood is not important
    d. Management strategies for parents will help
    e. Personality will be influenced by temperament and environment

### Key texts

Caspi A, Harrington HL, Milne B et al. (2003) The human personality shows stability from age 3 to age 26. *Journal of Personality*, **71**: 495–514.

Caspi A, Elder Jr GH, Herbener ES (1990) Childhood personality and the prediction of life-course patterns. In: Robins L, Rutter M (eds). *Straight and Devious Pathways from Childhood to Adulthood.* Cambridge: Cambridge University Press.

Lavigne JV, Arend R, Rosenbaum D et al. (1998) Psychiatric disorders with onset in the preschool years: I. Stability of diagnoses. *Journal of the American Academy of Child and Adolescent Psychiatry*, **37**: 1246–54.

Leibenluft E, Cohen P, Gorrindo T (2006) Chronic versus episodic irritability in youth: a community-based, longitudinal study of clinical and diagnostic associations. *Journal of Child and Adolescent Psychopharmacology*, **16**: 456–66.

Nigg JT (2006) Temperament and developmental psychopathology. *Journal of Child Psychology and Psychiatry*, **47**: 395–422.

Stringaris A, Cohen P, Pine DS, Leibenluft E (2009) Adult outcomes of youth irritability: A 20-year prospective community-based study. *American Journal of Psychiatry*, **166**: 1048–54.

Thomas MD, Chess S, Birch HG (1968) *Temperament and Behavior Disorders in Children.* New York: New York University Press.

# 31 *Crying*
## Christine Cornforth and Margaret Thompson

---

## Key concepts
- At three months of age, babies can be expected to cry for 2 hours in each 24 hours.
- At six months of age, crying should reduce to 1 hour in each 24 hours, with a slight increase to 1.3 hours in every 24 hours between the ages of seven and nine months.
- The rate of crying usually peaks during the first three months to approximately six months of age, followed by a rapid decline.
- Forty per cent of the total crying in the first three months takes place during the evening.
- As the first year progresses, the rates of crying rapidly reduce.
- The frequency of night-time crying increases with 'high criers', with persistent crying being defined as more than 3 hours crying in each 24 hours.
- There are no differences in crying between girls and boys or in relation to birth order.
- The impact on families can be severe.

---

## Introduction

A baby's cry can be very distressing for parents and, in many ways, it is meant to be. Sometimes parents can think that their infant cries more than other infants or more than they had expected. In such cases, it is important to explain a normal crying pattern in a young infant. There is a wide range of normal crying in infancy: some babies can cry much more than others for no clear reason. Based on a large number of maternal reports (St James Roberts, 1989), it is widely accepted that:

## Classification of crying syndromes in infants

There are four classic crying syndromes in infancy including: (i) colic; (ii) persistent mother–infant distress syndrome; (iii) the temperamentally difficult child; and (iv) the dysregulated infant (Barr, 1998). These are challenging for clinicians to define as they are difficult to identify, manage and treat. Furthermore, there is little evidence in the literature as to any relationship between them.

Interestingly, the concept of rhythmicity and ability to be soothed does not show genetic heritability (Tschann et al., 1996).

## Colic

This is normally defined as excessive bouts of prolonged, unsoothable crying, which typically take place in the late afternoon and evening. The child often displays behaviours suggesting that they are in pain (clenched fist, arched back, legs flexed over abdomen, flushing and passing of gas). Colic normally presents from around 2 weeks of age and resolves by the end of the fourth month. The bouts of crying are often referred to as paroxysmal (i.e. unpredictable and not related to the child's environment, including soothing attempts by parents).

## Persistent mother–infant distress syndrome

This is a syndrome whereby the normal interactive and co-regulatory behaviours of the infant and caregiver are disrupted. Infants present after the early crying peak (after two months of age) and show no reduction in crying rates. Such infants may have feeding and/or sleeping difficulties, developmental delay and other possible organic risk factors. Familial risk factors are typically present, for example maternal psychopathology and postnatal parental conflicts.

## Temperamentally difficult infant

Such infants often exhibit a predisposition to negative effect, greater intensity of reactions, poor adaptability and unpredictability. This does not represent a clinical classification but more a variant of normal behaviour in the early years. Such infants are more likely to continue to exhibit such predispositions throughout development, albeit through different behaviours depending upon their age.

## Dysregulated infant

The dysregulated infant often displays difficulties in many areas such as feeding, sleeping, motor activity, affect and attention, usually due to a central regulatory dysfunction. They usually present to clinicians after the age of six months with symptoms of irritability, poor self-calming, hypersensitivity, impulsivity and intolerance to change (Campos et al., 1989).

# Assessment

It is essential to obtain a good comprehensive history as the infant's crying problems can often merge with other issues, such as feeding and sleeping. Some babies who cry a lot can find it difficult to settle into a pattern of eating and sleeping. This can in turn impact the family, as everyone becomes overtired.

## Use of diaries

Diaries can be a useful source of clinical information when assessing a young infant. Ask the parent/s to keep a record of their child's behaviours. Record in 15 minute blocks throughout the day how much time the infant spends: (i) crying; (ii) fussing/grizzling; (iii) sleeping; (iv) feeding; (v) how much time has been spent comforting the infant; (vi) how the parent/s felt; and (vii) ask about other aspects of the child's behaviour, such as sleep and feeding patterns. This will provide a summary of the infant's sleep and wakeful states during a normal day.

## Parent–infant relationship

Psychodynamic issues are important when looking at infant crying. Daws (1989) suggests that it is equally interesting to assess what happens when the baby starts to cry during the session. It is possible that some of the mother's own feelings are expressed through her baby's cries. It is suggested that infants who are too young to understand words will cry as parents talk about traumatic events in their own lives (e.g. it has been observed that babies cry while their parents talk about difficulties in their marriage). Following this, we might think that, at times, baby's crying in the night could be connected with such feelings in the mother or that the mother's inability to comfort the crying infant stems from unresolved grief of her own.

## Family functioning

Take time to see how the infant's crying behaviour impacts on the family. It is very difficult to be patient with a crying baby, especially if he cries a lot. You might find that parents find themselves frustrated, angry, upset or distressed. These feelings cannot be ignored as they could prove to become a barrier to effective interventions.

# Interventions

Always consider the following in your strategy:

- develop an individual approach for each family based on the comprehensive assessment;
- apply developmental theory to behaviour;
- a 'no blame' attitude must be adopted;
- parents need to be reassured that any new approach needs time to work; and
- young infants go through a period of basic self-regulation and can need parents to help and guide them through it.

Intervention strategies usually depend on the key aims that will be worked out during the assessment. Some useful and commonly used interventions include:

- before soothing, wait 1–2 minutes, then intervene, so that the young infant can learn to find ways to soothe him or herself;
- reassure the parents that they may not be able to stop the crying every time, but as parents they need to do what they can to provide comfort and help their child learn to cope with the distress;
- flexibility is very important, for example do not feed a young child every time they wake and start crying, since they might be tired or in discomfort and not hungry;
- sometimes the infant is either over- or under-stimulated;
- whispering to young infants and children can sometimes secure their attention and stop them crying;
- soft rhythmic sounds or continuous machine noises (e.g. a hair dryer or washing machine) can soothe some young infants;
- some infants are more reluctant to be soothed, less rewarding and seem especially emotionally sensitive. They may be less good at attending, even in infancy. They do not pick up on maternal cues. These infants can seem nervous and agitated and might need a much quieter and more structured environment than other infants. In such circumstances, baby massage can be effective.

## Over-/under-responsive parents

- Some over-responsive parents will pick up their young child after every small murmur and, as a consequence, such infants rarely have a reasonable length of time asleep and become too tired to feed properly. Some infants need to be allowed to cry themselves to sleep (5–10 minutes of an intermittent 'tired' cry and not despair).
- Some parents can be under-responsive. Research has shown that when parents give comfort to their crying infants, such children may cry less when they are older.

## Strategies for the parents

- If there is someone else nearby who can help, suggest that the parent arrange for them to look after the child for a short while so that the parents can have a break.
- If the parent is alone, she still might need to take a break when she feels angry. In such situations, it is advisable that the parent puts the baby down in a safe place and then walks away from the child. Advise the parent to take some deep breaths, phone a friend for a few minutes or make a drink and then go back to the baby and try to settle him/her again.
- It is important that parents take care of themselves when they have a young child who depends on them. They should take up any offers of help and take some regular breaks if and when they can.
- If you suspect that the parent is feeling tearful and depressed and/or finding it difficult to enjoy their baby, it is important to talk this through with them and refer them for further help if necessary.

## Case study: Carol

Carol is 18 months of age and is a child who finds it difficult to be peaceful. She appears to become frustrated easily, for example, she did not like going from milk to solids and for a long time spat out lumps. She is cross if she is hungry or tired. She finds change difficult. She was also poor at settling. She was otherwise developing normally.

The health visitor helped her mother to understand that this was not just Carol being naughty or intentionally demanding, but that Carol found it difficult to self-regulate.

Her mother learned to try to keep life more calm and ordered (she was a busy teacher and was always chasing to get everything done, especially in the morning). She worked hard at getting herself more organized so that she could spend time keeping Carol calm in the morning. She helped Carol understand the day's timetable, and made sure there was more time for quiet times sitting playing and listening to music.

She tried to keep calm and encouraging when trying out different foods and when dressing her.

Gradually Carol cried less, and also began to settle better to sleep.

The relationship between the mother and child became more enjoyable.

## Multiple choice questions

1. Which is correct?

    a. At three months of age, babies can be expected to cry for 2 hours in each 24 hours
    b. Crying should reduce to 1 hour in each 24 hours, by six months
    c. Forty per cent of the total crying in the first three months takes place during the evening
    d. The rate of crying should decrease in the first year
    e. Boys and girls cry equally

2. Which are common causes of infant crying in the first year

    a. Colic
    b. Temperamentally difficult infant
    c. Dysregulated infant
    d. Persistent mother–infant distress syndrome
    e. Infant too hot

### Key texts

Barr RG (1998) Management of clinical problems and emotional care: Colic and crying syndromes in infants. *Pediatrics*, **102**: 1282–6.

Campos RG, Campos RG, Barrett KC (1989) Emergent themes in the study of emotional development and emotion regulation. *Developmental Psychology*, **25**: 394–402.

Daws D (1989) *Through the Night: Helping Parents and Sleepless Infants.* London: Free Association Books.

St James-Roberts I (1989) Persistent crying in infancy. *Journal of Child Psychology and Psychiatry*, **30**: 189–95.

Tschann JM, Kaiser P, Chesney MA et al. (1996) Resilience and vulnerability among preschool children: family functioning, temperament, and behaviour problems. *Journal for the American Academy of Child and Adolescent Psychiatry*, **35**: 184–92.

# Emotionality in children and young people and links to psychopathology

Georgia Chronaki

## Key concepts

- Emotionality is an important concept in understanding social adjustment and mental health in children and adolescents.
- Research and clinical practice have shown that individual differences in emotion processing are closely related to children's social adjustment.
- The ability to 'read' non-verbal cues of emotion in others, such as facial expressions, gestures, postures and tone of voice, is fundamental to children's social competence (Rothman and Nowicki, 2004).
- Children who are better able to understand non-verbal emotional cues in social interactions develop better social skills and form positive interpersonal relationships over time (Saarni, 1999; Trentacosta and Fine, 2010).

A number of mental health problems in children and adolescents are linked to inaccurate understanding of emotions. For example, emotion processing deficits, such as lower accuracy to perceive emotions in other people and a higher tendency to attribute hostility and anger (i.e. hostile attribution bias) to others intentions can place children at risk for heightened aggression (Schultz et al., 2004). Empathy, defined as accurate detection of others' emotional signals (Hoffman, 1991), has been linked to lower levels of aggressive and challenging behaviour in children (Zahn-Waxler et al., 1995). Children with inattention and hyperactivity show difficulties in understanding emotions from others' facial and vocal expressions, often because of inattentive, rapid and impulsive processing of such signals (Norvilitis et al., 2000; Kats-Gold et al., 2007).

Children with anxiety disorders are more likely to present avoidant behaviours (Barrett et al., 1996) and a bias towards negative or threatening emotional information (Bar-Haim et al., 2007). It is therefore essential to consider how children perceive emotions in other people in order to better understand children's social behaviour and adjustment.

In addition, although internalizing and externalizing disorders often co-occur in children,

there are different types of emotion processing mechanisms underlying each disorder type. For example, research from our laboratory has shown that a deficit to recognize an angry tone of voice in others may characterize children with externalizing behaviour, such as hyperactivity and conduct problems, but not children with internalizing symptoms. Children with externalizing problems tend to be more prone to anger and impulsivity, whereas children with internalizing symptoms are more prone to sadness (Ellis et al., 1997; Eisenberg et al., 2001).

In general, children with internalizing symptoms find it difficult to control negative emotionality, as indicated by rumination, sadness and elevated worry. Research suggests that children who present both externalizing and internalizing problems are more impaired in emotion processing, compared to children who present either condition alone (Manassis et al., 2007).

Neuroscientific methods, such as electroencephalograph (EEG) and event-related potentials (ERP), which represent changes in the electrical activity of the brain in response to specific stimuli, have been a focus of increasing interest during the last few years in understanding emotionality in children and young people and links to developmental disorders. Such methods can reveal emotion processing deficits which may not be evident in children's observable behaviour. For example, altered brain responses to social stimuli, such as facial emotional expressions, have been found in children with autism (Baron-Cohen, 1999; Dawson et al., 2004), psychopathic tendencies (Blair et al., 2009) and depression (Pine and Monk, 2009).

Although ERPs cannot currently be used for clinical purposes, individual differences in children's neural responses to emotional stimuli can contribute to a better understanding of developmental disorders in social processing (De Haan and Gunnar, 2009). Developmental social neuroscience perspectives can be very useful for clinicians and therapists working with children and adolescents in this area and hold promise in making great breakthroughs in our understanding of mental health problems in children in the future.

Finally, it is important to consider family factors when examining children's emotion processing. Early emotional experiences can have a major influence on emotional development. Parenting environments and parental psychopathology have been related to social information processing difficulties and biases in children. For example, children who have experienced abnormal parenting environments, such as physical abuse, show faster recognition of anger and delayed disengagement from angry faces in others (Pollak and Tolley-Schell, 2003; Pollak et al., 2009).

Similarly, children of mothers at elevated risk for depression selectively attend to sad facial expressions whereas children of never-disordered mothers attend to positive happy facial expressions (Joormann et al., 2007). High levels of maternal anger have been related to lower emotional knowledge in preschoolers (Halberstadt et al., 1999).

Early emotional experiences can influence the brain mechanisms underlying emotion processing in children. For example, maltreated children display greater frontal brain activation in response to threatening (i.e. angry) facial expressions compared to non-maltreated children (Cicchetti and Curtis, 2005). Similarly, children experiencing psychosocial deprivation, such as institutionalized care, show abnormal brain responses to emotional faces and such brain abnormalities can be remedied following foster care (Moulson et al., 2009).

In summary, emotions can provide a window offering a comprehensive view into children's mental health and adjustment. Future practitioners are encouraged to carefully consider children's understanding of emotion to better understand children's social behaviour.

## Multiple choice questions

1. Which statement is correct about emotion processing in children?

   a. Parental depression is bound to cause emotion processing abnormalities in children
   b. Children with internalizing and externalizing symptoms show identical impairments in emotion processing
   c. Children at higher risk for aggressive behaviour often tend to perceive others as hostile
   d. Empathy is not related to children's pro-social behaviour
   e. Mental health problems in children are a direct consequence of negative emotionality.

2. Which statement is correct about the neuroscience of emotion processing?

   a. ERPs can help uncover emotion processing abnormalities in children and young people with developmental disorders
   b. Children's brain activity patterns can be easily observed in children's behavioural performance during various tasks
   c. Clinicians should use only neuroscientific methods to assess emotion processing in children
   d. Difficulty to read others' emotions in children with autism is due to small brain size
   e. We can remedy children's negative emotionality by looking at how the brain works.

## Key texts

De Haan M, Gunnar MR (2009) *Handbook of Developmental Social Neuroscience.* New York: The Guildford Press.

Saarni C (1999) *The Development of Emotional Competence.* New York: The Guildford Press.

Trentacosta CJ, Fine SE (2010) Emotion knowledge, social competence, and behavior problems in childhood and adolescence: A meta-analytic review. *Social Development,* **19**: 1–29.

# 33 Juvenile disruptive behaviour disorders: oppositional defiant disorder (ODD) and conduct disorder (CD)

Christine Cornforth, Graeme Fairchild and Margaret Thompson

## Key concepts

- The behaviour of children with ODD or CD may persist over time.
- Intervention should be as early as possible.
- This behaviour can be severe and cause major stress to families.
- There is an increased risk of educational, social and criminal negative outcomes for these young people.
- Aetiology of the disorder is multi-factorial with a genetic component, temperament and parenting all contributing.
- There may be associated neuropsychological deficits with speech and language and executive function impairment.
- Co-morbidity is always found.
- The ratio of males to females is 2.5 with males more likely to have severe problems.

## Introduction

Oppositional defiant disorder (ODD) and conduct disorder (CD) are together considered as the disruptive behaviour disorders, and have in common the presence of socially difficult and antisocial behaviour. Children with these disorders are more likely to require chronic clinical interventions as often many of the presenting symptoms persist over time.

This chapter aims to describe the classification of ODD and CD, including symptomatology and subtypes. Following on from this, the prevalence and aetiology of the disorders are presented together with issues with assessment and diagnosis. Finally, a brief description of treatment and intervention options is provided.

## Classification of juvenile disruptive behaviour disorders

ODD involves a recurrent pattern of defiant and disobedient behaviour towards parents and other authority figures leading to impairment of day to day activities, and is typically viewed as a milder condition than CD. CD commonly involves behaviours which are pervasive across settings and against the law, such as physical assaults, serious theft and violations of societal norms (e.g. pathological lying or serious truancy). Although there is considerable overlap between these conditions, with many children with CD also meeting full criteria for ODD, and a proportion of those with ODD fulfilling sub-threshold criteria for CD, evidence from factor analytic studies suggests that these clusters of behaviour are at least partly separable.

There are also important developmental considerations for both of these disorders: ODD-type behaviours are more characteristic of younger children, whereas CD occurs more commonly in older children and adolescents (Loeber et al., 2000). Longitudinal studies that have followed children from a young age into adolescence and young adulthood have revealed that many children who fulfil criteria for ODD in childhood do not develop CD at a later stage, whereas almost all of those who meet criteria for CD previously fulfilled criteria for ODD.

It should be noted that there is considerable

overlap between CD, ODD and attention deficit hyperactivity disorder (ADHD), with approximately 50 per cent of those with CD or ODD also meeting the diagnostic criteria for ADHD and vice versa (Kutcher et al., 2004). Given this, the ICD-10 includes a specific diagnostic sub-group for this group of children referred to as 'hyperkinetic conduct disorder'.

# CD/ODD diagnostic criteria according to the WHO ICD-10

There are two classification systems for these disorders, the DSM-IV (American Psychiatric Association, 2000) and the ICD-10 (World Health Organization, 1996). However, both of these systems are relatively similar in terms of emphasizing the persistent duration of the behaviours and each takes a categorical approach to describing the presence of these disorders. They do, however, differ in that DSM-IV considers ODD and CD as separate conditions, whereas the ICD-10 symptom criteria are similar to the combined criteria for both the DSM-IV CD and ODD disorders.

According to the WHO ICD-10, to be classified as having either CD or ODD the following criteria need to be met:

- a repetitive and persistent pattern of behaviour has to be present, in which either the basic rights of others or age-appropriate societal norms or rules are violated;
- this pattern of behaviour must be present for at least six months, during which some of the following symptoms are present (individual sub-categories for rules or numbers of symptoms; WHO ICD-10 1993); and
- symptoms 11, 13, 15, 16, 20, 21 and 23 (see **Table 33.1** below) need only to have occurred once for the criterion to be fulfilled.

# Specification of possible sub-divisions ICD-10 (1996)

CD can be further categorized into the following subgroups; CD confined to the family context, unsocialized CD and socialized CD.

Table 33.1 Individual symptoms

| No | Symptom description |
|----|---------------------|
| 1. | Has unusually frequent or severe temper tantrums for his or her developmental level |
| 2. | Often argues with adults |
| 3. | Often actively refuses adults' requests or defies rules |
| 4. | Often, apparently deliberately, does things that annoy other people |
| 5. | Often blames others for his or her own mistakes or misbehaviour |
| 6. | Is often 'touchy' or easily annoyed by others |
| 7. | Is often angry or resentful |
| 8. | Is often spiteful or vindictive |
| 9. | Often lies or breaks promises to obtain goods or favours or to avoid obligations |
| 10. | Frequently initiates physical fights. This does not include fights with siblings |
| 11. | Has used a weapon that can cause serious physical harm to others (e.g. bat, brick, broken bottle, knife, gun) |
| 12. | Often stays out after dark despite parental prohibition (beginning before 13 years of age) |
| 13. | Exhibits physical cruelty to other people (e.g. ties up, cuts or burns a victim) |
| 14. | Exhibits physical cruelty to animals |
| 15. | Deliberately destroys the property of others (other than by fire-setting) |
| 16. | Deliberately sets fires with a risk or intention of causing serious damage |
| 17. | Steals objects of non-trivial value without confronting the victim, either within the home or outside (e.g. shoplifting, burglary, forgery) |
| 18. | Is frequently truant from school, beginning before 13 years of age |
| 19. | Has run away from parental or parental surrogate home at least twice or has run away once for more than a single night. NB: This does not include leaving home to avoid physical or sexual abuse |
| 20. | Commits a crime involving confrontation with the victim, including purse snatching, extortion, mugging |
| 21. | Forces another person into sexual activity |
| 22. | Frequently bullies others (e.g. deliberate infliction of pain or hurt, including persistent intimidation, tormenting, or molestation) |
| 23. | Breaks into someone else's house, building or car |

For 'CD confined to the family context' the following criteria must be met:

- the diagnostic criteria for CD must be met;
- three or more of the symptoms listed for CD

must be present, with at least three from items (9)–(23);

- at least one of the symptoms from items (9)–(23) must have been present for at least six months;
- conduct disturbance must be limited to the family context.

For 'unsocialized CD' the following criteria must be met:

- the diagnostic criteria for CD must be met;
- three or more of the symptoms listed for CD must be present, with at least three from items (9)–(23);
- at least one of the symptoms from items (9)–(23) must have been present for at least six months;
- there must be poor relationships with the individual's peer group, as shown by isolation, rejection or unpopularity, and by a lack of lasting close reciprocal friendships.

For 'socialized CD' the following criteria must be met:

- the diagnostic criteria for CD must be met;
- three or more of the symptoms listed for conduct disorder must be present, with at least three from items (9)–(23);
- at least one of the symptoms from items (9)–(23) must have been present for at least six months;
- conduct disturbance must include settings outside the home or family context. Peer relationships are within normal limits.

It is recommended that the age of onset be specified:

- Childhood onset type: at least one conduct problem before the age of ten years
- Adolescent onset type: no conduct problems before the age of ten years.

For determining a prognosis, the WHO guidelines suggest that 'severity' (indexed by number of symptoms) is a better guide than the precise type of symptomatology.

It is also recommended that cases be described in terms of their scores on three dimensions of disturbance, these include:

1. hyperactivity (inattentive, restless behaviour);
2. emotional disturbance (anxiety, depression, obsessionality, hypochondriasis);
3. severity of conduct disorder:

a. mild: few, if any, conduct problems are in excess of those required to make the diagnosis, and conduct problems cause only minor harm to others;

b. moderate: the number of conduct problems and the effects on others are intermediate between 'mild' and 'severe';

c. severe: there are many conduct problems in excess of those required to make the diagnosis, or the conduct problems cause considerable harm to others, e.g. severe physical injury, vandalism, or theft.

# Oppositional defiant disorder

- The general criteria for CD must be met.
- Four or more of the symptoms listed for CD must be present, but with no more than two symptoms from items (9)–(23).
- The symptoms must be maladaptive and inconsistent with the developmental level.
- At least four of the symptoms must have been present for at least six months.

## Prevalence

Epidemiological studies suggest that around 5 per cent of school-aged children meet criteria for either CD or ODD (Maughan et al., 2004). The prevalence of these disorders is difficult to quantify in the community, as many children will present with extremes of behaviour, but there are a number of factors that distinguish a child with ODD or CD. These include an extreme number of symptoms, the frequency of symptoms, chronicity and the degree of impairment for the child and/or their family.

Differences in prevalence for socioeconomic class are not pronounced (e.g. Tittle and Meier, 1990). Sex differences have been reported with a sex ratio of approximately 2.5 males for each female, with males furthermore exceeding females in terms of frequency and severity of symptoms (Moffitt et al., 2001). The causes of these disorders are generally the same for both sexes, however males experience more CD as they experience more of the risk factors (such as hyperactivity and cognitive deficits).

# Associated conditions

It has been estimated that approximately half of all referrals to child guidance clinics are for ODD/CD and furthermore half of these children have a dual diagnosis of either hyperactivity or ODD (Kazdin, 1995). Epidemiological studies have reported that more than 90 per cent of children with CD also meet the diagnostic criteria for other disorders (Moffitt, 2003). Furthermore, co-occurring behaviours include psychopathy (Lynam and Gudonis, 2005), autistic traits (Gilmour et al., 2004), bullying (Olweus, 1993) and adolescent partner violence (Ehrensaft et al., 2004).

Many children with ODD also have an emotionally labile temperament (with irritability being an important feature of the disorder) and their parents often find such children difficult to care for. Furthermore, children with ODD find it difficult to regulate their emotions and cope with challenging situations by being aggressive and oppositional.

Consequently, when CD is diagnosed, the clinician should also rule out any co-occurring behavioural or learning disorder, giving the opportunity for the long-term consequences of such a disorder to be prevented.

# Aetiology

## Genetics

There is increasing evidence from behavioural genetic studies for a role of genetic influences in the aetiology of CD/ODD, with 40–50 per cent of variance in these conditions explained by heritable factors, and a relatively large contribution of shared environmental factors relative to other psychiatric disorders (Rhee and Waldman, 2002). Heritability is even higher (60–70 per cent) for aggressive forms of CD and for CD with high levels of callous-unemotional or psychopathic traits (Viding et al., 2005). In terms of specific genes, a functional polymorphism in the monoamine oxidase A (MAOA) gene, which codes for an enzyme responsible for breaking down the neurotransmitters serotonin, noradrenaline and dopamine in the brain, has been implicated in the aetiology of CD. It appears to have only weak effects on the risk for developing CD when it occurs in isolation, but in combination with

exposure to childhood maltreatment, the low activity form of the MAOA gene appears to confer increased susceptibility to developing CD (Caspi et al., 2002). This gene is X chromosome-linked and its effects on vulnerability to negative rearing environments appear greatest in (or possibly confined to) males. It is likely that, as with other psychiatric disorders, many genes are involved in the aetiology of CD, and complex interactions between susceptibility genes and environmental factors will be the rule rather than the exception.

## Neuropsychology

Neuropsychological and neuroimaging studies have also provided important insights into the aetiology of CD/ODD. Children with conduct problems have been found to have increased rates of verbal and language-based deficits and poor executive functioning (e.g. Moffitt, 1993). It is therefore likely that such children have difficulties organizing their thoughts and expressing themselves. Consequently, such children may attempt to gain control over such situations by using aggression.

Children with these conditions have also been found to be more sensitive to positive or rewarding stimuli, and less sensitive to negative or punishing stimuli, when making decisions or learning than typically developing children (Fairchild et al., 2009a). They have also been shown to have weaker psychophysiological responses to punishing or painful stimuli (Luman et al., 2010). A number of brain imaging studies have revealed reductions in amygdala and anterior insula grey matter volume in the brains of children with CD compared to healthy controls (Sterzer et al., 2007; Huebner et al., 2008; Fairchild et al., 2011), which potentially helps to explain why they show deficits in empathy and facial expression recognition (Fairchild et al., 2009b). Functional brain imaging studies have also shown reduced amygdala responses to emotional facial expressions in adolescents with CD (Passamonti et al., 2010) or conduct problems and callous-unemotional traits (Marsh et al., 2008; Jones et al., 2009). It is likely that these changes in brain structure and function in children with CD contribute to their difficulties with social cognition, although longitudinal studies are needed to investigate whether these neural differences cause or contribute to the symptoms of CD, or are merely a secondary consequence of having this condition.

Attempts to link antisocial behaviours with neurotransmitters have been successful in adults (Nelson and Trainor, 2007); however, findings with children have not been consistent (Hill, 2002).

## Perinatal insults

Complications surrounding the time of birth (such as low birthweight; Brennan et al., 2003) are thought to be associated with some of the neuropsychological difficulties associated with CD and ODD. There is also evidence that maternal smoking during pregnancy is associated with increased risk of CD in offspring (Brennan et al., 1999). However, a direct causal link between smoking during pregnancy and CD has not been found (Fergusson, 1999).

## Temperament

The innate temperament of a child will make a difference to how they view the world and conversely how the world will view and interact with them.

Hyperactive children are difficult to parent and often exhibit behaviours that can escalate into chains of conflicts, which in turn can often result in coercive parenting (Patterson, 1982). This refers to a pattern of interactions whereby a parent may unknowingly reinforce coercive behaviours in their children by nagging, scolding and yelling when the child misbehaves. These behaviours initiate the coercive interaction. If the child continues to misbehave or even escalates the conflict despite the parent's aversive behaviours, the parent eventually reaches an exhaustion point. At this point, the child's misbehaviour is negatively reinforced when the parent fails to follow through with their promised consequences or ceases punishing them. Should the parent back down and fail to discipline the child adequately, the child quickly learns that they can manipulate the parent into meeting their needs by using coercive strategies.

Rule-breaking and apparent disobedience in children with poor listening skills and poor ability to predict the consequences of their behaviour can lead to punishment and negative reinforcement. A highly emotionally fragile child will be inappropriately sensitive to criticism and cry easily, thereby setting him/herself up to be teased and often used as a scapegoat. These are often children who tend to say 'no' rather than 'yes', creating situations for the development of ODD.

## Parental background

Parenting practices and attitudes will affect children with CD and ODD. Positive parenting practices foster good self-esteem, confidence and problem-solving techniques in children, while inconsistent, negative or 'coercive' parenting fosters the opposite. Children need predictability from parents together with consistent, clear and understandable limits. Inconsistent parenting is often present in families with a conduct disordered child, for example, extremes of lax to harsh and unpredictable discipline, with the child not knowing from one day to the next what is expected from him, or what punishment will follow should he transgress that day's rules. In addition, monitoring of the children's whereabouts may be poor. Mental illness and criminal behaviour in families, particularly fathers, is also highly correlated with conduct disordered children (Farrington, 1995; Kazdin, 1995).

The members of these dysfunctional families often lack empathy for each other, demonstrate little affection and have negative communication skills. There is often hostility and conflict between partners and, if it is a reconstituted family, there may be hostility and conflict towards the other natural parent, with the child caught in the middle.

## Other important factors

Children with CD or ODD are often from families who have financial difficulties, lack access to transport and live in overcrowded households and unsafe neighbourhoods.

Inevitably, such children are often in conflict with their teachers and other agencies, and the families might themselves find it difficult to work positively with professional agencies or healthcare workers. Consequently, a complex cycle then arises, with these difficulties inhibiting positive change. The child may then become the focus for perceived difficulties in the school, when that might not always be true. Children will target and scapegoat a child who annoys them, compounding the difficulties for the child. In some cases, teachers may do the same.

These children also have poorer peer relationships than non-disordered children. There is evidence to support that: (1) children's antisocial behaviours lead them to have peer problems; (2) their deviant peer relationships lead to antisocial behaviours; or (3) some common factor leads to both these factors (Moffitt and Scott, 2005). On the whole it is important to keep in mind the reciprocal manner in which conduct problems can influence who a child's friends are and in turn how such friends can promote the child's conduct problems.

# Treatment

Treatment methods have been developed for this group of children, but as the root causes of the disorder are complex and involve the child's temperament, family factors, the environment, the school and the child's peers, treatment techniques need to address more than one domain for lasting, effective change to happen.

Kazdin lays out a useful framework for considering whether a particular treatment is the correct one for a condition, bearing in mind that we should not be using treatments that have not been shown to produce change in well-conducted trials. This conceptualization of treatment is particularly helpful when we consider how best to change the behaviour of children with conduct disorder. Kazdin also discusses why some treatment approaches might not work (Kazdin, 1997; Kazdin et al., 1997; Kazdin, 2001).

## Framework for considering valid treatment approaches

- The disorder and the mechanisms underlying the disorder need to be conceptualized correctly in order to target treatment appropriately.
- Is there research to back up the above conceptualization? For example, is there clear research evidence that family factors correlate with the development of conduct disorder? Do particular family communication patterns correlate with the development of difficult behaviour in the children?

- Have there been sound controlled trials or well-evaluated treatment studies indicating that a particular treatment method works?
- Have there been studies looking at treatment targeted at the processes underlying the development of the disorder, e.g. the family communication pattern or the distorted cognitive processing mechanisms in children, and that have shown clinically, effective change in proportion to positive change in the processes?

The above criteria are very strict and no treatment can show change in all domains. The aim of treatment outcome for this group of children should be to improve the child's functioning in both the short and long term.

## Cognitive problem-solving skills techniques

How children perceive the outside world will depend on a variety of factors including their temperament and intelligence and the modelling and 'feedback experience' they have been exposed to from family, peers and other adults they encounter (e.g. teachers). As outlined earlier, these children often 'miscue' in social situations and incorrectly ascribe hostile intent in certain situations. This can lead to aggression on the part of the child.

The cognitive problem-solving skills techniques (CPSST) treatment approach addresses the different cognitive processes the child uses in everyday situations. Pro-social behaviour is encouraged by modelling and acting using a variety of techniques, for example paper exercises and role play. The therapist will guide the child and offer positive support. Moreover, positive reward systems with appropriate sanctions are built in with homework tasks for the child to work on.

Preliminary evidence of CPSST treatment suggests that positive results have been achieved in reducing aggressive and antisocial behaviours at home, school and in the community. Furthermore, gains have also been documented in the short and long term (one year) follow up. Finally, this treatment has been shown to be effective in clinic and non-clinic samples (Kazdin, 1997; Kazdin, 2001).

## Parent management training

As discussed previously, parenting will influence children's behaviour. However the relationship between the parent and child is a two-way process. Parents who have difficulty understanding why their child does not listen may find themselves in a very negative cycle with their child (i.e. children who are receiving little attention might behave badly to gain *any* attention, but, of course, this can produce an unpredictable result, reinforcing the negative cycle).

Parenting packages promote positive parenting, encouraging parents to recognize behaviours for what they are (i.e. reframing the problem). This enables the parents to anticipate the cycle of difficulties in order to learn to intervene with positive parenting strategies. Coercive and negative parenting strategies are discouraged (see above under Parental background, and Temperament p. 197). The family as a whole is encouraged to use positive rewards and plenty of praise with their children together with clear, well thought-out sanctions when necessary.

Parent training also emphasizes the importance of clear, consistent, predictable, parenting. It is often helpful for families with young children to bring them along to the session so that the therapist can demonstrate helpful techniques such as setting limits, and developing listening skills.

Such parent training for parents of children with CD/ODD has been well researched and the results look promising, with positive results at ten-year follow up (Forehand and Long, 1996).

## Functional family therapy

This therapeutic approach addresses how the family communicates. Its theoretical viewpoint draws together an understanding of family systems, underlying cognitive processes and behavioural functioning.

The aim of this approach is to help families understand individual family member's behaviour. This approach also focuses on how each family member's communication pattern affects the rest of the family. The therapist's task is to aid the learning process and reinforce positive approaches with praise and interpretation (both verbally and non-verbally).

Outcome studies indicate that this treatment method can be very successful, especially with delinquent children. Family processing does show change, and 'successful' families show positive change in communication style. These gains seem to remain present up to 2.5 years following treatment; however, research is still needed into predicting factors in families which would lead to positive change. For further information, please see Alexander et al. (2000).

## Multi-systemic therapy

It is often helpful to take a multi-systemic approach with children and their families as these children often cause distress to themselves, their families and their environment. The multi-systemic approach makes a positive decision to address the wider context and all the systems surrounding the individual. Such an approach will therefore address the child individually, the family (including the marital system), the peer group and the school. Although it uses many of the techniques already referred to, it is not simply an amalgamation of packages, but a positive attempt to offer a package to help resolve the difficulties. Outcome studies suggest that for children with extreme problems (e.g. those involved with the youth justice system), this approach works well (Henggeler, 1999).

## Medication

Medication has a place, in particular, with children with hyperactivity. Although stimulant medication might help the symptoms of extreme temper and aggression, it may not alter the conduct disorder behaviour (e.g. defiance, lying or stealing). Other types of medication have been used to try to target a variety of problems, but no clear benefits have been obtained. In the case of extreme aggression, clinicians often find that this is very difficult to control – mood stabilizers (e.g. carbamezipine or sodium valproate) have been found to be effective in such individuals. Risperidone has also been used in trials with conduct disordered children, most commonly in those with co-morbid intellectual disabilities. It appears effective in reducing aggressive symptoms in this group but should be used with caution, as it is associated with side effects such as extrapyramidal symptoms, somnolence, weight gain and dyspepsia in a significant minority of cases. The long-term side effects of this medication are still to be determined, thus base-line measures of blood sugar, cholesterol, liver function tests, and possibly lipids, should be taken and repeated if concerned, or at least every six months.

## What affects outcome?

Unfortunately, families with conduct disordered children often encounter a wide range of additional problems (as outlined earlier); such problems can often prove to be significant barriers to treatment. Therapists need to find ways of engaging family members as well as 'holding' them in therapy. Helping with transport issues, telephoning before appointments, engaging all family members separately, are important factors to consider and represent good practice.

Group work with children, all with similar delinquent problems, is not recommended, as the children tend to model each other's behaviour. If the group is mixed (i.e. including pro-social children), results seem to be better, as the children have pro-social norms from the non-conduct disordered child to follow.

Research has found that the factors, which mitigate *against* positive and lasting gains include:

- an early onset of the conduct disorder;
- aggressive behaviour;
- poor executive functioning in the child;
- being male and having an increased number of symptoms.

However, it should be noted that even in early-onset forms of conduct disorder, only 50 per cent of individuals go on to show serious forms of criminality and/or antisocial personality disorder in adulthood. Later onset of the disorder (at about age 15), which is characterized by less of a gender split, but by delinquent (theft or vandalism) rather than aggressive behaviour, has a better prognosis.

The best way to work with these children and families seems to be to assess carefully the domains in which the child has difficulties and whether there are any co-morbid problems present. Following this treatment can be targeted appropriately.

## Case study 1: Oppositional disorder
### Margaret Thompson

Harry, aged five, was very hard for his young parents to parent. He was referred into the CAMHS under five clinic as his school said that he was running the risk of exclusion. He would never finish his work, said 'no' when asked to put his work away and was constantly in trouble in the playground, fighting with other children and spoiling their games.

At home he always said 'no' when asked to do something and fought with his sister. He had frequent temper tantrums.

A careful history highlighted that he had been a dysregulated toddler, with a poor settling pattern to sleep, quite active and always crying and being irritable. His development of language was delayed.

Observation in the clinic indicated that the parents found it hard to be clear and firm with him in their messages to him. However, they clearly did love him but were puzzled and overwhelmed with how to parent him more successfully.

His behaviour in the clinic indicated that he was very active and had problems with language and understanding.

The nurse, who saw the family, asked the school to assess his behaviour and his language and pre-reading skills. The school filled out a Strength and Difficulties Questionnaire (SDQ). The school report suggested problems with learning and the SDQ showed problems across the whole questionnaire.

Following this she arranged for a cognitive assessment in the clinic. This indicated that Harry had a low verbal IQ and was very active. This was fed back to school.

The nurse explained to the parents the reasons behind his behaviour explaining his temperament, his overactive behaviour which meant he found it hard to sit still in the classroom. His problems with language contributed to him not being able to understand instructions and also this affected him socially.

She worked with the parents to change their parenting approach to be clearer and firmer, but to always make sure that Harry understood what was expected of him. Clear short messages were helpful. The parents were encouraged to join a parenting group which helped.

The school changed their teaching approach with him; he had work on language and pre-reading skills. He joined a nurture group with an ELSA (an emotional literacy support assistant) which he enjoyed and gradually his peer relationships improved.

## Case study 2
### Margaret Thompson

Dale, a 15 year old, was referred to the adolescent service by the Youth Offending Team (YOT) as he was stealing from shops and had pushed a shop assistant to the floor in the last episode of stealing.

Dale had had a long history of difficulties, with exclusion from school, difficulties with his parents as he was aggressive at home, he shoplifted with mates from the age of ten and had always been noncompliant.

His parents separated when he was 12 years of age, as his father was an alcoholic, aggressive and in and out of prison.

The worker from the YOT was concerned that as well as exhibiting severe conduct problems, Dale was very depressed and expressing suicidal thoughts.

The consultant who saw him was also concerned about him as Dale, although appearing on the surface as a boy who did not care about the world, did have insight into his problems and would have liked things to be different for him.

He was able to say that he had been sexually abused by his father from a young age until his father left the house, though had been unable to tell his mother or anyone else before.

The team in the behaviour support unit put together a programme within multi-systemic therapy: with individual work with Dale; undertook an educational and a cognitive assessment (indicating that he had learning difficulties in word processing and was dyslexic) and arranged for a referral to a pupil referral unit for one to one help; met with Dale's mother and gradually also with both Dale and her (a parent management programme with clear boundaries and curfews was set up, leading to functional family therapy including his brother and sister); a programme was started to help Dale with his smoking and heavy alcohol intake (he had never taken drugs).

His father was interviewed by social services and the police and charged.

Gradually Dale began to think that life could be different and he became less depressed. He made progress at school, changed his friendship groups and began to relate better with his family. He stayed out of trouble, and had stopped drinking and smoking. He was planning on going to college to do a course in car mechanics which he enjoyed and had managed to achieve a part-time job in a garage.

## Multiple choice questions

1. The division between conduct disorder – childhood onset and conduct disorder – adolescent onset occurs at what age?

   a. 14 years
   b. 12 years
   c. 10 years
   d. 11 years
   e. 13 years

2. What is the estimated prevalence of ODD and CD in school-aged children?

   a. >5 per cent
   b. 5 per cent
   c. 30 per cent
   d. 10–20 per cent
   e. 30–35 per cent

3. Which of the following is not a recommended treatment option for CD and/or ODD?

   a. Multi-systemic therapy
   b. Selective serotonin reuptake inhibitors (SSRIs)
   c. Cognitive problem-solving skills techniques (CPSST)
   d. Parent management training
   e. Functional family therapy

4. What is the current reported heritability for CD and ODD?

   a. <10 per cent
   b. 70–80 per cent
   c. 20–30 per cent
   d. >80 per cent
   e. 40–50 per cent

5. Which candidate gene has been particularly implicated in the aetiology of CD?

   a. BRCA1
   b. DAT1
   c. MAOA
   d. BDNF
   e. APOA5

## Key texts

Farrington DP (1995) The Twelfth Jack Tizard Memorial Lecture: The development of offending and anti-social behaviour from childhood: Key findings from the Cambridge Study in Delinquent Development. *Journal of Child Psychology and Psychiatry*, **360**: 929–64.

Henggeler SW (1999) Multi systemic therapy: an overview of clinical procedures, outcomes, and policy implications. *Clinical Psychology and Psychiatry Review*, **4**: 2–10.

Kazdin AE (2001) Treatment of conduct disorders. In: Hill J, Maughan B (eds). *Conduct Disorders in Childhood and Adolescents*. Cambridge: Cambridge University Press, 408–48.

Kazdin AE (1997) Psychosocial treatments for conduct disorder in children. *Journal of Child Psychology and Psychiatry*, **38**: 161–78.

Kazdin AE, Holland L, Crowley M, Breton S (1997) Barriers to Treatment Participation Scale: evaluation and validation in the context of child outpatient treatment. *Journal of Child Psychology and Psychiatry*, **38**: 1051–62.

# 34 Forensic child and adolescent psychiatry
## Suyog Dhakras

> ## Key concepts
> - The age of criminal responsibility in the UK is ten years.
> - There are a total of 2150 children and young people in custody in the country currently.
> - Of all convicted children, approximately 14 per cent are convicted of violent offences (e.g. assault) against the person.
> - The rate of recognized mental disorders in young offenders (mixed sample of offenders in custody as well as in the community) is 30 per cent – three times that seen in non-offender samples in the child and adolescent age group.
> - One in four 15–16 year olds admit to routinely carrying a knife.
> - Approximately 50 per cent of antisocial behaviour orders (ASBOs) are made for children and teenagers.

Forensic Child and Adolescent Psychiatry is a relatively new sub-specialty in Child and Adolescent Psychiatry dealing with issues of mental disorders and criminal and offending behaviour in children and adolescents.

Research into the causes of criminal behaviour in children and adolescents is a rapidly developing field. However, Forensic Child and Adolescent Mental Health Services (FCAMHS) lags behind Adult Forensic Psychiatric Services significantly in terms of the research evidence, as well as resources and development of services.

Studies in the UK and the USA show that rates of criminal and delinquent activity in adolescence are so high that they are statistically normative. The majority of young people who are violent/criminal in adolescence do not continue to offend in adulthood – studies show that approximately 75–80 per cent desist by the age of 21 years. Official crime rates in youth tend to peak at age 17 and then decline.

Moffitt et al. (1996) have suggested that patterns of aggressive and violent offences follow two distinct courses as follows.

## Life course persistent

- Five to 10 per cent of all young people who engage in violent offences and antisocial acts.
- Usually have other co-morbidities – attention deficit hyperactivity disorder (ADHD), oppositional behaviour, conduct disorder
- Early onset of criminal and antisocial activity – first arrest between 7 and 11 years strongly associated with long-term offending.
- Predisposition to antisocial behaviour remains stable.

## Adolescent limited

- More common.
- Antisocial behaviour begins and ends in the teenage years.
- At least 75–80 per cent will desist by early adulthood.
- Influence of delinquent peers is central.
- May usually maintain primary attachments and have capacity for empathy.

There are also some gender differences.

- Males commit the majority of violent crime (though the rates in young girls are rapidly rising).
- Most risk factors for violence apply similarly to boys and girls.
- Severely delinquent girls are more likely to be placed in care than males. They may also show early sexual maturation (menarche before 12.5 years) and peer relationships with older aggressive peers.
- Fire setting is seen more commonly in males – younger boys who set fires alone are likely to have learning disability (LD) while older youths may set fires as a part of group activity.

young people (especially males) with mild-moderate LD.
- Studies have shown that up to 15 per cent of young offenders with serious offences may have pervasive developmental disorders (PDD). Impaired social abilities and disruption of routines/rituals may lead to aggression. The lack of theory of mind may be perceived as lack of empathy and callousness.
- Rates of substance misuse, especially alcohol use, is likely to increase risk.
- Approximately one-third of all sexual offences against children are committed by other children and young people.
- Nearly half of youth with sexually offending behaviour began offences prior to age 12.

# Mental and behavioural disorders and offending behaviour

- High rates of co-morbidity between conduct disorder and ADHD – >50 per cent.
- High rates of low mood and depressive symptoms are seen in young people with a diagnosis of conduct disorder: 11–33 per cent.
- Adolescents with disruptive behaviour have a higher self-harm and completed suicide rate, even in the absence of depressive disorder.
- Early onset mania may involve high rates of aggression.
- Psychoses are rare in children and studies have shown that the predictors of violence are not significantly different from non-psychotic young people.
- Young people with anxiety are not prone to show violent and offending behaviour. However, rates of anxiety are higher in juvenile offenders in custody – 22–60 per cent.
- Post-traumatic stress disorder (PTSD) may be the exception to the above rule – higher rates of aggression may be seen.
- Approximately 25 per cent of young offenders have LD (i.e. IQ <70). However, if we consider borderline IQ scores, this figure rises to just over 50 per cent. Early literacy problems in boys at age seven – seen as 'gateway' to later conduct problems. Higher rates of fire setting and sexual offences have also been noted in

# Risk assessment in children and young people

- It may not be helpful or useful to use the concept of 'dangerousness' to denote risk. Dangerousness is a dichotomous concept, i.e. a young person could be seen as dangerous or not. Children and young people are not 'dangerous' all the time. It is more helpful to consider whether the risk to other people is high in certain circumstances and low or contained in other situations.
- The interplay between the static/historic risk factors and dynamic contextual risk factors must be considered.
- Adolescence is a period of profound and pervasive changes and the degree of risk factors may not remain stable.
- It is also important to consider protective factors; this is not merely the absence of a negative risk factor.
- Positive factors indicate the positive presence of a characteristic or person or circumstance (e.g. positive adult role model/confidante, positive engagement in education and other pro-social age-appropriate activity, compliance with treatment programme, high cognitive – especially verbal, intelligence) that can act to reduce the negative impact of one or more risk factors or otherwise directly buffer the risk. These positive factors may be inherent

to the young person, or related to development of appropriate social bonds, healthy normative social beliefs or clear standards of behaviour.

- There are useful risk assessment tools: SAVRY (Structured Assessment of Violence Risk in Youth, Borum et al., 2003); AIM 2 (for assessment of risk in sexual offences) – www.aimproject.org.uk. These tools are a good combination of actuarial and clinical risk assessment.

# Forensic CAMHS Services

Forensic CAMHS services are not uniformly commissioned across the UK. These services are mainly concentrated in centrally commissioned Adolescent Medium Secure Psychiatric In-Patient Units. There are currently six such units in England – based in Newcastle, Manchester, Birmingham, London, Northampton and Southampton. There are no community FCAMHS teams provided across the country. Community FCAMHS commissioning and development has remained patchy across the country.

Where such teams are present, they are highly specialist teams working closely with Specialist CAMHS, Local Authority Children's Services and Youth Offending Teams (in that particular area/region).

## An example of a community FCAMHS

The Hampshire and Isle of Wight Community FCAMHS Service started in April 2010. It consists of 0.8 WTE Consultant Psychiatrist, 0.3 WTE Clinical Psychologist and 0.6 WTE Trainee Consultant Nurse – covering the county of Hampshire (including the unitary authorities of Southampton City and Portsmouth City) as well as the Isle of Wight. The model of working involves close liaison with CAMHS, Local Authority Children's Services and Youth Offending Teams and the Youth Justice System; using consultation and advice for the majority of cases and taking on direct work with a small case load (currently stands at approximately 80 cases).

# Youth justice system

It is helpful to have knowledge about the pathway that a young person may take when he/she gets involved with the Youth Justice System (YJS).

The emphasis of the YJS is to work in a preventative way to divert young people away from prosecution and conviction if that is the most appropriate way forward (**Figures 34.1** and **34.2**).

## Youth Court

- It is a section of Magistrates Court.
- Deals with almost all cases to do with young people <18 years.
- It is a private arena – members of public not allowed.
- Presided over by District Judges or Magistrates (Panel of 3), *no jury.*
- Less formal than Magistrates Court.
- Court can hand down community sentences or Detention and Training Orders (DTOs).

## Crown Court

- Deals with both adults and children.
- Presided over by a Judge (Crown Court Circuit Judge or Recorder).
- It is a public arena – members of public can attend trial.
- Jury panel.
- Formal arena – judges wear robes, barristers wear wigs.
- Serious offences.

Custodial sentences may be spent in a Local Authority Secure Unit, a Secure Training Centre or in a Young Offenders Institution.

- The annual cost per young person of custodial incarceration in Government-run custody is approximately £60000.
- The cost of incarceration for one year in a privately run Secure Training Centre is £160000.
- The rate of re-offending within one year of release from custody is 75 per cent.

Young people in custody are referred to the Integrated Resettlement Service – they are seen 15 days prior to release and their needs (housing, education, mental health needs) are assessed.

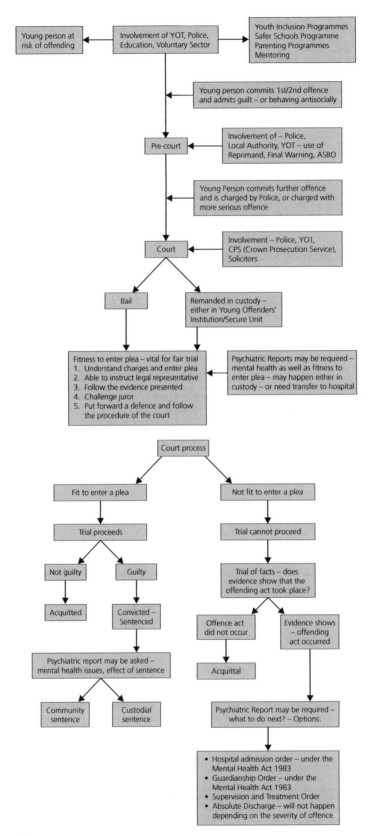

Figure 34.1 Prevention.

## Key texts

Borum R, Bartel P, Forth A (2003) SAVRY – *Manual for the Structured Assessment of Violence Risk in Youth.* Florida: University of Florida.

Moffitt TE, Caspi A, Dickson N et al. (1996) Childhood-onset versus adolescent-onset antisocial conduct problems in males: Natural history from ages 3 to 18 years. *Development and Psychopathology,* **8**: 399–424.

## Web page

www.aimproject.org.uk.

# 35

# *Substance misuse*
## Christine Hooper, Margaret Thompson and Claire Samwell

---

### Key concepts

- Young people are curious about drugs, but hear a confusing message: that drugs are good fun and give the user confidence and 'a better time' or that they are dangerous, illegal and cause drug-related crime and early death.
- Drugs can have interesting effects and change the way people feel. Alcohol and nicotine are easily available legal drugs, used for similar reasons, to be stimulating or comforting.
- Around 50 per cent of 16 year olds are estimated to have used drugs, if only occasionally.
- Young people are tempted to experiment with illegal drugs because of peer pressure and a desire to be accepted by their 'in-crowd'.
- The media tend to emphasize the unhelpful 'angle' about drug use and some young people caught up in the drug scene might feel ashamed, anxious and uncertain about asking for help. Others no doubt feel at ease with their drug use, enjoying the effects and the companionship of their friends.

---

## Introduction

Young people today are living in a drug-using culture. Pop stars, models, even professional athletes, admit to using drugs, to manage a pressured lifestyle where there is both the temptation and the funds to access drugs, to stay thin, to improve performance or simply to appear to be 'cool' and living dangerously.

## Why do children and young people use drugs?

Some young people are more vulnerable to the temptation of drugs because of:

- Temperamental traits, i.e. prone to risk-taking
- Impulsivity and tendency to run into trouble in school, be suspended and then end up on the streets unsupervised
- Unsupportive family
- Known to the care system
- Mixing with drug-taking peer group.

It is not difficult to buy drugs. The drugs business is consumer-driven and there are numerous outlets.

Although there may be a few Mr Bigs making huge fortunes and running huge risks (e.g. of being imprisoned for a long time or of being hunted down by rivals), most drug dealing takes place on a small scale, outside schools and colleges, in clubs, pubs and on the street among friends and associates.

Drug use begins as fun. Young people may be aware of the risks that adults and TV talk about, but rarely see their friends coming to harm and forget the risks in the excitement. Risk-taking is, in any case, one of the hallmarks of adolescence. No one would pay for drugs if they did not make them feel 'different'. Experiences are enhanced and shared. Sometimes drugs are used to reduce anxiety, increase energy or as self-medication for unhappiness, frustration and a fear of being 'left out'.

Other reasons for using drugs are status, i.e. 'the more I can use, the harder I am and the more I will be admired', rebellion, i.e. 'my parents would be horrified if they knew what I get up to' and creativity, i.e. 'I believe my song-writing, music or creative writing is more inventive when I am "stoned".' (Many famous writers and musicians have been frank about their drug use.) A minority will use drugs because they have become dependent and no longer enjoy them, but feel trapped and unable to break free.

# What drugs do young people use?

The most widely used drugs in our society, and those most likely to cause problems, are alcohol and nicotine. The risks of smoking are well understood and no one can be ignorant of them. The effects of alcohol misuse can be seen every day of the week in our inner cities, towns and villages and, particularly seriously, on our roads. It is important not to minimize the impact of alcohol and nicotine just because they are legal to buy, supply and use.

# Four categories of drugs

## Drugs that depress the central nervous system

This category includes those drugs usually described as 'downers'. Those that depress aspects of the central nervous system can have a beneficial effect used under medical supervision: others are alcohol, inhalants (i.e. glue-sniffing or butane gas use), minor tranquillizers and barbiturates. On the street, these drugs are used for 'coming down' from other drug use or to relax and feel disinhibited or to induce sleep.

Inhalants are cheap to buy and pose particular risks, even if used sporadically, because they inflame the upper respiratory tract and alter the electrical conductivity of the heart and, in addition, cause hallucinations and disinhibition, both of which can lead to reckless life-threatening behaviour.

Increased tolerance to these substances means that use has to be increased to bring about the same effects. When usage is reduced or stopped abruptly, psychological and physical discomfort develops, i.e. withdrawal symptoms, and continued and increased use seems preferable to the unpleasantness.

## Drugs that reduce pain

These drugs also depress certain functions of the central nervous system. The major drugs here are those derived from the opium poppy, i.e. morphine, heroin and codeine and synthetic drugs, i.e. methadone and buprenorphine (both of which are sometimes prescribed to help withdrawal from heroin, although methadone is more effective), oxycodone, dipipanone (Diconal), pethidine and Temgesic. The effects are of detatchment, euphoria and warmth. Again, they can be used medically to benefit patients. Regular use can result in dependence and these drugs are often administered by injection, thereby increasing the risks, not least of serious infection.

It seems that there has been an acceptance of heroin use among young people more recently, whereas for years, they were seen as the preserve of low-life 'junkies'. Heroin is being used to mitigate the 'high' of the over-use of stimulant drugs. As it becomes more popular, supply increases in response to demand and the price comes down. Heroin is usually smoked, i.e. 'chasing the dragon' initially but can escalate to being injected, which is more cost-effective and much more dangerous.

## Drugs that stimulate the central nervous system

These drugs are known as 'uppers' and apart from caffeine and nicotine, include amphetamines, cocaine and crack cocaine and some diet-enhancing drugs. These drugs suppress the appetite, and increase agitation, disturbing sleep patterns and inducing talkativeness and energy. They are used by 'ravers' as they help users to stay awake all night and are said to improve sexual performance. The after-effects include tiredness, excessive hunger and aggression.

The risks of prolonged use are weight loss, exhaustion and declining health and in some cases, paranoid-type psychosis. That declines once use is stopped. Amphetamines are the more common stimulants used by young people. Cocaine and crack cocaine are more expensive, have a briefer effect and are thereby more likely to induce physical and psychological dependence.

Ecstasy is a mix of stimulant and hallucinogen. It induces a sense of energy, confidence and empathetic warmth towards other people. The risks are due to the drug's effect of increasing body temperature, which can result in heat stroke and collapse. 'Ravers' are seldom without bottles of water to off-set this effect.

## Drugs that alter perceptual function

These drugs are hallucinogens and distort sensory processes. Cannabis is the most commonly used drug in this category. Cannabis is a mild hallucinogen, usually smoked either mixed with tobacco in a roll-up ('spliff' or 'joint' ) or through water-cooled pipes ('bung'). It can be eaten, baked into cakes and biscuits. Cannabis is used regularly by millions of young people and adults all over the world. Regular, heavy and early use can cause psychotic behaviour in vulnerable young people. There is a belief that cannabis users might be attracted to heavier end drugs by association with other users and dealers.

Teenagers may be unknowingly already suffering from a mental illness and use cannabis to calm those difficult symptoms. Conversely, others may be unaware of their heightened susceptibility to cannabis. There is concern currently about the incidence of cannabis-induced psychosis and schizophrenia. The younger an individual starts using cannabis and the heavier the use are both indicators for potential mental health problems. Pregnant women who use cannabis are more likely to give birth prematurely and for their baby to be of lower birth weight.

The government controversially downgraded cannabis from Class B to Class C under the Act. The wisdom of this has been disputed but cannabis remains a Class C drug. It is still illegal.

LSD belongs in this category. It has a significantly more potent effect than cannabis and used to be popular with young people and some bands and artists. However, the body develops a rapid tolerance to LSD and then more and more of the drug is needed to produce the earlier effects. LSD can induce altered thought processes, panic, depression and disorientation. Magic mushrooms have a similar effect.

## Levels of drug use

### Experimental

Some young people will be tempted to give drugs a try, if only to be seen to 'go with the flow' of their friendship network. Some will try it just once and either not like the effects or lose their nerve and feel anxious about the consequences. They will become non-users. Others will enjoy their first experience of drug use and the sense of acceptance by their friends; they may be more inclined to be risk-takers or be willing to work at enjoying drug use.

### Recreational

This heading will include the regular but controlled social use of street drugs in specific situations. Young people in this category do not necessarily see themselves as risk-takers or problem users, but as doing what everyone else is doing. Drug use is one aspect of their life with their friends. They may well abandon all drug use in adulthood when other commitments, e.g. career, marriage and children, take priority.

### Dependent

Once someone is reliant on a particular drug to help them to deal with uncomfortable feelings or emotions, disappointments, loss and anxiety or they fear the discomfort of withdrawal, they are likely to develop the spectrum of serious problems associated with out-of-control use and the need to fund their habit. They are likely to come to the attention of the police, the courts or the drug advisory services.

## What are the risks?

### Illegality

Most street drugs are controlled under the Misuse of Drugs Act. Possession of a prescribed drug is an offence and supply is a more serious offence, attracting a prison sentence. Some countries will refuse entry to anyone with a drugs conviction.

The Misuse of Drugs Act 1971, amended in 2005, divides drugs into three classes, depending on the perceived level of dangerousness:

- Class A refers to the most serious drugs and includes heroin, oxycodone, cocaine, crack, crystal meth, ecstasy, LSD, magic mushrooms prepared for ingestion and any Class B drug prepared for injection, e.g. amphetamines.
- Class B drugs include amphetamines.

- Class C drugs include minor tranquillizers, anabolic steroids, Ketamine ( a substance more commonly used to anaesthetize horses) and now cannabis.

Mephedrone (known as 'plant food' or 'meow meow') is a stimulant similar to amphetamines. It encourages a sense of euphoria and well-being. The side effects include sore nasal passages, nose bleeds, sore throats and mouths. Regular and heavy use can result in palpitations, blurred vision and, as with any other drug, can lead to psychological dependency. Until 2010, the drug was a 'legal high' but it is now classified as illegal.

Supplying or sharing a prescribed drug with another person, e.g. passing around a joint, is classed as supply. The 2005 amendment of the Act included Ketamine as a Class C drug and brought in the extended detention of suspected drug offenders. Being charged and found guilty of an offence under the Misuse of Drugs Act will result in a criminal record, with serious implications, for instance, for career choices and work permits to work abroad.

## Other drugs not currently illegal

### GHD
GHD (gammahydroxybutyrate, a medicine developed for use during surgery) can be used as an alternative to anabolic steroids.

### Poppers
Poppers (i.e. alkyl nitrates) are supposedly a prescription-only medicine. Users breathe in the vapour. They are used as a muscle relaxant and in sexual encounters.

### Khat
Khat is a plant often sold at greengrocers in Somali, Ethiopian, Kenyan and Yemeni communities in Britain, particularly in London. The fresh leaves and small stems are chewed to a pulp and spat out. The plant has a mild stimulant effect and serves a similar function in those communities as caffeine and alcohol in European communities. Khat is a controlled drug in the Republic of Ireland, Canada, USA, Norway and Sweden. Taking it into those countries would be against their laws. It is not currently illegal in the UK to use, possess or sell Khat.

## Over-doing it

This means being out-of-control, overdosing, taking risks in sexual behaviour and over-doing it in terms of frequency of drug use or use in dangerous situations, e.g. prior to driving.

## Individual differences

The strength and quality of the drug, physical and/ or mental health of the user, personal tolerance and the context and environment will all influence the outcome of an episode of drug use.

## Adulterants

Street drugs are not quality controlled. Very few are pure and most will have been adulterated to enhance the profit margin. Often the adulterant can be more dangerous than the original substance.

## Financial

Drugs can be expensive, especially if the user has become dependent. A £100 to £500 a week cost would not be uncommon. Even the costs of recreational use can mount up although they will simply be absorbed into the price of 'a good night out'. Money for drugs is not always obtained legally: stealing, dealing, fraud and in extreme 'need', prostitution, are all associated with drug use.

## Injection

Most drugs are taken orally or by smoking or 'snorting', but some users will choose injection. This carries higher risks and is the resort of addicted users who need to feel the effect of the drug as quickly as possible. Injection makes overdosing more likely and the adulterants and needles damage veins and spread infection, unless clean once-only use equipment is used.

Most young people will come through their period of drug use safely and unscathed, putting it behind them as they move into adulthood. Some of the more vulnerable will not and for them, drug use will scar their adult lives.

## What to look out for

The indicators of possible drug use are:

- Sudden mood swings, poor appetite, irritability and loss of interest in previously enjoyable hobbies, friendships and interests
- Deceitfulness, fidgetiness and secrecy, e.g. over mobile phone use, meetings arranged suddenly
- Money going missing
- Unusual smells, marks and stains on clothing, tablets and capsules hidden in bedrooms and obviously, drug-related items e.g. scorched tin-foil, 'bungs' (broken off bottles) or tubing
- Use of drug slang
- Loss of concentration and coordination
- Binge-eating ('the munchies' are a well-known feature of cannabis use)
- Unexplained absences from home
- Slurred speech.

Finding out that your teenager is involved in the drug scene is a serious shock for most parents. Local drug advisory centres can advise parents even if the young person is unwilling to make any contact with them.

If the young person is willing to engage with professionals, then referral to an adolescent unit or a drug advisory service should be considered.

## Assessment

In assessing the young person, consideration should be given to the following (see Chapter 22, Assessment of older children, young people and their families):

- Careful history of drug use, substance of choice, frequency of use including how the drugs have been paid for, using alone or with others, drug use situation

- Developmental history of the young person, medical and psychiatric background, e.g. any previous treatment, temperament, i.e. looking for any history of attention deficit hyperactivity disorder or conduct disorder (see Chapters 30, Temperament, 33, Juvenile disruptive behaviour disorders: oppositional defiant disorder (ODD) and conduct disorder (CD) and 36, Attention deficit hyperactivity disorder)
- Family background including any history of abuse and/or neglect
- School and college history including academic, social and behaviour difficulties
- Employment history
- Peer relationships
- Contact with other agencies including police or Youth Offending Teams.

## Intervention

Any intervention will depend on the young person's commitment to change (see Chapter 18, Engagement and motivation for Stages of Change model). The young person may need to be referred into a drug and alcohol misuse programme where they might follow a 12-step treatment programme (see Chapter 18, Engagement and motivation).

Other treatments that might be offered include:

- Family therapy (see Chapter 74, Family therapy models and practice)
- Cognitive behaviour therapy (CBT) (see Chapter 72, Cognitive behaviour therapy)
- If appropriate, substitute medication or a needle exchange scheme.

### Case study 1

Jensen, aged 15 years, was referred by his GP to the CAMHS clinic as an emergency. He was agitated and frightened as he thought he had strange feelings in his hands and feet, almost as if he had rings on his hands and feet.

On enquiry, the staff learned that he had been 'bonging' cannabis in a bottle with other boys, and bunking out of school. He was a boy who had learning difficulties and was easily led.

His condition deteriorated over the weekend and he became very paranoid believing that people were going to attack him. He had to be admitted over the weekend to an adult ward. He settled on Resperidone. Gradually his condition settled, he came off his medication and he was discharged home. He was assigned a nurse to work with him in order to help him understand the dangers of cannabis; to reintegrate back into school; and change his peer group. Family work was undertaken also. His mental state will have to be monitored in case his psychosis returns.

## Case study 2

Mary, aged 16 years, has become involved in the drug scene and become addicted to heroin. Her mother found a syringe and needles in her bedroom. She would not seek help as she did not think she had a problem. Her mother arranged to see a counsellor from the drug advisor service ( Dave). He learned about Mary and heard that she had always had problems at school, finding it hard to concentrate, never got her homework in in time, and was always falling out with her teachers. She, however, was a bright youngster. She was moved to a pupil referral unit, to try to assist her to stay within the school system. Unfortunately, she met up with a group of young people who were into the drug scene. Her mother realized that she was stealing money.

Dave arranged with Mary's mother to come to the house and her mother got Mary to agree to meet him. Gradually, Mary began to trust Dave and was able to discuss the possibility of trying to give up the drugs and to move to a different group of friends. She agreed to go into hospital to come off the heroin. When she came out she went back to her pupil referral unit. Cognitive testing indicated that Mary was dyslexic, and had ADHD (Chapter 36, Attention deficit hyperactivity disorder) with word processing problems (see Chapter 3, The role of the educational psychologist). With the educational psychologist's help, the unit worked out a package to improve Mary's ability to absorb educational material.

Dave worked with Mary using CBT techniques (Chapter 72, Cognitive behaviour therapy) to help her self-esteem and improve her life choices. Family therapy (Chapter 74, Family therapy models and practice) worked on family rules, honesty and monitoring movements.

## Multiple choice questions

1. Which is not correct?

   a. Cannabis is a Class C drug
   b. Cannabis is safe
   c. At least 50 per cent of young people have tried drugs at some point in their lives
   d. Cannabis can calm down young people when they are agitated
   e. Young people may move from cannabis to harder drugs

2. Children who are taking drugs may present with:

   a. Spots and rashes on face
   b. Need to eat a lot
   c. Sleeping a lot
   d. Psychotic behaviour
   e. Secretive behaviour

### Key texts

Gossop M (2000) *Living with Drugs*, 5th edn. Aldershot: Ashgate Publishing.
Department of Health (2002b) *Dual Diagnosis – Good Practice Guidance (Mental Health Policy Implementation Guide)*. London: Department of Health.

Department of Health (2002c) *Models of Care for Substance Misuse Treatment*. London: Department of Health.

### Web page

www.release.org.uk RELEASE: Drugs, The Law and Human Rights. The drug information charity.

# 36

# Attention deficit hyperactivity disorder

**Anan El Masry, Margaret Thompson and Wai Chen**
**Edited by David Daley**

---

## Key concepts

- Attention deficit hyperactivity disorder is a lifelong condition
- It is usually seen as a dimensional disorder
- There are a clear set of criteria to use for diagnosis
- It is the most researched condition in child and adolescent mental health
- ADHD is present in pre-school children
- ADHD usually presents with co-morbidity
- Functional changes can be seen in the brain of children with ADHD
- Neuropsychological differences present in some, but not all, children with ADHD
- Medication helps at least 70 per cent of the children
- Parenting and behaviour modification techniques should be introduced as treatment

---

Attention deficit hyperactivity disorder (ADHD) is a syndrome characterized by severe inattention, hyperactivity and impulsivity to a degree that is maladaptive or inconsistent with the developmental level of the child. To meet the DSM-IV criteria for diagnosis, symptoms should be pervasive across situations, persistent in time and start before the age of seven years (American Psychiatric Association, 2000). ADHD is present in approximately 6 per cent of the population (Schachar, 1991).

Some British clinics tend to use the stricter International Classification of Disease version 10 (World Health Organization, 1993) criteria for Hyperkinetic Disorder, which demands that onset be before the age of seven years, with a set number of symptoms of inattention, overactivity and impulsivity. ADHD affects around 6 per cent of the population (Barkley, 2006). Hyperkinetic disorder affects approximately 1 per cent of children at primary school age, with a male to female ratio of around 3:1 (Taylor et al., 1991).

Children with ADHD have an increased likelihood of having other medical, developmental, behavioural, emotional, social (with a financial impact on services due to educational and society breakdown) and academic difficulties (Mannuzza et al., 1998), and the disorder often severely affects family life (Barkley et al., 1990). These children can be very aggressive. Forty per cent of children with ADHD will continue to have problems in adulthood. Some may require referral to adult psychiatrists (Faraone et al., 2006).

## Aetiology: current thinking

The brains of these children are different.

Multiple studies of groups of children with ADHD compared to control groups have documented anatomical differences, for example reductions of about 10 per cent in size of the caudate nucleus, right frontal and cerebellar vermis regions of the brain.

Giedd et al. (2001) have proposed a cerebellar-prefrontal-striatal network, the cerebellar vermis, to fit with the findings of a smaller cerebellum. The cerebellum is associated with timing, cognition, affect and motor movement.

When scanning techniques are used, areas of the brain in children with ADHD function differently to the brains of children without ADHD.

# Neuropsychological findings

Different pathways are proposed to explain the way children with ADHD might present. Sonuga-Barke (2002) suggested a dual pathway:

- a dorso-lateral-striatal pathway which is associated with executive function difficulties, i.e. problems with planning, set-shifting and organization (Barkley and Murphy, 1998);
- a frontal-ventral striatal pathway which is involved with delay aversion and motivation, i.e. difficulty in waiting (Sonuga-Barke, 2002);
- Sonuga-Barke et al. (2010) propose the addition of a third neuropsychological pathway hypothesized to represent temporal processing deficits (TPD) in ADHD. Indeed, there is some evidence that ADHD children show TPD across a range of timing tasks (Smith et al., 2002).

The neuropsychology findings in pre-school children (Sonuga-Barke et al., 2003; Dalen et al., 2004) are the same as in older children with a similar dual neural pathway model proposed (Solanto et al., 2001).

# Genetic

Several genes may be implicated, but the dopamine and serotonin genes are the most researched, for example the DAT1 (dopamine transporter genes) and the DRD4 (dopamine receptor gene) (Ebstein et al., 1998; Di Maio et al., 2003; Todd et al., 2005). Gene–environment interaction is an important factor in causing the expression of the gene.

The importance of gene–environment interaction is stressed. ADHD is associated with low birth weight (Szatmari et al., 1990; Lou et al., 2004); toxins and infections in pregnancy, possibly mediated through the genetic profile of the baby; alcohol in pregnancy (Sood et al., 2001); drug abuse (Wilens et al., 2005); smoking (Kahn et al., 2003; Kotimaa et al., 2003; Thapar et al., 2003); infection in pregancy; stress in pregnancy probably mediated by cholesterol; exposure to other toxins, for example, lead, after birth.

# Persistence in symptoms

Persistence in symptoms will depend on ADHD symptoms and are more likely to persist if the disorder is severe (Sonuga-Barke et al., 1997 – community sample; Lahey et al., 2004 – clinical samples); if there is co-morbidity with behaviour problems; if there is neurodevelopmental delay and or neurocognitive delay; if the parenting style is hostile and coercive; if schools are not sympathetic.

# Co-morbidity

Children with ADHD have many problems, which may present in different ways, and by the time they are referred to CAMHS, they may have very complex problems. In the Multi-Modal Treatment Study of ADHD (MTA) study (Jensen et al., 1999) 11 per cent of the children had tics, 40 per cent had oppositional disorder, 14 per cent had conduct disorder, 34 per cent had anxiety disorder. Children with ADHD may have language disorder, reading disorder and tics.

# Nutrition

Evidence of whether nutrition is associated with ADHD is still equivocal. A recent trial reported in The Lancet suggested that preservatives can cause irritability in all young children (McCann et al., 2007). There may be gene–environment interaction, possibly the histamine gene (Stevenson et al., 2010). One or two fairly rigorous trials do suggest that nutrition may help hyperactive symptoms, but the hypothesis is not proven (Carter et al., 1993; Schnoll et al., 2003; Schab and Trinh, 2004).

# Is ADHD a categorical or a dimensional condition?

Current literature discusses whether the condition is categorical, i.e. if a child presents with a number of symptoms, will he definitely have the disorder or is it dimensional, i.e. that all children have some attention problems, but it becomes a difficulty for the child when he has problems in all the domains of ADHD (see below) and in all settings. Most professionals would recognize the problems as being dimensional.

# Pre-school children with ADHD

## Margaret Thompson

Parents may contact their general practitioners with concerns about very young children who seem to be overactive, especially if they are also non-compliant. By the time the child is referred to CAMHS services, the referred behaviour is usually non-compliant and aggressive, in addition to overactivity. The problems are generally both in school and at home.

## Symptoms

These will vary depending on any underlying neuropsychological difficulties and possible other co-morbid conditions. It is important that the initial assessment takes place within a developmental framework and observes the child in different settings:

- constantly 'on the go';
- dashing into obstacles, not watching where they are going. This differs from clumsiness, which can be a sign of dyspraxia, a potential co-morbid finding;
- attention and concentration problems (less obvious in young children, except perhaps at story time);
- poor at sharing;
- difficulty with waiting and turn-taking, wanting to do everything immediately.

Symptoms are often associated with problems with:

- negotiation skills;
- sleep pattern;
- early language;
- fine and/or gross motor skills.

## Current thinking about pre-school ADHD

- Prevalence in younger children is the same as that in older children, i.e. between 3 and 6 per cent (Egger and Angold, 2006)

- Hyperactivity is more common in younger children
- Inattention is more apparent as the child becomes older (Lahey et al., 2004)
- The behaviour differs from disruptive behaviour (Sonuga-Barke et al., 1997; Lahey et al., 1998)
- Fifty per cent of these children will still have symptoms at school entry (Campbell and Ewing, 1990; Lavigne et al., 1998).

A thorough assessment is necessary (see Chapter 19, Structured assessment of preschool children: observation of parent–child relationship, Chapter 21, Assessment of younger children and their families: individual interview of child and Chapter 23, Family assessment), paying special attention to the development of the child and speech and learning development.

The use of questionnaires can be helpful: (see Chapter 26, The use of questionnaires in the diagnosis of child mental health problems). General questionnaires would be Strength and Difficulties, 4–6 years, (Goodman, 1997; Conners, 1990).

Questionnaires that can be used for young children are the Routh modification of the Werry–Weiss–Peters (WPP) rating scale (a score of over 20) and Routh and the Emotionality Activity Shyness temperament scale (a score of over 4.5 on the activity subset) (Buss and Plomin, 1984).

In the New Forest Development Project (Thompson et al., 1996), a community project screening three-year-old children, 11.5 per cent of children were found to be overactive (a score of 20 or over on the WPP scale (Routh, 1978) and a score of 4.5 or over on the Emotionality Activity Scale (Buss and Plomin, 1984)). About half of the three year olds were found to have marked problems on further testing. Using only the WWP activity scale, 18 per cent will have a score of 20 or over; this is a useful community screening scale (see Chapter 9, Epidemiology of behaviour problems).

---

### Case study: James

James is four years old. His health visitor has referred him to the Young Child clinic. James seldom sits still to play, despite his mother's best efforts to encourage him. Pre-school staff have noticed the same behaviour at nursery and say that James has difficulty in sharing toys, becoming aggressive towards other boys at times. Management advice from both the health visitor and her nursery nurse has so far made no difference.

Following a careful assessment, the staff in the clinic thought that James was exhibiting signs and symptoms of pre-school ADHD.

James's mother was offered the New Forest Parenting Programme (Sonuga-Barke et al., 2001; Thompson et al., 2009), and she thought that the programme made a difference to James's behaviour. He settled well into his reception class.

---

## Treatment

Parenting work should be the treatment of first choice (Weeks et al., 1999; Sonuga-Barke et al., 2001; NICE, 2008; Thompson et al., 2009). For this to succeed, the work has to be delivered in an organized manner and the parents need to be motivated to be able to change, with few other problems in their life at the time. Parents who have ADHD themselves may cope less well (Sonuga-Barke et al., 2003).

Medication is effective in young children (see the preschool ADHD treatment study (PATS)) (Greenhill et al., 2006; Kollins et al., 2006; Daley et al., 2009) but there are more side effects associated with its use in young children. The most common of these are decreased appetite, emotional outbursts, difficulty falling asleep and weight loss (Wigal et al., 2006). Medication should be titrated slowly and in smaller doses than those used in older children.

# ADHD in the primary school child

## Anan El Masry

The primary school child with ADHD is frequently seen as being different. Although a sensitive teacher may be able to adapt the classroom to allow an able child with ADHD to succeed, more frequently the child experiences academic failure, rejection by peers and low self-esteem (Landgraf et al., 1999).

Difficulties at home and on outings with the family become more apparent at this age. Parents may find that family members refuse to care for the child, and that other children do not invite them to parties or out to play (Johnston and Mash, 2001).

Many children with ADHD have poor sleep patterns, and although they appear not to need much sleep, daytime behaviour is often worse when sleep is affected.

As a result, parents have little time for themselves; family relationships may become extremely strained and in some cases break down, bringing additional social and financial difficulties.

This may cause the child to feel sad or even to show oppositional behaviour (Harpin, 2005).

The siblings of children with ADHD report being victimized by aggressive acts of physical violence, verbal aggression and manipulation and control. In addition, siblings reported that parents expected them to care for their ADHD sibling because of the social and emotional immaturity associated with ADHD (Kendall, 1999). As a result, many siblings described feeling anxious, worried and sad. Indeed, siblings of children with ADHD are at an increased risk for conduct and emotional disorders (Szatmari et al., 1989).

Parents should let the school know if their child has been diagnosed and is receiving treatment for ADHD. If a child enters school and is experiencing difficulties that lead parents or the school to suspect he or she may be suffering with ADHD, then parents should ask the school to evaluate their child. A child may qualify for special education services once he has been diagnosed with ADHD. The school should assess the child's strengths and weaknesses and design an individualized educational programme (IEP). This should be ideally re-evaluated at each new school and stage of learning.

# ADHD in adolescence

## Anan El Masry

ADHD is the most common emotional, cognitive and behavioural disorder treated in youth. Though previously thought to remit in adolescence, a growing literature supports the persistence of the disorder and/or associated impairments into adulthood in a majority of cases (Goldman et al., 1998; Jensen et al., 1999).

ADHD is a major public health problem because of its associated morbidity and disability in children, adolescents and adults. Children with the disorder are at greater risk for longer-term negative outcomes, such as lower educational and employment attainment.

As children with ADHD grow older, the way the disorder impacts upon them and their families changes. The core difficulties in executive function seen in ADHD result in a different picture in later life, depending on the demands put on them by their environment, including school and family. This is affected by the insight and cognitive abilities of the child or young person (Harpin, 2005).

Adolescence may bring about a reduction in overactivity, but inattention and inner restlessness remain major problems (Spencer et al., 2007). Young people with ADHD are at an increased risk of academic failure, dropping out of school or college, teenage pregnancy and criminal behaviour (Harpin, 2005). When children enter high school, they have less adult supervision, multiple teachers, increased volume of homework, and more complex assignments and early academic problems may be amplified by the increased demands that are placed on children in high school (Barbaresi, 2007).

Driving poses an additional risk. Individuals with ADHD are easily distracted when driving slowly, but when driving fast they may be dangerous (Barkley et al., 1996; Woodward et al., 2008).

## Key features of ADHD in adolescence

- In adolescents there is a decline in hyperactivity/impulsivity
- Inattentive symptoms persist into adulthood
- Associated with school failure, emotional difficulties, poor peer relationships and trouble with the law

## Associated problems

The vast majority of co-morbidities with ADHD represent functional impairments and symptoms, which are not rooted in specific diseases.

# Oppositional defiant disorder and conduct disorder

ADHD and oppositional defiant disorder (ODD) or conduct disorder (CD) have been found to co-occur in 30–50 per cent of cases in both epidemiologic and clinical cases (see Chapter 33, Juvenile disruptive behaviour disorders: oppositional defiant disorder and conduct disorder for the diagnostic criteria for CD and ODD).

# Mood disorders

Lifetime rates of co-morbid depression in children with ADHD increased from 29 per cent at age 15 years to 45 per cent at a four-year follow up. A baseline diagnosis of major depression predicted lower psychosocial functioning, higher rates of hospitalization and impairments in interpersonal and family functioning (Biederman et al., 1992).

Recently it has been found that, although childhood ADHD increases the risk for adolescent depression, stimulant treatment for ADHD neither heightens nor protects against such risk (Staikova, 2010).

It is often difficult to differentiate adolescent onset mania from ADHD, CD, depression and psychotic disorders because of overlapping developmental features. However, the symptoms of ADHD may precede the first manic episode by many years.

The prevalence of mania in children with ADHD was found to increase from 11 to 23 per cent in a four-year follow up in an American study. Children with ADHD with co-morbid mania had other correlates, which are associated with mania, including additional psychopathology, psychiatric hospitalization, severely impaired psychosocial functioning and a greater family history of mood disorders (Spencer, 2007).

## Anxiety disorders

Childhood anxiety disorders are often not suspected in an overactive child, despite the fact that some of the behavioural features of anxiety include agitation, tantrums, and attention seeking behaviour. Children with ADHD and co-morbid anxiety disorder need more psychiatric treatment; they have more impaired social functioning and a greater family history of anxiety disorder (Biederman et al., 1996).

## Substance use disorders

Juveniles with ADHD are at increased risk of cigarette smoking and substance abuse during adolescence. Individuals with ADHD tend to maintain their dependence longer compared with their non-ADHD peers.

Treatment for ADHD with stimulant medication decreases the risk of substance use disorders by 50 per cent (Faraone and Wilens, 2003). Children diagnosed with ADHD mid-adolescence who were not treated with stimulants had the greatest occurrence of substance use disorders (SUDs). Studies have shown that 25–33 per cent of adolescents diagnosed with SUD meet the diagnostic criteria for ADHD (Biederman, 2003).

## School and cognitive performance

Children and adolescents with ADHD may perform less well than their non-ADHD classmates on standard measures of intelligence and achievement. In addition, they perform worse in school, with more grade repetitions, poorer grades in academic subjects, more placement in special classes and more tutoring. It may be that the school environment is especially aversive to hyperactive children and that different ways of learning may be more helpful (Spencer, 2007).

In children with ADHD there is an established and replicated weakness in neuropsychological executive functioning (EF). EF is broadly defined as the ability to regulate behaviour to context and maintain a response set. This involves inhibition and resistance to distraction, planning and goal directed acts, problem-solving and strategy development, flexible shifting of actions, persistence toward a goal state and self-awareness across time (Barkley, 2000). Children with ADHD show deficits in response inhibition, impairment in planning, set shifting and working memory.

### Case study: Peter

Peter is a 15-year-old boy, referred by his GP, as he was experiencing marked difficulties in keeping to task at school. Peter has always found school challenging, especially in keeping to task, and concentrating. When Peter was younger he found it difficult to sit still in class and required regular prompting from the teachers and teaching assistants. His mother has been able to manage him at home with the help of Peter's father, who is very supportive and firm. Sadly Peter's father had been recently diagnosed with cancer and he is less able to contribute. Peter's behaviour had undergone major changes, with him becoming increasingly angry, with violent outbursts and defiant behaviour.

## On assessment

Peter is an only child with older parents, but the pregnancy was normal, and the baby was healthy. He was breast fed for six months, and then began weaning. He was an easy baby but found it difficult to settle to sleep at night. As a toddler, Peter started at nursery, where he enjoyed playing with other children but he was always the one running around, dancing or knocking things over. Despite this, his nursery teachers felt he was a bright child who learnt to speak clearly and well early on.

At school, although clearly a bright child, Peter would often be restless in class, with constant fidgeting and he answered questions prematurely, interrupting other students. Nevertheless, he received very good support from school, with more intense input from the teaching assistants. Despite his difficulties, he clearly had a good grasp of the subjects taught, and performed exceptionally well in maths, art and music.

In senior school, Peter's fidgetiness seemed to lessen, although his ability to concentrate for long periods of time in class continued to be a problem. Although his grades had gone down, he was still doing well in his preferred subjects.

Since his father's illness, Peter's concentration in class seemed to have worsened, and he appeared less vivacious and lively in the classroom. At home, he would spend hours in his room, playing computer games and not attempting to achieve in his studies despite regular prompting from his parents. Indeed, their attempts to engage him have led to angry and verbally violent outbursts, which are out of character for him.

## Observation in clinic

Both parents attended with Peter. They seemed warm and genuinely concerned about him. Peter was sitting quietly most of the time, but he appeared to be fidgeting constantly with his jumper sleeves. He replied clearly and coherently to the questions.

Peter described feeling empty and unable to feel much for the last three months. His sleep, which is usually poor, continued to be a problem although lately he has started to have an interrupted sleep pattern. Peter described having lost his appetite, which was good before. Peter told us that he felt useless and hopeless about the future and saw no point in trying hard at school, as 'we were all going to die anyway'.

Peter described always having a sense of restlessness, although he feels this has improved with time. He said that he has always found it difficult to concentrate, but as the subjects were generally not too difficult, he could 'get away with' little work. Lately, he has not even been able to do that.

Following consent to contact the school, school staff were able to confirm many of the symptoms that Peter presented with at clinic.

A Conner's teacher and parent questionnaire confirmed high scores on inattention and poor concentration.

## Initial formulation

It seemed very possible from the history given that Peter had ADHD when younger. The hyperactivity symptoms seemed to have waned but the concentration problems were still an issue. Peter appeared to have managed well at school through the concentrated efforts of supportive schoolteachers, who saw his potential and through the loving and firm efforts of his parents.

Lately, however, there has been a marked shift in Peter's presentation, with symptoms suggestive of a major depressive illness, which was probably precipitated by his father's diagnosis. It was vital not to interpret all the difficulties facing Peter (and indeed any young person with ADHD) as being due to ADHD and not to consider any other precipitating factors (social, personal or educational) for additional mental health issues.

## Management plan

In this instance, treatment of the depressive illness was the initial step in the management of the symptoms. Anti-depressant medication (see Chapter 46, Mood disorders) was prescribed and Peter was referred for counselling to help him deal with the issues arising from his father's illness.

Following the improvement of his depressive symptoms, the option of medication for ADHD was discussed with Peter and the family, who declined the offer, as they felt Peter was able to manage better at school now that his mood had improved.

## Case study: Tania

Tania is a 13-year-old girl at a local school. She was referred to CAMHS due to her disruptive and defiant behaviour at school and at home. Tania has always had problems listening to instructions and keeping to task.

### On assessment

Tania lives with her mother, her stepfather and her younger brother, aged two.

Her parents separated when Tania was only three years old. She does see her father occasionally at weekends.

Tania was born when her mother was 18 years old. Her mother smoked for at least the first trimester. The pregnancy was uneventful but the delivery was prolonged and intervention via a Ventouse extraction was necessary. Tania required no special care.

Tania was a difficult baby to put down to sleep and often cried. As a toddler, she continued to have difficulties with her sleep, was constantly having accidents and was very difficult to manage. Tania went to nursery at age 3, and exhibited an obvious inability to sit still or engage gently with other children. This continued to be a problem when she went to primary school, with the teachers finding her very disruptive in class and very difficult to keep to tasks. At home, she exhibited defiant behaviour.

This pattern of problem behaviour continues till today. The defiant behaviour has escalated to aggression, both at school and at home. Tania's mother described how she was very similar to Tania as a child, but that, despite this, she found Tania very difficult to manage. She said that she often 'gave up' trying to promote discipline and would often give in to Tania's demands, which upset her husband who was trying to re-enforce the rules.

### Observation in clinic

Tania attended with her mother. She interrupted her mother constantly during the interview and would leave her seat regularly to fiddle with different toys and objects in the room. Tania was not keen to be seen on her own and her mother gave permission for us to contact the school.

The school report showed repeated incidents of disruptive behaviour and difficulty keeping to task. Conner's parent and teacher questionnaire revealed high scores on inattention, hyperactivity and oppositional behaviour.

### Initial formulation

The history and presenting symptoms suggest an early onset of behavioural manifestations suggestive of ADHD. There appears to be a family history of ADHD in the mother, in addition to the increased risk of developing ADHD due to maternal smoking.

The social circumstances, relating to parental separation and the different parenting styles adopted by Tania's mother and stepfather, may have assisted in the emergence of the ODD in recent years.

---

**Management plan**

Tania was started on an extended methylphenidate preparation, to help with her ADHD symptoms. This was regularly monitored and Tania's height, weight and blood pressure were measured regularly. Appointments with parents introducing them to parenting strategies were arranged and they eventually joined a parent ADHD group. Later on, the family began family therapy sessions to help improve family systems and dynamics. There was regular contact with the school to promote the understanding of Tania's problems and to assist the teachers in the development of management strategies in the classroom. Tania's mother sought a statement of special educational needs for Tania.

---

## Other treatment which may be helpful with children with ADHD

- Behaviour work with the young person on anger management and coping strategies
- Social skills training, especially if there are problems in social situations
- Family work, especially for adolescents where there may be relevant family stress issues and/or hostility towards the child
- Individual work (having first assessed for motivation), counselling, psycho-education
- Attention training, to help the child cope with delay
- Anger management: empathy, responsibility, turn taking
- Work with the school/college, for example work with reading, maths, writing, work study skills
- Speech programme
- Group work in school and/or clinic

# ADHD in adolescent transition and in adulthood

Wai Chen

## Persistence of ADHD into adulthood

Before the 1990s, ADHD was considered to be a disorder confined to childhood, undergoing spontaneous remission during the transition to adolescence and adulthood. The seminal longitudinal research studies derived from six major cohorts published in the 1990s showed that ADHD is a lifelong disorder in the majority of patients, persisting into adulthood with social, occupational and psychological impairments. These cohorts (and their representative authors) include those from: New York (Gittleman, Mannuzza), Montreal (Weiss, Hechtman, Milroy), Wisconsin (Barkley, Fletcher), California (Lambert) and East London (Taylor). Their fuller findings were reviewed by Chen and Taylor (2005). In brief, these studies suggested that about 30 per cent of childhood cases underwent spontaneous remission, 30 per cent persisted into adulthood with mild to moderate impairments, while the remaining 30 per cent developed severe impairments, with additional co-morbidities including substance misuse, depression, anti-social personality disorder and law infraction. Overall, conduct problems, impulsivity, low IQs, external locus of control (always blaming someone else for one's problems) and more negative self-esteem, predicted poorer outcomes.

In contrast to the earlier research, more recent works have focused on the impact of the definition of adult ADHD on the persistence rates of childhood ADHD. In other words, the thinking has moved away from applying the childhood criteria of ADHD to study persistence of adult ADHD. Biederman et al. (2000) found persistence rates to vary: at 40 per cent, if defined by childhood syndrome criteria; at 80 per cent, if defined by sub-syndromal presence of ADHD symptoms; and approaching 90 per cent, if defined by functional impairments. A meta-analysis (Faraone et al., 2006) of 32 follow-up studies showed a pooled persistent rate at around 15 per cent, if defined by the full syndromal criteria but around 65 per cent by the adult ADHD 'partial remission' criteria. Overall, ADHD is now regarded as a non-benign and lifelong disorder, rather than a self-limiting one confined to childhood.

## Other issues specific to ADHD in adolescence

There are several key themes relevant to ADHD transition in adolescence.

First, overt hyperactivity and impulsivity may desist to be replaced by a subjective sense of restlessness. It is not uncommon for the presentation of the 'combined' subtype of ADHD to evolve into that of the 'predominantly inattentive' subtype.

Second, some patients may present *de novo* in adolescence, because previously their high IQ and/or supportive family structure have protected them from developing significant impairments, despite displaying symptoms in childhood or primary school, whereas the increasing demands in secondary school and adolescence unmask their impairments.

Third, ADHD-related emotional dysregulation may become more prominent shading into 'adolescence turmoil' or an emerging adolescent affective disorder, when the prevalence of a mood disorder rises sharply.

Fourth, the influence of delinquent peers becomes more prominent when parental supervision and control recede, while ongoing educational failure or negative schooling experience accelerates the risk of conduct problems. This risk further superimposes upon the transient rise of delinquency in adolescence observed among even non-ADHD individuals.

Fifth, medication control may become out of control, mirroring the well-documented adolescent brittle diabetes, when rebellion and resentment intensify any non-adherence to medication.

Sixth, adolescence is a period of rapid maturity of executive function in non-ADHD adolescents. The development of executive function is delayed amongst ADHD subjects, lagging about 3–4 years behind their normative peers. The executive function deficit and lag further widen the gulf between ADHD and non-ADHD individuals, accentuating any behavioural and functional deviance.

Finally, the increasing autonomy associated with adolescence entails intensified conflicts with parental and adult authority, in addition to leading to a greater exposure to drugs, alcohol, reckless driving, sexuality and association with delinquent peers. Impulsivity and sensation-seeking traits amplify these risks, resulting in driving offences, crimes, substance misuse and increased rates of teenage pregnancies and contracting sexually transmitted disease and HIV. For some ADHD subjects, adolescence is a time associated with significant hazards presenting major challenges to their parents and clinicians. Specialist care is often indicated.

# *Issues specific to adult ADHD*

## Wai Chen

Patients may present to an adult ADHD service as a childhood ADHD 'graduate' or as a *de novo* adult referral seeking assessment and treatment for the first time, having come through childhood undiagnosed.

Alternatively, some parents of ADHD children self-diagnose themselves as having ADHD and come forward to seek treatment. Among these, some have marked disorganization and poor time management, leading to poor childcare and child protection concerns. The extreme cases could be involved in court proceedings where Social Services seek to remove their children from their care. A court assessment may thereby present another route of referral.

Recent surveys in prisons show that a significant

proportion of male adult inmates have undetected and untreated adult ADHD (Chitsabesan et al., 2006; Young, 2008). They may be referred for ADHD treatment via a forensic psychiatry service. Alcohol and substance misuse are common, because of their use as self-medication for primary ADHD symptoms and/or for secondary depression and anxiety arising from chronic ADHD impairments. Some adult patients are misdiagnosed as having a personality disorder or an affective disorder, including a bipolar disorder, because of their symptoms of impulsivity, emotional dysregulation and poor self-control. They may be referred as a long-standing psychiatric patient non-responsive to a series of treatments offered, because of misclassification.

In general, the impairments of adult ADHD are much more pervasive, affecting the functions in self-control, learning, occupation, organization, time-management, financial management, social and occupational relationships. Adult ADHD is a real, valid and debilitating condition and warrants a well-resourced service that provides both good quality assessments and comprehensive treatments.

# Medication

## Anan El Masry and Margaret Thompson

The MTA study (Jensen et al., 1999), the largest randomized control trial ever with children with ADHD, found that for most children with the disorder, medication alone was successful. However, the authors added important caveats that the medication should be carefully monitored and adjusted, to control symptoms appropriately.

The best results came from university clinics, where staff presumably had the special expertise and staffing resources to monitor their families frequently. Behaviour and family work alone, or as an added therapy, did not affect the efficacy but did influence the amount of medication that was necessary.

Some children with ADHD and co-morbid symptoms of anxiety and depression fared as well with behaviour work alone and possibly better in the long run (Jensen et al., 1999).

Interestingly, medicated children in community clinics improved in line with children offered behaviour and family work only, but less well than the children who attended the university clinics (Jensen et al., 1999; MTA, 1999).

During trials lasting between three and seven months, Schachar and Tannock (1993) found that stimulants were more effective at treating the core behavioural symptoms of ADHD than placebos, non-pharmacological treatments or no treatment. In addition, stimulants may improve cognitive performance and help to reduce conduct problems and peer relationship difficulties (Wolraich et al., 1990). In the long-term follow up, behaviour work was clearly helpful for those young people, who had major behaviour problems and/or anxiety and depression. ADHD symptoms were less well controlled as medication was adhered to less well without the benefit of the careful monitoring in university clinics.

In the UK, the prescription of stimulant medication is governed by law and clinical guidelines have been set down by the National Institute for Clinical Excellence (NICE, 2008). These guidelines recommend that medication was helpful for children with ADHD but stressed the importance of careful assessment, behaviour modification and regular monitoring to achieve optimum results.

The message seems to be clear that the appropriate children should be treated with the correct medication and that other work should be tailored to the needs of the children and the family. This is important, as assessing and treating children who are on the ADHD spectrum is becoming an increasing burden on CAMHS.

More in-depth assessment of parents, children and families might aid the decision about treatment pathways. Assessing the child and his/her parents understanding of the condition and the parents' empathy towards their child and the treatment process, might assist both parents and children to 'own' the treatment decisions and encourage compliance.

A thorough assessment should take place before

medication is started with baseline measurements of height, weight, pulse rate and blood pressure, at a minimum. It is important to take a history of baseline symptoms of stomach aches, headache, bruising and frequent nosebleeds, tics, sleep and eating patterns, as these symptoms may be present as side effects of medication.

A careful history should rule out a child and/or family history of heart disease, fits, tics and glaucoma (see European guidelines: Taylor et al., 2004; Banaschewski et al., 2006).

Regular monitoring (of blood pressure, pulse rate, height, weight and a list of possible side effects) should be carried out to determine whether to continue medication.

# Medication used

Stimulant medication (used in the United Kingdom at this time):

- methylphenidate (Ritalin): not licensed for use for children under six years of age;
- extended release: SR Ritalin, Concerta, Equasym XL, Medikinet (not licensed for use for children under six years of age);

- dexamphetamine (Dexedrine): licensed for use for children from three years of age.

Non-stimulant medication:

- atomoxetine.

Sometimes other medications might be helpful alongside medications for ADHD, for example:

- clonidine hydrochloride (Catapres, Dixarit), especially with concomitant tics;
- risperdal: could be used if the adolescent is exhibiting very aggressive behaviour;
- fluoxetine (Prozac): if the adolescent is depressed;
- carbamazepine (Tegretol); Sodium Valproate (for associated mood disorders).

## Medication use in adults

Medication is equally useful for adults with ADHD. As in younger people, a careful history has to be taken to exclude other psychiatric syndromes which might account for the symptoms or make it more complicated to treat. For example, bipolar disorder should be screened for, as should substance abuse.

Physical contraindications to medication should be established. Adults should receive ongoing care from their GP as well as an interested adult psychiatrist.

## Multiple choice questions

1. The prevalence of ADHD in the population is:

   a. 6 per cent of the population
   b. 20 per cent
   c. 30 per cent
   d. 15 per cent
   e. 25 per cent

2. Which is not correct?

   a. Inattention is the usual finding
   b. Medication is the treatment of choice for preschool ADHD
   c. Preschool hyperactivity is hard to diagnose
   d. Co-morbidity is not common
   e. The neuropsychology findings are different in preschoolers

3. Which is correct?

   a. A single gene has been identified in children with ADHD
   b. Tics are rarely found in young children with ADHD
   c. Behaviour modification should be started as first treatment, even when the symptoms are very severe
   d. High IQ will make no difference to outcome for children with ADHD
   e. In young children, the normal co-morbidity with ADHD is Oppositional Defiant Disorder

4. Which is not correct?

   a. ADHD may appear *de novo* in adolescence

   b. Medication is not effective with adults with ADHD

   c. Adults with ADHD are very likely to be smokers

   d. Driving offences occur more often in the population with ADHD

   e. Adults with ADHD may first present with problems at work

## Key texts

Barkley RA (2006) *Attention Deficit Hyperactivity Disorder: a Handbook for Diagnosis and Treatment*, 2nd edn. New York: Guilford Press.

Barkley RA, Murphy KR, Fischer M (2008) *ADHD in Adults: What the Science Says.* New York: Guilford Press.

Banaschewski T, Coghill D, Santosh P et al. (2006) Long-acting medications for the hyperkinetic disorders. A systematic review and European treatment guideline. *European Child and Adolescent Psychiatry*, **15**: 476–95.

Chen W, Taylor E (2005) Resilience and self-control impairment. In: Goldstein S, Brooks RB (eds). *Handbook of Resilience in Children.* Massachusetts: Kluwer Academic/Plenum Publishers.

Daley D, Jones K, Hutchings J, Thompson M (2009) Attention deficit hyperactivity disorder in pre-school children: current findings, recommended interventions and future directions. *Child: Care, Health and Development*, **35**: 754–66.

Faraone SV, Biederman J, Mick E (2006) The age-dependent decline of attention deficit hyperactivity disorder: a meta-analysis of follow-up studies. *Psychological Medicine*, **36**: 159–65.

National Institute for Health and Clinical Excellence (2008) Clinical guidance CG72. Attention deficit hyperactivity disorder: Diagnosis and management in ADHD in children, young people and adults. London: NICE. www.nice.org.uk/nicemedia/pdf/CG072NiceGuildelinesV2.pdf (last accessed 25/11/2010).

Taylor E, Dopfner M, Sergeant J et al. (2004) European Guidelines for hyperkinetic disorder-first upgrade. *European Child and Adolescent Psychiatry*, **13**: 7–30.

Thompson M, Laver-Bradbury C, Chen W, Sonuga-Barke (eds) (2009a) Directed by Phillips P, O'Riordan T. *Living with ADHD DVD.* Southampton: Southampton City PCT.

# 37 Epilepsy

Salvatore Rotondetto and Margaret Thompson

## Key concepts

- Epilepsy symptoms may be misconstrued as psychiatric symptoms and vice versa.
- The symptoms might reflect the position of the underlying focus for the seizure.
- Children may have cognitive impairments.
- Medication for epilepsy may produce side effects.

It is important for child psychiatrists to know how children, who could have epilepsy, might present. This is important in making diagnostic decisions with children who present with unexpected symptoms.

Keeping these symptoms in mind will help in identifying a child who is presenting for the first time with epilepsy, or to be able to recognize when the seizure control is not optimal.

## Presentation

Children with seizures may present with physical symptoms or emotional symptoms before the seizures happen or after. Equally, seizures could be confused with psychiatric symptoms.

Early seizure symptoms may present with warnings that could be misconstrued as psychosomatic symptoms. The children may say that their thoughts are racing, or they have strange tingling feelings in their hands, or butterfly feelings in their stomach. They might say they have an odd taste, or smell a strange smell. They sometimes talk about hearing sounds or having a feeling that something has happened before or deny something has happened (Déjà vu/Jamais vu).

Children can be very apprehensive with all these feelings and can become alarmed. However, sometimes they may report that the feelings are pleasant.

They can also present with physical symptoms of dizziness, headache, light-headedness, nausea and numbness in fingers or other places, for example the side of a face.

Sometimes seizures can also come with no warning.

The presentation of seizures symptoms may depend on where the seizure originates.

## Seizure symptoms presentation

### Sensory

- Confusion
- Deafness/hearing sounds
- Smell
- Electric shock feeling
- Loss of consciousness
- Visual loss or blurring
- Spacing out
- Out of body experience

### Emotional

- Fear or panic (especially in young children)

### Physical

- Chewing movements
- Tonic–clonic movements
- Difficulty in talking
- Drooling
- Eyelid fluttering
- Eye movements

- Drop attacks
- Apnoea

After a seizure children might have a memory loss that can be distressing. They might have difficulties in speech and gross and fine motor skills. They might be confused, fearful or embarrassed. They might be frustrated if they do not know what is happening to them. Children with epilepsy may feel different to other children, especially if the seizures happen in public, for example at school, and if the fear of seizures make it difficult for parents or teachers to let the children do the same things as other children, for example go swimming or boating. This can lead to sadness or depression. It is always more difficult for children if the epilepsy should occur for the first time at adolescence when normally a young person would be becoming independent.

Children may also suffer physical sequelae after an epileptic attack with bruising or injuries. They can feel nauseated, thirsty and weak, with headaches or painful muscles. Children may be very sleepy, exhausted and find talking difficult. Children may also have an urge to urinate or defecate.

## Types of seizures

- Self-limited seizure types
  - Generalized seizures
    - Tonic–clonic
    - Clonic (shaking)
    - Absence seizures ('staring')
    - Myoclonic absence
    - Tonic (stiffness)
    - Myoclonic (jerk movements)
    - Myoclonic atonic
    - Atonic (drop)
    - Reflex seizures
  - Focal seizures
    - Focal motor seizures
    - Gelastic seizures (laugh)
    - Hemiclonic seizures
    - Secondarily generalized seizures
- Continuous seizures
  - Generalized status epilepticus
  - Focal status epilepticus

In generalized epilepsies, the epileptic activity affects the whole brain from the onset. Patients can present with problems of impulsive behaviour, poor frustration tolerance and short attention span, likely to be linked to frontal lobe dysfunction. Children with secondary generalized epilepsy often have significant cognitive impairments and are more likely to present with depression, anxiety or attention deficit disorder.

During epilepsies of focal origin, the seizure activity starts from an identifiable cortical region. Reported psychiatric symptoms in these epilepsies depend on the area of the brain affected. Symptoms of depression and anxiety have been associated with seizures originating in the temporal lobe, frontal lobe or both.

Psychiatric symptoms can occur from 72 hours before a seizure occurring to 120 hours after it. They consist typically of irritability, poor frustration tolerance and impulsivity. Parents often can predict the occurrence of seizures as their child becomes more restless, impulsive and irritable. After the seizure the child may feel depression, anxiety or even experience psychotic episodes lasting several days.

Psychiatric symptoms may present between seizures and include low mood, anxiety and similar to behavioural disorders/attention deficit disorders. Differentiating these symptoms from psychiatric disorders in their own right may prove very difficult.

It is of importance to be able to differentiate epileptic seizure from non-epileptic seizure, a number of which are of psychogenic origin. These often mimic true epileptic attacks to a degree that are regularly misdiagnosed.

As mentioned above, alongside neurobiologic reasons in determining psychiatric symptoms, other factors may be responsible for behavioural disturbances. Effects on self-esteem and confidence in the social setting because of the possible occurrence of seizures in public places and parental over-protectiveness lead to social isolation and decrease involvement in academic activities. Other neurological disorders associated with the seizure disorder can also affect many areas of the child's general functioning (i.e. cerebral palsy).

## Anti-epileptic drugs and their side effects

All anti-epileptic drugs (AEDs) have potentially behaviour-changing effects on children, which are sometimes difficult to predict as they may depend on individual genetic and environmental factors. Some of these effects, which may vary in intensity, may also be opposite in quality. For example valproate, levetiracetam and vigabatrin may induce sedation in some subjects but can cause irritability and anxiety in others.

Sedative AEDs (barbiturates, benzodiazepines, valproate, gabapentin, tiagabine and vigabatrin) affect energy levels, impact with concentration and induce low mood, however they can be effective in controlling anxiety, mania and are hypnotics. Conversely, activating AEDs (e.g. felbamate and lamotrigine) can cause anxiety, insomnia and agitation but possess antidepressant effects and improve attention. AEDs with both inhibitory and excitatory properties (e.g. topiramate, levetiracetam and zonisamide) can cause anxiety, irritability and depression.

In children already in treatment, weaning off AEDs can trigger behavioural deterioration. This may happen because of the loss of the positive psychotropic effect of the pharmacological agent. For example, discontinuation of drugs which have mood-stabilizing properties, such as carbamazepine, valproate and lamotrigine, can unmask an underlying mood affective disorder.

Partial treatment ('outgrown dosage', poor compliance, pharmacological interaction, etc.) and response to treatment ('difficult epilepsies') are determinant factors for poor control in epilepsies which are associated with, and sometimes preceded by, behavioural disturbances.

# Diagnosis

The diagnosis of epilepsy remains a clinical one. A detailed and accurate history of presenting symptoms and past medical problems, together with a complete physical (including neurological) examination, are often more valuable than subsequent investigations. Witnessing a suspected seizure or viewing a video-recording by carers of the episode may be very informative towards a diagnostic formulation. A typical example is 'daydreaming' episodes of inattentive children, often confused with absence seizures and vice versa.

## Electroencephalography

Electroencephalography (EEG) may help in diagnosing epilepsy but only in relatively limited circumstances. It is important to remember that 44 per cent of children with epilepsy will have a normal first EEG. Sometimes a repeat EEG with or without sleep can increase the diagnostic yield. Conversely, misleading EEG abnormalities can be found on up to 10 per cent of routine EEGs. Only careful clinical and EEG correlation will improve diagnostic accuracy.

## Case study 1

Anna (14 years) was referred for behaviour problems at school, especially not wanting to finish tasks and not appearing to pay attention.

She had had epilepsy since she was five years of age and had always been reasonably well controlled and a good pupil in the past.

Careful observation in class indicated that actually her times of inattention might well be evidence of seizures, with confusion afterwards leading to apparent non-compliance.

An EEG indicated that her epilepsy was no longer well controlled and when her medication was increased her behaviour improved.

## Case study 2

Tom had just been diagnosed with temporal lobe epilepsy following a period of investigation for odd experiences of seeming to hear voices and experiencing odd tastes and smells. He then had a seizure at school.

He was embarrassed about the seizure at school, depressed that he would have to take medication and that he would not, at least for a while, be able to do the things he enjoyed, such as swimming and kayaking.

He and his parents met with the specialist epilepsy nurse who explained all the facts about epilepsy to them, and gave him sensible advice about looking after himself.

She also gave him time by himself to talk through his feelings and anger about his situation.

Gradually he was able to discuss with his friends, family and teachers how to allow him to carry on with his hobbies safely with sensible safeguards built in.

## Multiple choice questions

1. Which symptoms may be experienced by a child who could have epilepsy?

   a. Painful stomach
   b. Headache
   c. Nausea
   d. Tingling in hands
   e. Fear or panic

## Key text

Beattie M (2006) *Essential revision notes in paediatrics for the MRCPCH*, 2nd edn. Cheshire: PASTEST Ltd.

## Web page

Epilepsy Action www.epilepsy.org.uk

# 38 Tourette syndrome

## Catherine Thompson and Margaret Thompson

---

### Key concepts

- TS may be very mild and may pass unnoticed.
- It is more common in boys (a ratio of about 3:1).
- It may occur in around 1–10 in 1000 children.
- Co-morbidity may occur.
- It is not easy to treat.

---

Tics are common, about one in five children will have a simple tic at some point and this may last a few weeks. If the tic lasts less than a year it is benign (Transient Tic Disorder); if more than a year it meets the definition of a chronic tic (CT). If a child presents with tics that differ in severity and a history of both motor and vocal tics for at least a year (often in a waxing and waning pattern) the child may have Gilles de Tourette syndrome (TS) (DSM IV) (Pollak et al., 2009b).

The definition of TS is that more than two motor tics and one or more vocal tics have been present at some point in time, but not necessarily continuously; that the tics occur many times a day (in bouts), nearly every day for at least a year; other causes have been ruled out; the age of onset is before 18.

## Assessment

It is important to take a careful history of a child who presents with a tic or ask about tics if a child has other neurodevelopmental conditions, for example attention deficit hyperactivity disorder (ADHD). The parent might not have noticed the child shaking his head a lot or grunting or making noises, thinking it was a habit or the child was being naughty trying to attract attention. This is also relevant if the child is to start a course of stimulant medication as it is possible that if the tics worsen this could be blamed on the medication, although more recent trials show that this longstanding empirical belief may need to be revised (Bloch et al., 2011). Any ambiguity in post-treatment symptom change can be minimized by a thorough initial assessment of symptom patterns and possible co-morbidities.

A tic is a brief, repetitive, purposeless, non-rhythmic, involuntary movement or sound. Tics can be motor or vocal tics and the child may have both. The tics often occur in bouts. Simple tics would involve one group of muscles, for example face, head and neck or eye blinking. A vocal tic may be a simple sound or more complex, for example throat clearing, grunting, sniffing or coughing.

Complex tics involve a number of muscle groups in a coordinated movement. The child may touch objects or people, may jump up and down or spin around. He may involuntarily imitate the movements of another (echopraxia).

Sometimes the child will make inappropriate or taboo gestures (copropraxia).

When a child has complex vocal tics he may repeat one phrase over and over, a heard word (echolalia), his own words (palilalia), or use swear words, inappropriate words or derogatory remarks (coprolalia).

Some children may report internal tics sensations in their arms or fingers.

Why do tics occur? A tic may have a genetic component with variable expression of the gene and incomplete penetrance, and a child may inherit TS from a parent. For some children no cause may be found. It may be associated with prenatal smoking, drug use, alcohol, infections; post birth-infections, for example post-viral encephalitis; infections (as an autoimmune process, for example streptococcal infections, e.g. a condition called PANDAS); Sydenham's chorea (rapid uncoordinated movements affecting mainly the face, feet and hands resulting from a childhood infection with Group A beta-haemolytic streptococci); Wilson's disease (WD) or hepatolenticular degeneration. WD is an autosomal recessive genetic disorder in which copper accumulates in the brain and other tissues and usually presents between six and 20 years. Opthalmoscopic examination of the eye may reveal a Kayser–Fleischer ring on the edge of the iris if this diagnosis is the primary one (the abnormal movements seen in WD are not strictly 'tics'; dysteria and ataxia are common features in WD); tardive dyskinesia (involuntary repetitive movements, a condition that appears sometimes following antipsychotic medication or some medication for gastro conditions); stimulant medication (though important to check that the child did not have tics before medication); a head injury. Rarely it can be associated with Lesch–Nyhan syndrome, Huntington's chorea or neurocanthocytosis.

**Table 38.1** summarizes the family studies of probands and relatives with combinations of tic disorders, obsessive–compulsive disorder (OCD) and ADHD (O'Rourke et al., 2009; Pollak et al., 2009).

The tics are believed to occur because of an underlying disorder in the frontal cortex and the subcortical regions of the brain (the thalamus and basal ganglia – the dopamine circuits). The caudate nucleus and globus pallidus are decreased in size in medication-naive TS patients and the relative loss of volume correlates significantly with the symptom severity ratings in adults. Histological changes in post-mortem studies of the brains of TS patients have revealed significant and consistent changes in cell type and distribution of interneurones in these same areas (Bloch et al., 2011).

The (debated) finding of perinatal hypoxia being a predictor of tic severity, along with the correlation between maternal smoking (leading to chronic intrauterine hypoxia) and tic severity in TS offspring, suggests that TS aetiology may be mixed with neurodevelopmental and environmental factors playing significant and interactive roles.

TS is commonly also associated with ADHD or OCD, as well as clinical anxiety or depression. The child may also have a learning disorder which is often domain specific, for example dyslexia, a language disorder, Central Auditory Processing Disorder or a spatial problem.

The role of genetics in the pathology of TS and the possibility of overlap in the genotype of TS ADHD and OCD has been increasingly studied in the recent past.

Stresses and anxiety may make the condition worse, as will boredom or low concentration. Interestingly, if a child is happy or angry the tics are often less.

The tics normally start around 6–7 years of age and may wax and wane.

Although most children with TS attend normal classes at school it is found more commonly in children with learning difficulties who are attending special education classes (23 versus 7 per cent).

The tics will peak at about 10–12 years and the long-term prognosis is good; only about 20 per cent of individuals diagnosed with TS report functional impairment secondary to tics by age 20 years (Bloch et al., 2011). However, adults may report that tics have gone, but they often still present, albeit subclinically, and the tics may reoccur if the adult acquires a physical condition. Motor tic severity decreases in most individuals; however children with severe global tics are more likely to continue with it.

As already suggested, TS rarely occurs alone and may be associated with other neurodevelopmental disorders such as ADHD, autism, OCD or Central Auditory Processing Disorder.

The child or young person may also be prone to anger or rages, which may have an underlying neurodevelopmental focus. The child may also have other psychiatric conditions like anxiety, bipolar disorder or a major depression. It may also be associated with Conduct Disorder or self-injurious disorder.

The tics may be voluntary or involuntary. Some adults and older children can suppress them but they find they have to let them out at some point. Sometimes this can happen in a burst as the child having held them in all day 'lets go' on the way out of school. Children sometimes describe how they

Table 38.1 Family studies of probands and relatives with combinations of tic disorders, obsessive-compulsive disorder (OCD) and ADHD (O'Rourke et al., 2009; Pollak et al., 2009)

| | |
|---|---|
| Family studies | 10–100-fold increase in incidence of TS in first degree relatives versus general population |
| | Only 10–15 per cent of patients with TS have no other co-morbidities |
| | OCD and ADHD are the most common, each affecting over 50 per cent of TS individuals versus population baseline rates of 3.3 per cent (OCD) and 5 per cent (ADHD) in school age children |
| Primary diagnosis TS. Pattern of OCD incidence in probands and relatives | The incidence of OCD is raised in relatives of TS probands even if tics are not present and this increase is significant even if the proband does not have clinical OCD themselves |
| | Gender of the proband does not affect OCD or tic incidence in relatives. However, gender of the relative was a significant factor; females have an increased risk of developing isolated OCD while males develop tics more commonly |
| | It appears that TS chronic tics (CT) and some OCD forms may have underlying commonalities in genetic susceptibility |
| Primary diagnosis OCD. Pattern of TS incidence in probands and relatives | [The relationship is more complex] |
| | The relatives of probands with childhood onset OCD have an increased incidence of TS and CT |
| | Individuals with early onset OCD are more likely to develop tics than those with adult onset OCD |
| | Non-familial OCD seems not to be associated with TS and CT; relatives of OCD probands have a significantly higher incidence of TS and CT if the proband had a family history of OCD versus those probands who did not |
| | First degree relatives of probands with OCD and tics have a higher incidence of developing tics than probands with OCD alone |
| | These findings suggests only the pathology of early onset OCD is related to tic disorders with adult onset being a different genetic sub-type |
| ADHD versus TS/CT versus OCD | ADHD has a significant genetic component with 70–80 per cent of the risk believed to be attributed to genetic factors |
| | It is becoming clear that the most common form of ADHD does not have an underlying shared genetic susceptibility in common with TS or CT |
| | Rates of ADHD alone are not elevated in the relatives of TS probands unless the proband themselves has co-morbid ADHD |
| | Co-morbid diagnoses of TS and ADHD in a relative of a TS or ADHD proband is correlated with whether the proband also has an OCD diagnosis |
| | If a relative of a proband has TS or ADHD some OCD symptoms in that same individual tend to be found |
| | The co-morbidity of ADHD and OCD is higher in children with TS (44 per cent ADHD and 54 per cent OCD) versus those with CT (23 and 8 per cent) suggesting co-morbidity is associated with a more severe tic disorder |
| | 34 per cent of TS individuals were found to have co-morbid ADHD and OCD whereas the incidence of ADHD in individuals with TS but no OCD was only 10 per cent |
| | Individuals with TS and ADHD versus those with an ADHD diagnosis alone may present a distinct subset of ADHD symptoms with externalizing behaviour symptoms being more commonplace in those with ADHD and TS |

ADHD, attention deficit hyperactivity disorder; CT, chronic tic; OCD, obsessive-compulsive disorder; TS, Tourette syndrome feel the tic building up and they may or may not be able to control it. They sometimes feel an 'urge' to tic or move.

Socially the children may be teased at school and may become very distressed. If the child becomes more anxious about 'ticing' this may make the tics worse. There may be associated learning difficulties.

## Management

A careful history must be taken to establish the nature of the tics, and the severity, but also to exclude other morbidity.

Assessment of mood is also important. A family history of other neurodevelopmental conditions is helpful. A family assessment is important to establish how best to support, as often family relationships are under stress.

Individual work with the child will depend on assessment but might include work on anxiety, cognitive therapy and counselling. Some children can be taught to suppress the tics.

Other problems, if elicited, will need to be treated, for example ADHD or educational issues.

## Medication

Although most effective in the treatment of tic disorders, antipsychotic medications (large effect size showing good efficacy Cohen's '$d$' = 0.4–1.2) tend to be avoided in the paediatric population due to poor tolerance, weight gain and an increased risk of metabolic syndrome. Alpha-2 agonists such as clonidine are considered first line but their effect size is moderate at best ($d$ = 0.1–0.5). Clonidine has been shown to have equal efficacy versus methylphenidate in the treatment of ADHD symptoms in co-morbid TS patients. A recent study, as previously mentioned, has shown that the use of psychostimulant medication in patients with co-morbid tic disorders may significantly improve ADHD symptoms while at best improving, but not worsening, the child's tic symptoms. Other drug treatments more efficacious than alpha-2 agents with less side effects than neuroleptics in the younger population are actively being sought: dopamine agonists (Pergolide), monoamine transporter inhibitor (Tetrabenazine) and GABA neurotransmitter inducers (Topiramate) are drugs currently being trialled (Bloch et al., 2011).

Medication for anxiety may also be helpful.

A behaviouralist-based treatment, Habit Reversal Training, has shown promise as a non-invasive treatment of this often upsetting disorder. This is a structured therapy designed to make patients with complex tics gradually become aware at an early stage when their tics may be about to begin or worsen. By repetitively aiming to introduce contraction of the opposing muscle group (depending on the body area involved) it is theoretically possible for the patient to prevent or minimize the degree to which a bystander would notice the (motor) tic.

## Case study

Henry's tics started when he was four. They developed in severity, and waxed and waned. He struggled at school and was seen as a naughty child. On assessment in the children's unit his education problems were highlighted, but the school was not keen to take them seriously. He failed at secondary school despite efforts. His tics worsened, despite medication (clonidine), and he became very angry with constant rages.

Respirodine was started, but his weight rapidly increased and as his liver function tests were mildly impaired the medication was stopped.

He changed schools which helped as they were more sympathetic and he received support for his dyslexia and pragmatic language difficulties. He also had ADHD and this had to be treated with stimulant medication.

His parents were very supportive but they had their own problems with finance and neighbours who were not supportive. His mother was depressed and she had OCD. His brother had ADHD also. The family moved house and his mother sought treatment for herself and gradually the situation improved. Henry's tics settled as he became less anxious and he began to make friends and do better at school.

## Multiple choice question

1. Which is not correct?

    a. Simple tics are very common
    b. A child who grunts and make funny noises may have TS
    c. TS is associated with other disorders
    d. TS is not easy to treat
    e. Children with TS can be depressed

### Key texts

Bloch M, State M, Pittenger C (2011) Recent advances in Tourette syndrome. *Current Opinion in Neurology*, **24**: 119–25.
O'Rourke JA, Scharf JM, Yu D, Pauls DL (2009) The genetics of Tourette syndrome: A review. *Journal of Psychosomatic Research*, **67**: 533–45.

Pollak Y, Benarroch F, Kanengisser L et al. (2009b). Tourette syndrome-associated psychopathology: roles of comorbid attention-deficit hyperactivity disorder and obsessive-compulsive disorder. *Journal of Developmental and Behavioral Pediatrics*, **30**: 413–19.

# 39 *Autistic spectrum disorder*

Erika Harris and Josie Brown

---

## Key concepts

- Autism spectrum disorder (ASD) is regarded as a biologically based neurodevelopmental disorder.
- ASD is a lifelong disorder, although individuals can change and make considerable progress.
- Individuals on the autistic spectrum can present with a very wide range of difficulties, each of these difficulties presenting from mild to severe.
- Assessment is complex and involves a multidisciplinary approach.
- There is a range of treatment approaches.
- Management is focused on improving life for the individual and for their family.

---

## Introduction

The difficulties known as the 'autistic spectrum disorders' are defined in detail in the ICD-10 (International Classification of Diseases), compiled by the World Health Organization (WHO, 1993), where they are described under the umbrella term of Pervasive Developmental Disorders.

## History

### Background

Leo Kanner described his 'prototype of autism' in 1943 in the USA. In 1944, Hans Asperger, an Austrian physician, described the syndrome which bears his name.

The autistic spectrum disorders, or ASD, were first described by Lorna Wing in the 1970s, in what she called the 'Triad of Impairments', which is a broader concept than Kanner's original description of autism (Wing, 1993).

### Diagnostic criteria

People with an autistic spectrum disorder have difficulties in three key areas:

1. Social interaction

2. Communication (both verbal and non-verbal)
3. Restricted, repetitive interests and behaviour.

Problems in all three areas are required to make a diagnosis, but the way in which people with an autistic spectrum disorder present is hugely variable.

The diagnostic criteria for autism also includes abnormal development before the age of 36 months.

## Impairments in social interaction

Children on the autistic spectrum often make poor use of interpersonal social cues, for example facial expression, eye gaze, social smiling and gesture. They show a lack of awareness of, or an unusual response to, other people's feelings and sometimes to their own. These children find it difficult to develop relationships with other children, especially when young, and can appear disinterested in other children and adults, or only maintain interaction for a short period. Commonly, they become more sociable with age, but their behaviour may remain often socially inappropriate, with little understanding of social rules. They fail to develop Theory of Mind, i.e. the ability to place themselves in the shoes of another, and see the situation from someone else's point of view.

## Impairments in communication

These children often have delayed early speech development and sometimes do not develop the use of speech. In addition, their speech may be unusual with, for example, repetitive speech patterns, the use of stereotyped phrases, pronominal reversal (muddling up the use of I/me with you), and unusual intonation and vocal expression.

Commonly they do not use speech in a communicative, sociable way as much as people not on the autistic spectrum, for example it is often difficult to keep a conversation going with a child with autism (even if he/she has a well-developed use of speech), unless it is about one of the child's favourite interests.

Non-verbal communication is impaired, for example, children with autism do not make good use of gesture to communicate (e.g. young children do not readily point at objects that catch their interest). However, if they have marked speech delay, they can sometimes be taught the use of simple signing to communicate their wants.

Their play tends to be much less spontaneous and imaginatively varied than that of normal children, although some imagination may develop.

## Restricted, repetitive patterns of behaviour and interests

- These children may become preoccupied with certain interests which absorb them to an unusual degree, for example trains, numbers, buildings, car washes, etc. They can become fascinated by unusual objects such as toilets, plugs or street signs.
- Many children on the autistic spectrum show repetitive use of objects, for example repeatedly spinning wheels, lining up objects, dropping things from a certain height and so on. They may develop rituals and fixed sequences of behaviour.
- They may have unusual sensory interests, which occupy them for an unusual length of time, for example frequently feeling textures, peering at things from unusual angles, smelling things.

- They typically have problems with minor changes in their routine, for example they may strongly dislike taking different routes to places, dislike changes in their clothing or insist on eating only a limited range of food. They may dislike changes around them, for example how the furniture is arranged.

Some children develop repetitive motor mannerisms, for example hand flapping, finger flicking or body stereotypies such as repeated spinning of the whole body.

# Terminology

There is some confusion about the terminology used to define autistic spectrum disorders. Some of the confusion arises from different diagnostic criteria. Becoming 'bogged down' in the different terms is often unhelpful in clinical practice. It is more helpful to describe the child's strengths and weaknesses, for example in communication, sociability, non-verbal abilities and so on.

In ICD-10, the diagnostic system commonly used in the UK, Autistic Spectrum Disorders are included in the umbrella term 'Pervasive Developmental Disorders' and include:
- autism;
- Asperger's syndrome (see below);
- atypical autism (used when the onset is after three years of age or when problems are not present in all three of the diagnostic areas);
- Childhood Disintegrative Disorder (a rare condition when there is clear deterioration in a number of skills);
- Pervasive Developmental Disorder not otherwise specified ( development abnormal in all three of the key areas, but not to the same degree as in classical autism or Asperger's syndrome).

The next Diagnostic and Statistical Manual of Mental Disorders due out in 2013 (DSM-V) will include the various terms such as autism, Asperger's syndrome and pervasive developmental disorder not otherwise specified under one category: autism spectrum disorder. It will merge the three domains outlined above into two: social/communication deficits and fixated interests and repetitive behaviours. The language delay and specific language abnormalities are not included in the diagnostic criteria (although are clearly present in some autistic children), but more emphasis is placed on the unusual verbal and non-verbal communication of children on the autistic spectrum.

# Asperger's syndrome

Autism and Asperger's syndrome are on the same autistic continuum. The term Asperger's syndrome is used when the child's early language development was fairly normal (in contrast to autism, where there is a delay in speech and language development) and where the person has normal or above normal intelligence.

Individuals with Asperger's syndrome often speak with a good vocabulary and grammar and, when young, their speech may seem advanced for their years ('like a little professor'), but it can also appear stilted and pedantic, with poor reciprocity in communication.

Children with Asperger's syndrome show impairments in social interaction (but may become more sociable) and the development of repetitive patterns of behaviour (often having circumscribed interests in, and being very knowledgeable about, certain topics, for example bus timetables, a famous person, astronomy). These interests can be a strength for some individuals.

## Epidemiology

The epidemiology of autistic spectrum disorders is difficult to determine, because of the diagnostic dilemmas, and will depend on the diagnostic boundaries. One study gives estimates of an autistic spectrum disorder in a pre-school population of 45.8 per 10 000 (Chakrabarti and Fombonne, 2005). A study of Asperger's syndrome gives a rate of 36–71 per 10 000 (Ehlers and Gillberg, 1993). Severe classical autism is thought to affect around 6–9 individuals per 10 000 of the population.

Autism and Asperger's syndrome were once thought to be uncommon disorders, but recent studies have reported increased prevalence rates so autism spectrum disorder is now regarded as occurring in at least 1 per cent of the child population (Baird et al., 2006; Baron-Cohen et al., 2008).

Autistic spectrum disorders are diagnosed much more commonly now, than in the past, probably because of increased recognition and awareness, rather than a true increase in incidence.

There are no marked variances within social classes or ethnic groups. Males are affected more than females at an approximate ratio of 4:1 for classical autism, and at a ratio of 9:1 for Asperger's syndrome.

## Aetiology

This has been the subject of much debate over the years. For years, poor parenting was thought to be implicated, but this is most definitely not the cause. There is evidence for biological factors, as outlined below.

- Genetic factors have been found to be important. Several genes are thought to be involved, and work continues in this area. If one twin has autism then the chance of the other twin being autistic is much greater in monozygotic (identical) twins than in dizygotic (non-identical) twins. If one child in the family has autism, it is about 20 times more likely than the rate in the general population that those parents will have another child on the spectrum, although not necessarily of the same severity.
- Some other medical conditions are associated with autism, including tuberous sclerosis, phenylketonuria, congenital rubella.
- There is also a possible link with perinatal difficulties (hypoxia during labour, some pregnancy complications and so on), but such problems occur in a minority of autistic children and the significance is unclear.
- More recently, the MMR vaccine has been blamed for the development of the condition, but international research studies have disproved this causality.
- Abnormalities have been noted on brain scans (e.g. in the cerebellum and the ventricles), and electroencephalography (EEG), but the significance is unclear and the findings are not specific for autism. A raised level of serotonin, a neurotransmitter, has been found in a proportion of autistic children, but again the significance is unclear.

Much research continues in all these areas. In

summary, the disorder is regarded as a multi-factorial, biologically based neurodevelopmental disorder with a strong genetic influence.

## Assessment

The diagnosis of ASD is complex, and involves in-depth assessment. Various diagnostic tools have been developed, including the Autism Diagnostic Interview (ADI), developed by Lord et al. (1989). This interview is administered to the parents or carers by a trained professional, and takes around 3 hours to complete. Observation of the child is essential, and there is a tool for this, the Autism Diagnostic Observation Schedule (ADOS) (Lord et al., 1989). The Diagnostic Interview for Social and Communication Disorders (DISCO), developed by Lorna Wing is yet another interview schedule (Wing, 2003). The computerized 3Di interview developed by Professor David Skuse at Great Ormond Street Hospital is also recognized as valid and reliable for diagnostic purposes (Skuse et al., 2004).

As a screening tool for use in young children, the Checklist for Autism in Toddlers (CHAT) has been developed by Gillian Baird and Simon Baron-Cohen (Baron-Cohen et al., 1996). Designed for use by GPs and health visitors, this is a quickly administered questionnaire to screen for the presence of autistic traits at a very young age during routine clinic visits. For example, it asks whether the child uses finger-pointing to share their interest in something with the observer, as typically this does not occur in autistic spectrum children.

Specialist clinics will often have assessment protocols, including clinical opinions from a psychologist, speech therapist, paediatrician, psychiatrist, occupational therapist and so on. If the child is in an educational setting, observations from teachers and other staff will be sought, as these children's difficulties often come to light in these settings, often initially as 'non-conforming'. In practice, some children are not diagnosed until junior or senior school, especially as the social demands on the child increase. A later diagnosis is often regrettable, as intervention at an early age can lessen the impact on the child and family's life.

Comprehensive and detailed guidelines for the referral and diagnosis of children thought to have an ASD have been commissioned by the National Institute for Health and Clinical Excellence (NICE) and are due for publication shortly. These will be very helpful to those planning and commissioning services as well as to the professionals involved in referrals and diagnosis.

# The clinical picture

There is enormous variation among children on the autistic spectrum. Symptoms and signs vary along a continuum, and it is difficult to describe a 'typical' case. One certainly cannot tell just by looking. Some of the differences can be explained by the following factors.

## Intelligence

The cognitive abilities of children on the autism spectrum range from profound learning disability to above normal abilities. Intellectual disability (IQ <70) occurs in approximately 50 per cent of young people wth ASD (Charman et al., 2011). Other autistic children and children with Asperger's syndrome have normal or above normal non-verbal intelligence. The presence and degree of learning difficulty has a large impact on the child's behaviours and patterns of interests.

## Language

The amount of language acquired by children on the autistic spectrum varies enormously. Some children have no, or very little, functional use of speech, whereas others become very talkative (maybe with unusual speech patterns), but with limited social use of language.

## Age

Autistic children, like all children, change as they grow older. They tend to become more sociable and, sometimes, more communicative. Children with reasonable use of speech and normal non-verbal intelligence probably change the most with age.

## Sociability

Although all children on the autistic spectrum have, by definition, impaired social interaction, some are more sociable than others, although in an unusual way. Some may be very affectionate.

## Temperament

The temperament varies greatly. Some children are placid and passive, whereas others are very active. Some children with an autistic spectrum disorder are sunny-natured and easy going, but others are particularly prone to temper tantrums and may be aggressive towards others or themselves.

## Gender

The diagnosis is more easily missed in girls who tend to compensate for their social deficits better than boys. They copy their peers and can assimilate themselves thus without being detected, particularly if they are not aggressive in nature.

In the following are a few thumbnail sketches of individuals.

A nine-year-old boy described by his teachers as a 'loner', teased by his classmates for being a 'geek', spends his break-time in the library looking up obscure details of astronomy. He hates sitting on a table with other children, but if a subject can be found which interests him he will flap his hands up and down with excitement, making unusual crowing noises. People rarely invite him to their birthday parties. If he is told a joke, it can be guaranteed he will not understand it. He was in trouble with the headmaster, who told him he needed to 'pull his socks up' in class. The boy looked down at his socks, seemed puzzled and said 'No, I don't'.

A four-year-old girl in play school never speaks, but will scream for long periods if other children sit on the chair she regards as hers, or come within a metre of her when she is playing with her favourite Thunderbirds doll, of which she never seems to tire. She never makes eye contact with anyone, does not sit on the mat for 'snack time', but puts the teacher's hand on the tap when she wants a drink. Her favourite outdoor playtime activity is spinning herself round and round, even when it is pouring with rain. She tries to bite her teachers if they attempt to make her wear a coat, even in bad weather.

A 14-year-old boy prefers to spend every day of his school holidays, including weekends and bank holidays, at the local train station, writing down the numbers of trains he sees in a notebook. He has hundreds of these notebooks at home, which he keeps in chronological order, and attacks anyone who disturbs them. If he is asked the time for any train to London, leaving at any particular time of the day, even Sundays, he knows them 'off by heart', and is never wrong. He can recite all the 'Thomas the Tank Engine' stories from memory. In fact, it is virtually impossible to stop him once he has started.

# Co-morbid conditions and differential diagnoses

Individuals on the autistic spectrum have relatively high incidences of co-morbid conditions and may therefore have more than one diagnosis. Other problems may include: anxiety disorder, depression, obsessional compulsive disorder (OCD), Tourette syndrome, attention deficit hyperactivity disorder (ADHD), sleep disorders, self-injurious behaviour, for example self-biting, head-banging and aggressive behaviour. There may be marked dyspraxic symptoms, in comparison with the normal population.

Differential diagnoses include severe learning disability (without autism), speech delay without autism, elective mutism, institutionalized upbringing, attachment disorder and others.

# Management

There are four basic goals of management (Rutter and Taylor, 2002):

1. Fostering social and communicative development
2. Enhancing learning and problem-solving
3. Decreasing behaviours that interfere with learning and access to opportunities for normal experiences
4. Helping families to cope with autism.

Psychological interventions, for example behaviour analysis, social skills training, are used to promote learning, increase social communication and decrease maladaptive behaviour (e.g. aggressive outbursts, prolonged repetitive behaviour) (see Chapter 71, Applied behaviour analysis).

Interventions to facilitate better communication range from alternative methods of communication, such as the PECS programme (Picture Exchange Communication System), using picture cards to show to the child or for the child to show to others (used for children with little functional speech), to ways to improve social communication, for example the social use of language programme (see Chapter 41, Social stories for parents of autistic children).

Special educational methods have been developed, many using a high degree of structure and predictability. Programmes such as TEACCH (Treatment and Education of Autistic and related Communication-Handicapped Children) have been widely used and focus on communication and behaviour. Children on the autistic spectrum are educated in many different settings, depending on the needs of the child and ranging from special schools for autistic children and other special schools, to mainstream schools. Some level of additional support is usually needed, whatever the setting (see Chapter 40, Education for children on the autism spectrum).

Psychotropic medications are increasingly used, particularly to decrease maladaptive behaviour, for example aggressive outbursts and to treat co-morbid conditions such as marked obsessional symptoms, anxiety and ADHD. Typical drugs used include fluoxetine, methylphenidate and risperidone. The choice of drug and duration of use must be directed to a specific goal and be reviewed regularly.

Self-help groups can be very helpful to parents/carers or to the young people themselves, such as adolescents with Asperger's syndrome or to siblings of a child on the autistic spectrum. The National Autistic Society is often able to provide information (there will be local groups, for example in Hampshire, the Hampshire Autistic Society) (**Box 39.1**).

# Prognosis

The strongest predictors of outcome are the degree of language at age five years, the child's cognitive level, temperament and level of behavioural disturbance, for example the extent of aggressive behaviour or degree of rigidity and repetitive actions.

Children who have non-verbal abilities below 60 on cognitive testing and with markedly limited language at age five years are likely to require a high level of adult support throughout their life. Children with a high IQ and good verbal skills at a young age may make good progress in terms of social and communicative functioning. Children in between these two extremes may remain dependent on others as adults or may be capable of some degree of independent living. In adolescence and adult life, there is a greater susceptibility to psychiatric disorders, for example depression or anxiety, which may be easily overlooked. The emotional limitations and unusual behaviours of some individuals can result in difficulties in relationships and problems in the workplace.

Good and appropriate education, addressing behavioural problems and providing family support can all contribute to a better prognostic outcome.

Being able to exploit a special interest or 'gift' can be the key to social integration and recognition, for example the case of Professor Temple Grandin, a woman with autism, who is a world expert on cattle pen design. People with ASD are often quite skilled at working on computers. In some walks of life, for example academia, the ability to attend to detail, in a somewhat obsessive way, can be an enormous strength.

At the moment, there is still insufficient provision for children on the autistic spectrum, and little understanding of them as adults out in the wider community. This situation is improving however, thanks to campaigns by organizations such as the National Autistic Society and increasing public awareness. The 2009 Autism Act passed by the Government should improve the service provision across the age range for individuals with autistic spectrum disorders in the longer term.

## Multiple choice questions

1. Which one of the following is strongly suggestive of autism in a young child?

   a. An interest in tractor wheel nuts
   b. Delayed speech
   c. A preference for routine/sameness
   d. An unwillingness to hold eye contact
   e. Screaming to show excitement

2. Which of the following is not thought to play a role in the aetiology (causes) of autism?

   a. Genes
   b. Neurotransmitter dysfunction
   c. Poor parenting
   d. Perinatal difficulties, i.e. difficult birth
   e. Certain medical conditions

3. The principal reason ASD is diagnosed more commonly now is:

   a. Girls have it as much as boys
   b. The multi-ethnicity of modern populations
   c. Chemicals have caused damage *in utero*
   d. It is an advantage in the school setting to have ASD
   e. Increased awareness of the condition

4. Which of the following are well-validated diagnostic tools for ASD?

   a. ADI
   b. ADOS
   c. 3Di
   d. DISCO
   e. All of the above

5. Which one of the following conditions does not occur commonly with ASD?

   a. Attention deficit hyperactivity disorder
   b. Tic disorder
   c. Mania
   d. Learning difficulties
   e. Anxiety

### Key texts

Baron-Cohen S (2008) *Autism and Aspergers Syndrome: The Facts.* Oxford: OUP.

Frith U (2008) *Autism: A Very Short Introduction.* Oxford: OUP.

'Mental Health and Growing Up' factsheets published by the Royal College of Psychiatrists, 17 Belgrave Square, London SW1X.

MIND – information and support.

National Autistic Society – booklets and leaflets, as well as conferences and local support groups. www.nas.org.uk

OAASIS – Office for Advice, Assistance Support and Information on Special Needs www.oaasis.co.uk

Wing L (2003) *The Autistic Spectrum: A Guide for Parents and Professionals.* Robinson Publishing.

World Health Organization (1992) *The Tenth Revision of the International Classification of Diseases and Related Health Problems (ICD-10).* Geneva: World Health Organization.

# 40 Education for children on the autism spectrum

Sandy Teal

---

## Key concepts

When identifying the most appropriate programme or placement, variables to consider include:
- the nature of the curriculum and how it is delivered
- the experience of the staff
- the child to staff ratio
- the current peer groupings (ability and size)
- the involvement of parents
- the opportunity for specialist advisory support, therapeutic input (e.g. speech and language therapy, occupational therapy, music therapy)
- available resources
- the opportunity to spend time with peers (with or without an autism diagnosis) should be taken into account
- meeting the individual needs is paramount.

---

## Introduction

Education is an area that has received much attention of late, with changes that are far-reaching in the realm of special needs. Special education is in flux; funding implications impact on proposals for placements outside that of a named mainstream school. A growing number of local educational authorities are working to develop more inclusive policies and specialist 'in county' provision to accommodate the growing number of children with an autistic spectrum condition diagnosis. For those children with a diagnosis, the support needs are variable and sometimes very complex.

However, any individual educational programme needs to be mindful of the variable abilities, intellectually and socially, that this population can exhibit. This will then influence the type of educational package needed.

Many schools will attempt to identify and meet the needs of a child after initial 'in school' assessment. If a parent/carer or school feel that the needs of a child are not being addressed, they may apply to the Local Education Authority for a Statutory Assessment for a Statement. This statement is a legal document issued by a local authority, setting out the educational and learning needs of the child and specifying how these should be addressed. There is a time limit of 26 weeks for the assessment and the issue of a statement, should the local authority feel this is appropriate. If a local authority decides not to assess or issue a statement, the parents can appeal their decision.

Local Education Authorities need to be creative in their placement of children on the autistic spectrum, focusing on the overall needs of the individual child.

Effective types of provision for autism spectrum disorder (ASD) young people include:
- mainstream schools with trained support staff and ASD friendly ethos;
- mainstream schools with an ASD specialist unit attached;
- specialist day/residential provision for ASD/ Learning Difficulties with possible links to a local mainstream school;
- home-based learning programme.

Early Intervention programmes vary from outreach support for families provided by local authorities linking them to specialist services, to home-based programmes, which may receive funding from their local authority.

An effective early years programme would address the 'triad of impairments' and sensory needs and build positive relationships with those involved with the child.

The programme would focus on:

- communication;
- social interaction;
- play, leisure and life skills.

Access to a curriculum would include:

- structure, visual learning and modelling;
- direct teaching of social skills;
- understanding the functions of behaviour and teaching acceptable behavioural responses.

# Mainstream school

## Case study 1: Jim

Jim (9) was a quiet boy with a diagnosis of Asperger's syndrome and an extensive interest in airplanes. He was very compliant, eager to please and followed the school rules without question. The school were given training on ASD and were receptive to further professional support. Jim's teachers perceived him to be extremely polite and easy to manage. His peers were given training on ASD and others with different learning needs, developed a tolerance of Jim, seeing him as a bit of a 'geek', but non-threatening.

One other boy in the school described Jim as his best friend because they shared an interest in Pokemon. Jim found transitions challenging and large groups of people made him anxious. The school worked with Jim using social stories and supported him in identifying the most stressful situations, allowing him the opportunity to avoid these settings until he could tolerate them and learn how to cope.

Jim had an experienced Learning Support Assistant who had an understanding of ASD and his specific sensory needs. Initially, she worked with Jim 1:1 and then expanded her time to support other students with ASD, running a social skills group and offering 1:1 sessions with Jim twice weekly.

# Mainstream school with an ASD specialist unit attached

## Case study 2: Bob

Bob was a student with a diagnosis of High Functioning Autism who became extremely anxious when he moved from a small primary school to a large comprehensive school. He was very worried by the thought of the many changes associated with his change of school. Bob was motivated to attend a mainstream school, wanting to participate in the variety of lessons on offer. It was decided that to support Bob with this transition, he would be best suited to attending a school where there was an ASD base that he could use as a place of refuge and support when his anxieties dictated. Bob began at the school using the base for his first lesson to help him organize his day, relax and talk through his anxieties, practising strategies he could use throughout the day. He had an agreed exit strategy that the teachers supported, allowing Bob to leave a classroom when his anxieties rose to an unmanageable level.

During his first two terms, Bob had a Learning Support Assistant with him 1:1, with them fading their support during the latter part of the term. Bob is now in Year 10, receiving support from the ASD base through a social skills and life skills group, relaxation session and relationship/sex education lesson. He is on target to achieve his GCSEs at a high grade.

# Specialist day/residential provision for ASD/learning difficulties (with possible links to a local mainstream school)

## Case study 3: Beth

Beth (16) had a diagnosis of ASD and attended a residential specialist school for learning difficulties with a high proportion of the student population with ASD. Beth had some provocative sexual behaviours around males and became challenging with intervention by staff. It was felt that her needs and vulnerabilities warranted that she be educated within a secure setting. Beth's 24-hour waking day programme followed the national curriculum in addition to life skills, social skills training, sensory integration, behavioural interventions and specialist relationship/sexuality education.

Beth had a special interest in food preparation and participated in a local college link provision for catering, supported by a learning support assistant. She secured a placement in further education in food preparation and is on course to begin in September. She has been given an opportunity to develop a variety of activities bringing her into contact with peers her own age. She is directly taught and coached on appropriate social skills 1:1 when in these situations. Although Beth's lack of understanding about relationships/sexuality makes her vulnerable, she is developing an awareness of her own feelings and emotions.

# Home-based programme

## Case study 4: Joe

Joe (14) had a diagnosis of ASD and found any educational provision so anxiety-producing that he became a school refuser. His parents felt that the educational provision would need to be based at home if it was to support Joe.

The educational authority organized for Joe to have some of his programme delivered through a virtual school, accessing his computer with a tutor 1:1. He would progress onto joining a small group of three. Joe had the support of a specialist teacher in ASD who visited him to teach him life and social skills and an occupational therapist who identified his sensory needs, supporting him to develop coping strategies. During these sessions, Joe would be taught in a visual manner, helping him to explore social perspectives, social problem-solving and teaching him directly the skills needed in a variety of situations.

Joe had a support worker from social services who practised these skills with him out in the community. Joe joined a weekly exercise class. He joined a local scout group with the encouragement of his support worker, thereby beginning to build peer relationships. Joe attended sessions with the local CAMHS specialist ASD team to help him understand his feelings of anxiety, benefiting from a sensory profile to understand the difficulties he had in regulating his sensory input. This information, coupled with cognitive behaviour therapy (CBT) to address his anxiety, meant that Joe became aware of how to reduce his anxiety and practise coping strategies. Joe is currently investigating a small adult education class in Computing and Web Design.

Educational provision for ASD children is varied and benefits from having the needs of the individual as the main focus to identify the most appropriate programme or placement.

Box 40.1 Education provision

**Local Education Authorities** need to be creative in their placement of children on the autistic spectrum, focusing on the overall needs of the individual

**Effective early years programme** addresses the 'triad of impairments' and sensory needs; building positive relationships with those involved with the child

**The programme would focus on:**
Communication
Social interaction
Play, leisure and life skills
Access to a curriculum would include structure, visual learning, modelling and direct teaching of social skills
Understanding the functions of behaviour and teaching acceptable behavioural responses

# Related information

Autism Education Trust: The Autism Education Trust (AET) was launched in November 2007 with funding from the Department for Children, Schools and Families. It is dedicated to coordinating and improving education support for all children on the autism spectrum in England.

Inclusion Development Programme National Standards (IDP): Primary and Secondary: Teaching and supporting pupils on the autism spectrum: an e-learning course supports teachers in meeting the needs of pupils on the autism spectrum. The course is designed for teachers and teaching assistants, trainers and initial teacher training (ITT) providers, head teachers and leadership teams, support workers and student teachers in training.

The National Autistic Society is the leading UK charity for people with autism including Asperger's syndrome and their families. They provide information, support and services for those needing to be signposted to appropriate help.

The National Autistic Society's Early Bird Programme: a three-month programme for

the parents/carers of pre-school children on the autism spectrum. It is delivered by licensed trainers who work with parents/carers on how to encourage the best out of their child.

Autism Good Practice Guidance. This was developed by the Autism Working Group and gives practical advice to providers for children with autistic spectrum disorders, based on existing good practice, and helps them to reflect on their own practice and examples of good practice.

National Autism Plan for Children (NAPC) produced by the National Initiative for Autism: Screening and Assessment (NIASA). The Plan covers the identification, assessment, diagnosis and access to early interventions for pre-school and primary school-aged children with autistic spectrum disorders. The guidelines are for parents and all who work with children and were developed by a multidisciplinary group of core professionals from Health, Education, Social Services and representatives of parents and the voluntary sector.

Early Support Programme: the Government programme to achieve better coordinated, family-focused services for young disabled children and their families. Early Years Foundation Stage (EYFS) is a government initiative setting the standards for learning, development and care for children from birth to five. It brings together: Curriculum Guidance for the Foundation Stage (2000), the Birth to Three Matters (2002) framework and the National Standards for Under 8s Daycare and Childminding (2003) building a coherent and flexible approach to care and learning. All providers are required to use the EYFS to ensure that whatever setting parents choose, they can be confident that their child will receive a quality experience that supports their development and learning.

National Portage Association: a charity offering support and information to parents and professionals involved in Portage.

OAASIS – Office for Advice, Assistance, Support and Information on Special needs: a resource for parents and professionals caring for children and young people with Autism/ Asperger's syndrome and other learning disabilities.

Local Education Authorities need to be creative in their placement of children on the autistic spectrum, focusing on the overall needs of the individual.

Effective early years programme addresses the 'triad of impairments' and sensory needs; building positive relations with those involved with the child.

The programme would focus on:

- communication;
- social interaction;
- play, leisure and life skills;
- access to a curriculum would include structure, visual learning, modelling and direct teaching of social skills;
- understanding the functions of behaviour and teaching acceptable behavioural responses.

## Multiple choice questions

1. What considerations should be taken into account when identifying an appropriate placement for a child with ASD?

   a. The special advisory support
   b. Peer group sizes and abilities
   c. The opportunity to mix with ASD and non-ASD children
   d. The expertise of staff
   e. All of the above

2. What are the characteristics of an effective early years programme?

   a. Communication, social interaction, play, leisure and life skills
   b. Access to a curriculum would include structure, visual learning and modelling and direct teaching of social skills
   c. Understanding the functions of behaviour and teaching acceptable behavioural responses
   d. A, B and C
   e. Role modelling from peers that have no ASD diagnosis

### Key texts

Attwood T (1998) *Asperger's Syndrome: A Guide for Parents and Professionals*. London: Jessica Kingsley Publications.

Autism Education Trust (Accessed 30 March 2011) Available from the World Wide Website: www.autismeducation trust.org.uk/goodpractise/earlyyears

Jordan RR (2003) *Educational Provision: Making Mainstream Schools Autism-friendly and Inclusion*. Birmingham: School of Education, University of Birmingham.

Lawson W (2011) Adolescents, Autism Spectrum Disorder And Secondary School (Accessed March 28 2011) www. mugsy.org: The NAS (Surrey Branch)/cgi-bin/tp.pl

My Asperger Child (Accessed March 28 2011) www. MyAspergerChild.com/Help for parents with Asperger children developing social skills at home and school.

Sensory Integration (Accessed April 2 2011) www.autism. com/fam_page.asp?PID=372

Wing L (1993) The definition and prevalence of autism: a review. *European Child and Adolescent Psychiatry*, **2**: 61–74.

## 41 Social stories for parents of autistic children

Rachel Leeke

> ## Key concepts
>
> - Unique, tailor-made stories written in a specific format and from the perspective of the young person with autistic spectrum disorder (ASD).
> - To develop a better understanding of specific events, situations, skills or concepts, so that young people can work out how to respond or behave more appropriately.
> - As the aim is to develop understanding rather than just learning a rote response, the focus should always be on describing rather than directing.
> - Social stories can be used to help in any situation that is confusing, upsetting, or that the young person is struggling in.
> - Social stories are a specific technique designed to help improve the social understanding of young people with ASD.

## Introduction

Impairments in social understanding can mean that young people with ASD are often unaware of the unwritten social rules and what is or is not, expected in certain situations. Their difficulties with understanding and making sense of others can mean that they struggle to work out what other people might be thinking and feeling or why they are doing what they are doing. Social stories, originally developed by Carol Gray in 1991, are designed to help improve the social understanding of young people with ASD.

## What are social stories?

Social stories are short, unique, tailor-made stories written in a specified style and format (e.g. Smith, 2003). Each story focuses on a specific event, situation, skill or concept and aims to help the young person understand this better. Stories may draw attention to unwritten social rules or taboos, relevant social cues, others perspectives or the consequences of certain actions (see Gray and McAndrew, 2001 for examples).

## How do social stories work?

Increasing the social understanding of young people with ASD can decrease the frustration and anxiety that they experience in certain situations. It may reduce the inappropriate or challenging behaviour that not understanding a social situation, and/or experiencing high levels of distress, can result in. Increased understanding allows young people to adapt and modify their behaviour. Social stories can help other people see things from the point of view of the young person with ASD, thereby increasing their understanding of the young person (Gray et al., 2005).

The evidence-base for the efficacy of social stories with young people with ASD is growing; however, due to their highly specific, individual nature, most research comprises very small numbers of subjects, case studies or single case experimental designs.

## What do social stories look like?

Social stories are written in the first person, as though the young person with ASD is describing the event themselves. They describe situations in a series of logical steps. (Also see Chapter 73, Social Stories.)

Four types of sentences are used:

1. Descriptive (relevant factual information)
2. Perspective (information about others' thoughts, feelings, reasons and motives)
3. Directive (appropriate responses the young person could try) and
4. Affirmative (reassurance and motivation for the young person).

The basic ratio of 0–1 directive sentence for every 2–5 descriptive or perspective sentences (Gray, 2010) ensures that the focus of the story is to help develop young people's social understanding, rather than teaching them a rote response.

The length, vocabulary and style of writing are tailored to the young person's age and level of understanding. Illustrations, photos or symbols can be used for younger children and more creative adaptations, for example presenting them as a short film or in a multimedia format are possible.

Once written, social stories need to be read and re-read with the young person: frequent repetition facilitates the learning. Re-reading stories before a young person enters a specific situation is particularly helpful as the information about that situation will be fresh in the mind and can be applied straight away.

# When can social stories be used?

Social stories can be used in any situation that is confusing or upsetting for a young person. These could include introducing changes to routine, preparing for trips or visits and any other new situations that the young person needs help to understand. They can be used to describe social situations (e.g. clubs, break times) and expectations and appropriate behaviour for those or to help young people understand when and why to use specific social skills. Emotions, such as fear and anger, can be the topic of a social story, focusing on increasing the young person's ability to recognize, label and manage these emotions.

## Multiple choice question

1. Which of these statements about social stories is not true?

    a. Social stories aim to increase a young person's social understanding
    b. Social stories tell young people what they should do in certain situations
    c. Social stories are written from the point of view of the young person
    d. Social stories can be presented in a range of mediums
    e. Social stories can help others to understand young people with ASD better

### Key texts

Gray C, McAndrew S (2001) *My Social Stories Book*. London: Jessica Kingsley.

Gray C (2010) *The New Social Story Book*. Arlington: Future Horizons Inc.

Gray C, Howey M, Arnold E (2005) *Revealing the Hidden Secret Code: Social Stories for People with Autistic Spectrum Disorders*. London: Jessica Kingsley.

Smith C (2003) *Writing and Developing Social Stories: Practical Interventions in Autism*. Milton Keynes: Speechmark Publishing Ltd.

### Web page

www.thegraycentre.org

# 42 Behavioural problems in children with learning difficulties

Chantal Homan, Chris Hardie, Catherine Thompson and Ettore Guaia

## Key concepts

- Children and young people with learning disabilities (LD) are at an increased risk of developing mental health problems when compared to their typically developing peers.
- Challenging behaviour is often associated with mental health problems and is the most common reason for children and young people with learning disabilities to be referred to child and adolescent mental health services (CAMHS).
- Assessing the mental health needs of children and young people with learning disabilities requires a highly specialist set of skills involving an understanding of the relationship of genetic, neurological and social predispositions of this client group to mental health problems.
- Children with challenging behaviour, especially those with self-injurious behaviour (SIB), may have an underlying physical health problem. Remember diagnostic overshadowing.
- Children and young people with LD are more at risk from abuse which may in turn present with challenging behaviour.

Research has consistently demonstrated that children and young people with learning disabilities are at increased risk of developing mental health problems.

## Introduction

Rutter et al.'s (1976) Isle of Wight Study was one of the first to identify the increased prevalence rate of mental health problems in children with a learning disability, highlighting that children and young people with learning disabilities are 3–4 times more likely to develop mental health problems than their typically developing peers. Many studies have reached similar conclusions and it is now well accepted that approximately 40 per cent of children and young people with learning disabilities will develop mental health problems (Emerson and Hatton, 2007) with rates of conduct disorder, anxiety disorders, attention deficit hyperactivity disorder (ADHD) and autism spectrum disorders (ASD) being higher among children and young people with learning disabilities (Emerson, 2003). For many families it is the challenging behaviour,

which can be associated with mental health problems, that pose the largest challenge, impacting not only on the child's health and wellbeing, but on that of the family as a whole.

This chapter will give an overview of the factors relevant to the mental health of children and young people with learning disabilities, moving on to consider the assessment of need and interventions suited to the client group.

## Definition of learning disability

Learning disability, as defined by Valuing People (Department of Health, 2001b), includes the presence of a significantly reduced ability to understand new or complex information, to learn new skills (impaired intelligence) with a reduced ability to cope independently (impaired social functioning) and which started before adulthood, with a lasting effect on development.

A diagnosis of learning disability is traditionally applied in practice when an individual's IQ score falls below 70 on a psychometric assessment. The level of learning disability is defined based on an individual's overall score. A child may have a very unequal profile of strengths and weaknesses and a full scale IQ may not be especially helpful or a child may not have had a previous psychometric assessment. A diagnosis of learning disability may therefore be applied, based on an individual's level of impairment in social or adaptive skills (see **Table 42.1**).

Table 42.1 Levels of learning disability

|  | Mild | Moderate | Severe | Profound |
|---|---|---|---|---|
| ICD-10 | 69–50 | 49–35 | 34–20 | Less than 20 |

## Aetiology

The aetiology of learning disabilities is a combination of genetic, organic and psychosocial factors that impact upon development at the prenatal, perinatal and postnatal stages. The most common causes at each stage are highlighted in **Table 42.2**.

Table 42.2 Common causes of learning disabilities

| Prenatal | Perinatal | Postnatal |
|---|---|---|
| Chromosome disorders, e.g. Down syndrome | Premature birth and its complications | Environmental deprivation, e.g. psychosocial disadvantage, child abuse and neglect, chronic social and sensory deprivation |
| Autosomal deletion disorders, e.g. Cri du chat syndrome, 22q11.2 | Lack of oxygen causing asphyxia | Injury (accidental and non-accidental) |
| Triplet Repeat Expansion disorder, e.g. Fragile X | Complications through abnormal labour and/or delivery, e.g. haemorrhaging in the brain | Infection, e.g. meningitis, encephalitis |
| Gene mutation, e.g Tuberous Sclerosis (AD) | Hypoglycaemia | |
| Smith Lemli Opitz (AR) | | |
| Prenatal insults e.g. infection, CMV, rubella | | |
| Alcohol and substance misuse, e.g. Fetal Alcohol syndrome | | |

AD, autosomal dominant; AR, autosomal recessive.

## Definition of challenging behaviour

The most widely accepted definition of challenging behaviour is:

> 'Culturally abnormal behaviour of such intensity, frequency or duration that the physical safety of the person or others is likely to be placed in serious jeopardy, or behaviour that is likely to seriously limit use of, or result in the person being denied access to, ordinary community facilities'.
>
> **(Emerson, 1995)**

The most common challenging behaviours reported in children and young people with learning disabilities include:

- verbal and/or physical aggression;
- damage to property;
- self-injurious behaviour;
- non-compliance;
- stereotypical/ritualized behaviours;
- inappropriate urinating/defecating, including smearing;
- inappropriate sexualized behaviours.

Challenging behaviour is the most common reason for children and young people with learning disabilities to be referred to CAMHS. Emerson et al.

(1999) offered two suggestions as possible ways in which challenging behaviours may be associated with mental health problems:

1. Challenging behaviours may be an atypical presentation of an underlying mental health problem.
2. Challenging behaviours may be a secondary feature of mental health problems or underlying psychiatric symptoms may establish and maintain challenging behaviours.

In addition, the authors would propose that the presence of challenging behaviour indicates a level of emotional distress within the child/young person that needs to be recognized.

# Risk factors

Children and young people with learning disabilities face a multitude of biological, psychological and social risk factors affecting their mental health.

Psychological risk factors include:

- fewer coping strategies;
- low self-esteem;
- awareness of disability and difference to their typically developing peers;
- physical ill health in parents;
- mental ill health in parents. Emerson and Hatton (2007) found that 44 per cent of children with learning disabilities are cared for by a mother who has mental health difficulties, compared to 24 per cent of the typically developing population.

Social risk factors include;

- abuse;
- bullying;
- isolation;
- living in residential/institutional care;
- living in poverty. Approximately 55 per cent of families of children with disabilities have a low income (compared to 30 per cent in the

typically developing population) and the cost of bringing up a child with a disability is three times greater (Emerson and Hatton, 2007). There are more children with learning disabilities living within single parent families.

Biological risk factors include:

- physical disability;
- gastrointestinal (GI) problems, for example reflux and constipation;
- sensory impairments;
- epilepsy;
- specific genetic syndromes, for example Velocardiofacial syndrome.

## Behavioural phenotypes

The term behavioural phenotype refers to behaviours that are believed to be an integral part of certain genetic disorders. Nyhan (1972) first formally introduced the concept in connection with the self-harming behaviours that characterize Lesch–Nyhan syndrome. Flint and Yule (1993) have since provided a more thorough definition;

*'The behavioural phenotype is a characteristic pattern of motor, cognitive, linguistic and social abnormalities which is consistently associated with a biological disorder. In some cases, the behavioural phenotype may constitute a psychiatric disorder; in others, behaviours which are not normally regarded as symptoms of psychiatric diagnosis may occur.'*

**Table 42.3** provides a brief overview of the behavioural phenotypes, the genotype, medical conditions associated with them and associated psychiatric disorders for some of the more common syndromes. Not all children and young people will display all aspects of the behavioural phenotype. For a more comprehensive overview the reader should refer to specific genetic texts or to the Society for the Study of Behavioural Phenotypes (www.ssbp.org.uk).

Table 42.3 Overview of the behavioural phenotypes, the genotype, medical conditions associated with them and associated psychiatric disorders for some of the more common syndromes

| Condition | Comment | Physical findings | Behaviour/mental health |
|---|---|---|---|
| 22q11.2<br>Interstitial deletion | 1:4,000<br>Includes velocardiofacial syndrome and Di-George syndrome | Cleft palate<br>Congenital heart defects<br>Renal disorders<br>Lack of or underdeveloped thymus and parathyroid glands<br>Immunological dysfunction | Attention Deficit Disorder / Attention Deficit Hyperactivity Disorder<br>Exaggerated response to threatening stimuli<br>Fearfulness of painful situations<br>Autism spectrum disorder<br><br>In adolescence/early adulthood can develop-<br>Schizophrenia/ schizoaffective disorder<br>Manic depressive illness/ psychosis<br>Rapid or ultra rapid cycling of mood<br>Mood disorder, depression |
| Angelman<br><br>Autosomal deletion 68–75% (mother)<br>Uniparental disomy 2–7% (father)<br>Imprinting centre defects 2–5%<br>Mutation in UBE3A gene (8–11%%)<br>Some not found | 1;40,00 live births<br><br>Also known as happy puppet syndrome<br><br>15q11–13 | Hypopigmented hair, skin and eyes compared to other family members<br>Ataxic movements<br>Initial hypotonia to hypertonia<br>Over 80% develop seizures with a characteristic EEG appearance | Sleep difficulties<br>Increased levels of smiling, laughing and being happy<br>Excessive sociability<br>Hyperactivity and poor attention<br>Aggression |
| Cornelia de Lange<br><br>Gene mutation | 1:50 000<br>20–50% NIP-BL gene on chromosome 5<br><br>SMC3 on chromosome 10 and<br>X linked SMC1–5% and milder phenotype | Low birth weight<br>Short stature<br>Distinctive facies<br>Gastrointestinal disorders especially reflux and aspiration<br>Vision and hearing problems<br>Cardiac problems<br>Genitourinary problems | Shy and socially anxious<br>Selective mutism<br>Autism Spectrum Disorder (ASD)<br>Compulsive behaviour-tidying up, lining things up<br>Self-injurious behaviour (SIB) |
| Cri du chat<br><br>Autosomal deletion | Deletion of the short arm of chromosome 5 (5p-)<br>One of the most common deletion syndromes<br>Incidence 1/20 000 to 1/50 000 births<br>85% de novo | Cat-like cry<br>Feeding difficulties and failure to thrive in infancy<br>Microcephaly<br>Growth retardation<br>Gastro-oesophageal reflux<br>Respiratory tract infections<br>Ear infections | Sleep difficulties<br>Aggression<br>(SIB)<br>Hyperactivity |

| Condition | Comment | Physical findings | Behaviour/mental health |
|---|---|---|---|
| **Down syndrome**<br><br>Trisomy 21 (95%)<br><br>Translocation (2%)<br><br>Mosaicism (2%)<br><br>Chromosome rearrangements (1%) | Incidence: 1:7300 | Visual problems<br>Hearing difficulties – 38–78% individuals<br>Endocrine-hypo/hyperthyroidism<br>-diabetes<br>Congenital heart disease-incidence around 50%<br>Growth delay<br>Obstructive Sleep Apnoea-incidence: 30–75%<br>Gastrointestinal<br>Occur in about 5%<br>Cervical spine disorders-X-ray **not** predictive | Stubborn<br>Obsessional<br>Dislike of conflict<br><br>Under 20 years:<br>17.6% psychiatric disorder<br>ADHD<br>Anxiety<br>ASD<br>Conduct/<br>Oppositional<br>Aggression |
| **Fragile X**<br><br>Xq27.3<br><br>Triplet repeat-CGG<br>>200 Fragile X<br><br>55–100 pre-mutation | 1:4000–1:6000<br><br>Most common inherited form of LD<br><br>80% of males have LD | Can be difficult to detect clinically large head, long face and prominent ears<br>Connective tissue dysplasia leading to joint laxity and heart valve problems<br>Vision problems<br>Hearing problems<br>Problems with numeracy and visual spatial skills<br>Issues for both male and females with a pre-mutation | Social anxiety and aversion to eye contact<br>Anxiety<br>Hand flapping<br>ADHD<br>Aggression<br>ASD – 30% (SIB especially hand biting)<br>Those without autism said to be socially more responsive and affectionate |
| **Prader–Willi**<br><br>Autosomal deletion 70% (father)<br>Uniparental disomy 25% (mother)<br>Rest-imprinting centre defects and unbalanced translocations | Incidence: 1/29000<br><br>15q11-13 | Severe hypotonia at birth<br><br>Growth/nutrition – FTT in infancy and obesity due to excessive appetite and hyperphagia develops between 1 and 6 years of age<br>Hypogonadism | Changes in routine leading to temper tantrums leading to aggression and severe behavioural problems<br>SIB-skin picking<br>Obsessional traits<br>Impulsivity<br>ASD |
| **Rett**<br><br>95% due to MECP2 gene on the X chromosome | 1:10000–1:23000 | Breathing irregularities<br>Repetitive hand movements<br>Epilepsy (about 50%) with EEG abnormalities<br>Unsteady gait (about 50% become independently mobile), scoliosis<br>Muscles more rigid as age leading to joint deformity<br>Feeding difficulties and growth retardation<br>Gut-reflux and constipation | Self-injurious behaviour<br>Sleep difficulties<br>Anxiety<br>Mood changes<br>Teeth grinding |
| **Rubinstein–Taybi** | 1;125000<br>55% due to deletion in 16p13<br>5% due to changes in 22q13<br>Rest not known as yet | Feeding difficulties<br>Gastro-oesophageal reflux<br>CHD<br>Vision problems<br>Constipation<br>High pain threshold<br>Dislike loud noises | Sleep problems (? secondary to breathing difficulties)<br>Happy and friendly<br>Dislike change in routine<br>Short concentration span<br>Rock, spin and flap |

| Condition | Comment | Physical findings | Behaviour/mental health |
|---|---|---|---|
| Smith–Lemli–Opitz  Gene mutation- autosomal recessive | Incidence: 1/20 000 to 30 000 Mutations in DHCR 7 gene on 11q13 Inborn error of cholesterol synthesis | Webbing of toes Dysmorphic facial features Microcephaly CHD | Sleep difficulties  SIB  ASD |
| Smith Magenis  ? due to a single gene defect | Birth prevalence of 1;25 000  Deletion of 17p11 | Infantile hypotonia Failure to thrive (FTT) as an infant Congential heart disease (CHD) Vision and hearing problems 75% peripheral neuropathy resulting in insensitivity to pain | Severe sleep problems – settling, wakening and shortened length Severe challenging behaviour, temper tantrums and severe aggression Features of ADHD Self-mutilation |
| Tuberous sclerosis complex  Gene mutation | 1:6 000  Spontaneous mutation in 70% Autosomal dominant in 30% 2 genes – TSC1 (9q34) TSC2 (16p13.3) | Multi-system disorder Brain, kidneys, heart, eyes, skin, teeth, bone, lung and others 50–60% LD | Sleep difficulties 25% ASD ADHD SIB Adolescents/adults-anxiety and depression |
| Williams syndrome  Autosomal deletion | Incidence 1:7500– 1:20 000  Deletion of 7q11.23 | Hypercalcaemia in infancy (15%)  FTT, feeding difficulties and short stature Congenital heart disease- supravalvular problems Kidney problems Constipation Hyperacusis Cocktail chatter Dental caries | Abnormal attachment behaviours as infants Sleep difficulties Anxiety and fears Preoccupations and obsessions Highly sociable/overly friendly particularly with adults Overactivity, poor concentration and distractible |

# Assessment

Assessing the mental health needs of children and young people with learning disabilities, who often present with behavioural challenges, is a complex task. The child's ability to communicate their thoughts, feelings and experiences may be significantly impaired or altogether absent. Assessment therefore comprises information pulled together from a variety of sources, including:

- medical assessment and investigations to ensure that there are no underlying physical health problems which may be impacting on the child's behaviour, particularly if there is self-injury;
- observations across environments;
- interview with child/young person, when possible;
- parental knowledge;
- interviews with other professionals;
- use of standardized behavioural measures (where applicable) such as the Developmental Behaviour Checklist (Einfeld and Tonge, 1992);
- information gathering from previous assessments;
- any child protection concerns.

The professional will need to employ a range of strategies to engage the child/young person as much as possible in the assessment, taking into consideration factors such as any additional special needs of the child, for example sensory difficulties, communication style and ability.

The environment in which such assessments are undertaken should be afforded careful consideration. Often simply accessing unfamiliar environments, such as the CAMHS clinic or GP surgery, can be anxiety provoking for children and young people with learning disabilities. A more suitable environment may be the child's home or school environment, where they are familiar with the surroundings and the people supporting them.

A highly specialist set of skills is required to carry out such assessments. Alongside a thorough understanding of the needs of children and young people with learning disabilities, those involved in the assessment process should have an understanding of the genetic, neurological and social predispositions of this client group to mental health problems. A sound knowledge base of developmental disorders, particularly ADHD and ASD due to their high co-morbidity in children and young people with learning disabilities, is required (McDougall, 2006).

## Diagnostic overshadowing

This is where a child's presenting symptom(s) is attributed to their learning disability, rather than a potentially treatable cause. For example, if the child develops a new, troubling behaviour or a behaviour he already has becomes worse, consider:

- physical: pain from a tooth, ear infection, reflux, constipation or a deterioration in vision or hearing;
- psychiatric: depression, anxiety, psychosis;
- social: abuse, bereavement, change in carers.

## Interventions

While the evidence relating to the mental health needs of children and young people with learning disabilities is growing, it remains in its infancy. At present, there is no significant body of evidence relating to the effectiveness of interventions for treating the mental health problems of children and young people with learning disabilities. However, there is no reason to suggest that children and young people with learning disabilities will respond any differently to the biological, psychological, educational and social interventions currently employed for children and young people without learning disabilities.

Such interventions rarely refer to the age of the child. A CAMHS service working with children and young people between the ages of 5 and 16 is likely to cover a 'developmental range' from the four-year level to the 20-year level. Most young people with learning disabilities, despite their chronological age, are likely to fall within this developmental range: the exception being children and young people with severe and profound levels of learning disability.

Interventions can be made accessible in two ways (Gale, 2003):

1. Age-appropriate intervention is chosen and modified to make it developmentally appropriate.
2. Developmentally appropriate intervention is chosen and then modified to make it age appropriate.

In addition, many CAMHS interventions such as parental training and family therapy are directed towards parents and carers, rather than towards the child themselves. Such interventions are not dependent upon the child's ability to engage.

**Table 42.4** provides some examples of interventions considered effective for anxiety disorders and ADHD and how these may be modified to be accessible for children and young people with learning disabilities.

Treatment options for medical conditions associated with behavioural difficulties and learning disability are shown in **Table 42.5**.

## Case study: Amy

Amy, aged 10, has moderate learning disabilities, autism and epilepsy. She lives at home with her mother and younger sister and attends a mainstream school with additional support. Amy was referred to the local CAMHS team by her GP due to high levels of challenging behaviour that were placing her at risk of exclusion from her school placement. Amy's behaviour had a considerable impact upon her family. Her mother had given up work to provide additional care for Amy, placing extra financial stress upon the family, and she had been prescribed antidepressants by her GP. Amy's sister's sleep and education was affected by her behaviour. She experienced many sleepless nights and was falling asleep in her lessons at school.

A detailed assessment and functional analysis (see Chapter 71, Applied behavioural analysis (including children with learning difficulties)) led to the development of a behaviour programme that was implemented across environments. Changes to Amy's environment, introduction of communication systems, use of scheduling, teaching of relaxation skills and introduction of reward systems were some of the techniques used.

The interventions brought about positive changes in Amy's behaviour that both prevented an exclusion from school and increased the opportunities available to her because she was able to start accessing after-school activities. A more settled education placement meant that Amy's mother was able to seek part-time employment. Reduction in challenging behaviours at home meant that Amy's sister was able to settle into a healthy sleep routine, improving her alertness at school. A considerable increase in her academic achievement was noted. The all-round reduction of stress and anxiety meant that Amy's mother was able to speak with her GP about no longer needing antidepressants.

Table 42.4 Examples of interventions

| Condition | Interventions considered effective | Consideration for children and young people with learning disabilities |
|---|---|---|
| Anxiety disorder | Behavioural interventions and CBT are first line treatment (see Chapter 72, Cognitive behaviour therapy) | There is strong evidence for behavioural interventions with children and young people with learning disabilities and they are often the intervention of choice. Cognitive approaches will be affected by the child's ability but cognitive approaches can be used with children under 10 years of age |
| | Involvement of parents is recommended | |
| | Psycho-educational approaches for managing anxiety (see Chapter 36, Attention deficit hyperactivity disorder) | |
| ADHD | Behaviourally based parent management training | Parent management training is dependent upon engagement of parents, as with typically developing peers |
| | Behavioural interventions across settings | There is no evidence to suggest response to medication is any different for children with learning disabilities, although consideration would need to be given to its interaction with any other medication the child may be taking |
| | Alterations to environment | |
| | Medication (see Chapter 36, Attention deficit hyperactivity disorder) | |
| | Teaching of coping strategies to the child | |

# Case study: Joe

Joe, aged 4, has autism and Severe Learning Difficulty (SLD). His behaviour has always been difficult, but his head banging has increased over the last two months. He does not have any words and only situational understanding. A detailed history was taken from his mother and it appears that Joe has lost his appetite recently and, when examined, has not gained any weight. Although he has been opening his bowels every other day, his stools are 'like rabbit droppings' (Bristol Stool Chart Type 1). He has faecal masses when his abdomen is palpated.

Table 42.5 Treatment options

| Condition | Investigation | Treatment | |
|---|---|---|---|
| Reflux | pH probe | Environmental | Raise head of bed 6–8 inches |
| | Barium swallow and follow through | Drugs | Gaviscon, H2 blocker |
| | Endoscopy | | Domperidone/omeprazole |
| | | | Surgery |
| Unsafe swallow | Videofluoroscopy | Thicken liquids/mash food | Dietetic involvement |
| | | Gastrostomy | Surgery |
| Constipation | History | Fluids and dietary manipulation | NICE guidelines |
| | Rarely x-ray | Laxatives | |
| Pain | Dependent where? | Pain relief | |
| Dental pain | Dentist | Pain relief | Preventative-fluoride |
| | | Dental treatment | |
| Sleep problems | History | Good sleep hygiene | Straightforward: Vallergan/melatonin |
| | Investigations undertaken at home/overnight stay | Medication | More complex: Use of sedatives/atypical antipsychotics (i.e. risperidone) can be considered but under specialist supervision, high risk of side effects and possible worsening of the symptoms |
| | | Sleep clinic | |
| Epilepsy | Eye witness account of the episode(s) | Medication | |
| | Electroencephalogram (ECG) | Vagus nerve stimulation (VNS) | |
| | | Diet | |
| Visual difficulties | Ophthalmological opinion | Glasses | Special teacher advisor for children with visual impairment |
| | | | Special classroom aids |
| Hearing difficulties | Audiology opinion | Refer to Ear Nose and Throat specialist | Hearing aids |
| | | | STA children with hearing impairment |
| Sensory difficulties | Occupational Therapy sensory assessment | Sensory diet/programme | |
| Hyperacusis | Audiology/ENT assessment | Acoustic training | |

A dietary sheet and advice regarding fluids is given to his mother. Copies are given to his special school and his short break carer. Laxatives were started (as per NICE guidelines) and a bowel chart instituted. On review, Joe is now opening his bowels regularly, his self-injurious behaviour has greatly reduced and he is putting on weight. His diet remains restricted, but with occupational therapy and Speech and Language Therapy intervention, he has begun to extend the range of food he eats.

# Conclusion

Children and young people with learning disabilities are exposed to higher risk factors impacting upon their mental health than their typically developing peers. Awareness of this and an understanding of the epidemiology and aetiology of learning disability are crucial when considering the mental health and/or behavioural challenges of this population group. A thorough assessment of need requires a specialist skill set and input from many disciplines if an appropriate understanding of the difficulties is to be reached and an effective care plan developed.

## Multiple choice questions

1. A diagnosis of learning disability is traditionally applied in practice when an individual's IQ score falls below:

   a. 90
   b. 70
   c. 60

2. Approximately how many children and young people with learning disabilities will develop mental health problems?

   a. 40 per cent
   b. 30 per cent
   c. 10 per cent

3. Which mental health problem is higher among children and young people with learning disabilities?

   a. Psychosis
   b. Anorexia nervosa
   c. Anxiety disorder

4. Which intervention is often the treatment of choice when managing challenging behaviour in children and young people with learning disabilities?

   a. Pharmacological interventions
   b. Family therapy
   c. Behavioural interventions

## Key texts

Bernard S (2010) Epidemiology and aetiology. In: Raghavan R, Bernard S, McCarthy J (eds). *Mental Health Needs of Children and Young People with Learning Disabilities.* Brighton: Pavilion Publishing.

Department of Health (2001b) *Valuing People: A New Strategy for Learning Disability for the 21st Century.* London: The Stationary Office.

Emerson E (2003) Prevalence of psychiatric disorders in children and adolescents with and without intellectual disability. *Journal of Intellectual Disability Research,* **47**: 51–8.

McDougall T (2006) Nursing children and young people with learning disabilities and mental health problems. In: McDougall T (ed.). *Child and Adolescent Mental Health Nursing.* Oxford: Blackwell Publishing.

Society for the Study of Behavioural Phenotypes www.ssbp.org.uk

# 43 Anxiety and phobias

Roxanne Magdalena

## Key concepts

- Anxiety is seen as abnormal or pathological if it is out of proportion to the situation at hand, persisting or interferes with daily functioning or quality of life.
- Between 8 and 27 per cent of children and adolescents will meet the criteria for at least one anxiety disorder (Manassis et al., 2010). Point prevalence rates for anxiety disorders, for example prevalence rates over a six-month or year-long period, are not considerably lower than lifetime estimates, indicating their chronic and persistent nature.
- Anxiety presents as physical, emotional or behavioural disorders.
- Common childhood anxieties include separation anxiety and specific phobias and in adolescence as generalized anxiety disorder, social phobia, panic disorder and agoraphobia.
- There is good evidence for cognitive behaviour therapy (CBT), selective serotonin reuptake inhibitors (SSRIs) and venlafaxine. Relaxation techniques and bibliotherapy can play a role

Internalizing disorders in childhood and adolescence refers to a set of conditions whose central feature is disordered mood or emotions (Kovacs and Devlin, 1998). This chapter explores the significant internalizing disorders that may present in the CAMHS setting.

## Introduction

The term 'anxiety' describes a cluster of symptoms that includes worries and fears, but is different from stress. Anxiety can be a normal emotional response which is purposeful in certain situations, for example preparing the body for a 'fight or flight' response.

## Symptoms

- Physical: heart racing/pounding, sweating, shaking, dizziness, 'butterflies', nausea, vomiting, dry mouth, headaches, hyperventilation. In younger children, may present as somatic complaints, for example stomach ache.
- Emotional: Worry, fear, feeling 'on edge' or under threat, irritability.
- Behaviour: Avoidance of situation, maladaptive ways of coping with anxiety.

## Aetiology/risk factors

### Demographics

Wittchen et al. (1998) report that all anxiety disorders are around twice as frequent in females, with gender differences increasing with age. Higher rates are associated with reduced education status and low household income.

### Genetics

Children of parents with at least one anxiety disorder have an increased risk of having an anxiety disorder, with the risk increasing with the severity of that parent's condition (Schreier et al., 2008) and when both parents are affected (Johnson et al., 2008). Genetic heritability ranges from 30 to 40 per cent (Beesdo et al., 2009).

## Temperament

Personality traits, including neuroticism and behavioural inhibition (Kagan, 1989), may be important in the development of anxiety disorders. Behavioural inhibition is associated with shyness around strangers and fear in unfamiliar situations (Biederman et al., 2001).

## Psychological theory of conditioning

Previously neutral stimuli become associated with a frightening experience, subsequently leading to avoidance. The amygdala (part of the temporal lobe in the brain) is involved in learning to fear a previously harmless object.

## Parenting style

Parental overprotection and rejection is associated with higher rates of social phobia (Knappe et al., 2009). Social learning and parental modelling of anxious behaviour or avoidance may play a role (Ollendick et al., 2001).

## Trauma and adverse life events

Childhood adversity is linked to the onset of later difficulties; this is not specific to anxiety (Moffitt et al., 2007). Anxiety is related to threat events and smaller events may have a cumulative effect.

## Attachment theory

Separation anxiety arises from actual or threatened separation from attachment figures (see Chapter 12, Emotional development and attachment).

# Anxieties in childhood

## Separation anxiety

This occurs when anxiety over separation is developmentally inappropriate and impacts on the child's functioning. This affects 2–4 per cent of children and is the most common anxiety disorder in prepubertal children.

## Specific phobia

This is a fear associated with a specific object or event, which is out of proportion to the reality of the situation. The object is avoided or endured with intense anxiety. This results in significant social incapacity or distress. Specific phobias affect 2–4 per cent of children and adolescents and are more common in girls.

Different fears peak at different ages, according to Goodman and Scott (2002) and Beesdo et al. (2009), for example:

- fear of animals, thunder and lightning at age 2–4;
- fear of the dark and imaginary creatures at age 4–5;
- fear of illness and natural disasters at age 5–7;
- fear of war and negative social evaluation during adolescence.

# Anxieties in adolescence

- Generalized anxiety disorder: Symptoms include being fearful and worried most days, about various topics or minor events, or possibly worries about topics outside of conscious awareness. Prevalence is up to 0.8 per cent, with a later onset in boys.
- Social phobia: Prevalence is between 0.5 and 3.7 per cent. It typically emerges in late childhood and through adolescence with very few cases starting after age 25.
- Panic disorder, with or without agoraphobia: The age of onset is typically 15–19 years. Panic attacks occur, with or without identifiable triggers. Agoraphobia consists of anxiety in situations where escape would be difficult or embarrassing. It typically has a prevalence of up to 5.2 per cent and panic disorder up to 1.6 per cent.

# Interventions

## Cognitive behaviour therapy

A Cochrane review (James et al., 2007) demonstrated that CBT is an effective treatment for anxiety disorders. It can be adapted for the age of six years and upwards and can be delivered in individual, group and family formats. The review stated that CBT appears effective in just over 50 per cent of cases. CBT can be combined with relaxation techniques, including deep breathing, meditation and muscle relaxation (see Chapter 72, Cognitive behaviour therapy).

## Pharmacotherapy

A further Cochrane review (Manassis et al., 2010) suggests that psychotherapy remains the first line treatment for mild to moderate symptoms, with pharmacotherapy being considered for severe or treatment-resistant anxiety disorders. Manassis et al. (2010) found that SSRIs and venlafaxine were more effective than placebo for anxiety disorders. A combination of CBT and medication showed significant reductions in anxiety symptoms.

## Parent training

This may result in improved global functioning, but a study by Khanna and Kendall (2009) showed that it did not improve specific measures of child anxiety.

## Bibliotherapy/self-help

Rapee et al. (2006) showed that compared to children on a waiting list, use of written materials for parents resulted in around 15 per cent more children being free of an anxiety disorder diagnosis after 12 and 24 weeks.

---

## Case study 1: Dylan

Dylan is a six-year-old boy, who presented with nightmares, clinginess and ongoing difficulties with separation from his mother and who had started to refuse school. He initially reported a variety of somatic complaints, including daily headaches, stomach-aches, nausea and vomiting. Dylan has always been sensitive, particularly to the needs of his mother and to the fact that his parents had recently separated, but were still living together. Dylan's mother has a history of depression and anxiety. She allowed Dylan to stay off school because she was worried that forcing him to go would cause more distress and unhappiness.

### Initial formulation

Dylan shows symptoms of separation anxiety resulting in school refusal, in the context of family conflict. The situation is maintained by a misunderstanding of his symptoms of anxiety and avoidance of the situation.

### Assessment

Assessment involved taking a full developmental history, an understanding of Dylan's relationships with his parents, his temperament and coping mechanisms, an understanding of the impact of parental conflict and possible genetic factors. Dylan was seen on his own and with his parents.

### Treatment

The treatment involved liaising with school. It was explained to parents that avoidance maintains anxiety, so by not attending school or leaving his mother, Dylan did not have the opportunity to learn that his anxious thoughts and fears would not come true. Dylan's anxieties were formulated into a Cognitive Behavioural model and relaxation techniques were taught to him and his parents.

---

## Case study 2: Sally

Sally, aged 15, had always been shy and somewhat unassertive. She was assessed following a panic attack which occurred in public. She reported waiting in classrooms at school until her peers had left the corridors to avoid the crowds. In group situations, Sally felt that she was being judged and worried about what other people thought of her. When she had to speak in front of others, she felt her mouth go dry and her cheeks go uncontrollably red, so she avoided these situations. If she was forced to speak, she became very anxious and distressed. This had resulted in her falling behind in school, due to worries about asking questions in lessons and avoiding lessons involving group work. She had begun to spend less time with her friends in group situations and avoided going to parties.

### Initial formulation
Social phobia is associated with the avoidance of social relationships, particularly with unfamiliar people, and the intense fear of public scrutiny and humiliation.

### Assessment
Assessment involved a developmental history, an understanding of Sally's previous social relationships, coping skills and patterns of avoidance, enquiries about substance use and a family history.

### Treatment
Treatment with CBT included testing out her thoughts of being judged and helping her to understand that avoidance maintains social anxiety. The option of medication, for example using an SSRI, was considered due to the intensity of Sally's symptoms.

## Case study 3: Molly

Molly, a 10-year-old girl, had started to lose weight after changing her eating habits. Following a viral illness when she had been physically sick, Molly had drastically reduced her food and fluid intake. She explained that eating and drinking moderate amounts led to a feeling of fullness. She then worried that she would vomit the food. She interpreted her physical symptoms of anxiety as a sign that she was going to be sick and began to associate food with vomiting.

### Initial formulation
A phobia of vomiting, from a previous negative incident of being sick, can result in the association of a harmless object (food) with an uncomfortable experience.

### Assessment
Assessment involved taking a developmental and family history, including family attitudes to food and anxiety, exclusion of pathology indicating depression or an eating disorder and checking her physical health.

### Treatment
Exposure therapy, known as systematic desensitization, involved exposing Molly, in a safe and controlled way, to increased food and fluid intakes, first in her imagination and then in reality. This was coupled with testing out her negative thoughts and with relaxation techniques.

## Multiple choice questions

1. Which statement is correct regarding agoraphobia?

   a. Cannot occur with panic attacks
   b. Consists of anxiety in a situation where escape is difficult
   c. Is a fear of open spaces
   d. Typically starts in childhood
   e. Usually presents with somatic complaints

2. Which statement is correct regarding treatment of anxiety disorders?

a. SSRIs and CBT cannot be used together
b. Pharmacotherapy can be considered for severe disorders
c. Parent training is highly effective
d. Bibliotherapy/self-help has not been shown to be beneficial
e. CBT is effective in the vast majority of cases

3. Which statement is correct regarding the aetiology of anxiety disorders?

a. They are around 60 per cent heritable
b. Conditioning involves the frontal lobes
c. Smaller life events do not have an effect on anxiety
d. Social learning can contribute to anxiety disorders.
e. Personality traits are unrelated to anxiety

4. Which statement is correct regarding anxiety disorders presenting in childhood?

a. Separation anxiety presents in adolescence
b. Separation anxiety is thought to arise mainly from genetic factors
c. Specific phobias affect up to 4 per cent of children
d. Proportionate fears are part of specific phobias
e. Fear of negative social evaluation is common in young children

5. Which statement is correct regarding anxiety disorders in adolescence?

a. Panic attacks typically arise in late teens
b. Generalized anxiety disorder affects up to 4 per cent of children
c. Social phobia onset occurs equally throughout the lifespan
d. Panic attacks always have a trigger
e. Panic attacks have a prevalence of 10 per cent

## Key texts

Khanna MS, Kendall PC (2009) Exploring the role of parent training in the treatment of childhood anxiety. *Journal of Consulting and Clinical Psychology*, **77**: 981–6.

Manassis K, Russell K, Newton AS (2010) The Cochrane Library and the treatment of childhood and adolescent anxiety disorders: an overview of reviews. *Evidence-Based Child Health: A Cochrane Review Journal*, **5**: 541–54.

Ollendick TH, Vasey MW, King NJ et al. (2001) Operant conditioning influences in childhood anxiety. In: Vasey MW, Dadds MR (eds). *The Developmental Psycho-pathology of Anxiety*. New York: Oxford University Press, 231–52.

## Web pages

www.anxietyuk.org.uk/ General information on anxieties.

www.childanxiety.net/ The Child Anxiety Network.

www.kidshealth.org/teen/your_mind/mental_health/phobias. html Information on anxiety and phobias aimed at teenagers.

www.moodjuice.scot.nhs.uk/phobias.asp A self-help guide for phobias.

www.rcpsych.ac.uk/pdf/Sheet13.pdf Information leaflet from the Royal College of Psychiatrists on helping children to cope with anxieties.

# *Obsessive compulsive disorder*
Joanna Barker

## Key concepts

- OCD is a disorder that has been estimated to affect 0.25–2 per cent of children and adolescents.
- It is characterized by the presence of either obsessions or compulsions, but usually both.
- An obsession is defined as an unwanted intrusive thought, image or urge that repeatedly enters a person's mind. Although recognized as being their own thoughts, they are experienced as 'ego dystonic' (out of character, unwanted and distressing). In children and adolescents, the most common obsessions include fears of contamination, harm and death.
- Compulsions are repetitive behaviours or mental acts that the person feels driven to perform and hard to resist. A compulsion can either be an external action, such as checking that a door is locked, or internal action, such as repeating a certain phrase in one's mind. They are often intended to reduce the anxiety provoked by the obsessions. They are not enjoyable and do not result in the completion of any useful task. They are time-consuming, often interfering with social functioning and, in severe cases, may prevent the child from going to school. Children may involve their family in their compulsive acts, for example in checking, counting or cleaning, or may persistently demand reassurance.
- The symptoms can cause significant distress and disrupt social and academic functioning.
- If untreated, OCD generally persists, yet effective, evidence-based treatments are available.

## Introduction

Obsessive compulsive disorder (OCD) can be chronic, continuous or episodic. One in three children with OCD will make a complete recovery. Half of cases persist into adulthood and one in ten follow a chronic deteriorating course.

Most children with OCD have both obsessions and compulsions, although they can present with obsessions without overt rituals. They are often embarrassed by their symptoms and may try to keep them secret. It is thought that OCD can start at any time from preschool to adulthood and there are two peaks of presentation:

- between ages 10 and 12;
- between the late teens and early adulthood.

In childhood there are more boys with prepubertal onset (ratio is 3M:2F). The ratio then equalizes in adolescence.

OCD is thought to be associated with altered brain functioning in the basal ganglia and orbitofrontal cortex. OCD responds specifically to drugs that inhibit the synaptic reuptake of serotonin.

Evidence shows that early diagnosis and assertive treatment is likely to improve the outcome. To diagnose OCD the criteria shown in **Box 44.1** need to be met.

## Assessment

The NICE guidelines (2005a) recommend that if OCD is suspected, direct screening questions should be asked such as:

- Do you wash or clean a lot?
- Do you check things a lot?
- Is there any thought that keeps bothering you that you would like to get rid of but can't?
- Do your daily activities take a long time to finish?
- Are you concerned about orderliness or symmetry?
- Do these problems trouble you?

Box 44.1 ICD-10 definition of obsessive compulsive disorder

Either obsessions or compulsions (or both) present on most days for a period of at least 2 weeks. Obsessions (thoughts, images or ideas) and compulsions share the following features, all of which must be present:

- acknowledged as originating in the mind of the patient;
- repetitive and unpleasant;
- at least one recognized as excessive or unreasonable;
- at least one must be unsuccessfully resisted (although resistance may be minimal in some cases);
- carrying out the obsessive thought or compulsive act is not intrinsically pleasurable.

Detailed assessment should include:

- An accurate description of symptoms: content of thoughts, types of compulsions, onset, severity and frequency. The Children's Yale–Brown Obsessive Compulsive Scale (C/YBOCS) is a validated assessment measure that is widely used in specialist centres to rate symptom severity and functional impairment (Goodman et al., 1991).
- A consideration of the predisposing (e.g. genetic factors), precipitating (e.g. traumatic events), perpetuating factors (e.g. parental reinforcement) and protective factors (e.g. high self-esteem).

- Exclusion of other diagnoses (**Box 44.2**) and assessment of possible co-morbidity (**Box 44.3**) and family disturbance.
- It is vital to assess risk of self-harm and suicide, particularly if depression has already been diagnosed.
- Evaluation of family dynamics and the degree of family involvement in OCD.
- Assessment of parental anxiety and other mental illness.
- Consideration of developmental issues. Some superstitious behaviour and routines may be developmentally normal.

Box 44.2 Differential diagnoses

- Normal Developmental Variation; children commonly have routines/rituals that are normal up to the age of four, if not intense
- Primary depressive disorder with secondary obsessive/compulsive symptoms
- Tic Disorders; more likely to be touching, counting, blinking
- Pervasive Developmental Disorder; stereotypies can appear similar to rituals
- Neurological; brain injury, post-encephalitis, tumours
- PANDAS; Paediatric Autoimmune Neuro-Psychiatric Disorders associated with streptococcal infection, development of tics and OCD following confirmed streptococcal infection
- Body Dysmorphic Disorder
- Eating Disorders
- Psychosis

Box 44.3 Possible co-morbid conditions

- Depression (35 per cent)
- Anxiety Disorders (40 per cent)
- Tic Disorder/Tourette Syndrome (50–60 per cent of TS patients have OCD)
- Substance Misuse
- ADHD (30 per cent)
- Oppositional Defiant Disorder (43 per cent)
- Developmental Delay

## Treatment

The NICE (2005a) guideline on the treatment of OCD recommended a stepped care approach with increasing intensity according to clinical severity and complexity.

## Mild functional impairment

Guided self-help may be effective in early or mild OCD (see links below for resources). Psycho-education about the diagnosis should be given and the patient and family should be helped not to feel blame or shame. If self-help is refused or ineffective, the patient should be offered cognitive behaviour therapy (CBT).

## Moderate or severe impairment

CBT, and especially exposure plus response prevention, is an effective treatment for OCD and should be offered first. The patient makes a list of feared situations and starts with the least feared. He then practises facing the fear (exposure) without carrying out a ritual but noticing the anxiety and experiencing it lessening (response prevention). Understanding that repeated exposure leads to reduced anxiety is crucial. The family/carers should be involved and this may lead to greater success. Family involvement is essential for children under 11. Manual-based treatments can be usefully drawn upon (March and Mulle, 1998).

# Drug treatment

If CBT is ineffective or refused, a selective serotonin reuptake inhibitor (SSRI) should be considered after multidisciplinary review. The only SSRIs licensed for use in children and young people with OCD are sertraline (dose 25–200 mg) and fluvoxamine. However, where there is significant co-morbid depression fluoxetine should be used. Response may take up to 12 weeks, maximal doses may be required and improvements can continue for up to one year. Medication should be continued for at least six months after remission to reduce the risk of relapse. Maintenance therapy may be at a lower dose. Withdrawal from SSRIs should be very gradual to prevent discontinuation symptoms.

An SSRI should only be prescribed to children and young people with OCD following assessment and diagnosis by a Child and Adolescent Psychiatrist, who should closely monitor the medication and be involved in decisions about dose changes and discontinuation.

If CBT+SSRI combination is ineffective then switching to a different SSRI or augmentation with clomipramine or antipsychotic medication may be considered in a specialist setting (Heyman et al., 2006).

Inpatient treatment may be required in severe cases.

## Case study 1: Andrew

A mother presents to her local Tier 2 CAMHS service with her five-year-old son, Andrew. He has become obsessed with checking that the lights are off and the doors locked at night before he goes to bed. She has to reassure him endlessly and stays in his room until he goes to sleep. She is worried that he is developing OCD.

### Outcome

After careful history taking from both mother and Andrew, it becomes apparent that Andrew's father left the family home two months before and that these behaviours started when he left. There had been domestic violence and the boy was scared of his father. Andrew's mother is anxious and depressed. Andrew worries that his father will return and hurt his mother, but his thoughts are not of an obsessive nature as these worries are realistic. It is explained to Andrew's mother that it is likely that his worries are developmentally appropriate and adaptive in helping Andrew try to control a difficult situation.

It is recommended to Andrew and his mother that they read some books together about how to deal with anxiety and that he sees a therapist for individual work. His mother is given advice about where to seek help for herself. Andrew is able to talk through some of his worries in the sessions and enjoys using art. After six sessions he is feeling much better and is less reliant on asking his mother for reassurance.

## Case study 2: Jennifer

Jennifer (12) presented to her local GP with her highly anxious parents. She described having become anxious about a member of her family dying following her grandfather's funeral six months previously. She began to 'touch wood' for good luck when she had these thoughts to make sure that no one would die. This would calm her down. The thoughts then became more frequent and Jennifer found herself having to tap at least thirty times a day. She found it interfered with her school work and sleep. She described not feeling like herself anymore and she was worried she was 'going crazy'. Jennifer began to be worried that she herself may die and thought that if she washed her hands more thoroughly then she would not become ill from germs. This impacted on the time it took her to get ready for school in addition to time spent in the toilets at school.

### Outcome

Jennifer was diagnosed with OCD by the GP. The family were relieved to know what was wrong and that treatment was available. Genetic factors were discussed and time was spent helping the parents to understand that this was nobody's fault. Jennifer was referred to Tier 3 Child and Adolescent Mental Health Services and offered CBT. She attended sessions with her mother. She made a list of feared situations and with the help of her mother was able to work her way up the list keeping a diary of her thoughts and anxiety levels during these challenges. Jennifer made excellent progress and after 12 sessions of CBT was discharged. In the following year, Jennifer had a slight relapse following her cat's death and needed two 'top up' CBT sessions enabling her to renew her skills and prevent the return of ritualistic behaviours.

## Case study 3: Michael

Michael was a 15-year-old boy with Asperger syndrome who had always been obsessional and keen on routine, but this had been manageable in the past. He had been known to local CAMHS services for a long time and had been prescribed fluoxetine after becoming depressed two years previously. In the last year, his depression had eased and he had stopped taking his fluoxetine and no longer wanted to take any medication. He had now become increasingly more ritualistic. He was obsessed with numbers and had to do complex number counting in sets of fours whenever he was worried that something was not quite 'right'. Michael was worried about the presence of other people around him as they interrupted his thinking rituals and he could become very aggressive to his parents. He constantly asked his mother to make things right and was bothering her all night. Michael's mother tried to be firm and not do everything he asked of her, but she usually gave in. Michael stopped going to school due to the difficulty of going to sleep and then the amount of time it took him to be up and ready for school. If he was interrupted in the middle of his rituals, he would have to start all over again.

### Outcome

Michael was assessed at home by the Tier 3 CAMHS team. The team heard how his mother was at breaking point, as she was unable to sleep because Michael disturbed her all night. She was fragile and depressed herself. The team heard how sometimes Michael could be stuck in a cold bath for 2 hours, unable to come out due to his rituals. Michael spoke of how he hated his life, but he was not depressed. He reluctantly agreed to see a psychologist for CBT and to take medication.

Michael was started on sertraline at a dose of 25 mg OD, which was increased over a period of weeks to 100 mg OD. Michael did not engage well with CBT and only took his medication sporadically. His symptoms remained the same and the possibility of an inpatient admission was discussed, due to the severity of his illness. Michael was admitted to the local adolescent unit informally and improved dramatically. However, on weekend home leave his OCD was still very strong. The therapists worked closely with the family on how to respond to Michael's demands and worked with Michael on home visits. Gradually, Michael's OCD improved and he was discharged six months later on a dose of sertraline 150 mg OD.

## Multiple choice questions

1. In obsessive compulsive disorder (OCD), which of the following would be the true definition of compulsions?

   a. Repetitive or ritualized behaviour patterns that the individual feels driven to perform in order to prevent some negative outcome happening
   b. Repetitive thoughts about harming or distressing others
   c. Overwhelming desires to behave in an inappropriate fashion
   d. Ritualized worrying about negative outcome of events

2. In OCD the most important dysfunctional belief has been defined as inflated responsibility. This is:

   a. An inability to take responsibility for one's actions
   b. Delusions of grandeur
   c. The belief that one has power which is pivotal to bring about or prevent subjectively crucial negative outcomes
   d. Increased sense of self-importance

3. The most common treatment for OCD is exposure and ritual prevention. Part of the treatment is imaginal exposure. For example, for someone with compulsive washing, this involves:

   a. Suppressing thoughts about the ritual
   b. Imagining others touching a dirty dish
   c. Imagining touching a dirty dish
   d. Imagining negative consequences that will result from not washing

4. In children who have OCD, the most common obsession themes are:

   a. Contamination
   b. Harm to self/others
   c. Symmetry and exactness
   d. All of the above

5. Which of the following statements about obsessions and compulsions is true?

   a. Obsessional thoughts are recognized as originating outside of the body
   b. Obsessional thoughts/impulses do not have to be unpleasant
   c. Carrying out compulsive rituals is a means of avoiding anxiety
   d. Compulsions can lead to psychosis if resisted

### Key texts

Heyman I, Mataix-Cols D, Fineberg NA (2006) Obsessive-compulsive disorder. *British Medical Journal*, **333**: 424–9.

March J, Mulle K (1998) *OCD in Children and Adolescents: A Cognitive-behavioural Treatment Manual*. New York: Guilford Press.

National Institute for Health and Clinical Excellence (2005a) *Obsessive Compulsive Disorder: Core Interventions in the Treatment of Obsessive-compulsive Disorder and Body Dysmorphic Disorder (Clinical guideline 31)*. London: NICE.

### Useful resources for children, young people and families

Huebner D (2007) *What To Do When Your Brain Gets Stuck: A Kids Guide to Overcoming OCD*. Magination Press. An interactive self-help book for children and their parents.

March J (2007) *Talking Vack to OCD*. New York: Guilford Press. (A self-help guide for young sufferers and their families.)

Wever C, Phillips N (1996) *The Secret Problem*. Australia: Shrink-Rap Press. (Cartoon based book about OCD for young people.)

# 45 Body dysmorphic disorder

### Christopher Gale

*The Wolf Man neglected his daily life and work because he was engrossed, to the exclusion of all else, in the state of his nose (its supposed scars, holes and swelling). His life mattered on the little mirror in his pocket, and his fate depended on what it revealed or was about to reveal.*

**(Brunswick, 1928)**

## Key concepts

- Constantly checking oneself in the mirror
- Camouflaging with make-up
- Touching the body part
- Measuring the defect
- Excessive grooming
- Skin picking

## Introduction

The above observation reveals a case of what would now be described as body dysmorphic disorder (BDD). The ICD-10 Classification of Mental and Behavioural Disorders (WHO, 1992) defines BDD as: 'a persistent preoccupation with a presumed deformity or disfigurement, that causes persistent distress or interference in daily functioning and where the patient refuses to accept medical reassurance that there is no abnormality present'. This excludes body image concerns arising from an eating disorder, such as anorexia nervosa, or a mood disorder.

The preoccupation is most commonly centred on the hair, skin or facial features (Dyl et al., 2006; Labuschagne et al., 2010).

These behaviours can be very time-consuming (several hours in any one 'routine'), significantly impacting on a young person's attendance at school or work and on their ability to socialize with peers. A young person may wake exceptionally early in the day in order to perform the routines of checking or camouflaging, thus disturbing their sleep patterns and energy levels.

## Epidemiology

The prevalence of BDD ranges from 1 to 2 per cent (Arthur and Monnell, 2005) to 13 per cent (Biby, 1998) of the general population and 13 per cent of the psychiatric adult inpatient population (Grant et al., 2001). This range may be accounted for by the inclusion or exclusion of body image issues associated with eating disorders, in addition to the feelings of shame that prevent many BDD suffers from seeking professional help from mental health services (Grant et al., 2001; Veale, 2002). As adults, many will seek intervention from cosmetic surgeons as an alternative (Ashraf, 2000). This may explain the gap between age of onset of BDD, commonly held to be during adolescence, and its diagnosis and treatment, often during an individual's 20s or 30s.

Another explanation for the lack of identification in adolescence is the perceived crucial role of body image and issues of identity development, peer relationships, dating and sexuality (Levine and Smolak, 2002). This lack of identification would suggest that any prevalence rates in this age group are potentially underestimated (2.2 per cent; Mayville et al., 1999). The presentation of symptoms/

behaviours in adolescence does not appear to differ from that of adulthood (Phillips et al., 2006). There often is a chronic nature and course to the illness, with an average of 16 years' duration.

# BDD and other mental disorders

Frare et al. (2004) and Goldsmith et al. (1998) have compared the structural foundations of BDD and obsessive compulsive disorder (OCD), concluding that BDD could be seen as an obsessive compulsive spectrum disorder. The National Institute for Clinical Excellence (NICE) has grouped OCD and BDD together in its guideline for assessment and treatment (NICE, 2005a).

However, there are distinct differences, highlighted alongside the commonalities shown in **Table 45.1**.

Other co-morbid presentations include:
- borderline personality disorder (Semiz et al., 2008);
- depression (Labuschagne et al., 2010);
- anxiety (Labuschagne et al., 2010);
- suicidal thoughts or suicide attempts: 22–29 per cent in BDD sufferers (Arthur and Monnell, 2005).

Table 45.1  Similarities and differences between BDD and OCD

| Similarities between BDD and OCD | Differences between BDD and OCD |
|---|---|
| • Persistent and intrusive thoughts (is my nose to big? am I ugly?)<br>• Compulsive behaviours (grooming, mirror checking)<br>• Treatment approaches (SSRI anti-depressant medication and cognitive behaviour therapy) | • BDD suffers generally have poorer insight (Phillips et al., 1995)<br>• Checking behaviours increase rather than decrease anxiety (Phillips et al., 1995)<br>• BDD has a greater co-morbidity with depression and social phobia (Frare et al., 2004)<br>• BDD sufferers are less likely to form long-term relationships or hold down employment (Goldsmith et al., 1998) |

# Possible causal factors

Fully establishing the causal factors relating to BDD is difficult, as research in this area remains sparse and is conducted mainly with adult clinical populations, because of the feelings of shame that can delay presentation to mental health services. Mental health services do not routinely include body image screening questions during initial assessments. Despite these challenges, genetic, neurobiological and psychological causal factors have been proposed.

# Genetic

No twin studies have been completed for BDD, so answers relevant to the genetic causes of the illness are reliant on those completed in OCD research. Bienvenu et al. (2000) examined the relationship between OCD and possible spectrum disorders in a double blind trial. They concluded that certain somatoform disorders, especially BDD and pathologic grooming conditions, were transmitted within families with OCD.

# Neurobiological factors

No in-depth brain imaging or neurophysiologic studies have been conducted with BDD, although Phillips (1998) discusses well-documented body image disturbances related to brain damage. Injury to the occipital lobes, for example, can cause impairment to visual perception, including facial perception. Damage to the temporal lobes can result in a distorted view of body size and an inability to identify previously known faces, even their own. The positive effect of selective serotonin reuptake inhibitor (SSRI) medication on BDD symptoms might indicate disturbed brain chemistry.

Psychological causes can include:
- unconscious displacement of sexual or emotional conflicts, or feelings of guilt (Biby, 1998);

- inharmonious family backgrounds, with possible parental emphasis on perfectionism (Biby, 1998);
- frequent teasing, particularly about physical appearance (Phillips, 1998);
- childhood trauma abuse and neglect (Didie et al., 2006; Semiz et al., 2008);
- chronic low self-esteem (Phillips et al., 2004).

---

### Case study: Tilly

Tilly is a 15-year-old girl who has expressed concerns about her physical appearance since the age of five, asking her parents if she looked 'okay'. Her concerns have increased in the past three years since some boys in her class at school told her she looked like a horse. This has led her to carry out lengthy washing, make-up and grooming routines, for up to 3 hours at a time, in the morning and made a difference to her day-to-day life, as she was frequently late for school and social events. Her routines have left her physically and mentally exhausted and caused conflict with her parents and younger brother at home.

---

## Assessment

Because of the increased risk of suicidal behaviour in individuals with BDD, NICE (2005a) recommend that a thorough risk assessment and risk management plan is conducted at the earliest possible opportunity. As part of a CAMHS assessment, the following five questions should be included if BDD is suspected in a young person:

- Do you worry a lot about the way you look and wish you could think about it less?
- What specific concerns do you have about your appearance?
- On a typical day, how many hours a day is your appearance on your mind? (More than 1 hour a day is considered excessive.)
- What effect does it have on your life?
- Does it make it hard to do your work or be with friends?

Much of the literature about BDD emphasizes the importance of using diagnostic screening tools, for example the Body Dysmorphic Disorder Questionnaire (BDDQ), The Yale Brown Obsessive Compulsive Scale for BDD (BDD-YBOCS) and the Body Dysmorphic Diagnostic Module (BDDM).

Veale (2001) outlines the cognitive behaviour therapy (CBT) model for assessing BDD, looking at a trigger (i.e. reflection in the mirror) causing the processing of self as an aesthetic object, which leads to a negative appraisal of one's body image (depression or disgust) and the avoidance and safety behaviours (mirror checking or camouflaging).

In addition, it is important to consider the impact of the BDD symptoms on other members of the family: how does each family member respond when the young person is 'stuck' in their checking/grooming routine?

## Intervention

A clear feature of the NICE (2005a) recommended interventions with BDD are its links to OCD, which has a greater breadth and quality in the relevant research. Several studies have seen BDD as an obsessive compulsive spectrum disorder (Biby, 1998; Goldsmith et al., 1998; Bienvenu et al., 2000; Frare et al., 2004). As with OCD, the two key interventions in the management of moderate to severe BDD are the use of CBT, with the inclusion of exposure and response prevention strategies (see Chapter 72, Cognitive behaviour therapy).

Emphasis is placed on the importance of family/carers being involved in the therapeutic process and supporting experimental activities away from the therapeutic setting. As an adjunct, the introduction of an SSRI or clomipromine is suggested, especially if the young person is experiencing low mood. The stepped care model of intervention below outlines the appropriate treatment at each level of severity of the disorder (**Figure 45.1**).

The use of SSRI antidepressant medication with young people under the age of 18 is contentious, because of the perceived potential for an increased

| WHO IS RESPONSIBLE FOR CARE? | WHAT IS THE FOCUS? | WHAT DO THEY DO? |
| --- | --- | --- |
| **Step 6**<br>Inpatient care or intensive treatment programmes – CAMHS Tier 4 | OCD/BDD with a risk to life, severe self-neglect or severe distress or disability | • Reassess, discuss options, care coordination.<br>• SSRI or Clomipromine<br>• CBT including ERP<br>• Consider admission to hospital or special living arrangements. |
| **Step 5**<br>Multidisciplinary care with expertise in OCD/BDD – CAMHS Tiers 3/4 | OCD/BDD with significant co-morbidity, or severely impaired functioning and/or treatment resistance, partial response or relapse. | • CBT with ERP, then consider combined treatment with an SSRI or Clomipromine<br>• For younger children consider referral to specialist services outside of CAMHS |
| **Step 4**<br>Multidisciplinary care in primary of secondary care – CAMHS Tiers 2/3 | OCD/BDD with co-morbidity or poor response to treatment | • CBT with ERP, then consider combined treatment with an SSRI or Clomipromine |
| **Step 3**<br>GP, primary care team, primary care mental health worker, family support team – CAMHS Tiers 1/2 | Management and initial treatment of OCD/BDD | • Guided self-help (for OCD)<br>• CBT, including ERP<br>• Involve family/carers and consider involving the school. |
| **Step 2**<br>GP, practice nurses, school health advisors, general health setting (including hospitals) – CAMHS Tier 1 | Recognition and assessment | • Detect<br>• Educate<br>• Signpost voluntary support organisations<br>• Provide support to individuals/ families/school<br>• Refer to any of the other levels |
| **Step 1**<br>Individuals, public organisations, NHS | Awareness and recognition. | • Provide, seek and share information on OCD/BDD and its impact on individuals and families/carers. |

Taken from NICE (2005), p. 228.

Figure 45.1 The stepped care model of intervention with BDD (and OCD).

risk of suicidal ideation. The British National Formulary for Children (2010) recommends that when prescribing fluoxetine, the SSRI considered best tolerated in young people, a maximum dose of 20 mg daily is considered. For adults, the maximum dose is 80 mg for cases of severe depression or OCD. One of the few studies about the adolescent presentation of BDD (Phillips et al., 1995) saw a significant reduction of BDD symptoms after 10 weeks with a dose of only 60 mg a day. Veale (2004) suggests that these doses should be prescribed for at least 12–16 weeks before considering whether the medication has proved effective.

Although NICE (2005a) does not specifically recommend the introduction of family therapy with those children and young people experiencing BDD, as with many other mental disorders in under 18s, an exploration of its impact on the family and any possible maintaining influences within the family system should be explored (see Chapter 23, Family assessment).

## Summary

• BDD is a somatoform disorder, where the individual is excessively preoccupied with a perceived or minor bodily defect. It can have a chronic course and prognosis, if untreated.

- The prevalence in under 18s is difficult to ascertain, because of normal angst around body image experienced by many developing young people.
- The evidence base for the assessment and management of BDD is limited, especially so in

children and young people, and relies on wider research into OCD.

- The first line intervention with children and young people is CBT with exposure and response prevention (ERP), with an SSRI medication as an adjunct if deemed clinically appropriate.

## Multiple choice questions

1. What other mental disorder is BDD most commonly associated with?

   a. Schizophrenia
   b. Autistic Spectrum Disorder
   c. Depression
   d. Obsessive Compulsive Disorder
   e. Anorexia Nervosa

2. Which of the following is not a key feature of BDD?

   a. Constantly checking oneself in the mirror
   b. Camouflaging with make-up
   c. Pulling out of hair
   d. Touching the body part
   e. Measuring the defect

3. Which of the following statements would it not be true to say about BDD?

   a. BDD suffers generally have very poor insight
   b. Checking behaviours decrease anxiety
   c. BDD has a greater co-morbidity with depression and social phobia than OCD
   d. BDD sufferers are less likely to form long-term relationships or hold down employment
   e. BDD sufferers experience persistent and intrusive thoughts

4. Which two treatments are considered most effective in treating moderate to severe cases of BDD?

   a. A selective serotonin reuptake inhibitor (SSRI) medication
   b. Guided self-help/relaxation
   c. Cognitive behaviour therapy
   d. Cognitive behaviour therapy with exposure and response prevention
   e. Atypical antipsychotic medication

### Key texts

National Institute for Health and Clinical Excellence (2005a) *Obsessive-Compulsive Disorder: Core Interventions in the Treatment of Obsessive-compulsive Disorder and Body Dysmorphic Disorder.* London: The British Psychological Society and The Royal College of Psychiatrists.

Phillips KA, Didie ER, Menard W et al. (2006) Clinical features of body dysmorphic disorder in adolescents and adults. *Psychiatry Research,* **141**: 305–14.

Veale D (2002) Shame in body dysmorphic disorder. In: Gilbert P, Miles J (eds). *Body Shame: Conceptualisation, Research and Treatment.* Hove and New York: Brunner-Routledge, 267–8.

# 46 *Mood disorders*

### Ravi Mehendra, Nischint Warikoo and Christopher Gale

---

## Key concepts

- Depression is a common mental disorder that presents with depressed mood, loss of interest or pleasure, feelings of guilt or low self-worth, disturbed sleep or appetite, low energy, and poor concentration.
- Estimates of prevalence vary from just over 1 per cent in pre-school children (Domenech-Llaberia et al., 2009) to 4–25 per cent of children seen in secondary schools (Kessler et al., 2001).
- The reasons for the increase in prevalence after puberty, especially in females, are unclear, but may include hormonal changes, greater cognitive maturity, changes in social support, more life stresses and late genetic effects (Khalil et al., 2010).

---

## Introduction

Minor depressive episodes in childhood and adolescence have a good prognosis. They respond to outpatient treatment and do not tend to recur. More severe episodes and bipolar disorders are likely to recur. As with adults, poor pre-morbid personality seems to be a negative prognostic feature, as far as both treatment and recurrence go.

By comparison with non-depressed subjects, young people diagnosed as depressed are more likely to have subsequent episodes of depression. In addition, we know that adolescents with depression are at increased risk of depression in early adulthood, when compared with controls that had been matched on a large number of variables.

## Aetiology

Depression is most likely to be due to the interplay between genetics, biochemical and familial factors (Goodyer et al., 2000; Birmaher and Heydl, 2001; Hoffman et al., 2006). A family history of psychiatric disorder is important.

There are no firm conclusions with regard to race, social class or precipitating environmental factors.

Various models are used to understand the link between the environmental stressors and depressed mood. One of them is learned helplessness. It is postulated that the expectation of uncontrollable adverse events leads to depression, but only if the person attributes them to internal causes. For example, 'I failed the exam, because I am useless'.

The Amine hypothesis provides an organic model. It states that depression results from decreased activity of neurotransmitters, like monoamine, in the brain.

## Classification of mood disorders

As per the ICD-10 (WHO, 1992) a young person presenting with two core symptoms plus two or more additional symptoms can be diagnosed as being depressed.

### Core symptoms

- Low mood
- Anergia (lack of energy)
- Anhedonia (loss of pleasures in life)

## Additional symptoms

- Decreased concentration
- Reduced self-esteem
- Guilt
- Pessimism
- Sleep disturbance
- Appetite disturbance
- Suicidal thoughts

# Assessment of mental state

It is important that a careful assessment is made to determine the cause of the symptoms.

For younger children, the mental state is assessed during everyday conversation or while playing or painting. At the same time, an impression is formed of the mental state of the parents and all other family members present, including siblings. This is usually done informally. Although it is the child/young person who has been referred, it may be that another member of the family is more disturbed.

Family interactions and interrelationships are assessed at the same time. If possible, it is good practice to see the referred child on their own, briefly, in the case of very young children. This gives them the opportunity to speak about any private worries they may have.

For older children and adolescents the following should be explored (NICE, 2005b):

- social, family and educational context;
- quality of their peer relationships and social networks;
- presence of bullying or other abuse;
- alcohol or drug use;
- deliberate self-harm and suicidal ideas;
- co-morbidity with other mental disorders (Angold et al. (1999) found this to be the case for 40–70 per cent of depressed under 18s).

# Assessment scales

Assessment scales are useful for diagnosis, but are not a substitute for a thorough assessment. One of the scales used is the Children's Depression Inventory (CDI – Kovacs, 1992) which is a symptom-oriented instrument for assessing depression in children ranging from ages of 7 to 17 years. The short form of CDI can be useful for screening for depression.

# Differential diagnoses

It is important to consider organic causes before making a diagnosis of depression, for example, misuse of substances or organic brain disease. In addition, it is important to consider social problems, such as child abuse, bullying or neglect.

The list for differential diagnosis is extensive and includes every single psychiatric category in ICD-10. The following list is worth considering in children and adolescents:

- adjustment disorder with depressed mood;
- dysthymia (chronic mild depressive symptoms);
- bipolar disorder;
- anxiety disorder;
- attention deficit hyperactivity disorder (ADHD) with depressive symptoms;
- oppositional defiant disorder;
- substance misuse;
- attachment disorder (emotional and behavioural problems presumed to be caused by a lack of attachment to the main caregiver).

# Diagnostic difficulties

Diagnosing a child or young person can be challenging, particularly because:

- Certain manifestations of depression are more typical of depression in childhood than depression in adult life. Unlike depressed adults, a depressed pre-school child may not appear morbidly or obviously sad or withdrawn, and may have periods of brightening or apparently normal functioning during any given day. These features, as well as an inherent resistance to imagining that a pre-school child may be depressed, can make it more difficult to identify the disorder in young children.
- The transient mood changes in adolescence can result in difficulty distinguishing between normal sadness, unhappiness and depressive disorder.
- In the presence of family turmoil and chronic life stresses, it is difficult to evaluate the significance of depressive symptoms.

There are problems with the use of adult criteria of diagnosis in children because children can find it more difficult to verbally express their emotions and to give accurate historical data. Children with depression may present with:

- Mood which is irritable. This may appear as 'acting out', reckless behaviour or hostile, angry interactions.
- Vague physical complaints, sad facial expression or poor eye contact.
- Running away from home, separation anxiety (may present as school refusal), pain in head, abdomen or chest and/or hypochondriacal ideas, decline in school work or antisocial behaviour (mainly in boys).
- Failure to make expected weight gain rather than losing weight. Appetite may increase or decrease.
- Anhedonia or an inability to enjoy life, and social withdrawal.
- Additional non-verbal cues for potentially suicidal behaviour, such as giving away a favourite collection of music or stamps.
- Psychotic symptoms in severe major depression, if present, are more often auditory hallucinations (usually criticizing the patient).

## Interventions

Early diagnosis and management of depression is very important. Early treatment leads to better prognosis. It is important to consider education, impaired psychosocial functioning and co-morbid psychiatric disorders in a comprehensive management plan. All these problems need to be identified and the causes of each need to be assessed.

With mild depression the options are watchful waiting or psychological therapies. One of the following psychological therapies is offered for a limited period (around 2–3 months):

- guided self-help (GSH);
- individual non-directive supportive therapy;
- group cognitive behaviour therapy (CBT).

In addition, for moderate to severe depression, the following may be considered:

- individual CBT (see Chapter 72, Cognitive behaviour therapy);
- family (systemic) therapy (see Chapter 74, Family therapy models and practice).

There is a good evidence base for CBT, especially

for intelligent adolescents. CBT may be effective, especially if combined with antidepressants (NICE, 2005b).

## Medication

Fluoxetine has been shown to be useful for adolescents and is recommended initially (sertraline and citalopram are alternative second line treatments).

Careful assessment of the young person is necessary before commencing a selective serotonin reuptake inhibitor (SSRI) to assess and document suicidal ideation, as there have been historical concerns around increasing suicidality during the early stages of treatment. Full discussion should take place with the young person and their family about the side effects.

The young person should remain on medication for up to six months after the symptoms have resolved. Following that, medication should be withdrawn slowly to avoid side effects.

### Other medications

There is some evidence to support sodium valproate, carbamazepine, lithium and other augmentation medications. They should only be initiated by a specialist experienced in their use and would be recommended usually when it was suspected that the depression was part of a manic-depressive disorder.

### Electro-convulsive therapy

Finally, severe depressions in young people may respond to electro-convulsive therapy (ECT). ECT should be reserved for severe life-threatening disorders and only carried out in specialist centres.

## Summary

- Depression in children may manifest itself in a manner different from that in adults.
- Young children may not specifically complain of depressed mood or communicate their distress. But pre-school depression may be characterized by changes in sleep, appetite and activity levels.

- Overall, the best approach may be to identify age-appropriate signs and symptoms that take into account the child's level of functioning in various cognitive and affective domains.

- Depression in childhood should always be taken seriously.

## Case study 1: Jeremy

Jeremy is five years old and lives with his mother, Sandra (26), who has not worked since Jeremy was born. Sandra has experienced episodes of depression since adolescence and was particularly unwell during the first two years of his life. Jeremy's reception stage school teacher has raised concerns with the school nurse about his behaviour in class. Jeremy often appears withdrawn, isolating himself from other children and being irritable when they do try to engage him in play. The teacher reports that Jeremy has approached him on a number of occasions complaining that his 'head hurts' or his 'tummy aches'. When followed up with Sandra, she confirms the presence of these somatic complaints in addition to Jeremy's poor appetite.

Jeremy was referred to CAMHS, where a comprehensive assessment suggested that he may be experiencing depression. Jeremy was offered sessions with a play therapist who was able to explore why he might be feeling sad through the use of play materials. Work was carried out with Sandra and Jeremy to look at how Sandra could introduce more nurturing behaviours with her son. Crucially, Sandra was given advice and support about how to approach having her own mental health needs met, including local parent and child groups, to widen her network of support.

## Case study 2: Simone

Simone (16) is currently in her final year of GCSEs. She has noticed that her mood has been low for several months, ever since she had an argument with her group of friends at school. This resulted in her feeling excluded from the group, despite efforts by some of her friends to make contact. Initially, Simone withdrew from social life, explaining to her parents that she needed to focus on her studies. However, as time has gone on she has found it increasingly difficult to concentrate on her work and the school has noticed a dip in her marks.

Simone's mother has become increasingly concerned about her daughter's appetite and lack of sleep. She reports hearing Simone wandering around her room into the early hours and has brought Simone to the GP.

Simone is referred onto CAMHS, where she is offered a routine assessment appointment. At the appointment, when her parents are out of the room, Simone reveals that she has started self-harming by cutting the tops of her arms. On assessment, it is formulated that Simone is experiencing depression, triggered by school pressures and the difficulties with her peers. Because of the length of time she has experienced low mood and her clear cognitive difficulties, Simone is offered a trial of the SSRI medication fluoxetine combined with a course of CBT within the service.

Simone is seen on a regular basis by a psychiatrist to monitor her progress on the medication and she has fortnightly sessions with the CBT therapist. Within the CBT sessions, Simone's beliefs about herself and her peer relationships are explored and challenged. As part of the therapy, she is encouraged to make contact with those friends who were trying to contact her and test out some of her negative beliefs. To her surprise, several of them were pleased that she had been in touch and they have arranged to meet together soon.

## Multiple choice questions

1. Which of the following is not a core symptom of depression in young people?

   a. Low mood
   b. Irritability
   c. Deliberate self-harm
   d. Loss of pleasure in life
   e. Lack of energy

2. What is the estimated prevalence of depression in pre-school children?

   a. It does not exist
   b. 1 per cent
   c. 5 per cent
   d. 10 per cent
   e. 30 per cent

3. What intervention for moderate–severe adolescent depression has been found to be particularly effective?

   a. Cognitive behaviour therapy
   b. Antipsychotic medication
   c. CBT and antipsychotic medication
   d. SSRI medication
   e. CBT and SSRI medication

### Key texts

Angoxld A, Costello EJ, Erkanli A (1999) Comorbidity. *Journal of Child Psychology and Psychiatry*, **40**: 57–87.

Harrington RC (2008) Affective disorders. In: Rutter M, Taylor E (eds). *Child and Adolescent Psychiatry*, 5th edn. Oxford: Blackwell Publishing.

National Institute for Health and Clinical Excellence (2005b) *Depression in Children and Young People: Identification and Management in Primary, Community and Secondary Care.* London: NICE.

# 47 Bipolar disorder in children and young people

Matthew Fealey

---

## Key concepts

Three of the following symptoms need to be present for a diagnosis to be made:

- increased activity or physical restlessness
- increased talkativeness ('pressure of speech')
- flight of ideas or the subjective experience of thought racing
- loss of normal social inhibitions, resulting in behaviour that is inappropriate to the circumstances
- decreased need for sleep
- inflated self-esteem or grandiosity
- distractibility or constant changes in activity or plans
- behaviour that is foolhardy or reckless and whose risks the individual does not recognize, for example spending sprees, foolish enterprises, reckless driving
- marked sexual energy or sexual indiscretions.

---

## Introduction

Bipolar disorder or manic depression in children and adolescents has been the subject of huge debate in recent years, following a rapid rise in the rate of diagnosis in the United States (Moreno et al., 2007). There are a number of possibilities as to why this has occurred; a major area of ongoing debate is about diagnostic criteria. Bipolar disorder has always been considered a rare illness in children and adolescents. This has been confirmed by prevalence studies using the DSM IV criteria (Costello et al., 1996; Axelson et al., 2006). Others have argued that bipolar disorder presents differently in youths compared with adults and have made changes to the way the diagnostic criteria are applied in their research (Geller et al., 2006).

## Diagnostic criteria

A person's mood can be thought of as existing on a spectrum from high to low and the rate of change between these mood states varies, usually in response to what is happening in their life.

Individuals vary in their fluctuations of mood. In bipolar disorder the mood state is considered abnormal because of the duration and the intensity of the mood. The highs are manic or hypomanic episodes and combine usually with depressive lows. There can be mixed states where both extremes occur simultaneously.

According to ICD-10 research diagnostic criteria (WHO, 1992), in mania the mood must be predominantly elevated, expansive or irritable and definitely abnormal for the individual concerned. The mood change must be prominent and sustained for at least 1 week (unless it is severe enough to require hospital admission).

Hypomania is a mood state where the symptoms of mania are present, but usually less severe. The diagnostic criteria for depression in bipolar disorder are the same as for a depressive episode.

US researchers have suggested an alternative definition for the cycle of an abnormal mood episode. They use episodes of illness lasting longer than 2 weeks rather than a distinct continuously symptomatic period, with mood cycles within the episode only needing to be 4 hours in length (Geller et al., 2006; Leibenluft et al., 2006). This would obviously classify children in the UK that many would not see as having a mental illness as having bipolar disorder. Leibenluft et al. (2006) have operationalized criteria for severe mood and behavioural dysregulation (SMD) which apply to children and adolescents who experience severe, non-episodic irritability and symptoms of attention deficit hyperactivity disorder (ADHD). It is debated whether these individuals are a developmental presentation of bipolar disorder but research so far suggests that SMD is related to the development of major depressive disorder in early adulthood, not bipolar disorder.

## Case study 1: Justin

Justin is a nine-year-old boy who has been referred because of his behavioural problems. His mother complains that Justin is increasingly moody and difficult. She struggles to understand why he is in such a bad mood. He does not do as he is asked and cannot be reasoned with. He is up at night playing when he should be asleep. At school, Justin is easily distracted and does not do his work. He is struggling with friendships and has fallen out with his best friends following arguments and fights. He is in trouble with the teachers and will argue with them. His mother is worried that Justin has no friends and might be told to leave the school.

### Assessment

This is a typical presentation in this age group for a number of different disorders. It is important to interview parents, the child and their teachers. Parents often underestimate the severity of their child's anxiety symptoms, grandiose thinking, racing thoughts and less commonly, the extent of their child's psychotic symptoms (Baroni et al., 2009). A medical assessment will be needed to exclude an organic cause.

### Formulation

Bipolar disorder presents more commonly with irritability than with elation because parents are more likely to report irritability. This may be because children cannot use adult bipolar coping strategies, for example by skipping school or staying up late (Leibenluft and Dickstein, 2008). The NICE guidelines (2006) are clear, however, that mania must be present with euphoria to diagnose bipolar disorder in both pre-pubescent children and in adolescents.

   The key to diagnosing bipolar disorder is that there is a change from the child's normal behaviour, i.e. there is a distinct episode of a defined duration. In this case Justin had previously been a very active, talkative and adventurous boy who was popular at school but for the past 4 weeks he has been very irritable and not at all like himself. He has a reduced need for sleep, is up at night and does not feel tired. This is different from insomnia where a person cannot sleep, despite wanting to. Justin has shown a change to aggressive and argumentative behaviour, which is out of character. If he were normally like this as part of an ODD/conduct disorder presentation then they would not count as bipolar symptoms. It is the change that is significant.

   Justin was actually fighting with his friends because he believed he was a champion wrestler and they kept laughing at him. This is a grandiose delusion and is different from a childish fantasy because he truly believes he is a wrestler and becomes angry, if disbelieved. It can be much harder to distinguish grandiosity in children compared to adults. Justin's distractibility has been long-running and is not part of his manic presentation. He is hyperactive and impulsive, so ADHD would need to be considered and 70–90 per cent of bipolar children present with co-occurring ADHD (Singh et al., 2006). It is important to be aware of any history of physical, sexual or emotional abuse, substance abuse and undiagnosed learning disabilities.

## Intervention

The evidence base for the pharmacological and psychological treatment of bipolar disorder in children and adolescents is extremely limited (NICE, 2006). A meta-analysis of evidence in adults found evidence for the effectiveness of cognitive behaviour therapy (CBT), in combination with usual treatment, for relapse prevention in stable disorders. They found that group psycho-education is more effective than non-structured meetings (Saunders and Goodwin, 2010).

There is little information on the efficacy and safety of antipsychotic drugs in children and adolescents and treatment strategies are based on the extrapolation of adult data (The Joint Formulary Committee, 2010). No medication is indicated or licensed at Justin's age. If medication is thought necessary, then it would be appropriate to treat Justin's mania with an atypical antipsychotic such as risperidone or olanzapine. Height and weight are recorded and charted at baseline and during treatment. Prolactin levels are recorded. If there is an inadequate response then lithium treatment for females and valproate or lithium treatment for males should be considered (NICE guidelines, 2006). This would be the long-term treatment strategy for the prevention of relapse.

# Case study 2: Emily

Emily is a 16-year-old girl in Year 11 at school currently studying for her GCSEs. She has been referred by her GP who had been reviewing her for depressed mood when Emily disclosed that she has been thinking about killing herself. When seen, Emily describes low mood, feeling tired all the time, gaining no pleasure from her usual interests, inability to sleep, not eating and having recurrent thoughts of taking an overdose of paracetamol. She has felt like this for 3 weeks now. Before that, Emily was the best she had ever felt. She was out every night with friends until 1am and only needed 3 hours sleep at night to keep going. In fact she was 'buzzing', her mind was racing and she couldn't stop talking, which had been funny at first, but then became annoying to her friends. She had fallen out with her friends after she made sexual advances towards their boyfriends, which is totally out of character for her. Emily's attendance at school had become erratic and she was always in trouble with both teachers and pupils for inappropriate remarks and behaviour. This period of feeling 'high' lasted for 2 weeks.

## Assessment

As in the last case, the parents, the child and their teachers are interviewed. Rating scales such as WASH-U-KSADS, Child Behaviour Checklist, Parent Young Mania Rating Scale or Parent General Behaviour Inventory can be used. Organic causes need to be excluded.

## Formulation

Emily is presenting during a depressive episode but gives a clear history of an episode of mania with elated mood, pressure of speech, grandiosity, disinhibited behaviour and reduced sleep. Therefore, she has had the two mood episodes required by ICD-10 criteria. In addition, the NICE guidelines (2006) are clear that bipolar disorder is only diagnosed in the presence of mania with euphoria in children and adolescents.

In the adolescent age range, it is important to seek a history of substance abuse, as rates of the use of illegal substances are high and they can be responsible for a presentation like this. Substance abuse disorders are present in 60 per cent of adults with bipolar disorder (Cassidy et al., 2001) and 32 per cent of young people have a lifetime history of substance abuse disorder (Wilens et al., 2004).

Children presenting with mania are often misdiagnosed with schizophrenia (Carlson, 2000) as the agitation and flight of ideas of a manic state, plus the presence of psychotic symptoms, can resemble the positive symptoms of schizophrenia. The depressive symptoms can be mistaken as negative symptoms of schizophrenia (Baroni et al., 2009).

# Prognosis

Children with bipolar disorder spend more time depressed than manic. There is a much higher rate of suicidal ideation in bipolar disorder compared to the normal population, with 35 per cent having a life-time risk of attempting suicide (Axelson et al., 2006). Studies suggest that between 70 and 100 per cent of children experience remission, but recurrence has been reported in 80 per cent at four-year follow-up (Geller et al., 2004; Birmaher et al., 2006).

In the adult literature, long-term outcome in bipolar disorder has been studied in a number of cohorts, all of which support the notion that bipolar disorder is a lifelong illness (Saunders and Goodwin, 2010). A 40-year follow-up of the Zurich Cohort found that 16 per cent of those individuals had recovered (recovery defined as no episode for the past five years), but over 50 per cent were still experiencing recurrent episodes (Angst, 1980).

## Multiple choice questions

1. Which of the following are symptoms of mania?

   a. Being very happy
   b. Being up and down in mood through the day
   c. Not being able to stop talking
   d. Believing you have special powers
   e. Constantly irritable

2. Which other disorder of childhood has the highest co-morbidity with bipolar disorder?

   a. Substance misuse
   b. Oppositional defiance disorder
   c. Attention deficit hyperactivity disorder
   d. Anxiety
   e. Conduct disorder

3. Which of the following are possible risk factors in the development of bipolar disorder in children and young people?

   a. Attention deficit hyperactivity disorder (ADHD)
   b. Major pre-pubertal depression
   c. Anxiety
   d. Oppositional defiance disorder (ODD)/conduct disorder (CD)
   e. Tourette syndrome

4. Which of the following are recommended by NICE to treat mania?

   a. Sodium valproate
   b. Lithium

c. Fluoxetine

d. Risperidone

e. Olanzapine

## Key texts

Baroni A, Lunsford J, Luckenbaugh D et al. (2009) Practitioner Review: The assessment of bipolar disorder in children and adolescents. *Journal of Child Psychology and Psychiatry*, **50**: 203–15.

Leibenluft E, Dickstein DP (2008) Bipolar disorder in children and adolescents. In: Rutter M, Taylor E (eds). *Rutter's Child and Adolescent Psychiatry*, 5th edn. Oxford: Blackwell Science Ltd, 613–27.

National Institute for Clinical Excellence (2006) NICE Guideline CG38: *The Management of Bipolar Disorder in Adults, Children and Adolescents, in Primary and Secondary Care*. London: National Institute for Health and Clinical Excellence.

# 48 Deliberate self-harm and suicide
### Anthony Crabb

> ## Key concepts
> - Self-harm can mean a range of behaviours intended to cause pain for a young person, but not necessarily about suicidal intent.
> - The average onset for deliberate self-harm (DSH) behaviours is 12 years
> - When a young person presents with DSH, it is important to take a non-judgemental approach.
> - Key areas of assessment would include method, intent, previous history of DSH, precipitating events, thoughts/feelings after the event, ongoing support systems.

## Introduction

Self-harm in the adolescent age group is relatively common, but completed suicide is thankfully less so. The average age of onset for self-harm is 12 years old (Mental Health Foundation, 2006) and it is a symptom, rather than a cause or disease in its own right. Approximately 25 000 young people are admitted to hospital in the UK each year after deliberately harming themselves and most of these are from self-poisoning (Fox and Hawton, 2004).

Estimates of the prevalence of self-harm in community settings range from one in 10 (Hawton and James, 2005) to one in 15 (Mental Health Foundation, 2006) and the figures vary according to how the studies are done. In acute adolescent mental health inpatient settings, the rates have been reported to be upwards of 80 per cent (Ougtin and Zundelt, 2010). Self-harm is four times more common in girls than boys. Gathering accurate data can be difficult due to the stigma of self-harm and access to those that self-harm.

For each of those who actually self-harm, there are many more who have thoughts about it, but do not go on to actually do it. There is widespread misunderstanding about the causes and consequences of self-harm and a self-harming child can receive very negative responses from family, friends and professionals when self-harm is initially disclosed, reducing the likelihood of further disclosure.

## What is self-harm?

Self-harm can mean a range of behaviours that cause physical harm or pain to a young person. It can be hidden from others for a long period of time. Self-harm is usually intended to harm, not kill. According to Fox and Hawton (2004), 40–100 times as many young people engage in self-harm as those that actually complete suicide.

Self-harm can involve:
- cutting;
- burning;
- scalding;
- banging or scratching one's own body;
- breaking bones;
- hair-pulling;
- ingesting toxic substances or objects.

It can include not taking, or overdosing on, medications for illness, for example insulin for diabetes, in addition to drug or alcohol use (Mental Health Foundation, 2006).

Self-harm can be the presenting symptom of mental illness or distress but sometimes it can be difficult to identify a particular trigger. Sometimes it is viewed as an active coping strategy that reduces stress or anxiety in the short term and it can be a way of communicating distress when other forms of communication are either too difficult or have been tried without success. The relief from anxiety or tension that is provided by acts of self-harm is short lived, so that the self-harm needs to be repeated. This can set up an addictive cycle (Mental Health Foundation, 2006). For some young people physical pain can be easier to deal with than emotional pain (Fox and Hawton, 2004).

Some of the more common triggers of self-harm include:

- daily stressors – schoolwork/family arguments;
- feeling isolated;
- self-harm/suicide by peer;
- low self-esteem;
- relationship difficulties;
- bullying;
- emotional/physical/sexual abuse;
- mental health problems;
- physical health problems.

# Self-harm and suicide

Although the two are closely linked, there are some differences in attempted suicide and self-harm. Self-harm can occur in the absence of suicidal thoughts, i.e. the young person is distressed and wants to relieve that distress by self-harming, but has no suicidal intent. As described above, it can be seen as a way of managing distress. Some researchers refer to non-suicidal self-injury (NSSI).

Attempted suicide is a way of ending distress and thus has different motivation. Sometimes the distinction is difficult to tease out. The group of young people who self-harm are somewhat different to those that attempt, or complete, suicide.

Completed suicide is more common in males, who tend to use more violent and lethal methods. The most significant risk factor is a previous suicide attempt: 30× increased risk for males and 3× increased risk for females.

## Assessment

- Adopt a non-judgemental and respectful approach.
- Try to see the young person on their own if possible.
- Assess the young person in an appropriate setting.
- Respect confidentiality within the limits of the Children Act.

Assessment of young people who have self-harmed is usually undertaken in a hospital or in a community CAMHS (Child and Adolescent Mental Health Service) setting. It can be very difficult for young people to admit to self-harm as they are often afraid of negative reactions from parents, friends and professionals. Although most present with a parent or guardian, some may be alone and it is important to try to see the young person by themselves, unless they request otherwise.

## Key domains of assessment

- Method
- Intent/perceived lethality of self-harm
- Isolation
- Precipitating events
- Previous history of self-harm
- Ongoing intent to self-harm
- Mental health problems
- Physical health problems
- Substance use
- Social support
- Discharge/follow-up plans

## Method

The most common methods of self-harm reported in a UK study by Hawton and Rodham (2006) were self-cutting (55.3 per cent) and self-poisoning (21.6 per cent). It is important to take a detailed and accurate description of what harm has actually been done. You may need to ask for information from a friend or family member who was present at the time. Those young people who self-harm by cutting are much less likely to present to accident and emergency and many instances are unreported and are not known to CAMHS or accident and emergency. The method of self-harm is influenced by the availability of items such as tablets. The choice of method can indicate the seriousness of the intent. For example, superficially cutting one's forearm carries less risk of intent of suicide than hanging.

## Intent/perceived lethality

It is important to find out what the perceived lethality of the self-harm was. Did the young person think that the method used was likely to kill them? Most young people are aware of the potential for harm in differing methods; however, there is a common misperception that paracetamol is safe. Conversely, a self-harm episode that the assessor might consider to have little potential to be fatal may, in the young person's mind, have been likely to succeed. Subjective lethality is a better predictor of risk than objective lethality.

## Isolation

Sometimes referred to as the likelihood of discovery, it is important to ascertain who was around at the time of the self-harm. A self-harm episode in the company of friends and family carries less risk than one done in isolation. It is important to find out who sought help following the self-harm. Was it the young person, or was it a friend or family member? How soon after the episode of self-harm was help sought?

## Precipitating events

Were there any immediate triggers for the episode of self-harm and are these triggers persisting? Can any of the triggers be modified?

## Previous history of self-harm

Given that the most important predictor of future behaviour is past behaviour, it is necessary to obtain as much information as possible about previous episodes of self-harm.

## Ongoing intent to self-harm

Although some young people will find it difficult to disclose ongoing thoughts of self-harm, for many the desire to self-harm initially reduces after the act. Ongoing voiced intent to self-harm obviously increases the risk of future episodes.

## The future

Asking a young person about their plans for the future, such as college and work aspirations can help gauge any hopes/aspirations they may have and possibly indicate a lower risk of completed suicide.

## Mental health problems

Mental health problems increase the risk of further self-harm and may require specialist input from a CAMHS team.

## Physical health problems

Not only does chronic illness increase the risk of self-harm, it can provide the means for unusual methods of self-harm around both the illness itself and its treatment. Some treatments can be very dangerous if taken incorrectly, for example insulin.

## Social support

It is necessary to ascertain what social supports a young person has. Those in foster care or temporary placements are especially vulnerable.

## Discharge/follow-up plans

Ensure that there is a responsible adult to supervise the young person on their return home. Discuss limiting access to methods of self-harm on return home. Follow-up may need to be with a local CAMHS service.

## Person-specific risk factors for self-harm

- Previous self-harm or suicide attempt
- Mental illness
- Poor social support
- Physical illness, especially chronic illness
- Child abuse/bullying
- Substance abuse

## High risk groups

- Homeless/poor social supports
- Mental health problems
- Victims of abuse
- Mental health inpatients
- Those that are imprisoned
- Substance users
- Those with sexuality issues

## Prevention/intervention

There is no strong evidence base for specific interventions for self-harm. It is apparent that a 'one size fits all' approach cannot be taken and a tailored approach appropriate to the specific young person who has self-harmed is required.

School-based interventions, such as access to someone to talk to at school, has been cited by the national enquiry (Mental Health Foundation, 2006) as a possible preventative measure. Peer support schemes, anti-bullying strategies and a reduction in the sense of social isolation have all been suggested as interventions that could be helpful in reducing self-harm.

Self-help is crucial. Distraction techniques are important in addition to substitution acts, for example pinging a rubber band on the wrist to inflict pain or rubbing ice on skin.

## Case study 1: Jake

Jake (7 years old) ties a cord round his neck in front of his mother following an argument with her.

The younger a child is at the time of self-harm, the less likely the intent is to die, as they are less likely to have a fully formed understanding of what death is. Unfortunately, this group can be very impulsive and may sustain significant injury that is unintentional. Social factors need to be considered carefully as self-harm behaviour in this age group may be learned from observing others. Although the method used carries high risk, the isolation and the perceived lethality may be low; although this would need detailed enquiry.

## Case study 2: Melissa

Melissa (15 years old) takes 20 paracetamol tablets at her boyfriend's place after breaking up. She does this in front of him.

In this scenario it is more likely that the young person's intention is to communicate distress, rather than to die. Although the perceived lethality of the intent may be low, it is important that Melissa receives medical attention, as the risk of significant liver damage in untreated paracetamol overdose can be high.

## Case study 3: Richard

Richard (15 years old) repeatedly cuts his forearm to help 'reduce stress'.

Appropriate medical treatment needs to be given for any wounds, even if they are superficial, as poor healing can lead to permanent scars that outlast any emotional distress that precipitated the self-harm. Along with an assessment of mental state, work undertaken with the boy might include the suggestion of substitute acts, such as using a rubber band on his wrist to inflict pain.

## Case study 4: Jamie

Jamie (16 years old), out of school, with depression, goes into woods alone and takes 100 fluoxetine.

This scenario is one where the perceived lethality may have been high even though fluoxetine is safe in overdose. The degree of isolation is high, with less likelihood that Jamie would be found and help summoned. Jamie is already in a high risk group, as he is out of school and has a mental illness. This young person would warrant a very detailed assessment and a robust safety plan following hospital treatment.

# NICE guideline on self-harm: key points

All children and young people who have self-harmed should normally be admitted to a paediatric ward and be assessed the following day before discharge (NICE, 2004a).

CAMHS workers involved in the assessment and treatment of children and young people who have self-harmed should:

- be trained specifically to work with young people and their families after self-harm;
- be skilled in the assessment of risk;
- have regular supervision;
- have access to consultation with senior colleagues.

Initial management should include advising carers of the need to remove all medications or other means of self-harm available to the young person who has self-harmed.

## Multiple choice questions

1. Which statement is correct about self-harm?

   a. Rates of self-harm are decreasing in the UK
   b. Self-harm and suicide always have the same motivation
   c. It can be triggered by relationship difficulties
   d. Young people always report episodes of self-harm
   e. Self-harm is due to poor parenting

2. Which method of self-harm is the most common?

   a. Burning
   b. Cutting
   c. Overdose
   d. Hair pulling
   e. Hanging

3. Which of the following predict increased risk of self-harm?

   a. Social isolation
   b. Mental health problems
   c. Previous self-harm
   d. Substance use
   e. All of the above

4. Which of the following is true about boys that self-harm?

   a. They don't overdose on tablets
   b. Self-harm is more common
   c. They use more violent methods
   d. They have better outcomes than girls
   e. They don't use cutting

### Key texts

Fox C, Hawton K (2004) *Deliberate Self-harm in Adolescence.* London: Jessica Kingsley.

Mental Health Foundation (2006) *Truth Hurts. Report of the National Inquiry into Self-Harm among Young People.* London: Mental Health Foundation.

National Institute for Clinical Excellence (2004a) *Self-Harm: The Short-term Physical and Psychological Management and Secondary Prevention of Self-harm in Primary and Secondary Care,* CG16. London: National Institute for Health and Clinical Excellence.

## 49 *School refusal behaviour*
### Helen Mabey

---

## Key concepts

- School refusal behaviour (SRB) refers to any degree of repeated non-attendance or attempted non-attendance, regardless of the factors which motivate its onset and continuation.
- While historically schools have dealt with non-attendance by implementing a series of 'blanket' interventions, research shows the benefits of identifying the primary function of the behaviour and devising a tailored intervention based on this.
- Recent research for classifying school refusal behaviour favours Kearney's model:
- Type 1 – Avoidance of stimuli that provoke negative feelings
- Type 2 – Avoidance of aversive social or evaluative situations
- Type 3 – Attention seeking
- Type 4 – Pursuance of tangible reinforcement outside school.
- Best practice is to consider all cases individually and to devise a targeted and tailored management plan with the support of the pupil, family and school staff.
- Open lines of communication, and involvement where appropriate, with local authority agencies (e.g. Family Support Workers, Educational Psychologists and Education Welfare Officers) should also be ensured.

---

## Introduction

Recent government statistics have suggested that 50 000 pupils per day miss school without permission, resulting in a total of 7.5 million school days per year being missed (Department for Education and Skills, 2006). Kearney (2002) estimated that at any one time between 5 and 28 per cent of youth regularly miss school. Periods of school absence are more likely to occur after a weekend or school holiday, or school transitions – particularly primary to secondary. Males and females are equally likely to exhibit such behaviour and school refusal is relatively uncommon before adolescence, after which there is a significant and marked increase in prevalence (Berg et al., 1969; Berg, 1992).

School refusal has a significant impact on a child's social and educational development and is likely to give rise to many other negative consequences in addition to the possible prosecution of the parents (Lauchlan, 2003). In the short term, children who exhibit school refusal behaviour are more likely to have difficulties in their relationships with families and peers, while longer-term consequences may include academic underachievement, employment difficulties, greater risk of psychiatric illness and increased risk of criminal offending.

## What do we mean by school refusal behaviour?

Absenteeism has been discussed widely, with much disparity regarding the definition. Initially, a distinction was made between 'school phobics' and 'truants', with the term 'school phobic' describing children with a difficulty attending school associated with emotional distress, particularly anxiety or depression. 'Truants', however, were seen to be motivated by a lack of interest in school and a desire to engage in more attractive, often antisocial pastimes – thus emotional distress or anxiety about school was not seen as a key characteristic. A further distinction made between school phobics and truants was the tendency for truants to conceal their absenteeism from their parents, while school phobia was usually absence with the knowledge, perhaps even consent, of parents. This distinction, however, has proved simplistic as pupils are absent for a number of reasons, often complex, and may fall within both categories.

Kearney and Silverman (1999) proposed that rather than labelling children differently, the umbrella term 'school refusal behaviour' or 'SRB', should be used to describe all pupils exhibiting any attendance difficulties. SRB serves a number of different functions for different children and the factors which motivate its onset and continuation vary widely between children. Once a child has been identified as exhibiting SRB, the function of this behaviour can then be investigated and determined, in order to begin the management process.

Considering this inclusive definition of SRB, Kearney (2003) outlined a continuum, suggesting that children anywhere along this continuum could be classified as displaying SRB:

- attendance at school under duress and pleas for non-attendance;
- repeated misbehaviours in the morning to avoid school;
- repeated tardiness in the morning to avoid school followed by attendance;
- periodic absences or skipping of classes;
- repeated absences or skipping classes and mixed attendance;
- complete absence during a certain period of the school year;
- complete absence for an extended period of time.

# Identifying the function of SRB

The most widely accepted and utilized model of classifying the different functions of SRB is proposed by Kearney and Silverman (1990). This model outlines four different types of SRB:

1. Type 1 – Avoidance: Pupils who avoid situations which cause them anxiety or fear.

Examples may include avoiding a specific teacher or curriculum area; or anxiety about a specific location or aspect of the school routine (e.g. the playground at break time; the school bell or fire alarm).
2. Type 2 – Escape: This refers to pupils who appear to be avoiding any situation in which they may be negatively evaluated. Pupils who are bullied fit into this category as they are fearful of unfavourable social judgement, classification or ridicule. Other pupils may avoid tests or exam situations.
3. Type 3 – Attention seeking: This refers to pupils whose SRB is motivated by the attention they receive as a result of their non-attendance. This may include attention or special arrangements being made by members of staff at school, or the attention of a parent at home when they are not in attendance at school.
4. Type 4 – Tangible reinforcement: This type refers to those pupils who shun school in favour of the pursuit of more enjoyable activities outside school (e.g. television, shopping).

Within these classifications, Types 1 and 2 result mainly in internalizing behaviours and provide the child with negative reinforcement from not attending school. Types 3 and 4 result in externalizing behaviours and provide the child with positive reinforcement from their absenteeism.

# Assessment

Despite the identification of these types, it is important to note that the model does not 'box' children into one of the four types; rather, it allows for the fact that the function of a child's SRB may fall into more than one type, while allowing consideration of whether a predominant type might be identified for the purposes of informing and embarking on the intervention and management process. Similarly, the four types are not exhaustive and other factors may contribute to motivating a pupil's SRB. It is important to consider all cases and their unique characteristics and variables on an in-depth, individual basis.

To form hypotheses regarding the function of a pupil's SRB, it is necessary to consider information from a variety of sources, including the pupil, the pupil's family and members of teaching staff, and through a variety of media (e.g. observation, interview and discussion, analysis of attendance records, etc.).

Areas which warrant exploration may include:

- whether there is evidence of a key 'event' or incident which triggered, or preceded the period of school refusal;
- whether there are any patterns to the school refusal (i.e. is attendance linked to particular times of day, teachers, curriculum areas);
- what the pupil is doing when they are not in school;
- the quality and nature of the pupil's relationships with their peers;
- the quality and nature of the pupil's relationships with their family members;
- whether there is any history of SRB with other members of the family;
- whether there are any other areas of concern within the child's life; for example, is school the only area in which the behaviour manifests, or do they show difficulties in other areas (e.g. work, social situations);
- the level of attendance and the length of time that the SRB has persisted for.

Kearney and Silverman (1993) have devised the School Refusal Assessment Scale (SRAS), which was subsequently updated to form the SRAS-R (Kearney, 2002). This comprises pupil and parent/teacher questionnaires, each containing items to be rated on a seven-point Likert scale (from 0 to 6). Each item relates to one of Kearney's SRB types and scores are combined and calculated to indicate which type of SRB is predominant.

Both the SRAS and SRAS-R were reported to have good validity and reliability (Fremont, 2003). Again, this does not 'diagnose' pupils, but draws together information from various sources to suggest a primary motivation for SRB.

# Management and intervention

Various interventions for SRB have been researched and documented, including cognitive-behaviour therapy (CBT); play therapy, psychotherapy and family therapy, behavioural interventions such as flooding or gradual exposure, social skills training and implementing systems within school. Research into the efficacy of each of these has yielded inconclusive or unconvincing results and therefore many Educational Psychologists have reported uncertainty in knowing which intervention is best to recommend. As a result, schools have historically responded to cases by putting in place a series of 'blanket' interventions, including offering rewards to the pupil for attendance, or spending time with a key member of pastoral staff. Persistent cases are usually managed with the help of the school's Education Welfare Officer (EWO), who may or may not choose to pursue a legal course of action, with the possibility of prosecution of the parents.

As is widely accepted among psychology and behaviour professionals, it is necessary to consider the function of behaviour in order to implement an effective intervention. The nature of the research has indicated that this is particularly important for pupils exhibiting SRB, and pursuing the legal route for all persistent cases is not helpful and in some cases may exacerbate the situation. Many researchers have now emphasized the particular importance of linking a school refusal intervention to a functional analysis of behaviour (Kearney and Silverman, 1993; Elliott, 1999; Lauchlan, 2003). Such an intervention is termed a 'prescriptive intervention'.

Having developed the SRAS-R, Kearney (2002) developed some tentative guidelines suggesting interventions which might warrant consideration for each different type of SRB. These were as follows:

- Type 1 (avoidance) may be best targeted by a child-based approach; exposure to school through systematic desensitization or relaxation techniques to alleviate feelings of anxiety when presented with an anxiety 'trigger'.
- Type 2 (escape) may be best targeted by exposure to school as well as cognitive restructuring or social skills training to support the child in situations which produce anxiety.
- Type 3 (attention seeking) may be best targeted by focusing on implementing routine and providing training in parenting skills, to equip parents with the skills to deal with attention-seeking behaviour.

- Type 4 (tangible reinforcement) may be best targeted by family-based therapies or contingency contracts to provide positive reinforcement for desired behaviours. Forced school attendance may also be effective here.

Recent research into such prescriptive interventions which make use of these guidelines has shown encouraging results, particularly when compared to the historical 'blanket' intervention approach (Chorpita, 1996; Kearney and Silverman, 1999).

## Case study: Niall

Niall was 6 and in his third term of Year 1 at a large Primary School. He lived with his mother and younger brother. Niall's attendance at preschool was very good and he made a smooth transition into Primary School. He developed a good relationship with Miss Kennedy, his Reception teacher. Niall attended well in Reception and was a much liked member of the class, despite being shy and often quiet. He was of average ability and was keen to please Miss Kennedy and the class teaching assistant.

Niall's attendance became of concern a few weeks into Year 1. Niall initially settled in well to the new routines and the more structured approach to lessons, but often began to complain of stomach aches or feeling poorly towards the end of the morning. His attendance levels then fell rapidly, with Niall either going home poorly during the morning, or being absent for the day. His absences rose to 1 or 2 days per week.

Niall's mother reported that he appeared to enjoy school and when he attended, he came home happy and talkative, wanting to share his experience of his day. She was surprised by the sudden change in his behaviour in Year 1, and explained that some days there were no difficulties and other days, he complained of feeling poorly. When asked, he always told his mother and his teachers that there was nothing worrying him at school. On the occasions Niall was taken into school despite feeling poorly, he became very distressed, to the point where it became very difficult to calm him down. When Niall was home during the day, he occupied himself with his toys in his room and rarely chose to spend time with his family.

On analysis of Niall's attendance records, the majority of absences took place on a Monday, with very few absences on a Tuesday, Wednesday or Friday. It quickly became apparent that his absences usually occurred on a day with a whole school assembly, which took place each Monday and every other Thursday, after lunch. When information was shared between Year 1 and Reception staff, it emerged that while Reception staff usually accompany the class into assemblies and remain seated alongside the children, teachers of older classes usually return to the classroom. The Year 1 teacher noted that while Niall was a well-liked member of Year 1, he tended to spend his break and lunch times playing near the adults on duty. It was hypothesized that Niall found whole school assembly times difficult due to feeling overwhelmed, being part of a large student body size with no immediate familiar adult support.

Niall's SRB was considered predominantly Type 1, as he was avoiding the negative emotions he associated with large assembly times. While there were elements of attention-seeking behaviours, it was felt that this was not the primary function of his school refusal, as he did not seek the attention of the adults – rather, he sought reassurance of their proximity. As such, an intervention was planned in order to support Niall, whereby the Emotional Literacy Support Assistant (ELSA – a trained member of staff who supports pupils with emotional difficulties by working with them on an individual basis) worked with him. Some 'getting to know you' sessions were planned each week, and took place during assembly times. Following this, the ELSA would take him to assembly and remain there until the end. During the sessions that followed, Niall was able to talk a little about the things that frightened him and how he feels when he is in a large group of pupils – particularly older pupils. The ELSA worked with him on some visualization and relaxation techniques, which he could use to focus his thoughts or reassure himself. Particularly helpful for Niall was to locate a friend in his class and remember a good memory of their play, as this focused his attention onto one person within the crowd. A while after, a systematic desensitization process was then simultaneously employed, whereby the ELSA would explain to Niall that she would be leaving the assembly a little earlier over time. Niall is currently finding whole school assemblies easier to cope with and his attendance is reported to be very good.

## Case study: Lauren

Lauren was in Year 7 and moved to an independent Secondary School from her local Primary. Her attainment was above average and she was placed in the class for more able pupils. She attended well for the first few weeks and was a popular member of the class. Just before the first half term, she had a period of absence lasting a school week and following this, her attendance records showed that she averaged 1 or 2 days off per week. Initially, when Lauren attended school she coped well and appeared to enjoy her lessons and the company of her peers.

During the next term, Lauren's absences increased and she was often away for the whole week; perhaps attending for just one morning or afternoon. She arrived at school with her mother most mornings, but refused to go in, becoming very distressed and anxious, often hitting out when her mother attempted to leave. From the beginning of her attendance difficulties, Lauren developed an excellent relationship with the Deputy Head Teacher, who assumed the responsibility of coaching and supporting Lauren to separate from her mother at the start of the school day. As her attendance deteriorated, she was reluctant to leave the Deputy Head and spent what little time she was in school in the Deputy's office. Similarly to her mother, any of the Deputy's attempts to support Lauren to join her class were met with panic attacks, hyperventilation or upset and anger. On a few occasions, Lauren left the school without adult permission to return home.

It was felt that Lauren's SRB could be best described by Type 3 – attention-seeking behaviour. It did not appear that Lauren was avoiding anything in particular relating to school; on the contrary, she was very keen to maintain her role as 'classmate' and often invited the class back to her house for parties, which were successful. She attempted to go on all school trips, although this was not always successful, and where she did attend, she always returned home at night. When Lauren was not in school, she did not engage in any leisure activities – rather, she often complained of being bored as she had to attend her mother's office job with her. In addition, the issues around attendance also became apparent at Lauren's extracurricular activities (i.e. dance classes, going to other people's houses).

Lauren had a particularly close relationship with her mother. Her parents had separated and divorced in the previous academic year and it was hypothesized that this may have triggered the onset of separation anxiety with her mother and related attention-seeking behaviour. Without the attention of her mother at home, she sought the individual attention of the Deputy Head, which appeared to worsen the situation, as she no longer attended class. Although Lauren's mother had been threatened with legal action, this only appeared to add to Lauren's level of anxiety.

Due to the severe nature of Lauren's anxiety, she was referred to the Child and Adolescent Mental Health Service, through which she and her mother accessed some cognitive-behavioural based family therapy, which focused on working through issues around the separation of her parents as well as looking at the new routines in the home. Although the process was a lengthy one, her attendance rose over time and she was attending well by Year 10.

## Case study: Adam

Adam lived at home with his parents and older sister. He had attended three Primary Schools as his family moved due to their work. He previously attended school well, but his behaviour became difficult to manage when he was in Year 8. He received a number of fixed term exclusions for aggression and was permanently excluded from two Secondary Schools by the time he reached Year 10. He was placed on roll at the Local Education Centre/Pupil Referral Unit but his attendance was only around 25 per cent. During the time he was not in school, Adam was often picked up by the police who were carrying out 'sweeps' of the local area, looking for 'truanting' pupils. Although Adam would leave the house in the mornings promising to attend school, he would reply honestly when challenged about his whereabouts in the evenings. He tended to spend his time with a group of older children who had left school the previous year, and they would play video games or walk around the local shopping centre.

Adam was of average ability, but due to his attendance and approach to learning, his attainments were below average. He did not appear to be concerned about the effect his absences were having on his education or future prospects.

It was hypothesized that Adam's school refusal was primarily Type 4 – pursuit of tangible reinforcement outside of school. Due to the number of changes in school placement that Adam had experienced, the majority of his friends were people he had met in other circumstances – usually through his music activities and boxing club that he enjoyed attending. His behaviour was not seeking the attention of staff or other pupils, and when he did attend the Education Centre, he was a well-liked member of the class. There were no clear patterns to his attendance. The friendship group that he had chosen were not providing Adam with either a motivation to spend time in school away from them, a group in which he belonged, or with any positive role modelling around gaining qualifications or entering a working life.

Adam was reluctant to engage with the Connexions service, but did develop a positive relationship with an Assistant Psychologist, who was working in the centre with pupils on a programme designed to support pupils at risk of exclusion, and the centre's Family Support Worker. He appeared to enjoy the discussion and activity-based group sessions, designed to challenge thinking and encourage independence and was always in attendance for these. This proved the trigger for Adam to engage in decision-making around his future at the Centre, and he showed interest in a mechanics apprenticeship. The Education Welfare Service had become involved with Adam's family but were unable to engage them. The possibility of Adam's parents being prosecuted also proved motivating for Adam to reconsider his attendance. Although his attendance improved, he continued to need support to motivate himself and the Centre effectively used a contingency contract, in which Adam earned 'vouchers' for every session he attended, which could be exchanged for rewards or activities. By the end of Year 11, Adam's attendance had risen to 85 per cent and he earned a place at the sixth form college.

## Multiple choice questions

1. Which statement is correct about management of school refusal behaviour?

   a. All pupils who exhibit school refusal behaviour should be offered rewards to attend school
   b. It is important to ensure that all pupils who exhibit school refusal behaviour in a school are treated the same way
   c. It is important to consider the function of a child's school refusal behaviour, and plan an intervention tailored around this
   d. Given that it is the responsibility of the parent to ensure that a child attends school, all cases of school refusal should result in parents being threatened with prosecution
   e. Cognitive behaviour therapy is an effective intervention for all types of school refusal behaviour

2. Which statement is correct about school refusers?

   a. The majority of school refusers are female
   b. Pupils are more likely to exhibit school refusal behaviour in the middle of a school term or year

   c. School refusal is more prevalent in preschoolers than any other age group

   d. School refusers are often older siblings

   e. It is common for school refusers to experience academic underachievement, employment difficulties and increased risk of criminal offending

3. Which statement can be described as an example of school refusal behaviour?

   a. Attendance at school under duress and pleas for non-attendance

   b. Repeated tardiness in the morning to avoid school followed by attendance

   c. Complete absence during a certain period of the school year

   d. Complete absence for an extended period of time

   e. All of the above are examples of school refusal behaviour

4. Which statement is incorrect about the assessment of school refusal behaviour?

   a. The views of parents and staff should be sought, but the views of the school refuser are of limited value

   b. Information should be gathered from a variety of different sources and methodologies

   c. Information about areas of the pupil's life outside of school should be sought and taken into consideration

   d. It is important to consider what the pupil is doing when they are not in school

   e. Patterns in school attendance should be looked for and where they exist, should be explored

5. Which statement about school refusal is correct?

   a. School refusal is the result of poor parenting

   b. School refusal is often motivated by a number of different factors, but it is often useful to identify a possible primary or predominant motivation

   c. School refusal is evidence of a school's poor behaviour and attendance practices

   d. School refusal is interchangeable with the term truancy

   e. School refusal is solely a behavioural issue and not an emotional one

## Key texts

Kearney CA (2002) Identifying the function of school refusal behaviour: A revision of the school refusal assessment scale. *Journal of Psychopathology and Behavioural Assessment*, **24**: 235–45.

Kearney CA (2003) Bridging the gap among professionals who address youths with school absenteeism: Overview and suggestions for consensus. *Professional Psychology: Research and Practice*, **34**: 57–65.

Kearney CA, Silverman WK (1999) Functionally based prescriptive and nonprescriptive treatment for children and adolescents with school refusal behaviour. *Behaviour Therapy*, **30**: 673–95.

Lauchlan F (2003) Responding to chronic non-attendance: a review of intervention approaches. *Educational Psychology in Practice*, **19**: 133–46.

# 50 Psychosis
### Clair Henry

---

> ## Key concepts
>
> - Psychosis in young people is commonly encountered by CAMHS professionals.
> - There are few childhood psychiatric disorders that present as dramatically or with such devastating consequences as early onset psychosis.
> - The term 'psychosis' is used to describe a serious mental illness in which there is a degree of detachment from reality.

---

## Introduction

Despite advances in treatment, outcome in early onset psychosis is often poor with long-term difficulties in mental health and everyday functioning. Beginning treatment early can lead to a much better outlook. The impact on development and poor prognosis reinforce the need for early detection and prompt treatment. Childhood onset schizophrenia typically runs a chronic course with only a minority making a full recovery.

## Epidemiology

The lifetime prevalence of psychotic disorders is 2–3 per cent; schizophrenia accounts for just under half of these. Schizophrenia is extremely rare before the age of ten years but the incidence rises steadily through adolescence. Gillberg et al. (1986) calculated the age-specific prevalence for all psychoses in the age range 13–18 years. Forty-one per cent had a diagnosis of schizophrenia. At age 13 years, the prevalence for all psychoses was 0.9 in 10000 reaching a prevalence of 17.6 in 10000 at age 18 years.

The causes of schizophrenia are not clearly understood but the increased risk in relatives of sufferers suggests a genetic component (**Table 50.1**).

Table 50.1 Genetic risk of schizophrenia

| Relative with schizophrenia | Chance of developing schizophrenia |
|---|---|
| One parent | One in ten |
| One identical twin | One in two |
| One non-identical twin | One in 80 |

## Schizophrenia

In the prodromal phase of schizophrenia, the phase which precedes the onset of psychotic symptoms, there is a gradual decline in social and academic functioning, sometimes for several years. Often this phase is only recognized with the benefit of hindsight. Psychotic symptoms can be categorized into positive and negative symptoms.

### Positive symptoms

- Hallucinations are a false perception of something that is not really there. Auditory hallucinations (hearing voices) are most common. They can be addressing the young person directly (second person), discussing the patient (third person) or giving a running commentary on the patient's actions. Hallucinations can be in the form of sight, touch, smell or taste.

- Delusions are fixed false beliefs, which are not in keeping with the individual's religious, social or educational background. They can be a belief of being persecuted (paranoid delusions), a belief that events or the behaviour of others refer to oneself (delusions of reference), or a belief that one is being controlled by external forces (delusions of control).
- Passivity phenomena include a belief that one's thoughts can be read by others (thought broadcast), that thoughts are being inserted into one's mind (thought insertion) and thoughts are being removed from one's mind (thought withdrawal).
- Thought disorder is experienced as muddled thinking and may present with incoherent speech or neologisms (the invention of words with attached meaning).
- Disorganized behaviour and inappropriate affect can be positive symptoms

Positive symptoms in young people may first become apparent through behavioural changes such as:

- becoming irritable or isolative due to feeling paranoid;
- developing new interests or asking questions related to delusional ideas;
- appearing distracted or responding to hallucinations.

## Negative symptoms

- Reduced emotional reactivity with blunted affect and social withdrawal
- Poverty of thought and speech
- Non-specific behavioural changes can be early negative symptoms

For a diagnosis of schizophrenia, DSM-IV requires a six-month duration of disturbance, with ICD-10 requiring only one month duration.

# Differential diagnosis

In ICD-10, psychotic illnesses can be classified as:

- acute and transient psychotic disorders;
- schizoaffective disorders;
- psychotic disorder due to psychoactive substance use.

Other differential diagnoses of psychotic symptoms include mood disorders, anxiety disorders, autistic spectrum disorders, epilepsy and neurodegenerative disorders. It is important to consider an organic cause, including acute delirium or encephalitis.

# Cannabis and psychosis

Research suggests a causal relation in which frequent use of cannabis leads to a greater risk of psychotic symptoms through effects on the processing of dopamine in the brain (Fergusson et al., 2006; Moore et al., 2007). Continuation of cannabis use is associated with risk of persistence of psychotic symptoms in young people (Kuepper et al., 2011).

# Summary

- Eighty per cent of first psychotic episodes occur between the ages of 16 and 30.
- A prodromal phase often precedes the onset of psychotic symptoms.
- Positive symptoms include hallucinations, delusions, passivity phenomena, thought disorder and disorganized behaviour.
- Negative symptoms include reduced emotional reactivity and poverty of thought and speech.
- Prompt treatment leads to a better outcome.

## Case study 1: Peter

Peter is a 15 year old presenting at accident and emergency with deliberate self-harm by cutting his arms. He is distressed and frightened and denies using any psychoactive substances. His mother reports that over the past year, his school work has deteriorated; he has stopped socializing with friends and spends most of his time in his room. He admits to a two-month history of hearing an unknown male voice coming from outside his head telling him to harm himself. He believes that aliens are controlling his thoughts and that if he resists self-harming, he will be captured by alien forces and his family will be harmed.

Assessment of this case includes full mental state examination to assess for other psychotic symptoms and mood symptoms. A history of substance misuse and previous self-harming should be taken. The time course of his symptoms and change in functioning should be clarified and identification made of any possible precipitants. His past medical history and family history must be noted. Investigations include urine drug screen, electroencephalograph (EEG; records the electrical activity of the brain) and magnetic resonance imaging (MRI; used to scan for benign or malignant abnormal growths in the brain). A thorough risk assessment should be carried out to assess whether this young person can be managed in the community.

Peter is diagnosed with early onset schizophrenia. The focus of his treatment plan is to keep him safe while treating his illness using a multimodal treatment package. He requires psychoeducation to ensure that he and his family are fully informed about his illness along with individual therapy in the form of cognitive behaviour therapy (CBT) or counselling to help him understand and manage his symptoms. Family therapy will address any factors that may contribute to maintaining his illness or precipitate a relapse. Provision must be made to meet his social and educational needs. Hospital admission to an adolescent mental health unit may become necessary if Peter is thought to be at high risk in the community and antipsychotic medication remains the fundamental treatment.

Antipsychotic treatment should begin with an atypical antipsychotic (olanzapine, risperidone, quetiapine, amisulpride, aripiprazole). The aytpicals were introduced in the 1990s. Their mode of action involves various combinations of 5HT and dopamine blockade.

Young people are sensitive to the side effects of antipsychotic medications which can be severe. Extrapyramidal side effects (EPSEs) include dystonia (muscle spasm), akathisia (motor restlessness), pseudoparkinsonism (tremor, decreased body movement, rigidity) and tardive dyskinesia (abnormal movements). Atypical antipsychotics cause fewer EPSEs than older first-generation antipsychotics.

Other side effects include raised prolactin, reduced seizure threshold, postural hypotension, anticholinergic side effects (dry mouth, blurred vision, constipation), weight gain, diabetes and neuroleptic malignant syndrome (potentially fatal, presenting with fever, rigidity, confusion and elevated creatine kinase which is a potential marker of heart attack, acute renal failure or severe muscle breakdown).

## Case study 2: Selina

Selina (17) was diagnosed with early onset schizophrenia eight months ago. She was initially treated with an atypical antipsychotic which was ineffective. She experienced severe side effects and it was discontinued. She is currently prescribed another atypical antipsychotic but her psychotic symptoms remain. Selina is being treated in an inpatient unit as she is a risk to herself. She has persistent delusions that she is invincible and her body will regenerate. She believes that she will be 'taken by the devil' and experiences running commentary auditory hallucinations.

Algorithms for treating psychosis in young people are the same as those for adult patients. Patients unresponsive to two different antipsychotics, including one atypical, should be prescribed clozapine. Due to the association with neutropenia (reduced infection-fighting white cells in the blood; incidence 3 per cent), patients must be registered with an approved clozapine monitoring service and have blood tests weekly for the first 18 weeks, fortnightly until 52 weeks and monthly thereafter. Clozapine is effective in treatment-resistant schizophrenia in adolescents, although this population may be more prone to neutropenia and seizures than adults.

## Multiple choice questions

1. The majority of first psychotic episodes occur in which age group?

   a. Under ten years
   b. 10–15 years
   c. 16–30 years
   d. 25–50 years
   e. Over 40 years

2. The risk of developing schizophrenia if you have one parent with the diagnosis is:

   a. One in ten
   b. One in five
   c. One in two
   d. One in 50
   e. One in 80

3. An example of a negative symptom of schizophrenia is

   a. Delusions of control
   b. Third person auditory hallucinations
   c. Thought withdrawal
   d. Passivity phenomena
   e. Social withdrawal

4. Which statement is incorrect?

   a. The majority of patients with early onset schizophrenia make a full recovery
   b. Frequent cannabis use leads to greater risk of psychotic symptoms
   c. The prognosis of early onset psychosis is poor
   d. Psychotic symptoms can occur in epilepsy
   e. The prodromal phase of schizophrenia can last several years

5. Which statement is correct regarding antipsychotic medication?

   a. Typical antipsychotics are first line treatment for early onset psychosis
   b. Young people are resistant to extrapyramidal side effects
   c. Weight loss is a common side effect
   d. Clozapine does not require blood monitoring
   e. Neuroleptic malignant syndrome is potentially fatal

### Key texts

Gillberg C, Wahlstrom J, Forsman A et al. (1986) Teenage psychoses: Epidemiology, classification and reduced optimality in the pre, peri and neonatal periods. *Journal of Child Psychology and Psychiatry*, **27**: 87–98.

Kuepper R, van Os J, Lieb R et al. (2011) Continued cannabis use and risk of incidence and persistence of psychotic symptoms: 10 year follow-up cohort study. *British Medical Journal*, **342**: d738.

Tiffin PA (2007) Managing psychotic illness in young people: a practical overview. *Child and Adolescent Mental Health*, **12**: 173–86.

# 51   *Eating disorders*

Christopher Gale, Shilpa Balakrishna, Suyog Dhakras and Sarah Robotham

## Key concepts

- Eating disorders are split into three broad categories: Anorexia nervosa, Bulimia nervosa and Eating Disorders Not Otherwise Specified (EDNOS).
- Binge Eating Disorder fits under the EDNOS category.
- Anorexia nervosa is characterized by a morbid fear of gaining weight and concerted efforts to reduce weight through restricting food intake and in some cases, purging/vomiting and excessively exercising.
- Bulimia nervosa is characterized by episodes of bingeing on food, followed by concerted efforts to rid the body of food, through vomiting or use of purgatives.
- Binge Eating Disorder is characterized by episodes of bingeing on large quantities of food, followed by feelings of extreme guilt and self-loathing.
- Any intervention with an eating disorder should be carried out in partnership with the young person and their families.
- There is no one treatment of choice for eating disorders in children and young people: typically a combination of interventions is required to bring about a positive outcome.

## Introduction

Eating disorders usually develop in adolescence and early adulthood; more commonly in females, but increasingly in pre-pubertal children, older women and males. Cases that present in childhood or adolescence have a better prognosis than those that present or persist in adulthood. Anorexia nervosa, Bulimia nervosa and Binge Eating Disorder are subgroups of eating disorders. There are other subgroups that do not meet the threshold for these diagnoses and those that present differently.

## Anorexia nervosa

Anorexia nervosa was first described by Richard Morton in 1694; he called it 'Nervous Consumption'. The term 'Anorexia nervosa' was coined by the English physician, William Gull, in 1968; he emphasized the psychological causes of the condition, the need to restore weight and the role of the family.

It is marked by the determined efforts of the person to lose weight or to avoid weight gain, maintaining a weight that is below the expected range of weight for their height and age. Weight is lost or maintained at a low level by avoidance of certain foods, eating smaller portions and lower calorie food items, excessive exercise, self-induced vomiting and the use of medications, including laxatives.

There are abnormal thought processes in the form of excessive fear of fatness and weight gain. These individuals are preoccupied by misconceptions about the size and shape of their bodies. In the pre-pubertal age group, there is a failure to make the expected weight gain and growth. There may be a delay in pubertal development leading to delays in starting periods in girls. In the post-pubertal age group, there is disruption of the various hormonal systems in the body, for example in young women their periods may stop, known as amenorrhoea.

The incidence of Anorexia nervosa is reported to be between 0.08 and 8.1 per 100 000 per year. The prevalence of Anorexia varies from 0.5 to 1.0 per cent of the adolescent population. Though some studies have shown an increase in the rate of anorexia over the years, it is difficult to establish the exact numbers due to the secrecy displayed by young people around the illness and the rigidity of the diagnostic criteria.

## Diagnosis

Anorexia nervosa is diagnosed in the UK by using the ICD-10 (WHO, 1992).

For a definite diagnosis, all of the following are required:

- Body weight is maintained at least 15 per cent below expected weight, either lost or never achieved or the body mass index (BMI) is 17.5 or less. Pre-pubertal individuals may show a failure to make the expected weight gain during the growth period.
- Weight loss is self-induced by avoidance of 'fattening foods'. One or more of the following may be present: self-induced vomiting, self-induced purging, excessive exercise, use of appetite suppressants and/or diuretics.
- There is body image distortion whereby a dread of fatness persists as an intrusive, overvalued idea and the patient imposes a low weight threshold on him/herself.
- A widespread endocrine disorder involving the hypothalamic–pituitary–gonadal axis manifests in women as amenorrhoea and in men as a loss of sexual interest and potency. An exception is the persistence of vaginal bleeds in anorexic women on hormone replacement therapy, for example contraceptive pills. There may be elevated levels of growth hormone, cortisol, changes in the metabolism of thyroid hormones and abnormalities of insulin secretion.
- If onset is pre-pubertal, the sequence of pubertal events is delayed or even arrested; growth ceases, in girls, breasts do not develop and there is primary amenorrhoea; in boys, the genitals remain juvenile. With recovery, puberty is often completed normally, but menarche is late.

BMI is calculated as: BMI = weight (in kg)/height (in metre). Normal BMI falls within the range of 20–25. This can be a crude measure. It is an adult measure and does not allow for the varying rate at which children and young people physically develop, including body frame size. A more useful measure in children and young people would be weight for height charts.

The DSM IV-TR (American Psychiatric Association, 2000) further classifies Anorexia into:

- restricting type in people who restrict their dietary intake;
- binge eating/purging type in people who engage in binging and purging behaviours.

## Aetiology

Anorexia nervosa has a multi-factorial aetiology.

### Biological factors

The incidence of Anorexia is 6–10 per cent in the female siblings of patients, more so in identical twins than in non-identical twins. Apart from the genetic contribution, shared familial environment may be significant. Family genetic studies have shown that there is an association between eating disorders and mood disorders.

### Psychological factors

These young people are often struggling for control, a sense of identity and effectiveness with the relentless pursuit to achieve thinness as a result. They can be perfectionists, high achieving, conscientious, popular, successful, overly compliant and have low self-esteem. Often they struggle with expressing negative emotions, such as anger, sadness or anxiety, especially if these are not tolerated within the family system.

The bodily changes that return it to a pre-pubertal state or to maintaining one in younger children can be interpreted as a regression to childhood, escaping the emotional problems of older childhood and adolescence. This may include the process of developing an identity as a sexual being, particularly if there have been unwanted sexual experiences.

### Familial factors

There may be disturbed relations in the family. Patterns of relationships could include enmeshment, over-protectiveness, rigidity and lack of conflict resolution whereby strong negative emotions are not well tolerated. It is sometimes unclear whether these patterns of dysfunction predate the onset of the illness or are a response to it. The young person's illness and the need for closer supervision and care may be holding the family together, if it is perceived to be at risk of breaking down.

## Social factors

The cultural pressure on women to be thin and on men to be muscle-toned may be an important predisposing factor in the development of eating disorders. The disorder is predominantly seen in Western cultures. There are, however, reports of increased incidence of Anorexia in rapidly developing economies, such as India and China, where Western cultural influences are becoming more widespread.

Most adolescents and young women will diet at one time or the other. However, people with Anorexia nervosa usually come from a family or social background where weight, shape and eating concerns are promoted, for example family members dieting or consciousness about weight and shape. Those young people who aspire to enter certain sports or industries, such as dance, gymnastics or modelling, where a certain body shape is required, are at particular risk of developing the disorder.

## Physical and psychological signs/ problems

- Sensitivity to cold and possible hypothermia
- Constipation and slow gastric emptying
- Low blood pressure and low heart rate
- Vomiting and laxative abuse may lead to signs of electrolyte imbalances including severe hypokalaemia, i.e. low potassium levels in the blood, which may cause seizures and death by cardiac arrhythmia
- Hair becomes brittle and there can be the appearance of fine hairs on the face, arms and legs, known as lanugo, as the body attempts to maintain a safe core temperature
- Poor concentration and cognitive processing ability, which may increase the distress if the young person has historically been a high academic achiever
- Changes to mood and anxiety levels. Sufferers can become highly anxious and irritable/ angry, especially in situations involving food

- Increased social isolation in an attempt to avoid situations involving food

## Prognosis and the need for prompt treatment

In adolescence there is a critical growth period during which the young person completes vital physical development. This period is considered to be essential for optimum physical and mental growth as an adult. Any disruption at this stage may have serious long-term health implications, for example stunted growth and infertility and osteoporosis in women. In the shorter term, Anorexia is perhaps the most fatal of psychiatric disorders with a mortality rate up to 22 per cent.

In a systematic review of studies into Anorexia nervosa, Steinhausen (2002) found the following rates of recovery among adolescents ($n = 784$):

- full recovery 57.1 per cent;
- improvement after treatment 25.9 per cent;
- chronicity 16.9 per cent.

This does not account for those young people who do not access services to manage their illness. Some may cease the restricting behaviour but go on to develop Bulimia nervosa.

## Bulimia nervosa

Bulimia nervosa refers to episodes of uncontrolled excessive eating called 'binges' followed by vomiting or the use of purgatives. The onset of Bulimia nervosa is usually in late adolescence, often after a period of concern about weight and shape; following a period of food restrictions. Twenty-five per cent of patients have a past history of Anorexia. The number of episodes of bingeing increases over time, returning the weight to near normal.

### Diagnosis

ICD-10 (WHO, 1992) criteria for Bulimia nervosa:

- A persistent preoccupation with eating and an irresistible craving for food; the patient succumbs to episodes of overeating in which large amounts of food are consumed in short periods of time.
- The patient attempts to counteract the 'fattening' effects of food by one or more of

the following: self-induced vomiting, purgative abuse, alternating periods of starvation, use of drugs such as appetite suppressants, thyroid preparations or diuretics. When Bulimia nervosa occurs in diabetic patients, they may choose to neglect their insulin treatment.

- The psychopathology consists of a morbid dread of fatness. The patient sets him/herself a sharply defined weight threshold, well below the pre-morbid weight that constitutes the optimum or healthy weight in the opinion of the physician. There is often, but not always, a history of an earlier episode of Anorexia nervosa (in 25 per cent), the interval between the two disorders ranging from a few months to several years. The earlier episode may have been fully expressed, or may have assumed a minor cryptic form with moderate loss of weight and/or a transient phase of amenorrhoea.

The DSM IV-TR (APA, 2000) further classifies Bulimia nervosa into:

- purging type in people who have regularly employed self-induced vomiting/misuse of laxatives, diuretics or enemas;
- non-purging type in people who have used other compensatory mechanisms, for example starvation, excessive exercises.

## Other features

The young person may exhibit a profound loss of control. Episodes of bingeing can be brought about by stress or by the breaking of self-imposed dietary control. Binges usually occur when alone, with initial relief of stress followed by feelings of guilt and disgust. The young person may then induce vomiting or take laxatives. Co-morbid depression can occur, which may improve with the improvement of the eating disorder.

## Aetiology

The aetiology for Bulimia nervosa is in many ways similar to that of Anorexia nervosa, a possible exception being the dynamics within the family system. In contrast to the anorexic family, where strong negative emotions are not easily tolerated, bulimic families can often be high in conflict and distress (Wonderlich, 1992).

## Physical and psychological signs/symptoms

- Repeated vomiting can cause severe hypokalaemia, i.e. very low levels of potassium in the blood, resulting in weakness, kidney damage and potentially fatal cardiac arrhythmias (abnormal electrical activity in the heart leading to cardiac arrest). The mortality rate across all age ranges is approximately 0.4 per cent (NICE, 2004b).
- Decreased motility of the colon and constipation.
- Teeth may become pitted with gastric acid erosion due to repeated vomiting.
- It has been suggested that long-term vomiting can increase the risk of permanent damage to the oesophagus.

## Prognosis

The longer-term outcomes of bulimia nervosa are variable. With the most effective treatments, about 50 per cent of people across the age range can be expected to be symptom free between two and ten years after assessment. Twenty per cent are likely to continue with the full form of Bulimia nervosa, while the remainder (30 per cent) have a course of illness characterized either by remissions or relapses or persistent, but sub-diagnostic bulimia (NICE, 2004b).

# Binge Eating Disorder

Binge Eating Disorder is not yet fully recognized as a disorder in its own right; instead it is either listed under 'Overeating associated with other psychological disturbances' (ICD-10 – WHO, 1992) or 'Eating Disorders Not Otherwise Specified' (EDNOS – DSM IV-TR, APA, 2000).

However, the following symptoms/behaviours may be observed:

- recurring episodes of binge eating, where a larger than normal amount of food is consumed in a relatively condensed period of time, although the eating may be continuous over several hours;
- the individual has no control over the amount and type of foods they are eating;

- the individual may eat even when not hungry and feel uncomfortably full after an episode;
- the episodes may be hidden from others due to shame and embarrassment;
- an episode of bingeing is followed by feelings of guilt and disgust, which highlights a possible underlying depression or anxiety which may be the cause or the result of the disordered eating;
- the episodes need to have occurred over a significant period of time; it is different from occasional over-indulgence;
- there are no compensatory behaviours, such as vomiting, purging or exercise to rid oneself of the food consumed.

Binge Eating Disorder (BED) often begins in late adolescence or early adulthood, but because of the shame associated with bingeing and the stigma around obesity in Western societies, many do not seek help, if at all, until they are much older. This perhaps explains why there is virtually no research into BED with under 18s and why very few young people who may desperately need support and intervention are referred into CAMHS. Interestingly, a recent study in the United States revealed that more adult men and women met the above criteria for possible BED than both Anorexia and Bulimia nervosa combined (Hudson et al., 2007).

# Physical and psychological problems

- In adolescents and young adults, the impact is more likely to be psychological, i.e. low self-esteem, depression and anxiety.
- In addition, the longer-term problems are physical and associated with being overweight or obese, i.e. diabetes, high blood pressure, heart disease, stroke, increased pressure on bones and joints and some forms of cancer.

# Assessment of an eating disorder

A thorough assessment of the young person and their family is carried out by the multidisciplinary team, including a medical professional because of the seriousness of the disorder and the physical complications involved. The history obtained from the young person should be verified with the family, as the patient may be secretive. It should be considered that the family account may not be wholly reliable. It is important to:

- establish a rapport with the young person and family and clarify the problem;
- use a comprehensive assessment model to explore the biological, psychological, social and physical issues;
- establish the severity of the disorder and any physical complications to guide towards immediate, short- and long-term management plans;
- take a detailed history of the development of the illness, duration of the illness, weight prior to illness, current weight, rate of weight loss/fluctuations, menstrual cycles, methods used to lose weight, Anorexia nervosa or Bulimia nervosa: food restrictions in quantity and quality, avoidance of specific foods/fattening foods, exercises, medications, self-induced vomiting; management of weight loss so far;
- detailed diet history; quantity and quality of food taken per day;
- detailed personal, developmental, psychiatric history and family history of any psychiatric disorder;
- patient's and family's perception of the illness and their strength of belief, attitudes towards puberty, growing up and sexuality;
- the young person's mental state including co-morbid symptoms of depression, anxiety, obsessive-compulsive symptoms, any psychotic symptoms, suicidal thoughts and thoughts of self-harm;
- family dynamics including communication styles, conflict management and boundaries.

# Physical investigations

- Temperature, pulse, blood pressure
- Full blood count (FBC) to look for anaemia in suspected anorexia or bulimia
- Urea and electrolytes and liver function tests to look for effects of dehydration, starvation, induced vomiting and laxative abuse, in suspected anorexia or bulimia
- Hormonal tests, thyroid function tests and levels of sex hormones

- ECG to look for cardiac rhythm abnormalities, such as arrhythmias
- Pelvic ultrasound in females with Anorexia nervosa to look at the uterus and ovaries, which may have an immature appearance with lack of ovulation resulting from hormonal imbalance secondary to starvation and weight loss, leading to primary or secondary amenorrhoea. The scans can be repeated periodically alongside treatment. The uterus showing a mature appearance and ovaries with numerous follicles and at least one mature follicle is a good indicator of the adequate weight gain with hormonal balance restored
- Bone density scan to look at osteoporosis appearance, especially in chronic conditions and amenorrhoea lasting for more than a year in suspected anorexia
- Test for type 1 and 2 diabetes where binge eating disorder is suspected

## Management

NICE (2004b) states that there is no one treatment of choice available for eating disorders and that typically a combination of treatments is required.

# General principles of intervention for all eating disorders

- Assessment and intervention should be put in place at the earliest possible opportunity to improve the long-term outcomes for the young person and their family.
- Create a therapeutic alliance with the young person and the family.
- Provide information and psycho-education for the young person, the parents and other family members.
- Involve parents closely in the management and ensure that the adults, i.e. the parents and the professionals involved, take responsibility.
- In children and young people with eating disorders, growth and development should be closely monitored. Where development is delayed or growth is stunted, despite adequate nutrition, paediatric advice should be sought.

- Calculate a health target weight range, higher or lower, as an aim of treatment. BMI or child and adolescent average weight for height ratios can be used as a rule of thumb.
- Restoration of healthy eating patterns: parents and professionals must encourage the young person to have normal eating habits and patterns. The adults must provide supervision after meals, if there is a history of self-induced vomiting. Once the weight gain or loss is achieved, the young person can be encouraged to explore normal eating situations, for example eating in restaurants.
- Regular monitoring of physical health, especially if the young person is diabetic. This would include all the physical assessments highlighted earlier.
- For those with anorexia and bulimia nervosa who are vomiting regularly, advice should be given on dental hygiene with regular check-ups at the dentist.
- Where a young person is using laxatives, they should be advised to gradually reduce their usage. It is important to emphasize that the use of laxatives does not significantly reduce calorie absorption.

# Physical interventions specific to anorexia nervosa

## Refeeding

Refeeding must be gradual and begin with a slight increase on the current calorie intake. This avoids the potentially fatal complication of 'refeeding syndrome'. This may mean starting with only 1000 calories, perhaps a quarter or half a normal portion and gradually building up in increments of 200 calories per day to full portions. Meals should include all food groups, including fats, and essential nutrients. If the young person's diet is extremely restricted, for example to something like dried fruit, it might be a case of exploring with them how they might obtain their calories from this initially, while acknowledging that this will have to change.

The dietician is a useful member of the multidisciplinary team and can provide consultation. Refeeding should aim for a weight gain of up to 1 kg per week in hospital, but 0.5 kg in the community. It is useful to divide the daily food intake into three main meals, interspersed with three snacks.

## Nasogastric feeding

When the child's physical state demands immediate refeeding and it is not possible to achieve this orally, a nasogastric feeding programme should be started. The aim is to ensure an adequate daily diet of 2000–3000 calories. This programme should be closely coordinated between the paediatric team, nursing team, dietician and psychiatric team. Oral refeeding should be encouraged and restarted as soon as possible.

## Intravenous feeding

This is used for rapid rehydration and electrolyte replacement. Its use is restricted to emergency situations and for short periods. It can be implemented only on a paediatric ward.

## Psychotherapeutic treatment

Young people with eating disorders should have prompt access to a range of psychological therapies. The aim of psychological treatment should be to reduce the risk and symptoms related to the eating disorder, to encourage weight change and healthy eating and facilitate psychological and physical recovery.

## Individual psychotherapy

The therapeutic alliance or therapeutic relationship, a meaningful bond between the therapist and the patient, is an important feature across all the different types of individual psychotherapies. It is perhaps crucial in the treatment of eating disorders. Young people are typically unwilling to enter into treatment and are often described as 'resistant' when the treatment begins. Some of the treatments are described below:

- Psychodynamic psychotherapy: See Chapter 68, Child psychotherapy.
- Cognitive behaviour therapy (CBT): See Chapter 72, Cognitive behaviour therapy. For patients diagnosed with anorexia and bulimia nervosa, CBT can address overvalued cognitions about weight, shape and eating, and distorted body image, the treatment for

which involves cognitive restructuring and behavioural experiments. CBT adapted for binge eating disorder can be useful in exploring negative beliefs around self-image, guilt and disgust.

- Cognitive analytic therapy (CAT): CAT focuses on how the illness evolved and how the procedures devised to cope with their problems such as restricting or bingeing/vomiting, may be ineffective or even make the situation worse. The young person's problems are understood in the context of their personal histories and life experiences. The focus is on recognizing how these coping procedures originated and how they can be adapted and improved. Then, mobilizing the young person's own strengths and resources, plans are developed to bring about change (see www.acat.me.uk).
- Individual psychological work, such as counselling: See Chapter 69, Counselling children and young people and Chapter 70, Counselling psychology. The young person can work with members of the team on cognitive aspects of the eating disorder in addition to, for example, addressing self-esteem and issues around growing up.
- Cognitive remediation therapy (CRT) to address underlying neuropsychological deficits. There is evidence that individuals with Anorexia nervosa have problems with basic thinking skills, finding it difficult to multi-task and set-shift, i.e. switching from strategy to strategy. Therapeutic interventions such as cognitive remediation tasks aimed at addressing potential underlying neuropsychological deficits may be incorporated into the treatment of Anorexia nervosa.

## Family work/therapy and parental counselling

Family interventions that directly address the eating disorder should be offered. Parental counselling offers parents the opportunity to regain parenting skills, enables informed decision-making and maintains the link between parents and the treatment team.

Much of the research around family work/

therapy comes from the Maudesley group (Russell et al., 1987; Eisler et al., 2000; Eisler et al., 2007; Loeb et al., 2007), though their findings have been supported by other randomized control trials (Robin et al., 1999). A key finding from these studies has been the efficacy of family work with under 18 year olds being linked to reducing the chronicity of the illness, especially in Anorexia nervosa. The term 'family work' refers to an approach that avoids focusing on the young person and their illness as the problem, but rather explores it as a family difficulty that requires the combined effort and resources of all family members to address it effectively.

## Group therapy

Young people with eating disorders and their families can benefit from group work. Groups provide an atmosphere of mutual sharing where concerns can be aired and beliefs challenged in a supportive way. They bring people together to share problems and potential solutions. Examples of groups are psycho-education, activity focused, for example creative groups, parental or sibling support groups and community groups.

## Medication

There is little evidence to suggest that any medication is effective in treating the distorted cognitions related to Anorexia nervosa. There is some evidence to suggest that a selective serotonin reuptake inhibitor (SSRI), such as fluoxetine, can be useful in the reduction of symptoms related to Bulimia nervosa and binge eating disorder (NICE, 2004b; Brownley et al., 2007).

In eating disorders, SSRIs can often be prescribed to young people to treat co-morbid symptoms of depression and anxiety. It is important to recognize that these co-morbid symptoms often improve as weight is restored to a healthy range, especially in Anorexia nervosa.

## Indications for inpatient treatment

There is little evidence to suggest that young people with eating disorders who are admitted to hospital, whether that is to a paediatric ward for stabilization of their physical health or admission to a specialist eating disorder unit have better longer-term outcomes. However, there are situations in which the admission of a young person is unavoidable, such as:

- Acute physical complications that require specialist paediatric intervention, such as severe dehydration, dangerously low pulse and blood pressure, severe electrolyte imbalance, hypothermia, persistent vomiting and vomiting blood.
- When a young person is unable to take food orally and requires nasogastric tube feeding. Usually this takes place on a paediatric ward, but some specialist units can cater for it.
- The young person's weight to height ratio falls below 75 per cent or the third BMI centile (NICE, 2004b).
- The young person experiences marked depression, suicidal ideas or other severe mental disorders.
- Family engagement difficulties or exhaustion in the community setting.
- The community package of support has been unable to move the young person towards recovery, resulting in a sense of being 'stuck'.

In order to give the young person and family the best chance of a successful outcome after an inpatient stay, it is vital that the inpatient unit and community CAMHS team receiving them on discharge work closely together to formulate a robust package of post-discharge care: see Chapter 80, Inpatient services.

---

## Case study 1: Natalie

Natalie (16) was referred to her local CAMHS team for persistent weight loss. She had a history of dietary restriction for one year and had not menstruated for the past six months. Natalie lived with her mother and younger brother and had little contact with her father, whom her mother divorced when Natalie was ten. Natalie's father had moved to Australia soon after the divorce and was recently re-married.

## Assessment

Natalie reported feeling anxious and stressed about her exams and described withdrawing from her friends in order to spend her time revising. She talked about becoming more aware of her weight following a family holiday to Greece where she had been told she looked 'chunky' in a bikini. She described being preoccupied with thoughts of being fat and ugly.

Natalie's mother became concerned about Natalie's weight loss and encouraged her to eat, without success. At mealtimes, Natalie's mother would put a plate of food in front of Natalie and they would argue about whether or not she should eat it. Natalie's mother describing 'giving in' because she thought the arguments were upsetting for Natalie's younger brother, who sat with them at the meal table.

Natalie's mother encouraged Natalie's father to approach the issue of weight loss with her, but he insisted it was just a 'phase' that she would grow out of.

Natalie reported intensive physical activity, amounting to hundreds of star jumps and sit-ups each day.

## Physical examination

Natalie was mildly dehydrated with cold extremities and a weight for height ratio of 78 per cent.

## Intervention

Natalie and her mother were informed of her diagnosis of Anorexia nervosa and met with the dietician to agree a diet plan of three meals and three snacks a day to gain weight to her target healthy weight range; 95–105 per cent weight for height. Natalie was advised to stay at home until she was able to reverse her weight loss and the school liaised with her mother to provide homework and study, prior to Natalie's exams later that year.

Natalie was referred for individual psychotherapy but she initially refused to attend the sessions. Both Natalie and her mother attended family work and this helped to reduce the conflict at mealtimes. Natalie began to eat more. Eventually, Natalie asked to see her individual psychotherapist and explored themes of rejection and feeling 'left out' both in her family and in peer group relationships. Natalie's father joined family sessions once a month via Skype and Natalie reported feeling closer to her father, along with her mother, finding his support and understanding as a result of sessions helpful.

Natalie began to show significant cognitive changes and regained weight to the point where she began menstruating. She was motivated to continue her recovery. Natalie returned to school to take her exams and remained in contact with her therapist for a year following her initial assessment, to work through some of the interpersonal issues linked with her eating disorder.

## Case study 2: Noah

Noah is 15 years old and lives at home with his father, mother and younger sister. His older sister and closest family member is 19 and has recently left for university. Noah is an average–good achiever at school, whereas his older sister was very much a high-flyer. Noah and his younger sister have a reasonably good relationship, but she is the baby of the family and, in Noah's mind, receives more attention from their parents than he does.

Since Ruth left for university, Noah has been spending more time with a group of friends of whom his mother and father disapprove. Noah has returned home drunk on a few occasions, which has led to heated arguments, especially with his father. They have said he should not be spending time with these friends any longer.

For the past six months, Noah has been bingeing on food while everyone else is out, then making himself sick, three or four times a week. More recently, he has been going to the bathroom after meals and bringing up his dinner almost on a daily basis.

Noah has been seeing the school counsellor, to whom he has told everything. This includes thoughts that he may be gay and concern about how his parents would respond if they knew. The counsellor refers onto the local community CAMHS team after speaking with Noah and his mother.

## Assessment

At the assessment, Noah talks about 'not fitting in' within his family because he is neither the highest achiever nor the well-attended to youngest sibling. This feeling of alienation is heightened by the thoughts/feelings that he may be homosexual, as this would go against his father's idea of what a man should be. Noah reported feeling that he would feel out of control and binge and then vomit to regain a sense of control over himself. Unfortunately, this leaves him with feelings of guilt, shame and disgust and impacts on his mood. This cycle of behaviour is becoming a daily occurrence.

Noah's mother and father had recently noticed some odd behaviour, such as Noah disappearing to the bathroom soon after each meal and realized that food had been rapidly disappearing from the kitchen cupboards. However, their primary focus with Noah had been his association with 'undesirable' friends and the arguments this had caused.

Noah has stated that he does not use laxatives or any other purgatives.

## Physical examination

Noah's potassium level is low, but not at a dangerous level. There is some acid erosion to the enamel on his teeth and his fingers are sore from putting them down his throat to induce vomiting.

## Intervention

Although Noah experienced low mood, it was not felt that an SSRI medication was appropriate initially. He and his parents were advised that this be a future option should any therapeutic work be unsuccessful in moving Noah forward.

Noah agreed to a course of CBT during which he and the therapist explored the core beliefs underpinning his distorted cognitions and behavioural experiments, where he had to try to abstain from vomiting after meals. In the early stages of treatment, Noah was encouraged to spend at least 45 minutes in the company of another family member after each meal. At no time was he given the message that he had to stop vomiting completely, only to reduce it incrementally through the behavioural experiments.

Noah was advised to visit his dentist on a regular basis for check-ups and the best cleaning products available for weakened teeth.

Noah and his family, including older sister when she was home from university, were invited to family therapy sessions where all family members were given the opportunity to explore the dynamics within their family system and how this may have brought about or maintained the Bulimia nervosa. It was during these sessions that Noah's father was able to have his concerns around Noah's friends heard and for Noah to offer reassurance that he was able to discern the potential influences they may have and respond in a mature manner. Noah was able, with the encouragement offered in his individual sessions, to talk about his feelings related to his sexuality. Although initially shocked, his parents were able to accept Noah's current feelings around his sexuality and promised to support him in any way they could.

Within six months of initial engagement with CAMHS, Noah's bingeing and vomiting has virtually ceased, although he reports feeling an urge to resume those behaviours when something particularly stressful happens. As a family, they feel able to communicate in a better way, certainly when potential conflict arises, listening to one another's views and working towards a mutual resolution.

## Multiple choice questions

1. What does EDNOS stand for?

   a. Eating Disorder Not On the diagnostic Scale
   b. Eating Disturbance Not Otherwise Specified
   c. Eating Disorder Not Otherwise Specified
   d. Eating Disturbance Not On the diagnostic Scale
   e. Eating Dysfunction Not Otherwise Specified

2. One of the key diagnostic criteria of Anorexia nervosa is the maintenance of weight below:

   a. 5 per cent of ideal body weight for age and height
   b. 10 per cent of ideal body weight
   c. 15 per cent of ideal body weight
   d. 25 per cent of ideal body weight
   e. 50 per cent of ideal body weight

3. Repeated vomiting in Bulimia nervosa can cause hypokalaemia, i.e. low potassium levels in the blood. This can increase the risk of what?

   a. Brain haemorrhage
   b. Respiratory failure
   c. Muscle weakness
   d. Kidney damage
   e. Cardiac arrhythmias

4. Which of the following is not a key feature of binge eating disorder?

   a. Recurring episodes of binge eating, where a larger than normal amount of food is consumed in a relatively condensed period of time, although eating may be continuous over several hours
   b. The individual has no control over the amount and type of foods they are eating
   c. The episodes may be hidden from others due to shame and embarrassment
   d. An episode is followed by feelings of guilt and disgust, which highlights possible underlying depression or anxiety and may be the cause or the result of the disordered eating
   e. Eventually the young person will undertake compensatory behaviours, such as excessive exercise or vomiting and purging

5. Selective Serotonin Reuptake Inhibitors (SSRIs) can be useful in treating distorted cognitions in which eating disorder(s)?

   a. Anorexia nervosa only
   b. Bulimia nervosa only
   c. Binge Eating Disorder and Anorexia nervosa
   d. Binge Eating Disorder and Bulimia nervosa
   e. All three disorders

## Key texts

Brownley KA, Berkman ND, Sedway JA et al. (2007) Binge eating disorder treatment: a systematic review of randomized control trials. *International Journal of Eating Disorders*, **40**: 337–48.

Lask B, Bryant-Waugh R (eds) (2007) *Eating Disorders in Childhood and Adolescence*, 3rd edn. London: Routledge.

National Institute for Clinical Excellence (2004b) *Eating Disorders: Core Interventions in the Treatment and Management of Anorexia Nervosa, Bulimia Nervosa and Related Eating Disorders*. London: National Collaborating Centre for Mental Health.

Steinhausen H (2002) The outcome of anorexia nervosa in the 20th century. *American Journal of Psychiatry*, **159**: 1284–93.

# 52 · Behavioural sleep problems in children and adolescents

Catherine M Hill, Simone Holley, Angela Caulfield and
Cathy Laver-Bradbury

### Key concepts

- Sleep problems occur in one-quarter of all children.
- Children do not always grow out of their sleep problems.
- Sleep problems can have a detrimental effect on children's daytime behaviour.
- Careful assessment is required to rule out contributing factors.

## Introduction

Sleep problems are common with up to one-quarter of all children having difficulties at some time during their childhood (Mindell and Owens, 2003). As may be expected, sleep problems are most commonly reported in pre-schoolers with up to one-third having difficulties settling to sleep or waking at night. However, contrary to popular belief, children do not always grow out of their sleep problems and if they are ignored they can continue into later childhood and adolescence (Pollock, 1994). It is likely that sleep problems are indeed often overlooked in clinical practice as by their very nature they happen 'out of sight', during the night and are invisible to the clinician. Furthermore, sleep has historically been a blind spot in clinical training programmes (Mindell et al., 1994), often leaving clinicians feeling unconfident in their management.

This chapter will specifically consider behavioural insomnia of childhood – recently acknowledged by the International Classification of sleep disorders as a sleep disorder in its own right (American Academy of Sleep Medicine, 2005) as such disorders are very common in clinical practice and their management has a sound evidence base. However, practitioners need to be aware of the spectrum of sleep disorders that may present in childhood and that behavioural insomnias may coexist with other disorders such as sleep apnoea or parasomnias. For more information of the management of sleep disorders, the reader is referred to the recommended reading list.

In clinical practice children rarely present with an isolated sleep problem. More commonly they will also have behavioural and emotional difficulties during the day. There are a number of reasons why it may be appropriate to prioritize the management of the sleep problem. A growing body of research evidence now indicates the detrimental effect of sleep problems on children's daytime behaviour and ability to learn (Hill et al., 2007) as well as on the mental health of their parents and carers (Meltzer and Mindell, 2007). Put simply, exhausted parents will struggle to manage daytime behavioural problems in their child and exhausted children are likely to have daytime cognitive and behavioural difficulties – so addressing the sleep problem makes sense.

To what extent may daytime behavioural difficulties be associated with sleep problems? Research over the past decade in primary school-aged children has demonstrated significant associations between parental report of sleep problems and risk of behaviour difficulties in the day including: conduct problems (Holley et al., 2011), hyperactivity (Smedje et al., 2001), inattention and internalizing symptoms (Paavonen et al., 2009). At the other poles of the age spectrum, both in younger pre-school children (Goodlin-Jones et al., 2009) and adolescents, sleep problems have been associated with increased internalizing and externalizing problems. Furthermore in adolescent boys, shorter sleep times have been identified as a risk factor for delinquent behaviour (Meijer et al.,

2010). Importantly, sleep problems in childhood may have long-lasting effects. Anxiety, depression and aggressive behaviour later in life have been associated with parent report of sleep problems during school years (Gregory et al., 2008). In summary, there are good reasons to actively manage behavioural sleep problems and a reasonable expectation that for many children improving their sleep quality will have positive knock-on effects on their daytime mental health.

## Understanding behavioural sleep problems

Sleep is an active process comprising four stages (non-REM sleep stages I–IV) and REM sleep. Each sleep stage has quite distinct characteristics in terms of what is happening in both the brain and the body. Sleep stages occur in a predicable sequence during the night and are punctuated by brief awakenings (see **Figure 52.1**). Perfectly healthy and well-adjusted children, in satisfactory sleep environments, have routine wakeful moments every night. Few, if any, of these awakenings are remembered. A key concept in the management of behavioural insomnia of childhood is the notion that achieving a consolidated night's sleep is a learned process. In other words, a developmental task of early childhood is the learned ability to return to sleep independently after a spontaneous night waking.

Behavioural sleep problems fall into two basic categories which will be familiar to the practitioner:

1. Sleep onset association disorder
2. Limit setting.

Sleep onset association behavioural insomnia occurs where a child needs certain specific conditions to fall asleep independently at the start of the night and again following natural night-time awakenings. In other words, the child learns to associate falling asleep with certain conditions. The most common condition would be a parent/carer in the bedroom and, depending on the age of the child, may involve cuddling, stroking or rocking. Other 'associations' may include musical toys, soothing lights, warm milk and so on. With these conditions the child falls asleep quite easily at the beginning of the night and so may not present with a settling problem. However, when the child wakes up they will need to recreate the conditions they enjoyed at the start of the night in order to fall back asleep. In other words they cannot 'self-soothe' without these conditions. Invariably the child will awake fully and call on a parent/carer to help them again so parents present the child as repeatedly waking up at night, typically occurring in the late evening or after the hours of midnight when the parent is asleep.

Limit setting behavioural insomnia is another common difficulty for young children and children with developmental disorders. The child resists settling to sleep independently. This can set up a pattern of behaviour where bedtime becomes a protracted battle. Exhausted parents battling to settle their child to sleep may use inconsistent behavioural techniques to resettle the child. Not unusually, parents will have 'tried everything' to win this battle, causing high levels of stress at the end of the day and often giving in for a 'quiet life'.

The classification of the behavioural sleep disorders is useful in planning a logical approach to their management but it should be recognized that the two disorders often overlap (Box 52.1). For example, where a child has battled at bedtime the

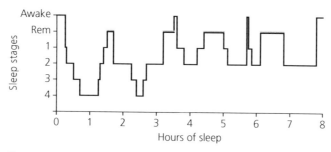

Figure 52.1 Hypogram illustrating a typical sequence of sleep stages during a night.

Box 52.1 Diagnostic criteria for Behavioural Insomnia of Childhood (American Academy of Sleep Medicine, 2005)

1. A child's symptoms meet the criteria for insomnia based upon reports of parents of other adult caregivers.
2. The child shows a pattern consistent with either the sleep onset association type or limiting setting type of insomnia described below:
   a. Sleep onset association type includes each of the following:
      i. Falling asleep is an extended process that requires special conditions
      ii. Sleep onset associations are highly problematic or demanding
      iii. In the absence of the associated conditions, sleep onset is significantly delayed or sleep is otherwise disrupted
      iv. Night-time awakenings require caregiver intervention for the child to return to sleep
   b. Limiting-setting type includes each of the following:
      i. The individual has difficulty initiating or maintaining sleep
      ii. The individual stalls or refuses to go to bed at an appropriate time or refuses to return to bed following a night-time awakening
      iii. The caregiver demonstrates insufficient or inappropriate limit setting to establish appropriate sleeping behaviour in the child
   c. The sleep disturbance is not better explained by another sleep disorder, medical or neurological disorder, mental disorder, or medication use.

defeated and exhausted parent may 'give in' and sleep alongside the child. This 'sleep onset association' then perpetuates signalling behaviour during natural night waking.

## Assessment of children with sleep problems

It can be tempting, as a professional, to give 'off-the-cuff' advice to a parent complaining of a child not sleeping. However, managing sleep difficulties needs to be very specific and effective treatment can only be achieved once a full assessment has been carried out and an accurate diagnosis has been made.

In assessing children with sleep difficulties it is important to gather information about the child's specific sleep problems and the psychosocial context within which they occur. It is essential to find out more about the individual child, his family, the environment and specific details relating to bedtime routines, night waking patterns and daytime sleeping habits.

Boxes 52.2, 52.3, 52.4 and 52.5 highlight the important factors to consider when assessing an individual family.

Other factors affect sleep in children and it is important that these are explored during the

Box 52.2 Child factors

- Any medical diagnosis
- Physical disabilities
- Description of additional needs
- Chronic illness
- Learning difficulties
- Means of communication
- Sensory impairments, e.g. vision/hearing
- Medication
- Equipment, e.g. sleep systems in children with cerebral palsy
- Feeding patterns
- Child's temperament

Box 52.3 Family factors

- Family members – who lives at home?
- Extended family/friends – who else is supporting the family?
- Parental age – young/unsupported?
- Parental mental/physical health
- Parenting styles
- Do parents agree how to manage the sleep problem?
- Attachment
- Parental perception of sleep problem
- Cultural beliefs

Box 52.4 Environmental factors

- Housing/garden/space
- Child's bedroom – is it full of toys? Is it dark? Is it shared?
- Income – is this a source of stress/does it impose practical limits on the family?
- Nursery/school – sleep and behaviour in other settings
- Transport to school – particularly for children accessing special education who can have long journeys and fall asleep
- Respite care – how does the child sleep in other settings?
- Social activities/opportunities
- Friendships
- Appointments – other demands on the family
- Neighbours – supportive network available to family

Box 52.5 Sleep factors

- Sleep history
- Activities carried out before bedtime
- Bedtime routine
- Settling procedure – does child fall asleep by himself, without distractions such as television or music
- Night waking – how often? What do parents do to resettle child?
- Morning routine – does child need waking?
- Other sleep-related behaviours
- Effect sleep problem is having on the family

assessment interview. The following list is not necessarily exclusive:

- breathing difficulties and snoring;
- obstructive sleep apnoea;
- recurrent ear, nose and throat problems;
- night-time cough or asthma;
- night-time seizures;
- enuresis;
- flare-up of existing medical problem, for example eczema;
- threadworms;
- scabies;
- abuse.

It may be that further investigations are required to clarify the situation before a behaviour management plan can be put in place. Video and audio tape recordings can be useful when interview alone yields confusing results, for example, when it is necessary to rule out night-time seizures. Actigraphy, where the child wears a small wrist-watch-like accelerometer device, can be employed to distinguish fairly accurately between periods of sleep and wakefulness.

Information from assessment interviews can be supplemented with sleep diaries. It is useful for parents to keep a sleep diary throughout the course of assessment and treatment so that improvement or deterioration in sleep problems is continuously monitored.

## Formulation

Once the assessment is complete, the salient features should be drawn together into a formulation that highlights the central features of the sleep problems and links these to pre-disposing, precipitating and maintaining factors. The strength and vulnerabilities of the family must also be considered, as these have implications for resolving the problem. Parents need to be emotionally robust to tackle a sleep problem. Treatment can fail if the timing is not right and may lead to a further erosion of parental esteem. It is also imperative that the professional involved can offer regular, structured support to the individual tailor-made programme that is drawn up in negotiation with the family.

# Principles of behavioural sleep management

Having identified that a child has a behavioural insomnia there are a number of therapeutic options that are available. Choice will be influenced by multiple factors. Important considerations will include:

- parent/carer's perspective: what is acceptable to one family will not be acceptable to another;
- the child's characteristics: including but not limited to their developmental stage, temperament and complicating health problems.

A range of strategies are available to the practitioner, each with their own strengths and limitations. The most important principle is that these are tailored to the individual and unique situation of the child and are sensitively negotiated with the family.

The first priority is to ensure that the child has good 'sleep hygiene'. This concept underpins all behavioural management techniques. Sleep hygiene includes three dimensions that influence sleep:

1. The sleep environment: a child's sleeping space should be a safe, comfortable, quiet place with low light or ideally complete darkness where they can lie down free from distractions. Many children in the developed world use their bedrooms as play spaces or study spaces in the day and as a consequence their sleeping space is stockpiled with toys and electronic media. A number of studies from around the world have clearly shown that when children use electronic media at bedtime they have reduced sleep quality (Olds et al., 2006; Li et al., 2007), largely explained by later bedtimes. Children need quiet time before they settle to sleep. Use of electronic media and stimulating activities should be avoided in the run up to bedtime.

2. Bedtime routines: promoting a consistent and calming bedtime routine exploits classical conditioning theory to teach a child to associate a predictable sequence of events (e.g. upstairs, bath, brush teeth, nightclothes, to bed, story time, etc.) with bedtime and sleep onset (Wiggs, 2009). These routines can usefully be linked to positive reinforcement approaches or 'special time activities' including story-telling, lullabies and close physical contact. Evidence clearly shows that when children lack consistent bedtime routines they have a shorter night-time sleep, indeed, almost 1 hour less in school-aged children (Mindell et al., 2009). See Box 52.6 for more details on an ideal bedtime routine.

3. Daytime activities: exercise is known to improve sleep quality. Children who exercise more fall asleep more rapidly and have the potential for a longer night's sleep (Nixon et al., 2009). One study has also shown that when adolescents exercise regularly for 8.5

Box 52.6 Good bedtime routine

- Lively play calms to quiet play
- Bedtime preparations in same sequence each night
- Use of clock to signal bedtime (even before the child can tell the time)
- Bedtime story, with clearly limited time, usually between three and 20 minutes, depending on age
- Nursery tapes/lullabies, limited and same time each night
- Hugs and kisses, between one and three minutes
- Dimmed light, corridor light (if necessary)
- No use of electronic media after lights out

hours per week they have more deep sleep than those who only exercise for 2 hours per week (Brand et al., 2010a). As well as exercise, sleep is influenced by diet. Caffeine blocks receptors in the brain that regulate sleep and promotes wakefulness and is associated with shorter sleep time in children. The Sleep in America Poll reported that 27 per cent of pre-schoolers and 41 per cent of school-aged children consumed at least one caffeine-containing drink per day (Mindell et al., 2009). Children with sleep problems would be well advised to avoid caffeine-containing food and drinks. It is also important that children do not go to bed feeling too full or too hungry. The gut naturally slows down in sleep and a full stomach at bedtime can cause discomfort.

There are a number of approaches to the management of behavioural insomnia that are supported by convincing research evidence for their effectiveness (Mindell et al., 2006).

## Unmodified extinction (cry it out technique)

This technique aims to 'extinguish' a child's learned behaviour by withdrawal of parental attention at bedtime. Parents are advised to completely ignore the child from 'lights out' to morning waking (other than safety checks if needed). This abrupt approach is likely to result in an 'extinction burst', in other words the child 'ups the stakes' and behaviours deteriorate in the short term. While undoubtedly this technique can be very effective for some children, parents need considerable persistence and strength of resolve to follow it through. Importantly, families need to understand that if they give in to the child's demands or cries this will act as a powerful reinforcement which will maintain the behaviour. Parents need to know that this strategy is stressful and may need time to think about it. Not surprisingly, extinction is not a popular technique with many parents and it seems at odds with concepts of nurturing parenting. It is crucial to understand how families would feel about this approach before recommending it. To address parental resistance to extinction techniques various modifications have been studied which have also been demonstrated to be effective.

## Graduated extinction (controlled crying/sleep training)

This modification popularized in the 1980s through self-help books, for example Ferber (1988) and more recently thorough television shows such as 'Super nanny'. The aim again is to negatively reinforce the child's bedtime protests by ignoring their cries. However, rather than do this indefinitely, the parent is instructed to return to the bedroom, provide brief and unrewarding reassurance at pre-set intervals. If the child attempts to leave the bedroom they are calmly returned to bed with minimal interaction. The parent is instructed to return the child to bed mechanically and unemotionally, with no kisses, conversation, angry words or refreshment. It is crucial that the child is returned every time. Sometimes gates at the door are helpful in breaking a pattern. Interval checks can be evenly spaced or gradually extended. There is no absolute right or wrong about the timing of intervals between checks, or whether a fixed (e.g. every 10 minutes) or incremental (5, then 10, then 15 minutes, etc.) regime is preferable. In clinical practice this is best negotiated with the parent depending on their tolerance limits.

## Extinction with parental presence

This is another modification of the extinction approach but the parent stays in the child's bedroom. It is useful where parents are in the habit of lying physically close to the child and allows a gradual 'distancing' programme.

The idea is to gradually increase the physical space between the parent and child while ignoring the child's requests for attention or physical contact. As for graduated extinction, if the child leaves the bed they should be returned calmly with minimal interaction. This technique may be particularly helpful in the school-aged anxious child or the child who does not tolerate rapid change, for example a child with autistic spectrum difficulties.

Importantly, the key concept underlying all of these techniques is to promote the child's ability to fall asleep independently at the beginning of the night so that when they experience their natural night wakings they are able to use the same learned techniques to self-soothe back to sleep independently.

## Stimulus control techniques

Children with long-standing difficult behaviour at bedtime 'learn' that this is a time of conflict and stimulation, as indeed do their parents. Extinction techniques may make this conflict worse in the short term. An alternate 'stimulus control' technique can be used for a child who has become very oppositional. It works well in children with limited awareness of 'clock' time. Having established what time the child usually falls asleep, expectations are changed so that this becomes the new bedtime for the start of the programme. So for example the child who is put to bed at 7 o'clock but won't fall asleep until 9 o'clock is instead settled into bed at the later time of 9 o'clock. If the child doesn't fall asleep within 20 minutes, they are removed from the bedroom and bedtime is delayed for a further agreed time, for example 30 minutes. Ideally this then removes the bedtime struggles and over-stimulation that goes along with these behaviours and reduces the level of conflict in between the parent and child. Stimulus control programmes need to be carefully supervised by the practitioner to gauge the child's response, support the parent and ensure early 'bail out' if the child continues to employ resistant behaviours which progressively delay bedtime. It is critical that sleep hygiene is maintained and that the child's settling routine is adjusted to the delayed bedtime. Once the child has learned to achieve struggle-free settling, the bedtime is incrementally adjusted to be 15 minutes earlier every day, such that a desirable bedtime is finally achieved. It is important that throughout the programme the child is woken at a regular time in the morning to maintain their biological clock.

## General considerations

Co-sleeping: For some families co-sleeping, where the child shares the parental bed, is a positive choice and part of normal routine. It is however, associated with sleep difficulties when it is used as a 'fall back' because the child will not sleep in their own bed (Touchette et al., 2005). The parental bed is the greatest 'reward' of all to a child. Exhausted parents who give in and allow the child to co-sleep during the night have undone all the hard work they have put in earlier in the evening teaching a child to settle to sleep. When a child creeps in silently while parents are sleeping, practical measures such as a bell on the door can alert the parent so that they can return the child to their own bed.

Timing: Only begin a sleep programme when parents have the resources to see it through, for example when a partner is about to be home for a long weekend, begin on a Friday evening.

Maximize parents strengths: For example, if father can cope more easily with crying than mother, then perhaps mother could go to a friend's house for four or five evenings, half an hour before child's bedtime, to allow father to make a start on the programme. Always acknowledge and resolve parental conflicts before the programme starts.

Take it a step at time: Where there are several difficulties, it is often a good idea to encourage the parents to work at part of the problem at first. Often they will choose to work on 'settling' problems first, as they feel stronger in the evening than in the middle of the night. Success at one stage builds up parental confidence, and leads to good results in the next phase.

Use positive reinforcement: When a child is able to understand what is expected of him, it can be useful to reward small and achievable goals using a star or picture chart for example. The chart will need to be fine-tuned to the interests and intellectual ability of the child, so that some success can be achieved early on.

## Medication

Families are often prescribed medication for a child's sleep problem as parents and physicians alike fail to recognize the behavioural nature of the difficulties. While such a 'quick fix' may appeal to exhausted parents and the busy physician, it fails to address the underlying problem and does no more than 'plaster over the cracks'. However, it is not logical to sedate a child that is expected to learn a new behaviour. The British National Formulary for children advises 'The prescribing of hypnotics to children is not justified. There is a risk of habituation with prolonged use and problems settling children at night should be managed psychologically'. A major limitation in the use of any medication for behavioural insomnia is the absence of good research data telling us exactly what can help, in what situation and at what dose. Nonetheless, most sleep clinics will use medication selectively. Crucially, however, it will always be used alongside sleep hygiene advice and behavioural management. For a helpful and full review of 'When to use drugs to help sleep' see Gringras (2008).

Prevention: As behavioural insomnia is so common, affecting 10–30 per cent of the child population (American Academy of Sleep Medicine, 2005), should more be done to educate parents when children are very young? Ideally, parents should understand some basic principles before a child reaches six months of age. From this time children begin to learn to sleep through the night as they no longer need night feeds. Research shows that when parents receive appropriate education antenatally and when their babies are young, their infants have improved sleep. Key messages include:

- sleep is a learned behaviour; babies need to learn to self-soothe to sleep at the start of the night;
- waking up at night is a normal part of sleep, crying for parental attention is a learned behaviour unless the child needs feeding or has a medical problem;
- children need healthy sleep environments, appropriate diets, exercise in the day and a bedtime routine to experience optimal sleep.

## Case study 1

Sam is 3 years old and recently began to have problems settling to sleep after starting playschool. His mother and father were exhausted because it was getting harder and harder for him to settle, he seemed to need one or the other of them to stay with him until he fell asleep. They had a fairly good routine established at the beginning of the evening, starting with a bath and then story time, however the story time was getting longer and longer and even after the stories had finished Sam became distressed when they tried to leave him. This resulted in Sam settling to sleep later and later and not wanting to wake up in the morning meaning he often missed playschool which he enjoyed.

Careful assessment was undertaken which showed Sam to be progressing well developmentally and to have no problems medically which reassured his parents. Discussion with Sam's parents about his sleep routine discovered that they were allowing Sam several stories which could be exciting and that following these he was awake and wanting more. Both parents found it hard to leave Sam to cry and so the extinction with parental presence approach was adopted as well as limiting the story both in the amount and the type. One or the other of his parents would sit next to Sam while he fell asleep gradually moving their position until he managed to fall asleep without their presence. This approach also meant that Sam was woken at the same time in order for him to attend playschool in the mornings. Sam's father found it easier to set the limits on stories and routines so he supported the mother with Sam. Within 3 weeks Sam's bedtime routine was well established and he was settling to sleep without his parents' presence after just one story.

## Case study 2

David aged 12 had been having problems settling to sleep for a number of years, leading to increased conflict at bedtime which included shouting and banging doors. His parents were desperate to get him to go to sleep, not only did they want some time to themselves but also they were sure David's sleep problems were having a knock-on effect to his schooling. He was often late to school because of the difficulties they had in waking him. Bedtime was dreaded by all as there was never a night when there was no conflict.

David has some developmental delay in that he is generally a couple of years behind in his development as compared to his peer group, because of this he has limited knowledge of time. His learning is being hampered by the fact he is reported to be tired in school, often wanting to go to sleep in lessons. Medically he also had some hearing problems in the past for which he received grommets to treat repeated ear infections.

Following careful assessment and a check of his hearing, which was normal, David's parents decided a stimulus control technique may be helpful and so this was instigated. David was being sent to bed at 8pm but actually was not falling asleep until 10pm. In this approach David was kept up until 10pm (the parents chose to start this approach during the half-term break so David's schooling was affected as little as possible). His evening routine was adjusted to the new sleep time. David was still woken at his normal waking time for school at 7.30am. At first David did not settle even at 10pm and so he was removed again from his bedroom until a further 20 minutes had passed and then taken back to bed. This was repeated on the first night until 11pm when finally he went to sleep. During the time when he was brought back downstairs no stimulus was given, no TV or games, his parents and David just waited until he wanted to try to go to sleep again.

The second night the same pattern was repeated. He was kept up until 11pm, however he was tired and asked to go to bed at 10.30pm. His parents agreed and he settled quickly. The following night he went to sleep at the same time. However, over the next few weeks his parents gradually reduced his bedtime by 15 minutes and within a few weeks David was settling to sleep at 9pm on a regular basis. Both David and his parents were happy with his progress.

## Multiple choice questions

1. Which statement about children's sleep problems is correct?

   a. Almost all children under the age of two years will have some kind of sleep problem
   b. Sleep problems in children over five years are the result of inappropriate parenting strategies
   c. All children will grow out of their sleep problem by the age of five
   d. All sleep problems in childhood need further investigation
   e. Child sleep problems are prevalent in up to 25 per cent of the population

2. Which statement about the consequences of sleep difficulties in children is true?

   a. All child behaviour problems are caused by child sleep difficulties
   b. Poor sleep does not have a negative effect on cognitive functioning
   c. All children with a sleep problem will also present with a behaviour problem
   d. Both learning and behaviour may be affected in children with sleep problems
   e. Sleep problems in childhood are not associated with emotional difficulties later in life

3. Which of the following statements about behavioural insomnia is correct?

   a. Limit-setting behavioural insomnia is common in children with developmental disorders
   b. Children with sleep-onset association do not always have problems settling at the start of the night
   c. There may be overlap between limit-setting and sleep-onset association
   d. Parental reports are important when assessing a child for behavioural insomnia
   e. All of the above

4. Which statement about infant sleeping is true?

   a. Infants should sleep through the night from birth
   b. Infants are unable to sleep through the night until 12 months
   c. Inappropriate parenting strategies are the cause of infant sleep problems
   d. Unmodified extinction is the best method to treat behavioural insomnia
   e. Controlled crying does not cause long-term emotional distress in the child

5. Which of these statements regarding the treatment of childhood sleep problems is true?

   a. Medication is never appropriate for children under five years
   b. Underlying physical problems should always be considered before embarking on behavioural management
   c. Medication should always be considered for children over the age of two years
   d. The use of positive reinforcement strategies are not effective
   e. Treatment does not always require a full assessment

## Key texts

### For practitioners

Mindell JA, Owens JA (2003) *A Clinical Guide to Pediatric Sleep: Diagnosis and Management of Sleep Problems.* New York: Lippincott Williams and Wilkins, 1–10.

### Recommended reading for parents

Ferber R (1988) *Solve Your Child's Sleep Problems: A Practical and Comprehensive Guide for Parents.* New York: Fireside.

Richman N, Douglas J (1988) *My Child Won't Sleep.* London: Penguin.

# 53 Feeding/eating problems in young children

Liz McCaughey, Sue Evans and Margaret Thompson

## Key concepts

- Eating problems in children are fairly common.
- Children who have developmental delay or neurological difficulties may need specialist help with feeding and eating problems.
- Support to the child and parent when instigating a management plan is essential.

This chapter is specifically written for children with normal or slightly delayed development. Children with neurological difficulties and severe learning difficulties may have additional needs which require a more specialist approach.

## Introduction

This is a common problem and may include:

- refusal of solids (texture);
- poor appetite/disinterest (quantity);
- faddiness (limited range);
- immature oral motor skills;
- poor table behaviour;
- lack of age-appropriate self-feeding (delayed development);
- eating of inappropriate objects (pica);
- failure to thrive.

## Prevalence

Over 30 per cent of five year olds are described as having mild or moderate eating or appetite problems (Butler and Golding, 1986), 16 per cent of three year olds had a poor appetite, and 12 per cent were thought to be 'faddy'.

## Aetiology

### Early aversive feeding experience

- Organic, for example vomiting, gagging, choking, reflux or pain associated with eating or drinking
- Force fed or reprimanded while eating
- Parent anxious/angry while feeding the child
- Experience of sensitivity reaction or bowel change (diarrhoea/constipation)

### Distortion of feeding experiences

- Lack of early oral feeding experience due to alternative feeding methods, for example early use of nasogastric tube, or gastrostomy feeding
- Immature oral motor skills or oral hypersensitivity
- Late introduction of solids (later than 12 months old)
- Parents' refusal to let the child self-feed

### Parental emotional state

- Frustration
- Depression
- Loss of confidence
- Anxiety

## Maintaining factors

- Parental management
- Parent/child relationship; family/marital problems
- Child's learned avoidance or fear of food
- Child's general behaviour problems

# Assessment

## Physical setting

- Seating arrangements
- Eating implements used
- Type and quantity of food offered/taken (food diary)
- Time taken for solids and drinks

## Child's behaviour/skills

- Symptoms
- Interest and anticipation
- Desire/ability to self-feed/drink
- Quantity, texture and range eaten
- Ability to concentrate and persevere with eating
- Oromotor skills
- Psychical parameters such as growth (height and weight) and nutritional state should be assessed (iron levels etc.)

## Parents' behaviour

- Control
- Management methods used, for example force, passive attitude
- Encouragement, distraction
- Emotional state, for example frustration, anger
- Awareness of child's needs and demands

Eating management involves:
- Dietary advice
- Enhancing oral motor skills
- Eating arrangements, i.e. seating, implements, social setting, etc.
- Eating management methods

# Behavioural management

## Graded approaches

- Introduce new foods (variety first then increase textures)
- Introduce solids (NB stage two foods are coarse puree, liquids plus lumps are mixed textures and more complicated to take/cope with)
- May be better to use mashed home food to give uniform texture (otherwise, lumps will be spat out)
- Increase quantity
- Improve concentration and sitting
- Encourage self-feeding
- Monitor oral motor control
- Reduce oral hypersensitivity

## Setting the scene

- Establish regular meal times (no snacks or not within 2 hours of meal – some children need snacks and can be useful for weight gain or developing oral skills)
- Expect the child to sit at the table to eat
- Family should eat together whenever possible
- Appropriate portion size
- Remove distractions (orientate child's attention to food, i.e. no TV)

## Reinforcement (positive praise, rewards and so on)

- Finishing
- Trying a new food
- Sitting down
- Eating solids
- Self-feeding

## Extinction

- Ignore non-eating
- Ignore demands for different foods or presentation
- Ignore disruption
- Time limits on length of meal (e.g. 30 minutes maximum)

NB Avoid aversive situation

# Pica

It is normal for infants and young children to mouth, and occasionally eat, strange things, but pica is when a child regularly and excessively eats inappropriate substances, for example soil, paper, wood, cloth, paint and so on.

The symptom has many causes, including adverse environmental circumstances and emotional distress. It may be associated with distorted developmental patterns and learning difficulty. Iron deficiency anaemia may result and lead levels may be elevated (previously this was associated with lead containing paints. Fortunately this is seen much less frequently now). These should be measured to exclude lead poisoning and its sequelae. Management of pica will depend on the nature of the problems, but should never be ignored.

# Feeding difficulties and failure to thrive

## Contributory factors

### Child factors
- Organic disorders including:
  - Metabolic disorders
  - Neuromuscular disorders
  - Immunological disorders
  - Medical factors (cardiac, renal)
  - Developmental level
  - Health status
  - Growth (height and weight)
- Feeding problems:
  - Neglect and abuse
  - Parental management
  - Lack of knowledge
  - Lack of oromotor skills
  - Lack of experience
  - Anxiety
  - Early feeding experience
  - Family discord
  - Depression

# Mealtime observations check list

- Environment:
  - Which room is used?
  - Are there distractions, for example TV, noise, room temperature too hot or too cold?
  - Behaviour of others, for example sibling 'playing up', mother cooking other food, other distractions?
- Child's seating:
  - Posture, support, head control
  - Is the child sitting in a high chair, on a booster seat on an adult upright chair, on a cushion on an upright adult chair, adult upright chair, easy chair or sofa, child's low chair?
  - Are the child's feet resting on the floor or a foot rest?
  - Is the child's plate on a table or food tray? If not, where is it?
  - How high is the table surface? Below waist/waist level/above waist
  - Does the child have to hold his/her arms up high to reach the plate?
- Child's implements:
  - Is the drink in a bottle, feeder cup or open cup? Is there a straw? Does the child hold the container or is that held by the person feeding the child?
  - Does the child have a bowl or a plate, and adult bowl or plate, teaspoon, child's knife, fork and spoon or adult cutlery?
  - Does the parent/carer cut/mash/feed the food?
  - Is there a non-slip mat, child's own placemat, keep-warm plate, finger food?
- Position of child:
  - Is the child fed or does he/she eat on their own?
  - Are other family members also eating?
  - Where are those other people sitting, around the same table? In the same room?
  - Is the parent/carer sitting next to/opposite/behind the child?
- Food and drink given:
  - Is the child's meal the same as the rest of the family?
  - Record what is offered and the amount
  - Is the texture mashed or whole?
  - How long is the child given to eat?
  - How long do the rest of the family spend eating?

- How much food does the child actually eat (e.g. mouthful/half the plateful)?
- Does the child feed him/herself or is he/she fed? No/a little/a lot?
- Child's behaviour:
  - Does the child refuse or delay coming to the meal?
  - Does the child seem uninterested in the food?
  - Is the child physically awkward feeding him/herself in that situation? Is he/she interested in feeding themselves?
  - Is the child easily distracted or finding it hard to concentrate?
  - Is the child fidgety?
  - Does the child refuse to eat when fed, for example keeps mouth closed, pushes spoon away?
  - In what way?
- Parent/s behaviour:
  - Does the parent offer encouragement? Positive or negative?
  - Is the parent tolerant/patient? Too much/adequately/too little?
  - Is there some opportunity for the child to eat independently? Too much/appropriately/too little?

- Is the parent aware of the child's needs and demands? Too much/appropriately/too little
- How does the parent try to intervene, for example feeding the child, forcing, distracting, playing games (e.g. 'airplane') encouraging, shouting, any other ways?
- Who is controlling the situation? Mostly the child/equally/mostly the parent?

# Progress recording sheet

Date:
Name:
People present:
Proposed task:
Success with the task:
What happened to make task a success?
List any new foods eaten, if appropriate?
Problems with the task?
What happened to hinder the task?
Observations of the session?
NEW TASK SET:
Review date:
Contact person/contact number:

## Multiple choice questions

1. When helping a family whose child has an eating problem, what routines may help?

   a. Allow the child to eat alone
   b. Establish a routine, eat together, ensure appropriate portion size and remove distractions
   c. Encourage them to sit still while eating
   d. Offer small amounts frequently

2. What should you observe during a mealtime observation?

   a. The environment, the implements
   b. The child's sitting position and the food and drink offered
   c. The parents and child's behaviour
   d. All of the above

3. What factors may contribute to a child developing a feeding or eating problem

   a. Organic difficulties
   b. Parental anxiety
   c. Abuse or neglect
   d. All of the above

## Key text

Dasha E, Nicholls RL, Russell M (2011) Viner Childhood eating disorder: British National surveillance study. *British Journal of Psychiatry*, **198**: 295–301.

# 54 *Enuresis, constipation and soiling*
### Melissa Bracewell

# Enuresis

## Key concepts

- Enuresis is very rarely deliberate or caused by behavioural/psychological problems, so all children with enuresis should be offered assessment and medical treatment before referral to/treatment by CAMHS.
- Children with enuresis commonly have low self-esteem, disturbed sleep which can worsen challenging behaviour, poor concentration in school/home (can mimic attention deficit hyperactivity disorder (ADHD)) or suffer bullying in school. Treatment of enuresis has been shown to improve all of these.
- NICE guidelines for treatment of Nocturnal Enuresis (2010a) recommend treatment with bed wetting alarms and/or desmopressin, both of which have good success rates and are tolerated well by children and their parents.

## Definition

Enuresis is the intermittent loss of urine at night or intermittent leakage of urine when asleep in a child of at least five years of age (International Children's Continence Society, 2007).

It can be primary when the child has never been dry at night, or secondary when the child has previously been dry at night for a continuous period of at least six months.

It can be monosymptomatic when there are no other urinary symptoms or non-monosymptomatic when there are other urinary symptoms, for example daytime urgency (inability to hold on) or frequency (voiding more than seven times in 24 hours).

There are no differences in the incidence of behaviour problems in children with enuresis and those who are dry at night (Hirasing et al., 1997), but children with enuresis have low self-esteem, suffer bullying and social isolation. Night wetting can affect performance in school and a study of children in Hong Kong showed an improvement in IQ of 10 points with successful treatment of enuresis.

## Prevalence

- 10 per cent of five year olds
- 5 per cent of 10 year olds
- 1 per cent of 19 year olds

Spontaneous resolution is common between the ages of five and seven years, but research has shown that five year olds who wet more than three nights a week and seven year olds with any wet nights are unlikely to get spontaneous resolution and should be referred for treatment (Yeung et al., 2006).

## Causes

All children with bed wetting are unable to wake at night to urinate in the toilet when their bladders are full. This poor arousal at night has been shown to be secondary to chronic tiredness from the enuresis disturbing sleep. Arousal, sleep and performance in school improve with treatment of the enuresis (Yeung, 2006).

Most children actually achieve dry beds while sleeping through the night, because the amount of urine produced overnight is held in the bladder until the morning.

Enuresis occurs when the amount of urine produced overnight exceeds the amount the bladder can hold and the child is unable to wake and urinate in the toilet.

There are therefore two subgroups of night wetting:

1. Nocturnal polyuria (large nocturnal urine production): Normal bladder function but large volumes of urine overnight, usually have abnormal circadian rhythm of ADH production (very occasionally have increased solute excretion). Approximately 70 per cent of cases.

2. Children with small nocturnal bladder capacity: Due to various types of bladder dysfunction, either only after sleep at night, or both during day and night-time. Approximately 30 per cent of cases.

There is a strong genetic predisposition with a positive family history in 63 per cent (Von Gontard et al., 2001).

## Assessment

### History

- Determine whether primary or secondary
- Record severity – how many wet nights a week
- Time of night wetting occurs (wetting prior to midnight–1am usually due to nocturnal polyuria)
- Amount of wetting (large wet patch usually due to nocturnal polyuria, small patch usually due to small bladder capacity)
- Number of wetting accidents a night (>1 usually due to small bladder capacity)
- Ask about drinking habits, especially in the evening
- Ask about sleeping arrangements, for example bunk or cabin beds, toilet access at night, fear of dark
- Any previous treatments tried
- Family history, past medical history, drug history and allergies
- Any developmental problems, special needs or behavioural problems which may influence treatment recommendations

## Examination

- Not required in primary monosymptomatic enuresis
- In non-monosymptomatic enuresis, if day symptoms do not resolve in three months with bladder training (good drinking and regular toileting during day) examine spine, lower limb neurology, abdomen and, if possible, genitalia

## Investigations

- None needed in primary nocturnal enuresis
- In secondary nocturnal enuresis, do urinalysis to exclude diabetes mellitus, urinary tract infection and renal disease

## Management

- Chart pattern of wet nights for 1–2 weeks
- Chart day drink volumes and day voided volumes (wee into measuring jug) for 24 hours
- Measure nocturnal urine volumes by:
  - waking child every 2–3 hours and recording voids in jug, sum and add first morning void; or
  - put child in nappy or pull-up until morning and measure first morning void in a jug – nocturnal urine volume = weight of wet nappy in grams – weight dry nappy in grams + first morning void in mL.

First-line:

- Remove nappy or pull-up at night and stop parents lifting child at night to use the toilet when not spontaneously roused by full bladder
- Ensure child is able to use toilet easily at night, for example not on top bunk, toilet nearby and not on different storey of house, light on between bedroom and toilet
- Stop blackcurrant, fizzy and caffeine containing drinks
- Stop any drinks for 2 hours before sleep time and improve day drinking habits (should drink two glasses at each meal and one in between)
- Promote regular toileting 1½–2-hourly during day. Child must void just before sleep.

Second-line:

- NICE guidelines (2010a) recommend treatment with desmopressin or alarms.

Logically, desmopressin should be used for children with nocturnal polyuria. It is an analogue of ADH and will, if taken at sufficient dose, reduce night urine volumes until they no longer exceed bladder capacity and the child will then be sleeping through dry. It comes in two formulations, tablets (preferred by over 12 year olds) and melts which dissolve under the tongue. Desmopressin nasal spray is no longer licensed for use in night wetting due to the variability in absorption from the nasal mucosa. Treatment is given every night for three months. Sixty per cent of children remain dry long term when desmopressin is stopped. The others go back on desmopressin for as long as it is required, having breaks off medication every three months to assess whether it is still needed. Every year 15 per cent will achieve long-term dry nights.

Alarm treatment should be used in children with small nocturnal bladder capacity. Historically it was assumed that alarm treatment worked by teaching the child to wake to the sound of the alarm, until gradually the child could wake before wetting and was then dry. However, research showed that in fact only 35 per cent of children achieved dry beds by waking to the alarm ringing, the remaining 65 per cent were dry and sleeping through the night without the alarm ringing (Bonde et al., 1994). Further research showed that bladder capacity increased in children using alarm treatment until large enough to hold a normal overnight urine volume, thus achieving dry nights (Hvistendahl et al., 2004; Taneli et al., 2004). Alarm treatment at night can also help those with day symptoms from small bladder capacity. Sixty per cent of children respond to alarm treatment but only half of them remain dry six months later.

The most important factor in deciding on which treatment to use is parental and child preference. Even if a child has obvious night polyuria there is no point in using desmopressin if the child/family do not want medication, likewise alarm treatment will not be used unless the child and family are prepared to wake to the alarm ringing.

It is common to combine treatments where one has not achieved dry nights.

Other treatments can be used in specialist centres.

## Case study 1

Lucy, aged 14 years, attends clinic after referral from her school nurse. She has always wet the bed, having only the occasional dry night. Her mother, who attends clinic with her, wet the bed until she was 15 years old so she never asked for help with Lucy's wetting.

Lucy was seen by her school nurse because school staff had become concerned by a change in Lucy's concentration, mood and attendance at school. When seen Lucy tells her school nurse that she has her first boyfriend and was anxious that he would find out about her bed wetting. She had told her best friend, who had laughed and teased her, and threatened to tell her classmates at school. Lucy has then been trying to avoid school and finds it difficult to concentrate as she is so anxious her classmates will find out about her bed wetting. Lucy had not told her mother about any of her concerns.

At clinic Lucy was delighted to hear that she could get treatment for her bed wetting. Her charts showed that she was following good drinking and toileting routines. She had measured her night urine volumes which demonstrated nocturnal polyuria. She was offered treatment with either desmopressin or an alarm but was not happy to use a bed wetting alarm as she felt she was 'too old' for it.

Lucy started treatment with desmopressin and returned to clinic three months later and was delighted to report that she was completely dry. Her school attendance and performance had improved.

Lucy had a trial of stopping the desmopressin but her wetting returned immediately, so she restarted the desmopressin for a further three months. Lucy was told that the desmopressin could continue for as long as it was needed so long as she had breaks off desmopressin every 3–6 months to see whether it was still needed.

Lucy continued to respond well to her treatment and was able to stop her desmopressin after one year and was discharged from clinic.

## Case study 2

Jim, age seven, attends clinic. He has a history of night wetting for the last year, having previously been dry from age three years. He is now wearing a pull-up. He has good drinking and toileting routines and no other medical problems. Screening tests exclude diabetes, UTI and other renal problems. His mother reports a pattern of a few months of Jim having dry nights and then a period of wet nights. For the last three months he has been wet every night. She and Jim do not know the time that he wets at night, nor the amount of wetting.

Jim is started on treatment with a bed wetting alarm and makes excellent progress and returns to clinic dry. His mother asks to be discharged.

Three months later Jim is referred back to clinic with a return of his night wetting and requests alarm treatment again. Jim and his mother are told about desmopressin but do not want to use medication so an alarm is issued. Jim again makes good progress with the alarm, sleeping through the night, but unfortunately relapses again.

Both parents attend Jim's next appointment. During the consultation, Jim has to be taken out of the clinic room by nursing staff when his mother starts shouting and behaving aggressively towards his father. His mother admits to mental health issues and agrees to approach her GP. His father agrees to take over the management of Jim's night wetting. Jim returns into the consultation room and is told very clearly that his mother is not angry with him or about his wetting, and that his wetting is not his fault and is not the cause of his mother's problems.

Jim returns to clinic with his father. A new start is made to his treatment and good information is provided by his father, which supports the use of a bed wetting alarm. After detailed discussion Jim and his father feel that they can manage alarm treatment again without worsening the family situation. Alarm treatment is well tolerated and gets Jim dry this time without any recurrence. His mother responds well to treatment of her mental health problems.

## Multiple choice questions

1. Night wetting (enuresis) has a significant financial impact on families: True/False

2. Night wetting is only treated from age seven: True/False

3. Treatment of night wetting improves self-esteem: True/False

4. Treatment for night wetting always starts with bed wetting alarms: True/False

5. Treatment with desmopressin can continue long term for many years and even into adulthood: True/False

### Key texts

Hirasing RA, van Leerdam FJ, Bolk-Bennink LB, Bosch JD (1997) Bedwetting and behavioural and/or emotional problems. *Acta Paediatrica*, **86**: 1131–4.

Yeung CK, Sreedhar B, Sihoe JD et al. (2006) Differences in characteristics of nocturnal enuresis between children and adolescents: a critical appraisal from a large epidemiological study. *BJU International*, **97**: 1069–73.

# Constipation and soiling

---

## Key concepts

- Soiling is usually caused by constipation and over flow but can result from fast bowel transit time with resulting loose stools and urgency of defecation, or poor wiping after bowels are opened.
- Medical treatment of the above conditions should always be started before or alongside behavioural treatments. Treatments include education, improvement in diet and toileting, as well as laxatives when constipation is present.
- Long-term soiling has a significant impact on self-esteem, behaviour and social isolation.

---

## Definition

Constipation is generally defined as passing a stool fewer than three times a week. Stools are usually hard, dry and difficult to pass.

The ROME III consensus (2006) gives a more detailed definition of constipation based on the presence of two or more of the following criteria in the previous two months in a child with a developmental age of at least four years:

1. Two or fewer defecations in the toilet a week
2. >1 episode of faecal incontinence (soiling) a week
3. History of retentive posturing or excessive volitional stool retention
4. History of painful or hard bowel movements
5. History of large diameter stools that may obstruct the toilet
6. Presence of large faecal mass in rectum

Soiling is the involuntary passage of small amounts of stools, resulting in staining of underwear.

Encopresis is the active passage of stools in inappropriate places after the age when bowel control is normally expected. In older children encopresis is sometimes associated with oppositional defiant disorder, conduct disorder or sexual abuse. Constipation, soiling and encopresis must be assessed and treated in primary care and/or secondary paediatric services for constipation and soiling before referral to child mental health services.

## Incidence/prevalence

Worldwide prevalence of childhood constipation in general population ranges from 0.7 to 29.6 per cent in both boys and girls (NICE guidelines, 2010a). It becomes chronic in more than one-third of children (Van der Berg et al., 2006).

## Causes

In 95 per cent of children with constipation, no pathological cause is found. The following underlying causes should be considered but rarely need to lead to investigations:

- Anatomical – imperforate anus, anal stenosis, Hirschprung's disease, etc.
- Metabolic – hypothyroid, hypercalcaemia, hypokalaemia, cystic fibrosis, poorly controlled insulin-dependent diabetes mellitus (IDDM)
- Gastroenterologic – coeliac disease, inflammatory bowel disease
- Neurological – abnormal spinal or lower limb neurology, muscle weakness/wasting disorders
- Drugs – including iron, anticholinergics, opioid analgesics, some antihistamines and anticonvulsants.

Soiling is rarely a psychological problem and should always be assessed for causes below before referring to psychology services:

- Constipation and stool holding with leakage of runny stools around impacted faecal mass. Soiling is involuntary and child often unaware. Stool is often very offensive smelling to all but the child
- Fast bowel transit time leading to loose stools per rectum and urgency toileting, with stool leakage before toilet is reached
- Poor wiping after defecation.

## Assessment

### History

- Age of onset of problem – if constipation started at one month old or less and any delay in passage of meconium >48 hours needs referral to hospital paediatric service.
- How long has child had problem with stools?
- Stool pattern:
  - <3 per week, type 1–2 stools on Bristol Stool chart suggests constipation. Child may have soiling with type 6–7 stools.
  - Two or more stools per 24 hours with type 5–6 stools suggest fast bowel transit time
- Ask about defecation, any pain, straining, blood on paper. Ribbon-like stools suggest possible bowel pathology.
- Ask about fluid intake and diet.
- Drug history is very important as medications can cause constipation.
- History of any problems with toilet training.
- Any recent change in family circumstances, for example change school/nursery, move of house, parental separation.
- Family history.

### Examination

- All children must have height and weight measured and plotted on growth charts. Any faltering growth suggests possibility of inflammatory bowel disease, celiac disease, hypothyroid, cystic fibrosis, etc.
- Abdominal examination, particularly for palpable faeces.
- Inspection of anus (if child is happy to be examined and child/parent gives informed consent) but digital rectal examination should only be performed by those who can interpret findings (Van der Berg et al., 2006).
- Inspection of spine, sacral area, gait and lower limb neurology.
- General examination of other systems.

### Investigations

- These are rarely needed but may include blood tests: full blood count, U+E, LFT, ESR, TFT, coeliac screen, immunoglobulins.
- Abdominal x-rays should not be performed in constipation.
- Marker transit study x-rays should not be performed except in specialist centres.
- If any suggestion of infective cause for loose stools, send stool for culture.

### Management

- Soiling and constipation will only resolve with treatment of the constipation with laxatives.
- Movicol Paediatric Plain is the recommended first laxative to be used in all children, some needing disimpaction regimes before regular doses (Van der Berg et al., 2006).
- If not tolerated, stimulant laxatives, usually senna, can be substituted or added into the Movicol when highest doses are ineffective.
- Rectal preparations are not normally recommended in the treatment of constipation and should only be used by specialists.
- Diet and fluid management (increasing fruit and vegetables and good fluid intake) should be given once constipation is improving to help prevent the problem recurring, but should not be first line management.
- Child must be encouraged to sit on the toilet regularly, at least daily, in correct posture (child toilet seat, foot stool). Praise and encouragement should be given for sitting to try to defecate.

To help the child understand the difficulties they are experiencing, a narrative approach can be helpful such as 'beating sneaky poo', a booklet designed to help children cooperate when establishing toileting routines. See Chapter 25, Narrative therapy.

---

## Case study 1

Leo, aged 11 years, has mild learning difficulties and poor school attendance. He has had constipation and soiling since he was first toilet trained. He has been seen by three different services for his problem and has had an admission to an inpatient unit for two months when he was six years old, where he initially had good progress but relapsed on discharge.

Leo's mother died when he was five years old and he now lives with his father and paternal grandmother. Leo has given up any hope of getting better. He is bullied at school and often refuses to attend.

When he attends clinic, he is found to be taking senna syrup intermittently and refuses to accept any advice or change in management. After several appointments where Leo has the cause of his soiling explained using diagrams and internet education programmes, he agrees to start filling in simple bowel charts and to take his senna regularly.

Several sessions later, Leo has had his senna dose adjusted to produce a soft daily stool each morning after breakfast. His school attendance improves. The school staff support Leo well with dealing with any bullying. Leo starts to lead the clinic appointments showing his charts and discussing his medication.

Sadly, Leo's grandmother who has been attending clinic becomes unwell and attendance at clinic declines. The family is contacted, and Leo's father agrees to take over supporting Leo with his management. It is difficult for Leo's father to attend clinic, so further contact is made by telephone and Leo continues to do well.

## Case study 2

Brian, aged 7, a looked after child, moves into the area to be with new foster parents. He has daily soiling. He refuses to undress or wash for the first 4 weeks in his new placement. He is seen regularly by a child psychologist and his looked after children (LAC) nurse and after 4 weeks is undressing and bathing daily. His soiling continues despite good drinking, diet and regular toileting.

Brian will not discuss how often he has his bowels open, nor his stool type. Constipation is suspected by his LAC nurse and with advice from the consultant paediatrician, senna and movicol PP are started. Brian is seen weekly by his LAC nurse and starts to make some progress with his soiling. Eventually Brian allows the LAC nurse to palpate his abdomen and he is found to have obvious faecal impaction. Treatment is started with movicol PP disimpaction regime. Brian finds this a difficult process but is supported well by his foster parents. Following disimpaction with regular senna and movicol PP, Brian stops soiling and starts to slowly wean his laxatives.

Over the summer holidays when the LAC nurse is on annual leave, Brian starts soiling again. His foster mother makes telephone contact with the consultant paediatrician who advises an increase in laxative doses. Social services arrange an appointment with a private child psychiatrist who believes Brian's soiling is behavioural and stops all of Brian's laxative medication.

Brian's soiling worsens markedly. His foster mother is confused by the conflicting advice given, but feels that as Brian's soiling had improved with laxative treatment to contact the LAC nurse. The laxative treatment is restarted and Brian makes good progress. He is able to start school in the autumn and has continued support for his constipation from his LAC nurse and for his behavioural issues from CAMHS.

## Multiple choice questions

1. Soiling is usually a behavioural problem: True/False

2. Soiling can result in low self-esteem and poor school attendance: True/False

3. Children are often not aware when they have soiled their underwear: True/False

4. NICE guidelines recommend treatment of constipation with senna and Movicol Paediatric Plain: True/False

5. Suppositories are commonly used in children with faecal impaction: True/False

## Key texts

International Children's Continence Society. www.i-c-c-s.org

Internet site for parents and children (sponsored by pharmaceutical company) www.childhoodconstipation.com

NICE guidelines (2010a) *Constipation in Children and Young People*. London: NICE.

NICE guideline www.nice.org.uk

Van der Berg MM, Benninga MA, Di Lorenzo C (2006) Epidemiology of childhood constipation: a systematic review. *American Journal of Gastroenterology*, **101**: 2401–9.

# 55 *Psychosomatic disorders; dissociative disorder and psychological disorders*
### Jason Phillips

---

## Key concepts

- There is a strong interplay between psychological and physical symptoms in psychosomatic disorders.
- Repeated presentation of physical symptoms in spite of negative findings is known as a somatoform disorder.
- Assessment using predisposing, precipitating, presenting, perpetuating and protective factors can be helpful.
- Management of psychosomatic disorders often involves the multidisciplinary team.

---

## Terms and definitions

- Psychosomatic: A broad term used to describe conditions in which there is a strong interplay and inseparability between physical and psychological components.
- Somatoform disorder: A disorder in which the main feature is 'repeated presentation of physical symptoms, together with persistent requests for medical investigations, in spite of repeated negative findings and reassurances by doctors that the symptoms have no physical basis' (ICD-10, WHO 1992).

In the International Classification of Diseases-10, somatoform disorders include:

- Somatization disorder, in which the main feature is the presentation of symptoms for which there is insufficient or no underlying medical cause (common in children).
- Hypochondriacal disorder, in which the essential feature is a persistent preoccupation with the possibility of having a serious physical disorder (very rare in children).
- Dissociative (conversion) disorder: where there is a partial or complete loss of the normal integration between memories of the past, awareness of identity and immediate sensations, and control of bodily movements, for example paralysis of a limb, loss of sensation, inability to talk and blindness.
- Psychogenic disorder: where the disorder has a psychological origin.
- Factitious disorder (Munchausen's syndrome): symptoms are initiated voluntarily (unlike all of the above where symptom production is thought to be unconscious) by the patient, who has no obvious goal other than to enter the sick role.

## The connections

Lask and Fosson (1989) suggest that the interplay between psychological and physical symptoms can be conceptualized in the form of a continuum from predominantly psychosocial aetiology on the one hand, to predominantly organic on the other (**Figure 55.1**).

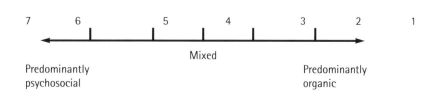

Figure 55.1

Thus some conditions, for example congenital heart disease, may have a clearly organic aetiology and would be placed at position 1, while others, for example school phobia, would be at position 7, having a marked psychosocial influence. Conditions such as asthma may lie between the two, being influenced by lung structure and function and infections, in addition to poor social circumstances and stress.

# Common somatization disorders in children

- Abdominal pain
- Headaches
- Limb pains
- Nausea and vomiting
- Fatigue

Different symptoms seem to occur, according to developmental stages, for example pre-pubertal children present more often with abdominal pain (this symptom peaks around age nine years), and older children with headaches (peaking at age 12 years). Adolescents are more likely to present with limb pain, fatigue or neurological symptoms.

## Recurrent abdominal pain

- Occurs in 10–20 per cent of children (Apley et al., 1978). Only 5 per cent of these have an organic cause. Organic causes are suggested by localized pain and occurrence at non-specific times, for example at night.
- Non-organic cause is more likely if the pain is vaguely localized or diffuse. Other indications of non-organic cause include associations with specific times, for example Sunday evenings or school day mornings, or coinciding with unpleasant circumstances.
- Is one of the most commonly presenting symptoms in childhood, most frequently in 5–12 year olds, and equally distributed between boys and girls.
- Thirty per cent of children continue to have abdominal pain in adulthood, a further 30 per cent develop migraine or recurrent headache, while the rest 'grow out of it'.

## Headache

- A common symptom occurring in slightly older children. Eleven per cent of 10–11 year olds had headaches at least once a month in the preceding year (Rutter et al., 1970). In one study of children with headache (Jerrett, 1979), 66 per cent had no organic cause. Organic causes included infected sinuses, febrile illnesses, dental caries, hypertension, brain tumours, and so on. It is important to note that non-organic headaches and migraine are uncommon in children under the age of five and, therefore, an organic cause should be carefully looked for in this age group (Graham, 1991).
- Migraine is another cause of headache, and may occur in about 5 per cent of all children at some time, usually at age eight years or older. A family history of migraine, plus typical symptoms of throbbing headache, photophobia, visual disturbance and nausea, point to this diagnosis.
- Non-organic headaches are characterized by a tight feeling around the head, and there may be associations with emotive situations ( similarly to recurrent abdominal pain), for example school days.

## Adolescents

- Physical symptoms are common, especially in girls (Eminson et al., 1996). In Eminson's epidemiological study, common symptoms were the feeling of a lump in the throat, dizziness, heart pounding, limb pains, headaches and chest pains.
- Of the adolescents reported, 8.3 per cent experienced 13 or more symptoms and, again, this was more common in girls than in boys.
- The more symptoms the adolescents reported, the more likely they were to have serious concerns about illnesses (hypochondriacal beliefs) and a preoccupation with health. In some adolescents, the symptoms had a significant effect on lifestyle, for example preventing the adolescent from going to school or enjoying themselves. Thus, in some adolescents, somatization is associated with significant disability in terms of general functioning.

- An important aim in treatment must be to prevent this from becoming chronic.

# Dissociative disorders

The term 'dissociative' came from the presumption that the psychological mechanisms occurring in these disorders were the dissociation of one part of the individual from the rest, and 'conversion' from the conversion of emotional conflict into physical symptoms.

- Disorders characterized by loss of function in any modality.
- Seen from middle childhood onwards, more commonly in adolescence and in girls.
- Complaints may be limb weakness, inability to see, talk or hear, unusual movements and epileptiform fits ('pseudoseizures'). Pseudoseizures may be more common in children who actually do have epilepsy.
- Examination and observations may show that the symptoms and signs do not correspond to known disorders, rather the symptoms correspond to the patient's idea of physical disorder, which may not coincide with physiological or anatomical principles, for example an area of loss of feeling on a limb may display 'glove or stocking' distribution of anaesthesia, rather than corresponding to the anatomy of the nervous system.
- There may be inconsistencies in the symptoms and signs, for example the child cannot weight bear when asked, but is observed to when not watched directly. Often the adolescent shows a striking lack of distress about the symptoms (known as 'la belle indifference').

## Management

- Assessment: a detailed history including predisposing, precipitating, perpetuating and protective factors and an examination of the family beliefs about illness
- Reassurance: when investigations show negative findings
- Explanation: the family is given some understanding of the role of psychological factors in the presenting illness
- Treatment: methods vary according to the assessment

## Assessment

- Professionals involved must work collaboratively
- Joint assessments can be beneficial, so that physical, developmental, psychological and social aspects can be considered in parallel, rather than the family being 'shunted around' professionals
- It is essential to acknowledge the validity of the child's symptoms and not to dismiss them out of hand or suggest that the child is deliberately 'making them up'
- It is usually unproductive to challenge the patient's subjective reality of the complaint
- It is important to acknowledge the family's concerns, and to engage the family. With the family engaged, the history taking is carefully continued

## Predisposing, precipitating, perpetuating and protective factors

- Predisposing factors: These include biological vulnerability, for example bronchial hyper-reactivity in asthma; early life experience, for example previous exposure to illness or parental over-concern with bodily functions or minor illnesses; temperament, for example an anxious child is more likely to develop somatic symptoms, than a 'happy-go-lucky' child and socio-cultural influences. In some cultures, physical ill health may be more 'acceptable' than psychological ill health.
- Precipitating factors: These include events such as falling out with friends, being bullied, parental ill health (physical or psychological); a physical illness, for example a chest infection or viral illness; disruption of an attachment relationship (loss and bereavement) and traumatic experiences, for example accidents, assault or homelessness.
- Perpetuating factors: What precipitates distress may also perpetuate it, for example continued bullying or family discord. There may also be a gain for the child in expressing the symptom and the symptom may be thereby perpetuated. Gain can be considered as being primary or secondary (Lask and

Fosson, 1989). Primary gain is the relief of anxiety by symptom production. Secondary gain is the benefit obtained from the symptoms, often the avoidance of undesirable situations (consider an 11-year-old child who is anxious about attending school. The onset of abdominal pain draws attention from the anxiety (primary gain) and if the child misses school, then this can be seen as secondary gain).

- Symptoms may be perpetuated by reinforcement, for example if the parents only give positive attention to the child when they appear unwell, the child is more likely to continue expressing the symptom.
- Protective factors: Some factors may protect children exposed to stress, for example adaptability, good self-esteem, good peer relationships and good family relationships with open communication.

It may be necessary to undertake physical investigations on the basis of the detailed history taken. If negative, they can be reassuring to the child and to the family. Repeated and prolonged investigation is often unhelpful and can perpetuate the problem unnecessarily.

Having gathered the necessary information, the next step is to formulate an explanation for the family to explain what may be going on. It is sometimes helpful to use analogies, for example the idea of a tension headache being brought on by stress, a concept that most people would understand and accept.

- Treatment methods vary according to the assessment in each case.
- It is important to form a good therapeutic relationship with the family, whatever the treatment approach.
- Family therapy, individual therapy, including cognitive behaviour therapy (CBT), behaviour therapy, group therapy and relaxation could all be helpful.
- Medication, for example antidepressants, may be tried. It has been suggested that they are of benefit in adults with somatoform pain disorders. However, there is a lack of evidence to suggest that they are effective in children and of course, they are themselves occasionally associated with side effects such as nausea, anxiety and headache.
- Physical treatments, for example physiotherapy, and dietician advice may be helpful.
- Several treatment methods can be used at any one time, but only if this approach is planned, with good communication between the professionals.
- It is important to consider the social circumstances of the child, for example there may be a need for liaison with the child's school, especially if there has been a prolonged absence, and a planned reintroduction is essential.

## Case study

Christina, aged eight, was taken to her GP by her mother because of concerns about her recurrent abdominal pain. This had increased in frequency causing serious worry in the family and leading to poor school attendance.

Christina is a quiet, sensitive and shy child, who lives at home with her parents and two-month-old baby sister. Christina's mother suffers from migraine and her father, who works as a travelling engineer, is often away from home.

The GP could not find a physical cause for the pain, but acknowledged Christina's very real distress and the fact that she was not 'putting it on'. The GP suggested that the local Child and Adolescent Mental Health Service was ideally well placed to provide a comprehensive assessment and an effective treatment programme.

The assessment then considered that Christina's temperament might have predisposed her to this presentation. Precipitating factors included the increasing lack of her mother's attention as she attended to the new baby and the worry of her father succumbing to a terrorist attack. The condition was thought to be perpetuated by the 'reward' of avoiding school and therefore receiving more care from her mother. It had also meant that Christina's father had cancelled a couple of his long distance trips in order to help out at home.

The reassurance and explanation of what might be going on for Christina was enough to enable the parents to acknowledge her stress, and to pay more attention to her in a positive way. It also prompted them to consider communication patterns in the family. Christina was kept more clearly informed as to her father's movements. Liaison with her school helped to provide a smooth return, and the school was reassured that Christina's previous symptom of abdominal pain was not considered life threatening.

## Multiple choice questions

1. What are some of the common symptoms seen in children presenting with somatizing disorders?

    a. Abdominal pain
    b. Headaches
    c. Limb pains and fatigue
    d. Nausea and vomiting
    e. All of the above

2. What percentage of children presenting with abdominal pain in childhood continue to have symptoms in adulthood?

    a. 10 per cent
    b. 50 per cent
    c. 30 per cent
    d. 20 per cent
    e. None

3. What factors may be helpful in assessing children with psychosomatic disorders?

    a. Predisposing factors
    b. Precipitating factors
    c. Protective factors
    d. Perpetuating factors
    e. All of the above

### Key texts

Eminson DM (2001a) Somatising in children and adolescents. 1. Clinical presentations and aetiological factors. *Advances in Psychiatric Treatment*, **7**: 266–74.

Eminson DM (2001b) Somatising in children and adolescents. 2. Management and outcomes. *Advances in Psychiatric Treatment*, **7**: 388–98).

Lask B, Fosson B (1989) *Childhood Illness: The Psychosomatic Approach: Children Talking With Their Bodies*. Chichester: John Wiley and Sons.

# 56 An example of a therapeutic group intervention for children and adolescents with chronic medical conditions: The IMPACT Group

**Kirsteen Stevenson**

The IMPACT Group was set up in 1997 in Portsmouth and SE Hampshire (population 580 000) to meet the needs of children and adolescents with long-term medical conditions presenting with psycho-social adjustment difficulties, particularly for those not meeting the criteria for general Child and Adolescent Mental Health Services (CAMHS). The decision to provide a therapeutic group intervention was based on the concept of peer support providing a protective factor, promoting resilience and as a predictive factor for later functioning. The CAMHS Paediatric Liaison team (five professionals) have facilitated two groups per year, concluding the optimum number of young people is eight in a group within 2–3 years of each other. We ensure patients from junior and secondary schools are not combined in one group. The structure has evolved using qualitative feedback from parents and young people and now is offered on four consecutive full days during half-term and holidays. A parents' meeting is facilitated at the start and end of each group.

We take a non-categorical approach to inclusion criteria on the premise that these patients share more similarities than differences in their experience of their conditions and treatment. It permits those with rare conditions and physical disabilities to be included. Those requiring wheelchairs can be accommodated, unless they require more specialist equipment. Young people with mild learning disability and autism spectrum disorders can access the therapeutic process of the groups but those with more significant difficulties require specialist provisions. The diversity of conditions promotes reflection by the young people on inclusion, and helping and adapting to the needs of others. As anticipated, we received more referrals than the number eventually attending the group. We are mindful of the risks others have identified as inherent in offering such group interventions, for example creating a sub-culture of patients identifying themselves as ill and handicapped, although this has not been our experience.

Theoretical models used are psychodynamic theory, group theory and some elements of social learning theory. Our aim is to create a therapeutic milieu that is safe and containing, promotes group cohesion and identity, encourages trust and validation and provides an opportunity for expression of feelings both conscious and unconscious using a range of creative materials and activities. Our hope is that the positive experience in the group is internalized and hence improves the young person's self-esteem and self-acceptance. The tools at our disposal include games, graded from low risk of exposure to those enabling group cohesion and those requiring trust. Facilitated activities include, for example, creating a safe place, working with stories and creating group paintings. Throughout the group, reflection and understanding of the group processes by staff, facilitated by daily supervision, allows flexibility in responding to the needs of each group. We ensure decisions are made collectively, for example agreeing how to respond to an absent member.

Certain themes arise in each group: Feeling different with the belief they are the only one (experiencing problems), bullying and lack of understanding and acceptance at school, sadness and anger about missing out and why the medical condition has happened to them, difficulty maintaining peer friendships, guilt about the impact on their families and fear and anxiety about the future. The end of the group is marked by celebration and goodbye ceremonies. The young people release a helium balloon with the group members' names attached, exchange mobile telephone numbers and emails, and exchange cards with affirming statements.

Marked changes can be observed in some of the young people over the 4 days, examples include experimentation with different roles, improved affect, reduced anxiety and increased self-esteem. This is often accompanied by improved posture. Some examples of specific individual changes include exposing affective skin, removal of a cap hiding alopecia and wearing a skirt to expose a leg splint, normally covered by trousers. These changes seem to indicate increased self-acceptance, and are key in instilling hope and more positive thoughts about the future.

In the first parents' meeting we provide the means for private expression of negative feelings about their child's condition in a non-judgemental manner. Once given the opportunity to reflect on difficult feelings, they are free to accept more positive relationships with their children. The final ceremony involves everyone and parents are given the opportunity to express all their positive feelings about their children, witnessed by other parents, staff and children, a powerful validation of the young person.

We have been unable to provide empirical evidence for the cost-effectiveness of the groups or outcomes over time. We obtain qualitative feedback from the young people and parents using feedback forms, while acknowledging the limitations of these. Some examples of positive comments by the young people – 'this is the best thing I have ever done', 'the IMPACT Group is a good place to be', 'I'd love to come to the group again, we might need more help'. The young people regularly express the desire for the group to continue reflecting the chronicity of their conditions. Positive comments from parents – 'never seen such confidence in her as this week', 'he hates going to school but he has been up and ready every morning to come here'. Less positive comments received relate to the distance needed to travel in order to attend the group, 'need time to judge overall benefits to whether the family felt it was helpful'.

# 57 Chronic fatigue syndrome/myalgic encephalomyelitis in children and adolescents

Sally Wicks

> ## Key concepts
> - Children and young people have better outcomes than adults.
> - Poorer outcomes are associated with: low socioeconomic status; chronic maternal health problems; lack of well-defined acute physical triggers.
> - Fifty to 75 per cent make a full recovery or a marked improvement.
> - Symptoms can persist in some.
> - Many young people show a dramatic improvement.

## Introduction

Chronic fatigue syndrome (CFS) is the name for a condition with the principal symptoms of fatigue and easy fatiguability. The other recognized name is myalgic encephalomyelitis (ME) (or encephalopathy).

CFS is recognized in children and adolescents, where it can have profound effects on physical, emotional, social and academic functioning.

## Demography

- Prevalence under 18 years of age: approximately 0.07 per cent although some studies suggest higher rates. Mean age of onset in clinic samples is 11–15 years, perhaps lower in community samples.
- Some studies report a higher proportion of girls.
- Social class in clinic samples: more from higher socioeconomic classes.

## Diagnostic criteria and symptomatology

Below are the symptoms listed in the NICE clinical guideline (53) for chronic fatigue syndrome/ myalgic encephalomyelitis. This guideline applies to the diagnosis and management of the illness in both adults and children. Diagnosis should not be made on the basis of symptoms alone as it is important to first perform investigations to exclude other conditions. The guideline recommends the diagnosis not being made until the illness is of four months' duration in adults, but advises earlier diagnosis, at three months, in children and adolescents.

## Chronic fatigue syndrome symptoms

Fatigue with all of the following features:
- new, or had a specific onset (i.e. not lifelong);
- persistent and/or recurrent;
- unexplained by other conditions;
- has resulted in a substantial reduction in activity level characterized by post-exertional malaise and/or fatigue (typically delayed, for example by at least 24 hours, with slow recovery over several days).

And one or more of the following:
- difficulty with sleeping, such as insomnia, hypersomnia, unrefreshing sleep, a disturbed sleep-wake cycle;
- muscle and/or joint pain that is multi-site and without evidence of inflammation;
- headaches;
- painful lymph nodes without pathological enlargement;

- sore throat;
- cognitive dysfunction, such as difficulty thinking, inability to concentrate, impairment of short-term memory, and difficulties with word-finding, planning/organizing thoughts and information processing;
- physical or mental exertion makes symptoms worse;
- general malaise or 'flu-like' symptoms;
- dizziness and/or nausea;
- palpitations in the absence of identified cardiac pathology.

Some further points about diagnosis of CFS/ME in children and adolescents:

- depressive and/or anxiety symptoms may be present and do not exclude the diagnosis of CFS, especially if they appear after the onset of fatigue;
- school phobia/refusal can be common in CFS, but may also be a differential diagnosis.

# Assessment

History from child and parent should include:

- presenting complaint: principal symptoms, length of illness, school attendance, withdrawal from activities, typical day (weekday and weekend), current level of functioning and independence;
- past medical history: previous illnesses and course of recovery, allergic history;
- family history: illness in other family members, including CFS and psychiatric, family adaptation to current illness, description of family relationships and communication style, current family stresses;
- social history: usual activities, peer relationships, degree of independence, school performance, enjoyment of school, previous school attendance;
- illness history: previous treatment and treatment experiences, child and family belief about the illness and effect of activity, dietary habits and beliefs;
- psychological history: mental health problems, especially anxiety, depression, and school refusal, temperament.

It is essential when taking the history to validate the child's complaints.

Children with CFS and their families are extremely sensitive to a dismissive attitude on the part of professionals. A trusting relationship between the family and professional is very important in subsequent management and the professional's acknowledgement of and concern about the symptomatology at the outset helps to foster such a relationship. Children and families may have experienced repeated investigations, delay in referral and diagnosis or ineffective treatments. They may have fears about undiagnosed serious organic conditions. They may need explanation and support in understanding why a mental health team is involved. Joint paediatric and psychiatric assessments have been shown to be useful.

## Physical examination

Physical examination is important to exclude other pathology and to reassure the child and family. Marked physical abnormalities are rare in CFS and should be investigated.

## Investigations

There is no specific diagnostic test. Investigations should be carried out to exclude other diagnoses suggested by the history or clinical examination and should be kept to a minimum. Investigations can be reassuring to children and parents but, once completed, further investigations should be avoided as this continues to raise parents' anxiety about possible misdiagnoses.

## Investigations in CFS

Full blood count, erythrocyte sedimentation rate, C-reactive protein, urea and electrolytes, serum calcium, liver function, serum creatinine, creatine kinase, thyroid function tests, random blood glucose, serum ferritin, screening blood tests for gluten sensitivity, serological testing if there is a history indicative of infection, for example for glandular fever, toxoplasmosis, etc. Occasional other tests as clinically required, to exclude specific diagnoses, for example inflammatory bowel disease.

## School report

A report from the child's school should be obtained with details of the child's academic achievements, social functioning, attendance record and any concerns the school may have.

Other useful assessments: These may only be possible in specialized treatment centres:

- Cognitive assessment: Formal testing of the child's cognitive/intellectual abilities, plus level of functioning in, for example, reading and spelling. Children with CFS may in the past have pushed themselves to do well. A comprehensive assessment of their abilities can ensure help is targeted and expectations are realistic.
- Physiotherapy and Occupational Therapy assessment: An initial assessment of the child's muscle tone, muscle power, exercise tolerance, balance and coordination is useful in providing the baseline for the child's graded exercise programme. An occupational therapy assessment may be helpful in picking up subtle problems, for example poor fine motor control.
- Detailed psychological assessment: Children who show very significant impairment in functioning, a long duration of illness or clear depressive/anxious symptomatology, should have a further assessment from a professional in the mental health field.

# Aetiological factors

Aetiology of CFS in children, adolescents and adults remains controversial. The 1996 report from the Royal Colleges stressed a multi-factorial (biological, psychological and social) approach in defining the predisposing, precipitating and perpetuating factors in each patient. It is not helpful to view CFS as either purely physical or purely psychological and it is often unhelpful to enter into long debates with the family and young person about this issue.

Examples of aetiological factors in children and adolescents are given below. For a detailed discussion of the role of infection as a precipitating and/or maintaining factor, see report from the Royal Colleges.

# Physical factors

Viral illness may precipitate CFS. In particular, fatigue may follow infection with the Epstein–Barr virus (EBV), although less than 10 per cent of EBV sufferers develop CFS.

Fatigue and weakness is exacerbated by excessive rest and inactivity. It is very important for the young person and family to understand this.

# Effects of excessive rest and inactivity

- Significant effects occur within 1–4 weeks of bed rest
- Reduced muscle volume and strength
- Reduced muscle protein and increased connective tissue
- Reduced bone mineral density
- Joint stiffness
- Reduced BMR
- Altered white cell function
- Changes in immune response
- Affect on mood and circadian rhythm

# Psychological factors

Once out of normal activities, children can quickly lose confidence in their physical and social activities and become anxious or miserable about loss of time in school and reduced contact with their peers.

Many of these young people are compliant and perhaps perfectionist by nature and find failure hard to tolerate, so returning to school after a prolonged absence is difficult. A professed desire to return to school does not mean there are no problems in this area.

Some young people with CFS may become depressed and the depression may be a perpetuating factor of CFS. Symptoms of depression in adolescents include irritability and anger, as well as the more commonly recognized depressive symptoms.

Psychological difficulties such as the effects of bullying and/or poor peer relationships may be predisposing, precipitating or perpetuating factors.

Abuse or major life events are not often found to be aetiological factors.

# Family factors

The family's response to the illness, and beliefs about the cause of the illness, are important. In particular, families who put a great deal of energy into pursuing an entirely physical cause, with an insistence on a large number of physical investigations, may be contributing to the perpetuation of the symptoms.

Family dynamics are often relevant, for example overprotection of the child (possibly as a result of the illness rather than present before the onset); identification with another sick member of the family; and a change in family roles such as a mother, who has altered her work pattern to look after the child.

# Treatment

A combined approach addressing the physical and psychological issues together is best, for example in primary care or combined paediatric/psychiatric clinics. It is essential to believe the child and family's description of the symptoms and to establish a trusting relationship between the child, family and professionals. The child should be central to any decision-making about management.

A positive approach to treatment and outcome is vital with an emphasis on good prognosis, although full recovery may take some time.

The concept of gradual rehabilitation should be introduced, i.e. a steady and controlled increase in physical activity, social activities and school work.

A rehabilitation programme should consist of a structured daily timetable:

- Complete a daily timetable to structure the day with clear periods for rest, eating, sleeping and activity. Discourage sleeping during rest periods, if sleep pattern at night is affected.
- Start the timetable at the child's current level of functioning with small increases (5–10 per cent weekly). Stress the need to go at a pace agreed between the clinician and the child and family, neither too fast nor too slow. As the child's tolerance improves, the increases in activity can increase.

Graded exercise programme:

- Activity includes: exercise programme. Exercise should not be short bursts of very strenuous activity, but more gradual exercises, carried out daily.
- Mental activity, for example school work, reading, social activity.
- Review goals regularly.

## Individual support for the young person

Some young people may require more intensive psychological treatment than general counselling or supportive therapy. Cognitive Behaviour Therapy (CBT) has been shown to be effective in the treatment of adults with CFS and is generally suitable and effective in young people for a variety of conditions, including CFS. Treatment of co-morbid psychiatric conditions should be addressed.

## Family support

Regular liaison and involvement of the family in the rehabilitation programme is essential. Work with the family to address identified issues of family dynamics may be important. Gaining the family's confidence by working with and acknowledging their concerns is a priority. Family therapy can be helpful in exploring factors maintaining illness or more serious underlying family dysfunction.

As family life, and life outside the home for the parents, may have ceased because of the worry about the young person, encourage the parents to pick up life again. This may include the mother returning to work when possible.

## Friends

Young people who are off school, for any length of time, often lose friendships. Encourage the young person and the family to keep contact with friends by phone and visits, so that he/she can keep in touch with the gossip and friendship groups. This loss of friendships often makes it more difficult to return to school.

## School

Discourage home tuition for any length of time, if possible, as this may perpetuate the illness. Encourage a very gradual return to school, if necessary with a tutor who goes with the child into a school or small school unit. Good liaison between the school, parents and other professionals is essential. Any discrepancies found on cognitive testing and any specific school-related problems, for example bullying, need to be addressed. Young people are often very anxious about time in school and careful attention to managing details of the school day, for example carrying heavy bags, helps progress.

# Drug treatment

There is no systematic evidence for any drugs benefiting the core disorder. However, pain relief, for example paracetamol, and non-steroidal anti-inflammatory drugs, may occasionally be necessary for headaches and muscle pain. Anti-depressant therapy may be indicated, if there are clear depressive symptoms, for example low mood with irritability and lack of pleasure in activities. There is, as yet, no clear evidence for alternative therapies offering substantial long-term benefits. It is important to anticipate set-backs and difficult transitions. It is important to maintain encouragement and an optimistic attitude.

# Treatment setting

Some young people can be managed as outpatients, with combined input from primary care, education, paediatric and child mental health services. Good liaison between all professionals involved is essential with regular (for example weekly) goal-setting and monitoring.

Inpatient or day-patient treatment is necessary, in some cases, especially if there is a lack of progress, a long duration of illness, or if the child is particularly affected, for example not attending school at all or housebound. A specialist unit with experience in the treatment of CFS in young people and with access to a number of professionals (e.g. paediatricians, child psychiatrists and psychologists, physiotherapists, occupational therapists and nurses) is desirable, so that there is a multidisciplinary approach to assessment and management

## Case study 1

C, a 12-year-old girl, was referred to the paediatric liaison team with a four-month history of fatigue and headaches and a fluctuating school attendance. C was trying to continue to attend school on a regular basis, but frequently had to return home early or would have days when she felt too ill and tired to manage to get in at all. She was not able to participate in the sports she normally enjoyed. The weekend before she was seen a friend had come over for a sleepover, which she very much enjoyed but which kept her up later than usual. This left her with worsened symptoms of fatigue and headache for several days afterwards.

C and her mother were asked to keep a diary for 2 weeks, showing in 30 minute chunks all her activity and grading this as low energy activity, high energy activity or rest. There was some discussion of how to categorize different activities and the need for rest to be true rest and not watching television or texting to friends. This exercise showed something of a 'boom and bust' cycle, with C being much more active for 2–3 days at a time, then showing very much reduced activity for the next few days due to redoubled symptoms. The information was used to find a baseline for activity levels, and a structured plan including short periods of high and low energy activities and rest was constructed. C's school was happy to agree to C attending school each day for a much shorter length of time with an expectation that this would be manageable and could be increased with time. A very short walk was included daily. C initially found it difficult to have periods of absolute rest during the day, but soon found that these did help her to feel better. She found it very frustrating not to be allowed to do more with friends on days that she felt better, but did understand the rationale for this. Once it was clear that C was able to cope with her baseline plan, small changes were introduced every 1–2 weeks to increase activity and reduce some of her rests, with careful attention paid to how C coped with each change. She was gradually able to increase her time in school, but a brief relapse on returning to full-time schooling showed that the pace of change had become too fast, and she reverted to attending for a little less than a full school day for an extended period of time before successfully managing full-time attendance. C continued to have a short rest on return from school each day. She became able to have some participation in sports again, but on a less competitive level than previously.

## Case study 2

B, a 15-year-old girl, started with a period of a few months when she had a series of sore throats, at times with fever. She managed to attend school through much of this time, but on one return to school after time off, still fatigued, she had to return home the same day due to her feeling of exhaustion. Her parents were alarmed at how pale she appeared. A number of investigations failed to reveal any abnormality, and as the fatigue, headaches and intermittent sore throats continued in spite of rest, a diagnosis of Chronic Fatigue Syndrome was made.

B had increasing difficulty with mobility, only leaving the house in a wheelchair, and although home tuition was arranged, was only able to participate minimally in this. Her mother was taking extended periods of leave from work, which was a source of stress for the family. B was not improving with an outpatient approach and so was admitted for a period of rehabilitation.

A daily timetable was drawn up which matched her levels of activity at the time, with careful structuring to spread activity and rest across the day. Daily physiotherapy was included involving stretches and some gentle muscle strengthening exercise. Time with a psychologist was also included, initially for only 15 minutes at a time. B was able to cope with this baseline programme, and subsequently small increases in activity and decreases in rest were made each week. She started to attend the unit's school and gradually started to walk short distances outside as well as inside the unit. B's rehabilitation continued for several months before a plan was made for school reintegration. A discharge date was agreed, after which physiotherapy input was maintained on an outpatient basis, for some time.

## Multiple choice questions

1. Chronic fatigue syndrome is often precipitated by a viral illness: True/False

2. Children with chronic fatigue syndrome have a higher recovery rate in comparison with adults: True/False

3. Graded exercise is often recommended in the treatment of chronic fatigue syndrome: True/False

### Key texts

Garralda ME, Rangel L (2002) Annotation: Chronic Fatigue Syndrome in children and adolescents. *Journal of Child Psychology and Psychiatry*, **43**: 169–76.

National Institute for Health and Clinical Excellence (2007) *Chronic fatigue syndrome/Myalgic encephalomyelitis (or encephalopathy); Diagnosis and Management.* CG53. London: National Institute for Health and Clinical Excellence.

Rangel L, Rapp S, Levin E, Garralda ME (1999) Chronic Fatigue Syndrome: updates on paediatric and psychological management. *Current Paediatrics*, **9**: 188–93.

# 58 *Chronic illness in children and young people*

Julie Waine

---

## Key concepts

- Chronic illness is a stressor that increases the risk to children of both developing a mental disorder and of impeding their developmental trajectory.
- Family functioning is an important mediator of outcome for the child.
- Adolescence is characterized by thinking in the 'here and now' and risk-taking behaviour, both of which may interfere with treatment adherence.
- Education alone does not increase adherence.
- A multidisciplinary paediatric liaison team can provide timely, evidence-based interventions in order to minimize the impact of chronic illness on a young person's mental health.

---

## Introduction

There is no universally agreed definition of chronic illness. Van Der Lee et al.'s (1970) systematic review of this area found that most research definitions took into account both the duration of symptoms and their impact on daily life. The prevalence of chronic illness in children in the developed world has increased partly as a consequence of the increase in survival rates from serious congenital and acquired illness (Zylke and DeAngelis, 2007).

Studies have shown an association between physical illness and behavioural and emotional difficulties. Parents of children with chronic illness report behavioural and emotional difficulties at least twice as often as do the parents of healthy controls (Mrazek, 2002). This incidence rises if the illness directly affects the brain.

The Office for National Statistics survey of the mental health of children and adolescents in Great Britain found that 4 per cent of all 5–15 year olds sampled had an emotional disorder. The prevalence of any mental disorder was 37 per cent in young people with epilepsy and one in six in children (17 per cent) with a life-threatening illness (Meltzer et al., 2000).

At follow up, three years later, physical illness was found to be a predictor of the persistence of an emotional disorder. Of the group who had a physical illness when originally sampled in 1999, 6 per cent fulfilled criteria for an emotional disorder. This compared to only 2 per cent of the group with no physical disorder (Meltzer, 2003).

Chronic illness can be viewed as a stressor, which may prevent a young person reaching their developmental potential, but happily this is not the most common outcome (Eiser, 1983). Gannoni and Shute (2010) used focus groups to ask parents and children about adaptation to illness. They found parents and children taking positive steps to cope with their challenges by, for example, using problem-focused coping strategies.

## Possible mental health consequences of chronic illness in children

There are common themes to living with any chronic illness and those which are disease specific (Wallander and Varni, 1998). Whether the illness is life threatening or life limiting, static or progressive, predictable or of uncertain prognosis, acquired, genetic or inherited will have an effect on how the young person, and their family, views and lives with the illness.

The most common psychiatric diagnosis made is that of an adjustment disorder, after the diagnosis is made. An adjustment disorder is defined as emotional symptoms and/or behaviour, which are temporarily linked to a life event and which subsequently resolve within six months of the life event.

One study showed 36 per cent of newly diagnosed diabetics, aged 8–13 years, had an adjustment disorder within the first three months after diagnosis. The symptoms were mainly of depression but, within a year, 93 per cent of the children no longer had diagnosable psychiatric disturbance (Kovacs et al., 1985).

Young people with physical illness may develop depression. Diagnosis of depression can be complicated by the misattribution of somatic symptoms, such as tiredness, weight loss and sleep disturbance, to the physical illness rather than as due to depression.

Mental distress may influence a physical illness. For example, stress has been associated with acute exacerbation of asthma (Sandberg et al., 2000).

The mental effects of a physical illness may remain dormant for several years, until a later stress activates them, for example pre-school serious illness is thought to be a risk factor for later depressive symptoms at age 15.

# Physical illness and maladjustment

Young people with chronic illness have the same developmental needs and health concerns as their healthy peers. They have the same coping strategies (Abbott, 2003). Children will have their own temperamental characteristics which will influence how they and their family cope with the demands of the illness. In addition to factors within the child, family functioning predicts adjustment to illness.

Chronic illness increases the burden of care for the child by the family. As well as responsibility for outpatient attendance and possible hospital admissions, care may be needed beyond that generally expected for a child of that age, for example needing to toilet a middle childhood child. This is alongside needing to administer or supervise medication and/or therapy.

It is important to help the family find a workable balance between providing the care that is needed for the optimum health of the young person and fulfilling the family's ordinary everyday needs

# School

School attendance is an important measure of the impact of an illness. Children with chronic illness miss school through illness and planned hospital attendances and this can limit their academic potential. School phobia after time in hospital is recognized. School can have an important influence on the young person's successful adjustment to their illness. Schools within hospitals can be particularly beneficial for children with chronic illnesses, both in helping them to keep up to date with their schoolwork and also by liaising with the child's school.

Poor support from classmates has been associated with low self-esteem and an increased risk of depression in young people with cancer (Noll et al., 1991).

This research demonstrates that intervention by improving the child's social skills may help improve their peer relationships and lower the risk of subsequent depression. Chronic illness is a vulnerability factor for bullying (Pittet et al., 2010).

A further possible difficulty can arise if teachers inappropriately lower their expectations of the child's academic performance. A nurse specialist may have a role to play in visiting the school. They can educate the school community about the needs and abilities of the young person, in addition to facilitating realistic discussions about the possible health and safety risks.

# Chronic illness at different stages of childhood

There is some evidence to suggest that the diagnosis of a chronic illness before the age of five years is associated with a negative impact on later cognitive performance (Eiser and Lansdown, 1977). This finding was noted in survivors of childhood cancer, but has also been shown in young people with early onset diabetes. It is thought to be due to the adverse effects of the illness process, for example the effect of hypoglycaemia in diabetes, the use of radiotherapy for brain tumours.

Early diagnosis of chronic illness can be associated with delayed developmental milestones. The impact of separation on attachment as demonstrated in Robertson's film 'A two year old goes to hospital' (1952) led to a change in hospital policy so that parents were encouraged to stay with their child in hospital.

Chronic illness developing early may limit the child's opportunities to socialize. This may then have an impact on the child's ability to socialize later at school.

During middle childhood, time missed at school may set a pattern for later poor attendance.

---

## Case study: Vicky

Vicky is 14. Insulin-dependent diabetes was diagnosed two years ago after a short viral illness. Vicky's diabetic control is suboptimal and she needed an emergency admission to hospital in ketoacidosis in the past couple of months. The psychologist from the multidisciplinary paediatric liaison team is working with Vicky using a motivational interviewing approach in order to help her integrate diabetes into her self-image.

---

Adolescence is traditionally thought of as a time of emotional turbulence, as the young person grows emotionally and physically towards becoming a mature adult. Separation from the family and increasing autonomy are viewed as the tasks of adolescence, along with maturation into a sexual being. In general, the opinion of friends and acceptance into a peer group increase in importance.

It is not difficult to imagine how a chronic illness could interfere with these important developmental changes. Integrating illness into a positive self-view may be difficult. Self-esteem could be affected if physical appearance is altered beyond the normal range of peers. Cystic fibrosis, for example, may slow growth and delay puberty. Delayed puberty itself can lower self-esteem, particularly in boys, and result in the adolescent being treated in an inappropriately immature way (Suris et al., 2004).

Adherence with treatment may become more of a problem during the teenage years, although non-compliance with treatment plans is not solely the domain of young people. Many factors influence treatment adherence. Adherence may be seen as on a spectrum rather than an all-or-nothing phenomenon (Lask, 1994).

# Why might an adolescent not adhere to a treatment plan?

Most physicians caring for adolescents would hope that the young person themselves would become increasingly responsible for completing their treatment, ideally with a gradual handover of responsibility from their parents. For this to be successful, both parent and child must negotiate the change at a pace they are both happy with and with a degree of acceptance as to the seriousness of the illness.

For a young person, the daily care necessary to treat their illness is a daily reminder of being different and unwell. Adolescence is a time of risk-taking and feelings of invincibility, which are recognized aspects of normal adolescent thought processes. This might not contribute to adherence and chronic illness is associated with an increase in risk taking behaviour (Suris et al., 2008).

Non-conformity with a treatment regime may mirror non-conformity in other aspects of the adolescent's life. The young person may choose not to adhere, thereby taking back some control over their life. In assessing adherence, it is always important to exclude depression as a possible cause. A young person struggling with accepting a life-limiting illness may currently decide that rigid adherence to a strict treatment regime is not a priority for them, as they will die anyway, just a bit younger than some of their peers (Esmond, 2000).

# Effect on siblings

The research findings on the effects of chronic illness on siblings are mixed. An excess of somatic symptoms and attention-seeking behaviour has been found, as have increased rates of pro-social behaviour. Understandably, siblings have been found to be concerned about their brother or sister, but also about their own risk of illness and the effect of the illness on their parents. Siblings may suffer from the effects of social isolation, as the illness isolates the family, for example infection risk may deter parents from allowing their children to attend playschool.

# Long-term outcome

The long-term outcome for young people with chronic illness is difficult to assess. A significant volume of available research is based on young people treated at specialist centres. This may not be able to be generalized to the outcomes of young people who receive care from less specialist centres (Gledhill et al., 2000). In general, most young people remain well-adjusted, although women who remain chronically ill seem at most risk of psychiatric sequelae.

## What can be helpful?

The following list gives some suggestions as to possible areas of intervention, in order to strengthen resilience factors in the young person and their family.

- Family: Have the parents themselves come to terms with the illness? Are they ready to allow you to discuss it with the child? Work out together what the parents are happy with you saying to the child. Make an assessment of the parents' mental health and coping strategies.

- Explain the illness to the child: Use age-appropriate language. Young children may view illness as a punishment. It is useful to reassure explicitly that the illness is not their fault.
- Talk to the young person and encourage their questions: Asking questions is a step on the path to assuming responsibility for self care. Prepare the child for specific procedures and the likely questions of others. Disease-specific web-sites, role play and literature from patient support groups may be helpful.
- Use of play therapy: If the child has problems coping with procedures and pain, play therapist or psychologists can be very helpful in talking through procedures and role playing. Use of social stories can be useful: see Chapter 73, Social stories.
- Educate the parents about the illness: Although there is no direct correlation between illness knowledge and subsequent adherence with treatment, it may provide the parent with realistic expectations of healthcare professionals and provide the child with an adult, who can answer some of their illness-related questions.
- Enable the parents: It is important that their child can talk to them without fear of them becoming overly upset or disproportionately negatively judgemental.
- Encourage the family to lead as normal a life as possible: Setting age- and ability-appropriate limits and boundaries and giving responsibility for household chores are all important for normal emotional development.
- Encourage the parents to look after themselves and their adult relationships: Facilitate this by encouraging the acceptance of offers of help.
- Allow the child as much choice in their life as possible: Chronic illness removes choice in many aspects of life.
- Model a collaborative relationship with other healthcare professionals: Collaboration, particularly a shared therapeutic goal between the young person and their medical team, has been shown to positively influence treatment adherence.

## Multiple choice questions

1. Chronic illness in childhood

   a. Is a well-defined entity
   b. Has decreased in prevalence in the developing world
   c. Is invariably associated with behavioural or emotional disturbance
   d. Is more likely to cause emotional disturbance if the illness directly affects the brain
   e. Is most often dealt with by parents and children using emotion-focused coping strategies.

2. Mental health consequences of chronic illness

   a. The least common is an adjustment disorder
   b. Are easy to distinguish from symptoms of the physical illness
   c. Usually persist into adulthood
   d. Parents are a potent source of infection so should be discouraged from remaining with their children during a hospital stay
   e. The attachment between a parent and child can be affected by chronic illness

3. Chronic illness and school

   a. Repeated absences are unlikely to be a major issue for a junior school-aged child
   b. It is usually appropriate for staff to lower their expectations of the child's attainment
   c. Intervention to improve social skills is rarely helpful
   d. Chronic illness may be a vulnerability factor for bullying
   e. School attendance is not a useful marker of the impact of an illness

4. Chronic illness in adolescence

   a. Is unlikely to interfere with the adolescent's sense of self
   b. Is unlikely to interfere with the developmental processes associated with adolescence
   c. Is rarely associated with non-compliance with treatment
   d. Low self-esteem may result from delayed puberty
   e. Usually adherence is all or nothing to a treatment regime

5. Helpful suggestions for families dealing with chronic illness include

   a. Not discussing the illness for fear of upsetting the young person
   b. Advising against parental research on the internet
   c. Telling the adolescent robustly what to do
   d. Usually exempting the affected adolescent from household chores
   e. Addressing necessary procedures with the adolescent

## *Key texts*

Eiser C (1983) *Growing up with a chronic disease: The impact on children and their families.* London: Jessica Kingsley.

Gannoni AF, Shute RH (2010) Parental and child perspectives on adaptation to childhood chronic illness: A qualitative study. *Clinical Child Psychology and Psychiatry,* **15**: 39–53.

Gledhill J, Rangel L, Garralda E (2000) Surviving chronic physical illness: psychosocial outcome in adult life. *Archives of Disease in Childhood,* **83**: 104–10.

Wallander JL, Varni JW (1998) Effects of pediatric chronic physical disorders on child and family adjustment. *Journal of Child Psychology and Psychiatry,* **39**: 29–46.

Zylke JW, DeAngelis CD (2007) Paediatric chronic diseases-stealing childhood. *JAMA,* **24**: 2765–6.

# 59 Gender identity disorder

Josie Brown and James Walker

## Key concepts

Children with gender identity disorder commonly show:

- A persistent desire to be, or insistence that he or she is, the opposite sex. This includes the child calling him or herself an opposite sex name. Some children have a strong belief that they will grow up to become the opposite sex.
- Dressing in a manner typical of the opposite sex, for example boys wearing or simulating wearing female clothes, including underwear; in girls, a strong preference for male clothing and a resistance to wearing feminine clothing.
- Persistent desire for the toys, games, etc. of the other gender.
- Strong preference for cross-gender roles in make-believe play.
- Strong dislike and discomfort with his or her sexual anatomy. A boy may have a marked aversion to his penis and testes and may pretend not to have a penis and sit to urinate. Girls approaching puberty may dread the development of breasts, often binding their breasts to minimize them, and the onset of periods. In adolescents, the wish to be rid of his or her primary and secondary sex characteristics may become an overwhelming preoccupation.

## Introduction

Gender identity disorder (GID) is best understood as a natural, but unusual, variation in human development. It is a term used to describe individuals whose gender self-identification (gender identity) does not match their assigned gender, i.e. their assignment as male or female based on their sex appearance at birth. Other terms commonly used to describe gender identity disorder are 'transsexualism' and 'gender variance'. A transsexual male is a person who has a gender identity that is female and a transsexual female has a gender identity that is male.

The broader term 'transgender' is an umbrella term for individuals who do not conform to the accepted gender roles and includes people with a gender identity disorder and people who identify as being part of a third or middle sex. Sexual orientation is sometimes confused with gender identity. Sexual orientation means being sexually attracted to men, or to women, or both, or, occasionally, to neither and people with gender identity disorder can show any of these sexual preferences.

Individuals with gender identity disorder suffer from gender dysphoria, the term describing the aversion to the person's physical characteristics and social role associated with his or her biological sex.

Gender identity disorder individuals are often socially stigmatized and can suffer very significant difficulties such as harassment, bullying, abuse and rejection by families and peers.

Children establish a solid sense of their gender in pre-school years and disturbances of gender identity may be apparent from pre-school or primary school years, shown by the persistent cross-gender behaviour described above. Most adolescents and adults with GID say that they showed cross-gender behaviour and can remember experiencing gender dysphoria as a younger child. However, many children who prefer to wear the clothes of the opposite sex and may be thought to have a GID when they are pre-pubertal do not subsequently have a GID as adults; they may become bisexual, homosexual or heterosexual and the gender variant behaviour may disappear. However, those who have strong gender dysphoria at puberty, and subsequently in adolescence, are very likely to become transsexual adults.

Many children and adolescents with a GID are teased or taunted by their peers and other family members and can become isolated and rejected. Some hide their wish to be the opposite sex and experience profound loneliness. Children may withdraw from social activity and experience marked anxiety.

Adolescence is a particularly vulnerable time with the young person's marked aversion to their bodily changes coupled with, in some cases, rejection and harassment from others. Some gender dysphoric adolescents have significant mental health issues such as depression, suicidal thoughts and substance misuse.

## Epidemiology

The prevalence of GID is very difficult to determine. Population-based studies are challenging to undertake because of the stigma often associated with having a GID and the secrecy some people employ. Previous estimates of prevalence have been based on those individuals seeking treatment, but there is a large hidden population. There are more transgender males than females and the estimates of prevalence are increasing over time. The prevalence stated in DSM-IV, 1:30000 males and 1:100000 females, has been shown to be a marked underestimate. In the UK, the total number of adults who have sought help for gender dysphoria is around 10000, of whom about half have undergone full transition to the opposite sex, including surgery, but there are probably many more adults who do not present to the medical profession or seek treatment overseas or from the internet.

## Causation

No decisive causal factors have been identified in GID. Research includes looking at intra-uterine hormone exposure, differences in brain structure and genetics, and the examination of child–parent relationships. Mostly, child–parent relationships are good and families are supportive of their child. Concern has been expressed that disorders of gender identity may arise in children brought up in families with same-sex parents, but there is no evidence to support this.

## Management

Management in childhood involves:
- information and education to families and schools;
- advice and support to parents;
- treatment of secondary problems of distress in the child;
- appropriate advice about the child's behaviour.

The family obviously plays a crucial role and helping families with their own feelings about their child, which can range from shock, anger, disgust, grief and worry to acceptance, understanding and pride, is an essential part of management. Different family members commonly have very different views and feelings. There is no role for aversive treatment to deter the child from his or her preferred gender identity and these have been shown to be harmful and to result in increasing distress.

Rather, the aim of management should be to provide a supportive, understanding and accepting environment which is not judgemental and does not discourage or condemn the child's preferred identity, but allows the child to develop a clear sense of self with good self-esteem and aims to minimize any feelings of rejection and isolation. In childhood there should be a 'wait and see' approach which tolerates the child's exploration of his or her preferred gender, but does not actively promote it beyond the child's own pace and wishes, as their feelings may change at adolescence. There may need to be appropriate limit-setting to the child's behaviour, for example establishing where it is appropriate for the child to cross-dress and to explain that the wish to cross-dress is not a secret and is not shameful, but is private.

Guidance to families and schools may include practical and specific advice and the exploration of issues such as wearing certain clothes to school, the use of toilets and changing rooms and a discussion about what name normally to call the child.

Adolescence is a very challenging and often distressing time for young people who continue to have gender dysphoria. In puberty, those males who identify as girls can become very upset about their pubertal changes, i.e. voice deepening, development of facial hair, growing tall, experiencing erections and so on. Similarly, those females who identify as boys strongly dislike the development of breasts and periods. Ongoing supportive help to the young person and family, including liaison with the school and practical guidance, as above, is often welcomed. In some cases it is important to monitor for any signs of substance misuse, clear depression, anxiety or suicidal ideas. Some adolescents may engage in high-risk sexual activity, including identifying themselves as their preferred sex on the internet.

Medical treatment of these adolescents frequently involves discussion about which hormonal or surgical treatments may be available. There is no medication or hormones that will reverse the feeling someone has of gender dysphoria. For example, giving testosterone to a boy who feels he is a girl makes no difference to his gender identity.

If hormonal and ultimately surgical treatments are to be used, the stages and ages in the UK when this is considered in some cases are discussed below.

## Hormonal blocking drugs

The drugs used are gonadotrophin releasing hormone (GnRH) analogues which put the physical changes of puberty on hold. In addition to allowing time for the young person to make decisions about their preferred gender identity, the blocking drugs prevent the irreversible changes that occur during puberty and can be so distressing, for example voice changes and the development of large hands and feet in individuals born as males. The GnRHs should not be given too early: there are possible complications, such as unusual and inadequate bone development if given too early in puberty.

The timing of this treatment varies from country to country. In the US and in the Netherlands, hormone blockers can be given when Tanner Stage 2 of pubertal development has been completed, although, in practice, in the US they are often given later. In the UK, hormone blocking treatment is not currently offered until the young person is over 16 and there has been full pubertal development: there is concern that earlier intervention may result in unsatisfactory pubertal development and possible psychological harm. There is currently debate in the UK about whether in some cases earlier intervention

would be indicated. One advantage is that this would decrease some of the irreversible changes that occur if full pubertal development is completed, for example the voice changes in biological males.

## Cross-gender hormone therapy

The effects of cross-sex hormones include, for example, some development of breast tissue with oestrogen and stimulation of the growth of facial and body hair with male hormonal treatment. In the UK, cross-sex hormone is not offered before the age of 16.

## Gender reassignment

The decision to have surgery which alters the body so it conforms as nearly as possible to the person's preferred gender is clearly an enormous one and the procedures are irreversible. Surgery is never contemplated before the age of 18 and is undertaken after considerable psychological and physical assessment.

At all stages of medical treatment the decision-making process and the consent of the young person and parents must be very carefully considered. The guidelines and legal parameters on consent (for example, who has parental responsibility? is the young person Fraser competent?) must be adhered to.

Children and adolescents can be referred to the UK specialist treatment centre: the Gender Identity Development Unit at the Tavistock and Portman NHS Foundation Trust. Young people can be referred to the adult NHS gender identity clinics once they are aged 18 or over.

## Summary

In gender identity disorder there is no known aetiological cause and management is not aimed at prevention or at changing the child's thinking or functioning in childhood. Professionals have a role in trying to alleviate any severe psychological distress such as marked depression and in helping the child, family and others, including school, to a satisfactory point where decisions about adult gender identity and sexual adjustment can be achieved without undue external pressures.

## Case study

From the age of two Tom showed a preference for playing with dolls, play kitchens, etc., rather than more traditional boys' toys such as action men type figures and weapons. From this age also he liked to wear his mother's high heel shoes and to put things such as towels on his head to pretend they were his hair. At school he showed a strong preference for playing with girls and continued in his liking for playing with more traditional girls' toys. At the age of seven he started calling himself 'Lisa' and wanted his parents to do the same, which they felt uncomfortable about at that time. He periodically said he wanted to be a girl or said he was a girl. He continued to wear his mother's and his older sister's clothes when he could and to try on their make-up. He started to refuse to use public urinals and his parents realized that he would sit to urinate.

When Tom started to develop pubertal changes he became distressed, especially about the development of facial and pubic hair, and spent long periods of time trying to erase all signs of facial hair. He spent his pocket money on female clothes and make-up and dressed in female clothes, including underwear, most of the time he was at home. He began to want to go out of the house dressed as a girl. He was increasingly insistent on his parents calling him Lisa. He became more withdrawn, spending long periods of time in the bathroom or in his room. Having previously been quite a sociable child, he now had few friends and social activities were rare. Tom was very stressed on school days when he had PE and often complained of various aches and pains on those days. His parents were very worried that Tom was significantly depressed.

Tom's parents sought help and Tom and family were seen by the local CAMHS clinic and subsequently referred to the national service at the Gender Identity Development Unit so there was shared care between these two services. School meetings were held and these were helpful in addressing some of the school's concerns and some of the issues for Tom in school. Tom and his parents were seen, sometimes together, sometimes separately and were given literature on Gender Identity Disorder. After the age of 16 Tom decided to start hormonal treatment: initially GnRH analogues (hormone blocking drugs) and then oestrogen. His parents were supportive of this and the family consistently called him Lisa and referred to him as 'her'. Lisa was then considering whether to undertake the long process of full gender reassignment.

### Key texts

Department of Health Publications (2008) *Medical care for gender variant children and young people: answering families' questions; A guide for young trans people in the UK; A guide to hormone therapy for trans people.* London: HMSO.

Olsen J, Forbes C Belzer M (2011) Management of the transgender adolescent. *Archives of Pediatrics and Adolescent Medicine,* **165**: 171–6.

Zucker K (2002) Gender Identity Disorder. In: Rutter M, Taylor EA (eds). *Child and Adolescent Psychiatry,* 4th edn. Oxford: Wiley-Blackwell.

# Management of grief, loss and bereavement
## Sue Ricketts

---

### Key concepts

- CAMHS clinicians need to be aware of how an unresolved experience of loss can present itself in often disguised form: physical, psychological and behavioural.
- Certain states of mind as shown form part of the experience of grief, they do not follow a neat consecutive path but may return repeatedly.
- Helping individuals feel contained enough to safely explore their loss through verbal or non-verbal means requires a consistent and reliable setting but not necessarily a clinic base as long as it can be a reliable setting, along with appropriate supervision for the practitioner.
- The loss of a child is not a normal experience and places those involved under the most extraordinary emotional and psychological distress. Grief reactions in bereaved parents are often more extreme and can include suicidal thoughts and feelings.
- Untreated difficulties with a loss are very likely to lead to depression and anxiety which may present itself and require more serious intervention at a later date.

---

## Theoretical underpinnings

We are living in a time where our knowledge of the experience of loss and how it affects us psychologically is increasingly sophisticated; the Western understanding of grief believes that successful mourning means that the bereaved must disengage from the deceased. Carrying on with an attachment to the dead person can be seen as denying the reality of the loss. It was Freud (1917) in his paper 'Mourning and Melancholia' who said 'when the work of mourning is completed the ego becomes free and uninhibited again'. He believed it was the work of mourning to detach from those who went on living hopes and memories from those who have died. Following on, John Bowlby (1997) wrote about how understanding grief is intrinsically linked to what happens when attachments are broken and the strong emotional reactions that will ensue, such as distress, anger and withdrawal. All have a place in the process of grieving.

Bereavement is the loss by death of someone significant to you.

- Bereavement is what happens

- Grief is what one feels in relation to the bereavement
- Mourning is what one does to express grief
- To be deprived of someone of value implies attachment; the level of attachment will determine the degree of loss experienced which leads to grief.

It was then Colin Murray-Parkes (2010) who developed the idea that grief contained a predictable set of behaviours that were to be gone through in phases before the final acceptance of the loss was accepted. More recently, works by Judd (1995) and Leader (2008) have helped to deepen our understanding of grief reactions and the importance of helping those who are bereaved to mourn their loss. Leader suggests that without this work of mourning being adequately carried out, clinical depression and low mood may result. Thanks to the work of Judd we know more about the workings of a child's mind who is faced with death and how best those around them can support the individual and family (Judd, 1995).

The experience of loss is a normal part of the human experience. The grief we feel as a result of a loss is expressed in many different ways by adults and children. Services such as CAMHS become involved in this normal emotional process when the process of mourning a loss has in some way become unhelpfully altered or suspended in some way. In the day-to-day work of CAMHS, one is often faced with a range of symptoms which once explored can be seen to be linked to the experience of loss. Symptoms may present themselves, often much later, in the form of sleeplessness, angry outbursts, headaches and various anxiety states. The CAMHS clinician needs to be alert in the initial assessments to the losses that the individual may have experienced, but which may have been overlooked or have been unavailable to attend to until now.

There are many forms of loss that we encounter during our work; from the loss that parents feel during pregnancy when they are told that their unborn child may have a disability. Here a process of mourning is required for the healthy longed for child that is now not expected to arrive. Children may have suffered birth trauma which results in a limit to their abilities and so the parents will need to make huge adjustments, often not just emotionally, but also practically in caring for a child with special needs. Siblings may be living in the knowledge that a sister or brother may not live on with them. All these scenarios can be encountered in the daily work of a CAMHS clinician and even though some may arrive as a clear referral for bereavement work, it often emerges over time that it is the experience of loss that is the root to current difficulties.

Our views on grief and bereavement changed over time and the cultural practices described to them range from Queen Victoria's remaining in black at the loss of her beloved husband to the introduction of jazz bands and colour at funerals. Black (1978) writes: 'the combination of a heavy death toll by the end of World War 2 and medical treatment breakthroughs led to a taboo on talking about death, for doctors consider death a failure'. We are now at a time where there is an interest in the processes surrounding loss and bereavement and fortunately bereavement counselling is far more available. Psychologically that which occurs in old age at its right time and place, however painful, is different from the death of a child or an unexpected death of a parent which shocks us to the core and tests all our emotional and psychological resilience.

Through the work of those such as Murray-Parks, we began to think about a recognized emotional process connected with loss and bereavement. There are five or six main areas which are numbness, the news of death, denial that it will happen, exploration of this can allow the patient and family to accept the change in life expectations and the possibility that death may occur.

- Regression: Earlier patterns of behaviour are often brought to the fore in relation to the loss. Returning to an earlier stage of development is quite common in children who are experiencing loss.
- Depression: It is appropriate to have depressed feelings at the prospect of loss. However, as Winnicot says 'depression at the normal end is a common almost universal phenomenon and relates to mourning'. The CAMHS clinician needs to be alert to what we would term a 'normal' experience of depression in relation to a loss where it becomes a 'clinical depression' that requires psychiatric treatment.
- Bargaining: Kubbler Ross delineates this stage as an attempt to postpone the death. Superstition and ritualized or obsessional behaviour can often occur in this theological state.
- Acceptance: With some acceptance of death it may be possible to maximize the remaining time before death and following on from death the person who has died can be remembered, commemorated and treasured in concrete and emotional ways.

These outline the major states of mind that individuals travel through when coming to terms with loss and bereavement. Whereas previously we thought these followed a rather neat consecutive path, it has become far more evidenced latterly that different states of mind such as these are visited and revisited in the process of coming to terms with bereavement.

Far more is now known about the different age groups of children and how they think about death and loss. Through the work of clinicians such as Dorothy Judd we now know far more about how children think about death and dying.

Again, Judd (1995), in her excellent book 'Give Sorrow Words' says 'children can both know and deny the existence of death'.

## Case study

### Pre-school

Jenny was a four year old who was referred into CAMHS by a pre-school nursery worker as she had missed a good number of play sessions and her mother was concerned that her complaint of continual tummy pains which had been investigated physically may have some kind of emotional root. Her mother and father were happy for CAMHS to become involved. CAMHS began the work by meeting with the parents in order to gain a more comprehensive understanding of the family which included Jenny's early history. During the discussion it emerged that Jenny's grandmother, who at different times in Jenny's young life had lived with them, had died very suddenly nine months earlier. We discussed with the parents their own experience of this bereavement, for instance had grandma been talked about in the family since, was she remembered through photos etc. We found that Jenny's father was also having periods of time off work with unexplained back problems. The parents had felt that Jenny was too young to be spoken to about this loss, but through discussion with the nursery workers, had begun to hear that Jenny was playing a repetitive game in the dolls house at the nursery which was centred around people suddenly disappearing. With the parents' permission we invited the nursery worker to come and meet with them and ourselves in order to think about what Jenny might be expressing in her play and how it linked with the loss of grandma. It was clear that the nursery worker was both very sensitive and able to offer Jenny some individual play time and then meet with us in order to discuss what she observed. The parents also began to mention grandma's name at home and observe how Jenny reacted to this. The nursery worker would offer Jenny some special time to play in the dolls house once a week and this work continued for 6 weeks. She then liaised with CAMHS to discuss and receive some supervision on her observations. After several weeks Jenny was attending playschool regularly and she was no longer complaining of stomach aches. Being able to talk with Jenny about the figures in the dolls house disappearing and having the permission of the parents to link this with the 'disappearance of her Grandma' seemed to have brought about relief for Jenny and the disappearance of the stomach aches.

### Junior school

Stephen was a nine-year-old boy who was referred to CAMHS for increasingly aggressive outbursts both at home and at school, inability to concentrate and complaining of headaches, and he seemed listless at home. He had been a keen footballer in the local team, but had recently been making excuses not to attend training sessions. He was referred by the GP as his mother was becoming increasingly worried, as were school. An initial appointment was sent to meet with his mother who was the main carer and his father who lived in a separate household. Prior to the appointment, CAMHS was given permission by his mother to have a discussion with school in order to form a more complete picture. On taking a full family history in the first appointment, it emerged that the relationship between mother and father had broken down two years after the birth of Stephen's younger sister who had been diagnosed with a rare genetic disorder which over the years had required intensive hospital visits and they were now faced with the decision regarding major surgery which could enhance or indeed endanger her life. Father had left the family home when Stephen was four years old, but his love of football was connected with contact with his father and a genuine shared interest. It emerged during the initial appointments at CAMHS that Stephen had been present at many of the medical discussions which had taken place about his sister and this had led him to become acutely aware of the life and death issues around her, and the real possibility that she may not live for many more years. While the parents had attempted to shield him from some of these discussions, it had been very difficult to protect him from them all due to practical difficulties of him needing to be at the appointments due to lack of childcare. The Nurse Therapist who carried out these initial appointments thought that Stephen may have signs of attention deficit hyperactivity disorder (ADHD), but wanted to do a more general assessment with him in order to consider these other issues, i.e. the impact of the loss of his father and the separation of his parents, but also the very significant knowledge and experience of living with a sister with a life-limiting illness. A discussion took place with the Child Psychotherapist within the team who then met with the family, both together and then with Stephen on his own. Over a period of four individual sessions, Stephen gradually began to talk and play, with the cars and a football game, about his life at home and the heavy worries which he carried in relation to his sister, but also his mother's ability to cope. Through the play it was clear that he had very powerful angry feelings towards his father for having left him at home with so many difficult issues to try and deal with. In the play, the little boy whom they came to recognize as Stephen later was able to say 'I just don't think I can do anything to help'. He was also able to show through some of the play and speech that he did believe his sister's genetic illness could be infectious and despite having been told repeatedly and very clearly that this was not the case, he had a morbid fear that he carried the same life-limiting illness. It was through this gradual process and the extending of the assessment with the Child Psychotherapist into some longer-term work that he came to understand that his anger really was an attempt to hide his sadness and by acting as the 'the man of the family' who wanted to take control of a situation that was completely out of his control. It was possible during this time for the Nurse Therapist to be meeting with the parents and talking with them about appropriate boundaries and information for Stephen to be aware of in regards to his sister and how vitally important it was that father was in good consistent contact with him and made time to listen to any worries he may have.

This work involved a Nurse Therapist in CAMHS and a Child Psychotherapist who were able to work together to support the members of the family. Work for Stephen continued weekly over a period of three terms until it was felt Stephen's work had come to an end. His mother continues to be seen within CAMHS as she is still coping with many of the issues surrounding anticipatory grieving for her daughter.

This was a little boy who had not just suffered the loss of his father leaving the family home, but was living with a sister who, in all likelihood would die within the next couple of years. He continues to be monitored by school and it may well be that CAMHS will be needed to offer him support again at a different developmental point depending on circumstances at home.

## Senior school

Julie is a 15-year-old girl with muscular dystrophy who is increasingly multiply disabled. She was referred by a community nurse for vomiting. This had been extensively investigated with no physical cause found. The family had been known for a considerable time within the area as Julie required home visits from community staff following various operations which she had to endure during the course of her life. She was well known by the members of staff who had good relationships with the family and a thorough understanding of the pressures and strains they were under in caring for a child such as Julie. The parents were invited to CAMHS and it became evident quite quickly that they were both suffering with mental health difficulties, mother with anxiety and father with intermittent clinical depression. They were clear that they did not feel robust enough to undergo family sessions, but fully supported individual work for Julie and were happy to support in any way they could.

The CAMHS clinician, with the consent of Julie's parents, consulted with both her paediatrician and consultant in the acute service in order to ascertain the likely prognosis for her and also any possible interventions that might be needed within the next year. Much thought was given in the CAMHS team as to how to offer Julie a way of expressing herself as her physical mobility was now so limited. The CAMHS clinician who met with Julie was quickly made aware that despite her physical disability, she was very able in her mind and well able verbally to convey thoughts and feelings. She talked animatedly about her love of the 'soap operas' and was completely absorbed in the issues they presented such as infidelity, abortion, murder, etc. What emerged through the series of assessment sessions was that Julie was almost 'overdosing' psychologically and emotionally on these adult issues and was often left feeling highly stimulated by what she had seen and heard and was unable to talk to anybody about this.

The appropriateness of some of these issues was questionable for a girl of her age and it seemed that she was allowed to watch everything and anything that she wanted with no limits. It was decided following several early assessment sessions to meet with the parents again in order to talk with them about this aspect of Julie's life. Through group supervision within the CAMHS clinic it was felt that Julie was unable to process much of what she was witnessing on the television and that the vomiting may well have been connected with being emotionally unable to digest some of these very adult issues. This was creating a lot of anxiety for her and little opportunity to either explore or discharge it. Crucially, it also linked to many major underlying issues for Julie about the shortening of her life and the hopes that she had to actually live long enough to experience some of the issues she was witnessing on the screen. The result of offering Julie individual work was that the vomiting ceased, but it was very clear that she needed some safe psychological space in order to explore some of the thoughts and feelings which were emerging for her around her illness. While the parents understood the possible consequences of her watching such programmes and did make attempts to limit this, they were also caught, as many parents are with children in this condition, to allow them to have every apparent enjoyment they wish as the awareness of a life cut short is ever present in the family.

The outcome in this situation is that the family remains under the care of CAMHS, both children and parents.

## Multiple choice questions

1. What is essential information to gather in the assessment period?

   a. Number of siblings

   b. Grandparents' ages

   c. Losses the child or young person may have suffered in their life

2. Is supporting the bereaved person best carried out by?

   a. Teacher

   b. Nurse

   c. Professional who knows the individual well and who can access skilled supervision in this area of work

   d. Professional bereavement counsellor

3. What does the author claim is crucial in bringing about the best possible outcome for the patient?

   a. Timing of the intervention

   b. Setting

   c. Training

   d. Both a and c

4. How many of these are true in what we know about the stages of grief? They:

   a. Follow in sequence

   b. Cannot occur without assistance

   c. Do not follow a set sequence

   d. Are completed in a set time period

### Key texts

Black D (1978) The bereaved child. *Journal of Child Psychology and Psychiatry*, **19**: 287–82.

Judd D (1995) *Give Sorrow Words*. Oxford: Haworth Press.

Leader D (2008) The New Black, Mourning, Melancholia and Depression. London: Hamish Hamilton.

# Introduction

## Christopher Gale

The issues surrounding equality and diversity in today's UK culture are wide ranging and should be comprehensively addressed in the services offered to children, young people and families. This section begins to explore some of these issues, focusing on cultural competence in CAMHS, the needs of young carers from different backgrounds, asylum seeking, refugee and homeless young people, and finally those young people who may be exploring their emerging sexuality.

# 61 Working with diversity – cultural competence in child and adolescent mental health (CAMHS)

## Karen Davies

---

### Key concepts

The Department for Race Equality (DRE) report (Department of Health, 2005) delivered a vision for mental health services that includes:
- Decreased fear of services
- Increased satisfaction and effective communication
- Better management of challenging situations
- A more balanced range of effective interventions
- A workforce that is capable of delivering appropriate and responsive services to black and minority ethnic (BME) communities
- All professionals must strive and continue to grow to deliver a service that is innovative, patient centred and increases access for all through understanding inequalities, increasing awareness, implementing fresh and creative approaches and delivering appropriate and responsive care to meet the diversity of the needs of children, young people and families within our locality.

---

# Introduction

Working with diversity in child and adolescent mental health requires that individuals understand difference and the need to develop the capacity to deliver culturally competent care. When one is able to move beyond the limits of one's own cultural experiences to incorporate the perspectives of other cultures, one has begun the journey of cultural competence.

The term 'cultural competence' has become frequent in many care services language and settings and first appeared in social work and counselling psychology literature beginning in the early 1980s (Gallegos, 1982; Pedersen and Marshall, 1982). Although cultural competence has been referred to as a theory by some (Wu and Martinez, 2006; Lum, 2010), there has been ongoing debate as to whether cultural competency meets the criteria for a theory or whether the description of cultural competence fits more comfortably as a model, framework, skills or perspective (Gallegos et al., 2008).

Cultural competence refers to the ability to interact effectively with people from different cultures and essentially comprises four components:

1. Awareness of one's own cultural worldview
2. Attitude towards cultural differences
3. Knowledge of different cultural practices and worldviews
4. Cross-cultural skills.

Dalrymple and Burke (1995) stated that 'unless clients are considered as true partners, culturally sensitive care is not being achieved; equal partnership involves trust, acceptance and respect as well as facilitation and negotiation'.

The Delivering Race Equality in Mental Health Care action plan (Department of Health, 2005) identifies drivers and the following acts and guidelines underline the clinical necessity of incorporating the cultural competence and equality agenda:

- Race Relation Act (Amendment ) (HM Government, 2000)
- Delivering Race Equality (Department of Health, 2005)
- Every Child Matters (Department for Education and Skills, 2003)
- NICE Revised Equality Scheme and Action Plan: 2010–2013 (NICE, 2010b)
- National Service Framework for Children, Young People and Maternity Services (Department of Health, 2004a).

They all identify:

- appropriate and responsive services;
- engaged and more accessible communities;
- better information and communication;
- cultural competency training available to all staff.

All children, young people and their families have their own individual identity and each come with their own life experiences that have informed their independent beliefs, attitudes and values regarding culture, faith and community. Some communities may have a different perception of mental health and fear the stigma of a diagnostic label or have concerns around possible discrimination within services. Therefore, practitioners require training and skills development to implement culturally

competent principles in all aspects of their work with culturally diverse clients, as well as a thorough knowledge of the legislative requirements.

*Cultural sensitivity requires a commitment from health care professionals to understand and be responsive to the different attitudes, values, verbal cues and body language of those with a different cultural heritage*

**(Goldsmith, 2000)**

The Tier 2 Community CAMHS service in Southampton was a multidisciplinary team which served three locality areas in the city. As each team incrementally rolled out across the city, a scoping exercise took place to identify the predominant needs and concerns within each community; the service has in turn modelled the care delivery to meet these needs.

The North Central team which served the areas of the city with the highest number of BME residents recognized that there were significant gaps in services and numerous barriers to effectively meeting the needs of BME communities within the city. In response, the team undertook Cultural Competence training supported by CSIP (Care Services Improvement Partnership) and completed a cultural self-assessment tool (the CAMHS Cultural Competence in Action Tool – 'CCATool' – Papdopoulos et al., 2006, 2008). This was a key component of a national project which aimed at promoting cultural competence within CAMHS. The training supported further learning and increasing the knowledge base of the team through identifying issues of stigma and shame around mental health within some cultures, provided guidance on how to tackle racism and prejudice; increased understanding of cultural issues and the impact of personal values and belief on how we perceive problems and difficulties.

The team goals were to engage with communities and deliver culturally appropriate interventions with young people and their families. The team believed in being proactive, taking responsibility, being equipped and trained; 'getting the questions right', understanding the barriers such as gender, disability, beliefs, faith, context, representation, locality, diversity and exclusion, having a keen awareness of misconceptions and assumptions and 'not being afraid to ask what you do not know'.

There are always challenges and risks for practitioners and an area that became apparent early on was the fear of what an appointment may entail. There is anxiety regarding confidentiality and whether one can trust professionals with one's thoughts and feelings; there is an increased stigma and shame surrounding mental ill health in some ethnic communities and some community workers were so conscious of these attitudes that they chose not to refer clients whom they felt may benefit because they were afraid that they would choose not to attend.

The CAMHS teams have been able to effectively promote CAMHS to the BME population in Southampton and there is an increase in the number of referrals from the community and the number of children and families accessing CAMHS.

Saucepans North Central Community CAMHS team are proud that as a Culturally Competent team we are committed to implementing practices that promote engagement, involvement, responsiveness, equity, participation and collaboration with communities in Southampton. The team actively engaged in learning and being open to other cultures and worked in partnership to develop projects to target under-represented groups to help increase access to support within the community. Project Honour – Cultural Fusion, an award winning film project undertaken by young people of Southampton, grew from a team of people who believed in reducing inequalities, challenging assumptions and hearing the voices of young people and their families. Following a Commissioning service review, Solent West CAMHS has been re-designed as an Integrated service. The staff teams previously known as Saucepans are no longer operating as a Tier 2 team but are integrated within the new service model. The skills and expertise in the delivery of Culturally competent care will be embedded in practice throughout the service. This document will therefore reflect the ongoing ethos and approach of the practitioners in the delivery of culturally competent care in CAMHS.

*What I liked about the project is that people communicated, cooperated and others listened to our thoughts and ideas.*

**(Ikram, 'Project Honour – Cultures Fusion' 2008).**

Cultural competence does more than provide a non-discriminatory service to clients; it includes a policy framework which supports a culturally sensitive response, a collaborative model with ethnic and minority communities and agencies to ensure that specific ethnic groups are understood, needs addressed and partnerships developed. Assessment and intervention processes which take account of the culturally defined needs of young people, their families and community need to be implemented. Papadopoulos et al. (1998) devised a model for the development of 'Transcultural competence' and offered that the model aims 'to help us deliver culturally competent care, that ultimately ensures high quality care for all'.

Cultural competence is not an 'add on' and must be integrated into effective, quality mental health service provision.

## Multiple choice questions

1. What are the four guiding principles for culturally competent practice?

   a. Professionalism, Beliefs, Equality, Knowledge
   b. Awareness, Attitude, Knowledge, Skills
   c. Communication, Challenge, Anti-discriminatory practice, Attitudes
   d. Respect, Values, Judgements, Understanding

2. Which statement is correct about cultural competence?

   a. Cultural competence predicts behaviour
   b. Cultural competency is providing resources in different languages
   c. Cultural competence is a developmental process that evolves over an extended period.
   d. Cultural competence is treating everyone equally

3. Who is responsible for implementing and delivering culturally competent practice within agencies/ services?

a. Managers and policy development team
b. It is for individuals to research if they have a BME client
c. It is part of professional training modules for different disciplines, for example nursing or social work
d. Every individual has a responsibility to continue to learn and develop their practice

## Key texts

Lum D (2010) *Culturally Competent Practice: A Framework for Understanding Diverse Groups and Justice Issues*, 4th edn. Pacific Grove, CA: Brooks/Cole.

National Institute for Clinical Health and Excellence (2010b) *Revised Equality Scheme and Action Plan: 2010–2013.* London: NICE.

Papadopoulos I (2006) The Papadopoulos, Tilki and Taylor model of developing Cultural Competence. In: Papadopoulos I (ed.). *Transcultural Health and Social Care: Developing Culturally Competent Practitioners.* Oxford: Elsevier.

# Young carers
### Charlotte Pyatt

## Key concepts

- It is estimated that one in four of the UK population will experience mental illness at some point in their lives (Royal College of Psychiatrists, 2004).
- Many children will grow up with a parent who experiences mental illness.
- The 2001 census found 175000 young carers in the UK of which 5000 were aged between five and seven years (Dearden and Becker, 2004). Most of these cases will be mild or short-lived. The family adapts, learns to cope and the episode ceases.
- However, some children live with a parent who has a long-term problem or a severe mental illness.

## Introduction: about the author

I am a Registered Mental Health Nurse. Since qualifying in 2007, I have worked for Hampshire Partnership NHS Foundation Trust (now Southern Health NHS Foundation Trust). I was a carer for my mother at times throughout my adolescent years during her episodes of depression. My contribution to this book uses both my personal and professional experiences of caring for an individual with mental ill health.

When I was a caring for my mother, I never even realized I was a carer. Young carers are defined as:

> Children and young persons under 18 years old who provide, or intend to provide, care, assistance or support to another family member. They carry out, often on a regular basis, significant or substantial caring tasks and assume a level of responsibility, which would usually be associated with an adult.
>
> (Becker, 2000)

My mother experienced episodes of depression for some time. After my father and two older sisters left home, she found it increasingly difficult to cope. I helped much more around the house: small jobs like cooking, cleaning or looking after my little sister. I remember calling my mother's employer to report her off sick when she was too unwell to be there and I would go food shopping. I would sit and chat with my mother giving emotional support. I enjoyed doing all of those things. It made me feel important and special to my mother and sister. Caring can sometimes help cement bonds between parents and children, as children who care feel both valued and included (Aldridge and Becker, 2003a).

There is support available for children and young carers. It is vital that young carers are identified. If a family is unsupported in this situation, they may struggle to cope and rely on children within the family to take on inappropriate caring responsibilities (Frank and McLarnon, 2008). Even if identified, the degree of their caring role and the impact it has on the young carer's own development may not be identified quickly or assessed thoroughly (The Children's Society Young Carers Initiative, 2006). It is not inevitable that children are at risk of significant harm because they care for a parent with a mental illness. For various reasons, young carers can remain hidden and their needs and those of the person that they care for are only identified in a crisis.

There are many reasons why children and young carers may remain hidden. In my case, I did not view my situation as different or unusual. My mother's depression was undiagnosed and untreated, largely due to her fear of the stigma associated with mental illness. Other young carers are so loyal that they do not want to ask for help or may fear their family will be split up. Children who are exposed to mental illness in the family may display the following:

- social withdrawal or isolation;
- anxiety;
- find it difficult to concentrate on their schoolwork, leading to underachievement in education and limited life opportunities;
- low self-esteem and depressed mood;
- a fatalistic acceptance of their life situation;
- behavioural difficulties, violent or self-destructive behaviour;
- paranoid or suspicious behaviour if they believe their parents' delusions;
- many children are teased or bullied because of their unwell family member.

Some children have periods of separation from their parents, who are admitted to hospital, which can be a confusing and stressful time. Healthcare professionals need to consider what arrangements are made for visiting and to identify and meet the needs of the child or young person arising from loss and separation (Barnardos, 2008). Daily routines may be changed, education disrupted and siblings separated, all of which have an impact on the child.

The child may need to be offered or referred for an assessment following the Common Assessment Framework (CAF) guidance (www.everychildmatters.gov.uk). Evidence shows that a major issue for families who have a parent with a mental health problem is a lack of joint working between adult mental health teams and children's services (Social Care Institute for Excellence, 2005). Social Care Institute for Excellence (2005) states that Local Authorities should have 'a protocol, shared between adults and children's services, for identifying and assessing young carers.

Research has shown that many mental health professionals are unaware that their patients are parents (Aldridge and Becker, 2003a). This in turn raises questions for adult mental health services to consider. Mental health professionals should find out if their patients are parents, documenting names and dates of birth of children; enquiring about the impact their illness is having on other family members. The key to change is the development of a whole family approach (Leadbitter, 2008; Social Care Institute for Excellence, 2009).

For the children themselves, the following needs should be addressed:

- Someone whom they trust to talk to, preferably one key worker who will respond promptly and positively when they ask for help. This is often a difficult step to take.
- Children and young people may have important information about the person with the mental illness; they need to know they will be listened to and their perspective taken into account in care plans.
- Help in recognizing the behaviour signs that indicate their parent/sibling is becoming ill.
- They need to know what is not acceptable behaviour from an adult and they will need to know who to contact at any time for help.
- Additional support at school, such as learning support, access to counselling or education welfare. They may wish to keep school and friends separate from their caring responsibilities, which must be respected.
- For pre-school age children, there are alternative options for support. When working with a child under five, the health visitor should be contacted as the first port of call for support and signposting: information about who this is can be found through the GP surgery. Referrals to Children's Social Services may be beneficial for the assessment of the required level of support.
- Providing practical support to the family, such as shopping and domestic chores, can reduce the stress for the child or young person.
- Evidence suggests that what young carers often require most is recognition of their caring contribution, alongside practical support (Aldridge and Becker, 2003b) (see **Figure 62.1**).

If a family is unsupported in this situation they may struggle to cope and rely on children within the family to take on inappropriate caring responsibilities (Frank, J and McLarnon, J 2008).

It is not inevitable that children are at risk of significant harm if they care for a parent with a mental illness but being exposed to mental illness in the family may impact on the child.

When young carers are identified they may need to be offered or referred for an assessment following the Common Assessment Framework (CAF) guidance.

It is crucial for professionals working with an adult with a mental illness to identify young carers and their needs.

Young Carers Projects run nationally and have been found to be invaluable by young carers. Recognition and practical support go a long way.

It is so important to listen to children and young carers about how they think and feel about their situation; interacting with individuals according to their age and understanding with warmth and empathy.

Adult mental health teams and children's services must work together in supporting the whole family.

Figure 62.1 Young carers: summary points. Young carers are defined as: 'Children and young persons under 18 years old who provide, or intend to provide care, assistance or support to another family member' (Becker 2000).

## Case study 1: Isabelle

Alice was experiencing an episode of psychotic depression. Her four-year-old daughter, Isabelle, was her carer at times. Alice was a single mother and while her ex-partner Steve was involved in the care of Isabelle and Alice, the couple did not live together. Working with the well parent and the extended family can help support the child or young carer. When appropriate, it is helpful to include children in discussions about their caring responsibilities and consult with them about their family's needs. When very young children are involved they must be made to feel comfortable, relaxed and supported by professionals interacting with them at their level.

During a visit one day by the community mental health practitioner, Isabelle would not leave the room, intent on being present, despite her young age. Children and young carers' predominant feelings may be of fear or guilt regarding the ill person, while anger and embarrassment tend to be more common among adolescents (The Children's Society, 2008). It is likely that Isabelle was seeking reassurance by staying with Alice during the visit and by protecting her, as young carers do. She stood next to Alice, holding and stroking her hand. Alice was talking about her lack of sleep due to panic attacks when Isabelle said 'I climb into bed with mummy to make sure nothing bad happens to her, I wait until she goes to sleep and then I can go to sleep'. During the visit Isabelle fetched a glass of water for Alice saying 'Please drink this mummy, it's good for you'. The practitioner began to talk to Isabelle about what she likes to play with and Isabelle brought her favourite doll. This interaction was playful and caring and Isabelle responded very well. It is crucial that children can still be children despite the mature caring role they may have adopted. Importantly, the health visitor should be made aware of

Isabelle's needs as a young carer, because children and young people need to be looked after themselves as well as the person they care for and will need 'time out' for themselves. A referral to Social Services would be appropriate for an assessment of Isabelle's needs.

## Case study 2: Tom

Children who observe a family member experiencing symptoms of mental illness may be confused about the illness. This can leave them feeling scared or angry and feeling powerless to change the situation. Tom was nine years old and could not understand what was happening to his mother, Rachel. He knew she was sometimes happy and sometimes sad and would ask the community mental health practitioner 'why is mummy sad sometimes?'

Rachel is diagnosed with bipolar affective disorder. Explaining the illness to Tom in an age-appropriate manner may help him to understand her emotions and reduce any feelings of fear, guilt or anger. Research indicates that giving information to young carers helps them to cope (The Children's Society, 2008). An additional source of support with the caring role may be accessed through a Young Carers Project group. Young carers can meet with other children and young people who have had similar experiences. The projects run various social activities and offer emotional support. Young Carers Projects have been found to be invaluable, appreciated by young carers their families and professionals (Aldridge and Sharpe, 2007).

## Case study 3: Oliver

Oliver (15) was beginning to fall behind in his schoolwork; he struggled to concentrate because he was worried about his father who had been admitted to hospital. Oliver was going out with his mates; he started smoking cannabis and stayed up late; as a result, his education was disrupted. It is imperative that schools are able to identify and support young carers. 'Schools might find it helpful to have one member of staff to act as a link between young carers, the education welfare service, social services and young carers projects. Their role would be one of liaison with the relevant services. This would be a proactive way of recognizing the difficulties faced by young carers and getting help to them, both within and outside the school. Young carers may need the opportunity to talk to someone at school, perhaps their teacher or someone else with the right skills, in a way which is confidential and sensitive' (The Children's Society, 2010).

## Multiple choice questions

1. How can a young carer be defined?

    a. Children and young persons who visit a relative in a care home every week
    b. Children and young persons under 18 years old who provide, or intend to provide, care, assistance or support to another family member
    c. Children and young persons who walk to school with their parent to collect an older sibling

2. How many young carers were found in the UK in the 2001 census?

    a. 125 000
    b. 150 000
    c. 175 000

3. What major issue has been identified for families who have a parent with a mental health problem?

    a. Lack of joint working between mental health teams and children's services

    b. They don't want any support

    c. There are no issues

4. Young carers can remain hidden, which of these are possible reasons?

    a. There is no support available for young carers

    b. Young carers aren't hidden

    c. Loyalty, stigma, unaware the situation is unusual

5. What can mental health professionals do to ensure young carers are identified?

    a. Look at the patient's notes

    b. Find out if their patients are parents, documenting names and date of birth of children, enquiring about the impact their illness is having on the family

    c. Assume other professionals have obtained this information

## Key texts

Aldridge J, Becker S (2003b) *Children Caring for Parents with Mental Illness. Perspectives of Young Carers, Parents and Professionals.* Bristol: The Policy Press.

Frank J, McLarnon J (2008) *Young Carers, Parents and their Families: Key Principles of Practice. Supportive practice guidance for those who work directly with, or commission services for, young carers and their families.* London: Young Carers Initiative, The Children's Society.

Social Care Institute for Excellence (2009) *Think Child, Think Parent, Think Family: A Guide to Parental Mental Health and Child Welfare.* London: SCIE.

# 63 Asylum seeking, refugee and homeless young people and families

Pam Campbell, Ann Spooner and Sarah Gale

---

## Key concepts

- Asylum seekers can be defined as people who have moved to a country in order to seek asylum.
- A refugee is someone who has arrived in another country, sought asylum, and been granted either a fixed or indefinite period of leave to remain.
- Definitions of homeless vary considerably, but include having no security of tenure in rented accommodation, living in bed and breakfast housing, hostels and refuge houses for people fleeing from domestic violence.
- In working with both asylum seeking and homeless children and young people the most important factor is to build trust by being caring and honest.
- Professionals should seek to understand mental health issues in the context of the young person's whole life and not in isolation.

---

## Introduction

For both young asylum seekers and homeless people the common theme is that they have lost their home. It may be, particularly in the case of young homeless people, that they never had anywhere which was stable, warm and loving to call home and that this concept of home does not exist for them.

## Asylum seekers and refugees

For young asylum seekers home is another country, often literally a whole world away. It is important to recognize that this is the only factor which asylum seekers and refugees have in common. They are a diverse group. Asylum seekers can be defined as people who have moved to a country in order to seek asylum. They are offered accommodation (sometimes in detention) while awaiting the outcome of their claim. If it is rejected they are deemed to be in the UK unlawfully and will have to leave. The alternative to this is destitution and a life below the radar of authorities and all that this

implies. If their asylum claim is successful they will be allowed to remain in the UK, sometimes for a fixed length of time. At this point they assume the status of a refugee. A refugee is a person who is living outside of their country of nationality and who cannot return because of fear of persecution. Both asylum seekers and refugees are fully entitled to NHS services.

For asylum seekers the seeds of their mental distress have usually been sown in their own countries. They have had, or are fearful of having, experiences which mean they have to leave homes, extended family and everything they know. In extreme cases both adults and children may suffer from post-traumatic stress disorder. In all cases there will be a sadness and pain at who and what has been left behind. The circumstances of their travel usually mean that asylum seekers are not able to take many possessions with them. The journey itself can often be hazardous.

Once here in the UK there are other difficulties and issues which can cause or exacerbate mental health issues:

- Asylum seekers find themselves dispersed to a place which may not be of their choosing and placed in accommodation which may be quite poor.

- Often the key issues for the clients are homesickness, social anxiety, and managing the difficulties of living in the system here (Cavill, 2000).
- There is a considerable uncertainty inherent in being an asylum seeker and people do not know when their asylum claim will be heard and are anxious about its outcome.
- Families must get used to a new culture, learn a new language and navigate the local school and healthcare systems; all of which can be extremely daunting.
- Children may also suffer from their parents being heavily reliant on them to interpret for them and support them (Woodhead, 2000). This is often an additional burden on a young person who is trying to integrate into a new culture, a new school and make new friends.

Many asylum seeking children come to the UK as part of a family unit but some young people are unaccompanied. Hodes (2008) highlights that: 'Lone asylum seeking children are at much greater risk of mental health problems, such as post-traumatic stress symptoms, than their accompanied peers'. Unaccompanied asylum seekers are more likely to be suffering from the after effects of extreme experiences in their home countries, such as being involved in combat or being tortured, or possibly being the one individual elected to leave the home and escape death or imprisonment. On arrival in the UK they are often placed in temporary accommodation rather than a more supportive environment such as foster care.

A Mental Health Foundation report (Stephens, 2002) considers that insecure accommodation damages both mental and physical health. A lack of stable housing means that young people and/or families are likely to be moved regularly, often into housing which may not be entirely suitable. An example may be having only a single room for a family, having to share a bathroom and kitchen with others, having a lack of furniture and basic household items. There is often a stigma attached to living in these circumstances and children may experience bullying at school. Moving house may require changing schools and the consequent loss of friends and familiarity. There may be considerable anxiety about the future. Children may feel an obligation to care for parents who may themselves be suffering from mental health problems or have substance misuse problems.

Young people who have been forced or chosen to leave 'home' (this may be temporary accommodation or local authority care) are often vulnerable. Substance misuse may occur in conjunction with mental health problems. Self-harm is an extremely common presentation in young homeless people. For some people self-harm and substance misuse can be a form of self-medication for psychological damage sustained by child abuse. These young people have a lack of opportunities: educational, employment and social. This often leads to a lack of self-esteem. There are also difficulties in transferring from child to adult services, particularly for those with mental health or behavioural problems such as attention deficit hyperactivity disorder (ADHD).

# Homeless young people and families

One study has demonstrated that homeless children and their mothers have a high level of mental health problems (Vostanis et al., 1998). There are many reasons for this; Vostanis (2002) has found that 'the majority of families become homeless because of domestic violence'. Witnessing domestic violence can cause behavioural and mental health problems in young people, such as anxiety and post-traumatic stress disorder. In some cases children also experience abuse and may choose to leave home because of it.

# Summary

For all homeless people, including asylum seekers, use of health services may be difficult. There are barriers to using mainstream services. These include not attending appointments due to the chaotic nature of their lifestyles, not receiving post (due to having no address or a shared address), illiteracy and mistrust of statutory services. For asylum seekers there is the specific issue of not speaking English and it is vital that health professionals obtain an independent interpreter and do not expect the client to bring a friend or family member to interpret. It is also important to recognize potential religious and cultural issues (please see Chapter 61, Working with diversity – cultural competence in child and adolescent mental health (CAMHS)). For example, in some cultures there is no concept of depression and people present with physical manifestations, such as all over body pain.

## Case study 1: Asad

Asad was born in Somalia and fled the violent conflict in his home country at the age of 16 and arrived in the UK seeking asylum. Upon arrival he was placed in a young asylum seekers home provided by the Home Office. In his early years in the UK he was very quiet and mistrusting of others, especially those who represented the government (including the police and social workers).

Once he turned 18, Asad was granted indefinite leave to remain (refugee status). This change in status and his age meant that he was no longer able to remain in the young person's project and became street homeless.

Asad was very anxious about living on the streets, especially as his English was still quite limited. However, he was equally worried about moving into hostel accommodation, because of rumours he had heard about violence in those settings. Eventually Asad presented himself to the local street homelessness prevention team, who worked with him for some time in order to persuade him to move into a hostel. It was crucial not to pressurize Asad into hostel accommodation, but build up a trusting relationship with him. He opened up about his interests and stated that he had a flair for art. His support worker was able to identify a smaller hostel where his artistic talent could be encouraged, which they visited on several occasions in order for him to feel more comfortable with the idea of being there.

Asad began to settle well. However, after a few weeks an argument between two other residents triggered traumatic flashbacks from the violence he had witnessed in Somalia. He left the hostel and was found by his street homelessness worker asleep in a local car park. With encouragement, he, his worker and the hostel manager met away from the hostel to discuss his fears and concerns. An action plan was formulated between the three of them, which involved him spending time with a member of the hostel staff if another confrontation occurred until he felt calmer. Asad was also referred to his GP to discuss a possible psychological report around the flashbacks he had experienced.

## Case study 2: James

James (16 years old) had lived in a family where high conflict had been present throughout his entire life. Until the age of 10 he had witnessed his mother experiencing domestic violence at the hands of his father. On one occasion his mother became extremely violent towards his father and after that the physical abuse ended. The verbal aggression continued.

As James grew older and developed physically, he had begun to respond to verbal aggression from his parents with similar responses and on a few occasions with his father it had become physical. The situation came to a head when James got into a fight with his father and broke two of his father's fingers. James was immediately thrown out of the house by his father and told never to return.

James was able to stay on the sofas in friends' houses for a few weeks, but his friends' parents would eventually say that he needed to move on. Eventually an adult friend took James to the local homeless unit. After the homeless unit tried and were unable to reach a resolution with James' parents, he was placed in emergency accommodation until a room in a young person's project could be found.

Once at the youth housing project, staff observed James displaying unusually high levels of verbal aggression towards other young people, normally in response to the smallest of triggers. This had resulted in a fight with another male resident, which put his tenancy at risk. James confided in a staff member, saying that he hated getting angry so quickly, but felt unable to manage himself. James was referred by the project to the local community CAMHS team, where he was assessed and allocated an individual therapist to begin exploring his experiences and their impact on his current behaviour.

After a course of sessions James was able to identify conflict situations and his patterns of response to them. With the therapist he was then able to explore alternative responses in those situations, which he tested out and reported a positive outcome. With the support of his therapist he was able to make contact with his mother and father and meet them to begin rebuilding their relationship. James stated that he would not return home, but wished to find accommodation of his own once he turned 18.

Once more settled, James was able to enrol on a course in plumbing at his local college.

## Multiple choice questions

1. Which of the following should be considered when assessing an asylum seeking child/young person?

   a. Whether they speak English or not
   b. Cultural issues and religious beliefs
   c. Whether or not they are entitled to NHS services
   d. Past experience of traumatic events
   e. All of the above

2. According to Vostanis (2002), what is the main cause of homelessness for mothers and children?

   a. Being made redundant
   b. Domestic violence
   c. Harassment from neighbours
   d. Relationship breakdown
   e. Rent arrears

3. Which of these is a young homeless person most likely to experience?

   a. Schizophrenia
   b. Self-harm
   c. Anxiety
   d. Bi-polar disorder
   e. Substance misuse

## Key texts

Hodes M (2008) Risk and resilience for psychological distress amongst unaccompanied asylum seeking adolescents. *Journal of Child Psychology and Psychiatry*, **49**: 723–32.

Stephens J (2002) *The Mental Health Needs of Homeless Young People. Bright Futures: Working with Vulnerable Young People*. London: The Mental Health Foundation.

Vostanis P (2002) Mental health of homeless children and their families. *Advances in Psychiatric Treatment*, **8**: 463–9.

## 64 Young carers from black and minority ethnic communities

Julia Pelle

---

### Key concepts

- Children and adolescents from BME communities not only experience the impact of a parent, sibling or other family member with a mental health problem, but may have to endure the added stigma of perceived cultural stereotypes.
- Some young carers belong to first generation migrant families who find themselves adapting to a very different way of life in Great Britain (Green et al., 2008). Other young carers are part of the second generation migrant community and although they have acculturated to what is their birth place, they can be vulnerable to inequalities within education, social exclusion, racial discrimination, insecure housing and the criminal justice system (Fatimelehin, 2007).
- People from black and minority ethnic (BME) communities are more likely to experience poverty, discrimination and unemployment.
- Individuals, from the Black African and Black Caribbean communities are more likely to be given a diagnosis of schizophrenia and bipolar disorder and are less likely to be diagnosed with depression and anxiety (Sharpley, 2001; Bhugra, 2002; Wordsworth, 2008).
- These individuals experience higher rates of admission to in-patient units and compulsory detention (National Black Carers and Carers Workers Network, 2002; Department of Health, 2003c; Department of Health, 2005; National Black Carers and Carers Workers Network, 2008).

---

## Introduction

A number of Department of Health reports in the UK have acknowledged the integral role young carers play in the recovery of parents and other family members with mental health problems (Department of Health, 1999, Department of Health, 2003, Department of Health, 2005, Department of Health, 2007a, Department of Health, 2009a).

The term BME (black and minority ethnic) includes people from Black-African, African-Caribbean, South Asian and Chinese heritage in addition to individuals from white communities who have a heritage different from that of the majority population, for example Irish, Gypsy and Travelling communities and Eastern European migrants (e.g. Lithuanian, Latvian, Russian, Polish and Slovakian communities).

For young carers, parental and sibling mental health problems can have a negative impact on their development, breakdown in family relationships, interrupted and incomplete education and risk of child abuse. Young carers can find it uncomfortable to discuss family matters with those people whom they perceive to be 'outsiders', such as teachers, mental health nurses or social workers. Some young carers may take on a role as an interpreter and translator for their relatives, giving them access to information that can lead to increased distress. They may become more vulnerable as a result of isolation from their peers, experiencing health problems of their own and poor communication between child and adult mental health services (Grant et al., 2008; Greene et al., 2008).

# Case study 1: Aisha and her brother, Khaleel

Aisha (9) lives at home with her parents, Youssuf and Afsana, and five other siblings. Aisha's oldest brother Khaleel (16) has drug-induced psychosis and has recently been diagnosed with schizoaffective disorder. Aisha remembers when Khaleel used to look after her, play with her and protect her but now he can be very angry over any little thing: she and her other siblings are scared of being around him. Aisha says she sometimes sees Khaleel talking to himself and wonders who he is talking to. Aisha knows that sometimes Khaleel has to go to hospital and her mother and father have to spend time with him. All the siblings in the family are bi-lingual. However, neither of Khaleel's parents speaks very good English and they are reliant on their older daughter, Eiliyah (14), to be their interpreter.

Mark is Khaleel's key worker and is a Child and Adolescent Community Nurse; he arranges to visit the family a week after Khaleel's discharge from the local mental health unit. Mark observes that both parents are very distressed and Aisha seems to be hiding behind the door in the hallway: Khaleel is somewhat withdrawn. Both parents express their concern about the number of young black men they have seen in the mental health hospital when they visited Khaleel and are adamant that they do not want him to be re-admitted to the hospital.

## Assessment

- Explain to the parents the reason for the visit and explain the importance of finding out how Khaleel thinks he is managing since returning home.
- Explain and discuss the usefulness of first speaking to Khaleel by himself and then speaking to both parents.
- After speaking to Khaleel, discuss with his parents how the family care for Khaleel and find out how they are coping.
- What contact do the parents have with their local GP, when caring for their son? Identify what support they have from their GP.
- Explore with the parents what their everyday experience is of caring for their son.
- Complete Carer Assessment Form with the family.
- Establish during conversation any cultural preferences that Khaleels' parents have.
- Review the discharge plan and establish whether both parents and Khaleel are still happy with the discharge plan.
- Discuss what support the community mental health services can give to the family and to Khaleel.
- Evaluate the relationship between a) Khaleel and his siblings and b) between Khaleel and his parents.

## Possible interventions

- Education for parents about drug-induced psychosis.
- Consider which education material would be useful for both Khaleel and his siblings.
- Check with the family if they have computer access and 'signpost' them to user-friendly information which further explains mental health problems and could identify local carer support groups and service user groups.
- Identify how the parents can explain Khaleel's mental health problem to Aisha, as the youngest child, and to his other siblings.
- Discuss opportunities to have leisure time as a family, for example meeting with other families who care for a child with a similar mental health problem.
- Consider accessing the interpretation services for future meetings.
- Family Centred Work.

## Outcomes

- Carers often complain about the lack of information on mental health problems and the lack of support when caring for a family member with a mental health problem.

- By signposting the family to local community support networks, this can make it easier to meet with others experiencing the same difficulties and offer opportunities to share better ways of accessing information and managing issues around caring.
- By empowering parents with the information they need about their son's mental health problem, they can then explain this to other family members.
- It is important to ensure that parents are aware of any other local support networks, other than the statutory mental health services.

# Case study 2: Jade and her mother, Monique

Jade (12) has been caring for Monique since she was ten years old. Monique has been diagnosed with paranoid schizophrenia. Jade has an older sister, Joleesa, who is now 18. Joleesa found their mother 'too weird' and left to live with their grandparents. When Monique is very unwell, she 'sees' people who are not there and hears voices .She has been known to experience tactile hallucinations. Jade does most of the cooking during these times and is able to cook a number of traditional Caribbean dishes. She helps her mother with the weekly shopping. Monique has accused Jade of trying to poison her when Jade tries to encourage her to take her medication. Often what follows is that Monique threatens to throw Jade out, but Jade knows this is because she is unwell. Monique struggles with trusting health professionals but she has agreed to meet with Sharon, her keyworker, although she worries that Jade will be taken away from her. During the meeting Jade speaks 'Patois' to her mother and then transfers to English when speaking to Sharon.

Sharon meets with Jade and Monique and observes that their relationship is a very loving one; both have a great sense of humour. Sharon observes that Jade looks very tired and appears to be underweight. Sharon discusses the possibility of respite care for Jade, but Monique becomes notably upset.

## Assessment
- Young Carer assessment form.
- Identify what supports Jade already has.
- Review how she manages school work and home/housework and looking after Monique.
- Monitor how Jade takes care of herself each day; review any barriers to her own self-care.
- Jade already cooks traditional Caribbean meals for her mother, explore what other aspects of culture are important to her.
- Assess what leisure activities Jade engages in a) with Monique and b) with others.
- Review the relationship between a) Jade and her sister, Joleesa and b) Monique and Joleesa. Jade may be feeling like a 'go between' or 'piggy in the middle' in that relationship.
- Discuss with Jade what her understanding of her mother's mental health problem is and ask if she would like more information. If she does, offer useful educational material appropriate for Jade's age that could help her recognize triggers with Monique and help her to build self-esteem around her caring skills.
- Build on which aspects of Caribbean culture both individuals identify with.
- The change in Monique's mental state can have a negative impact on Jade's self-esteem, particularly when Jade tries to help Monique with taking her medication.

## Intervention
- Continue to build up trust with Jade and Monique. Discussions about cultural identity can be initiated through asking about the Caribbean dishes that Jade cooks.
- Provide information on respite care and types of respite care for Jade and her mother to read about together.

- Explain that some respite time for Jade would help Monique in the long term.
- Consider activities where Jade and Monique can have leisure time together.

## Outcomes

It is important to build up a trusting relationship with both carer and the person cared for. Understanding their daily routine helps the mental health nurse to see where there may be barriers to the caring relationship and to consider what options are available to overcome those barriers.

Finding out about the cultural identity of the young carer and their parent or relative can help put them at their ease, demonstrate an interest and this may lead to information on how best to support this family.

Some parents are concerned about their children receiving respite care because:

- they may perceive this as an opportunity for their children to be taken away from them;
- of concerns about how they will cope when the young carer is not around;
- they are unable to trust anyone else to give them the care they need and in the way they like to be cared for;
- of concerns that the young carer may decide they no longer wish to care for their parent or relative.

The mental health nurse needs to reassure the parent or relative that respite is really for the short term and will be jointly discussed with them. However, it is important to reiterate the need for young people to have the opportunity to be 'young' and enjoy childhood; that this is a chance for young carers to meet other carers going through similar experiences and that it is good for the physical and mental well-being of the young carer. This can only help the young carer to develop more confidence in their caring abilities and extend their scope for support.

## Case study 3: Evelina

Evelina is 17. She looks after her younger brother Alexander (8) and her mother Viktorya. Alexander has attention deficit disorder (ADD) and Viktorya suffers with severe depression. Evelina's father left the parental home shortly after the family arrived in England from Russia, four years ago. Evelina and Alexander speak very good English, but Viktorya's English is very limited so Evelina fills out any forms they need to complete and helps her brother and mother be ready for each day. Alexander attends a special school 5 days a week but Evelina finds him difficult to manage at the weekends. Evelina says life is easier now that she is not at school, although she attends the local college where she is studying music and art. Viktorya has been very well recently: she no longer wants to take medication and wants to do more around the house and look after her son herself. She feels guilty that Evelina has to do so much for her and is missing out on her youth.

Joan is Viktorya's key worker and meets with the family for a weekly visit. Evelina looks particularly tired and drawn and is preoccupied with her brother, Alexander. Viktorya mentions to Joan that she wants to stop the medication she is currently prescribed, because she wants to be more in control and fulfil her role as a mother.

### Assessment and intervention options
- Young Carer assessment form.
- Identify what supports Evelina already has.
- Discuss with Evelina how she manages her college work and home/housework in addition to looking after Viktorya and Alexander.
- Assess what leisure activities Evelina engages in, if any, or establish what she would like to do, if she had time to herself.

- Review the relationship between Evelina and a) her brother and b) her mother.
- Discuss with Evelina her understanding of Viktorya's mental health problems and ask if she would like more information. If she does, offer useful educational material for Evelina and maybe explore whether Evelina would like to have the information in her native Russian language or in English.
- Establish during conversation any cultural preferences that Evelina and her family may have.
- Discuss with both Evelina and Viktorya the importance of not abruptly stopping medication.
- Family Centred Work.

## Outcomes

For some young carers, caring for a parent or relative can lead to dropping out of the educational system to become full-time carers and missing out on developing opportunities for themselves. For those young carers who do go on to further education, the challenge can be how they balance studying with caring and any other activities. The mental health worker should review how a young carer is currently managing to balance the various responsibilities and consider different support mechanisms.

Not all members of the BME community necessarily want to have close links with others from their community: there may be a sense of shame about having to care for a relative with mental health problems and they may wish to keep this private. It is useful to explore who they would like to receive support from, both within the mental health services and within the community.

When young carers are caring for more than one member of the family, this brings an added burden to their everyday lives. Discussing the opportunities for respite care can be important as a way to help relieve some of the burden of care.

## Multiple choice questions

1. Individuals from black African and Caribbean communities are more likely to receive a diagnosis of:

    a. Schizophrenia and bipolar disorder
    b. Depression and anxiety
    c. ADHD
    d. Anorexia nervosa
    e. Emotionally unstable personality disorder

2. Individuals are less likely to receive a diagnosis of:

    a. Schizophrenia
    b. Mood disorder
    c. ADHD
    d. Anorexia nervosa
    e. Emotionally unstable personality disorder

3. Which of the following would present a key challenge to young carers from the BME community?

    a. Completion of a young Carers Assessment form?
    b. Contacting the family's heritage community for support.
    c. Being provided with information to young carers around the illness.
    d. Being provided with information around statutory and voluntary sources of support
    e. Offer Family Centred Work.

## Key texts

Department of Health (2009a) *Delivering Race Equality in Mental Health Care: A Review.* London: HMSO.

Grant G, Repper J, Nolan M (2008) Young people supporting parents with mental health problems: experiences of assessment and support. *Health and Social Care in the Community,* **16**: 271–81.

Greene R, Pugh R, Roberts D (2008) *Black and Minority Ethnic Parents with Mental Health Problems and their Children, Research Paper.* London: Social Care Institute for Excellence.

# 65

# Emerging sexuality
### Charlotte Young

## Key concepts

- Research has shown that half of lesbian and bisexual women under 20 have self-harmed compared to one in 15 of the general population (Stonewall, 2007).
- Young people who identify themselves as non-heterosexual are more likely to have attempted suicide than young people identified as heterosexual (Fish, 2007).
- Exacerbating mental health difficulties, young lesbian and bisexual females are more likely to smoke and drink alcohol excessively than their heterosexual counterparts (Fish, 2007).
- Young gay and bisexual males are more likely to misuse illegal substances (Fish, 2007).
- Research has not identified a causal relationship between non-heterosexuality and mental health problems, despite the fact that homosexuality was once considered a mental disorder. The development of mental health difficulties in this group of young people is more likely to be the consequence of living in a society that is predominantly heterosexual and the resultant isolation, prejudice, hostility and potential violence experienced (Kitts, 2005).

## Introduction

It is well known that adolescence can be a turbulent period of identity formation. Part of this involves developing sexual identity and the consequent feelings of sexuality. It seems as though young people are experiencing this at younger ages. Research has shown that the average age for 'coming out', when a person discloses their sexuality, is 15 years (Stonewall, 2010). This is a pertinent issue for CAMHS as evidence shows that those young people who are questioning their sexuality or consider themselves not to be part of the 'expected' heterosexual group have difficulties maintaining their mental health.

Particular challenges that are faced by young people considering being open about their sexuality may include:

- they or their family hold beliefs that reject their sexuality as immoral;
- they may live in an isolated setting where sources of support, such as other non-heterosexual young people or organized support groups, may not be available;
- their family or social groups may not represent their sexuality (Morrow, 2004);
- they may perceive their family and friends to be homophobic and they fear parental rejection (Morrow, 2004);
- experiencing conflict around their sexuality leading to denial or living a 'double life', lying to friends and families about their relationships.

For those young people who are questioning their sexuality, this is a traumatic and difficult time. Two-thirds of lesbian, gay and bisexual (LGB)-identified young people experience homophobic bullying at school (Hunt and Jensen, 2007).

Young people who are questioning their gender identity often come to CAMHS presenting with gender identity disorder (GID). Historically, transsexual people would mix with the lesbian and gay community and often use the same support groups. However, GID is not a sexual orientation but a gender orientation. Individuals with GID are at high risk for mental health problems, suicidal ideation and attempts (Gibson and Catlin, 2010).

CAMHS policy in this area is clear. The National

Service Framework (NSF) for Children Young People and Maternity Services (Department of Health, 2004a) states that services should be provided regardless of a young person's sexuality or gender. Legally, young lesbian, gay, bisexual and transsexual (LGBT) people's rights are protected in law. The recent Equality Act (HM Government, 2010) protects against discrimination on the grounds of sexuality in the provision of business and public services. This covers both schools and healthcare provision. Equality is further recognized with the age of consent for sexual intercourse being 16 for both homosexual and heterosexual young people.

## Definitions

- Bisexual: a person who is sexually, romantically and emotionally attracted to persons of both the same and the opposite gender.
- Gay/homosexual: A person who is sexually, romantically and emotionally attracted to persons of the same gender.
- Lesbian: A female homosexual.
- Gender identity disorder: discomfort in one's gender identity, characterized by the desire to be the opposite gender.
- Homophobia: Fear of homosexuality in others or oneself.
- Heterosexual/straight: A person who is sexually, romantically and emotionally attracted to persons of the opposite gender.
- Transsexual: A person who feels they are the wrong sex

## Case study 1: Andreas

Andreas (16) was initially referred to CAMHS by his GP due to bulimic behaviours and emotional dysregulation. On assessment, it was clear that Andreas was coming to terms with his sexuality. He later identified himself as gay. Creating an environment where questions on sexuality were actually asked offered an environment in which Andreas could 'come out' (Meckler et al., 2006). This was in a non-judgemental way and Andreas felt comfortable to open up to the practitioners (Kitts, 2005). A practitioner was assigned to work with him and a colleague to work with his mother.

Andreas' worker was able to work with him on his eating difficulties. Young non-heterosexuals are more likely to experience eating disorders (Busseri et al., 2006). It was important to distinguish between 'coming out' and emerging personality dysfunction.

Emerging sexuality issues can provoke uncomfortable emotions in practitioners and clinical supervision is essential. It is important for practitioner and supervisor to examine their attitudes/beliefs around sexuality and how this may impact on their practice (Dootson, 2000). By providing a positive and accepting environment, Andreas was able to express his worries about his sexuality (Morrow, 2004). Providing literature about local support groups for LGBT youth and posters advertising inclusivity enabled Andreas to be supported in his environment (Kitts, 2005).

Confidentially was key, as his family were initially unaware of his sexuality. The practitioner supported Andreas in developing coping strategies to respond to whatever reaction his parents had to his 'coming out'. His family had strong religious beliefs that viewed homosexuality as morally wrong. The practitioner did not challenge them on the issue but allowed them to explore their worries and fears. Part of this role was to prepare them for family therapy where this was further explored.

## Case example 2: Nicole

Nicole (15) was referred to CAMHS after an overdose that warranted admission to a local hospital. The practitioners who assessed her were careful to use inclusive language, and Nicole felt able to disclose the worries about her emerging sexuality that had precipitated the overdose (Kitts, 2005). It transpired that Nicole had been subject to homophobic bullying at school. It was important not to use the words 'lesbian' or 'gay' as Nicole was not yet ready to label herself. Her parents had begun to be aware of her sexuality and were supportive to Nicole. This improved her self-esteem and sense of well-being (Ryan, 2010).

A practitioner worked with Nicole to explore the association between her enduring low mood and coming to terms with her sexuality. Nicole self-harmed and this was explored in relation to the anger at her sexuality and about not feeling 'normal'. Careful risk assessment was carried out with Nicole because of the risk of further self-harm, arising from the psychosocial stressors associated with her sexuality (Morrow, 2004; Kitts, 2005). With her permission, the CAMHS team liaised with Nicole's school to highlight the homophobic bullying and ensure that it was addressed. Nicole was put in touch with local youth LGBT support groups.

## Case study 3: Harry

Harry was taken to his GP by his mother, presenting with gender non-conformity. He was born female. Harry was referred by his GP into CAMHS due to his low mood about this issue. With Harry, it was important to have a non-judgemental approach. It was vital to see gender from Harry's perspective and not the 'norms' of society (Singh et al., 2011). It was important to not use terms like 'gay' but words like 'attraction to females'. Harry received counselling to help with low mood, explore identity and, as it later transpired, to cope with bullying at school and the subsequent social isolation in addition to the family difficulties over acceptance (Gibson and Catlin, 2010). School was liaised with over Harry's difficulties (Gibson and Catlin, 2010). Practitioners encouraged Harry to join a local support group. These interventions and supportive counselling work helped Harry through his difficulties (Singh et al., 2011).

### Outcomes

Prognoses for LGBT people tend to be poorer than for heterosexuals or for people with a clear gender identity. This is due in part to the heterosexual-centric society in which young people live and the psychosocial stressors that will be placed on them. Family acceptance predicts better outcomes for LGBT people (Ryan, 2010).

## Multiple choice questions

1. Should transsexualism be seen as related to:

   a. Gender orientation
   b. Sexual orientation
   c. Neither
   d. Both

2. What is the legal age of consent for adolescents to engage in sexual intercourse?

   a. 16 for both heterosexual and homosexual sex by males and females
   b. 18 for homosexual sex and 16 for heterosexual sex
   c. 16 for male homosexual and heterosexual sex, 18 for female homosexual sex and 16 for heterosexual sex
   d. 16 for both heterosexual sex and male homosexual sex, no age of consent for female homosexual sex

### Key texts

Busseri M, Willoughby T, Chalmers H, Bogaert AR (2006) Same-sex attraction and successful adolescent development. *Journal of Youth and Adolescence,* **35**: 563–75.

Ryan C, Russell ST, Huebner R et al. (2010) Family acceptance in adolescence and the health of LGBT young adults. *Journal of Child and Adolescent Psychiatric Nursing;* **23**: 205–13.

Troiden R (1987) Homosexual identity development. *Journal of Adolescent Health Care,* **9**: 105–13.

## Web pages

www.stonewall.org.uk – A charity that campaigns on behalf of LGB people. It has excellent guidance on working with young people who identify as LGB.

www.mermaidsuk.org.uk/index.html – For families of those with children and young people who have gender identity issues.

www.queeryouth.org.uk/community/ – An internet community and support site for young LGBT identified people and those questioning.

# Introduction
## Christine Hooper

When making decisions with children, young people and their families around the most appropriate intervention, the primary consideration must be their ability and motivation to engage with what is offered. Although practice policy and guidance around therapeutic interventions should be and often have an empirical evidence base to support their efficacy, the values base of the individual child/young person and/or family is central (Woodbridge and Fulford, 2004). This may mean considering the use of alternative treatment approaches that may 'fit' with them. Alongside this it is important that any intervention is age appropriate for the child/young person. For example, play therapy may be more beneficial for younger children, who may not have developed the appropriate language to express their emotions, whereas a more talking therapy approach may suit older children and adolescents (although this is not always the case).

This section is divided broadly into three parts; Creative Therapies, Individual Talking Therapies and Systemic Therapies, although in reality some cannot easily fit into one category; for example, Solution Focused Therapy can be used with individuals and family groups.

## Creative therapies

All of the creative therapies (whether using art, drama, play or music) involve a therapeutic relationship between the therapist and the individual, within the framework of a clinical setting. The visual images and objects are the medium for the development of the relationship, allowing for alternative means of communication and enabling individuals to explore the emotions and feelings relating to their difficulties, in a safe and containing environment. Children, especially, often find it difficult to articulate their feelings verbally. Play, drama, art or music offer a more natural non-verbal language for them to express distress or unhappiness.

All creative therapists working within the statutory agencies must have completed post-graduate diplomas and be registered with their appropriate professional body.

## Drama therapy

Drama therapists are seldom found in CAMHS teams or, indeed, in adult mental health settings. 'Drama' in ancient Greek, meant the thing that is acted out or lived through. It does not need a stage, costumes or props, but it does need an individual or group of people who use action or speech to create a story or scene.

Children use drama from an early age. Through imitation and experimentation, they learn to take on a role, for example imitating sounds before they can talk and using objects in imaginative play. In a clinical setting, drama can be used to express conflict or distress. Several key processes lie at the heart of drama therapy, illustrating how the healing potential of drama and play can be realized. They include dramatic projection, therapeutic performance process, embodiment (i.e. dramatizing the body), playing and transformation.

# 66

# Art therapy
**Margaret Josephs**

## Key concepts

- Clients learn to use artwork as a way to express inner thoughts, feelings and conflicts. From this creative expression, various levels of conscious and subconscious issues emerge. These can be worked with at the depth and pace that is appropriate for the client at the time.
- The ratio of time spent between producing artwork and talking is the client's choice.
- The process of working with art materials, and the ensuing images, can release clients from their traditional ways of thinking and behaving. This can facilitate a new way of exploring difficult issues.
- Art therapy can promote self-awareness and increase self-esteem.
- Art therapy offers an opportunity for the client to actively structure his or her own therapy.
- Both adults and children, of all ages, can benefit from all of the creative therapies.

## Introduction

Art Therapy is a clinical practice involving a psychodynamic and psychotherapeutic relationship between the art therapist and the client, working either 1:1 or in a group setting. At the heart is the artwork, which helps to develop a trusting relationship and communication between the client and the therapist.

All creative therapists (including music therapists) working within the statutory agencies must have completed post-graduate diplomas and be registered with their appropriate professional body.

When looking for the origins of using art in therapy, Tessa Dalley (1996) in 'Art as Therapy' suggests its consideration in the context of the arts generally. 'Art is an indigenous feature in every society', she writes. Odell-Miller, Learmouth and Pembrooke (2003) state that creativity is part of human problem-solving. It is used as a resource for dealing with distress and disturbance: it is common sense to put creativity, through the inclusion of creative therapies, at the service of improving mental health.

Creative therapy, in particular art therapy, differs from other psychological therapies in that it is a three-way process between the client, the therapist and the image or artefact, offering a third dimension to the process. The art activity provides a concrete, rather than verbal, medium through which the client can achieve both conscious and unconscious expression. It can be used as a valuable agent for therapeutic change.

Art therapy is practised in a variety of both residential and community settings, within health, social services, education, and the voluntary and private sector. Clients are seen individually with their families and in groups.

## Art therapy groups for adolescents

Art therapy in a group setting can be helpful for:

- Young people, aged between 12 and 16 years, who find it difficult to express their feelings, struggle with relationships and are not felt to be fulfilling their potential.
- Young people who protect themselves by withdrawing from the world, either refusing/not being able to go to school, not mixing with their peers or losing themselves in the care they provide for others.

- A high proportion of referrals have a parent with a diagnosed mental health problem, or parents who are fragile for a variety of reasons, for example being victims of violence, or abusive or broken relationships, and who have depended on the support of their child.
- Young people who are suffering long-term illnesses, for example degenerative loss of hearing and brain tumours.

In 'Playing and Reality', Winnicott (1971) discusses the creative spark that develops between mother and child. His concept of the intermediate area between mother and child, in which a healthy interaction is one of playful creativity, is central to the development of the 'potential space' that is created by the three-way process between the client therapist and materials (see **Figure 66.1**).

- Within art therapy groups, the group therapists are seen as the facilitators of that space.
- The process is intended to be collaborative and as transparent as possible, from beginning to end. Great importance is placed on engaging and negotiating what each person, their family and the referrer are hoping to gain from the young person's attendance in the group.
- Each group runs for an academic year, and meetings are held with the group facilitators, young person, family, referrer and, if appropriate, any other involved professionals, to assess their appropriateness for the group and to set outcome targets.
- These are reviewed and updated at further meetings halfway through and when the group has finished.

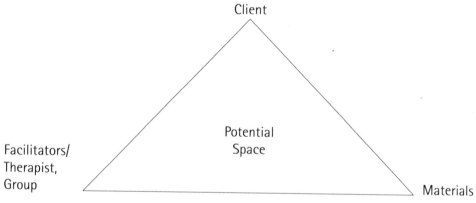

Figure 66.1 The potential space created by the three-way process.

For many of these group members, it may be the first time they have had an experience in a group that they can relate to. Saying goodbye is inevitably challenging and can be painful. Often young people's previous experiences of endings have been to withdraw themselves before the end, to protect themselves, or to behave in such an unacceptable way as to be excluded. The end result is the same, i.e. the avoidance of the end and saying goodbye. The group, therefore, spends most of the final term preparing for finishing and has developed several methods for addressing the issues around leaving:

- A range of art materials are available.
- Group members are encouraged to use the art materials in a way that encourages the development of free expression.

- The amount of art work and discussion varies from week to week, depending on the needs of the group.
- The way the work is created also varies, i.e. working individually, or in pairs, small groups or larger groups.

Over the years the importance of 'messy painting' has increased and noted to be significant in the development of group members ability to emerge as individuals within the group.

If young people are to develop in ways that allow them to find their own identity through their feelings, recognize themselves as separate from others, and recognize and relate to others and develop reciprocal relationships, they must first go through the process of 'immersing' themselves in the materials, in a way that allows them to 'let go' of previously held pre-conceptions about themselves, giving them the freedom to explore new ways of developing as individuals.

Issues about boundaries and containment emerge. Fears of being overwhelmed can be explored through the metaphor of the paint on the paper. What happens to the messy paintings is always a matter for discussion, as they can take days to dry. The paintings are usually photographed in their original state and then stored in plastic boxes (see **Figure 66.2**).

Figure 66.2  An example of a 'messy' painting.

## Case study: Sophie

A CAMHS (Child and Adolescent Mental Health team) colleague referred Sophie to the art therapy group. Sophie was described as presenting with clinical depression, frequently experiencing suicidal ideations. She complained of sleep disturbance and early morning waking. Sophie described herself as a 'psychotic neurotic'. A psychiatric assessment had been requested to discuss medication.

Both Sophie's parents had been treated for depression in the past and she believed she would inherit it.

Sophie came to our initial meeting accompanied by the CAMHS worker. Her parents were unable to attend.

The group uses a rating system to evaluate progress. Sophie scored herself at 1 out of 10 for how she felt about herself. She said she would like to be between 7 and 9 out of 10. Her aims for attending the group were to be happier, more expressive, better at explaining things and able to go out more.

Sophie spent most of her time on her computer, staying up well into the night. She was in her last year at school, where there were issues of bullying.

From the start of the group, Sophie used the materials in a very creative way, immediately painting pictures to describe how she was feeling. She described herself as 'mad'. She would often talk about being let down by other adults, including her GP, teachers and mental health workers.

Her early pictures describe being 'stuck in the dark' and 'standing on the edge looking on' (see Figures 66.3 and 66.4).

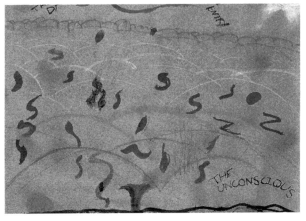

Figure 66.3  'Stuck in the dark'.

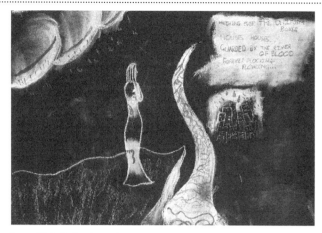

Figure 66.4 Under the surface.

Sophie spoke about hitting her head on her desk when everything was too much for her and about how coming to the group and painting helped her and her school feel she was doing something about her situation. Sophie did not talk about her family until late into the group. She began to wonder out loud about being depressed, and started to show visible signs of distress, becoming withdrawn and tearful.

Sophie found it better to focus on her artwork, which she found easier to share, and she joined in with the discussions about others feeling overwhelmed and overwhelming. She would describe herself as 'dead 'and as needing more than anyone could offer. She was still spending much of her time on the Internet, where she felt she could be herself because she could not be seen. She began to talk about arguing with her parents and resisted attempts by other group members to meet up outside the group, although she would sometimes communicate with a group member by email and text.

The group was exploring issues around safety and either drew or made models of a place where they could feel safe. Sophie made what she described as a padded cell out of modelling material to which, she said, she had swallowed the key. She described being afraid of hurting others more than hurting herself, which was an issue shared by several others in the group. The last time she could remember feeling safe was when she was seven years old and her father was working a night shift. Then she would be allowed into bed with her mother to watch TV and have 'lots of cuddles'.

Sophie's use of the materials helped her to identify what she was experiencing, looking for and feared, in a way that could be discussed openly within the group.

Unfortunately, neither Sophie's parents nor the referrer could attend the mid-group review. This fuelled Sophie's feelings of loss and rejection. She attended on her own and was very distressed. This allowed for the issues to be addressed and then, with her permission, shared within the group.

From then onwards, Sophie became noticeably more playful and relaxed. She engaged in group discussions and used the materials much more freely. In a group discussion preparing for the end of the group, the group members described her, among other descriptions, as caring, understanding, trustworthy, serious, sensitive, funny and a good listener. This seriously challenged Sophie's previous view of herself.

Sophie's parents attended the final meeting. They were very positive about the changes they had seen in her. They described their daughter's mood as 'up'. Sophie was being more sociable, less tired, more energetic and with a much-improved sleeping pattern.

Sophie now rated herself as between 7 and 8 out of 10. She had plans to attend a local college after finishing school. She had been able to hold onto the feedback from the group and was letting go of her previous self-perceptions. There had been no incidents of self-harm since the group began.

Sophie's involvement in the art therapy group shows how the facilitation of a space where thoughts and feelings can be explored, at the client's pace and in a way that encourages exploration and development through the use of art materials, can result in a whole new way of experiencing oneself and the world. Unconscious material surfaces through images and words. It is the therapist's task to help the young person make sense of it. Clear boundaries and limits make the group a safe experience for intense and powerful feelings to be expressed and worked through. The groups are hard work and can be hectic, disruptive and angry, or thoughtful, reflective, sharing and supportive. The young people's commitment is admirable and the feedback from parents and schools indicates the level of change that can be achieved.

## Multiple choice questions

1. Which young people may particularly benefit from art therapy in a group setting?

   a. Young people who find it difficult to express their feelings and struggle with relationships?
   b. Young people who protect themselves by withdrawing from the world and not mixing with others?
   c. Young people who have a particular artistic talent?
   d. Young people whose parents are very dependent on them through issues such as mental ill health or domestic violence?
   e. Young people who are suffering long-term illnesses such as degenerative loss of hearing and brain tumours?

2. DW Winnicott states that the three-way process between client, therapist and materials is central to the development of what?

   a. The therapeutic area
   b. The potential space
   c. The artistic landscape
   d. The therapeutic milieu
   e. The healing process

## Key texts

Dalley T (1996) *Art as Therapy*. London: Routledge.

Winnicott DW (1971) *Playing and Reality*. London: Penguin.

# 67 Play therapy

Sarah Holden and Susie Dutton

## Key concepts

- Play Therapy is suitable for children aged 2.5–12 years.
- Play and toys are a child's primary form of communication.
- Materials are selected: a) to match developmental stages of play; and b) to encourage children to express feelings.
- Change happens through the therapeutic relationship with the therapist.
- Given the opportunity, children have an innate desire to resolve difficulties.
- Play Therapy can help presenting problems such as aggression, impulsivity, isolation, low mood arising from, for example, loss, trauma, abuse, neglect, illness, disability.
- Treatment can be short or long term, non-directive or with a focused approach.
- Consistency is vital. Sessions should be with the same Play Therapist at a regular time and in the same place.
- Active work with parent/carer alongside Play Therapist is desirable.

## Introduction

- Play is central to human development and enables a child to express bodily activity, repetition of experience and demonstrate fantasy in preparation for life.
- Through play, children develop motor and cognitive skills, language, emotional and behavioural responses, social competence and morals, as well as coping and problem-solving skills, in the context of the ecological environment.
- The British Association of Play Therapists defines play therapy as: 'The dynamic process between child and play therapist, in which the child explores, at his own pace and with his or her own agenda, those issues past and current that are affecting the child's life in the present. The child's inner resources are enabled by the therapeutic alliance to bring about growth and change. Play therapy is child centered, whereby play is the primary medium and speech is the secondary medium.'

Play therapy practice has developed in the UK over the past 25 years, with post-graduate level training established around 1993. Trained Play Therapists can apply for full membership of two regulating bodies, British Association of Play Therapists (BAPT) and Play Therapy UK (PTUK), who are currently seeking joint membership of the Health Professionals Council.

Play Therapy training is underpinned by theories and research that help the therapist make sense of the child's play as it unfolds. They include, for example, normal and atypical child and adolescent development (Meadows, 1992), trauma (Van Der Kolk et al., 1999), attachment theory (Bowlby, 1973), neuroscience (Panksepp, 2004), and theories of play therapy (Axline, 1989; West, 1996; Landreth, 2002). Non-directive play therapy is rooted in person-centred therapy (Rogers, 1976) and developed further in the UK by, among others, Cattanach (2008a; Cattanach, 2008b), Jennings (1999) and Wilson and Ryan (2005).

## Who can benefit?

Play therapy can be helpful for youngsters of all ages, but is most often used for children aged 2.5 to about 12 years, whose development is delayed or arrested as a result of presenting problems such as:

- trauma, neglect, abuse;
- loss through bereavement, family breakdown or separation from culture of origin;
- witnessing/experience of domestic abuse or parental substance misuse;
- behaviour/emotional difficulties arising from their experiences.

## What happens in play therapy?

Current Play Therapy practice, although rooted in the non-directive approach (Axline, 1989) can be on a continuum from non-directive to focused therapy. Those who use focused activities, for example with a bereaved child, may choose a storybook with a relevant theme, a board game or a creative activity to help the child make sense of their loss.

### Assessment

Play Therapy assessment is undertaken to ensure that it is the most appropriate form of treatment for the child and that the carer(s) can commit to supporting the child through therapy. Ideally, another professional works in parallel with the carers to help them manage any issues arising from the child's sessions. Sometimes the carer is trained to replicate the therapeutic play relationship after therapy ends with the child (Van Fleet and Gurney, 2003).

Good communication with the wider network is important and consistency and reliability is vital for the child to gain maximum benefit from the therapy. The sessions are weekly, at the same time and venue, with planned holiday breaks. Depending on the referral, play therapy can be 6–10 sessions, or can last up to, or over, a year. Regular reviews are held and endings are always carefully planned.

### Why 'play' in therapy?

Play is a vital part of child development promoting socialization, gross and fine motor skills, emotional and social intelligence, empathy, reflection, problem solving, creativity, initiative and resilience to stress.

The therapy room is equipped with a variety of toys and creative art materials selected to match developmental stages of play and to encourage children to express feelings. The child is not judged or rushed and can experiment without fear of criticism, thereby giving them control over their healing.

He/she is free to play about issues and may choose materials as symbolic representation of people and events:

- clay, playdoh slime, sand and water encourage sensory play, allowing the child to regress to preverbal experiences and to express emotions difficult to articulate;
- art and craft allows the child to externalize and represent inner feelings;
- projective play and use of puppets, little figures, toy animals and dolls, help children to make up stories and offer the opportunity to explore real life experiences at a safe distance, using metaphor and symbolism;
- role play and dressing up offers them the chance to play out scenes and take control of the narration;
- musical instruments are useful for all children, but particularly those with limited verbal ability or learning difficulties;
- carefully chosen books with themes relating to the child's own experiences can help them identify with the story and validate their feelings.

## Outcomes

Outcomes will vary depending upon each child's situation and the support offered in his wider environment.

The aim is that therapy will lead to changes in the child's behaviour and a more positive view of themselves, promoting self-esteem, confidence, emotional regulation, healthier relationships with others and a greater ability to problem solve, innovate and be willing to experiment. The child can try out different scenarios until they reach a healthier understanding of their experiences.

There is a growing body of research and evidence from the US and UK which supports the beneficial effects of Play Therapy, when assessed as an appropriate treatment (Mining Report, 2011) and

research on eliciting the child's view of therapy (Jaeger, 2010).

---

## Case study 1: Megan

Megan (8) was referred to CAMHS because of her distractible, impulsive behaviour, difficulty in relationships and angry outbursts in her foster home. The psychiatric assessment considered the presenting behaviour alongside her traumatic early experiences, which had led to her being accommodated by the local authority for four years. Megan had witnessed her drug-dependent father severely abuse her mother and had suffered long periods of neglect when she was not fed or nappy changed. A possible diagnosis of attention deficit hyperactivity disorder (ADHD) was ruled out and, with a belief that her difficulties stemmed from attachment issues and early trauma, she was referred for Play Therapy.

During 18 months of therapy, Megan played out what she had seen, and worked through the developmental stages of play; making up for what she had missed in the parental home. These experiences were witnessed, acknowledged and validated by the therapist. The first 12 weeks consisted of extreme 'messy play,' mixing red paint and sand and enjoying the sensations. Later Megan used the dolls houses and figures to make sense of her current situation in the foster home and her contact with her mother (projective play). Finally, she used role play, making up scenarios which she controlled and in which she directed the therapist to follow her lead.

In parallel with the therapy, the foster carers were encouraged to allow Megan's play to regress at home. They gave her regular access to sand, water and 'gunge'. Work was undertaken with the carers and school staff to help them understand Megan's behaviour within the context of her early experiences. A gradual improvement in her behaviour at home was replicated at school, her concentration improved and she began to attend after-school clubs and cope with the social relationships this involved. At the close of individual therapy the carer was trained to continue to offer regular play sessions based on non-directive Play Therapy principles (Van Fleet and Gurney, 2003).

---

## Case study 2: George

George (4), who was already being treated by his Psychiatrist for ADHD, was referred for short-term Play Therapy following the sudden death of a favourite uncle. The concern was that his preoccupation with death went beyond the normal grief processes and his parents requested help to manage his behaviour, which included a disrupted night-time routine, periods of inconsolable crying and complete withdrawal from activities and peers at pre-school.

George was seen by the play therapist for six sessions, during which he played exclusively with dolls and figures, initially burying them all in the sand. He named each as members of his family, including his uncle. Gradually, those representing the people who were alive remained on top of the sand, while the 'uncle' was buried. The therapist then extended the work to include his parents, who were encouraged to allow George to express his feelings through these media at home. At the conclusion of therapy, his distress was less and his sleep patterns improved.

---

## Multiple choice questions

1. What is the primary role of a Play Therapist?

   a. To have fun in the play room with the child
   b. To help the child make sense of difficult life experiences and relationships
   c. To show parents how to play with their child
   d. To find out whether a child has been abused
   e. To show a child how to use the different toys and media

2. Who can benefit most from Play Therapy?

    a. All children up to age 16 years
    b. Any child who has experienced trauma and neglect
    c. Children with a learning difficulty
    d. Children aged 2.5–12 years who have difficult life experiences
    e. Children who have behaviour difficulties at school

3. Why Play Therapy rather than talking therapy?

    a. The Play Therapist prefers playing to talking
    b. Playing helps the child feel in control
    c. Play is the child's primary form of communication
    d. Expecting a child to sit and talk for an hour is unrealistic
    e. Children should have every opportunity to play.

4. What media would a Play Therapist make available to help the child access pre-verbal memories?

    a. Story books
    b. Sensory materials such as 'gunge' and sand
    c. Dressing up clothes
    d. Little animals
    e. Dolls

5. What were the original theoretical approaches underpinning non-directive Play Therapy?

    a. Lots of different theories
    b. Child/person centred
    c. Psychodynamic
    d. Social constructionist
    e. Systems theory

## Key texts

Cattanach A (2008a) *Narrative Approaches in Play Therapy with Children*, 2nd edn. London: Jessica Kingsley.

Cattanach A (2008b) *Play Therapy with Abused Children.* London: Jessica Kingsley.

Jennings S (1999) *Introduction to Developmental Play Therapy.* London: Jessica Kingsley.

# 68 Child psychotherapy

Miranda Passey

---

## Key concepts

- Projection and containment
- Transference
- Introjection

---

## Introduction

Child Psychotherapy derives from the ideas and psycho-analytic theories first created by Sigmund Freud and later elaborated on by Melanie Klein and others (see Appendix). The professional association was founded in 1949 and the first formal training was presided over by Dr John Bowlby at the Tavistock Clinic. Today, Child Psychotherapists form part of the multidisciplinary team in many Child Guidance settings.

## Projection and containment

We all use projection. It is the mechanism whereby painful feelings are transferred from ourselves to others, to rid ourselves of those feelings or sometimes, to communicate our distress in a primitive way. For example, a baby crying is projecting the feeling that 'someone must do something to help me'. We are meant to find this unbearable and be moved to action. Similarly, in therapy, the child may project all kinds of feelings into the therapist in the hope that his experience will be received and understood. Because traumatized children may have had terrible experiences, which they have not been able to make sense of, they are left terrorized and in the grip of often unbearable states of mind, acute mental pain or confusion.

The therapist's task is to attempt to contain and hold in mind these feelings, while refraining from

action. This is often extremely difficult as with very disturbed children projection of feelings may involve shouting, screaming or physical violence, all designed to give the therapist a taste of how it might feel to be a terrorized child. When the therapist creates a space to think, these experiences can be reflected on and, when appropriate, shared with the child. However, the first crucial therapeutic tool is this capacity to receive and contain in oneself the distress, muddled confusion or despair of the child, and not to set some premature 'task', goal or activity, which would serve to keep the 'message' at arms length. The experience of being contained can be some children's first experience of someone struggling to understand and give meaning to their most raw experiences. This, by itself, is therapeutic.

## Transference

Unthought-about, unprocessed events that have frightened or troubled us remain with us. They emerge in unexplained fears, in nightmares or in apparently random fixed likes or dislikes. A child psychotherapist pays careful attention to the living relationship, or lack of it, created with her by her patients. They can expect that the child's earliest important relationships will be re-enacted and repeated in the present, transferred onto the therapist and re-experienced by the child in therapy. This process is facilitated by the fact that the therapist is receptive and open to what the child brings, rather than directing what happens or shaping what the child chooses to do. As Hunter (2001) puts it 'the child is not jollied out of their hostility or seduced from their distrust', but instead negative feelings are acknowledged and accepted when they emerge. Over time, by means of the new, constantly re-examined relationship that the psychotherapist makes with the child, the child's way of seeing the world and his expectations of it can be changed and modified.

Children who have been sexually abused, for example, will often at some time demonstrate that they expect (often with weary cynicism), to be abused in the therapy. This 'transference' can provide powerful, living evidence of the child's experiences. Faced with a child inviting her to abuse them, a therapist's task is to put into words what the child expects and fears. The therapist might find herself saying something like: 'I think you are showing me that deep down, this is what you feel all adults want from you. And you feel I am no different'. Or 'You can't imagine that there might be any different way to be with a grown-up who is interested in you'.

It may take many months, or even years, before such a child can begin to trust, to reconstruct painful memories and experience rightful anger, outrage and sorrow. While being understood brings relief, it often brings emotional pain, as the capacity to feel is rediscovered. Re-visited painful experiences will show themselves in disturbances or outbursts in the therapy room. However, a child who has become more 'emotionally alive' is freed to experience life in a much richer way, for example to become more able to learn, to respond to parental love and concern, to take in ideas at school and to make fulfilling friendships.

can begin to believe that knowing about other people's minds is worthwhile. His painful experiences, once mourned, cease to have their destructive impact on the present and can be allowed to recede to the past, allowing more room for the relationships of the here and now.

Freud described how mental pain is expressed as anxiety. This anxiety causes us to develop defences against the pain. These defences in turn can cause symptoms. A Child Psychotherapist may be asked to help when a child is suffering from serious emotional problems which cannot be easily understood or resolved, which are inhibiting normal healthy development and spoiling relationships. The work involves trying to understand and describe the child's defences and helping the child to become more aware of the hidden pain these defences were designed to conceal or avoid. Slowly the child can develop a greater understanding of himself and of his fears and feelings and reclaim buried experiences. The primary focus of the work is the unconscious: the hidden, inner world of feelings and experiences that lies inside all of us but is not available to conscious awareness. This inner world is usually only known to us through our dreams.

Many of the children we see are suffering from developmental trauma in response to deprivation, separation or loss, and many are 'looked-after' children. By understanding and bringing to light buried pain and confusion, and exploring the unique meanings which each child has attached to their experience, Child Psychotherapy can help the child to see reality more as it is. As a result, they are more able to learn and to use the support on offer from parents or other carers, because they are no longer 'locked' in the grip of their past experiences.

## Introjection

Over time, if therapy goes well, the child discovers a greater capacity to think and understand. He can struggle more and more to make sense of his feelings and notice his different states of mind. This capacity comes from the experience of his relationship with a therapist, who has struggled to understand him and has not enacted his fears and expectations of relationships (e.g. that he would be misunderstood or rejected), but has given him something different. The child can use his mind and

## The setting for therapy

Crucial attention is paid to the setting for child psychotherapy. Children are seen in the same room, at the same time each week, over a sustained period of months or years. The room is safe and as free as possible from any of the therapist's personal possessions and with minimal 'no-go areas', to allow for exploration. There is often access to water and/or sand. Each child is provided with a sturdy box in which to keep the play materials for their exclusive use. These materials form part of the child's 'language' or 'tool box' for therapy, facilitating exploration and the opportunity to make sense of their experience.

Typically the box will contain paper, pens and crayons, family dolls, wild and domestic animals, building blocks or Duplo, fences, small cars and trucks, string, glue, sellotape, scissors, plasticene or playdoh and a soft ball. Whatever the child creates stays in the box. The meaning that is attached to whatever is made resides within the therapy. It may often be revisited as the child begins to change and can reflect in a different way and notice his different feelings. The room becomes a safe, private place where deep feelings can be explored and held. The therapist ensures the safety of the child and of herself, for example sometimes having to stop sessions until the next time, if the child's violence or fear of his feelings cannot allow him to continue within safe bounds for that day.

It is crucial for the success of therapy that there is both support for the child and regular support for his parents or carers. A child needs an ally who will help him to come for regular sessions, even when he is reluctant or apprehensive. This may be a social worker or family support worker. Parents need to feel there is someone to help them to make sense of what they are feeling and what their child is going through, and to keep pace with changes in the child.

## What happens in the therapy session

### Assessment

A child will have three or more assessment sessions to establish whether this work may be of help to him and give him a taste of what psychotherapy involves. Children who come for psychotherapy will often have had previous forms of intervention, perhaps in a family context, which in itself can be a form of screening.

Child psychotherapists aim to allow the child to express and describe his unique picture of the world and his relationships within it, by means of play, drawing, words or other behaviour in the therapy room. They believe that this internal picture of our world is not just created by our actual experiences, but that it is also altered by what we have made of them, because of the unconscious ideas (known as 'phantasies') that we have attached to that experience.

Psychotherapy can bring these phantasies to light. For example, a child who has suffered the loss of a parent or sibling often secretly believes that they caused this loss or damage, because of their own behaviour. This belief can be compounded by the even more unconscious knowledge that he has, at times, felt full of hatred and anger towards that lost person or indeed at times wished, for example, that his infuriating sibling had not even been born. Once this unconscious version of events can be seen, described and shared, it can also be thought about by both therapist and child. Once it has been thought about, traumatized children can slowly begin to think about themselves and their states of mind, rather than just reacting to anticipated events, or remaining convinced that their version of events is the only one, or automatically 'blocking out' the attempts of concerned adults to get through to them. In the words of Hunter (2001) they can become 'master of their own house'.

Because many disturbed and traumatized children cannot 'play', Child Psychotherapists have to use their capacity to observe minute details of behaviour and shifts of feeling, in addition to interpreting the meaning of play or drawings, in a more conventional way. They often find themselves treating children who are so disturbed, for example autistic and severely learning disabled children (Sinason, 1992), that other forms of therapy from other professionals, which rely on more traditional forms of communication, have not been helpful for them. Child psychotherapists work with parents, families, mother–infant couples and groups, children and adolescents, and not only one-to-one with patients.

They can offer support and consultations to foster parents and groups of staff working with troubled children and young people.

## Training

Child Psychotherapists undergo a long and rigorous post-graduate training. An MA followed by four years clinical training and a doctorate leads to membership of the Association of Child Psychotherapists. This is the regulating body for standards and ethics in the UK.

## Personal therapy

The fundamental core of the training is the trainee's own intensive personal psychotherapy. This ensures that, so far as possible, undigested issues from the therapist's own experience and history are not transferred into their work with their patients. In-depth work with deeply troubled children can stir up very powerful and primitive feelings and anxieties. Therapists have to prove over this long training that they can contain, and struggle to think about, extremely disturbing events and states of mind that their patients bring to them.

## Supervision

All Child Psychotherapists have regular supervision so that their work can be shared and explored. This remains an essential part of good practice.

Alongside the study of formal theory and technique, the third cornerstone of the training is the Infant and Young Child Observation. This is the detailed observation, for an hour a week, of the first two years of an infant's life, within the context of his family and relationships. An under-five-year-old child is also observed for one year. Written-up observations are discussed in weekly seminars, providing a lived experience of each child's unique emotional development. Here the student also develops the capacity for in-depth detailed observation and learns a richer understanding of the unconscious meaning behind our actions and responses.

## Case study 1: Work with a school-age child (Tracey)

Tracey was six years old when I started work with her. The work lasted for two years. She had been left in the care of a mentally ill and sexually abused mother when she was two and her parents separated. During this time, she was sexually abused by the maternal grandfather and left with a mother who was alternately groggy with medication or 'smothering', insisting that Tracey sleep in her bed. When the abuse and inadequate care came to light, Tracey was removed into local authority care and eventually, aged five, placed with her father, who had returned to the area. Tracey's father had severe health problems of his own. Tracey was referred for help because she was failing to learn at school and had inappropriately touched other children. She suffered from nightmares.

In therapy, Tracey presented a brittle, superior, almost manic facade, keeping up a running commentary 'look at me how clever I am', and being frantically busy, making imaginary meals, doing acrobatics and singing and dancing. It felt as though this was to ward off any kind of sadness, any real contact or dialogue with me, or any awareness of her own limitations. By contrast, I felt heavy and stupid, and often unable to think or follow what was happening. I wondered if I was being 'made' to feel like a drugged, mentally ill mother or like a confused impotent and bewildered Tracey, faced with behaviour she could not make sense of.

Because Tracey had been abused and terrified as a small child, life experience had taught her to be cynical about adults and to fear any real close connection with them. She showed me that it did not feel safe to stop for a moment or relax her guard. She could not allow anything 'in' from me, because it might turn out to be abusive or dangerous. This closed-off quality accordingly severely impeded her capacity to learn. At times, I felt under great pressure to join in and admire her as a miracle 'performing child' and to forget the embracing sadness I felt when I was with her, and that she could not read or write or even do simple sums. The painful task was to help her make more contact with her fear and terror and underlying sadness, and to remember some of the frightening and confusing experiences she had undergone. She could then be helped to differentiate between then and now and to make more use of me to help her think and become more reflective about her real needs and difficulties.

In one moving session, after many months of manic activity, Tracey made a 'bed' for herself with the rug and pillow I had provided for her. She allowed herself to lie quietly and to have an experience of being contained and thought about, as I sat at a safe distance and spoke to her gently.

As some of her past experiences could be played out, and thought about, Tracey became more able to take things in and learn at school. As she changed, her father became more aware of the real vulnerability beneath her brittle, premature grown-up facade, and began to feel braver to challenge her and provide firmer boundaries, to which Tracey responded with relief. She began to heal and to be able to trust again.

## Case study 2: Parent–infant work (Jane)

Jane came for help because she felt depressed and overwhelmed by her six-month-old daughter who she felt cried without stopping and 'did not like her'. When she began to explore her own experience of mothering in childhood with the therapist a painful story emerged of her own depressed and overwhelmed mother, who sent Jane away to be cared for by an aunt for the first year of her life. Jane experienced her baby's gestures towards her as hostile and would flinch when her baby reached out to touch her face. Slowly the therapist helped Jane to separate out her past experience of being given up by her own mother and voice her fears about her mother's dislike of her, so that she could distinguish between these experiences and her own real six-month-old daughter. Their relationship began to improve with mutual enjoyment and the little girl began to thrive and cried much less.

## Case study 3: Work with an adolescent (Sarah)

Sarah came for help because she was struggling with self-harm and furious outbursts at school and at home. Her parents had separated and she could not accept her mother's new partner or find her place in two newly constituted families. With the therapist's support, she was able to come to terms with her powerful jealousy and possessiveness and to understand her wish to control everything because of her fear of being abandoned. Gradually she could allow herself to be more separate from her mother, to develop and learn more at school, to voice her fears and worries rather than expressing them by means of cutting her arms, and her relationships improved.

## Multiple choice questions

1. Child Psychotherapy addresses what is going on in:

    a. The external world of the child
    b. The internal world of the child
    c. Both external and internal

2. Child Psychotherapy attempts to help the child explore and change:

    a. Other people
    b. Their own view of the world and relationships
    c. Learn coping strategies

3. Child Psychotherapy training lasts for:

    a. One year
    b. Three years
    c. Six to eight years

4. Child psychotherapy draws on:

    a. The work of Freud and Melanie Klein
    b. The work of John Bowlby on attachment
    c. Both the above

*Key texts*

Hunter M (2001) *Psychotherapy with Children In Care: Lost and Found*. Hove, East Sussex: Brunner-Routledge.

Lanyado M, Horne A (eds) (1990) *The Handbook of Child and Adolescent Psychotherapy*. London and New York: Routledge.

Sinason V (1992) *Mental Handicap and the Human Condition*. London: Free Association Books.

For further information, contact the Association of Child Psychotherapists, at 120 West Heath Road London NW3 7TU or www.acp-uk.eu

# 69 Counselling children and young people

Jacquie Kelly

---

## Key concepts

- A belief that each individual has the potential to make positive changes.
- A holistic approach, considering the whole person, rather than a specific problem or diagnosis.
- Understanding the young person's way of seeing their experiences, suspending own judgements and opinions.
- Openness and honesty, relating to a young person as a real human being.
- A trusting relationship, being reliable, consistent and clear about limits of confidentiality.
- Challenge when appropriate.
- Awareness of own power as an adult in the relationship.
- Regularly reviews with the young person how counselling is progressing.

---

Although the term 'counselling' can be used for a wide range of helping activities, and many professional disciplines, such as nursing and social work, might include counselling in their role, counselling itself is a specific kind of therapy, which is widely used with young people. Counsellors are trained according to a variety of different theories which have been developed since the 1940s, growing out of the traditions of psychoanalysis. Ways of categorizing counselling usually distinguish the theoretical approach used, and a broad distinction might be between psychodynamic, cognitive–behavioural and humanistic approaches. An integrative counsellor might use any of these, depending on their training, and on what they feel would benefit the client.

There is some debate about the distinction between counselling and psychotherapy, because many practitioners use the terms interchangeably, while others would distinguish counselling as shorter-term work or involving shorter training than psychotherapy.

In Britain, the biggest national body for counsellors is the British Association for Counselling and Psychotherapy (BACP), which has its own process of accreditation for counsellors, supervisors and training courses, and a code of practice called the 'Ethical Framework for Good Practice in Counselling and Psychotherapy' (BACP, 2010).

Counselling training involves between three and five years part-time study, leading to qualification at Diploma, Degree or Masters Level. Trainees are required to complete at least 100 hours of supervised counselling practice, and most courses require students to undertake their own personal therapy.

All counsellors are required to receive regular supervision where they can discuss their work, and to keep their practice updated with regular professional development.

## Humanistic counselling

There are several counselling approaches which fall within the category of Humanistic counselling, including Person-Centred, Gestalt, Transactional Analysis and Existential. These approaches share a belief in the individual client's potential for positive change, what Carl Rogers, the founder of the Person-Centred Approach, calls the 'self-actualizing tendency' (Rogers, 1961). Rogers believed that it is a counsellor's responsibility to provide the environment for a relationship to develop in which the client can achieve this potential, and he identified essential qualities ('Core Conditions', see Box 69.1) which enable the counsellor to provide this environment.

Box 69.1 Rogers' Core Conditions

- Empathy: understanding the client's experience, meanings and world view
- Unconditional Positive Regard: accepting and validating the client as an individual person, suspending judgements, opinions and values
- Congruence: being open, being themselves and challenging when appropriate

# Counselling children and young people

The BACP Ethical Framework highlights the specialized nature of work with young people:

*The practitioner is required to consider and assess the balance between young people's dependence on adults and carers and their progressive development towards acting independently.*

**(BACP, 2010, p.6)**

A key part of humanistic counselling is understanding and working with the power dynamics within the relationship, to empower the client to make their own decisions and take autonomous responsibility for themselves. Young people have little control in many aspects of their lives; they are financially dependent on others and, developmentally, the younger they are, the less maturity they have to make decisions. This means that issues of power are central and developing life-skills in decision-making and negotiating relationships is crucial. Humanistic counselling provides an ideal way of helping young people to make sense of their lives and their relationships with family, teachers and peers.

It is important that the young person can understand the counselling process and be sufficiently able, cognitively and in terms of maturity, to talk about what they are experiencing. For young people who find it difficult to express themselves, and particularly with younger children, counsellors use creative techniques, art materials, toys or worksheets (using these media is not the same as Play Therapy or Art Psychotherapy – see Chapter 66, Art therapy and Chapter 67, Play therapy), and it is essential to assess when one of these other interventions may be more appropriate). Specialist counsellors offer counselling to young people with learning disabilities, taking into account the client's cognitive and verbal abilities, and ensuring that they can take an autonomous part in the therapy.

# Counselling and mental health

Counsellors take a holistic approach to problems that a client is facing, exploring physical, environmental, emotional and psychological factors. Therefore, mental health problems are seen in the context of the whole person, and this is particularly important in working with children and young people, where developmental issues have such an impact. For instance, a counsellor working with a young person showing symptoms of depression might help them to understand how environmental, interpersonal and emotional factors affect their mood, while considering the hormonal changes of adolescence and other aspects of growing up, for instance changing relationships with parents.

Counselling is not helpful for young people with impaired cognitive functioning (such as may be associated with severe anorexia), who do not have a sufficiently clear sense of self (as with psychosis), or where the expression of feelings may exacerbate symptoms (e.g. obsessive–compulsive disorder (OCD), phobias).

# The counselling process

Counselling forms a one-to-one relationship, based on developing increasing trust. The safer a young person feels, the more honestly they can express themselves and the more effective counselling will be in addressing their real issues. If they understand how counselling works, they can be active and feel safe in the therapeutic process. Sessions are held in private, at a regular, agreed time, usually on a weekly basis. Counsellors begin by explaining limits of confidentiality, practical arrangements, and how the counselling will be reviewed and end.

Using active listening skills, the counsellor encourages the young person to tell their story in their own way and at their own pace. The counsellor tries to understand how they see their problems, what brings them to counselling now and what they would like to achieve. Through this exploration, the client understands themselves and their problems more clearly and is supported to make decisions about changes or action they want to take in their lives.

Regular reviews help the counsellor and client see how the counselling is progressing. This involves feedback from the young person and the counsellor, relating back to the goals agreed at the beginning. This will inform whether further sessions are required, or whether some other interventions are indicated in addition to, or instead of, counselling. Work with young people may be short or long term. Endings are part of the counselling process, and counsellors offer the opportunity to review and say goodbye.

## Outcomes

Outcomes will depend on what the young person wants to achieve, but in general would include increasing their:

- understanding of themselves, their problems and others;
- ability to make links between experiences, feelings and behaviour;
- ability to make decisions and take responsibility in their lives;
- development of interpersonal and relationship skills;
- self-esteem and self-confidence.

### Case study: Emily

Emily is a 17-year-old girl, referred to an adolescent mental health service, and assessed as suffering from low mood. She cut her arms, and had taken two overdoses of paracetamol. Her mother had died from cancer two years before, and she lived with her father and younger brother.

She was referred to Jo, a counsellor in the team. Jo started by trying to understand how Emily saw the issues in her life. Emily explained that she was struggling with her college work, felt low in confidence and self-esteem, and had left home, and was staying at various friends' houses. She felt very low because she didn't feel she belonged anywhere and didn't feel like she had a future.

Over the next few months, Emily attended her counselling sessions sporadically, and Jo found it difficult to contact her because she had no permanent address and didn't have money for credit on her phone. Emily missed many appointments, but gradually she was able to explain more of her story. Her relationship with her father, which had been good when Emily was a child, had deteriorated since her mother's death, as her father had found it hard to cope and was himself suffering from depression. Emily felt her friends didn't understand how she felt and she was unable to talk to anyone about how she was feeling.

Through talking with Jo, Emily realised the importance of sharing her feelings and how isolated she had become since her mother's death. Jo explained to her about the emotional effects of bereavement, and Emily was able to see how these had affected not only her, but her father and brother as well. They explored ways of opening up ways of communicating with her family and getting support from friends and tutors at college.

At first Emily found it very difficult to talk about her self-harm, but through counselling she came to understand that it was a coping mechanism she was using to communicate how bad she was feeling when she couldn't talk directly to her friends and family. As her relationships with other people improved, Emily decided to stop self-harming and she found ways to express her difficult feelings to others more directly.

When she finished counselling, Emily said that she had gained more understanding of herself, and learnt that her feelings and behaviour were natural reactions to the traumatic loss of her mother. She also had more understanding for her father and brother and together they were rebuilding their family relationships, with Emily staying at home a few nights a week. Emily said that the most important thing about counselling for her was that Jo did not judge her behaviour, and that she stuck by her and didn't stop the sessions when she found it difficult to attend. She said that Jo was 'there for her' and that she felt better about herself because Jo treated her like a worthwhile person, even if she didn't always feel that about herself.

## Multiple choice questions

1. One of the counsellor's main aims is to:

   a. Sort out a young person's problem for them
   b. Give a young person advice about their problem
   c. Understand how the young person sees their problem
   d. Assess what is wrong with the young person
   e. Make a clinical diagnosis

2. A counsellor creates a trusting relationship with a young person by:

   a. Agreeing with the client
   b. Being honest and being themselves
   c. Promising to keep everything confidential
   d. Giving them their personal mobile phone number, in case they need to talk to someone between the counselling sessions
   e. Telling the child's parents what they talked about in their counselling session

3. Which of the following is not true?

   a. A young person can benefit from counselling, even if they don't know what their problem is
   b. If a young person doesn't want to speak to anyone, they should still be made to attend counselling
   c. People with learning disabilities can benefit from counselling
   d. Counselling is not appropriate for children and young people who can't understand cognitively what counselling is
   e. Counselling may not be appropriate for young people with severe anxiety, such as OCD

4. A key outcome for counselling with children and young people is:

   a. They will definitely get solutions to their problems
   b. They will learn that they need to let their parents make important decisions in their lives
   c. They will realize their problems are not as bad as they thought
   d. They will have a greater understanding of themselves and their relationships with other people
   e. Their bad behaviour will improve

## Key texts

BACP (2010) *Ethical Framework for Good Practice in Counselling and Psychotherapy*, revised edn. Lutterworth: British Association for Counselling and Psychotherapy.

Culley S, Bond T (2004) *Integrative Counselling Skills in Action*, 2nd edn. London: Sage.

Geldard K, Geldard D (2008) *Counselling Children: A Practical Introduction*, 3rd edn. London: Sage.

Rogers C (1961) *On Becoming a Person: A Therapist's View of Psychotherapy*, London: Constable.

## Web pages

www.bacp.co.uk
www.youthaccess.org.uk

# 70 Counselling psychology

Sarah Robotham

**Key concepts**

- An emphasis on the helping relationship as a significant and powerful variable in promoting and facilitating therapeutic change, with a specific focus on the quality of the relationship within the therapeutic endeavour.
- A movement towards a humanistic and existential value base that stresses the validity of subjective experience, self-determination and individual responsibility.
- A focus on facilitating well-being rather than responding to illness and pathology.

## Introduction

Psychology is the scientific study of the human mind and behaviour. Counselling Psychology examines mental health difficulties and disorders and explores the underlying problems that may have caused and contributed to these.

Counselling Psychology in the UK is a relatively new area of professional applied psychology. It has a longer and more established history in the United States.

Counselling Psychologists are concerned with the integration of psychological theory and research with therapeutic practice, in the role of scientist–practitioner that demands the acquisition of skills in research and practice and scientific methods underpinning Counselling Psychology. The scientist–practitioner model also demands that these skills be integrated coherently, using continual self-reflection and self-improvement.

## Settings

Counselling Psychologists work across a wide variety of settings: in education, industry and commerce, the prison service and healthcare. Approximately 50 per cent of all trained Counselling Psychologists undertake clinical work in health and social care in the public sector and increasingly work in private practice. They are employed to work

as lecturers, teachers, supervisors and researchers in academic settings or work as consultants. Counselling Psychologists are employed to work not only directly with individuals but also with families, couples and groups.

## What do Counselling Psychologists do?

The practice of Counselling Psychology demands a high level of self-awareness and self-reflection in the application of psychological theory to clinical practice. Knowledge of interpersonal dynamics and the ways in which these affect the therapeutic relationship or context are important.

Counselling Psychologists are trained to undertake a number of key tasks that vary according to their role within the organization in which they work. These include the following.

### Psychological assessment

An assessment of needs and current risk. This may also include psychological testing and feedback of results.

### Psychological formulation

A hypothesis of the person's difficulties, drawing upon psychological theory:

- therapeutic work: planning and implementation;
- record keeping;
- report writing;
- outcome and audit evaluation;
- supervision and training;
- research.

Responsibilities can involve:

- working as part of a multidisciplinary team;
- management duties;
- service organization and development.

Different approaches to Counselling Psychology exist. The major paradigms are broadly defined as humanistic, psychodynamic, cognitive–behavioural, existential–phenomenological and systems approaches. Other approaches include feminist, transpersonal, constructivist, eclectic and integrative ways of working. Counselling Psychologists differ as to the ways in which they view well-being and emotional disturbance, with the preferred theoretical orientation influencing the kind of therapeutic intervention the professional makes.

## The therapeutic relationship

For the Counselling Psychologist, regardless of therapeutic orientation, the therapeutic relationship, also known as the working alliance or therapeutic alliance, is undisputedly central to the work. Roger's (1951) work on the therapeutic relationship characterizes a helping relationship as one in which core conditions of empathy, acceptance and congruence are vital. Counselling Psychologists adhere to these values.

At the heart of Counselling Psychology lies the belief that the interaction within the therapeutic relationship ultimately helps clients in therapy to live more fulfilled and symptom-free lives, while enabling them to be self-directive in fulfilling their developmental goals. Rather than simply undertaking a prescribed course of treatment, Counselling Psychologists advocate a collaborative exploration of subjective experience within the therapeutic relationship where a greater understanding of difficulties is sought. Strawbridge and Woolfe (2003) note that: 'the notion of doing-something to clients is replaced by that of being-with clients'. In the therapeutic relationship the Counselling Psychologist does not assume superior

knowledge but is a collaborator in the therapeutic process.

## The scientist–practitioner model

The scientist–practitioner model in Counselling Psychology demands that the professional be adept at applying psychological knowledge to their clinical practice and synthesize research and practice in an integrated and scientific way. They must be capable of reflecting on their practice using a combination of supervision, continuing professional development, a self-critical stance and openness to experience (Strawbridge and Woolfe, 2003). While it may appear that the values of Counselling Psychology, for example valuing subjective experience are at odds with this model, the resulting creative tension offers opportunities for Counselling Psychologists to develop their professional identities and is an area of ongoing debate (Blair, 2010).

## Reflective practice

Reflective practice is a necessary and important part of Counselling Psychology training and professional development. It involves monitoring professional practice in process, both individually and with other practitioners, in addition to a commitment to personal development, where reviewing one's work with the application of self-awareness and an understanding of the subjective experience between the psychologist and the client is vital.

## Training

Counselling Psychologists undergo a rigorous postgraduate training that involves research, study, clinical work, supervision and personal psychotherapy. Basic counselling skills training and an undergraduate degree in Psychology that is recognized by the British Psychological Society (BPS) are often entry requirements for Counselling Psychology training.

Counselling Psychologists are registered with the Health Professionals Council (HPC), an independent, UK-wide health regulator which sets and maintains standards of professional training and performance across several healthcare professions. Requirements for registration with the HPC involve completion of a Professional Doctorate in Counselling Psychology or equivalent that has been approved by the BPS.

# Personal therapy

Self-development and personal therapy are significant components of the training. Together, these provide the Counselling Psychologist with an opportunity to explore potential vulnerabilities or 'blind spots' in the work which may stem from personal experiences. The level of emotional and psychological distress the Counselling Psychologist is likely to be exposed to through the work may be significant: an exploration of personal vulnerabilities and experiences is important and may lead to an increased understanding of the vulnerabilities of the client or patient (Jennings, 1996).

# Supervision

All Counselling Psychologists undertake supervision where work is shared and explored. The relational dynamics between supervisee and supervisor may mirror those within the relationship between the client and the psychologist. Supervision is an independent means of reviewing professional work so that insights can be gained. It is a setting in which ethical issues and the need for specialist support can be discussed, along with further opportunities for professional development such as learning by modelling and toleration of and learning from mistakes.

## Case study: Maria

Maria (15) was referred to CAMHS presenting with marked features of depression, including a lack of pleasure and interest in many areas of her life and a pattern of sleep disturbance. She had recently been prescribed anti-depressant medication by her local GP.

Maria met with the Counselling Psychologist for an initial assessment session. Maria revealed that she had experienced low mood for several months and that she was desperate to try anything that might help her feel differently. Maria stated she was not considering suicide and could not think of any recent events that might have caused her depression.

The Counselling Psychologist explained her way of working to Maria. It was explained that Maria's individual therapy was a place where she could share her thoughts and concerns and they could explore these together in order to help her understand more about the meaning of her troubles. They agreed to meet for 10 weeks of individual therapy at the same time each week and then review the work together at the end. Working as a humanistic Counselling Psychologist, in this initial meeting they looked at Maria's readiness and willingness to change and the Counselling Psychologist felt Maria was motivated to explore herself in the sessions

Together Maria and the Counselling Psychologist drew a family tree to better understand Maria's biographical context. Maria's father had died of cancer seven years ago and she lived at home with her mother, Sarah, and sister, Ruth (12). Maria described a good relationship with her sister but a poor relationship with her mother since the age of 12.

Throughout the course of the therapy the Counselling Psychologist listened actively to Maria's story and experiences, mindful of Carl Rogers' necessary conditions for therapeutic change; acceptance, empathy, and congruence. The Counselling Psychologist took a phenomenological stance in the work, valuing the meaning of the content Maria provided in the sessions.

They worked together at Maria's pace and followed the direction she wanted to explore. This seemed to allow Maria to open up and develop insight into her difficulties: she talked about experiencing a great deal of guilt over seemingly forgetting her father and a feeling of being a 'bad' daughter and sister. After a number of sessions, Maria asked the Counselling Psychologist directly about her own experiences within a mother–daughter relationship and, according to the humanistic approach, which perhaps permits more openness and transparency than other theoretical orientations, the Counselling Psychologist was able to reveal some of her personal feelings and values to Maria. This seemed an important turning point in the work, as Maria told the Counselling Psychologist it was at this stage she began to think of her as an individual rather than an 'expert', which facilitated Maria to start seeking her own answers to her difficulties.

Maria and the Counselling Psychologist started to think about her depression as stemming from unresolved loss and grief following the death of her father. Maria began to mourn his loss with the Counselling Psychologist and focus on her individual needs and hopes for the future, which included a more positive relationship with her mother.

Maria attended a total of 40 therapy sessions. In the latter phase of the work she became more focused on her own needs and set herself a number of tasks and goals, including talking to her mother about their relationship and spending more time with her mother and sister together as a triad to build relationships between them. At this stage of the work the Counselling Psychologist reflected at length on the ways in which Maria was approaching her problems in different and creative ways, in order to convey empathic understanding. The Counselling Psychologist was able to make some suggestions to Maria as she became more active and self-directive outside of the individual work.

At the end of the therapeutic work Maria's symptoms of depression had significantly reduced. She told the Counselling Psychologist that she had found the work valuable and that the Counselling Psychologist's willingness to be known by her had helped her more than she had hoped for. She felt she was beginning to look forward to things in her life again. Maria's involvement within the therapy and specifically as part of the therapeutic relationship demonstrates how Counselling Psychology working within the humanistic paradigm, and specifically the therapist's use of self and empathic understanding, can be applied to therapeutic work with depression.

## Multiple choice questions

1. Which of the following concepts is considered to be central to the work of a Counselling Psychologist?

   a. Diagnosis of a problem or a specific difficulty
   b. The therapeutic relationship
   c. Behavioural therapy

2. Which statement below best describes Reflective Practice in Counselling Psychology?

   a. The monitoring of professional practice in process, both individually and with other practitioners.
   b. Talking to the patient or client about the process of therapy
   c. The presentation of clinical cases to others

3. What are the core conditions that Carl Rogers (1951) believed characterized a therapeutic relationship as a helping relationship?

   a. Understanding and sympathy
   b. Empathy, acceptance and congruence
   c. Caring and empathy

### Key texts

Hammersley D (2003) Training and professional development in the context of Counselling Psychology. In: Woolfe R, Dryden W, Strawbridge S (eds). *Handbook of Counselling Psychology*, 2nd edn. London, UK: SAGE Publications, 637–55.

Walsh Y, Frankland A (eds) (2006) *Counselling Psychology Review*, 21(1). Special Edition: The First 10 Years. London: The British Psychological Society.

### Further information

British Psychological Society, St Andrews House, 48 Princess Road East, Leicester LE1 7DR. Tel: +44 (0)116 254 9568 Web: www.bps.org.uk Email: enquiries@bps.org.uk

# 71 *Applied behaviour analysis*
## Hanna Kovshoff

---

## Key concepts

- Functional analysis: understanding what is maintaining the child's behaviour
- In ABA, reinforcement is a more effective and long-term solution to problem behaviour than punishment
- In keeping with functional analysis:
- Change maintaining contingencies or add new contingencies to improve problem behaviour
- Use reinforcement of other behaviour
- Use 'extinction': ignore problem behaviours so they no longer produce reinforcement
- Use a 'time-out' procedure: remove the child from the situation in which he/she is creating a problem, and then return him/her without comment
- Children are less difficult to manage if a programme offers them consistency, predictable routines and clear boundaries.
- Give short and clear messages when something has to happen
- Anticipate difficult situations and give warnings
- Work hard to use positive ways of helping him/her to increase self-esteem
- Reinforce desired behaviour: positive praise for good things that have been achieved will encourage good behaviour

---

This chapter outlines the theory and practice of applied behaviour analysis (ABA).

## Understanding the functions of behaviour in applied settings

The key to understanding why certain behaviours occur in applied settings is an evaluation of the contingencies (the relationship between antecedents, behaviour and consequences; explained below) which promote and maintain behavioural repertoires within the environment. This interaction between behaviour and the environment in applied settings sits at the core of ABA methods. ABA is based on the principles of operant conditioning: behaviours which have particular (or reinforcing) consequences are selected, and will be repeated, become stronger, and endure for as long as they continue to produce reinforcement, even if the reinforcement does not occur reliably after every instance of the behaviour.

| EOS: | A | B | C |
|---|---|---|---|
| (Establishing Operations) | (Antecedent) | (Behaviour) | (Consequence) |

Each behaviour has a function. The consequences of a behaviour can increase, decease or leave unchanged, the likelihood of the behaviour occurring.

Antecedents refer to the environmental trigger, event or condition that sets the occasion for the occurrence of the behaviour. These antecedent stimuli control most of what we think of as 'everyday' behaviours. Antecedents are effective because they also predict the consequences of behaviour. Consequences follow behavioural instances and predict the probability that the particular behaviour will reoccur. These reinforcing stimuli are always dependent on the performance of the behaviour.

Through assessing and collecting information about antecedents, behaviours and consequences, along with modifying the environment, you can become aware of establishing operations. These are the social or behavioural conditions of satiation or deprivation that affect the reinforcing value of a consequence, and thus the power of antecedent cues that signal reinforcement's availability. An understanding of establishing operations is imperative to assessing or attempting to modify behaviour as it takes into account all of the social and biological conditions which may impact upon the relationship between antecedents, behaviours and consequences. For example, if you discovered that chocolate buttons were reinforcing for a child and attempted to use the buttons to encourage him to engage in a specific behaviour, the chocolate may not be reinforcing if the child had just eaten their lunch or indeed, had just polished off a packet of chocolate buttons!

Thus, behaviour can be changed either through manipulating the establishing operations, the antecedent stimuli, or the response to the behaviour, all of which can increase (reinforce) or decrease (punish) the probability of a behaviour occurring.

# Behavioural assessment

A comprehensive assessment of a child's behaviour must provide unambiguous information about the behaviour that is to be increased or decreased, and this behaviour must be observable and measurable. If a target behaviour is absent from the repertoire, the potential to observe and measure the behaviour must be possible. It is important to create an operational definition of the problem, maladaptive or absent target behaviour in objective and clear terms, including specific instances and examples of the behaviour as well as inclusion and exclusion criteria. For example, if the behaviour of biting other children in the playground is to be reduced, an operational definition may be: closing teeth and jaw on any part of another child's body and includes both instances of biting that do not cause damage and those that lead to pain, red marks or breaking of another child's skin. This excludes instances when the child opens their mouth and bares their teeth without making contact with another child's skin. Information (data) needs to be collected about the frequency (how often) and context in which the behaviour occurs (which environments, with which people, under what conditions). In doing so, one seeks to establish the functional relationship between establishing operations, antecedents and consequences and the behaviour in question. This can be achieved through conducting a functional analysis.

# Functional analysis

## Why conduct a functional analysis?

A functional analysis aims to identify what purpose a behaviour serves through identifying the environmental determinants of target behaviours. When initiating a functional analysis, it is important to identify the predominant problem or maladaptive behaviour and be mindful of establishing operations. ABA is most effective when a limited number of behaviours are targeted at any one time. In addition, a functional analysis can be most informative when the behaviour targeted for change is complex and the function is not so easily identifiable. If the behaviour is multipart, a task analysis may be conducted which seeks to break down complex sequences of behaviour into component parts whereby each part behaviour may be targeted for change in turn. For example, in teaching a child to wash their hands one would identify all of the component parts to washing the hands and teach each separately (e.g. turn on water tap, wet hands, squeeze soap dispenser, rub soap on both sides of hands, rinse soap from hands, turn off the water tap, dry hands with towel or hand dryer).

Typical functions of maladaptive behaviours usually include:

- escape/task avoidance;
- attention seeking/initiation of social interaction;

- tangibles – gaining desired objects or activities;
- sensory stimulation.

It is important to note that the target behaviour might serve multiple functions. In addition, while one function might be dominant, it is important to acknowledge and target any other lesser functions served by the behaviour to maximize the benefit of intervention.

# Identify behaviour

The identification of those behaviours most in need of change can be done through formal assessment or discussion with parents, teachers and significant others. Ideally, one would use systematic procedures to uncover the antecedent and consequent events that are leading to, and maintaining, the behaviour. This way, hypothesized reinforcement contingencies which control or maintain variables can be tested, manipulated and evaluated. In all cases, assessment must include direct observation of the individual displaying the behaviour. Not only must the maladaptive behaviour be identified clearly, but a desirable outcome must be agreed upon. Outcomes must be realistic and achievable. By producing an operational definition or description of the behaviour, the effectiveness of the intervention is maximized and the propensity of accurate and consistent measurement of the behaviour is increased.

# Recording

It is important first to identify any potential internal cause(s) of the behaviour to ensure that the behaviour is not a direct result of, for example, medical conditions (and/or medication), disrupted sleep patterns, emotional responses to traumatic events (bereavement, abuse) and so on. For accurate record-keeping, it is useful to identify whether the behaviour is pervasive, i.e. manifests itself in all aspects of the individual's life, or whether there are situations in which it is more likely to occur.

To establish an accurate function of the behaviour, observe and record the frequency, intensity and duration of each episode, along with the antecedents and consequences (ABCs) of each episode. When recording behaviours, be as creative

as is necessary to gain the relevant information which can later be tested through more systematic procedures, for example discuss the behaviours informally with teachers, parents and significant others. ABC charts can be completed by the practitioner, a significant other, and ideally by more than one individual for reliability purposes. It is also useful to record the time and date, the location of the incident, and who was present when the behaviour occurred, along with the antecedent, behaviour and consequence, in order to identify any significant patterns or trends.

If possible, the behaviours targeted for intervention should be observed on a number of separate occasions, and in as many situations as the behaviour occurs, noting of course that behaviour can be situation-specific. There is no specific length of time recommended over which to conduct these observations. However, recording should continue until a clearer understanding of the behaviour has been obtained. Behavioural assessment must also include assessment of the child's skills, particularly those skills which do, or might with encouragement, serve the same function for the child as the problem behaviour, by achieving similar results.

# Establishing function

Once a satisfactory amount of observation data has been recorded, look for trends in the frequency, intensity and duration of the behaviour targeted for change. In addition, look to see if there are any consistent establishing operations, antecedents and/or consequences, for example:

- Are the temper tantrums occurring when the child is tired/hungry/overstimulated?
- Do temper tantrums regularly follow a demand made by the parent to the child?
- Are the child's temper tantrums controlled by the removal of any demands?
- Do the temper tantrums occur when the parent's attention is on another child?

Once a hypothesized formulation has been developed, informal discussion with the child's significant others can be helpful in reaching a consensus. Meetings attended by professionals involved in the case can provide an opportunity to discuss the formulation with those who know the child well.

# Avenues for intervention

## Methods for increasing appropriate behaviour

One of the most frequently observed methods of modifying behaviour involves the use of reinforcement. Reinforcement can be defined as any consequence which, when it follows a behaviour, strengthens the probability of that behaviour re-occurring. Crucially, reinforcement is not the same thing as 'reward'. What is reinforcing for a particular child may not be for another (e.g. a shy child may not be positively reinforced through the use of social praise, and in actuality this may have detrimental effects). Reinforcers can be primary, secondary or social. A primary reinforcer is an immediate, tangible reward, for example food, drink, toys, hugs, high-fives and so on. A secondary reinforcer is a 'means to an end' form of reinforcement whereby, for example, the individual 'earns' tokens or money which can then be exchanged for primary reinforcers. Secondary social reinforcement includes attention for appropriate behaviour.

When selecting a reinforcer for use in an intervention programme, it is often advisable to collaborate with the individual to design a realistic and meaningful reinforcement system. It is imperative that the reinforcement used in the intervention programme is meaningful to the individual to maximize its reinforcing potential; otherwise it will not function as a reinforcer. A reward that has little significance or reinforcing value to the child will be ineffective in producing the desired change in behaviour and results will be negligible. The reinforcing value of a particular reward may vary over time and with establishing operations, so it is important in designing intervention programmes to consider that reinforcers may need to be modified.

## Positive reinforcement

When a positive reinforcer follows a behaviour, the behaviour is strengthened. Examples of practical applications of positive reinforcement in the modification of maladaptive behaviours include differential reinforcement of other behaviour programmes (DRO, see below), and token economies.

# DRO/DRA/DRI programmes

These intervention programmes involve the positive reinforcement of more appropriate responses to antecedents or consequences, which ordinarily would have pre-empted the undesirable behaviour. For example, if a child has previously learned that getting out of his seat in class and throwing a temper tantrum is effective in gaining attention from a teacher, the implementation of a DRO programme (differential reinforcement of other behaviour) would involve reinforcing behaviour other than the tantrum. In other words, reinforcement would occur if the target behaviour is not occurring. This would most likely be paired with the 'planned ignoring' of temper tantrum behaviour. However, this procedure would not necessarily teach the child appropriate behaviour to use to gain attention in place of the tantrum behaviour.

A DRI programme (differential reinforcement of incompatible behaviour) would seek to positively reinforce behaviours that are physically incompatible with the target behaviour. In the example above, the child may be actively reinforced for sitting in his seat, a behaviour incompatible with getting out of his seat. With a DRA programme (differential reinforcement of alternative behaviour) more appropriate methods of gaining a desired outcome are reinforced such that in the example above, positive methods of gaining attention such as raising a hand in class would be reinforced. Note that selecting alternative behaviours that are already in the child's repertoire aids the rapid learning of new, adaptive responses. Differential reinforcement programmes are often used within schools and clinical settings as they allow teachers and clinicians to gain effective control over a maladaptive behaviour without specifically intervening on the problem behaviour. Moreover, the use of positive reinforcement to develop skills and appropriate behaviour is very effective, and these methods have been used with a wide range of problem behaviours including antisocial, disruptive and self-injurious behaviours.

# Token economies

These programmes involve the use of small tokens or marks that are exchangeable for a bigger reward at a later date. Appropriate behaviour is rewarded with a token either during pre-arranged time-periods, or to reinforce specific behaviours independent of a time period (e.g. putting toys away, cleaning teeth, etc.). Using the information gathered in the functional analysis regarding the frequency of the maladaptive behaviour, an action plan can be developed to divide a task into manageable segments appropriate to that child. For example, if a child displays a challenging behaviour on an hourly basis, it would be appropriate to provide a token to the child for each hour in which the behaviour was not displayed. These tokens are effective in maintaining the child's attention and focus on their behaviour in order to receive a bigger reward. However, to maximize the effect of intervention it is often useful to provide a choice of rewards whereby the child selects what they will be working towards. The child must also be provided with clear information regarding which behaviours (or absence thereof) are rewarded with tokens and the number of tokens which must be collected before the larger reward is gained.

Common practical resources involved in intervention programmes using the positive reinforcement principle include star-charts, which serve as secondary reinforcers, recording progression towards achieving a pre-defined goal.

# Methods for decreasing inappropriate behaviour

## Extinction

This strategy is similar in principle to DRO techniques. However, whereas DRO aims to reduce a target behaviour by replacing it with another, extinction is based on the theory that the target behaviour will gradually decrease, following the removal of the consequences which maintain it. The essential difference here is that extinction does not support the development of alternative behaviours. For example, in the classroom example given earlier, an extinction strategy would aim to reduce temper tantrums by simply taking no notice of such behaviour. Specifically, the teacher might remove eye contact, stay silent and move away from the child.

One has to be aware and prepare for the possibility that within extinction protocols, behaviour that was previously strongly reinforced in the past but is no longer gaining reinforcement may result in an extinction burst. An extinction burst involves a temporary escalation in the frequency, duration and/or severity of the problem behaviour (or other/new forms of behaviour that may serve the same function) before the target behaviour is eliminated entirely. Often intervention programmes are abandoned at this point as people can wrongly assume that the intervention is not working because the problem behaviour is increasing. Conversely, this is evidence that the procedure is working and should not be abandoned or one risks reinforcing the new or more extreme form of problem behaviour. A common example of an extinction burst is a broken vending machine. Vending machines provide a continuous reinforcement schedule such that each time you insert your coins and press a button to make a selection, you receive your chosen snack. However, if you insert your coins, press a button, and nothing comes out, you might become frustrated and insert more coins, or press the buttons more heavily. If this still does not result in the machine releasing the snack, you may start to hit, kick or shout at the machine (i.e. have an extinction burst). Once you realize that no amount of physical or verbal abuse directed at the vending machine will result in the release of the snack, you will eventually give up and walk away.

# Developing interventions

## Preparation

All professionals involved with the child should be made aware of the ABA programme. Professionals should decide upon the length of the programme, based on the frequency and intensity of the behaviour targeted for change. Ensure that all members of the team involved in implementing the programme are fully briefed in its employment. This will ensure the programme's consistency and maximize its efficacy.

## Execution

The recording process initiated in the functional analysis should continue throughout the programme to record progress and identify any areas requiring revision. For example, reinforcers initially identified as desirable by the child may gradually lose their potency. In this case, discuss with the child or parents/caregivers and agree upon a more meaningful reward.

## Review

At the end of the allocated period of time, the team should gather to review the effectiveness of the programme. If the desired changes have not been achieved at this point, the programme may be refined and reactivated.

## Case study: Kate

Kate is a four-year-old girl with a history of emotional and behavioural difficulties, including temper tantrums, inappropriate use of language, disturbed sleep patterns and poor eating habits. Kate's father, Paul, does not live in the family home and makes irregular contact with Kate and her younger brother, Joseph. This is the first time that Kate's mother, Janet, has sought help for her daughter's behaviour, following a referral from her GP. While problematic at home, staff at Kate's pre-school do not report similar behaviours. However, Janet remains concerned that Kate's behaviours will lead her into difficulties at her new school, which she is due to start in reception year in September.

Through discussion, Kate's most difficult piece of behaviour would be identified and, in this case, her temper tantrums were targeted for intervention. The tantrum behaviour was operationalized as instances where Kate began to cry, yell or shout while stomping her feet, and/or pounding her fists and/or throwing herself on the floor. The functional analysis revealed that 90 per cent of her tantrums occurred when Joseph was occupying Janet's full attention; when Janet was doing something with Joseph and Kate began to tantrum, Janet then intervened and directed her attention towards Kate in an effort to get her to stop the tantrum. The analysis of frequency and duration of behaviour revealed that Kate's temper tantrums occurred regularly throughout each day (at least one every 2 hours). On the occasions when Janet was not present, Kate's inappropriate behaviour was significantly less likely. It was therefore hypothesized that Kate's temper tantrums (behaviour) were a means by which she could gain attention (consequence) from her mother whenever her brother was around (establishing operation) and Janet was attending to him (antecedent). Janet would then intervene, thus providing Kate with the attention that she desired; this giving of attention was observed to reinforce the tantrums.

The intervention was designed to reduce Kate's temper tantrums by removing Janet's positive reinforcement of the inappropriate behaviour. Janet and Kate discussed the programme and agreed upon a reinforcer that Kate could earn for improving her behaviour – a trip to a swimming pool where Janet and Kate could spend some quality time together, without the distraction of Kate's younger brother. DRO and DRA programmes were subsequently developed. In practice, this meant that Janet was asked to ignore Kate's temper tantrums when they occurred. When a more appropriate method of initiating contact with her mother when she was involved with Joseph was displayed, Kate would be reinforced with praise. Furthermore, a star-chart was used to record Kate's improved behaviour and maintain her motivation and interest. For every 2-hour interval where no tantrum-like behaviour was displayed, Kate would receive a sticker on her star-chart. Kate and Janet agreed that when she had earned 25 stickers they would go on their special trip together.

The ABA programme was successful for several weeks, during which Kate and Janet went on four trips to the swimming pool. However, Janet reported that she had recently noticed a gradual increase in the tantrum-like behaviour. By talking this through with Kate, Janet learned that Kate no longer wanted to go to the swimming pool as much as she did when the programme had begun. However,

Janet learned that Kate wanted to change the quality time she spent with her mother at the pool to a trip to the funfair. With a renewed interest in the programme, and regular changes to the reward, Kate's inappropriate temper tantrums reduced at a consistent rate, until the behaviour became an infrequent occurrence.

## Multiple choice questions

1. Behaviour is shaped and maintained by:

    a. Antecedent stimuli
    b. Parents and caregivers
    c. Its consequences
    d. Establishing operations
    e. The environment

2. A comprehensive behavioural assessment must provide:

    a. Details about the A-B-C contingency
    b. How establishing operations affect the behaviour
    c. Measurable and operational information about the target behaviour
    d. Information about the context in which the behaviour occurs
    e. All of the above

### Key texts

Cooper J, Heron TE, Heward WL (2007) *Applied Behavior Analysis*, 2nd edn. Upper Saddle River, NJ: Prentice-Hall.

Kearney AJ (2007) *Understanding Applied Behavior Analysis: An Introduction to ABA for Parents, Teachers, and Other Professionals.* London: Jessica Kingsley Publishers.

Williams BF, Williams RL (2011) *Effective Programs for Treating Autistic Spectrum Disorders: Applied Behavior Analysis Models.* New York: Routledge.

# 72 Cognitive behaviour therapy

### Rachel Leeke

---

## Key concepts

- At the core of CBT is the principle that it is the interpretation of events, not the events themselves, that is crucial.
- What we think in any given situation influences what we feel, our psychological reaction and how we respond.
- In turn, our feelings (both emotional and physical reaction) and our behaviour impact on our thinking and what we do in future situations.

---

## Introduction

Cognitive behaviour therapy (CBT) emerged in the late 1960s, melding theories and principles from behaviour therapy into a cognitive, information-processing model. Since then, research supporting both the basic tenets and assertions of the cognitive–behavioural model and the efficacy of therapy based on this model, has continued to grow. Although the research relating to CBT with adults is more substantial than that for children and young people, the evidence-base for CBT with this population is rapidly expanding. There is currently good evidence for the efficacy of CBT in treating children and young people with anxiety disorders (including panic/agoraphobia, generalized anxiety disorder, specific phobias, separation anxiety, social phobia and obsessive–compulsive disorder (OCD)), depression, post-traumatic stress disorder (PTSD), bulimia nervosa and some physical symptoms (including pain, chronic illness, chronic fatigue and psychosomatic disorders). Evidence for the efficacy of CBT with anorexia nervosa and psychosis is emerging but currently limited (BPS, 2006).

CBT can be delivered in a range of ways, including in individual and group formats, in a structured and manualized or highly individualized manner, in face-to-face appointments or through self-help materials, such as books and computerized therapy programs. The evidence base and flexibility of delivery mean that CBT features heavily within numerous NICE guidelines.

Within a CBT framework, mental health problems are characterized by unhelpful, distorted thinking patterns, which affect how situations are interpreted. These thinking patterns are thought to have their roots in early experiences, which affect a person's view of themselves, the world, and others. Negative experiences increase the likelihood that a person will develop negative beliefs such as 'I'm useless' or 'the world is a dangerous place'. These beliefs are known as 'core beliefs' or 'schema' and are at the core of how an individual views life, but are not usually easy to access verbally, because they are at a deeper level of consciousness than usual everyday thoughts.

The layer of thinking that surrounds these is known as 'assumptions' or 'rules for living'. These may have benefits at some level but are generally dysfunctional. If somebody with the core belief, say, 'I am a failure' develops the assumption that 'If I can achieve A-grades then it means that I am a success (and not a failure)'; they might work hard, achieve good results and do well in their studies. However, when the work becomes harder or life events interfere with accomplishing their goals, they may interpret situations when they gain a B rather than an A as meaning that they are 'useless' or 'not good enough'. Such thoughts are then triggered automatically in specific situations. They are the easiest to access verbally and are known as 'negative automatic thoughts'.

CBT focuses on challenging dysfunctional thoughts and changing behaviour.

## Example

You see someone you know walking along the street and wave to them, but they do not acknowledge you. If you think 'they are probably busy, stressed, and didn't notice me' you may feel concerned about them, experience some mild symptoms of anxiety and ring them later that evening to check that they are okay. This, in turn, may mean that you hear all about their problems and reaffirm your confidence in that particular friendship. If, however, you think 'they're ignoring me because no-one likes me', you may feel upset and low in mood, be tearful and become more lethargic and consequently withdraw, go home and avoid people. This may mean that you never find out that they did not notice you because they were busy or stressed. You continue to believe it was because they (and everyone else) do not like you and both your confidence and the effort you make to socialize are affected.

## CBT in practice

### Therapeutic approach

As with most therapies, engagement and developing a therapeutic alliance are key. CBT therapists adopt a non-expert position. The young person is the expert on their own thoughts, feeling and life, while the therapist has knowledge and experience of CBT models and techniques. CBT is collaborative and a process of joint exploration and discovery (see Friedberg and McClure, 2002 for further information). Rather than telling the young person what they think, what they do wrong or what they need to do, the therapist helps the young person discover it for themselves. This is a process known as guided discovery. Socratic questioning, which involves asking young people to assimilate potentially contradictory information into their existing beliefs, is another useful technique.

### Assessment

A CBT assessment will involve the young person and other people close to them, people they live with and teachers at school. The child's difficulties must be understood in context and other people can be helpful with ideas and support at the treatment stage. A CBT assessment will focus on situations that trigger the young person's difficulties or a worsening of them. Problems and difficulties are broken down into cognitive, emotional, physiological and behavioural components, with questions being asked to elicit what the young person thought in that situation, what emotion he felt, how he felt physiologically, what he did and what the impact was.

The young person will be asked what he would like to be different. This helps to establish motivation for change and is used as the basis for setting specific therapy goals.

Standardized questionnaires are frequently used as part of the assessment and information-gathering process. These provide additional information about young people's symptoms and difficulties and how severe they are. They serve as a baseline measure, which can be re-administered at the end of treatment to measure improvement.

## Formulation

Within CBT, formulations are developed collaboratively, with the young person and the therapist working together to develop a shared understanding of the difficulties. These formulations are continuously revised and elaborated on throughout the therapy process as more information emerges about how the different components of the presenting problem interact.

There are two main types of formulation within CBT: onset formulations, which take into account how the problem developed and maintenance formulations, which focus on the here and now and how the problem is being maintained (see **Figures 72.1** and **72.2** below). Although it may be useful to think about how and why the problem developed, it can be more useful to think about what keeps it going. Maintenance formulations serve as the initial basis for tailoring therapy techniques to the young person's difficulties.

## Intervention

The formulation and goals that the child wants to reach will help inform what intervention might be useful; this is a highly individualized process. The therapy process is structured: this involves a contract for the therapy at the outset and agreeing frequency of sessions (usually weekly, at least in the early stages), the number of sessions before reviewing progress and agreeing goals to be worked towards. Therapy sessions take a structured format with each session starting with an update ('mood check' or 'review of difficulties') and the setting of an agenda for that session. This agenda is drawn up collaboratively with both the therapist and the young person suggesting items for it.

The overall aim of therapy is to break the young person's negative cycles of thoughts, feelings and behaviour and to establish more helpful and adaptive patterns. This involves drawing on skills training, techniques from behaviour therapy or cognitive strategies and using specific strategies, depending on the young person's individualized formulation (Graham, 2005). Skills training involves developing and applying specific skills, such as assertiveness skills, emotional regulation skills and problem-solving skills and is often used when young people lack an alternative, more appropriate behavioural response in key situations.

Specific skills are taught and rehearsed, if the young person has not yet fully developed them. Behavioural and cognitive therapy techniques both involve applying skills that have already been mastered. Behavioural therapy strategies may include relaxation, systematic desensitization and behavioural activation through scheduling of activities. Cognitive strategies include cognitive restructuring, i.e. learning to evaluate situations in a more objective and balanced way, challenging distorted thinking patterns, and behavioural experiments, where additional evidence to confirm or challenge specific thoughts, is looked for.

Homework (often called 'practice tasks' or 'jobs' to avoid school work associations) is given between sessions. This can include rehearsing new skills, gathering evidence on particular issues and trying out ways to do things differently. A review of the homework set (and any problems with completing it) is put on the agenda for the next session. This helps to underline the importance of these activities and 'reinforces' the young person for doing it.

# Monitoring and reviewing outcome

This stage is about reviewing the young person's progress to ensure that treatment has been helpful and therapy goals achieved. It can be useful to complete the questionnaires again during or after treatment, to enable the therapist and the young person to see what progress has been made. As always, it is helpful to ask the young person and those around them what they feel has improved, so that a comprehensive view of treatment outcome is identified.

# Additional considerations when working with children and young people

The issue of the extent to which to include parents or carers in CBT for children and young people needs careful consideration. Many clinicians consider including parents in CBT for children to be beneficial, but evidence related to whether this enhances efficacy is mixed. Parental involvement may be indicated when parents occupy a central role in their child's difficulties, as with separation anxiety or when they are involved in the maintenance of difficulties (e.g. by providing reassurance or 'rescuing' their child from potentially distressing situations). Parents can be involved in CBT as co-therapists, which includes being taught how to manage and address their child's anxiety using CBT strategies. Parental support with reward systems tied to completing specific tasks can help promote desired behaviours and increase the motivation for therapy tasks. A separate parent/carer session can be useful if the formulation suggests that factors such as parental expectations of the child or the way in which 'problematic' behaviour is modelled or reinforced are maintaining the difficulties.

There is emerging evidence that children as young as three and four years may benefit from CBT. However, while younger children (e.g. those under the age of seven or eight years) are able to identify thoughts, they may struggle with this, unless the therapist is very creative and able to adapt their approach to the young person's developmental abilities. If younger children are struggling with the cognitive components of CBT, more behavioural and skills-training based approaches may still be useful.

# Summary

It is how we interpret events, not the events themselves that is key. Mental health problems are characterized by distorted thinking patterns. Mental health problems arise as a result of negative or difficult early experiences, which increase the likelihood of:

- developing negative views of ourselves, the world and others (core beliefs);
- creating dysfunctional assumptions or unhelpful rules for living life;
- negative thoughts automatically popping into consciousness in potentially difficult situations.

Distorted thinking patterns are maintained by our emotional, physiological and behavioural responses to them.

Therapy, which is problem specific, goal-oriented and focuses predominantly on the here and now, aims to challenge dysfunctional thoughts and change behaviour.

## Case study 1: Theresa

Theresa, a 14-year-old girl, was referred to CAMHS by her GP as she was not attending school or leaving her house.

### Assessment

Assessment consisted of clinical interviews with Theresa and her family and standardized questionnaires (e.g. The Spence Children's Anxiety Scale, Spence, 1994) (see Chapter 26, The use of questionnaires in the diagnosis of child mental health problems).

Theresa had taken some examinations four months before. She had experienced a panic attack during one of these, when she was unable to answer a question. Since then, she had increasingly refused to go to school or see friends, as she felt embarrassed and worried that the panic attack would happen again. Her biggest fear was that if this did happen, other people would ultimately reject her. Questionnaire measures highlighted several symptoms of panic/agoraphobia.

Theresa's parents had divorced when she was much younger and she had interpreted that as meaning 'I'm unlovable' and 'others will leave me' (i.e. core beliefs). This had, in turn, contributed to her adopting the 'rule for living' that 'If I am perfect and please people all the time, they won't reject or leave me'. Theresa had therefore put all her efforts into her schoolwork and received high grades throughout her childhood.

Theresa's main goal was to return to school as soon as possible.

## Formulation

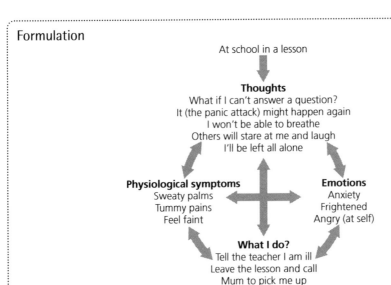

Figure 72.1 Theresa's formulation.

## Situation

Theresa was 'catastrophizing' what might happen if she could not answer a question at school. These thoughts triggered unpleasant emotional and physiological responses and led her to escape from, and avoid, the situation that had provoked her anxiety. She interpreted the physical symptoms that she experienced when she began to feel anxious as evidence that the panic attack was going to happen again. Her 'coping strategy' of leaving, while making her feel better in the short term (and therefore making it more likely that she would choose this option again in the future), prevented her from learning that the things she was worried about were highly unlikely to happen. This prevented her from gaining evidence to 'disconfirm' her predictions and her difficulties were thereby maintained within a vicious cycle.

## Intervention

Key areas of intervention with Theresa included:

- Challenging the distorted thinking and tendency to 'catastrophize' in situations. Theresa was encouraged to think in a more balanced way by collecting evidence for and against her worries being likely to come true, and then weighing this up to arrive at an objective conclusion. This technique resulted in thoughts such as 'if I can't answer a question then everyone will stare and laugh and I'll be left alone,' being re-evaluated and replaced by the conclusions 'nobody's perfect all of the time' and 'if I get it wrong the teacher will move onto the next person and I can then try my best to answer the next question'.
- Relaxation exercises: These were introduced to help Theresa manage the physiological arousal that she experienced when anxious and to break the pattern of misinterpreting this as a sign of an impending panic attack.
- Systematic de-sensitization: Theresa drew up a hierarchy of the least to most anxiety-provoking steps involved in working towards her goal of returning to school. She then started with the least scary, and when feeling more comfortable with that and her ability to cope, moved on to the next scariest. Her school needed to be involved and allowed her to start reintegration into school with 1 hour a day.

- Family involvement: Theresa's mother set up a reward system to reward her for completing her goals each week and to increase her motivation to undertake difficult, anxiety provoking tasks.

## Outcome

By the end of therapy, Theresa was attending school on a part-time basis, seeing friends regularly, and going on trips with her family. She was anxious at school, but 'nowhere near as anxious' as before therapy. Her scores on standardized questionnaire measures had reduced significantly.

## Case study 2: Daniel

Daniel (9) was referred to CAMHS due to concerns about his low mood, which had 'worsened steadily over the last nine months'.

### Assessment

Assessment included clinical interview and standardized questionnaires (e.g. The Children's Depression Inventory).

Daniel had always struggled academically at school and around nine months ago his best friend had moved away, leaving him feeling isolated. He had begun experiencing verbal bullying. He had gradually withdrawn from activities, such as cubs that he had previously enjoyed, saying that he 'couldn't be bothered'. He was described as tearful and unhappy, and his parents expressed concern that he had no enthusiasm and had 'lost his sparkle'. Daniel scored highly for symptoms of depression on questionnaire measures, but not for anxiety.

Daniel's goals were to feel happier (currently 2/10 for mood) and to enjoy things again (current enjoyment rated as 3/10)

### Formulation

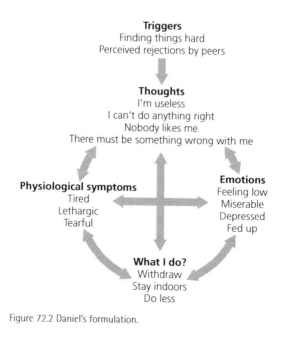

Figure 72.2 Daniel's formulation.

Daniel's experiences had led him to develop a negative view of himself ('I'm useless', 'I'm not good enough'), others ('others do not like me/will be horrible to me') and the world ('life is hard and unfair'). His negative thinking was activated when he found work (or other tasks) hard or when he perceived others as rejecting him, with negative automatic thoughts such as 'nobody likes me' and 'I'm useless' resulting in him feeling low, miserable, upset and fed up. This was accompanied by a worsening of his physical symptoms, such as lethargy and tearfulness. Behaviourally, he would then withdraw and not engage in activities. This pattern of response meant that he was doing fewer fun things, losing contact with friends and struggling even more to do work. This, in turn, reinforced his beliefs that he was useless and nobody liked him.

## Intervention

Key areas of intervention with Daniel included:

- Activity scheduling: Daniel's withdrawal was targeted by asking him to record what he did each day and how much fun (pleasure) and achievement (mastery) he gained from each activity. Activities that increased his pleasure and mastery were then increased.
- Thought challenging: This was used to help Daniel look for evidence for and against his thoughts being true and to help him generate alternative, more balanced perceptions of himself.
- Problem-solving: Problem-solving skills were taught to help Daniel find ways of coping with difficulties, such as bullying, in a more proactive way. Potential solutions were generated, the pros and cons of each considered, and chosen strategies rehearsed in session.
- Family involvement: Techniques and strategies were shared with Daniel's parents so that they could coach him to use these when triggers arose.

## Outcome

At the end of therapy, Daniel reported feeling happier (mood 8/10) and enjoying things more (enjoyment in pleasurable activities 9/10). His parents reported that he was doing more, seemed more able to cope with his peers and had 'got his smile back'. Standardized questionnaires suggested that Daniel's symptoms had improved considerably.

## Multiple choice questions

1. Which of these is not a principle of CBT?

    a. Events determine how we feel
    b. It is the interpretations of events, not events themselves which determine how we feel
    c. Thoughts influence, and are influenced by, emotions, physiological reactions and behaviour
    d. Our early experiences impact upon how we interpret and perceive situations

2. CBT can be delivered:

    a. Only on a one-to-one basis
    b. On a one-to-one basis or in groups
    c. On a one-to-one basis, in groups, or through self-help materials
    d. None of the above

3. Which of the following statements is not true? In CBT sessions, the therapist:

    a. Prioritizes engagement and the therapeutic alliance
    b. Tells people what to think
    c. Focuses initially on the here-and-now
    d. Uses a process of joint exploration and discovery

4. Formulations in CBT:

   a. Are written collaboratively with the young person and help develop a shared understanding of the young person's difficulties
   b. Are written collaboratively in the first session and are set in stone
   c. Are written by the therapist in-between sessions and the young person does not see it
   d. All of the above

5. Possible interventions in CBT include:

   a. Establishing more helpful and adaptive patterns of functioning
   b. Teaching the young person new skills, which serve as coping strategies
   c. Behavioural strategies, such as relaxation techniques
   d. All of the above

## Key texts

Freidman RD, McClure JM (2002) *Clinical Practice of Cognitive Behaviour therapy with Children and Adolescents: The Nuts and Bolts*. London: Guilford Press.

Graham P (2005) *Cognitive Behaviour Therapy for Children and Families*, 2nd edn. Cambridge: Cambridge University Press.

Spence SH (1994) Spence Children's Anxiety Scale. In: Yule W (ed.). *Child Psychology Portfolio: Anxiety, Depression and Post-Traumatic Stress Disorder in Childhood*. UK: Nfer-Nelson.

## 73 Social Stories™

Liz Smith

### Key concepts

- A Social Story describes a situation, skill or concept in terms of relevant social cues, perspectives, and common responses in a specifically defined style and format (Gray, 2008).
- Social Stories are short personalized stories designed to teach children how to manage their own behaviour during a particular social situation that they find challenging or confusing (Gray and Garand, 1993).
- The story describes the context of a specific social situation and includes detail relating to where the activity takes place, when it will occur, who will be participating, what will happen, how other people may be feeling and why the child should behave in a given manner.
- A Social Story is written from a first person perspective and uses positive language.

## Introduction

A Social Story™ is a short story that helps teach a child how to manage their own behaviour during a particular social situation that they find challenging or confusing (e.g. dinner time, bed time, play time with a brother or sister). The goal of a Social Story is not to change an individual's behaviour but it is hoped that improving the child's understanding of social events and expectations will lead to more effective responses (Gray, 2007). The visual presentation of social rules is thought to be less confusing, compared to other methods of teaching social skills, for example social skills groups, where children may struggle with the high verbal demands (Rust and Smith, 2006). Social Stories are tailored to each individual child in accordance with their level of understanding, relating to a particular area of difficulty that they are experiencing and can incorporate themes and characters that relate to their interests. The idea is to increase the child's level of interest and motivation.

There are four basic sentence types commonly used in social stories, each of which is designed to fulfil a separate function (Gray, 2000).

| Sentence type | Description of sentence |
| --- | --- |
| Descriptive | These are truthful, opinion-and-assumption-free statements of fact. They identify the most relevant factors in a situation or the most important aspect of the topic. Examples include; 'my name is ...' and 'Sometimes my brother reads to me at home'. |
| Perspective | These are statements that refer to or describe a person's internal state, their knowledge, thoughts, feelings, beliefs or physical condition. Examples include; 'My sister usually likes to play on the piano'. |
| Directive | These statements identify a suggested response or choice of responses to a situation. Examples include; 'I will try to put my hand up if I want to ask the teacher a question'. |
| Affirmative | These statements enhance the meaning of surrounding sentences, are used to stress an important point or reassure the individual and usually follow directly after a descriptive, perspective or directive sentence. Examples include; 'This is a good idea' and 'This is very important'. |

Gray (2000) suggested using a balanced ratio of at least 2:5 descriptive, perspective and/or affirmative sentences to every directive sentence.

# Writing a Social Story

## Step 1: Identify the target situation

What is the situation that the child has difficulties with? (e.g. bath time, bed time, going to the hairdressers, etc.). The author translates social information into meaningful text and illustrations, describing abstract concepts and ideas with visual, concrete references and images. The priority is to share relevant social information in a meaningful way.

## Step 2: Gather information

This includes when and where the situation occurs, who is involved, how events are sequenced, what occurs and why. This information can be gathered through direct observation and/or discussions with school staff and parents.

## Step 3: Personalize the text

The author customizes the text to the learning style, needs, interests and abilities of the child. Some generic stories are available (Gray, 2000; Gray and White, 2001) and these can be a helpful starting point covering a range of topics such as sharing, going to the hairdressers and so on.

A Social Story has the following defining characteristics:

- describes expected behaviours;
- answers 'wh' questions, such as who is involved, where and when a situation occurs, what is happening, how it happens and why;
- written from a first person perspective;
- is matched to the child's interests and ability level, and is literally accurate;
- uses positive language;

- uses four different sentence types and a ratio of between two and five descriptive, perspective or affirmative sentences to every directive sentence.

Phrases such as 'I will try', 'sometimes' and 'usually' are good to use in stories.

Social Stories are good because they:

- are visual;
- provide a consistent, concrete message;
- are permanent, providing a support for the child's memory;
- are individualized;
- are practical;
- provide an opportunity for children to practice skills before attempting the real situation;
- may provide additional support for use with parents with learning and/or memory difficulties.

# How to use them

Identify an appropriate focus, and then create a Social Story. Make them individualized and think about yourself in the child's shoes. Make them visual if need be, by using illustrations or any symbols the child is using.

Try reading the story once a day, if possible, immediately before the situation in question.

The use of the story should be reviewed after about 2 weeks. Do you think it is working? What are you going to look for to tell you if it is? If it has not been working, do you have the right focus for the story? Will you keep using stories with a particular child? What might be your next focus? How will you store the stories and celebrate achievement?

# Example stories

These stories can be adapted to fit your own child by inserting photographs/pictures/drawings of them doing the different activities. Also, all the text in italic can be altered to fit your own situation better, for example your child might not hit or pinch, but they might bite or pull hair.

## Helpful hands

My name is _____ and I am __ years old. This is a photo of me

I have two hands that help me do lots of things

Most times my hands do good things like *help with tidying up the toys, or getting dressed on my own in the morning, or having fun, drawing with my sister/brother* _____

Sometimes my hands might do things that are not kind and can make people sad like *punching or hitting someone*, or *pinching my friends or family*. If my hands do naughty things like these, it can hurt people and sometimes make them cry. If I use my hands to do naughty things then I will *get told off*, and my friends might not want to play anymore. I will try to make sure that my hands do good things like *drawing with my sister*, or *helping mummy with the cooking*. When I am doing these things I am using my helpful hands. When I use my helpful hands my friends and family will be pleased with me. Mummy will be really pleased and I might get *a special sticker on my chart*.

## Bedtime

My name is _____. This is a picture of me.

At about *6.30pm* I normally eat my tea

After tea I might *play with my toys or watch some TV.*

Five minutes before I need to go upstairs mum will give me my timer and tell me that it is nearly time to for bed.

When the timer has run out *first I might have a bath.*

Then I brush my teeth and put my pyjamas on ready to go to bed. Most of the time *mummy* reads me a bedtime story. I enjoy this time together

When it is time for me to go to sleep *mum* usually gives me a hug and a kiss and then she says 'goodnight'. This means that it is time for me to close my eyes and try to go to sleep.

*Sometimes daddy also gives me a hug and a kiss. Daddy cannot always give me a hug and a kiss goodnight because he is not always at home when it is my bedtime. This is okay because I will get to see him in the morning at breakfast.*

After *mum or dad* has said goodnight to me I will try to stay still and quiet in my bed until I fall asleep. This will make *mummy and daddy* very pleased with me.

*Mummy will turn my bedroom light out. This is okay because the landing light will be left on and this will make it easier for me to fall asleep.*

Here I am going to sleep on my own!

Good morning _____ Mummy wakes me with a big cuddle and a kiss for settling down to sleep quietly and staying in my bed. She is really pleased with me.

Well done _____ !! What a good *boy/girl* you are for settling down to sleep quietly – *you can have a special sticker for your chart.*

## Multiple choice questions

1. Which of the following is not one of the four common sentence types used in Social Stories?

   a. Perspective
   b. Affirmative

    c. Cathartic

    d. Descriptive

    e. Directive

2. Which of the following is not a defining characteristic of Social Stories?

    a. Answers 'wh' questions

    b. Written in the third person

    c. Written in positive language

    d. Follows the use of the four different sentence types

    e. Uses a smaller ratio of directive sentences compared to the other three types

## Key texts

Gray C (2000) *The New Social Story Book,* illustrated edition. Arlington: Future Horizons Inc.

Gray C, White WL (2001) *My Social Stories Book.* London: Jessica Kingsley Publishers.

## Web page

www.thegraycenter.org

# 74

# Family therapy models and practice
Christine Hooper

## Key concepts
- Symptoms are seen as the individual's responses to their situation and environment.
- Any intervention must 'fit' with the family's beliefs and values.
- Family members are both part of the problem and of the solution.

## Introduction

The ideas that govern family therapy are mainstream now but in the 1960s they were seen as an innovative and untried approach to what had hitherto been seen as problems belonging solely to the individual presenting with the symptoms. This chapter looks at the early practitioners who first attempted to place individual difficulties into a systemic context. Over recent years these ideas have been adapted and modified and family therapists no longer adhere to the only one 'pure' approach. Family therapy is a flexible evolving approach to treating child and adolescent mental health, one that is respectful and inclusive.

## Early family therapy practitioners

### Salvador Minuchin (1960s)

As director of the Philadelphia Child Guidance clinic, Salvador Minuchin worked with families living in disadvantaged conditions and often with only one parent in the home. In 1967, he published 'Families of the Slums' explaining the techniques he had developed over time. His approach became known as Structural Family Therapy.

The main features were:
- establishing a comfortable rapport with the family, often visiting at home;
- identifying the 'executive system' of adults, and sometimes older children, and a 'sub-system' of younger children;
- enactment: encouraging the acting out of the problem in the session to understand how other family members react to it;
- intensification: 'turning up the heat' on the problem to highlight its seriousness;
- unbalancing: allying with different family members in turn to allow everyone to express themselves;
- identifying alliances (when two family members are unusually, perhaps dangerously, close) and coalitions (where two or more family members gang up against another);
- enmeshment: when all family members rally enthusiastically around even a relatively minor problem, often involving extended family and neighbours;
- disengagement: where the child has to escalate the problem behaviour before anyone in the family takes any notice.

Structural family therapy became linked to a 'masculine', problem-solving approach to therapy, whereby the therapist took responsibility for change. It fell out of favour during the 1970s as feminist ideas gained ground. Nevertheless, some of the techniques may still underlie (however unconsciously) current practice.

### Strategic family therapy (1970s)

This approach arose from the collaboration of several significant practitioners (Jay Haley, Don Jackson, Gregory Bateson, John Weakland and Paul

Watzlawick, among others) working at the Mental Research Institute in Palo Alto, California. The key concept was that of looking at a family as a 'cybernetic system', governed by unwritten and not necessarily overt, rules of interaction.

The main features were:

- the use of warfare terminology: tactics, planning, strategy and resistance;
- uncommon solutions: interventions were tailormade to each family;
- compliance-based interventions, direct and transparent suggestions for change and defiance-based paradoxical interventions whereby the family were expected to defy the suggestions. Indeed, if they were to comply with them, the outcome would be the opposite of what was desired;
- feedback: is what shapes and maintains social relationships over time;
- complementarity: where one person responds to another with the opposite behaviour, for example where one is aggressive, the other is passive;
- symmetry: where one person responds to the other with the same behaviour, for example when one shouts, the other shouts louder.

Both symmetry and complementarity have the potential to spiral out of control, known as 'runaway'.

Strategic family therapy was criticized for its assumption that families would be resistant to change and that devious means would need to be employed to effect change. Family therapy today is more transparent and 'honest'.

## Milan Systemic therapy (1980s)

This approach was the concept of four psychotherapists (Cecchin, Boscolo, Selvini-Palazolli and Prata) working in Milan. These practitioners began to feel disillusioned with the individual approach of psychotherapy. They initiated a formal framework for a therapeutic session. Two of the team would interview the family and their two colleagues would watch from behind a one-way screen to offer a distanced analysis of the family interaction. The observer position was called 'second order cybernetics'. The theory was that the interviewing therapist was always at risk of being 'pulled into' the family's interaction and less

able to offer a sophisticated impartial intervention. The session would be structured with a hypothesizing section, the observed interview, a break for team discussion, delivery of the message to the family and the wash-up discussion once the family had left.

The main features were:

- Hypothesizing: making a guess about the family interaction based on information from other sources, for example, referral letter, statutory agencies or school and testing out the hypothesis in the session, revising or confirming it, as the session progressed.
- Curiosity: letting questioning flow freely, based on feedback, known as the 'feedback loop'.
- Neutrality: the therapist remains impartial.
- Reframing: finding an equally valid explanation for the presenting problem that would 'fit' into the family's relationship context, rather than the problem belonging to the 'symptom-carrier'.
- Positive connotation: framing the problem behaviour as a rational response to the situation.
- Circular questioning: asking each family member to comment on the relationship and behaviour of any two others. The idea is that it is easier to talk about someone else's behaviour than one's own.
- Invariate prescription: a standard intervention of telling the parents to go out together on a regular basis both to strengthen their own relationship and to emphasize to the children how together they are as a couple.
- Messages: each session ended with a message delivered coolly to the family, often written out for them to take home, sometimes read out aloud and sometimes written but with instructions for it to read at home, perhaps over a meal (very Italian!) or with other family members present.

The sense of Milan systemic family therapy is of an intervention delivered from above, at a distance and by experts. Genograms were used extensively to help illuminate family relationships.

Some of these early techniques have survived into the newer, more collaborative, family therapy approaches more popular nowadays, most especially, the use of family trees, circular questioning and re-framing. It fell out of favour as an approach because of the expert stance taken and the distant, rather than egalitarian, position adopted by the therapist. In addition, there are too few therapists and too heavy caseloads now to allow for half a day and a four-man team to be set aside for just one appointment.

## Case study 1: John

John (aged 11) lives at home with his parents and his paternal grandmother. His mother is white British and his father is Indian. John's mother suffered two miscarriages before John was born. John had some language delay as a young child and saw a speech therapist for a few sessions. He did not settle at nursery and starting new schools has been a challenge for him. John's mother works full time in the home and his father works long hours for an IT company. The couple are isolated from their wider family, who live in a town 40 miles away. The grandmother's presence in the home is a source of tension between the couple.

John has told his parents about being teased at school over the past few months. John's attendance at school has fallen below 80 per cent and the Education Welfare Officer is now involved. John's absences have been due to a series of illnesses, related to abdominal pain and headaches. The GP does not believe there is a physical cause for his symptoms and thinks they may be anxiety-related. There is a family history of abdominal pains and anxiety. The GP referred John to the CAMHS Clinic.

John enjoys attending a local Youth Club at weekends and sees a Youth worker for support.

### Treatment plan

John and his mother are seen in the clinic and a picture emerges from the initial appointment of racial bullying at school. John feels anxious in the morning at the thought of leaving his mother at home, in case she becomes ill. As John has difficulty going off to sleep, his mother says he can recuperate in the morning and sleep in at weekends. According to John's mother, his grandmother believes he is a lazy boy, who won't do as he is told and is disrespectful towards her. The family therapist begins to externalize the anxiety (see Chapter 25, Narrative therapy) and to look at times when John manages to keep the anxiety at bay.

A network meeting is convened with the Education Welfare Officer, the Head of Year from school, the Youth worker, the parents and John. A careful systemic assessment is carried out to identify the anxiety triggers and to look at the obstacles to anxiety control and school attendance. The racial bullying is spoken about with the Head of Year, who agrees to take this up following the school's procedures on bullying.

A Return to School plan is formulated, which includes an individual component for John and a family-based component. Following a FRIENDS programme, John begins to learn skills to manage his anxiety. These include relaxation, cognitive coping skills and using social support. The Youth worker helps John to practise these skills at the Youth club.

The parents begin to understand the family's behaviour patterns of distress being expressed through physical symptoms. John's father relates this to a culture of expressing distress through the body, but nevertheless wants his son to receive help from the CAMHS services. The Family Therapist sees the couple by themselves to focus on rewarding John's use of anxiety management skills. They talk about their understandable fears for their son growing up. The family therapist agrees that these are fears shared by most parents of adolescents. Ways that the parents can manage their anxiety are discussed. It has been difficult for them to communicate as a couple, due to their living arrangements, and ways to manage this using the support of their local church are suggested.

John gradually returns to school on a more regular basis.

# Case study 2: Rosie

Rosie is a 15-year-old white Caucasian girl. Her mother is a health professional and her father runs his own business. She is the elder of two girls. Rosie's mother and grandmother both had eating difficulties as teenagers and a paternal aunt has been treated in hospital for obsessive compulsive disorder.

Rosie is a quiet, hardworking and conscientious girl who enjoys ballet and wants to be the best in the class. She exercises by swimming twice a week, horse-riding, PE and gym at school and sit-ups at home each morning. All the family enjoy exercise.

Rosie was a faddy eater when she was young, eating only a limited range of foods. For the past two years she has been counting calories and reading food labels to check the fat content of foods. It can take up to 2 hours for Rosie and her mother to buy the weekly food shop. She prepares the evening meal for the family, but with different food for herself. Her periods stopped a few months ago.

Rosie compares herself unfavourably to her peers and does not like to eat lunch at school in front of the other girls.

Due to her father's work, the family have moved home every year for the past three years. She began to restrict her eating after the second move.

Rosie has lost seven kilos in the last three months. Rosie's mother is concerned about her weight loss, although her father does not see it as an issue. The family have private health insurance and saw a Child and Adolescent Psychiatrist for assessment, who suggested inpatient treatment. This was not covered by insurance and the family were referred to the local CAMHS team.

## Treatment plan

At the initial assessment, Rosie is seen both on her own and with her parents.

Rosie's mother is apprehensive about attending the initial appointment, fearing she will be blamed for her daughter's eating problem. The family state that they do not like to talk about difficult emotions, preferring to keep these private.

In the family session, the family therapist is interested in trans-generational stories of girls struggling with weight and shape issues in adolescence. The several house moves have meant a series of peer relationship losses for Rosie. The family therapist learns that independence is very important and an organizing belief for the family.

The family motto is 'daily exercise keeps you healthy', which they all strive to do. Recent bereavements in the family have undermined this belief and they have been struggling to cope with their feelings of loss. According to her mother, it is easier for the family to talk about Rosie's eating problem than their distress over the losses.

In engaging the family, the Family Therapist explores their motivation to attend sessions and their attitude towards professional help.

The family's goals for therapy are to be able to eat together and to enjoy mealtimes with less stress. Rosie states she both wants to get better and wants things to stay the same.

When a secure rapport has been established with the family, the family therapist works with the parents to help them to regain their executive position in the family system by taking control of buying food, preparation and presentation. In the beginning phase of treatment, it is often necessary for parents to take charge of meals. This is difficult for Rosie who initially loses weight because she leaves the table quickly after supervised eating to go to the bathroom. When the parents support Rosie for 20 minutes after eating, to help her to tolerate the distress of eating, her weight slowly increases.

Family therapy provides a space where the difficulty in managing Rosie's anxious and challenging behaviour can be worked on. Support for the family and consideration of other family members relationships to the eating disorder are considered.

Family therapy is integrated with individual therapy and psychiatric input. Rosie's physical state is monitored regularly at the GP practice.

After a period of three months when Rosie's weight is back within a healthy range, Rosie begins to feed herself. The family begin to look at how their responses to the eating disorder, for example, trying to ignore it, may have left 'it' room to take over Rosie's thinking. The family sessions are a safe containing space where the family can begin to talk about difficult emotions. The eating disorder has had an isolating effect, whereby the family found it difficult to socialize with friends and other family members. Bereavements were named and worked through, celebrating the positive memories and influences, while acknowledging the losses.

The family looked at changing relationships in the family in the context of Rosie developing into a young woman. Rosie was encouraged to talk about the dilemmas of independence and the losses this means for her. Communication was enhanced by setting aside a specific time each day for family members to 'check in' with each other how everyone was managing their day. Rosie joined in with some family activities and began socializing again with close friends. New patterns of relationships were negotiated in the family, and the family altered its belief about exercise.

As the work with the family advanced, the family therapist focused on adolescent issues and relapse prevention strategies.

The family attended weekly sessions initially, extended to fortnightly sessions after four months. There were monthly reviews with the family, to plan relapse prevention strategies and to consolidate the changes in the family. Rosie was discharged after an 18-month intervention.

## Multiple choice questions

1. Which of these techniques is especially associated with Milan Systemic therapy?

   a. Enactment
   b. Circular questioning
   c. Paradoxical intervention
   d. Intensificationn

2. Which family therapy approach is associated with Salvador Minuchin?

   a. Strategic
   b. Milan Systemic
   c. Structural

3. What is a 'hypothesis'?

   a. A random guess
   b. An intervention
   c. The referrer's definition of the problem
   d. A framework for thinking before seeing the family
   e. The family's definition of the problem

4. Why did Structural family therapy fall out of favour?

   a. It didn't work
   b. It was too complicated to master
   c. It was seen as too directive and 'masculine'
   d. Families didn't like it
   e. New ideas are always better than old ones

## Key texts

Carr A (2006) *Family Therapy: Concepts, Process and Practice.* London: Wiley.

Dallos R, Draper R (2010) *An Introduction to Family Therapy*

*Systemic Theory and Practice*, 3rd edn. Oxford: Oxford University Press.

Dallos R, Vetere A (2006) *Systemic Therapy and Attachment Narratives.* Oxford: Oxford University Press.

# 75

# Solution focused brief therapy
Jonathan Prosser

## Key concepts

- Getting what we want in life is not necessarily dependent on resolving problems that seem to stand in the way.
- Therapeutic conversations that generate richly described visions of their preferred future can provide clients with high levels of motivation and achievable goals to aim for.
- Techniques which draw attention to day-to-day variations in behaviour and experience, to exceptions to the 'rules' of problems and to the skills, strengths and qualities of the people experiencing those problems, seem to result in rapid behavioural change and hope for future change.
- Paying attention to the positive attributes in one's life tends to enhance the maintenance of those attributes, while declining (or forgetting) to continually 'rehearse' problem narratives, habits, ways of thinking and patterns of relating tend to improve the client's sense of well-being and mastery over their life.
- Problems often resolve without direct attention being paid to them in therapy.

## Introduction

The experience of 'well-being' in people can be seen as the relative balance between the negative effects of problems and the positive effects of desirable qualities in their lives.

Problem focused approaches to therapeutic work are underpinned by the idea of understanding how problems 'work' and helping individuals, families or groups to reduce those problems, or their impact, in some way.

The solution focused approaches, including Brief Solution Focused Therapy, aim instead to increase the desirable qualities of life, by building an awareness of, and sense of competency to achieve, the kinds of changes that are desired. By focusing in concrete, observable, specific detail on the 'preferred future' of individuals and by noticing which aspects of that vision are already present in some way, and building on them, the energy of the individual (or family) is devoted to the achievement of that preferred future, rather than being spent on combating 'problems' that are apparently preventing that brighter future.

Clearly, there are some problems that it is very effective to focus on directly. In the event that I have a heart attack, I do not wish to meet a physician who asks me to conceptualize how my life might be better without the heart attack! I want to have my heart attack promptly diagnosed and appropriately treated.

Solution focused therapists contend that many, if not most, of the psychological 'problems' that people face in their lives and relationships, especially the chronic ones that are often brought to therapy, are not easily resolvable, if they are resolvable at all, by a direct focus on them. This is where the solution focused approach is at its most helpful.

## History of the approach

Solution Focused Brief Therapy was developed in the United States over 25 years ago, by Steve de Shazer and Insoo Kim Berg. They drew on the innovative work of Milton Erickson and the 'problem-solving' approaches of the Mental Research Institute in Palo Alto.

The solution focused approach was said to have been empirically derived by de Shazer and his team, who having discarded, one by one, ineffective psychotherapeutic strategies from the range of problem-solving and Ericksonian techniques, noticed that the remaining effective techniques just happened to be outcome oriented and competency focused in nature. Further, they noticed that the duration of such therapeutic encounters, led by the client, was brief.

The practice of Solution Focused Brief Therapy has evolved alongside the many other therapeutic approaches that have developed over the intervening years, such that similarities can be seen between techniques from solution focused approaches, cognitive behavioural therapy approaches, family therapy approaches, narrative therapy approaches and other therapies, including motivational interviewing.

## Therapeutic relationship

In common with other therapeutic approaches, outcomes improve when the therapist can engender a sense of trust, hope and expectation of change in their clients. The universal therapeutic factors of respect, warmth and genuineness, combined with careful listening to the client's account, allows the formation of a therapeutic relationship that creates an environment in which clients will attempt full and honest answers to any questions asked of them.

In the solution focused approach, the therapist shows respect, warmth and genuineness to the client, but instead of listening carefully to information about the problem (which the client will almost invariably present), he listens out for any evidence in the account of what the client wants, what they already have that may be healthy and positive and what skills, strengths or qualities they might possess which may be of use in building their preferred future.

## Goal focused questioning

After listening to only so much of the problem that is required to establish credibility in the client's eyes

(and perhaps to reassure themselves that there are no 'heart attack' type problems that demand a different, or even non-therapy, response) the therapist enquires how the client hopes that their life will be different in the future after the problem is solved or lessened in some way.

All of the early influential texts on Solution Focused Brief Therapy will make reference to 'the Miracle Question' and many practitioners use this question as a mainstay of their practice. Many other solution focused practitioners generate similar conversations with less obviously 'artificial' outcome orientated questions. In either case, the aim of the therapist is for the client to imagine, articulate and reflect on their own preferred future.

In the miracle question, one asks 'Suppose you were to leave here ... and do whatever it is you normally do for the rest of today and tonight you go to bed, and go to sleep. And while you are asleep, a miracle happens ... so that all your problems are solved, instantly, but because you are asleep, you can't know that a miracle just happened. When you wake up, how do you suppose you will discover that a miracle happened in the night?'

Other outcome focused questions that can lead to similar conversations might include:

- How will you know that this problem has resolved?
- How will you know that things are better than they are now?
- How would you like things to be, when the problems you have just described have become a thing of the past?

Initially, most clients will describe their preferred future in terms of 'not having' specific problems. If a goal is negatively expressed, the questioner should ask what the client wants to have happen instead. Where a goal is positively expressed, but is non-specific, the questioner should ask what concrete signs will tell them that that their non-specific goal has been achieved. If a goal is expressed as a desirable change in someone else, the questioner should ask what difference that would make to the client and how the client behaves. If a client seems to be fixated on a goal that they have not so far been able to achieve, the questioner should instead focus on what difference it would make if that goal was achieved.

> **Example of a sequence of goal focused questioning:**
>
> Q: How will you know that a miracle happened in the night?
> A: I wouldn't feel depressed any more
> Q: What will you feel when you no longer feel depressed?
> A: Just normal
> Q: How will you tell that you are feeling normal again?
> A: I will be happy
> Q: What are the signs of you being happy? Who will notice? What will they notice?
> A: Me smiling
> Q: What else?
> A: Maybe opening the window to smell the garden
> Q: And how else will you be able to tell that you are feeling normal again?

Particular attention should be paid to the many different areas of the client's life, and to the perspectives of other important people in their lives, so as not to be restricted to the areas of life in which the problems are dominant. For example, if home life is brought as 'the problem' and there are 'no problems' at work, the client should be asked what will be different at work when the problems at home have been solved.

The aim of this sequence of questioning is for the client to hear themselves describe, in concrete observable detail, a preferred future that, when they reflect upon it, they really like the sound of and which they thus have a high degree of motivation to work towards.

# Making progress

When a clear vision of a preferred future has emerged, the nature of which is motivating for the client, questions can be asked which uncover evidence of aspects of the preferred future already in place, of factors in the past and the present which are likely to be of use in the realization of the preferred future and of skills, qualities, attributes and relationships of the client, which will make the outcome more likely.

The most common technique for doing this involves the use of scaling questions, although questions eliciting exceptions to the 'rule' of the problem, coping questions (when things have been bad), and 'problem-free talk' can all be used to fill in the gap between where the client feels they are now and where they would like to be in the future.

> **Example of a scaling question:**
>
> Q: If 10/10 represents the way things are on the miracle morning and 0/10 means that there isn't a single positive thing to be said about any aspect of your life at the moment, what score would you give to your life at the current time?
> A: 3/10
> Q: What lets you give it 3/10 rather than 0/10? What is better than zero right now?
>
> Follow up questions may include:
>
> When did your score last go higher than 3/10? How did that happen?
> When did you last notice a score lower than 3/10, but somehow the score returned back to 3/10? How did you do that?
> How will you know for sure that the score has reached 5/10 for the first time?
> What score out of ten would you settle for? How will you know you have got there?

## Break and feedback

In formal Solution Focused Brief Therapy, the session is structured with a short break taken two-thirds of the way through, after which a feedback message is given to the client/family. During the break, the client can be asked to reflect on what they have talked about that has been helpful and what ways forward they may have decided upon, while the therapist, ideally with the assistance of a reflecting team who have observed the session so far, formulate a feedback message incorporating key aspects of the preferred future that has been articulated, what is already known about the partial achievement of the preferred future and what compliments the client would probably accept as obviously true of themselves.

Very few solution focused practitioners have the luxury of a reflecting team and many contexts for solution oriented conversations would not generally allow for a specific break to be taken. It may nevertheless be helpful for the solution focused practitioner to cultivate a habit of recapping, clarifying, feeding back and complimenting the client, which can all serve to 'strengthen' the account of the preferred future and the ability of the client to achieve it.

## Evidence based

The evidence base for the efficacy of the solution focused approaches is growing and broadly indicates that they are of at least equivalent efficacy to other effective therapy approaches. For an excellent online summary of solution focused therapy research findings, go to www.solutionsdoc.co.uk/sft.html.

Since a core feature of the solution focused approach involves not paying attention to the nature of the problem and since trials of psychotherapy are usually constructed around their efficacy for one particular, carefully defined problem or another, there is a paradigmatic problem for most solution oriented therapists in generating research that will sit alongside efficacy studies of other approaches to specific problems. Indeed, it is one of the attractions of the approach that a natural suspicion of apparent certainty of diagnostic categories is seen as a positive advantage for the therapist.

It would be true to say that the popularity of the approach has spread much more as a result of therapist to therapist 'contagion' than via compelling research evidence, nevertheless, such are the results of some of the larger scale implementations of the approach, particularly in the criminal justice sector, education sector, and health sector that there is an increasingly recognized role for solution focused thinking in the strategies of many public, private and voluntary sector organizations.

---

## Case study: Smith family
### Christine Hooper

Mrs Smith sought specialist help for her nine-year-old son, describing his behaviour as 'out of control.' Evan agreed that his behaviour was sometimes unacceptable and that his teachers probably agreed with his mother. He complained that his mother treated his younger brother better than him and that she was unfair in her judgements about him.

After carefully 'listening' around the problem, during which it was agreed by all that Evan was a talented footballer and that his mother had unbelievable levels of energy as a mother, the answer to the miracle question revealed that both Evan and his mother wanted a 'calm and peaceful' house in which both Evan and his mother would be 'happy'. Evan's mother would know he was happy when she heard him whistling tunes to himself around the house and acting 'grown up' like he did recently at a family wedding, even though his younger brother happened to be in a whining mood. Mrs Smith imagined herself smiling at both of her sons much more in a 'miracle' and feeling like wanting to spend time with both of them. She could even see herself looking forward to taking Evan out of the house for 'special time' on his own every week.

If he was happier, Evan thought he would experience successful schooldays which would see him coming home in a good mood, possibly even playing with his younger brother (which is something that already happened from time to time) and 'being nice' when his parents made reasonable, if unwanted, requests of him, like he did sometimes with his teachers at school.

If that miracle state was 10/10, Evan and his mother agreed that the current average would be 4/10. They thought that some days certainly reached 1/10, but occasionally they said they managed 6/10 together. They were not sure how those 6/10 days happened and they agreed it would be important to find out.

The next two meetings involved listening respectfully to Evan and his mother who brought accounts of when the problems had reappeared, but picking up on, and specifically asking for, exceptions to these examples, perhaps of the kind of behaviour (both in Evan and his mother) that they had been looking for and for evidence of the kind of relationship they both wanted to have with each other.

Special attention was paid to one particular day that had reached 8/10, which apparently came about when Mrs Smith, deciding that she was fed up of shouting at Evan for yet again causing his younger brother to cry, instead put a scribbled note in his hand stating that she was looking forward to the next time she and Evan could score a 6/10 or more together. This had made Evan smile, despite his stormy mood at the time and Evan's smile had made his mother smile. The day 'just seemed to get better' after that.

At the end of the third session and numerous explorations of exceptions and small successes, both Evan and his mother felt they knew how to reach a 6/10 whenever they wanted to and could see no reason why things could not continue to improve from that point onwards. They did not feel they needed to arrange a further appointment.

## Summary

The solution focused approach, whether or not one chooses to adopt the core techniques of formal Solution Focused Brief Therapy, is a simple and often refreshing model for conducting helpful conversations with individuals, groups and families.

If one can avoid the pitfalls of an unnecessary focus on 'the problem' without becoming 'problem phobic' in the process, and if one can resist the perils of 'solution forced therapy' in which clients or families are actively encouraged to accept something as positive that they really do not regard as positive, then significant change in previously 'stuck' situations is often possible.

## Case study: Liam

Liam is ten years old and was referred to the clinic because of occasional spells of school refusal. He attends school generally, but there are times when he misses a week or more. Liam explained that he often felt ill, with headaches and stomach aches. Liam's mother works full-time and his father is in charge of the home and childcare. There is an older sister, Claire. Claire is a high-achiever and expects to go on to university. Liam has moderate dyslexia and struggles at school.

Liam's parents both attended the appointments. Liam's father was inclined to be more lenient with Liam. He said he knew him well and believed Liam would not say that he was ill if he wasn't. Liam's mother was more confrontational. She was afraid Liam would not make a successful transition to secondary school.

With careful questioning, it was clear that Liam's school refusal was initially in the context of his mother either working from home, or going to work later in the day. Once he was out of the routine of school, it was difficult to persuade him to return. When Liam was reluctant to go to school, his parents found themselves arguing about it, and sometimes, Claire would try to help out by supporting her mother's position. It was as if Liam had three parents all saying different things.

His mother's answer to the Miracle Question was that she would like Liam to bring her a cup of tea in bed, already dressed for school. It was important for Liam's parents to decide how they would handle Liam on those days he was not keen to attend school. They were obviously able to negotiate and had done so when they had to choose which of them would work outside the home. Liam's answer to the Miracle Question was that he would wake up on a Saturday and learn that he would be spending it with his mother, and without his sister, Claire. With further questioning, he was able to describe exactly how he would spend that day. Liam's father just wanted his wife to respect his instincts about the children and to make time to go out with him once a week, rather than prioritizing her work. This would help Claire to recognize that her parents were in charge of decisions about Liam and she could relax her own position with regard to helping her parents deal with him.

Liam began secondary school in the September term. He has attended regularly and now has special help for his reading and writing difficulties, and a school mentor.

## Multiple choice questions

1. Which of the following are key questions asked of the client within solution focused therapy?

   a. The problem question
   b. The miracle question
   c. Scaling questions
   d. The responsibility question

2. With whom can solution focused therapy be used?

   a. Individuals
   b. Families
   c. Groups
   d. All of the above

### Key texts

George E, Iveson C, Ratner H (1999) *Problem to Solution: Brief Therapy with Individuals and Families.* London: BT Press.

O'Connell B, Palmer S (eds) (2003) *Handbook of Solution-Focused Therapy.* London: Sage Publications.

O'Hanlon WH, Weiner-Davis M (2003) *In Search of Solutions: A New Direction in Psychotherapy,* revised edn. New York: W.W. Morton.

# 76

# *Parenting programmes*
Cathy Laver–Bradbury

---

## Key concepts

- Different parenting programmes target different difficulties.
- Choose the programme most suitable to the child difficulties and parents' needs.
- Parents often need 'top up's' post-parenting programmes in order to maintain progress.
- The parent–child game enables parents to develop more nurturing interactions with their children by teaching an increased use of Child-Centred Behaviours (alpha commands) and a decreased use of Child-Directive Behaviours (beta commands).

---

This chapter covers:
- parenting programmes used with parents;
- the parent/child game.

## The background to parenting programmes

The use of parent training in treatment for behaviour problems has gained in popularity over the last 15 years. Various governments have been investing in both preventative and intervention programmes. A high profile example of this has been the establishment of 'Sure Start' areas, in which a variety of services are available for families to support their parenting. These are often found in areas of deprivation and poverty, both factors which are known to be associated with behaviour problems in children.

More recently, the Department of Health publication 'Delivering Better Mental Health Outcomes for People of all Ages' (Department of Health, 2011) discusses the use of parenting interventions for early intervention with young people presenting with mental health difficulties.

In 2007, The National Academy of Parenting Practitioners (NAPP) received Government funding for a number of functions which included listing and evaluating the parenting programmes being used in practice in England. The Academy was also funded to commission the training of practitioners

to be able to deliver parenting programmes to ensure that in each area there were staff trained to support parents in need of help. NAPP produced a Tool Kit for commissioners to provide information about these programmes (www.commissioning toolkit.org/). NAPP researchers also rated the programmes on a number of factors, one of these being that the research evidence available for the programmes indicated their suitability for different age groups and presenting problems. Higher ratings were given to those programmes which were evaluated in randomized controlled trials.

The Tool Kit allowed commissioners access to the programmes with the most robust evidence. This led to a significant amount of training for practitioners being commissioned throughout the UK. Predominantly these were the Incredible Years Programmes imported from the USA, which helps children with conduct disorder (Webster-Stratton, 1991; Jones et al, 2007) and the Triple P Parenting Programme from Australia (Bor et al., 2002); both of which have demonstrated evidence in improving children's behaviour problems.

NAPP encouraged training on a smaller scale, for a number of other programmes aimed at specific groups such as Mellow Parenting for parents with relationship problems with their children (Puckering, 2004), and The New Forest Parenting Programme (Sonuga-Barke et al., 2001), which is an early intervention parenting programme for preschool children presenting with attention deficit hyperactivity disorder (ADHD) difficulties. These programmes were seen as specialist programmes targeting specific difficulties rather than a more general approach of 'catch all'.

NAPP work ceased in 2010 when the funding came to an end. This work is now being continued under the Children's Workforce Development Council (CWDC) which is currently re-evaluating some of the programmes.

There are a considerable number of parenting programmes available for families. These range in cost, length of delivery and the age group of the children to whom they apply. They can be delivered on an individual basis or in a group setting. They are facilitated by voluntary workers, as well as by members of the statutory services, including social workers, health visitors, school nurses and educational psychologists and teachers, and more recently by parenting practitioners usually employed by local government.

Alongside the research in the parenting programmes there has also been some significant research regarding which attributes in parents may make accessing a parenting programme difficult; for example parental ADHD (Sonuga-Barke et al., 2002), and also what support is needed in order to maintain engagement and motivation (Routh et al., 1995; Green, 2006; Kazdin et al., 2006; McCurdy et al., 2006).

## Theoretical background

Most parenting programmes use the same underlying behaviour principles. Parents are encouraged to look at an analysis of the underlying problem and be the prime agents for change. They are encouraged to understand that behaviour is learned and can be changed and to work on trying to change the child's non-compliance. Techniques are taught around shaping behaviour; ignoring bad behaviour in order to lead to extinction; using clear commands, especially 'do' commands rather than 'don't' commands; 'catching the good'; using alpha and beta commands (see the parent–child game); using the '5 second rule' so as to give the child time to respond; use of house rules and clear boundaries.

Parenting programmes also try to help the parents develop proactive rather than reactive parenting, teaching parents strategies around

assessing their children and anticipating problems and intervening early. An example of this would be setting up children with play to keep them occupied before the parents have to do a task (Gardner et al., 1999).

## What to consider when recommending a parenting programme

It is important for the therapist to have the knowledge and experience of a programme, as well as understanding the particular problems the child has before recommending a parenting programme to a family. This means the therapist is able to outline to a parent why a particular programme could help the parent and her child and what she would gain from attending.

In addition to this, an assessment of the parent's particular parenting style would be useful, for example, if a parent had a very authoritative parenting style then a programme which is primarily aimed at discipline may not be helpful, equally a programme based on play, for parents who always play with their child, may not bring about a change in behaviour or the willing participation of the parents.

When choosing how to deliver a parent training programme as a professional, it is important to consider whether this is best done on an individual basis or within a group setting. Sometimes, it is a combination of both approaches that helps parents. Initially seeing a parent at home may help the parent transition to a group if she has already met the professional who will be running the group.

## Group delivery of parenting programmes

### Advantages

- Positive interactions between parents
- Parents can learn from each other
- A chance to socialize
- Can facilitate programme delivery to a large number of parents at once

- Possibility of fewer distractions
- Possible use of creche
- Can be fun
- May provide additional encouragement for both parents to attend

## Disadvantages

- Better to work with a co-therapist, so expensive and requires planning and discussion
- Finding a suitable venue, with appropriate equipment and chairs
- Cost of venue
- Staff to run creche
- Possibility of being side-tracked
- Managing different views within the group
- Reliant on people turning up regularly
- Confidentiality for group members
- Location of venue may not suit everyone, and times of sessions may be inconvenient
- Reliant on advertising for group members
- Too many in a group
- Parents may be intimidated by other group members

# Individually delivered parenting programmes

## Advantages

- Could be in family's own home
- Chance to 'model' some of the interactions with the child
- More personalized approach
- Appointments can be tailored to the family's schedule, which may mean parents are more likely to attend
- A chance to practice advice in own situation
- Easier to 'hold' through change
- Can begin the sessions straight away, do not need to wait to make up numbers for a group

## Disadvantages

- Staff travel time, if in family's home
- Less chance of learning from others doing same programme

- Can be difficult, if child is present, especially if parent is being negative
- Less in control of environment (e.g. visitors, TV, safety factors and so on)
- There may be less commitment from parent

The professional must consider what the purpose of offering a parenting programme is? For example:

- Has the parent approached you for help or is it that you feel they may benefit from some of the advice available? This can affect compliance. Is there an education aspect to the programme?
- Are you aiming to offer support rather than advice? Which do you feel may be more effective at this time?
- How you can assess whether the programme is having the desired outcomes? For you? For the family? For the child?

Research confirms that group-run parenting packages are effective (Webster-Stratton, 1991; Jones et al., 2007). However, even the best researched parenting packages have a drop-out from the intervention offered, sometimes as high as 50 per cent. This implies that for 50 per cent of families, it was not helpful. There have been a number of reasons given for this. These include parental factors and child factors, in addition to some of the disadvantages listed above.

# Why parenting programmes may not work

## Parent factors

- Often only one parent attends the session, so the approach taken may be inconsistently applied and there may be a lack of partner support for the parent attending
- Parental depression
- Parental ADHD
- Wrong timing for parent emotionally, for example too much else going on to focus on changing behaviours (e.g. domestic violence, divorce)
- Lack of motivation
- Dislike of having to do 'homework'
- Parental attributions
- Physical illness in parent(s)
- Mental illness in parent(s)

## Child factors

- Parenting advice may not suit temperament of child
- Undiagnosed developmental disorder (ADHD, Autistic Spectrum Disorder, speech and language disorder)
- Emotionally sensitive child
- Physical illness in child
- Mental illness in child

# Reflection and evaluation

Whichever programme is used with a family, it is important after each session the practitioners reflect on how the session went. This can be done with the parent(s) and alone, and can be done in a number of ways. Reflecting back to the parent acts as a summary of what has been said and offers an opportunity for the parent to say if she thinks something has been particularly helpful. Often written information is used to back up what has been said, as people absorb different amounts of information. Using diaries to monitor behaviour can be useful, especially if the diary is designed with a 'how did you resolve this' type question. This can often demonstrate how the parent has interpreted the advice given and checks her understanding of it.

Questionnaires can be used at the beginning and end of the programme as a way of evaluating the effectiveness. However, consideration should be given to how these are used. Is the parent to complete them in the presence of the professional? This could have an influence on how the parent completes them.

Ideally, the evaluation should be given or sent, after the parenting programme intervention, with a stamped addressed envelope provided for return and parents anonymity assured, if required. This may allow for more freedom in the information received. However, the return rate for questionnaires is often very low.

The compromise is to give the parents the questionnaire, to fill in anonymously which can then be placed in a sealed envelope.

However, if it is possible, have a colleague give the parent numbered questionnaires at the beginning and at the end of the course which can then be looked at to measure change.

If working with a colleague, it is possible to review each other's cases. This would involve a possible focus group or interview, to explore with the parent what she gained from the intervention. This is a means of giving parents a chance to say what may have been more helpful or what they would have liked more of, without offending the professional involved in the work.

Personal reflection can be very useful, especially if you are able to recognize what may be transference or counter-transference. Understanding and recognizing emotions that may not originate with the practitioner can be a vital skill when working with parents. It enables emotions to be brought into the room, which may be necessary to explore before strategies can be used.

There often appears to be a period for parents of grieving for the child they wanted (often a quiet compliant one), as opposed to the child they have (e.g. a busy 'into-everything' one). This may happen half-way through a programme.

Parenting advice is based on helping the parent accept the child they have, with their particular temperament, in order to find a way to work with the child to change behaviours. This includes acknowledgement of the child and the role the parent plays with that child. This may be difficult, and may cause a variety of emotions within the parent. This is especially so if the child has other difficulties, such as ADHD when a more specialist programme may be of use (Thompson et al., 2009).

# The Parent/Child Game

The Parent/Child Game is an innovative intervention designed to help parents who feel they have lost control of their child's behaviour 'to regain loving control without resorting to physical punishment' (Jenner, 1999).

The technique, originally devised in America in 1981, following the research of Professors Rex Forehand and Robert McMahon, enables parents to develop more nurturing interactions with their children by teaching an increased use of child-centred behaviours (alpha commands) and a decreased use of child-directive behaviours (beta commands).

Forehand and McMahon (1981) showed that an excess of child-centred behaviours could:

- enhance a child's individual development;
- reduce their non-compliance;
- improve the quality of the parent/child relationship.

However, an excess of child-directive behaviours was associated with:

- an adverse developmental impact on the child;
- raised levels of non-compliance;
- an impoverished parent/child relationship.

Child-centred behaviours meet a child's emotional needs, giving them a positive message, while child-directive behaviours demand a response from the child, or enforce a restriction on their behaviour (**Figure 76.1**).

When a referral has been made for Parent/Child Game, parents and children are invited to attend for 12 weekly sessions. On the first session, a pre-treatment baseline of the parent's child-centred and child-directive behaviours is taken.

The parent then plays with their child for a 10 minute session in another room, wearing an 'ear-bug', through which the therapist can speak to them, prompting and rewarding them for being child-centred rather than child directive towards their child. The therapist watches their interaction from behind a two-way mirror, creating an environment in which the parent and child can interact more naturally.

The first 6 weeks: 'The Child's Game', are spent working with the parents on increasing child-centred behaviours and decreasing child-directive behaviours. On the sixth session a midpoint baseline is taken. Then the following six sessions: 'The Parents Game', are spent dealing with non-compliance through the use of effective commands. On the 12th session, a post-treatment baseline is taken.

During the intervention parents are asked to spend at least 10 minutes a day practising child-centred behaviours at home, during what is often called 'Special Time' (Pentecost, 2000).

| Child Centred Behaviours | Child Directive Behaviours |
| --- | --- |
| Attends<br>Describing out loud, with warmth and enthusiasm, what the child is doing | Questions<br>Asking the child questions about what they're doing, what they know and so on |
| Praise<br>Clearly expressing approval and delight towards your child | Criticism<br>Complaining about the child, scolding them, reminding them of past failures |
| Smiles<br>Making eye contact and smiling right into the child's eyes in a loving and friendly way | Negative Looks<br>Looking at them in a cold, bored, angry, disapproving or threatening way |
| Imitation<br>Copying the child's actions, words or noises with enthusiasm | Teaching<br>Giving the child advice or facts that they have not asked for |
| Ask to Play<br>Asking the child what they would like you to do, how they would like you to play with them | Commands<br>Giving the child instructions, calling out their name, telling them to look at something |
| Positive Touches<br>Giving the child a warm affectionate hug, kiss, pat or stroke | Negative Touches<br>Touching the child in a way that they do not like or is considered unacceptable by most people |
| Ignoring 'Minor Naughties'<br>Not responding and turning your head away when the child is misbehaving in a non-dangerous way | 'No'<br>Saying 'No!' to the child as a threat or a warning. |

Figure 76.1 Key child-centred and child directive behaviours.

## Case study: Samuel

Samuel was five years old when he was referred for extreme verbal and physical aggression, and non-compliance, both at home and at school. He was only allowed to attend school part time as a result of his behaviour.

Samuel's parents were separated. He was living with his mother and had only very sporadic contact with his father. Until his father left when he was four years old, Samuel had witnessed countless acts of domestic violence, which involved his father attacking his mother, both verbally and physically.

Both parents believed Samuel to have ADHD and were waiting for a diagnosis.

### Pre-treatment baseline

Samuel's mother scored nine child-centred behaviours (cc) and 67 child-directive behaviours (cd): a ratio of 1 cc:7.4 cd.

Samuel's father scored five child-centred behaviours and 79 child-directive behaviours: a ratio of 1 cc:15.8 cd.

### Post-treatment baseline

Samuel's mother scored 82 child-centred behaviours (cc) and 12 child-directive behaviours (cd): a ratio of 6.8 cc:1 cd.

Samuel's father scored 76 child-centred behaviours and 19 child-directive behaviours: a ratio of 4 cc:1 cd.

The radical change in parenting style that can be seen in the post-treatment baseline scores had an equally radical effect on Samuel. During and following the intervention, his parents noted enormous changes in his behaviour, both at home and at school. He was happier, less anxious, no longer violent or aggressive, and could concentrate for longer periods of time at school. His parents no longer felt he had ADHD, and the school were now happy for him to attend full-time.

For Samuel, the most important change was the shift in his parents' relationship. As they had been working together on the same goal for the 12 weeks, they had learned the need to cooperate for Samuel's sake in the future.

Research has shown that after the intervention of the Parent/Child Game, relationships between parents and children become more positive, and tension and stress between family members is reduced. 'Children's acting out behaviour decreases in response to their parents increasing confidence in providing clear boundaries and emotional nurturing. These benefits have been found to last for many years without the need for further professional input' (Jenner, 1999).

In families where there is a significant cause for concern, the Parent/Child Game can also work as an assessment tool. Family relationships can be evaluated, and an objective assessment made of whether professional input is likely to be successful in enabling parents to make changes in order to meet their children's needs more effectively.

## Multiple choice questions

1. What should you consider when recommending a parent to attend a parenting programme?

    a. Suitability of the programme to meet the parent's needs?
    b. The location
    c. The parental motivation
    d. All of the above

2. The National Association of Parenting Practitioners role has been taken over by?

    a. The NHS
    b. Education

c. Children's Workforce Development Council

d. Social Services

3. When trying to find information regarding the evidence base for parenting programmes the best place to look is?

a. www.commissioningtoolkit.org/

b. The Internet

c. University libraries

d. Focus

## Key texts

Forehand R, Long N (1996) *Parenting the Strong Willed Child: The Clinically Proven Five Week Programme for Parents of 2–6 year olds.* Chicago: Contemporary Books.

Jenner S (1999) *The Parent/Child Game.* London: Bloomsbury Publishing.

Kazdin AE, Whitley M, Marciano PL (2006) Child–therapist and parent–therapist alliance and therapeutic change in the treatment of children referred for oppositional, aggressive, and antisocial behavior. *Journal of Child Psychology and Psychiatry,* **47**: 436–45.

Pentecost D (2000) *Parenting the ADD Child.* London: Jessica Kingsley Publishers.

Thompson MJJ, Laver-Bradbury C, Ayres M et al. (2009) A small-scale randomised controlled trial of the revised New Forest Programme for Pre-schoolers with Attention Deficit Hyperactivity Disorder. *European Child and Adolescent Psychiatry,* **18**: 605–16.

Webster-Stratton C (1991) Annotation: Strategies for helping families with conduct disordered children. *Journal of Child Psychology and Psychiatry Newsletter,* **32**: 1047–62.

# 77 *Principles of group work*
### Stuart Gemmell

## Key concepts

- Step one: need for groups
- Step two: co-workers
- Step three: co-workers planning and identify supervisor
- Step four: advertise group
- Step five: referral stage
- Step six: individual assessments and plenary session
- Step seven: group up and running
- Step eight: group evaluation and exit interviews

## Introduction

Groups can be a significant therapeutic tool and a particularly helpful approach for young people. Where possible, the group should be time-limited and closed. There should be co-workers running the group and they must identify a supervisor. The co-workers must ensure that they are freed by their employing organization to ring-fence the group work time. Where possible, the group should be of mixed gender. A common unifying need for the group must be identified. Group members must be willing to explore new skills and coping mechanisms with others in a group setting.

There is a very clear step-by-step approach that needs to be identified and acted upon to ensure effective group work. Anything short of this process and the group itself becomes at best unmanageable and at worse counter-productive to the group member's needs and well-being.

## Step one: Identify need for group

*Many emotional problems involve difficulties in relating to others... Although the therapist can help to work out some of these problems, the final test lies in how well the person can apply the attitudes and responses learned in therapy, to relationships in everyday life. Group therapy permits clients to work out their problems in the presence of others, observe how other people react to their behaviour and to try out new ways of responding when old ones prove unsatisfactory.*
### (Edward et al., 2000)

Atkinson's notion that groups can act as a training environment for the individual to 'practice' new coping mechanisms is supported further by Doel and Sawdon (2001) who state: 'Groups can provide a more effective environment to experience empowerment because they can be used to replicate or simulate the larger society; in many respects they are microcosms of the wider society'.

## Step two: Identify co-workers

There are many benefits to co-working, such as the ability to enhance practice, learn new interventions from another professional, receive instant feedback on the delivery of an intervention and share an experience that is all too often lost in the individual work. However, Doel and Sawdon (2001) caution that: 'Co-working a group can be a bit like parenthood; as a twosome everything has been going fine, but when the children come along you suddenly discover you have very different views about how to raise them!'

# Step three: Co-workers planning and identifying a supervisor

## Planning

The organizational background of the group is important. Facilitators need to ascertain whether or not there is enough support from colleagues and management to allow the group to take place. At this stage, the objectives of the group need to be made clear so that all stakeholders, including potential group members, are aware of the functions and outcomes of the group.

Details of group composition, size (6–12 is ideal), timing, accommodation and transport are to be flagged up at this stage of planning, as are any requirements for special facilities, materials and equipment (Doel and Sawdon, 2001). Dedicated time should be allocated for co-worker reflection and supervision.

There is a very practical and stress-reducing exercise co-workers should consider undertaking at this stage of the planning; spending time individually to create a 'What If' list in relation to scenarios that may arise in the group. Examples may be:

What if......... I can't make it one week, will you run the group alone?

What if......... I don't agree with a statement you make in the group? Do I challenge you there and then or wait for our wash-up time or at supervision?

What if......... I plan to go on holiday during the time span of the group?

What if......... I have different attitudes to you? Say, about swearing?

The more 'What Ifs' that are raised, the more preparation and contingency plans are identified, thus reducing anxieties should any arise.

## Supervision

A supervisor is vital for the well-being of the co-workers. The supervisor should have previous experience of group work and appreciate the 'marriage of convenience' the co-workers have entered into. This is not to say that a supervisor should be seen as an 'expert' in a particular group theme, but that their supervision skills be sought due to their understanding and experience in such areas as: system theory, co-working and recognition of dynamics that operate within groups.

Supervision can help:

- resolve any difficulties in the complex co-leadership relationship;
- manage the anxieties and demands of group work;
- discuss issues raised within the group;
- monitor the effectiveness of the work;
- develop the skills and knowledge of the workers;
- share responsibility for the group.

# Step four: Advertise group

Groups do not exist in a vacuum and to a very large degree rely on the wider community or organization giving the identified group validity and sanction.

To this end the first task facing the co-workers is the engagement of the organization and wider community, ensuring that:

1. Individuals are supported outside the group by the organization, often by a key worker.
2. The organization openly supports the group's aims and objectives.
3. The organization recognizes the boundaries of the group in a practical manner, such as a dedicated room which will not have interruptions from staff or other visitors.
4. The co-workers are given protected time for the organization and planning of the group.

## How to advertise

There are a variety of ways to advertise the group, including:

- presentations to the organization's meeting including the Aims and Objectives, practical matters and protocols, which will include a referral form;

- a written memo or flyer to each relevant organization member detailing the points highlighted above.

# Step five: Referral stage

Once the group has been advertised it is anticipated that referrals will begin to reach the co-workers and they may consider the following:

1. There are identified criteria for the group and they should both be satisfied that each referral meets those criteria.
2. Making themselves available to possible referrers to talk through appropriate referrals.
3. Visualizing the referred individual in the group setting.
4. The composition of the group in relation to age, gender, race and presenting difficulty. It is unrealistic to expect a single female or male to attend a group of six or seven members of the opposite sex. This is not a criterion for exclusion, but rather the need for that particular individual to be made aware that they might be the only male/female.

The letter is often the first contact between the co-workers and the individual referred. As such it is important that the letter is clear, concise and friendly. The letter should include a brief statement regarding the aims of the group and include practical statements with regard to the frequency and timing of the group.

# Step six: Individual assessments and plenary session

## Individual assessments

The whole notion of holding individual assessment interviews allows both the referred person and the co-workers the opportunity to look at the viability of working together. It is important that the individual being interviewed voices their own perceived benefits and concerns about attending such a group. It is vital that practical considerations are highlighted, such as how the person is to travel to the group.

One aspect the co-workers may consider voicing at the point of initial interview is that they are not expecting the interviewee to commit to the group until they have experienced the plenary session.

## Self-evaluation forms

There are many ways to evaluate group work, but probably the most rewarding is a self-evaluation form that group members use to monitor their own sense of development. Despite it being a self-assessment tool, the by-product may be used in auditing the effectiveness of the group.

## Plenary session

It is the function of the plenary session to achieve three distinctive goals:

1. To give prospective group members a 'taster' of the group the co-workers hope to run.
2. To give all those attending the plenary meeting the opportunity to familiarize themselves with the other group members.
3. At the end of the plenary session individuals 'sign up' to the group. This allows the formation of the group to be undertaken and group trust to be initiated through a sense of ownership.

# Step seven: Group up-and-running

Members have a right to expect that the co-workers will have a clear plan of how the group will run and operate in terms of content and style. Time spent by the co-workers before and after each group will allow negotiation of changes to take place so that the material, methods and pace of the group can be constantly adapted to suit the needs of its members.

Such meetings can reduce stress on the partnership by highlighting worker differences, the allocation of group tasks including who opens or closes the group, who introduces what and when in the group and the administration and record-keeping surrounding the group.

## Step eight: Group ending

*The best way to achieve a concerted closure is to ensure that everybody knows when that is.*

**(Doel and Sawdon, 2001)**

The ending of a group is as crucially important as the beginning and should be planned by the co-workers and group members well in advance.

The following is a list of useful considerations when planning the end of the group:

- Ensure that the group ends in the same environment as it began. This will enable the membership to say goodbye both practically and (as importantly) psychologically.
- Ensure that any graphics or written work produced by the group is on display. This will help with the group evaluation process and encourage individuals to recall the journey they have undertaken in the group's lifetime.
- That while the co-workers hope that the members may keep in contact with each other for added ongoing support, the group is ended and will not be repeated in this format.

## Group evaluation

It is important to recognize that while members remain individuals they, including the co-workers, have shared a unique experience and will need to validate and evaluate that experience as a group.

Evaluating the group as a whole permits all the membership to grasp the uniqueness of the group's experience.

## Exit interviews

*Members enter a group as individuals and they leave as individuals... It is important that they are given space to express their opinions and concerns as individuals.*

**(Doel and Sawdon, 2001)**

When the group is ended, the co-workers and individual group members meet up for one last time to consider the progress the individual has made in relation to the group experience they have just completed.

At this interview the self-evaluation form is once again completed and reviewed alongside the earlier pre-group form. It is important that the individual identifies what has changed for them and how this change has occurred.

The co-workers should be aware that many individuals find it very difficult to attend the exit interviews, regardless of how positive or even negative they have viewed their own participation in the group to be.

One way of maximizing the potential for this final exit interview is to arrange exit interviews in the final group session.

In the final interview, it is important that the co-workers make reference to the participation of the individual and express openly and with conviction that the uniqueness of the group was down to the participation of that individual being present in the group.

## Case study: Sarah

Sarah (13) is a young carer and lives with her disabled mother.

As a result of bullying, Sarah has become more and more isolated and would rather stay at home looking after her mother than attend school. The school referred Sarah to the Peer Support Group, due to her isolation and with growing concerns leading up to GCSE options. Both her mother and the school report that Sarah is a bright student and should do well if she takes her exams. This ambition is being challenged by the bullying and by Sarah's erratic school attendance.

### Outcome

Through an individual assessment with the group's co-workers, Sarah was offered a place in the Peer Support Group, which she attended for the full 12 sessions. Through direct interventions on issues such as anxiety management, self-esteem, confidence-building and assertiveness, Sarah was able to 'practise' new ways of challenging, managing and sharing her worries.

The outcome was rewarding both for Sarah and for her fellow peer group members. She became more open to discussing her fears with her mother and with her peers. Sarah is taking her GCSEs and now attends school regularly, receiving ongoing support from the Young Carers Association. Her mother has a support worker.

## Multiple choice questions

1. What is the ideal number of individuals to have in a group setting?

   a. 4–5
   b. 5–7
   c. 6–12
   d. 8–14
   e. 0–16

2. Which of the following is not an essential consideration when setting up a group?

   a. Identifying the need for a group
   b. The group identifying a common need once established
   c. The group co-workers identifying a supervisor
   d. The group and co-workers being of the same gender
   e. The group co-workers having time away from their organization to facilitate the group

### Key texts

Doel M, Sawdon C (2001) *The Essential Group Worker in Teaching and Learning Creative Group Work*, 2nd impression. London and Philadelphia: Jessica Kingsley.

Edward E, Bem DJ, Nolan H, Smith S (2000) *Hilgard's Introduction Psychology*, 13th edn. San Diego: Harcourt College Publishers.

Whitaker DS (1987) *Using Groups to Help People*. New York and Hove: Routledge (reprinted 1992).

# Group work for parents of children with ADHD: The New Forest Parenting Programme

Cathy Laver-Bradbury

---

## Key concepts

- Group programmes for parents whose children have attention deficit hyperactivity disorder (ADHD) should target the neuropsychological deficits seen in ADHD.
- The group should include psycho-education about ADHD and this should be individually tailored to the parents' child.
- Groups can provide much needed support for parents whose child has ADHD.

---

## Why a different type of parent group for those with a ADHD diagnosis?

Having worked with many different types of parenting programmes over the years, many of them were not specific enough to help parents whose children have ADHD. Trying to adapt programmes to cover issues that are particular to children with ADHD in an existing programme is possible but often this led to frustration in the parents and in the professional trying to facilitate the group.

Parents with a child who has ADHD have different needs than parents whose children have other difficulties. They need to understand what are ADHD behaviours, i.e. the behaviour the child cannot help and those behaviours which are not linked to ADHD. They also need to recognize the characteristics in their child and have specific strategies to target the neuro-psychological deficits.

## What is different about the New Forest Parenting Programme?

This New Forest Parenting Programme (NFPP) group programme has been developed over a number of years with the help of many parents and professionals. Its aims are to improve the parents' knowledge of what ADHD is and how it affects their child and give them ways of helping their child with these specific difficulties. Helping parents understand ADHD is fundamental to the programme, as is targeting the areas of difficulty their child has. The group allows parents to highlight specific areas of difficulties that they recognize in their child and therefore often provides specific as well as general ADHD knowledge. The programme can be used alone or with the DVD 'Living with ADHD' (Thompson et al., 2009). The DVD is particularly useful if parents have difficulty with literacy or for parents whose learning style is visual. It is worth asking parents discreetly if they need any help with reading any literature. Experience tells us that often parents with literacy difficulties will have someone who they trust who will read important information to them. If this is not the case then alternative arrangements need to be identified.

The benefit of the DVD is that it provides a focus for discussion and can be shown in sections each week to reinforce the strategies being discussed. Additionally, on week one when parents can be nervous at attending the group and speaking out, it can give a visual reinforcement that they are not the only ones experiencing difficulties, as parents talk about their children on the DVD. DVDs can be lent to partners or grandparents not able to attend the group to provide a consistent approach for the child.

## Evidence base for the NFPP

This group programme has been developed from the NFPP which is a one-to-one home-based intervention (Thompson et al., 1999; Sonuga-Barke et al., 2001), for use in a group format. The benefits of a group intervention are to enable parents to support one another, to share concerns and perhaps importantly for parents to realize they are not the only ones having difficulties. Parents whose children have ADHD are often isolated and feel under-skilled as parents. The group aims to raise the self-esteem of parents and empower them in being their child's advocate in a variety of settings in addition to increase their knowledge and understanding of ADHD. This approach has been subject to evaluation (Laver-Bradbury and Harris, 2008).

## Age appropriateness of the NFPP

The NFPP-group programme is not age specific; the core ADHD characteristics often remain similar after pre-school up until adolescence (and arguably into adulthood!). The main difference in adolescents is that the hyperactive symptoms in the child reduce and the young person is seen as fidgety and internally restless rather than hyperactive, but the need to understand the characteristics is crucial in both helping a young child as well as a teenager with ADHD. The children and teenagers need to understand themselves and their good and less good points as well as learning to problem solve for themselves. The strategies that parents of adolescents can use are very similar if not the same as in younger ADHD children but they need to be adapted to fit the teenage years, for example in how the strategies are initiated perhaps using humour to allow the adolescent to understand their difficulties without feeling humiliated or ridiculed. From experience it is often valuable to have mixed age groups of children whose parents attend the group and as long as they are not the only one with a teenager it seems to work well. (This does depend on the teenagers having ADHD without conduct disorder; If the teenager is exhibiting conduct difficulties it can be very worrying for parents of younger children to hear the young person's problems, so be mindful of this when organizing the group. It may be better to run a group specifically for those parents whose children have ADHD and conduct disorder as their needs will be different.)

## Length of the NFPP

The NFPP-group programme is a minimum of 6 weeks (preferably 8). It is designed so that weeks can be interchanged to meet the specific needs of the group of parents you are working with. At the beginning of the group it is important for parents to tell the group leaders what they are hoping to get from the group. This helps parents feel that they are being listened to and their concerns are being taken seriously, rather than 'this is a programme for parents of ADHD children' approach. Our experience when running the groups has been that those parents, when asked, say they want to know how to manage their child's temper outbursts as well as their own, how to keep calm, and how to deal with outside pressures. They appear to have some understanding of the characteristics of ADHD but have difficulty in seeing these characteristics in the behaviours their child may be exhibiting. By really exploring and highlighting the characteristics throughout the sessions, as parents give examples, this appears to enhance their understanding and allows them to discriminate between what are ADHD characteristics and what are not, and then explore how to deal with difficult issues.

## Practicalities

Each week has an outline of what should be covered and this is based on the NFPP-Step by Step – helping your child with ADHD (Laver-Bradbury et al., 2010), which is given to parents at the beginning of the group. However, there is some flexibility in how the sessions can be ordered. The order of the weeks depends on the group requirements which can be ascertained on week one. The outline of the contents of the next 5 weeks can then be completed and linked to the manual, and a copy given to the parents so they have a rough outline of what will happen each week and this also helps the group leaders to remain focused. Additional problems can be discussed as the group progresses or extra sessions added. We have found that review groups approximately 6–8 weeks after the end of the 6–8 week programme allows the group to meet up again and support each other as well as serving as a reminder on the strategies. We use a simple question and answer paper for parents as a starting point for discussion.

It is anticipated that group leaders will have in-depth knowledge of the NFPP and will familiarize themselves with the contents prior to running a course. The group programme is set out in weekly sessions with handouts needed for each session included. Basic evaluation measures are undertaken at the beginning and end of the group.

## Multiple choice questions

1. What do you think a group programme for parents of children with ADHD should include?

    a. Support for the parents
    b. A chance to educate the parents to fully understand what ADHD is?
    c. Tailored strategies to meet the parents' needs
    d. All of the above

2. What considerations should be taken into account when running a group?

    a. How to teach parents?
    b. Parents' learning style?
    c. Making sure everyone agrees?
    d. That it is short

### Key texts

Laver-Bradbury C, Harris H (2008) Advanced Nurse Practitioners for Attention Deficit Hyperactivity Disorder (In) Department of Health. *New Ways of Working in Child and Adolescent Mental Health*. London: Department of Health.

Laver-Bradbury C, Thompson M, Weeks A et al. (2010) *Step by Step Help for Children with ADHD*. London: Jessica Kingsley.

Sonuga-Barke EJS, Daley D, Thompson M et al. (2001) Parent based therapies for pre-school Attention/Hyperactivity Disorder: a randomized controlled trial with a community sample. *American Academy of Child and Adolescent Psychiatry*, **40**: 402–8.

Thompson M, Laver-Bradbury C, Weeks A (2009) *Living with ADHD a DVD for Parents and Professionals*. University of Southampton Media Services.

## 79 Group work with adolescents: Safe House

**Charlotte Young**

---

### Key concepts

- Groups have been set up in CAMHS to help adolescents experiencing, for example, anxiety or depression.
- In groups, adolescents can learn new skills, such as how to better manage their depression using cognitive behaviour therapy (CBT) and practise social skills through peer interaction. These skills increase self-esteem and confidence.
- In a group, some of the perceived difficulties can be normalized as part and parcel of adolescence.
- Group work can be more effective in teaching new skills rather than individual work.
- Research and anecdotal evidence indicates that peer support is vital when young people are experiencing mental health problems (Smith and Leon, 2001; Garcia et al., 2007).
- Group work can be cost-effective when compared with individual work.
- The national service framework (NSF) for young people, children and maternity services (Department of Health, 2004a) recommends multi-agency working in CAMHS and new ways of working with children and young people.

---

## Introduction

Teen Safe House in Southampton is an example of a group for adolescents. It is a comprehensively supervised, referral-only group for 13–19 year olds. It is held weekly for 2 hours after the school/college day, with the primary aim of providing a safe group environment to improve self-esteem, develop social skills and ultimately promote mental well-being.

The group is run in partnership between CAMHS and a local young person's information advice and counselling service (with mixed voluntary and statutory funding) called No Limits. CAMHS provide a mental health worker and supervision to the team. No Limits provide a worker, administrative support and management of the group. Grants from CAMHS and charities finance the group and the Local Authority provides the venue free of charge. Volunteers from education and youth charities facilitate the weekly sessions, alongside nursing and social work students.

Referrals come from both CAMHS and No Limits.

Participants in the group can have a mix of learning and mental health needs. Adolescents must be socially isolated, with difficulties in socializing and interacting with their peers, to be referred to the group.

As in any therapeutic process, groups need boundaries and rules, for example expectations of behaviour and rules for attendance, guidance about referral criteria, the group's therapeutic aims and how to join the group. It is most important that both the group and the group leaders are well-supervised. Young people can be highly emotional. Testing the boundaries is common and healthy in adolescence. The group leaders need a safe space to off-load the issues raised.

'Every Child Matters' (Department of Health, 2003b) recommends that young people make a positive contribution to society by engaging in community activity. Safe House offers the opportunity for community engagement and community activities. Improved mental well-being is another key recommendation.

## Case study 1: Karen

Karen is 15 years old. She was initially referred by CAMHS because she had been bullied at school and was socially isolated, with few friends. When she joined the group, it was noticed that she had significant social anxiety and that she was anxious about trying out new things, for example when cutting out pictures for a group collage, she was afraid of 'getting it wrong'. Through CBT-based techniques led by the mental health worker, she was able to engage in new challenges and lessen her anxiety. This helped improve her self-esteem. Karen was able to practise the CBT skills immediately in a group setting, for example trying out new tasks that previously she would have avoided.

Because the group listened to her, Karen was able to find her own 'voice' (McDonald et al., 2009). The positive feedback from her peers when she expressed herself increased her self-esteem. Being able to practise these new communication skills and receive positive feedback from her peers in a safe environment, Karen felt more confident to try them out beyond the group setting.

## Case study 2: Ali

Ali is 14. He was referred to Safe House via CAMHS, by his psychiatrist, because of his difficulties in mixing with other young people and regulating his emotions in response to them. Ali had a diagnosis of ADHD and oppositional defiance disorder (ODD), meaning he presented as quite challenging in the Safe House group setting. Team supervision for Safe House workers was highly important in this instance, enabling a consistent group response. Safe House works on a tight structured 2-hour session. This was supportive and containing for Ali.

During one group session Ali reported being bullied at school. In response the No Limits worker was able to refer him to the No Limits drop-in service at his school. In addition, Ali felt safe enough in the group environment to share his experience of being bullied; something he had felt uncomfortable talking about before (Steen and Bemak, 2008). By allowing Ali to talk about his concerns and setting the agenda for the group discussion, his confidence improved and this in turn improved his mental well-being. When Ali spoke about his concerns, the group members were able to help him to problem solve.

Given the opportunity to engage in shared problem solving and ultimately help another young person, the self-esteem of the other group members increased.

## Case study 3: Chris

Chris was referred by No Limits. He and his mother had asked for social activities in the local area that would meet his needs. Chris had had difficulties in previous groups due to his 'challenging behaviour'. In the group, Chris exhibited his anxiety through disruptive behaviours, such as dominating the group and challenging the boundaries, for example, speaking on his mobile phone during the session. He had a diagnosis of Asperger's syndrome.

To help Chris to develop the theory of mind skills, i.e. the ability to recognize that others think differently to oneself, he was engaged in group activities, such as discussions and games (Mackey et al., 2007). This was especially useful for him as he could model the responses of young people without Asperger's syndrome. Research has demonstrated that groups are effective in improving social communication in young people with Asperger's syndrome (Mackay et al., 2007).

Chris initially adopted the role of 'trouble maker' in the group. Through the workers recognizing his needs and adapting their responses to him, the other group members modelling pro-social behaviour and their gentle challenging of his behaviour, Chris was able to abandon that role. The group encouraged him by responding more positively towards him as he became more pro-social. During a residential weekend, Chris was able to generalize the skills learnt to a real-life situation (Mackay et al., 2007), for example talking to other people there, including the activity organizers.

## Outcomes

Karen went on to college, joined in activities based there and no longer required Safe House. Ali was able to attend a 'mainstream youth group'. Chris developed more social skills and identified some behaviours he wished to work on.

Through Safe House, most young people gain in confidence and many have commented that they learnt how to better manage their anger. The group members have developed friendships with each other outside the group, greatly reducing their social isolation (McDonald et al., 2009). They have developed 'life skills', for example managing a night away from home.

In summary, groups can provide a safe environment where adolescents feel able to express themselves. They must be appropriately supervised and the staff must have regular clinical supervision. A group like Safe House can provide a cost-effective intervention that improves an adolescent's mental health, self-esteem and social skills.

For multiple choice questions please refer to Chapter 77, Principles of group work.

### Key texts

Dwivedi KN (ed.) (1993) *Group Work with Children and Adolescents: A Handbook*. London: Jessica Kingsley Publishers.

Mackay T, Knott F, Dunlop A-W (2007) Developing social interaction and understanding in individuals with autism spectrum disorder: a group work intervention. *Journal of Intellectual and Developmental Disability*, **32**: 279–90.

Malekoff A (2004) *Group Work with Adolescents: Principles and Practice*, 2nd edn. New York: Guilford Press.

# 80

# Inpatient services

**Mary Mitchell and Christopher Gale**

---

## Key concepts

- Inpatient services provide a safe environment to assess and treat the most severely mentally ill children and young people.
- They can pose disadvantages, such as institutionalizing the child/young person, separating them from their community and support network.
- The last decade has seen the emergence of intensive community-based CAMHS services to work in partnership with Tier 4 inpatient and traditional community services.

---

## Introduction

When a young person with a severe mental illness has difficulties that cannot be managed by the family or community services, admission to an inpatient psychiatric unit may be considered. The usual reasons for an inpatient stay include:

- the severity of the illness;
- the need to try complex medication regimes such as Clozapine (an atypical anti-psychotic requiring close monitoring and weekly blood tests);
- risk of suicide and/or risk to others;
- when families can no longer cope;
- when there is uncertainty about the diagnosis and a period of assessment is required.

Inpatient psychiatric units vary across the country with differing age ranges, criteria for admission, therapies on offer and average length of stay. The research evidence regarding inpatient care is difficult to interpret because of methodological problems in making comparisons between such different services. Little is known about the factors influencing hospital admission, the quality of care in hospital, optimum duration of stay and outcome.

The Bridge over Troubled Waters report from the Health Advisory Service (1986) identified serious weaknesses and inequalities in in-patient services for adolescents. There has since been extensive evidence of increasing fragmentation and inadequacies of planning (McDougall et al., 2008; Kurtz, 2009).

The Department of Health directed the Mental Health research Initiative to commission the National Inpatient Child and Adolescent Psychiatry Study (NICAPS; O'Herlihy et al., 2001), which demonstrated:

- lack of emergency beds;
- insufficient numbers of beds;
- poor provision for high-risk groups;
- poor liaison with other services.

There are only 80 inpatient units for children and adolescents in England and Wales, including private sector facilities, fewer than there were ten years ago and further closures are planned.

The Royal College of Psychiatrists (2005) recommended the following numbers of psychiatric inpatient beds per population:

- For adolescents:
  - 6–9 beds/100 000 young people under the age of 18.
- For children:
  - 2–4 beds/250 000 population;
  - 3–6 beds/100 000 young people under the age of 18.

There are large regional variations in the number of beds available to young people with psychiatric illness, including those in the private sector. In south-east England there are currently approximately 12.9 beds/100 000 population under the age of 18, whereas in the south-west, there are about four beds/100 000 and in Wales, there are approximately three beds/100 000 young people under the age of 18.

The NICAPS survey (O'Herlihy et al., 2001) demonstrated that children and young people admitted to inpatient units have multiple, co-morbid diagnoses and severe disorders. The most common diagnoses in male children included conduct disorder, hyperkinetic disorder and mood disorders. In female children, the most common diagnoses were eating disorders and mood disorders. In male adolescents, the most common diagnoses included psychotic illnesses (35 per cent), mood disorders (22 per cent), conduct disorders (22 per cent) and eating disorders (6 per cent). In female adolescents, the most common diagnoses were eating disorders (33 per cent), mood disorders (19 per cent) and psychotic illnesses (14 per cent). In most units, the average length of stay is three months.

There are wide variations in the numbers and skills of the staff in inpatient units: 72 per cent of the staff are nurses, 34 per cent of whom are unqualified; 65 per cent of units have a social worker; 60 per cent have a psychologist; 45 per cent an occupational therapist; 40 per cent a family therapist and only 28 per cent child psychotherapists.

The NICAPS study attempted to measure the number of young people admitted to other facilities, such as adult psychiatric wards and paediatric wards, due to the lack of appropriate beds in adolescent units. Nine health authorities reported 26 inappropriate adolescent admissions to their 18 adult wards. From this snapshot figure, it was estimated that more than 500 inappropriate admissions of young people with mental illness to adult wards were occurring annually. There are likely to be another 200–300 inappropriate admissions of young people to paediatric wards.

While there is constant demand for emergency admission to inpatient beds, it is not feasible to keep a bed empty for emergencies. Therefore, in most areas, psychiatric units for young people are functioning at full capacity and it is rarely possible to admit in an emergency.

Although there is little research in this area, it is likely that many of the requests for urgent inpatient psychiatric beds are inappropriate. Often the young person needs a safe place and a brief period of assessment, following which it is more apparent that the young person does not have severe psychiatric illness, but emotional disturbance secondary to complex social or educational problems or dangerous conduct-disordered behaviour. In instances like these, the young person may require a multiagency approach, coordinating the support of CAMHS, social services and education. It is unlikely that psychotherapeutic treatments will be sustainable or effective while the environment in which the young person lives remains the primary cause of the problem.

Young people are frequently admitted to paediatric wards, following presentation in accident and emergency departments with deliberate self-harm. This is in accordance with the guidelines of the Royal College of Psychiatrists (1998) which recommend that any young person under the age of 16 should be admitted to hospital after any episode of self-harm so that a psychiatric assessment can be arranged. These young people may remain on the ward beyond the time necessary to manage the medical aspects of the self-harm, to wait for the psychiatric assessment from the local CAMHS service, which may not have the manpower to provide a rapid response. The young person may be obliged to wait in an inappropriate setting, where nursing staff do not have the training to manage psychological problems, and where they are at risk of hospital-acquired infection. The process of prolonged admission might reinforce the self-harming behaviour, as a way of problem-solving or obtaining emotional support.

There may be a widespread expectation, among hospital staff, that the individual should be admitted immediately to an inpatient psychiatric unit for young people. However, just as is the case for adults, not all young people presenting in crisis with deliberate self-harm are suffering from a severe psychiatric illness requiring admission to an inpatient psychiatric hospital. Work by Chitsabesan et al. (2003) demonstrated that approximately one-third of these young people have self-harmed because of a problem they cannot solve, for example, school-related difficulties, relationship breakdown, fear of pregnancy. One-third of young people may have moderate psychiatric illness, which could be manageable in the community, following the interventions of CAMHS. Finally, one-third may present because of complex difficulties, secondary to alcohol or drug abuse, chronic social deprivation and mental illness, requiring a multiagency approach.

# Advantages to inpatient admission

When a young person is a risk to themselves, because of strong suicidal urges, or when a young person is a risk to others, because of the effect of severe mental illness on their behaviour, hospital admission can provide safety. Close supervision and modifications to their environment in hospital will keep them safe and protect other people. Once safely held in this manner, a thorough assessment of psychiatric and psychological processes can be made and intensive treatments commenced. These might include psychopharmacological treatment and psychotherapy.

In hospital, the young person may benefit from contact with other young people in similar circumstances. The group process can be used for therapeutic purposes, as in the case of eating disorders, whereby the group effect is helpful in encouraging the individual to eat.

The young person often benefits from some separation from the family, who may require respite following the conflict and turmoil that accompanies mental illness in a family member. However, there can be disadvantages in this separation and the family should be included, wherever possible, in treatment planning and provision.

Hospital admission provides an opportunity to complete physical assessments and investigations, which may be very relevant to the cause of the mental illness. It allows complex psychopharmacological treatment regimes to be introduced safely in a controlled environment.

# Disadvantages of inpatient admission

There are risks to inpatient admission and some research evidence that admission to an inpatient unit is associated with worse outcome.

## Disempowerment

On a practical level, the admission process can disempower parents, who have made considerable efforts to manage the difficulties presented by their child at home. This is particularly evident in the cases of young people with anorexia nervosa. Young people who have refused to eat and who have lost weight to a dangerous degree at home often eat regularly with peer group support in hospital. With the assistance of highly skilled staff, the young people frequently make surprisingly rapid progress. Unless parents are involved in this recovery process from the beginning of the inpatient admission, with early and increasing periods of weekend leave during which they can practice the lessons learnt from staff, it is unlikely that this progress will be transferred home after discharge. The parent may feel alienated and disempowered and become increasingly reliant on hospital support, thus potentially aggravating the situation.

## Splitting

The members of staff who work in psychiatric hospitals are very aware of the difficulties inherent in managing young people with relationship difficulties. It is not unusual, for example, for a young person to relate to one member of staff more easily than to others. Often this results in the young person seeking out their special member of staff, paying less heed to other staff, which, if it goes unrecognized, can lead to staff tension and differences in approach, which may be detrimental to the treatment programme. This is known as 'splitting' and is frequently misinterpreted as manipulative behaviour, for example a young person struggling with anorexia nervosa may relate particularly well to one member of staff and, as a result of that close relationship, may induce a less rigid stance around dietary issues and avoid eating adequately as a consequence. If the staff team works well, these potential pitfalls are anticipated and avoided by establishing clear boundaries around the professional relationship with the patients and staff.

'Splitting' is often played out between staff and parents, or between staff in the community or staff in different agencies, and can lead to a breakdown in the therapeutic alliance if it is not recognized early and managed appropriately. It is good practice to warn parents of these blocks to effective treatment and to encourage parents to contact staff to discuss their complaints before sharing them with their son or daughter, so as not to undermine the staff. The family, whenever possible, should be seen as part of the therapeutic team.

## 'Copycat' behaviour

It is not unusual for the young people who spend several months in inpatient units to copy the abnormal behaviours they witness on the unit, for example superficial cutting, food avoidance, non-compliance and 'hearing voices'. There are several possible ways of interpreting these copycat behaviours:

- often, superficial cutting is copied in order to join with the peer group;
- food avoidance may be a way of obtaining the 'privileges' of the eating disorder group, often seen as an elitist group;
- threats to self-harm or reports of 'hearing voices' may be an expression of the young person's wish to remain in a therapeutic setting, or fear of discharge.

It is important to remember these potential hazards when assessing a young person for admission as the admission process may cause more problems than it solves. This is particularly important in the cases of young people who have suffered chronic trauma, for example in child sexual abuse, who require long-term therapeutic care. A brief admission to an acute inpatient unit may result in further painful relationship breakdown and copycat behaviour.

## Institutionalization

The admission of a young person to a hospital setting, where all their needs are taken care of, may interfere with the development of independence, which is particularly crucial at this stage in the young person's life. Young people can become dependent on staff supervision and support. If a young person has a lengthy stay in hospital and has required very close attention, because of suicide risk or poor eating, it is important to challenge their sense of autonomy early in the therapeutic process, actively encouraging them to seek out staff support, to voice their needs and to resist the temptation to self-harm or to have thoughts of being rejected by staff or family. It is important to re-establish contact with the family through weekend leave, so that the young person and the family members share the responsibility for protecting the young person well before discharge planning.

Young people suffering from mental illness may have experienced poor care in their early years. Having found consistent and 'unconditional' care in the therapeutic setting, it may be very difficult for the young person to contemplate independence. Rather than ignoring the potential hazards in this difficult area, it is often better to challenge the young person by including them in discussion about their risk management and to avoid long periods of close supervision, whenever possible.

## Patient mix

Some young people with severe mental illness suffer from conduct disorder or associated substance misuse. Young people with conduct disorder find enormous difficulty in adjusting to the rules and regulations necessary in adolescent inpatient units. If the young person has a long history of anti-authoritarian and anti-social behaviour, it is not easy for him or her to begin to consider the needs of the other young patients on the unit and to moderate their behaviour accordingly. In fact, it is often the case that the young person influences the others to act in a disruptive and un-cooperative manner.

To maintain the safety of the unit, members of staff inevitably become preoccupied with the challenges of these behaviourally disturbed patients to the detriment of the other patients. Staff attention is drawn from the patients who are seeking support and accepting therapy to control the disruptive behaviour of the less compliant and disaffected conduct disordered patients. Similarly, it is very difficult to treat young people who are regularly using illegal substances, which have an effect on mood and behaviour and which interfere with the effects of pharmacological interventions. In this situation, young patients may be disadvantaged because of the behaviour of other patients on the unit and this would have to be considered when weighing up the pros and cons of admitting a young person onto the unit.

# Tier 4 inpatient services and the interface with intensive community-based services

The concept of Tier 4 CAMHS in the last decade has moved away from purely inpatient provision, possibly with an attached day service, to a range of multiagency services offering extensive intervention in the community as well as in hospital. Service models have included intensive home services, crisis resolution and home treatment, assertive outreach, multi-systemic therapy (MST) and treatment foster care (TFC) (Green and Worrall-Davies, 2008; McDougall et al., 2008: Kurtz, 2009). The purposes of these community-based services have been to:

- reduce the need for unnecessary inpatient admissions by preventing crises in young people's mental health and family breakdown;
- meet the needs of groups of children and young people who would not traditionally be admitted to a Tier 4 inpatient unit (i.e. those with conduct disorder/challenging behaviour);
- reduce the length of stay for young people in inpatient settings;
- provide a 'bridge' of support on discharge from the inpatient setting, maintaining a level of intensity unsustainable in traditional Tier 3 specialist CAMHS.

Green and Worrall-Davies (2008) conclude that there is an increasing body of research to support the efficacy of alternatives to inpatient care. However, this by no means negates the need for robust inpatient services to provide care for those most severe and complex children and young people, for whom management in the community would not be safe or efficacious. Instead it points to a more integrated approach to care delivery where the needs of different groups of children, young people and their families are placed at the very centre of the treatment plans.

## Multiple choice questions

1. Which of the following is not a common reason why a child or young person may be admitted to a Tier 4 inpatient setting?

   a. The severity of mental ill health
   b. The child/young person's family being no longer able to cope at home
   c. It is far more effacious than treatment in the community for mental illness
   d. There is a significant risk to self and/or others posed by the young person
   e. There is uncertainty about the diagnosis and an intensive period of assessment is required

2. How many beds per 100 000 of the population do the Royal College of Psychiatrists recommend for adolescents?

   a. 1–3
   b. 3–6
   c. 6–9
   d. 9–12
   e. 12–15

3. Which of the following is not a key purpose of intensive community-based treatment services?

   a. To reduce the length of inpatient stay
   b. To prevent unnecessary hospital admissions
   c. To meet the needs of complex young people who may not traditionally enter Tier 4 services, i.e. those with complex health, social and education issues
   d. To gradually phase out inpatient units and provide a purely community model of care
   e. Provide a 'bridge' of support from the inpatient setting to traditional community CAMHS services

## Key texts

Kurtz Z (2009) *The Evidence Base to Guide Development of Tier 4 CAMHS.* London: Department of Health & National CAMHS Support Service.

McDougall T, Worrall-Davies A, Hewson L et al. (2008) Tier 4 child and adolescent mental health services (CAMHS): inpatient care, day services and alternatives: An overview of tier 4 CAMHS provision in the UK. *Child and Adolescent Mental Health,* **13**: 173–80.

O'Herlihy A, Worrall A, Banerjee S et al. (2001) *National inpatient Child and Adolescent Psychiatry Study.* London: College Research Unit of the Royal College of Psychiatrists and the Department of Health.

# 81

# *Example of a children's residential unit – Bursledon House, Southampton*

## Sally Wicks

---

### Key concepts

- Bursledon House is an example of a unit that meets the needs of children and young people with complex psychiatric/emotional/behavioural and or physical health problems.
- Due to the complexity of presenting children, it is staffed by a range of health and education specialists.
- Children and young people are commonly referred from CAMHS or community/inpatient paediatric services.
- Once admitted, children, young people and their families are offered an individualized package of care including individual and family-based work.
- Close contact is maintained with the wider professional network around the child/young person, especially when reintegrating them into their own school.

---

## Introduction

Bursledon House is located in the grounds of Southampton General Hospital. It is a 12-bedded residential unit for children and adolescents, with therapy/meeting rooms, kitchen and dining room, lounge, single and multiple bedrooms, a playground, and with an integrated school, divided into junior and senior level classrooms. It is open from Monday to Friday. The children go home at weekends with report forms to encourage their parents to feedback weekend progress to staff. Parents usually bring the child in on a Monday morning and take them home on Friday afternoons. Some children (up to five or six at a time) attend as day patients, usually at the end of an inpatient stay as part of a school reintegration plan.

## Staffing

This unit lies within the Child Health Department, with all patients being admitted under the care either of a Child Psychiatry Consultant or a Paediatric Consultant (either hospital or community based). There is daily medical input from an Associate Specialist in Paediatrics and from the Child Psychiatry team including an ST3 and at times an ST4-6 as well as Consultants. There is cover from nursing staff 24 hours a day, Monday to Friday. In addition, there is a comprehensive multidisciplinary team including psychologists, occupational therapists, physiotherapists, play specialists, a dietician, teaching staff and administrative staff.

## Patient group

Bursledon House is for children with psychiatric/emotional/behavioural problems and/or physical problems, which have impacted severely on day-to-day life and normal functioning, for example causing difficulties over school attendance or with family relationships. Common physical problems include constipation and soiling, wetting, feeding problems, chronic pain syndromes and children requiring neuro-rehabilitation. There is usually a mix of physical and emotional/behavioural difficulties in these children. Children who are too young for an adolescent psychiatric unit may be admitted with a range of mental health problems, including anorexia nervosa, obsessive compulsive disorder, depression and anxiety.

Patients can be admitted from infancy to age

sixteen. Infants would be admitted with a parent/guardian, while school age children do not have their parents resident.

# Referral process

Patients are referred to the team by clinicians, such as hospital consultants, community paediatricians or CAMHS consultant psychiatrists, by letter. The referral is discussed at the referral meeting. A decision is taken about which team members should carry out a pre-admission assessment with the family. This would be one member of the nursing staff with between one and four other members of the team, including at least one doctor. The play specialist would usually also be involved.

At the pre-admission assessment, a decision is taken as to whether the child, or adolescent, is a suitable candidate for admission, i.e. whether the admission would help the family and whether they want to go ahead with it, or whether there may be other, more appropriate, management methods. Following this assessment, a detailed letter is sent to the referrer regarding the information gained and, if admission is felt to be appropriate, funding from commissioners in the patient's area is sought and then the patient is placed on the waiting list. If the child is to be admitted, the pre-admission assessment appointment is an opportunity for the family to familiarize themselves with the unit, so that when the admission day arrives, it is not as anxiety-provoking as it might otherwise have been. Sometimes a further visit might be arranged for this purpose.

The time spent on the waiting list may be several months. Urgent cases must take priority and it is important to have the right inpatient mix at any time to maintain a positive therapeutic environment.

# Admission and management

On admission, the family is seen for a 'catch-up' assessment of the ongoing problems. These are then documented in the notes. The team will discuss the new patient at the ward round and a management plan will be agreed.

Management will consist of a combination of the following, as deemed appropriate to that particular case:

- Individual work with the child/adolescent, which may consist of supportive counselling, anger management, self-esteem work, cognitive behaviour therapy-based approaches, anxiety management provided by psychology or psychiatry.
- Play sessions, particularly with younger children
- Sessions with the parents/family to look at their concerns and at the issues which will need to be considered, and to enable the family to work collaboratively with the staff in helping their child/adolescent
- Physiotherapy assessment and treatment
- Occupational therapy assessment and treatment in daily living activities, fine and gross motor coordination, perceptual and sensory difficulties. Establishing child's developmental level of functioning.
- Dietary information and advice
- Psychological assessment, including cognitive and neuropsychological assessments and psychology-based individual work
- Assessment of ability in Bursledon House school
- Observation and assessment of interaction with other children and with staff, and of general behaviour
- Assessment of sleep patterns, eating habits, self-care and mental state
- Reintegration into the child's own school if appropriate
- Support and advice to the parents/carers and own school staff
- Close liaison with family/school/other professionals involved in the case
- Multidisciplinary meetings at appropriate intervals and pre-discharge meeting
- Full discharge summary to referring clinician, parent and other professionals involved, including clear follow-up plan in the community.

## Case study 1: Stefan

Stefan, a 12-year-old boy, was admitted for rehabilitation following a head injury in a road traffic accident. Problems included:
• right-sided limb weakness;
• behavioural difficulties;
• memory impairment;
• parents having difficulty accepting the severity of some of the changes.

### Rehabilitation plan
• A structured weekly timetable including defined periods of time in the on-site school and periods of rest.
• Strategies to assist memory put in place including use of a memory book and signs on doors initially.
• Physiotherapy input twice daily with a particular focus on improving mobility.
• Occupational therapy directed at improving arm function and independence with Activities of Daily Living.
• Regular liaison with Paediatric Neurology team.
• Behavioural management strategies devised between Child Psychiatrist, Psychology and nursing staff.
• Ongoing psychological support for parents.
• Individual psychological support with Stefan.
• Neuropsychology review with full assessment at six months post-head injury.
• Attention deficit hyperactivity disorder (ADHD) assessment by Child and Adolescent Psychiatrist.
• Liaison with own school leading to reintegration.

### Progress
Stefan's behaviour improved after transfer from the paediatric wards, showing a good response to having a more structured timetable and nursing staff providing clear boundaries. The decision was made to carry out an ADHD assessment. History from parents did not suggest this diagnosis prior to the accident. It was felt that the poor concentration, over activity and impulsiveness that had been present in the recovery period were becoming less prominent, so a policy of watch and wait was adopted. Eventually the decision was made that methylphenidate would not be required. With ongoing physiotherapy, Stefan became progressively steadier on his feet and in time was able to walk unaided. Less progress was made with the upper limb, but some functional use was regained. Stefan's parents initially found it difficult to accept that there were some cognitive/memory deficits and changes in temperament which were likely to be ongoing. They were supported in coming to terms with this. Multidisciplinary team meetings were held to give professionals in the community a clear idea of Stefan's needs. A statementing process was initiated with plans for one-to-one support in school and follow-up arranged from local physiotherapists and occupational therapists. Stefan then had a reintegration to school and was discharged home.

## Case study 2: Holly

Holly, an eight-year-old girl, was admitted with concerns about her eating. Problems included:
• longstanding narrow range of foods with poor intake and anxiety around food;
• slow weight gain;
• maternal stress due to poor eating and slow weight gain.

## Management plan

- Occupational therapy assessment for sensory and oral motor issues.
- Play programme including messy play and play with food to make food fun.
- Regular meetings with family to share progress and make plans for the weekend.
- Psychology input including anxiety management strategies and devising a hierarchy of new foods to try.
- Reward system involving stickers and prizes for trying new foods and for eating good amounts.
- Dietician's advice to staff and to family.

## Progress

The occupational therapist's assessment did not show any significant sensory or oral motor issues. Holly made the decision alongside the psychologist working with her that she wanted to try new foods outside mealtimes, supported by one member of staff. At mealtimes, Holly was observed to be anxious but this gradually improved with only familiar foods being offered initially and with gentle encouragement being given by staff. The distraction of social interaction with peers also appeared helpful. Holly soon began to earn stickers by eating greater quantities of familiar foods and also by eating very small amounts of new foods in individual sessions. With time it became possible for a couple of the 'new' foods to be incorporated at mealtimes. Parents were invited in to join some mealtimes and initially were observed to inadvertently be placing pressure on Holly to eat, but with advice from and modelling by nursing staff this improved. Eating at home at weekends improved, and Holly gained weight during the admission. At discharge parents were happy to know that Holly could eat reasonable amounts of food and had gained weight. They felt confident that the range of foods she would eat could gradually increase over time with a more relaxed approach to mealtimes.

## Multiple choice questions

1. Which of the following physical complaints in children and young people would commonly be seen in a unit such as Bursledon House?

   a. Soiling and bed wetting
   b. Feeding problems
   c. Chronic fatigue problems
   d. Neurological problems
   e. All of the above

2. Which of the following professionals/services would not commonly refer directly into specialist units such as Bursledon house?

   a. Paediatric wards
   b. Community paediatricians
   c. Social services
   d. Community CAMHS
   e. All would commonly refer

*Key texts*

Department of Health (2003c) *Every Child Matters*. London: HMSO.

Department of Health (2004a) *National Service Framework for Children, Young People and Maternity Services*. London: HMSO.

# 82

# Forensic CAMHS: Bluebird House
## Lee Bradley and Clare Campbell

---

## Key concepts

- Bluebird House is a Tier 4 CAMHS provision, a secure forensic mental health unit for young people between the ages of 12 and 18. It is one of six similar NHS units in a network of Secure Forensic Mental Health Services for Young People (SFMHSfYP). These units are commissioned by the National Specialised Commissioning Team who are themselves informed by The Advisory Group for National Specialised Services.
- Tier 4 services need a highly specialized staff team to treat serious mental health problems and very challenging behaviour (Department of Health, 2007b). Provision may offer intensive outpatient services, outreach, inpatient psychiatric provision, residential and secure accommodation, specialized assessment, consultation and intervention.
- Young people admitted to Bluebird House do not have to have committed an offence. The need is for a secure and safe environment to contain, manage and treat the difficult and challenging behaviour they present.
- A key aspect of the nursing care of the young people is the assessment and management of the risk they pose to themselves and others.

---

## Introduction

Forensic nursing is a sub-branch of mental health nursing and requires a specific knowledge base centred on risk management, offending behaviour and certain sections of the Mental Health Act (Department of Health, 1983): 'the recipients of forensic care are a diverse group, they span the range of mental health problems and diagnosis, often their needs are complex and involve a number of agencies' (McCann, 1999).

There will always be a need for young people whose behaviour is extremely challenging, and perhaps unlawful, to be kept safe and as free as possible from the risks of harm to themselves or to others.

## Description of the unit

Bluebird House is a 20-bed unit and can admit an equal number of male and female patients. There are three wards, two with seven beds and the other with six beds. All three wards can take both male and female admissions. There is a Learning and Therapy Centre, to meet the educational and occupational therapy needs of the young people, a gym and fitness suite, games room and all-weather pitch, a multi-faith room, relaxation suite and family therapy suite. In addition, there are two separate high care areas for young people requiring a period of increased support in a low stimulus environment.

Bluebird House admitted their first young person early in 2008 and 42 young people have since been admitted. Fifty-seven per cent of these young people had a primary diagnosis of 'psychosis' including paranoid schizophrenia, drug-induced psychosis and brief psychotic episode. Twenty-four per cent had a primary diagnosis of borderline personality disorder. The rest had diagnoses of conduct disorder, bipolar affective disorder, autistic spectrum disorder and illicit substance misuse.

## Background

Estimates of the number of young people requiring these beds at any given point vary enormously, ranging from 204 (Vaughan, 2002) to 1256 (Kurtz, 1998). The majority of young people referred to Bluebird House come from either other mental health units ill-prepared for managing the risks posed by these young people or from another secure establishment. It is estimated that there are around 3000 young people under the age of 18 held within the 45 establishments that make up the secure estate in England and Wales (Department of Health, 2007b). This includes the 19 Young Offenders institutions (YOIs), which are part of the prison service; four secure training centres, run by private operators; and 22 secure children's homes, almost all run by local authorities. The YOIs hold the majority of the young people in custody (Tunnard, 2008).

The mental health care needs of young people in secure settings is considerably higher than in the general population and within care as a whole, for example among 15–17 year olds placed in secure children's homes, two-thirds were assessed as having a mental health disorder (Office for National Statistics, 2002).

In a study of mentally disordered offenders, the Reed committee (Department of Health and Home Office, 1992) commented that the problems often begin in childhood or adolescence, but that there has been little understanding of the prevalence of mental disorder among juvenile offenders. In addition, the NHS Health Advisory Service et al. (1994), in reviewing the service offered by the Gardener unit in Manchester, found that the unit was ill-equipped to deal with the needs of young people with mental disorder. In response, the study by Kurtz et al. (1998) found that 'the mental health needs of young people who are highly disturbed, may be a danger to themselves and to others and may be in trouble with the law are not well recognized, widely understood or adequately met'. Children with severe mental illness should not be held in custody but should be transferred to an appropriate hospital or a unit of the SFMHSfYP (Department of Health, 2007b). The admission criteria by which referrals are assessed are as follows:

- The young person is under 18 years of age at the time of referral

AND
- The young person is liable to be detained under either Part 2 or Part 3 of the Mental Health Act 1983 (excluding the categories of mental impairment/severe mental impairment only).

AND/EITHER
- The young person presents a risk to others of one or more of the following:
  - direct violence liable to result in injury to people
  - sexually aggressive behaviour
  - destructive and potentially life-threatening use of fire

OR
- The young person is in custodial care and presents a serious risk of suicide and/or severe self-harm

AND
- The referrer can give evidence that serious consideration of alternatives has already been considered or tried prior to referral, indicating that the case has exceeded the ability of available mental health services to meet the need.

Violence and aggression towards others and property is a significant feature within the patient group in Bluebird House. Deliberate self-harm is common. Assessing and managing these risks for day-to-day management and ultimately assessing and managing the risks leading up to discharge, is a highly complex endeavour. 'The practice of assessing risk for future violence has been a highly controversial issue in the past. The validity of predictions of dangerousness has been riddled with methodological problems' (Monahan, 1984). Furthermore, Harrison (1997) comments, 'key workers and consultant psychiatrists face a unique challenge in attempting to balance the therapeutic needs of their patients against the risks of personal criticism in the present climate of public anxiety about community care'. Even though risk assessment is a controversial issue, units such as Bluebird House could not function safely without the continuous assessment and planning for risk management. Heilbrun (2003) supports this view 'it is fair to be critical of the process of risk reduction strategies, but it needs to be acknowledged that they are enormously important endeavours to be practiced (and must be practiced), whatever the science'.

Staff within units such as Bluebird House have a constantly changing role, especially those nursing staff working face-to-face with the patients for many hours each day. Working with adolescents, who may use violence to communicate distress, solve problems or compete for adult attention, requires a careful balance of authority, responsibility and therapeutic risk-taking (McDougall, 2000). This task is further complicated when the histories of many of the young people within the unit are taken into account. 'Powerful interpersonal dynamics occur within nurse-patient relationships in forensic settings. Patients disadvantageous early life experiences with attachment figures shape their expectations of current care givers, furthermore, forensic mental health nurses, with their conflicting roles of control and care, can too easily replicate their patients relationships with abusive or neglecting early care givers' (Aiyegbusi, 2004).

The successful treatment of the young people admitted to Bluebird House depends on how well the multidisciplinary team works together. Fully integrated multi-agency working is now seen as a prerequisite for the delivery of effective mental health care for those patients with complex mental health care needs. The Care Programme Approach (Department of Health, 1990) underpins the coordination of mental health services for individuals with mental health illnesses and disorders. It is the framework for the systematic assessment of the individual's needs, the shaping of care and crisis plans and the completion of risk assessments.

The emphasis is on collaborative working across all disciplines involved in delivering health and social care interventions. The Children Act 2004 aimed to encourage integrated planning, commissioning and delivery of services and to improve multidisciplinary working, remove duplication, increase accountability and improve the coordination of individual and joint inspections in local authorities. It is the legal force which supports the five outcomes for children and young people outlined in Every Child Matters: Change for Children (2004). The National Service Framework for Mental Health (Department of Health, 1999b) was explicit in its intention to ensure that each person with severe mental illness receives the range of mental health services they require.

The multi-disciplinary team (MDT) within Bluebird House is well equipped to meet the highly complex needs of the young people. The clinical staff are solely based within the service and comprise the following disciplines:

- nursing staff (registered nurses from the fields of mental health, learning disabilities and children's nursing, plus unqualified health care support workers);
- security and clinical risk liaison nurses;
- medical staff, including consultant psychiatrists and junior doctors;
- occupational therapists;
- social worker;
- clinical psychologists and assistant psychologists;
- family therapist;
- creative therapist;
- teaching staff;
- speech and language therapist.

The MDT within Bluebird House has a wealth of experience and expertise in the specialist field in which the service operates and can meet the priority needs that Liberman et al. (2001) identified as key to a well-functioning team. They stated that 'there must be specialists with expertise in critical areas, e.g. the assessment and treatment of medical disorders, psychopharmacology, reliable diagnosis and on-going assessment of the psychopathology of severe mental illness, functional assessment, management of substance abuse, skills training, employment services, housing, family psycho-education and access to entitlements and benefits'.

Interventions are delivered within what has been termed 'The Structured Day', the main aspect of which is the five 1-hour sessions timetabled between 09.30 and 17.00 Monday to Friday (see daily plan below). All plans are individualized to maximize the benefit for all young people. An example of an individual timetable is provided below. Education sessions take account of each young person's skill, ability and current mental state. Therapeutic interventions are timetabled around the education sessions. This ensures a balance between the therapeutic and educational needs of the young people.

The structured day continues after 17.00 and includes weekends. Apart from the five core 1-hour sessions on weekdays, the timetable offers flexibility and the young people are encouraged to use this time for family visits, community/home leave and relaxation.

Figures 82.1 and 82.2 outline a structured day plan for Bluebird House and an example individual plan for a young person:

| INDIVIDUAL TIMETABLE | | | | | |
|---|---|---|---|---|---|
| | Monday | Tuesday | Wednesday | Thursday | Friday |
| Session 1 09:30–10:30 | Hair and Beauty | English | Ward Emotional Coping Skills Group (DBT informed) | English | Maths |
| BREAK – RETURN TO THE WARD | | | | | |
| Session 2 11:00–12:00 | Mental Health Act Review Tribunal | Maths | History | Ward Community Meeting | 1:1 with psychologist |
| LUNCH – RETURN TO THE WARD and ROOM TIME | | | | | |
| Session 3 13:15–14:15 | Science | 1:1 with creative therapist | Sport | 1:1 with social worker | Occupational therapy – Relaxation room |
| BREAK – RETURN TO THE WARD | | | | | |
| Session 4 14:45–15:45 | Tutorial – personal development | Science | 1:1 with family therapist | Information Technology | English |
| BREAK – RETURN TO THE WARD | | | | | |
| Session 5 16:00–17:00 | Ward Community de-brief and goal setting meeting | Family visit | Community leave | Occupational therapy Walking Group | Ward Community de-brief and goal setting meeting |

Figure 82.1 Example individual timetable for a young person.

## Case studies

The two case studies described here give examples of the presenting issues in a young person that may warrant an admission to a secure forensic unit, such as Bluebird House.

## Case study 1: Anna

Anna's behaviour changed dramatically at the age of approximately two years, despite an unremarkable birth and meeting her early milestones. She broke things, ran into the garden and took her clothes off and would turn taps on or go downstairs to eat sugar and teabags in the night.

Throughout her early years, her mother was subjected to domestic violence at the hands of her partner (Anna's stepfather). At the age of eight, Anna lived with her biological father for a year, but following concerns that she was being neglected, she returned to stay with her mother and stepfather. Aged ten, she was left with a young couple while her mother and stepfather went on holiday. During

| DAILY PLAN | |
|---|---|
| 07:45 | Morning wake up call. (Young people can be on ward from 07:30a.m. if they choose) |
| 08:30 | Everybody to be in the lounge |
| 08:30–09:00 | Breakfast in the dining room |
| 09:00 | Medication |
| 09:20 | TV off: prepare for session 1, tidy room, do washing and so on |
| 09:30 | **Session 1** (as per individual timetable) |
| 10:30 | Break on the ward and access to courtyard |
| 11:00 | **Session 2** (as per individual timetable) |
| 12:00–12:30 | Lunch in the dining room |
| 12:30 | Medication |
| 12:40–13:10 | Room Time |
| 13:15 | **Session 3** (as per individual timetable) |
| 14:15 | Break on the ward and access to courtyard |
| 14:45 | **Session 4** (as per individual timetable) |
| 15:45 | Return to ward |
| 16:00 | **Session 5** (as per individual timetable) |
| 16:00–16:30 | Room time (if not involved in session 5) |
| 17:00 | Dinner in the dining room |
| 17:00–18:30 | Access to telephone |
| 18:30–19:00 | Room Time |
| 19:00–19:30 | Optional Room Time (access to telephone between 19:00 and 20:00) |
| 19:30–20:00 | Leisure time: if not engaged in an activity, expected to be in ward areas |
| 20:00 (or 21:00) | Supper |
| 20:15 | Winding down time: can choose to retire to bed. Access to music. TV off in bedroom at 9p.m. |
| 21:00 | All security items to be handed in |
| 21:30<br>22:30<br>22:30 | Under 16's Bedtime and access to music<br>Over 16's Bedtime and access to music<br>Ward TV off |
| 22:00<br>23:00 | Under 16s – Music off and Lights Out<br>Over 16s – Music off and Lights Out |

Figure 82.2 Example individual daily plan for a young person.

this time, she reported that the male carer made her drunk and sexually assaulted her.

Soon afterwards, her mother reported that Anna 'locked up her emotions' and would not cry. She became worried about germs and about being touched and would shower three times a day, often for an hour each time. She began to be in serious trouble in school, including exclusions for fighting.

Anna was charged with numerous criminal offences including robbery, burglary and arson in her early teens. Aged 17, she was convicted of robbery and actual bodily harm and was sent to a Young Offenders Institute. Here, she was assessed by the mental health team because of her low mood and an escalating pattern of deliberate self-harm. Anna was referred and subsequently admitted to a secure mental health service for young people with the aim of clarifying her diagnosis and instigating an individualized treatment plan in place.

## Case study 2: Ben

Ben walked early, at nine months, but was a slow talker and only used babyish talk until he was about seven. He seemed to be different from other children of his age and was excluded from three or four playgroups. He would draw pictures of people impaled on stakes and other violent scenes on the walls of his bedroom. He used to say 'they are watching me' about his pictures.

Ben was excluded from several primary schools for biting and hurting other children, and for oppositional behaviour. He became involved with the Youth Justice System when he was 11 and was seen in CAMHS after his mother raised concerns about his behaviour.

At age 16, Ben was arrested when a neighbour made a call to the police describing Ben's bizarre and threatening manner on the street outside his house. Ben was said to be making threats to harm someone. When the police attended, he assaulted two officers by punching and head butting. He received a custodial sentence and was sent to a YOI.

Shortly afterwards, he was seen wandering around at night on the wing, talking incomprehensibly. He was assessed by a psychiatrist and reported hearing a male and female voice arguing in his head about whether he is gay or straight, and feeling as though staff on the other side of the wall were watching him and talking about him. He reported poor sleep and reduced food intake and he had cut his left wrist. He presented as somewhat confused about how long he had been at the YOI, believing he had only been there for 2 days, when in fact, it had been almost exactly a month.

Ben was transferred to a secure forensic young person's unit, where he could be fully assessed. The early formulation was that Ben was experiencing a first psychotic episode and he was prescribed Respiridone to alleviate some of the distressing symptoms he had been experiencing. Ben was supported around increasing his food intake and maintaining a positive sleeping pattern. Once settled on the unit Ben was able to meet with a therapist individually to explore some of the distress experienced around his psychotic symptoms.

## Multiple choice questions

1. It is estimated that how many young people are in prison or another secure setting at any one time in the UK?

   a. 2000
   b. 3000
   c. 4000
   d. 5000

2. Bluebird House and similar units sit within which tier of CAMHS?

   a. Tier 2
   b. Tier 3
   c. Tier 4
   d. Is a specialist service, so does not sit within the tier system

3. Admission to Bluebird House or similar units across the UK is via:

   a. Secure Forensic Mental Health Service for Young People
   b. Young offenders institutions
   c. Local community CAMH teams
   d. Youth offending teams

4. Which of the following is not a criterion for admission to a secure forensic unit?

   a. The young person is under the age of 18
   b. The young person is detained under a section of the Mental Health Act

c. The young person poses serious risk to others through physical or sexual violence, or destructive behaviours

d. The young person is in custodial care and is at serious risk of suicide or deliberate self-harm

5. Would a young person have had to commit an offence in order to access a service such as Bluebird House?

a. Yes

b. No

c. Yes, but only if the offence is committed while already in a custodial setting and linked directly to mental ill health.

d. Yes, but the offence must ordinarily carry a custodial sentence of three or more years.

## Key texts

Aiyegbusi A (2004) Forensic mental health nursing. Care with security in mind. In: Pfafflin F, Adshead G (eds). *A Matter of Security The Application of Attachment Theory to Forensic Psychiatry and Psychotherapy*. London: Kingsley, 167–90.

Department of Health (2007b) *Promoting Mental Health for Children Held in Secure Settings: A Framework for Commissioning Services*. London: Department of Health.

Vaughan PJ (2002) *Secure Care and Treatment Needs of Mentally Disordered Adolescents. Report to the National Specialist Commissioning Advisory Group of the Department of Health*. London: Department of Health.

# Appendices

# Appendix

## Drawing and using a family tree

SYMBOLS

Males $\square$  Females $\bigcirc$  Unknown gender $\triangle$

Married ——— Co-habiting – – – – Death $\times$

Divorced // Separated / Adopted or fostered child ⁞

EXAMPLE

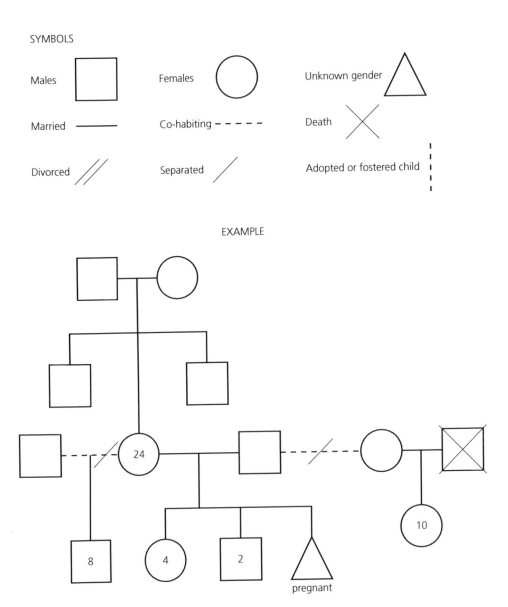

**2** *Appendix*

# Family life cycle

Adapted from Carter B, McGoldrick M (1989) *The Changing Family Life Cycle: A Framework for Family Therapy*, 2nd edn. Boston: Allyn and Bacon.

| Family life cycle | Transitional processes | Developmental changes |
|---|---|---|
| **Leaving home:**<br>**single young adult** | Accepting emotional and financial responsibility | Differentiation from family of origin<br>Intimate peer relationships<br>Work and independence |
| **Coupling up** | Commitment to new relationship | Division of labour<br>Relationships with extended family and friends |
| **Starting a family** | Sharing partner<br>Financial constraints<br>Childcare/work issues | Re-aligning roles with parents and grandparents<br>Responsibilities<br>Loss of singledom |
| **Family with adolescents** | Negotiating independence | Midlife and career issues<br>Care of elderly parents |
| **Launching family and**<br>**moving on** | Multiple exits and entries into and out of family | Re-negotiate marital system as a twosome<br>Develop adult:adult relationships with children<br>Disability or death of (grand) parents |
| **Families in later life** | Shift in generational roles | Maintaining own and/or couple function in face of old age and infirmity<br>Preparation for death<br>Widow(er)hood |

# 3 Appendix

## CAMHS initial interview

Name:................................................. Date:.................................................

Address:................................................. Tel:.................................................

DOB:................................................. School:.................................................

Family members present:                Clinicians present:

Referred by:
GP/HV/Other (State)                     GP:

Problem on referral:                    Duration
                                        3/12
                                        6/12
                                        6/+
                                        1 year
                                        Birth

Main concerns as described by parents on
assessment:

Child's view of difficulties

Have you any ideas as to why the problem(s) started?
Duration of the problem?

Family background: (can include brief family tree)

Pregnancy and developmental history

Other pregnancies:

Mother's health during pregnancy (Presenting child)

Smoking?                                             Yes/No

Alcohol?                                             Yes/No

Illicit Drug use?                                    Yes/No

Other medical problems?


Type of delivery:

Spontaneous vaginal delivery

Instrumental delivery

Elective caesarean section

Emergency caesarean section

Other

Birth weight:


Gestation:


SCBU                                                 Yes/No


Neonatal period:


Mother's feelings about the birth and early months:


Development milestones:

Gross and fine motor skills Age appropriate?         Yes/No

Language development Age appropriate?                Yes/No

                                                     ?SALT involved?

Understanding

Pronunciation/clarity


Behaviour: (early years)

Any unusual/fixed repetitive behaviours


Child's experience of play and what types of play he/
she likes (imaginative/concrete)

Ability of child to play with other children:

Can the child perceive things from another person's
point of view and are they able to reflect on their own
thoughts and actions?:

Are they able to take responsibility for their actions?   Yes/Sometimes/not often/no
Perceive that it is their fault?

Mood level (?sensitive ?anxious)

Feeding and eating: (including diet responses/
changes)

Sleep and settling:

Is your child difficult to settle to sleep?

How long does he/she take to fall asleep (30 minutes
or more)?

Does your child have the sensation of fidgety
legs? (Restless legs syndrome is characterized by
uncomfortable sensations in the legs resulting in
motor restlessness to relieve the symptoms. This may
occur at anytime during the night)

Does your child wake during the night?

Does he/she snore?

Is he/she a restless sleeper?

Is your child difficult to wake in the morning?

Separation issues:

What age?

How long for?

Difficult to separate?

Is child cuddly:

Towards everyone or just mother?

Is child sensitive, e.g. to loud noises or touch, i.e.
increased sensory awareness? Child's medical history
(include hearing probs/wetting

Heart problems                                                          Yes/No (if yes what)

| | |
|---|---|
| Hearing problems | Yes/No |
| Fits | Yes/No |
| Visual difficulties | Yes/No |
| Operations | Yes/No |

Medications (please list)

Allergies (please list and record in folder section 4)

A and E attendance

Child's educational history:

Pre-school

Current school

Global learning disability (i.e. less than average)

Special needs – has the child a statement of special
educational needs

Special needs support provided by school?

Educational psychology involvement?

Parental background and upbringing:

Parents' childhood (please comment unhappy/
average/very happy

Mother's

Father's

Other partners relevant to child

Comments

| | |
|---|---|
| Do parents work together? | Yes/No/Average |

Marital communication

The history of family's physical and mental health

Parental mood (please describe)

Mother's

Father's

Siblings

Other history:

Domestic violence?

Substance misuses in family (alcohol/drugs)?

Parental education history (any learning difficulties?)

Criminality within the family?

Relationship of child with siblings

Child's peer relationships and support network

Self-esteem

Hobbies and interests

Strengths and abilities

What has the family tried to do to help the difficulties?

What has worked?

What hasn't and why?

What would the family like to happen now?

Formulation

Care plan – agreed with parents

Signed                                                    Date

Designation

Risk assessment

|  | High | Medium | Low |
|---|---|---|---|
| Currently suicidal | Plan, expressed wish | Strong feelings wish | None expressed |
| Self-harming | Frequent, severe | Often, moderate | Occasional/None |

| | | | |
|---|---|---|---|
| Previous self-harm | Yes, serious | Yes, mild | No |
| Family history | Severe mental illness | Some mental health problems | No relevant history |
| Peer family support | None | Some | Good |
| Previous professional involvement perceived as | Unhelpful | Neutral/no previous involvement | Helpful |
| Other: | | | |

**4** *Appendix*

# ADHD Assessment Sheet (based on NICE Sept 2008)

| | |
|---|---|
| Name: | |
| DOB: | NHS no: |
| Concerns following choice assessment | |
| Current concerns – parent | |
| Current concerns – child/young person | |
| Overview of everyday life – parents' view | |
| Home | |
| School | |
| School reports obtained | YES/NO |
| Meeting expected educational milestone | YES/NO |
| Peer relationships | |
| Overview of everyday life – child/young person's view | |
| Home | |
| School | |
| Peer relationships | |

| | |
|---|---|
| Birth and developmental history (may have been covered in choice app) | |
| Prenatal | |
| Birth | |
| Postnatal | |
| Developmental milestones | |
| Walking | YES/NO |
| Speech and language | YES/NO |
| Early behaviour problems | YES/NO |
| Child's medical history | |
| Heart problems | YES/NO |
| Breathlessness | YES/NO |
| Exercise syncope | YES/NO |
| Epilepsy or fits | YES/NO |
| Tics | YES/NO |
| Hearing problems | YES/NO |
| Thyroid problems | YES/NO |
| Iron deficiency | YES/NO |
| Medications: | |

| | |
|---|---|
| Allergies | |
| Child psychiatric history (inc mental state if appropriate) | |
| | |
| Substance abuse | |
| | |
| Addictive behaviours | |
| | |
| Family medical history | |
| | |
| Family history of ADHD | |
| | |
| Family history of medical problems (particularly heart problems and fits) | |
| | |
| Family psychiatric history (inc criminality) | |
| | |
| Symptoms of hyperactivity/attention deficit disorder NB Hyperactivity is the term used in ICD-10 classification. Attention deficit disorder (ADD) or attention deficit disorder with hyperactivity (ADHD) is the term used in the DSM-IIIR classification (American classification). ADD/ADHD is a broader concept than hyperactivity. | |
| | |
| Use ICD-10 criteria to elicit symptomatology. Do not give to parents to fill in, but ask parents for descriptions of behaviour covering the various areas. | |

## Inattention

[At least six of the following have persisted for at least six months, to a degree that is maladaptive and inconsistent with the developmental level of the child]

1. Often fails to give close attention to details, or makes careless errors in schoolwork, work or other activities (slapdash, sloppy). Please give examples:
2. Often fails to sustain attention in tasks or play activities. Please give examples:
3. Often appears not to listen to what is being said to him/her. Please give examples:
4. Often fails to follow through on instructions or to finish schoolwork, chores, or duties in the workplace (not because of oppositional behaviour or failure to understand instructions). Please give examples:
5. Is often impaired in organising tasks and activities Please give examples:
6. Often avoids or strongly dislikes, such as homework that require, sustained mental effort. Please give examples:

7. Often loses things necessary for certain tasks or activities, such as school assignments, pencils, books, toys or tools. Please give examples:
8. Is often easily distracted by external stimuli. Please give examples:
9. Is often forgetful in the course of daily activities (but memory okay on testing). Please give examples:

# Overactivity

[At least three of the following symptoms have persisted for at least six months, to a degree that is maladaptive and inconsistent with the developmental level of the child]

1. Often fidgets with hands or feet or squirms on seat (adolescents – often overtalkative). Please give examples:
2. Leaves seat in classroom or in other situations in which remaining seated is expected. Please give examples:
3. Often runs about or climbs excessively in situations in which it is inappropriate (in adolescents or adults, only feelings of restlessness may be present). Please give examples:
4. Is often unduly noisy in playing or has difficulty in engaging quietly in leisure activities. Please give examples:
5. Exhibits a persistent pattern of excessive motor activity that is not substantially modified by social context or demands. Please give examples:

# Impulsivity

[At least one of the following symptoms of impulsivity has persisted for at least six months, to a degree that is maladaptive and inconsistent with the developmental level of the child

1. Often blurts out answers before questions have been completed. Please give examples:
2. Often fails to wait in lines or await turns in games or group situations. Please give examples:
3. Often interrupts or intrudes on others (e.g. butts into others' conversations or games). Please give examples:
4. Often talks excessively without appropriate response to social constraints. Please give examples:

Extracted from the World Health Organisation (WHO) (1992) The ICD-10 Classification of Mental and Behavioural Disorders: Clinical Descriptions and Diagnostic Guidelines. Geneva: World Health Organisation

## Additional information to be collected from parents at assessment

Strengths and Difficulties – Parent and child version if appropriate
*additional form

## Additional Information to collected from School post Assessment

Strengths and Difficulties – Teacher version
*additional form

# Onset of the disorder is thought to be no later than the age of seven years

## Pervasiveness

The criteria should be met for more than a single situation, e.g. the combination of inattention and hyperactivity should be present both at home and at school, or at both school and another setting where children are observed, such as a clinic. (Evidence for cross-situational difficulties will ordinarily require information from more than one source; parental reports about classroom behaviour, for instance, are unlikely to be sufficient.)

The symptoms above cause clinically significant distress or impairment in social, academic or occupational functioning.

There may be symptoms of other problems (co-morbidity) so important to ask about these in more detail if appropriate e.g. conduct/oppositional – defiant disorder. If both hyperactivity and conduct disorder are present then hyperactivity has usually preceded conduct disorder.

# Conduct disorder or oppositional disorder

To be classified as having either conduct disorder or oppositional disorder there has to be present a repetitive and persistent pattern of behaviour, in which either the basic rights of others or major age-appropriate societal norms or rules are violated, lasting at least six months, during which some of the following symptoms are present (see individual subcategories for rules or numbers of symptoms).

Note: The symptoms in 11, 13, 15, 16, 20, 21 and 23 need only have occurred once for the criterion to be fulfilled.

# The individual

1. has unusually frequent or severe temper tantrums for his or her developmental level;
2. often argues with adults;
3. often actively refuses adults' requests or defies rules;
4. often, apparently deliberately, does things that annoy other people;
5. often blames others for his or her own mistakes or misbehaviour;
6. is often 'touchy' or easily annoyed by others;
7. is often angry or resentful;
8. is often spiteful or vindictive;
9. often lies or breaks promises to obtain goods or favours or to avoid obligations;
10. frequently initiates physical fights (this does not include fights with siblings);
11. has used a weapon that can cause serious physical harm to other (e.g. bat, brick, broken bottle, knife, gun);
12. often stays out after dark despite parental prohibition ( beginning before 13 year of age)
13. exhibits physical cruelty to other people (e.g. ties up, cuts or burns a victim);
14. exhibits physical cruelty to animals;
15. deliberately destroys the property of others (other than by fire setting)
16. deliberately sets fires with risk or intention of causing serious damage;
17. steals objects of non-trivial value while confronting the victim, either within the home or outside (e.g. shoplifting, burglary, forgery,);
18. is frequently truant from school, beginning before 13 years of age;
19. has run away from parental or parental surrogate home at least twice or has run away once for more than single night (this does not include leaving to avoid physical or sexual abuse);
20. commits a crime involving confrontation with the victim (including purse snatching, extortion, mugging);
21. forces another person into sexual activity;
22. frequently bullies other (i.e. deliberate infliction of pain or hurt, including persistent intimidation, tormenting or molestation);
23. breaks into someone else's house, building or car.

Extracted from the World Health Organisation (WHO) (1992) The ICD-10 Classification of Mental and Behavioural Disorders: Clinical Descriptions and Diagnostic Guidelines. Geneva: World Health Organisation

# Summary of findings

DSM-IV or ICD-10 Score

| Impulsivity | Overactivity | Inattention |
|---|---|---|
| Pervasive | YES/NO | |

Co-morbidities (tick if present)

| | | | |
|---|---|---|---|
| ASD symptoms | Tics | Oppositional Defiant Disorder | Dyspraxia |
| Learning Difficulties, specific or general | Anxiety | Conduct Disorder | Other: |
| Psychological Testing Indicated | | | YES/NO |
| If diagnosis confirmed treatment discussion with parents and child/young person | | | |
| Parents' wishes | | | |
| Child's wishes (consider age of consent) | | | |
| Handouts given: Information for parents re ADHD | | | YES/NO |
| Information for child re ADHD | | | YES/NO |
| Consider: self-help manual | | | |
| Group interventions | | | |

# Treatment plan

| Confirm diagnosis to school | YES/NO |
|---|---|
| Booklet sent | YES/NO |
| Confirm diagnosis to GP | YES/NO |
| Shared care agreement sent | YES/NO |
| Shared care agreement confirmed | |
| Further physical examination (if indicated) | YES/NO |

| | Offered (date) | Completed (date) |
|---|---|---|
| 1:1 ADHD specific parenting advice | | |
| ADHD Support Group | | |
| Confirmation to school of diagnosis | | |
| Psychometric testing (if indicated) | | |
| Medication (take baseline measures) | | |

# Management of Co-morbidities (if present)

| | Offered/discussed | Intervention/Ass | Completed (date) |
|---|---|---|---|
| ASD | | | |
| Anxiety | | | |
| Conduct disorder | | | |
| Oppositional defiant disorder | | | |
| Learning disabilities (general) | | | |
| Dyspraxia | | | |
| Specific learning difficulties | | | |
| Sensory issues | | | |
| Other paediatric problems (please list) | | | |
| Sleep issues | | | |

 *Appendix*

## Initiation of medication

Child's name ............................................................................ Date ........................

Present (inc clinicians) .........................................................................

Shared Care agreement                                              YES/NO

Prior to commencing medication
Medical history reviewed
Heart probs                                                              YES/NO
Fits                                                                     YES/NO
Exercise syncope                                                         YES/NO
Thyroid probs                                                            YES/NO
Iron deficiency                                                          YES/NO
Hearing probs                                                            YES/NO
Information for parents Medication booklet given                         YES/NO
Information for child Medication Booklet given                           YES/NO
Consent obtained                                                         YES/NO
Side effects discussed                                                   YES/NO
Contra-indications discussed                                             YES/NO
Over the counter meds discussed                                          YES/NO

Medication targets
Parent ...............................................................................
Child ...............................................................................
Medication prescribed ...............................................................................
Child's baseline monitoring (plot on centile charts)
B/P ........................ Pulse ........................ Ht ................ Weight ...............................................
!st Review date: ........................................... with whom: ...............................................

# Consent form

Please ensure you have read the whole booklet before signing. It is important that parents understand why medication is being considered and have the chance to discuss medication fully.

The following are questions to check that it is safe to prescribe medication for your child.

| | |
|---|---|
| 1. Is or has your child received medication for any illnesses? | Yes/No |
| 2. Has your child attended your GP recently? | Yes/No |
| If so what for | |
| 3. Have you a family history of fits or convulsions? | Yes/No |
| 4. Has your child ever had any fits or suffer from epilepsy | Yes/No |
| 5. Has your child or any family member had any heart problems? | Yes/No |
| If so, were they referred? | Yes/No please give details |
| 6. Is your child allergic to any medication? | Yes/No |
| If so what | |
| 7. Has your child ever had any facial tics or jerky movements | Yes/No |

I/We have been given the literature on medication and have read it and understand what I/we have read, and have been given the opportunity to discuss any concerns or questions. I am the child's legal guardian.
I hereby give my consent to my child
Name.............................................................................
D.O.B.
Receiving medication in treatment for his/her ADHD symptoms.

Signed                                                          Date

Parent/Guardian

# Appendix

## MCQ answers

### Chapter 2

1. c) A baby is predisposed to attach to any caregiver (not just its mother) at birth, with a special preference for one or two usually developed by one year of age. Attachment patterns are learnt behaviours that have a lasting impact throughout a person's life, such as their ability to express emotions and develop relationships.
2. d) The FNP is a programme for vulnerable first-time young parents from pregnancy until their child is two years old. Family nurses develop a therapeutic relationship with their client, but do not provide therapy or prescribe medication. Family nurses are highly skilled, specially trained nurses whose background is usually health visiting or midwifery, not social care. Family nurses focus attention on the importance of a parent's awareness and attitudes towards their baby and the development of secure attachments.

### Chapter 3

1. c)
2. b)
3. d)
4. d)
5. a)

### Chapter 5

1. c)
2. b)
3. c)
4. c)
5. All of the above

### Chapter 10

1. d)
2. b)
3. b)
4. e)
5. a)

### Chapter 12

1. a) Transference refers to the intense emotions expressed during a session and perceived by the patient as inspired by the clinician, but actually are pre-existing emotional experiences directed, or caused by, other characters in the patient's life. The emergence of these feelings are the aim of psychodynamic psychotherapy, but would not be 'forced' by the therapist/clinician.
2. c) Role reversal is not a main attachment pattern/representation, but a possible attachment disorder whereby the child becomes the secure base for their parent/carer, so there is no one to provide the same for them when they are feeling distressed or threatened. This is especially important to consider when working with young carers for parents experiencing disability or mental ill health. The child may have an avoidant/dismissive pattern of attachment, as they have learnt to be self-reliant and internalize their distress.

### Chapter 13

### Emotional wellbeing and emotional literacy

1. b) Mathematically ability would be part of cognitive intelligence.
2. a) For children and families living in poverty it is often a struggle, therefore children will find it harder to deal with other life stresses.

## Emotional literacy

1. c)
2. b)
3. d)
4. c)
5. c)

## Chapter 14

1. b)
2. c)
3. c)

## Chapter 15

1. a) and d)
2. c)
3. d)

## Chapter 16

1. c)
2. d)

## Chapter 17

1. a), c) and d)
2. a)

## Chapter 18

1. b)
2. c)
3. c)

## Chapter 19

1. d)
2. a)
3. d)

## Chapter 21

1. b)
2. d)

## Chapter 22

1. d)
2. d)
3. b)

## Chapter 23

1. (d)
2. (e)
3. (a)
4. (d)

## Chapter 26

1. b)
2. b)
3. d)
4. e)
5. c)

## Chapter 27

1. a)
2. d)
3. c)
4. a)
5. d)

## Chapter 28

1. b)
2. d)
3. a)
4. f)
5. d)

## Chapter 29

1. The main occupational roles of a child would be play and socialization but can include anything within a child's day (i.e. personal care, eating, toileting, etc.), attending school and leisure pursuits. Within these would be all the gross, fine and sensory skills required to function. Roles within the family and wider community would also be considered.
2. The ability to break down an activity and consider its component parts in relation to physical, social and psychological demands. Then to change, adapt and modify the activity or environment so that it is purposeful, achievable, motivating and holds the right level of challenge for the child or young person.
3. Using tools, i.e. pencil, scissors, art activities, computer skills, maintaining sitting posture, negotiating the classroom environment i.e. standing in line, dressing/undressing for gym (list is not exhaustive).
4. Taking into consideration all aspects of a child's being – physical, social and psychological needs, within the contexts of their environment and wider network.

5. An OT will assess a child in any setting which is appropriate to the child, i.e. home/school/nursery (including playground, gym class) and clinic environment.

## Chapter 30

1. c)

## Chapter 31

1. All of them
2. All of them

## Chapter 33

1. c)
2. b)
3. b)
4. e)
5. c)

## Chapter 35

1. b)
2. All of them

## Chapter 37

1. All of them

## Chapter 38

1. d)

## Chapter 39

1. a) The other characteristics are quite often seen in young children with normal development, whereas this interest would be particularly unusual.
2. c) This has been excluded as a cause whereas the other four possibilities are implicated.
3. The principal reason ASD is diagnosed more commonly now is (e). The first four options are not proven assertions.
4. e) All four tools listed are validated for reliable assessment for ASD.
5. c) Co-morbid conditions a, b, d, and e occur not uncommonly in individuals with ASD. Mania can occur but is far from common.

## Chapter 40

1. e)
2. d)

## Chapter 41

1. e)

## Chapter 42

1. c)
2. a)
3. c)
4. c)

## Chapter 43

1. b)
2. b)
3. d)
4. c)
5. a)

## Chapter 44

1. a)
2. c)
3. c)
4. d)
5. c)

## Chapter 45

1. d)
2. c)
3. b)
4. a)

## Chapter 46

1. b) and c)
2. b)
3. e)

## Chapter 47

1. c), d) and e)
2. c)
3. b), c) and d)
4. a), b), c) and d)

## Chapter 48

1. c)
2. b)
3. e)
4. c)

## Chapter 49

1. c)
2. e)
3. e)
4. a)
5. b)

## Chapter 50

1. c)
2. a)
3. e)
4. a)
5. e)

## Chapter 51

1. c)
2. c)
3. c), d) and e)
4. e)
5. d)

## Chapter 52

1. e)
2. d)
3. e)
4. e)
5. b)

## Chapter 53

1. b)
2. d)
3. d)

## Chapter 54

### Enuresis

1. True – Research shows that the presence of bed wetting costs on average £20 a week
2. False – Children with more than three wet nights a week are unlikely to grow out of their night wetting and should be treated from the age of five years
3. True – Research shows a significant improvement in self-esteem and school performance when successfully treated
4. False – NICE guidelines support treatment with both alarms and desmopressin. Choice of treatment depends on the cause of wetting but child/family preference is the most important factor in determining which treatment is used
5. True – Desmopressin is licensed for use from 5 to 65 years and can be used long term so long as breaks off medication for 1 week are taken to see if wetting has resolved

## Constipation and soiling

1. False – Soiling is most commonly a result of constipation and overflow
2. True – This has been confirmed in several research projects
3. True – Overflow soiling results from loose stool leaking out of the anus undetected and the child is often unable to smell the faeces
4. True – These laxatives are first line treatment of constipation
5. False – NICE guidelines recommend that suppositories are only used by specialists. Children dislike the use of suppositories

## Chapter 55

1. e)
2. c)
3. e)

## Chapter 57

1. True
2. True
3. True

## Chapter 58

1. d)
2. e)
3. d)
4. d)
5. e)

## Chapter 60

1. c)
2. c)
3. a) and b)
4. c)

## Chapter 61

1. b)
2. c)
3. d)

## Chapter 62

1. b)
2. c)
3. a)
4. c)
5. b)

## Chapter 63

1. a), b) and d)
2. b)
3. b) and e)

## Chapter 64

1. a)
2. b)
3. b)

## Chapter 65

1. a)
2. a)

## Chapter 66

1. a), b), d) and e)
2. b)

## Chapter 67

1. b)
2. d)
3. c)
4. b)
5. b)

## Chapter 68

1. c)
2. b)
3. c)
4. c)

## Chapter 69

1. c)
2. b)
3. b)
4. d)

## Chapter 70

1. b)
2. a)
3. b)

## Chapter 71

1. c)
2. e)

## Chapter 72

1. a)
2. b)
3. b)
4. a)
5. a)

## Chapter 73

1. c)
2. b)

## Chapter 74

1. b)
2. b)
3. d)
4. c)

## Chapter 75

1. b) and c)
2. d)

## Chapter 76

1. d)
2. c)
3. a)

## Chapter 77

1. c)
2. d)

## Chapter 78

1. d)
2. b)

## Chapter 80

1. c)
2. c)
3. d)

## Chapter 81

1. e)
2. c)

## Chapter 82

1. b)
2. c)
3. a)
4. b)
5. b)

# References

## A

Abbott J (2003) Coping with cystic fibrosis. *Journal of the Royal Society of Medicine*, **96**(Suppl. 43): 42–50.

Abramson LY, Seligman ME, Teasdale JD (1978) Learned helplessness in humans: Critique and reformulation. *Journal of Abnormal Psychology*, **87**: 49–74.

Achenbach TM (1991a) Integrative Guide to the 1991 CBCL/4-18, YSR, and TRF Profiles. Burlington, USA: University of Vermont, Department of Psychology.

Achenbach TM, Edelbrock C, Howell C (1987) Empirically-based assessment of the behavioral/emotional problems of 2–3 year old children. *Journal of Abnormal Child Psychology*, **15**: 629–50.

Achenbach T (1992) *Manual for the Child Behavior Checklist/2-3 and 1992 Profile*. Burlington, VT: University of Vermont, Department of Psychiatry.

Achenbach TM (1991b) *Manual for the Teacher's Report Form and 1991 profile*. Burlington, VT: University of Vermont, Department of Psychiatry.

Achenbach TM, Edelbrock C (1983) *Manual for the Child Behavior Checklist and Revised Child Behavior Profile*. Burlington, VT: Queen City Printers.

Ainsworth MDS, Blehar MC, Waters E, Wall S (1978) *Patterns of Attachment: A Psychological Study of the Strange Situation*. Hillsdale, NJ: Erlbaum.

Aiyegbusi A (2004) Forensic mental health nursing. Care with security in mind. In: Pfafflin F, Adshead G (eds). *A Matter of Security The Application of Attachment Theory to Forensic Psychiatry and Psychotherapy*. London: Kingsley, 167–90.

Aldridge J, Becker S (2003a) *Children who Care*. London: Zero2nineteen (www.zero2nineteen.co.uk).

Aldridge J, Becker S (2003b) *Children Caring for Parents with Mental Illness. Perspectives of Young Carers, Parents and Professionals*. Bristol: The Policy Press.

Aldridge J, Sharpe D (2007) *Pictures of Young Caring*. Loughborough: Young Carers Research Group, Loughborough University.

Alexander JF, Pugh C, Parsons BV, Sexton TL (2000) *Functional Family Therapy*. Boulder, CO: University of Colorado, Center for the Study and Prevention of Violence.

Allen JP, Land D (1999) Attachment in adolescence. In: Cassidy J, Shaver PR (eds). *Handbook of Attachment: Theory, Research, and Clinical Applications*. New York and London: Guilford Press, 319–35.

American Academy of Sleep Medicine (2005) *International Classification of Sleep Disorders*, 2nd edn. Westchester, IL: American Academy of Sleep Medicine.

American Psychiatric Association (2000) *Diagnostic and Statistical Manual of Mental Disorders*, 4th edn. Text Revision. Arlington, Va: American Psychiatric Association.

Anderson JR (2000) *Learning and Memory: An Integrated Approach*, 2nd edn. Hoboken, NJ: John Wiley and Sons.

Angold A, Costello EJ, Erkanli A (1999). Comorbidity. *Journal of Child Psychology and Psychiatry*, **40**: 57–87.

Angst J (1980) Course of unipolar depressive, bipolar manic-depressive and schizoaffective disorders. Results of a prospective longitudinal study [in German]. *Fortschritte der Neurologie, Psychiatrie, und ihrer Grenzgebiete*, **48**: 3–30.

Apley J, McKeith R, Meadow R (1978) *The Child and His Symptoms: A Comprehensive Approach*. Oxford: Blackwell.

Appleby L (2004) *The National Service Framework for Mental Health, Five Years on*. London: Department of Health.

Appleton P (2000) Tier 2 CAMHS and its interface with primary care. *Advances in Psychiatric Treatment*, **6**: 388–96.

Appleton P (1990) Interventions by health visitors. In: Stevenson J (ed.). *Health Visitor Based Services for Pre-School Children with Behaviour Problems*. Occasional Papers No. 2. London: ACPP.

Appleton P, Hammond-Rowley S (2000) Addressing the population burden of child and adolescent mental health problems: a primary care model. *Child Psychology and Psychiatric Review*, **5**: 9–16.

Arcos-Burgos M, Castellanos FX, Pineda D et al. (2004). Attention deficit hyperactivity disorder in a population isolate: linkage to loci at 4q13.2, 5q33.3, 11q22, and 17p11. *American Journal of Human Genetics*, **75**: 998–1014.

Arthur GK, Monnell K (2005) *Body Dysmorphic Disorder*, USA: eMedicine (online). Available from: www.emedicine.com/MED/topic3124.htm

Arundale J, Bandler Bellman D (eds) (2011) *Transference and Countertransference. A Unifying Focus of Psychoanalysis*. London: Karnac.

Asghari V, Sanyal S, Buchwaldt S et al. (1995). Modulation of intracellular cyclic AMP levels by different human dopamine D4 receptor variants. *Journal of Neurochemistry*, **65**: 1157–65.

Ashraf H (2000) Surgery offers little help for patients with body dysmorphic disorder. *Lancet*, **355**: 2055.

Attwood T (1998) *Aspergers Syndrome: A Guide for Parents and Professionals.* London: Jessica Kingsley Publishers.

Audit Commission (1999) *Children in Mind: Child and Adolescent Mental Health Services.* Portsmouth: Audit Commission.

August GJ, Braswell L, Thuras P (1998) Diagnostic stability of ADHD in a community sample of school-aged children screened for disruptive behavior. *Journal of Abnormal Child Psychology,* **26**: 345–56.

Autism Act, 2009. Available from: www.autism.org.uk/AutismAct

Autism Education Trust (Accessed 30 March 2011) Available from: www.autismeducationtrust.org.uk/goodpractise/earlyyears

Axelson D, Birmaher B, Strober M et al. (2006).Phenomenology of children and adolescents with bipolar spectrum disorders. *Archives of General Psychiatry,* **63**: 1139–48.

Axline V (1989) *Play Therapy.* London: Churchill Livingstone.

## B

BACP (2010). *Ethical Framework for Good Practice in Counselling and Psychotherapy,* revised edn. Lutterworth: British Association for Counselling and Psychotherapy.

Baddeley A, Hitch G (1974) Working memory. In: Bower GA (ed.) *Recent Advances in Learning and Motivation,* vol. 8. New York: Academic Press, 47–60.

Baird G, Simonoff E, Pickles A et al. (2006) Prevalence of disorders of the autism spectrum in a population cohort of children in South Thames: the Special Needs and Autism Project (SNAP). *Lancet,* **368**: 210–15.

Banaschewski T, Coghill D, Santosh P et al. (2006) Long-acting medications for the hyperkinetic disorders. A systematic review and European treatment guideline. *European Child and Adolescent Psychiatry,* **15**: 476–95.

Bandura J (1977) *Social Learning Theory.* Englewood Cliff, NJ: Prentice Hall.

Barbaresi W, Kaustic S, Cilligan R et al. (2007) Long term school outcomes for children with Attention-deficit/ hyperactivity disorder: A population based perspective. *Journal of Developmental and Behavioural Paediatrics,* **28**: 265–73.

Bar-Haim Y, Lamy D, Pergamin L et al. (2007) Threat-related attentional bias in anxious and non-anxious individuals: A meta-analytic study. *Psychological Bulletin,* **133**: 1–124.

Barkley RA (2006) *Attention Deficit Hyperactivity Disorder: a Handbook for Diagnosis and Treatment,* 2nd edn. New York: Guilford Press.

Barkley RA (2000) Genetics of childhood disorders: XVII. ADHD, Part 1: The executive functions and ADHD. *Journal of American Academy of Child and Adolescent Psychiatry,* **39**: 1064–8.

Barkley RA, Murphy KR (1998) *Attention-Deficit Hyperactivity Disorder: A Clinical Workbook,* 2nd edn. New York: Guildford Press.

Barkley RA, Murphy KR, Fischer M (2008) *ADHD in Adults: What the science says.* New York: Guilford Press.

Barkley RA, Murphy KR, Kwasnik D (1996) Motor vehicle driving competencies and risk in teens and young adults with ADHD. *Paediatrics,* **98**: 1089–95.

Barkley RA, DuPaul GJ, McMurray MB (1990a) Comprehensive evaluation of attention deficit disorder with and without hyperactivity as defined by research criteria. *Journal of Consulting and Clinical Psychology,* **58**: 775–89.

Barkley RA, Fischer M, Edelbrock CS, Smallish L (1990b) The adolescent outcome of hyperactive children diagnosed by the research criteria: 1 and 8 year prospective follow-up study. *Journal for the American Academy of Child and Adolescent Psychiatry,* **29**: 546–57.

Barkmann C, Schulte-Markwort M (2005) Emotional and behavioral problems of children and adolescents in Germany – an epidemiological screening. *Social Psychiatry and Psychiatric Epidemiology,* **40**: 357–66.

Barnes J, Ball M, Meadows P, Belsky J (2011) *Nurse-Family Partnership Programme: Wave 1 Implementation in toddlerhood and a comparison between Waves 1 and 2a implementation in pregnancy and infancy.* London: DCSF.

Baron-Cohen S (2008) *Autism and Asperger Syndrome: the Facts.* Oxford: Oxford University Press.

Baron-Cohen S, Scott FJ, Allison C et al. (2009) Autism spectrum prevalence: a school-based UK population study. *British Journal of Psychiatry,* **194**: 500–9.

Baron-Cohen S, Ring H, Wheelwright S et al. (1999) Social intelligence in the normal and autistic brain: an fMRI study. *European Journal of Neuroscience,* **11**: 1891–8.

Baron-Cohen S, Cox A, Baird G et al. (1996) Psychological markers in the detection of autism in infancy in a large population. *British Journal of Psychiatry,* **168**: 158–63.

Baron-Cohen S, Wheelwright S, Cox A et al. (2000) Early identification of autism by the Checklist for Autism in Toddlers (CHAT). *Journal of the Royal Society of Medicine*, **93**: 521–5.

Baron-Cohen S, Allen J, Gillberg C (1992) Can autism be detected at 18 months? The needle the haystack and the CHAT.*British Journal of Psychiatry*, **161**: 839–43.

Baroni A, Lunsford J, Luckenbaugh D et al. (2009) Practitioner Review: The assessment of bipolar disorder in children and adolescents. *Journal of Child Psychology and Psychiatry*, **50**: 203–15.

Barr RG (1998) Management of clinical problems and emotional care: Colic and crying syndromes in infants. *Pediatrics*, **102**: 1282–6.

Barrett PM, Rapee RM, Dadds MR, Sharon M. (1996) Family enhancement of cognitive style in anxious and aggressive children. *Journal of Abnormal Child Psychology*, **24**: 187–203.

Barthélémy C, Roux S, Adrien JL et al. (1997) Validation of the Revised Behavior Summarized Evaluation (BSE–R). *Journal of Autism and Developmental Disorders*, **27**: 139–53.

Barthélémy C, Adrien JL et al. (1990) The Behavioral Summarized Evaluation:Validity and Reliability of a Scale for the Assessment of Autistic Behaviors. *Journal of Autism and Developmental Disorders*, **20**: 189–204.

Beattie M (2006) Essential revision notes in paediatrics for the MRCPCH, 2nd edn. Cheshire: PASTEST Ltd.

Beck AT, Ward CH, Mendelson M et al. (1961) An inventory for measuring depression. *Archives in General Psychiatry*, **4**: 561–71.

Becker S (2000) *The Blackwell Encyclopaedia of Social Work*. London: Blackwell.

Bee HL (1994) *Lifespan Development*. New York: HarperCollins College Publishers.

Beesdo K, Knappe S, Pine DS (2009) Anxiety and anxiety disorders in children and adolescents: developmental issues and implications for DSM-V. *Psychiatry Clinics of North America*, **32**: 483–524.

Bentovim A (2003) Theories of family interaction and techniques of intervention. *Journal of Family Therapy*, **1**: 321.

Berg I (1992) Absence from school and mental health. *British Journal of Psychiatry*, **161**: 154–66.

Berg I, Nichols K, Pritchard C (1969) School phobia – its classification and relationship to dependency. *Journal of Child Psychology and Psychiatry*, **10**: 123–41.

Bernard P, Garralda E, Hughes T et al. (1999) Evaluation of a teaching package in adolescent psychiatry for general practitioner registrars. *Education for General Practice*, **10**: 21–8.

Bernard S (2010) Epidemiology and aetiology. In: Raghavan R, Bernard S, McCarthy J (eds). *Mental Health Needs of Children and Young People with Learning Disabilities*. Brighton: Pavilion Publishing.

Berry D, Courtenay M, Bersellini E (2006) Attitudes towards, and information needs in relation to supplementary nurse prescribing in the UK; an empirical study. *Journal of Clinical Nursing*, **15**: 22–8.

Bhugra D (2002) Ethnic factors and service utilization. *Current Opinion in Psychiatry*, **15**: 201–4.

Biby EL (1998) The relationship between body dysmorphic disorder and depression, self-esteem, somatization and obsessive-compulsive disorder. *Journal of Clinical Psychology*, **54**: 489–99.

Biederman J (2003) Pharmacotherapy for attention deficit/hyperactivity disorder (ADHD) decreases the risk for substance abuse: findings from a longitudinal follow up of youths with and without ADHD. *Journal of Clinical Psychiatry*, **64**(Suppl. 11): 3–8.

Biederman J, Faraone SV (2005) Attention-deficit hyperactivity disorder. *Lancet*, **366**: 237–48.

Biederman J, Hirshfeld-Becker DR, Rosenbaum JF et al. (2001) Further evidence of association between behavioral inhibition and social anxiety in children. *American Journal of Psychiatry*, **158**: 1673–9.

Biederman J, Mick E, Faraone SV (2000) Age-dependent decline of symptoms of attention deficit hyperactivity disorder: impact of remission definition and symptom type. *American Journal of Psychiatry*, **157**: 816–18.

Biederman J, Farone SV, Mick E et al. (1996) ADHD and Juvenile mania: An overlooked co morbidity? *Journal of the American Academy of Child and Adolescent Psychiatry*, **35**: 997–1008.

Biederman J, Farone SV, Keena K et al. (1992) Further evidence for family-genetic risk factors in ADHD. Patterns of co morbidity in probands and relatives in psychiatrically and paediatrically referred samples. *Archives of General Psychiatry*, **49**: 728–38.

Biederman J, Faraone SV, Keenan K et al. (1990) Family-genetic and psychosocial risk factors in DSM-III attention deficit disorder. *Journal of the American Academy of Child and Adolescent Psychiatry*, **29**: 526–33.

Bienvenu OJ, Samuels JF, Riddle MA et al. (2000) The relationship of obsessive-compulsive disorder to possible spectrum disorders: results from a family study. *Biological Psychiatry*, **48**: 287–93.

Big Society. Available from: www.cabinetoffice.gov.uk/sites/default/files/resources/building-big-society_0.pdf

Bird HR (1996) Epidemiology of childhood disorders in a cross-cultural context. *Journal of Child Psychology and Psychiatry*, **37**: 35–49.

Birleson P (1998) Building a learning organisation in a child and adolescent mental health service. *Australian Health Review*, **21**: 223–40.

Birmaher B, Axelson D, Strober M et al. (2006) Clinical course of children and adolescents with bipolar spectrum disorders. *Archives of General Psychiatry*, **63**: 175–83.

Birmaher B, Heydl P (2001) Biological studies in depressed children and adolescents. *International Journal of Neuropsychopharmacology*, **4**: 149–57.

Black D (1978) The bereaved child. *Journal of Child Psychology and Psychiatry*, **19**: 287-82.

Blair L (2010) A critical review of the scientist-practitioner model for counselling psychology. *Counselling Psychology Review*, **25**: 19–28.

Blair RJ, Finger E, Marsh A (2009) The development and neural bases of psychopathy. In: De Haan M, Gunnar MR (eds). *Handbook of Developmental Social Neuroscience*. New York: Guilford Press, 419–434.

Bloch M, State M, Pittenger C (2011) Recent advances in Tourette syndrome. *Current Opinion in Neurology*, **24**: 119–25.

Bloom L, Lahey M (1978) *Language Development and Language Disorders*. New York: Wiley.

Bonde HV, Andersen JP, Rosenkilde P (1994) Nocturnal enuresis: change of nocturnal voiding pattern during alarm treatment. *Scandinavian Journal of Urology and Nephrology*, **28**: 349–52.

Bondy B (2011) Genetics in psychiatry: are the promises met? *World Journal of Biological Psychiatry*, **12**: 81–8.

Bor W, Sanders MR, Markie-Dadds C (2002) The effects of the Triple P-Positive Parenting Program on preschool children with co-occurring disruptive behaviour and attentional/hyperactive difficulties. *Journal of Abnormal Child Psychology*, **30**: 571–87.

Borum R, Bartel P, Forth A (2003) *SAVRY – Manual for the Structured Assessment of Violence Risk in Youth*. Florida: University of Florida.

Bowlby J (1969) Attachment and loss, Vol. 1: Attachment. New York: Basic Books.

Bowlby J (1997) Attachment and Loss 1–3, 2nd revised edn. London: Pimlico.

Bowlby J (1988) *A Secure Base: Clinical Applications of Attachment Theory*. London: Routledge.

Bowlby J (1973) *Attachment and Loss*, volumes 2 and 3. New York: Basic Books.

Box S, Copley B, Magagna J, Moustaki E (1981) *Psychotherapy with Families: An Analytic Approach*. London: Routledge and Kegan Paul.

Bradbury E, Wain P, Nolan P (2008). Putting mental health prescribing into practice. *Nurse Prescribing* **6**: 15–21.

Bradley E, Campbell P, Nolan P (2005) Nurse Prescribers: who are they and how do they perceive their role? *Journal of Advanced Nursing*, **51**: 439–48.

Brand S, Gerber M, Beck J et al. (2010a) Exercising, sleep-EEG patterns, and psychological functioning are related among adolescents. *World Journal of Biological Psychiatry*, **11**: 129–40.

Brennan PA, Grekin ER, Mednick SA (1999) Maternal smoking during pregnancy and adult male criminal outcomes. *Archives of General Psychiatry*, **56**: 215–19.

Bretherton I. (1985) Attachment theory: Retrospect and prospect. *Monographs of the Society for Research in Child Development*, **50**: 3–35.

Brisch KH (2002) *Treating Attachment Disorders: From Theory to Therapy*. New York, London: Guilford Press.

British Medical Association and the Royal Pharmaceutical Society of Great Britain (2009) *British National Formulary*, 58th edn. London: BMJ Publishing Group.

British Paediatric Association (1996) The Future Configuration of Paediatric Services. London: British Paediatric Association.

British Psychological Society (2006) Drawing on the evidence: Advice for mental health professionals working with children and adolescents. Available from: www.bps.org.uk/dcp-cyp/documentations/publications.cfm

Britton R (1981) Re-enactment as an unwitting professional response to family dynamics. In: Box S, Copley B, Magagna J, Moustaki E (eds). *Psychotherapy with Families*. London: Routledge and Kegan Paul.

Broadbent DE (1958) *Perception and Communication*. London: Pergamon.

Bronfenbrenner U (1979) *The Ecology of Human Development*. Cambridge, MA: Harvard University Press.

Brown L, Hammill DD (1990) *Behaviour Rating Profile: Examiner's manual*, 2nd edn. Austin, TX: Pro-Ed.

Brownley KA, Berkman ND, Sedway JA et al. (2007) Binge eating disorder treatment: a systematic review of randomized control trials. *International Journal of Eating Disorders*, **40**: 337–48.

Brunswick RM (1928) A supplement to Freud's 'History of an infantile neurosis'. *International Journal of Psychoanalysis*, **9**: 439–76.

Bryan K (2004) Preliminary study of the prevalence of speech and language difficulties in young offenders. *International Journal of Communication and Language Disorders*, **39**: 391–400.

Burnham J (1986) *Family Therapy: First Steps Towards a Systemic Approach*. London: Routledge.

Burns D, Bulley R, Curphey P (2002) Nurse prescribing: extended prescribing powers: three views. *Nursing Times*, **98**: 37–8.

Buss AR, Plomin R (1984) *Temperament: Early Developing Personality Traits*. Hillsdale, NJ: Lawrence Erlbaum.

Busseri M, Willoughby T, Chalmers H, Bogaert AR (2006) Same-sex attraction and successful adolescent development. *Journal of Youth and Adolescence*, 35: 563–5.

Bulter NR, Golding J (eds) (1986) *From Birth to Five: A Study of the Health and Behaviour of Britains Five Year Olds*. London: Pergamon Press.

Byng-Hall J (1995) *Rewriting Family Scripts: Improvisation and Systems Change*. New York: Guilford Publications.

## C

Campbell SB (1995) Behaviour problems in preschool children: a review of recent research. *Journal of Child Psychology and Psychiatry* 36: 113–49.

Campbell SB, Ewing LJ (1990) Follow up of hard-to-manage preschoolers: adjustment at age 9 and predictors of continuing symptoms. *Journal of Child Psychology and Psychiatry* 31: 871–89.

Campos JJ, Campos RG, Barrett KC (1989) Emergent themes in the study of emotional development and emotion regulation. *Developmental Psychology*, 25: 394–402.

Cantwell DP (1975) Genetic studies of hyperactive children: psychiatric illness in biologic and adopting parents. *Proceedings of the Annual Meeting of the American Psychopathological Association*, 63: 273–80.

Cardno AG, Marshall EJ, Coid B et al. (1999) Heritability estimates for psychotic disorders. *Archives of General Psychiatry*, 56: 162–8.

Care Services Improvement Partnership (2005) *Our Choices in Mental Health*. London: CSIP.

Carlson G (1990) Annotation: child and adolescent mania – diagnostic considerations. *Journal of Child Psychology and Psychiatry*, 31: 331–41.

Carr A (2006) *Family Therapy: Concepts, Process and Practice*. London: Wiley Series in Clinical Psychology.

Carr A (1998) Michael White's narrative therapy. *Contemporary Family Therapy*, 20: 485–503.

Carter B, McGoldrick M (1989) *The Changing Family Life Cycle: A Framework for Family Therapy*, 2nd edn. Boston, MA: Allyn and Bacon.

Carter CM, Urbanowicz M, Hemsley R et al. (1993) Effects of a few food diet in attention-deficit disorder. *Archives of Disease in Childhood*, 69: 564–68.

Caspi A, Harrington HL, Milne B et al. (2003) The human personality shows stability from age 3 to age 26. *Journal of Personality*, 71: 495–514.

Caspi A, McClay J, Moffitt TE et al. (2002) Role of genotype in the cycle of violence in maltreated children. *Science (New York)*, 297: 851–4.

Caspi A, Moffitt TE, Newman DL, Silva PA (1996) Behavioral observations at age 3 years predict adult psychiatric disorders. Longitudinal evidence from a birth cohort. *Archives of General Psychiatry*, 53: 1033–9.

Caspi A, Elder Jr GH, Herbener ES (1990) Childhood personality and the prediction of life-course patterns. In: Robins L, Rutter M (eds). *Straight and Devious Pathways from Childhood to Adulthood*. Cambridge: Cambridge University Press.

Cassidy F, Ahearn EP, Carroll BJ (2001) Substance abuse in bipolar disorder. *Bipolar Disorders*, 3: 181–8.

Castle J, Beckett C, Rutter M, Sonuga-Barke E (2010) Post-adoption environmental features. *Monographs of the Society for Research in Child Development*, 75: 167–86.

Castle J, Groothues C, Bredenkamp D et al. (1999) Effects of qualities of early institutional care on cognitive attainment. E.R.A. Study Team. English and Romanian Adoptees. *American Journal of Orthopsychiatry*, 69: 424–37.

Catalano RF, Berglund ML, Ryan JAM et al. (2002) Positive youth development in the United States: Research findings on evaluations of positive youth development programs. *Prevention and Treatment*, 5: 15.

Cattanach A (2008a) *Narrative Approaches in Play Therapy with Children*, 2nd edn. London: Jessica Kingsley.

Cattanach A (2008b) *Play Therapy with Abused Children*. London: Jessica Kingsley.

Cavill S (2000) Psychology in practice: welfare of refugees. *The Psychologist*, 13: 552–4.

Chakrabarti S, Fombonne E. (2005) Pervasive developmental disorders in preschool children: confirmation of high prevalence. *American Journal of Psychiatry*, 162: 1133–41.

Charman T, Jones CRG, Pickles A et al. (2011) Defining the cognitive phenotype of autism. *Brain Research*, 1380: 10–21.

Chen W, Taylor E (2005) Resilience and self-control impairment. In: Goldstein S, Brooks RB (eds). *Handbook of Resilience in Children*. New York: Kluwer Academic/Plenum Publishers.

Chess S (1977) Report on autism in congenital rubella. *Journal of Autism and Childhood Schizophrenia*, 7: 68–81.

Children Act (1989) Chapter 41. London: HMSO.

Children Act 1989 Regulations and Guidance (updated).

Children and Young People in Mind: the Final report of the National CAMHS Review (2008) DOH.

Children's Health Care Collaborative Group (1992) Romanian health and social care system for children and families: Future directions in health care reform. *British Medical Journal*, **304**: 556–9.

Children's Workforce Development Council (2009) *The Common Assessment Framework for Children and Young People: A Guide for Practitioners*. London: CDWC.

Chitsabesan P, Kroll L, Bailey S et al. (2006) Mental health needs of young offenders in custody and in the community. *British Journal of Psychiatry*, **188**: 534–40.

Chitsabesan P, Harrington R, Harrington V, Tomenson B (2003) Predicting repeat self-harm in children: how accurate can we expect to be? *European Child and Adolescent Psychiatry*, **12**: 23–9.

Chomsky N (1957) *Syntactic Structures*. The Hague: Mouton.

Chorpita BF, Albano A, Heimberg RG, Barlow DH (1996) A systematic replication of the prescriptive treatment of school refusal behaviour in a single subject. *Journal of Behaviour Therapy and Experimental Psychiatry*, **27**: 281–90.

Chugani HT, Behen ME, Muzik O et al. (2001) Local brain functional activity following early deprivation: A study of postinstitutionalized Romanian orphans. *Neuroimage*, **14**: 1290–301.

Ciaranello AL, Ciaranello RD (1995) The neurobiology of infantile autism. *Annual Review of Neuroscience*, **18**: 101–28.

Cicchetti D, Curtis WJ (2005) An event-related potential study of the processing of affective facial expressions in young children who experienced maltreatment during the first year of life. *Developmental Psychopathology*, **17**: 641–77.

Claude D, Firestone P (1995) The Development of ADHD boys. A 12 year follow up. *Canadian Journal of Behaviour Science*, **27**: 226–49.

Clegg J, Hollis C, Rutter M (1999) *Life Sentence – What Happens to Children with Developmental Language Disorders in Later Life?* London: Royal College of Speech and Language Therapists Bulletin November.

Cohen IL, Sudhalter V (2005) *The PDD Behaviour Inventory*. Lutz, FL: Psychological Assessment Resources, Inc.

Conners CK (2008) *Conners Comprehensive Behaviour Rating Scales Manual*. Toronto, Ontario, Canada: Multi-Health Systems.

Conners CK (1990) *Conners Rating Scales Manual*. New York: Multi-Health System.

Constantino JN, Gruber CP (2005) *Social responsiveness scale (SRS)*. Los Angeles, CA: Western Psychological Services.

Cook EH Jr, Stein MA, Krasowski MD et al. (1995) Association of attention-deficit disorder and the dopamine transporter gene. *American Journal of Human Genetics*, **56**: 993–8.

Coolidge FL, Thede LL, Young SE (2000) Heritability and the comorbidity of attention deficit hyperactivity disorder with behavioral disorders and executive function deficits: a preliminary investigation. *Developmental Neuropsychology*, **17**: 273–87.

Cooper J, Heron TE, Heward WL (2007) *Applied Behavior Analysis*, 2nd edn. Upper Saddle River, NJ: Prentice-Hall.

Costello EJ, Angold A, Burns BJ et al. (1996) The Great Smoky Mountains Study of Youth. Goals, design, methods, and the prevalence of DSM-III-R Disorders. *Archives of General Psychiatry*, **53**: 1129–36.

Coughlan BJ (2010) *Critical Issues in the Emotional Wellbeing of Students with Special Educational Needs*. Available from: www.ssatrust.org.uk/pedagogy/networks/specialschools/CLDD/Pages/ThinkPiece6.aspx

Courtney M, Carey NJ (2009) Nurse prescribing by children's nurses: views of doctors and clinical leads. In one specialist children's hospital. *Journal of Clinical Nursing*, **18**: 2668–75.

Creedon R, O'Connell E, McCarthy G, Lehane B (2009) An evaluation of nurse prescribing. Part 1: a literature review. *British Journal of Nursing*, **18**: 1322–7.

Crittenden P (2008) *Raising Parents: Attachment, Parenting and Child Safety*. Cullompton, UK: Willan Publishing.

Crossley ML (2000) *Introducing Narrative Psychology: Self, Trauma and the Construction of Meaning*. Buckingham: Open University Press.

Culley S, Bond T (2004) *Integrative Counselling Skills in Action*, 2nd edn. London: Sage.

**D**

Dalen L, Sonuga-Barke EJS, Remmington RE et al. (2004) Inhibitory deficits, delay aversion and preschool AD/HD implications for the dual pathway model. *Neural Plasticity*, **11**: 1–11.

Daley D, Jones K, Hutchings J, Thompson M (2009) Attention deficit hyperactivity disorder in pre-school children: current findings, recommended interventions and future directions. *Child: Care, Health and Development*, **35**: 754–66.

Dalley T (1996) *Art as Therapy*. London: Routledge.

Dallos R, Draper R (2010) *An Introduction to Family Therapy Systemic Theory and Practice*, 3rd edn. Oxford: Oxford University Press.

Dallos R, Vetere A (2006) *Systemic Therapy and Attachment Narratives: Applications in a Range of Clinical Settings*. Hove, East Sussex and New York: Routledge.

Dalrymple J, Burke B (1995) *Anti-Oppressive Practice. Social Care and Law*. Buckinghamshire: Open University.

Dasha E, Nicholls RL, Russell M (2011) Viner Childhood eating disorder: British National surveillance study. *British Journal of Psychiatry*, **198**: 295–301.

Davidson PW, Myers GJ, Cox C et al. (1998). Effects of prenatal and postnatal methylmercury exposure from fish consumption on neurodevelopment: outcomes at 66 months of age in the Seychelles Child Development Study. *Journal of the American Medical Association*, **280**: 701–7.

Davis H, Spurr P, Cox A et al. (1997) A description and evaluation of a community child mental health service. *Clinical Child Psychology and Psychiatry*, **2**: 221–38.

Davis H, Spur P (1998) Parent counselling: an evaluation of a community child health mental service. *Journal of Child Psychology and Psychiatry*, **39**: 365–76.

Davison F, Howlin P (1997) A follow-up study of children attending a primary age language unit. *European Journal of Disorders of Communication*, **32**: 19–36.

Daws D (1989) *Through the Night: Helping Parents and Sleepless Infants*. London: Free Association Books.

Dawson G, Webb SJ, Carver L et al. (2004) Young children with autism show atypical brain responses to fearful versus neutral facial expressions of emotion. *Developmental Science*, **7**: 340–59.

Dearden C, Becker S (2004) *Young Carers in the UK – the 2004 Report*. London: Carers UK.

De Haan M, Gunnar MR (2009) *Handbook of Developmental Social Neuroscience*. New York: Guilford Press.

De Kloet ER, Sibug RM, Helmerhorst FM, Schmidt M (2005) Stress, genes and the mechanism of programming the brain for later life. *Neuroscience and Biobehavioral Reviews*, **29**: 271–81.

Department for Children, Schools and Families (2010a) *IRO Handbook: statutory guidance for Independent Reviewing Officers and local authorities on their functions in relation to case management and review for looked after children*. London: The Stationery Office.

Department for Children, Schools and Families (2010b) *Short Breaks: statutory guidance on how to safeguard and promote the welfare of disabled children using short breaks*. London: The Stationery Office.

Department for Children, Schools and Families (2010c) *Working Together to Safeguard Children – A Guide to Inter-agency Working to Safeguard and Promote the Welfare of Children*. London: The Stationery Office.

Department for Children, Schools and Families, Department of Health (2009) *Aiming High for Disabled Children; best practice to common practice*. London: The Stationery Office.

Department for Children, Schools and Families, Department of Health, NHS (2008) *Aiming High for Disabled Children: Transforming Services for disabled children and their families*. London: The Stationery Office.

Department for Children, Schools and Families (2007) *Vol 1: Court Orders*. London: The Stationery office.

Department for Education (2010a) *Vol 2: Care Planning, Placement and Case Review*.

Department for Education (2010b) *Vol 3: Planning Transition to Adulthood for looked after children*.

Department for Education and Skills (2006) *Sure Start Children's Centres Planning and Performance Management Guidance*. Crown copyright. Available from: www.everychildmatters.org.uk

Department for Education and Skills/Department of Health (2005) *National Healthy Schools Status: A guide for schools*. London: DH Publications.

Department for Education and Skills (2003) *Every Child Matters*. London: DfES.

Department for Education and Skills (2004) *Every Child Matters: Change for Children*. London: DfES.

Department of Constitutional Affairs (2007) *Mental Capacity Act 2005 Code of Practice*. London: TSO.

Department of Health (2011) *Delivering Better Mental Health Outcomes for People of all Ages*. London: HMSO.

Department of Health (2010) *Keeping Children and Young People in Mind. The Governments Response to the independent review of CAMHS*. London: HMSO.

Department of Health (2009a) *Delivering Race Equality in Mental Health Care: A Review*. London: HMSO.

Department of Health (2008a) *Children and Young People in Mind*. The Final report of the National CAMHS Review. London: HMSO.

Department of Health (2008b) *Mental Health Act 1983 Code of Practice*. London: TSO.

Department of Health (2008c) *Refocusing the Care Programme Approach: Policy and Positive Practice Guidance*. London: Department of Health.

Department of Health (2007a) *Positive Steps: Supporting Race Equality in Mental Health Care*. London: HMSO.

Department of Health (2007b) *Promoting Mental Health for Children Held in Secure Settings: A Framework for Commissioning Services*. London: HMSO.

Department of Health (2005) *Delivering Race Equality in Mental Health Care Action Plan*. London: HMSO.

Department of Health (2004a) *National Service Framework, for children, Young People and Maternity Services*. London: Her Majesty's Stationary Office.

Department of Health (2004b) *Patient and public Involvement in Health: The Evidence for Policy Implementation*. London: The Stationary Office.

Department of Health (2003a) *Child and Adolescent Mental Health Service (CAMHS) Grant Guidance 2003/2004 HSC2003/003*: LAC 2. London: HMSO.

Department of Health (2003b) *The green paper 'Every Child Matters and the Children's Bill'*. London: HMSO.

Department of Health (2003c) *Every Child Matters*. London: HMSO.

Department of Health (2003d) *Inside Outside: Improving Mental Health Services for Black and Minority Ethnic Communities in England*. London: HMSO.

Department of Health (2002a) *Improvement, expansion and reform: the next three years: the Priorities and Planning framework*. Available from: www.doh.gov.uk/planning (2003-2006).

Department of Health (2002b) *Mental Health Policy Implementation Guide: Dual Diagnosis Good Practice Guide*. London: Department of Health.

Department of Health (2002c) *Models of Care for Substance Misuse Treatment*. London: Department of Health.

Department of Health (2001a) *The Children Act Now Messages from Research*. London: HMSO.

Department of Health (2001b) *Valuing People: a new strategy for learning disability for the 21st century*. London: HMSO.

Department of Health (2000) *Consultant Nurses*. London: HMSO.

Department of Health (1999a) *National Strategy for Carers*. London: HMSO.

Department of Health (1999b) *National Service Framework for Mental Health: Modern Standards and Service Models*. London: HMSO.

Department of Health (1995a) *Modernisation funding*. London: HMSO.

Department of Health (1995b) *Child Protection Messages from Research*: London: HMSO.

Department of Health (1990) *Caring for People. The Care Programme Approach for People With a Mental Illness Referred to Specialist Mental Health Services*. London: HMSO.

Department of Health and Social Security (1986) *Neighbourhood nursing: a focus for care* (Cumberlege Report).

Department of Health, Home Office, Department for Education and Employment (2000) *Framework for the Assessment of Children in Need and their Families*. London: The Stationery Office.

Department of Health Publications (2008): *Medical care for gender variant children and young people: answering families' questions*; *A guide for young trans people in the UK*; *A guide to hormone therapy for trans people*. London: HMSO.

Department of Health (2009) *New Horizons: A Shared Vision for Mental Health*. London: HMSO.

Department of Health, Home Office (1992) *Review of Health and Social Services for Mentally Disordered Offenders and Others Requiring Similar Sservices*. London: HMSO.

Department of Health (1983) *Mental Health Act*. London: The Stationery Office.

Desmond MM, Wilson GS, Melnick JL et al. (1967). Congenital rubella encephalitis: course and early sequelae. *Journal of Pediatrics*, **71**: 311–31.

DeYoung A, Kenardy J, Cobham V (2011) Trauma in aarly childhood: A neglected population. *Clinical Child and Family Psychology Review*, **14**: 231–50.

DeYoung CG, Getchell M, Koposov RA et al. (2010) Variation in the catechol-O-methyltransferase Val 158 Met polymorphism associated with conduct disorder and ADHD symptoms, among adolescent male delinquents. *Psychiatric Genetics*, **20**: 20–4.

Dick DM, Aliev F, Krueger RF et al. (2011) Genome-wide association study of conduct disorder symptomatology. *Molecular Psychiatry*, **16**: 800–8.

Didie ER, Tortolani CC, Pope CG et al. (2006) Childhood abuse and neglect in body dysmorphic disorder. *Child Abuse and Neglect*, **30**: 1105–15.

Diesendruck G (2007) *Mechanisms of Word Learning*. Oxford: Blackwell Publishing Ltd.

Di Maio S, Grizenko N, Joober R (2003) Dopamine genes and attention-deficit hyperactivity disorder: a review. *Journal of Psychiatry and Neuroscience*, **28**: 27–38.

DiMaio S, Grizenko N, Joober R (2003) Dopamine genes and attention-deficit hyperactivity disorder: a review. *Journal of Psychiatry and Neuroscience*, **28**: 27–38.

Doel M, Sawdon C (2001) *The Essential Group Worker in Teaching and Learning Creative Group Work*, 2nd impression. London and Philadelphia: Jessica Kingsley.

Domenech-Llaberia E, Vinas F, Pla E et al. (2009) Prevalence of major depression in preschool children. *European Child and Adolescent Psychiatry*, **18**: 597–604.

Dootson LG (2000) Adolescent homosexuality and culturally competent nursing. *Nursing Forum*, **35**: 13–20.

Duncan J (1980) The locus of interference in the perception of simultaneous stimuli. *Psychological Review*, **87**: 272–300.

Durand CM, Betancur C, Boeckers TM et al. (2007) Mutations in the gene encoding the synaptic scaffolding protein SHANK3 are associated with autism spectrum disorders. *Nature Genetics*, **39**: 25–7.

Dwivedi KN (ed.). (1993). *Group Work with Children and Adolescents: A Handbook*. London: Jessica Kingsley Publishers.

Dyl J, Kittler J, Phillips KA, Hunt JI (2006) Body dysmorphic disorder and other clinically significant body image concerns in adolescent psychiatric inpatients: prevalence and clinical characteristics. *Child Psychiatry and Human Development*, **36**: 369–82.

## E

Early Years Foundation Stage (2007) Department for Education and Skills.

Eaves LJ, Silberg JL, Meyer JM et al. (1997) Genetics and developmental psychopathology: 2. The main effects of genes and environment on behavioral problems in the Virginia Twin Study of Adolescent Behavioral Development. *Journal of Child Psychology and Psychiatry*, **38**: 965–80.

Ebstein R, Levine J, Geller V et al. (1998) Dopamine D4 receptor and serotonin transporter promoter in the determination of neonatal temperament. *Molecular Psychiatry*, **3**: 238–46.

Edelbrock C, Costello AJ (1988) Structured psychiatric interviews for children. In: Rutter M, Tuma AH, Lann IS (eds). *Assessment and Diagnosis in Child Psychopathology*. New York, London: Guilford Press, 87–112.

Edelbrock C, Rende R, Plomin R, Thompson LA (1995) A twin study of competence and problem behavior in childhood and early adolescence. *Journal of Child Psychology and Psychiatry*, **36**: 775–85.

Edvardsen J, Torgersen S, Røysamb E et al. (2008) Heritability of bipolar spectrum disorders. Unity or heterogeneity? *Journal of Affective Disorders*, **106**: 229–40.

Edward E, Bem DJ, Nolan H, Smith S (2000) *Hilgard's Introduction Psychology*, 13th edn. San Diego, CA: Harcourt College Publishers.

Egan G (2002) The Skilled Helper: *A Problem-management and Opportunity-development Approach to Helping*, 7th edn. Pacific Grove, CA: Brooks/Cole.

Egger HL, Angold A (2006) Common emotional and behavioral disorders in preschool children: Presentation, nosology, and epidemiology. *Journal of Child Psychology and Psychiatry*, **47**: 313–37.

Egly R, Driver J, Rafal RD (1994) Shifting visual attention between objects and locations: Evidence from normal and parietal lesion subjects. *Journal of Experimental Psychology: General*, **123**: 161–77.

Ehlers S, Gillberg C (1993) The epidemiology of Asperger syndrome. A total population study. *Journal of Child Psychology and Psychiatry*, **34**: 1327–50.

Ehrensaft MK, Moffitt TE, Caspi A. (2004) Clinically abusive relationships in an unselected birth cohort: men's and women's participation and developmental antecedents. *Journal of Abnormal Psychology*, **113**: 258–70.

Einfeld SL, Tonge BJ (1992) *Manual for the Developmental Behaviour Checklist (Primary carer Version; DBC-P)*. Melbourne: School of Psychiatry.

Eisenberg N, Cumberland A, Spinrad TL et al. (2001) The relations of regulations and emotionality to children's externalizing and internalising problem behaviour. *Child Development*, **72**: 1112–34.

Eiser C, Lansdown R (1977) A retrospective study of intellectual development in children treated for acute lymphoblastic leukaemia. *Archives of Diseases in Childhood*, **52**: 525–9.

Eiser C (1983) *Growing up with a Chronic Disease: The Impact on Children and their Families*. London: Jessica Kingsley Publishers.

Eisler I, Simic M, Russell GFM, Dare C (2007) A randomised controlled treatment trial of two forms of family therapy in adolescent anorexia nervosa: a five year follow up. *Journal of Clinical Psychology and Psychiatry*, **48**: 552–60.

Eisler I, Dare C, Hodes M et al. (2000) Family therapy for adolescent anorexia nervosa: the results of a controlled comparison of two family interventions. *Journal of Child Psychology and Psychiatry*, **41**: 727–36.

Elliott JG (1999) Practitioner review: School refusal: Issues of conceptualisation, assessment and treatment. *Journal of Child Psychology and Psychiatry*, **40**: 1001–12.

Ellis CR, Lindstorm KL, Villani TM et al. (1997). Recognition of facial expressions of emotion by children with emotional and behavioural disorders. *Journal of Child and Family Studies*, **6**: 453–70.

Eluvathingal TJ, Chugani HT, Behen ME et al. (2006) Abnormal brain connectivity in children after early severe socioemotional deprivation: A diffusion tensor imaging study. *Pediatrics*, **117**: 2093–100.

Emde RN, Hewitt JK (2001) *The Transition from Infancy to Early Childhood: Genetic and Environmental Influences in the MacArthur Longitudinal Twin Study*. New York: Oxford University Press.

Emerson E (2003) Prevalence of psychiatric disorders in children and adolescents with and without intellectual disability. *Journal of Intellectual Disability Research*, **47**: 51–8.

Emerson E (1995) *Challenging Behaviour: Analysis and Intervention in People with Learning Disabilities.* Cambridge: Cambridge University Press.

Emerson E, Hatton C (2007) *The Mental Health of Children and Adolescents with Learning Disabilities in Britain.* Lancaster University: Foundation for People with Learning Disabilities.

Emerson E, Moss S, Kiernan C (1999) The relationship between challenging behaviour and psychiatric disorders in people with severe developmental disabilities. In: Bouras N (ed.). *Psychiatric and Behavioural Disorders in Developmental Disabilities and Mental Retardation.* Cambridge: Cambridge University Press, 38–48.

Eminson M, Benjamin S, Shortall A, Woods T (1996) Physical symptoms and illness attitudes in adolescents: an epidemiological study. *Journal of Child Psychology and Psychiatry,* **37**: 519–27.

Eminson DM (2001a) Somatising in children and adolescents. 1. Clinical presentations and aetiological factors. *Advances in Psychiatric Treatment,* **7**: 266–74.

Eminson DM (2001b) Somatising in children and adolescents. 2. Management and outcomes. *Advances in Psychiatric Treatment,* **7**: 388–98.

Eriksen B, Eriksen C (1974) Effects of noise letters upon the identification of a target letter in a nonsearch task. *Attention, Perception, and Psychophysics,* **16**: 143–9.

Ernst M, Fudge JL (2009) A developmental neurobiological model of motivated behavior: Anatomy, connectivity and ontogeny of the triadic nodes. *Neuroscience and Biobehavioral Reviews,* **33**: 367–82.

Esmond G (2000) Cystic fibrosis: adolescent care. *Nursing Standard,* **14**: 47–52.

Evans J, Fowler R (2008) *Family Minded: Supporting Children in Families Affected by Mental Illness.* London: Barnardos UK.

Evaluation of Sure Start Centres. Available from: www.ness.bbk.ac.uk.

Every Child Matters website. Further information on the Every Child Matters. Change for Children programme and Sure Start children's centres can be accessed on the Every Child Matters website at the following address: www.everychildmatters.org.uk

Eyberg S, Pincus D (1999) *Eyberg Child Behavior Inventory and Sutter-Eyberg Student Behavior Inventory - Revised.* Odessa, FL: Psychological Assessment Resources.

Eysenck HJ, Sybil BG (1964) An improved short questionnaire for the measurement of extraversion and neuroticism. *Life Sciences,* **3**: 1103–9.

Ezpeleta L, de la Osa N, Domenech JM et al. (1997) Diagnostic agreement between clinicians and the Diagnostic Interview for Children and Adolescents--DICA-R--in an outpatient sample. *Journal of Child Psychology and Psychiatry and Allied Disciplines,* **38**: 431–40.

Ezzati M, Lopez AD (2004) Regional, disease specific patterns of smoking-attributable mortality in 2000. *Tobacco Control,* **13**: 388–95.


## F

Fairburn CG, Beglin SJ (1994) Assessment of eating disorders: interview or self-report questionnaire? *International Journal of Eating Disorders,* **16**: 363–70.

Fairchild G, Passamonti L, Hurford G et al. (2011) Brain structure abnormalities in early-onset and adolescent-onset conduct disorder. *American Journal of Psychiatry,* **168**: 624–33.

Fairchild G, van Goozen SH, Stollery SJ et al. (2009a) Decision making and executive function in male adolescents with early-onset or adolescence-onset conduct disorder and control subjects. *Biological Psychiatry,* **66**: 162–8.

Fairchild G, Van Goozen SH, Calder AJ et al. (2009b) Deficits in facial expression recognition in male adolescents with early-onset or adolescence-onset conduct disorder. *Journal of Child Psychology and Psychiatry, and Allied Disciplines,* **50**: 627–36.

Fallon K, Woods K, Rooney S (2010) A discussion of the developing role of educational psychologists within Children's Services. *Educational Psychology in Practice,* **26**: 1–23.

Faraone SV, Doyle AE (2001) The nature and heritability of attention deficit hyperactivity disorder. *Child and Adolescent Psychiatric Clinics of North America,* **10**: 299–316, viii-ix.

Faraone S, Wilens T (2003) Does stimulant treatment lead to substance use disorders? *Journal of Clinical Psychiatry,* **64**(Suppl. 11): 9–13.

Faraone SV, Biederman J, Mick E (2006) The age-dependent decline of attention deficit hyperactivity disorder: a meta-analysis of follow-up studies. *Psychological Medicine,* **36**: 159–65.

Faraone SV, Perlis RH, Doyle AE et al. (2005) Molecular genetics of attention-deficit/hyperactivity disorder. *Biological Psychiatry,* **57**: 1313–23.

Farrington DP (1995) The Twelfth Jack Tizard Memorial Lecture. The development of offending and antisocial-behavior from childhood – key findings from the Cambridge Study in Delinquent Development. *Journal of Child Psychology and Psychiatry, and Allied Disciplines*, **36**: 929–64.

Fatimelehin IA (2007) Building bridges in Liverpool: Delivering CAMHS to black and minority ethnic children and their families. *Journal of Integrated Care*, **15**: 7–16.

Ferber R (1988) *Solve Your Child's Sleep Problems: A Practical and Comprehensive Guide for Parents*. New York: Fireside.

Fergusson DM (1999) Prenatal smoking and antisocial behavior. *Archives of General Psychiatry*, **56**: 223–4.

Fergusson DM, Poulton R, Smith PF, Boden JM (2006) Cannabis and psychosis. *British Medical Journal*, **332**: 172–5.

Fergusson DM, Horwood IJ, Lawton JM (1990) Vulnerabilty to childhood problems and family social background. *Journal of Child Psychology and Psychiatry, and Allied Disciplines*, **31**: 1145–60.

Fish J (2007) Getting equal: the implications of new regulations to prohibit sexual orientation discrimination for health and social care. *Diversity in Health and Social Care*, **4**: 221–8.

Fisher SE, Francks C, McCracken JT et al. (2002) A genomewide scan for loci involved in attention-deficit/hyperactivity disorder. *American Journal of Human Genetics*, **70**: 1183–96.

Flanagan DP, Kaufman AS (2009) *Essentials of WISC-IV Assessment*. Hoboken, NJ: Wiley & Sons.

Flaskas C, Perlesz A (1996) *The Therapeutic Relationship in Systemic Therapy*. London: Karnac.

Flint J, Yule W (1993) Behavioural phenotypes. In: Rutter M, Hersov L (eds). Child and Adolescent Psychiatry. Oxford: Blackwell Scientific.

Folstein S, Rutter M. (1977). Genetic influences and infantile autism. *Nature*, **265**: 726–28.

Forehand R, Long N (1996) *Parenting the Strong Willed Child: The Clinically Proven Five Week Programme for Parents of 2–6 year olds*. Chicago: Contemporary Books.

Forehand R, McMahon R (1981) *Helping the Non-Compliant Child: A Clinician's Guide to Parent Training*. New York: Guilford Press.

Fox C, Hawton K (2004) *Deliberate Self-harm in Adolescence*. London: Jessica Kingsley.

Frank J, McLarnon J (2008) *Young Carers, Parents and their Families: Key Principles of Practice. Supportive practice guidance for those who work directly with, or commission services for, young carers and their families*. London: Young Carers Initiative, The Children's Society.

Frare F, Perugi G, Ruffolo G, Toni C (2004) Obsessive-compulsive disorder and body dysmorphic disorder: a comparison of clinical features. *European Psychiatry*, **19**: 292–8.

Freidman RD, McClure JM (2002) *Clinical Practice of Cognitive Behaviour Therapy with Children and Adolescents: The Nuts and Bolts*. London: Guilford Press.

Freitag CM (2007) The genetics of autistic disorders and its clinical relevance: a review of the literature. *Molecular Psychiatry*, **12**: 2–22.

Fremont W (2003) School refusal in children and adolescents. *American Family Physician*, **68**: 1555–60.

Freud S (1915) *Mourning and Melancholia*. London: Vintage.

Frick P, Lahey B, Loeber R et al. (1992) Familial risk factors to oppositional defiant disorder and conduct disorder: Parental psychopathology and maternal parenting. *Journal of Consulting and Clinical Psychology*, **60**: 49–55.

Frith U (2008) *Autism: a Very Short Introduction*. Oxford: OUP.

## G

Gale F (2003) Towards a Comprehensive CAMHS Child and Adolescence Primary Mental Health

Gale F, Vostanis P (2005) Case Study, the primary mental health team – Leicester, Leicestershire and Rutland CAMHS. In: Williams R, Kerfoot M (eds). *Child and Adolescent Mental Health Services: Strategy, Planning, Delivery, and Evaluation*. Oxford: Oxford Press, 439–44.

Gale F, Vostanis P (2003) Developing the primary mental health worker role within child and adolescent mental health services. *Clinical Child Psychology and Psychiatry*, **8**: 227–40.

Gale I (2003) Is there a general evidence base for child and adolescent mental health problems applicable to children and young people who have learning disabilities? Northgate and Prudhoe NHS Trust.

Gallegos J (1982) The ethnic competence model for social work education. In: White BW (ed.) *Color in a White Society*. Silver Spring, MD: NASW Press.

Gallegos J, Tindall C, Gallegos S (2008) The need for advancement in the conceptualization of cultural competence. *Advances in Social Work*, **9**: 51–62.

Gannoni AF, Shute RH (2010) Parental and child perspectives on adaptation to childhood chronic illness: A qualitative study. *Clinical Child Psychology and Psychiatry*, **15**: 39–53.

Garcia I, Vasiliou C, Penketh K (2007) *Listen up! Person Centred Approaches to Help Young People Experiencing Mental Health Problems.* London: Mental Health Foundation.

Gardner F, Sonuga-Barke EJS, Sayal K (1999) Parents anticipating misbehaviour: An observational study of strategies parents use to prevent conflict with behaviour problem children. *Journal of Child Psychology and Psychiatry*, **40**: 1185–96.

Gardner H (1983) *Frames of Mind: The Theory of Multiple Intelligences.* New York: Basic Books.

Garralda ME, Rangel L (2002) Annotation: Chronic Fatigue Syndrome in children and adolescents. *Journal of Child Psychology and Psychiatry*, **43**: 169–76.

Gazzaniga MS, Ivry RB, Magnum GR (1998) *Cognitive Neuroscience: The Biology of the Mind.* New York: W.W. Norton.

Geldard K, Geldard D (2008) *Counselling Children: A Practical Introduction,* 3rd edn. London: Sage.

Gelhorn HL, Stallings MC, Young SE et al. (2005) Genetic and environmental influences on conduct disorder: symptom, domain and full-scale analyses. *Journal of Child Psychology and Psychiatry, and Allied Disciplines.* **46**: 580–91.

Geller B, Tillman R, Bolhofner K et al. (2006) Controlled, blindly rated, direct-interview family study of a prepubertal and early adolescent bipolar I disorder phenotype: morbid risk, age of onset, and comorbidity. *Archives of General Psychiatry*, **63**: 1130–8.

Geller B, Tillman R, Craney JL et al. (2004) Four-year prospective outcome and natural history of mania in children with a prepubertal and early adolescent bipolar disorder phenotype. *Archives of General Psychiatry*, **61**: 459–67.

George E, Iveson C, Ratner H (1999) *Problem to Solution: Brief Therapy with Individuals and Families.* London: BT Press.

Gerhardt S (2004) *Why Love Matters: How Affection Shapes a Baby's Brain.* London and New York: Routledge.

Ghuman JK, Ginsing GS, Subramaniam G et al. (2001) Psycho stimulants in preschool children with attention deficit-hyperactivity disorder: Clinical evidence from a development disorders institution. *Journal of the American Academy of Child and Adolescent Psychiatry*, **40**: 516–24.

Gibson B, Catlin AJ (2010) Care of the Child with the desire to change Gender – Part 1. *Paediatric Nursing*, **36**: 53–9.

Giddan JJ, Milling L, Campbell NB (1996) Unrecognised language and speech deficits in pre-adolescent psychiatric inpatients. *American Journal of Orthopsychiatry*, **66**: 85–92.

Giedd JN, Blementhal J, Molloy E, Castellanos FX (2001) Brain imaging of attention deficit/hyperactivity disorder. *Annals of the New York Academy of Sciences*, **931**: 33–49.

Gillberg C, Wahlstrom J, Forsman A et al. (1986) Teenage psychoses: Epidemiology, classification and reduced optimality in the pre, peri and neonatal periods. *Journal of Child Psychology and Psychiatry*, **27**: 87–98.

Gilmour J, Hill B, Place M et al. (2004) Social communication deficits in conduct disorder: a clinical and community survey. *Journal of Child Psychology and Psychiatry*, **45**: 967–78.

Gizer IR, Ficks C, Waldman ID (2009) Candidate gene studies of ADHD: a meta-analytic review. *Human Genetics*, **126**: 51–90.

Glass N (1999) Sure Start: The Development of an Early Intervention Programme for Young Children in the United Kingdom in Children and Society, Vol 13: 257–264.

Gledhill J, Rangel L, Garralda E (2000) Surviving chronic physical illness: psychosocial outcome in adult life. *Archives of Disease in Childhood*, **83**: 104–10.

Golden MH (1994) Is complete catch-up possible for stunted malnourished children? *European Journal of Clinical Nutrition*, **48**(Suppl. 1), S58–70.

Goldman L, Genzel M, Bezman R, Slanetz P (1998) Diagnosis and treatment of ADHD in children and adolescents. *Journal of the American Medical Association*, **279**: 1100–7.

Goldsmith O (2000) Culturally competent health care. *The Permanente Journal*, **4**: 1–7.

Goldsmith T, Shapira NA, Phillips KA, McElroy SL (1998) Conceptual foundations in obsessive compulsive spectrum disorders. In: Swinson RP, Antony MM, Rachman S, Richter MA (eds). *Obsessive Compulsive Disorder: Theory, Research and Treatment.* New York and London: Guilford Press, 57–72.

Goleman D (1998) *Working with Emotional Intelligence.* New York: Bantam Books.

Goleman D (1995) *Emotional Intelligence.* New York: Bantam Books.

Goodlin-Jones B, Tang K, Liu J, Anders TF (2009) Sleep problems, sleepiness and daytime behavior in preschool-age children. *Journal of Child Psychology and Psychiatry*, **50**: 1532–40.

Goodman R (1997) The Strengths and Difficulties Questionnaire: A research note. *Journal of Child Psychology and Psychiatry*, **38**: 581–6.

Goodman R, Scott S (2002) *Child Psychiatry.* Oxford: Blackwell Publishing.

Goodman R, Scott S (1999) Comparing the strengths and difficulties questionnaire and the child behavior checklist: Is small beautiful? *Journal of Abnormal Child Psychology*, **27**: 17–24.

Goodman R, Scott S (eds) (1997) *Child Psychiatry*. Oxford: Blackwell Science.

Goodman WK, Price LH, Rasmussen SA et al. (1991) *Children's Yale-Brown Obsessive Compulsive Scale (CY-BOCS)*. New Haven, CT: Yale University.

Goodyer IM, Herbert J, Tamplin A, Altham PM (2000) Recent life events, cortisol, dehydroepiandrosterone and the onset of major depression in high-risk adolescents. *British Journal of Psychiatry*, **177**: 499–504.

Gottesman II, Shields J (1971) Schizophrenia: geneticism and environmentalism. *Human Heredity*, **21**: 517–22.

Government White Paper (2007) Care Matters: Time for Change Cm 7137.

Government White Paper (2003) Every Child Matters Cm 5860.

Gowers SG, Harrington, RC, Whitton A et al. (1988) Brief Scale for measuring the outcomes of emotional and behavioural disorders. *British Journal of Psychiatry*, **174**: 413–16.

Graham P (1991) *Child Psychiatry: A Developmental Approach*, 2nd edn. Oxford: Oxford Medical Publications.

Graham P (2005) *Cognitive Behaviour Therapy for Children and Families*, 2nd edn. Cambridge: Cambridge University Press.

Graham P, Rutter M (1973) Psychiatric disorder in the young adolescent: A follow-up study. *Proceedings of the Royal Society of Medicine*, **66**: 1226–9.

Grandjean P, Weihe P, White RF et al. (1997) Cognitive deficit in 7-year-old children with prenatal exposure to methylmercury. *Neurotoxicology and Teratology*, **19**: 417–28.

Granger B, Tekaia F, Le Sourd AM et al. (1995) Tempo of neurogenesis and synaptogenesis in the primate cingulate mesocortex: Comparison with the neocortex. *Journal of Comparative Neurology*, **360**: 363–76.

Grant G, Repper J, Nolan M (2008) Young people supporting parents with mental health problems: experiences of assessment and support. *Health and Social Care in the Community*, **16**: 271–81.

Grant JE, Kim SW, Crow SJ (2001) Prevalence and clinical features of Body Dysmorphic Disorder in adolescent and adult psychiatric patients. *Journal of Clinical Psychiatry*, **62**: 517–22.

Gray C (2010). *The New Social Story Book*. Arlington, VA: Future Horizons Inc.

Gray C (2008) Social Stories. Retrieved August 14, 2008, from www.thegraycenter.org

Gray C (2007) How to write social stories. Retrieved December 10, 2007 from www.thegraycenter.org

Gray C (2000) *The New Social Story Book*, Illustrated Edition. Arlington, VA: Future Horizons Inc.

Gray CA, Garand J (1993) Social stories: Improving responses of students with autism with accurate social information. *Focus on Autistic Behaviour*, **8**: 1–10.

Gray C, McAndrew S (2001) *My Social Stories Book*. London: Jessica Kingsley.

Gray C, White WL (2001) *My Social Stories Book*. London. Jessica Kingsley.

Gray C, Howey M, Arnold E (2005) *Revealing the Hidden Secret Code: Social Stories for People with Autistic Spectrum Disorders*. London: Jessica Kingsley.

Green J (2006) Annotation: The therapeutic alliance – a significant but neglected variable in child mental health treatment studies. *Journal of Child Psychology and Psychiatry*, **47**: 425–35.

Green J, Worrall-Davies A (2008) Provision of intensive treatment: in-patient units, day units and intensive outreach. In: Rutter M, Bishop D, Pine D et al. (eds). *Rutter's Child and Adolescent Psychiatry*, 5th edn. London: Blackwell Publishing, 1126–42.

Greenberg BD, Li Q, Lucas FR et al. (2000) Association between the serotonin transporter promoter polymorphism and personality traits in a primarily female population sample. *American Journal of Medical Genetics*, **96**: 202–16.

Greene R, Pugh R, Roberts D (2008) *Black and Minority Ethnic Parents with Mental Health Problems and their Children, Research Paper*. London: Social Care Institute for Excellence.

Greenhill L, Kollins S, Abikoff H (2006) Efficacy and safety of immediate-release methyphenidate treatment for preschoolers with hyperactivity. *Journal of the American Academy of Child and Adolescent Psychiatry*, **45**: 1284–93.

Greenough WT, Black JE (1992) Induction of brain structure by experience: Substrates for cognitive development. In: Gunnar MR, Nelson CA (eds). *Developmental Behavioral Neuroscience*. Hillsdale, NJ: Erlbaum, 155–200.

Gregory AM, Van der Ende J, Willis TA, Verhulst FC (2008) Parent-reported sleep problems during development and self-reported anxiety/depression, attention problems, and aggressive behavior later in life. *Archives of Pediatrics and Adolescent Medicine*, **162**: 330–5.

Grindley GC, Townsend V (1968) Voluntary attention in peripheral vision and its effects on acuity and differential thresholds. *The Quarterly Journal of Experimental Psychology*, **20**: 11–19.

Gringras P (2008) When to use drugs to help sleep. *Archives of Disease in Childhood*, **93**: 976–81.

Guest DE, Peccei R, Rosenthal P et al. (2004) *An Evaluation of the Impact of Nurse, Midwife and Health Visitor Consultants.* King's College, London.

Gunnar MR (1998) Quality of early care and buffering of neuroendocrine stress reactions: Potential effects on the developing human brain. *Preventive Medicine,* **27**: 208–11.

Gunnar MR, Morison SJ, Chisholm K, Schuder M (2001) Salivary cortisol levels in children adopted from Romanian orphanages. *Development and Psychopathology,* **13**: 611–28.

## H

Haberstick BC, Lessem JM, Hopfer CJ et al. (2005) Monoamine oxidase A (MAOA) and antisocial behaviors in the presence of childhood and adolescent maltreatment. *American Journal of Medical Genetics. Part B, Neuropsychiatric Genetics: The Official Publication of the International Society of Psychiatric Genetics,* **135B**: 59–64.

Halberstadt AG, Crisp VW, Eaton KL (1999) Family expressiveness: A retrospective and new directions for research. In: Philippot P, Feldman RS, Coats E (eds). *The Social Context of Nonverbal Behavior.* New York: Cambridge University Press.

Haley J (1973) *Uncommon Therapy: Psychiatric Techniques of Milton H Erickson, MD.* New York: W.W. Norton.

Haley J (1976) *Problem Solving Therapy.* New York and London: Harper-Colophon.

Hammersley D (2003) Training and professional development in the context of counselling psychology. In: Woolfe R, Dryden W, Strawbridge S (eds). *Handbook of Counselling Psychology,* 2nd edn. London, UK: SAGE Publications, 637–55.

Hampshire Educational Psychology Service Statement (2008).

Harchik AE, Harchik AJ, Luce SC, Jordan R (1992) *The Special Educational Needs of Children with Asperger Syndrome.* University of Hertfordshire: Educational Research Into Autism Group.

Harley T (2001) *The Psychology of Language: From Data to Theory.* London: Taylor and Francis Group.

Harlow HF, Zimmermann RR (1959) Affectional responses in the infant monkey. *Science,* **130**: 421–32.

Harpin VA (2005) The family, and community from preschool to adult life. *Archives of Disease in Childhood,* **90**: 2–7.

Harrington RC (2008) Affective disorders. In: Rutter M, Taylor E (eds). *Child and Adolescent Psychiatry,* 5th edn. Oxford: Blackwell Publishing.

Harrison G (1997) Risk assessment in a climate of litigation. *British Journal of Psychiatry,* **32**: 37–9.

Hart and Risley (1995) Meaningful Differences National Strategies Every Child a Talker Project 2008–2011.

Hawi Z, Dring M, Kirley A et al. (2002) Serotonergic system and attention deficit hyperactivity disorder (ADHD): a potential susceptibility locus at the 5-HT(1B) receptor gene in 273 nuclear families from a multi-centre sample. *Molecular Psychiatry,* **7**: 718–25.

Hawton K, James A (2005) Suicide and deliberate self-harm in young people. *British Medical Journal,* **330**: 891–4.

Hawton K, Rodham K (2006) *By Their Own Young Hand. Deliberate Self Harm and Suicidal Ideas in Adolescents.* London: Jessica Kingsley.

Health Advisory Document DoH (1995) *Together We Stand: A Thematic Review of Mental Health Services in England and Wales.*

Health Advisory Service (1995) *Child Psychiatry – The Future.* Department of Health.

Health Advisory Service (1986) *Bridge over Troubled Waters.* London: Health Advisory Service.

Heilbrun K (2003) Violence risk: From prediction to management. In: Carson D, Bull R (eds). *Handbook of Psychology in Legal Contexts,* 2nd edn. London: John Wiley and Sons, 127–43.

Henggeler SW (1999) Multi systemic therapy: an overview of clinical procedures, outcomes, and policy implications. *Clinical Psychology and Psychiatry Review,* **4**: 12–10.

Henry G (1974) Doubly deprived. *Journal of Child Psychotherapy,* **3**: 15–28.

Hewitt K, Appleton P, Douglas J et al. (1990) Health visitor based services for pre-school children with behaviour problems. *Health Visitor,* **63**: 160–2.

Heyman I, Mataix-Cols D, Fineberg NA (2006) Obsessive-compulsive disorder. *British Medical Journal,* **333**: 424–9.

Higgs J, Jones M (2000) *Clinical Reasoning in the Health Professions,* 2nd edn. Oxford: Butterworth Heinemann.

Hill CM, Hogan AM, Karmiloff-Smith A (2007) To sleep, perchance to enrich learning? *Archives of Disease in Childhood,* **92**: 637–43.

Hill J (2002) Biological, psychological and social processes in the conduct disorders. *Journal of Child Psychology and Psychiatry, and Allied Disciplines,* **43**: 133–64.

Hirasing RA, van Leerdam FJ, Bolk-Bennink LB, Bosch JD (1997). Bedwetting and behavioural and/or emotional problems. *Acta Paediatrica (Oslo),* **86**: 1131–4.

Hirschhorn JN, Lettre G (2009) Progress in genome-wide association studies of human height. *Hormone Research*, **71**(Suppl.): 5–13.

HM Government (2011) *No Health Without Mental Health: A Cross-government Mental Health Outcomes Strategy for People of all Ages.*

HM Government (2000) *Race Relations Act (Amendment).* London: HMSO.

HM Treasury and Department for Education and Skills (2007) *Aiming High for Disabled Children: better support for families.*

HM Government (2000) *Race Relations (Amendment) Act 2000.* London: HMSO.

Ho TP, Leung PWL, Luk ESL et al. (1996) establishing the constructs of childhood behavioural disturbances in a Chinese population: a questionnaire study. *Journal of Abnormal Child Psychology*, **24**: 417–31.

Hodes M (2008) Risk and resilience for psychological distress amongst unaccompanied asylum seeking adolescents. *Journal of Child Psychology and Psychiatry*, **49**: 723–32.

Hoffman M (1991) *Empathy, Social Cognition and Moral Action.* New Jersey: Lawrence Erlbaum.

Hoffman C, Crnic KA, Baker JK (2006) Maternal depression and parenting: implications for children's emergent emotion regulation and behavioral functioning. *Parenting: Science and Practice*, **6**: 271–95.

Holley S, Hill CM, Stevenson J (2011) An hour less sleep is a risk factor for childhood conduct problems. *Child: Care, Health and Development*, **37**: 563–70.

Home Start. Available from: www.home-start.org.uk/about/what_we_do

Hougaard E (1994) The therapeutic alliance: A conceptual analysis. *Scandinavian Journal of Psychology*, **35**: 67–85.

Hubel DH, Wiesel TN (2005) *Brain and Visual Perception.* Oxford: Oxford University Press.

Hubel DH, Wiesel TN (1965) Binocular interaction in striate cortex of kittens reared with artificial squint. *Journal of Neurophysiology*, **28**: 1041–9.

Hudson JI, Hiripi E, Pope HG Jr, Kessler RC (2007) The prevalence and correlates of eating disorders in the National Comorbidity Survey Replication. *Biological Psychiatry*, **61**: 345–58.

Hudziak JJ, Derks EM, Althoff RR et al. (2005) The genetic and environmental contributions to oppositional defiant behavior: a multi-informant twin study. *Journal of the American Academy of Child and Adolescent Psychiatry*, **44**: 907–14.

Huebner D (2007) *What to do When Your Brain gets Stuck: A Kids Guide to Overcoming OCD.* Washington DC: Magination Press.

Huebner T, Vloet TD, Marx I et al. (2008) Morphometric brain abnormalities in boys with conduct disorder. *Journal of the American Academy of Child and Adolescent Psychiatry*, **47**: 540–7.

Humphreys GW, Quinlan PT, Riddoch MJ (1989) Grouping processes in visual search: Effects with single- and combined-feature targets. *Journal of Experimental Psychology: General*, **118**: 258–79.

Hunt R, Jensen J (2007) *Stonewall School Report: The Experience of Young Gay People in Britain's Schools.* London: Stonewall.

Hunter M (2001) *Psychotherapy with Children in Care: Lost and Found.* Hove, East Sussex: Brunner-Routledge.

Huttenlocher PR, Dabholkar AS (1997) Regional differences in synaptogenesis in human cerebral cortex. *Journal of Comparative Neurology*, **387**: 167–78.

Hvistendahl GM, Kamperis K, Rawashdeh YF et al. (2004) The effect of alarm treatment on the functional bladder capacity in children with monosymptomatic nocturnal enuresis. *Journal of Urology*, **171**: 2611–14.

**I**

I Can DVD (2007) Available from: www.ican.org.uk

Impagnatiello F, Guidotti AR, Pesold C et al. (1998) A decrease of reelin expression as a putative vulnerability factor in schizophrenia. *Proceedings of the National Academy of Sciences of the United States of America*, **95**: 15 718–23.

Inclusion Development Programme Supporting children on the autism spectrum: Guidance for practitioners in the Early Years Foundation Stage (2009) Published by the Department for Children, Schools and Families.

International Childrens Continence Society (2007). Available from: www.i-c-c-s.org

International Molecular Genetic Study of Autism Consortium (IMGSAC) (2001a) A genomewide screen for autism: strong evidence for linkage to chromosomes 2q, 7q, and 16p. *American Journal of Human Genetics*, **69**: 570–81.

International Molecular Genetic Study of Autism Consortium (IMGSAC) (2001b) Further characterization of the autism susceptibility locus AUTS1 on chromosome 7q. *Human Molecular Genetics*, **10**: 973–82.

International Molecular Genetic Study of Autism Consortium (IMGSAC) (1998) A full genome screen for autism with evidence for linkage to a region on chromosome 7q. International Molecular Genetic Study of Autism Consortium. *Human Molecular Genetics*, **7**: 571–8.

Isaacs JB (2007) Impacts of Early Childhood Programs. First Focus making children and families the priority. Available as a PDf from tomorrowsyouth.org.

## J

Jaeger J (2010) *Experts in Play: The Development and Use of Play-based Evaluation Methods in Facilitating Children's Views of Non-Directive Play Therapy.* York: PhD thesis, University of York.

James A, Soler A, Weatherall R (2007) Cochrane review: Cognitive behavioural therapy for anxiety disorders in children and adolescents. *Evidence-Based Child Health: A Cochrane Review Journal*, **2**: 1248–75.

Jenner S (1999) *The Parent/Child Game.* London: Bloomsbury Publishing.

Jennings C (1996) Training the reflective professional: the practice of supervision. In: Jennings C, Kennedy E (eds). *The Reflective Professional in Education.* London: Jessica Kingsley.

Jennings S (1999) *Introduction to Developmental Play Therapy.* London: Jessica Kingsley.

Jensen P, Kettle L, Roper M et al. (1999) Are stimulants over prescribed? Treatment of ADHD in Four US communities. *Journal of American Academy of Child and Adolescent Psychiatry*, **38**: 797–804.

Jerrett W (1979) Headaches in general practice. *Practitioner*, **222**: 549–55.

Jewell D, Tacchi J, Donovan J (2000) Teenage pregnancy, whose problem is it? *Family Practice*, **17**: 522–8.

Johnson JG, Cohen P, Kasen S et al. (2008) Parental concordance and offspring risk for anxiety, conduct, depressive, and substance use disorders. *Psychopathology*, **41**: 124–8.

Johnson M, Wintgens A (2001) *The Selective Mutism Resource Manual.* Milton Keynes: Speechmark Publishing Ltd.

Johnston C, Mash E (2001) Families of children with attention deficit/hyperactivity disorder: Review and recommendations for future research. *Clinical Child and Family Psychology Review*, **4**: 183–207.

Johnston C, Mash EJ (1989) A measure of parenting satisfaction and efficacy. *Journal of Clinical Psychology*, **18**: 167–75.

Jones AP, Laurens KR, Herba CM et al. (2009) Amygdala hypoactivity to fearful faces in boys with conduct problems and callous-unemotional traits. *The American Journal of Psychiatry*, **166**: 95–102.

Jones K, Daley D, Hutchings J et al. (2007) Efficacy of the Incredible Years Basic parent training programme as an early intervention for children with conduct problems and ADHD. *Child Care, Health and Development*, **33**: 749–56.

Joormann J, Talbot L, Gotlib IH (2007) Biased processing of emotional information in girls at risk for depression. *Journal of Abnormal Psychology*, **116**: 135–43.

Jordan RR (2003) *Educational Provision: Making Mainstream Schools Autism-friendly and Inclusion.* Birmingham: University of Birmingham, School of Education.

Judd D (1995) *Give Sorrow Words.* Oxford: Haworth Press.

## K

Kagan J (1989) Temperamental contributions to social behavior. *American Psychology*, **44**: 668–74.

Kahn RS, Khoury J, Nichols WC, Lanphear BP (2003) Role of dopamine transporter genotype and maternal prenatal smoking in childhood hyperactive-impulsive, inattentive, and oppositional behaviors. *Journal of Pediatrics*, **143**: 104–10.

Kanner L (1949) Problems of nosology and psychodynamics in early childhood autism. *American Journal of Orthopsychiatry*, **19**: 416–26.

Kanner L (1943) Autistic disturbances of affective contact. *Nervous Child*, **2**: 217–50.

Kats-Gold I, Besser A, Priel B (2007) The role of simple emotion recognition skills among school aged boys at risk of ADHD. *Journal of Abnormal Child Psychology*, **35**: 363–78.

Kazdin AE (2001) Treatment of conduct disorders. In: Hill J, Maughan B (eds). *Conduct Disorders in Childhood and Adolescents.* Thousand Oaks, CA: Sage, 408–48.

Kazdin AE (1997) Psychosocial treatments for conduct disorder in children. *Journal of Child Psychology and Psychiatry*, **38**: 161–78.

Kazdin AE, Whitley M, Marciano PL (2006) Child-therapist and parent-therapist alliance and therapeutic change in the treatment of children referred for oppositional, aggressive, and antisocial behaviour. *Journal of Child Psychology and Psychiatry*, **47**: 436–45.

Kazdin AE, Holland L, Crowley M, Breton S (1997) Barriers to Treatment Participation Scale: evaluation and validation in the context of child outpatient treatment. *Journal of Child Psychology and Psychiatry*, **38**: 1051–62.

Kazdin AE (1995) *Conduct Disorder in Childhood and Adolescence*, 2nd edn. Thousand Oaks, CA: Sage.

Kearney AJ (2007) *Understanding Applied Behavior Analysis: An Introduction to ABA for Parents, Teachers, and Other Professionals*. London: Jessica Kingsley Publishers.

Kearney CA (2003) Bridging the gap among professionals who address youths with school absenteeism: Overview and suggestions for consensus. *Professional Psychology: Research and Practice*, **34**: 57–65.

Kearney CA (2002) Identifying the function of school refusal behaviour: A revision of the school refusal assessment scale. *Journal of Psychopathology and Behavioural Assessment*, **24**: 235–45.

Kearney CA, Silverman WK (1999) Functionally based prescriptive and nonprescriptive treatment for children and adolescents with school refusal behaviour. *Behaviour Therapy*, **30**: 673–95.

Kearney CA, Silverman WK (1993) Measuring the function of school refusal behaviour: The school refusal assessment scale. *Journal of Clinical Child Psychology*, **22**: 85–96.

Kearney CA, Silverman WK (1990) A preliminary analysis of a functional model of assessment and treatment of school refusal behaviour. *Behaviour Modification*, **14**: 340–66.

Kendall J (1999) Siblings' account of ADHD. *Family Process*, **38**: 117–36.

Kessler RC, Avenevoli S, Ries MK (2001) Mood disorders in children and adolescents: an epidemiologic perspective. *Biological Psychiatry*, **49**: 1002–14.

Kessler RC, Chiu WT, Demler O, Walters EE (2005) Prevalence, severity, and comorbidity of 12-month DSM-IV disorders in the National Comorbidity Survey Replication. *Archives of General Psychiatry*, **62**: 617–27.

Khalil AH, Rabie MA, Abd-El-Aziz MF et al. (2010) Clinical characteristics of depression among adolescent females: a cross sectional study. *Child and Adolescent Psychiatry and Mental Health*, **4**: 26.

Khanna MS, Kendall PC (2009) Exploring the role of parent training in the treatment of childhood anxiety. *Journal of Consulting and Clinical Psychology*, **77**: 981–6.

Kitts RL (2005) Gay adolescents and suicide: understanding the association. *Adolescents*, **40**: 621–8.

Kitzman HJ, Olds DL, Cole RE et al. (2010) Enduring effects of prenatal and infancy home visiting by nurses on children – follow up of a randomised trial among children at age 12. *Archives of Pediatric and Adolescent Medicine*, **164**: 412–24.

Knappe S, Lieb R, Beesdo K et al. (2009) The role of parental psychopathology and family environment for social phobia in the first three decades of life. *Depression and Anxiety*, **26**: 363–70.

Knudsen EI (2004) Sensitive periods in the development of the brain and behavior. *Journal of Cognitive Neuroscience*, **16**: 1412–25.

Kollins S, Greenhill L, Swanson J et al. (2006) Rationale, design and methods of the preschool ADHD treatment study (PATS) *Journal of the American Academy of Child and Adolescent Psychiatry*, **45**: 1275–83.

Kotimaa AJ, Moilanen I, Taanila A et al. (2003) Maternal smoking and hyperactivity in 8-year-old children. *Journal of The American Academy of Child and Adolescent Psychiatry*, **42**: 826–33.

Kovacs M (1992) *Children's Depression Inventory (CDI)*. New York: Multi-Health Systems Inc.

Kovacs M, Feinberg TL, Paulauskas S et al. (1985) Initial coping responses and psychosocial characteristics of children with insulin dependent diabetes mellitus. *Journal of Paediatrics*, **106**: 827–34.

Kranowitz C (1998) *The Out-of-Sync Child: Recognising and Coping with Sensory Integration Difficulties*. New York: Perigree Books.

Kreppner J, Kumsta R, Rutter M et al. (2010) Developmental course of deprivation-specific patterns: early manifestations, persistence to age 15 and clinical features. *Monographs of the Society for Research in Child Development*, **75**: 79–101.

Kübler-Ross E (1973) *On Death and Dying*. London: Routledge.

Kuepper R, van Os J, Lieb R et al. (2011) Continued cannabis use and risk of incidence and persistence of psychotic symptoms: 10 year follow-up cohort study. *British Medical Journal*, **342**: d738.

Kumsta R, Stevens S, Brookes K et al. (2010a) 5HTT genotype moderates the influence of early institutional deprivation on emotional problems in adolescence: evidence from the English and Romanian Adoptee (ERA) study. *Journal of Child Psychology and Psychiatry*, **51**: 755–62.

Kumsta R, Rutter M, Stevens S, Sonuga-Barke E (2010b) Risk, causation, mediation and moderation. *Monographs of the Society for Research in Child Development*, **75**: 187–211.

Kumsta R, Kreppner J, Rutter M et al. (2010c) Deprivation-specific psychological patterns. *Monographs of the Society for Research in Child Development*, **75**: 48–78.

Kurtz Z (2009) *The Evidence Base to Guide Development of Tier 4 CAMHS*. London: Department of Health and National CAMHS Support Service.

Kurtz Z (1996) *Treating Children Well. A Guide to Using the Evidence Base in Commissioning and Managing Services for the Mental Health of Children and Young People.* London. The Mental Health Foundation.

Kurtz Z, Thornes R, Bailey S (1998) Children in the Criminal Justice and Secure Care Systems: how their mental health needs are met. *Journal of Adolescence,* **21**: 543–53.

Kutcher S, Aman M, Brooks SJ et al. (2004) International consensus statement on attention-deficit/hyperactivity disorder (ADHD) and disruptive behaviour disorders (DBDs): clinical implications and treatment practice suggestions. *European Neuropsychopharmacology,* **14**: 11–28.

## L

Labuschagne I, Castle DJ, Dunai J et al. (2010) An examination of delusional thinking and cognitive styles in body dysmorphic disorder. *Australian and New Zealand Journal of Psychiatry,* **44**: 706–12.

Lacey I (1999) The role of the child primary mental health worker. *Journal of Advanced Nursing,* **30**: 220–8.

Lahey BB, Pelham WE, Loney J et al. (2004) Three year predictive validity of DSM-IV Attention-Deficit/Hyperactivity Disorder in children diagnosed at 4–6 years of age. *American Journal of Psychiatry,* **161**: 14–20.

Lahey B, Pelham W, Stein M et al. (1998) Validity of DSM-1V attention-deficit/hyperactivity disorder for younger children. *Journal of the American Academy of Child and Adolescent Psychiatry,* **37**: 695–702.

Lamb JA, Barnby G, Bonora E et al. (2005) Analysis of IMGSAC autism susceptibility loci: evidence for sex limited and parent of origin specific effects. *Journal of Medical Genetics,* **42**: 132–7.

Laming BH (2009) *The protection of children in England: A progress report.* London: The Stationery Office.

Landgraf JM, Abetz L, Ware JE (1999) *The CHQ Users Manual,* 2nd edn. Boston: Health Act.

Landreth G (2002) *Play Therapy, The Art of the Relationship.* New York: Brunner Routledge.

Lanyado M, Horne A (eds). (1990). *The Handbook of Child and Adolescent Psychotherapy.* London and New York: Routledge.

Lask B, Bryant-Waugh R (eds). (2007) *Eating Disorders in Childhood and Adolescence,* 3rd edn. London: Routledge.

Lask B, Fosson B (1989) *Childhood Illness: The Psychosomatic Approach: Children Talking With Their Bodies.* Chichester: John Wiley and Sons.

Lask B (1994) Non-adherence to treatment in cystic fibrosis. *Journal of the Royal Society of Medicine,* **87** (Suppl. 21): 25–7.

Lasky-Su J, Anney RJ, Neale BM et al. (2008) Genome-wide association scan of the time to onset of attention deficit hyperactivity disorder. *American Journal of Medical Genetics. Part B, Neuropsychiatric Genetics: The Official Publication of the International Society of Psychiatric Genetics,* **147B**: 1355–8.

Latter, S, Courtney M (2004) Effectiveness of nurse prescribing: a review of the literature *Journal of Clinical Nursing,* **13**: 26–32.

Lauchlan F (2003) Responding to chronic non-attendance: a review of intervention approaches. *Educational Psychology in Practice,* **19**: 133–46.

Laver-Bradbury C, Harris H (2008) *Advanced Nurse Practitioners for Attention Deficit Hyperactivity Disorder (In) Department of Health, New Ways of Working in Child and Adolescent Mental Health.* London: Department of Health.

Laver-Bradbury C, Thompson M, Weeks A et al. (2010) *Step by Step Help for Children with ADHD.* London: Jessica Kingsley.

Lavie N (2005) Distracted and confused? Selective attention under load. *Trends in Cognitive Science,* **9**: 75–82.

Lavie N (1995) Perceptual load as a necessary condition for selective attention. *Journal of Experimental Psychology: Human Perception and Performance,* **21**: 451–68.

Lavigne JV, Arend R, Rosenbaum D et al. (1998) Psychiatric disorders with onset in the preschool years: I. Stability of diagnoses. *Journal of the American Academy of Child and Adolescent Psychiatry,* 37: 1246–54.

Law J (ed.). (1992) *The Early Identification of Language Impairment in Children.* Boca Raton, FL: Chapman and Hall.

Lawson W (2011) Adolescents, Autism Spectrum Disorder And Secondary School (Accessed March 28 2011). Available from: www.mugsy.org: The NAS (Surrey Branch)/cgi-bin/tp.pl

Leadbitter H (2008) *Whole Family Pathway.* London: The Children's Society.

Leader D (2008) *The New Black, Mourning, Melancholia and Depression.* London: Hamish Hamilton.

Le Grand R, Mondloch C, Maurer D, Brent HP (2001) Neuroperception: Early visual experience and face processing. *Nature,* **410**: 890.

Leibenluft E, Dickstein DP (2008) Bipolar disorder in children and adolescents. In: Rutter M, Taylor E (eds). *Rutter's Child and Adolescent Psychiatry,* 5th edn. Blackwell Science Ltd, 613–27.

Leibenluft E, Cohen P, Gorrindo T et al. (2006) Chronic versus episodic irritability in youth: A community-based, longitudinal study of clinical and diagnostic associations. *Journal of Child and Adolescent Psychopharmacology*, **16**: 456–66.

Leon-Carrion J, Atutxa AM, Mangas MA et al. (2009) A clinical profile of memory impairment in humans due to endogenous glucocorticoid excess. *Clinical Endocrinology*, **70**: 192–200.

Lesch KP, Bengel D, Heils A et al. (1996) Association of anxiety-related traits with a polymorphism in the serotonin transporter gene regulatory region. *Science*, **274**: 1527–31.

Levine MP, Smolak M (2002) Body image development in adolescence. In: Cash TF, Pruzinsky T (eds). *Body Image: A Handbook of Theory, Research and Clinical Practice*. New York: The Guilford Press, 74–82.

Li S, Jin X, Wu S et al. (2007). The impact of media use on sleep patterns and sleep disorders among school-aged children in China. *Sleep*, **30**: 361–7.

Liberman RP, Hilty MD, Drake RE, Tsang HWH (2001) Requirements for multi-disciplinary teamwork in psychiatric rehabilitation. *Psychiatric Services*, **52**: 1331–42.

Liu JH, Raine A, Venables PH, Mednick SA (2004) Malnutrition at age 3 years and externalizing behavior problems at ages 8, 11, and 17 years. *American Journal of Psychiatry*, **161**: 2005–13.

Liu JH, Raine A, Venables PH et al. (2003) Malnutrition at age 3 years and lower cognitive ability at age 11 years: Independence from psychosocial adversity. *Archives of Pediatrics and Adolescent Medicine*, **157**: 593–600.

Loeb KL, Walsh T, Lock J et al. (2007) Open trial of family-based treatment for full and partial anorexia nervosa in adolescence: evidence of successful dissemination. *Journal of the American Academy of Child and Adolescent Psychiatry*, **46**: 792–800.

Loeber R, Burke JD, Lahey BB et al. (2000) Oppositional defiant and conduct disorder: a review of the past 10 years, part I. *Journal of the American Academy of Child and Adolescent Psychiatry*, **39**: 1468–84.

Lomas C (2009) Nurse prescribing: The next steps. *Nursing Times*, 14 July 2009.

Lord C, Rutter M, Goode S et al. (1989) Autism diagnostic observation schedule: a standardized observation of communicative and social behavior. *Journal of Autism and Developmental Disorders*, **19**: 185–212.

Lord C, Rutter M, Couteur A (2003) Autism Diagnostic Interview-Revised: A revised version of a diagnostic interview for caregivers of individuals with possible pervasive developmental disorders. *Journal of Autism and Developmental Disorders*, **24**: 659–85.

Lorenz K (1979) *The Year of the Greylag Goose*. New York: Harcourt Brace Janovich.

Lou HC, Rosa P, Pryds O et al. (2004). ADHD: increased dopamine receptor availability linked to attention deficit and low neonatal cerebral blood flow. *Developmental Medicine and Child Neurology*, **46**: 179–83.

Lougher L (2001) *Occupational Therapy for Child and Adolescent Mental Health*. Edinburgh: Churchill Livingstone.

Lum D (2010) *Culturally Competent Practice: A Framework for Understanding Diverse Groups and Justice Issues*, 4th edn. Pacific Grove, CA: Brooks/Cole.

Luman M, Sergeant JA, Knol DL, Oosterlaan J (2010) Impaired decision making in oppositional defiant disorder related to altered psychophysiological responses to reinforcement. *Biological Psychiatry*, **68**: 337–44.

Lynam DR, Gudonis L (2005) The development of psychopathy. *Annual Review of Clinical Psychology*, **1**: 381–407.

## M

Mackay T, Knott F, Dunlop AW (2007) Developing social interaction and understanding in individuals with autism spectrum disorder: A groupwork intervention. *Journal of Intellectual and Developmental Disability*, **32**: 279–90.

Macmillan HL, Wathen CN, Barlow J et al. (2009) Interventions to prevent child maltreatment and associated impairment. *Lancet*, **373**: 250–66.

Maestrini E, Pagnamenta AT, Lamb JA et al. (2010) High-density SNP association study and copy number variation analysis of the AUTS1 and AUTS5 loci implicate the IMMP2L-DOCK4 gene region in autism susceptibility. *Molecular Psychiatry*, **15**: 954–68.

Maher BS, Marazita ML, Ferrell RE, Vanyukov MM (2002) Dopamine system genes and attention deficit hyperactivity disorder: a meta-analysis. *Psychiatric Genetics*, **12**: 207–15.

Main M, Goldwyn R, Hesse E (2002) Adult Attachment Scoring and Classification Systems, Version 7.0. University of California at Berkeley: Unpublished manuscript.

Malekoff A (2004) *Group Work with Adolescents: Principles and Practice*, 2nd edn. New York: Guilford Press.

Manassis K, Russell K, Newton AS (2010) The Cochrane Library and the treatment of childhood and adolescent anxiety disorders: an overview of reviews. *Evidence-Based Child Health: A Cochrane Review Journal*, **5**: 541–54.

Manassis K, Tannock R, Young A, Francis-John S (2007) Cognition in anxious children with attention deficit hyperactivity disorder: a comparison with clinical and normal children. *Behavioral and Brain Functions*, **3**: 4.

Mannuzza S, Klein R, Bessler A et al. (1998) Adult psychiatric status of hyperactive boys grown up. *American Journal of Psychiatry*, **155**: 493–8.

March J (2007) *Talking back to OCD*. New York: Guilford Press. (A self-help guide for young sufferers and their families)

March J, Mulle K (1998) OCD in children and adolescents: a cognitive-behavioural treatment manual. New York: Guilford Press.

Marsh AA, Finger EC, Mitchell DG et al. (2008) Reduced amygdala response to fearful expressions in children and adolescents with callous-unemotional traits and disruptive behavior disorders. *American Journal of Psychiatry*, **165**: 712–20.

Maslow AH (1943) A theory of human motivation. *Psychological Review*, **50**: 370–96.

Mason B (1993) Towards positions of safe uncertainty. *Human Systems*, **4**: 189–200.

Maughan B, Rowe R, Messer J et al. (2004) Conduct disorder and oppositional defiant disorder in a national sample: developmental epidemiology. *Journal of Child Psychology and Psychiatry, and Allied Disciplines*, **45**: 609–21.

Mauriac F (1952) *The Desert of Love*. New York: Bantam.

Mayer J, Salovey P (1997) *Emotional Intelligence*. NPR.

Mayville S, Katz RC, Gipson MT, Cabral K (1999) Assessing the prevalence of body dysmorphic disorder in an ethnically diverse group of adolescents. *Journal of Child and Family Studies*, **8**: 357–62.

McCann D, Barrett A, Cooper A et al. (2007) Food additives and hyperactive behaviour in 3-year-old and 8/9-year-old children in the community: a randomised, double-blinded, placebo-controlled trial. *Lancet*, **370**: 1560–7.

McCann G (1999) Care of the mentally disordered offenders. *Mental Health Care*, **3**: 65–7.

McCurdy K, Daro D, Anisfield E et al. (2006) Understanding maternal intentions to engage in home visiting programs. *Child Youth Service Review*, **28**: 1195–212.

McDonald L, Conrad T, Fairtlough A et al. (2009) An evaluation of a groupwork intervention for teenage mothers and their families. *Child and Family Social Work*, **14**: 45–57.

McDougall, T. (2006) Nursing children and young people with learning disabilities and mental health problems. In: McDougall T (ed.). *Child and Adolescent Mental Health Nursing*. Oxford: Blackwell Publishing

McDougall T (2000) Violent incidents in a forensic adolescent unit: a functional analysis. *Nursing Times Research*, **5**: 363.

McDougall T, Worrall-Davies A, Hewson L et al. (2008) Tier 4 child and adolescent mental health services (CAMHS): inpatient care, day services and alternatives: An overview of tier 4 CAMHS provision in the UK. *Child and Adolescent Mental Health*, **13**: 173–80.

McEwen BS, Lasley EN (2002) *The End of Stress*. Washington, DC: Joseph Henry Press.

McKinnon J (2004) The importance of patient-centered planning in prescribing practice. *Nurse Prescribing*, 2:

Meadows S (1992) *Understanding Child Development*. Hove: Routledge.

Meaney MJ, Szyf M (2005) Environmental programming of stress responses through DNA methylation: Life at the interface between a dynamic environment and a fixed genome. *Dialogues in Clinical Neuroscience*, **7**: 103–23.

Meckler GD, Elliott MN, Kanouse DE et al. (2006) Nondisclosure of sexual orientation to a physician among a sample of gay, lesbian, and bisexual youth. *Archives of Paediatric and Adolescent Medicine*, **160**: 1248–54.

Mehta MA, Golembo NI, Nosarti C et al. (2009a) Amygdala, hippocampal and corpus callosum size following severe early institutional deprivation: The English and Romanian Adoptees study. *Journal of Child Psychology and Psychiatry*, **50**: 943–51.

Mehta MA, Gore-Langton E, Golembo N et al. (2009b) Hyporesponsive reward anticipation in the basal ganglia following severe institutional deprivation early in life. *Journal of Cognitive Neuroscience*, **22**: 2316–25.

Meijer AM, Reitz E, Dekovic M et al. (2010) Longitudinal relations between sleep quality, time in bed and adolescent problem behaviour. *Journal of Child Psychology and Psychiatry*, **51**: 1278–86.

Meltzer H, Gatward R, Goodman R, Ford T (2000) *Mental Health of Children and Adolescents in Great Britain*. London: HMSO.

Meltzer LJ, Mindell JA (2007) Relationship between child sleep disturbances and maternal sleep, mood, and parenting stress: a pilot study. *Journal of Family Psychology*, **21**: 67–73.

Meltzer H (2003) *Persistence, Onset, Risk Factors and Outcomes of childhood Mental Disorders*. London: The Stationery Office.

Mental Health Foundation (2006) *Truth Hurts: Report of the National Inquiry into Self-Harm among Young People*. London: Mental Health Foundation.

Merikangas KR, Low NC (2004) The epidemiology of mood disorders. *Current Psychiatry Reports*, **6**: 411–21.

Mick E, Faraone S (2008) Genetics of attention deficit hyperactivity disorder. *Child and Adolescent Psychiatric Clinics of North America,* **17**: 261–84, vii–viii.

Millar JK, Wilson-Annan JC, Anderson S et al. (2000) Disruption of two novel genes by a translocation co-segregating with schizophrenia. *Human Molecular Genetics,* **9**: 1415–23.

Miller J, Cohen E (2001) An integrative theory of prefrontal cortex function. *Annual Review of Neuroscience,* **24**: 167–202.

Mindell JA, Owens JA (2003) *A Clinical Guide to Pediatric Sleep: Diagnosis and Management of Sleep Problems.* New York: Lippincott Williams and Wilkins, 1–10.

Mindell JA, Meltzer LJ, Carskadon MA, Chervin RD (2009) Developmental aspects of sleep hygiene: findings from the 2004 National Sleep Foundation Sleep in America Poll. *Sleep Medicine,* **10**: 771–9.

Mindell JA, Kuhn B, Lewin DS et al. (2006). Behavioral treatment of bedtime problems and night wakings in infants and young children. *Sleep,* **29**: 1263–76.

Mindell JA, Moline ML, Zendell SM et al. (1994) Pediatricians and sleep disorders: training and practice. *Pediatrics,* **94**(2 Pt 1): 194–200.

Mining Report – May 2011. Available from: http://www.a4pt.org/download.cfm?ID=29310

Minuchin S, Fishman HC (1981) *Family Therapy Techniques.* New York: Harvard University Press, 149.

Moffitt TE (1993) The neuropsychology of conduct disorder. *Development and Psychopathology,* **5**: 135–51.

Moffitt T, Scott S (2005) Conduct Disorders of Childhood and Adolescence.

Moffitt TE, Caspi A, Harrington H et al. (2007) Generalized anxiety disorder and depression: childhood risk factors in a birth cohort followed to age 32. *Psychological Medicine,* **37**: 441–52.

Moffitt TE, Caspi A, Rutter M, Silva PA (2001) *Sex Differences in Antisocial Behaviour.* Cambridge, MA: Cambridge University Press.

Moffitt TE, Caspi A, Dickson N et al. (1996) Childhood-onset versus adolescent-onset antisocial conduct problems in males: Natural history from ages 3 to 18 years. *Development and Psychopathology,* **8**: 399–424.

Moffitt TE (2003) Life-course-persistent and adolescence-limited antisocial behavior: A 10-year research review and a research agenda. Causes of conduct disorder and juvenile delinquency. In: Lahey BB, Moffitt TE, Caspi A (eds) *Causes of Conduct Disorder and Juvenile Delinquency.* New York: Guilford Press. 49–75.

Monahan J, Steadman HJ, Silver E et al. (2001) *Re-thinking Risk Assessment. The MacArthur Study of Mental Disorder and Violence.* Oxford: Oxford University Press.

Moore T, Zammit S, Lingford-Hughes A et al. (2007) Cannabis use and risk of psychotic or affective mental health outcomes: a systematic review. *Lancet,* **370**: 319–28.

Moreno C, Laje G, Blanco C et al. (2007) National trends in the outpatient diagnosis and treatment of bipolar disorder in youth. *Archives of General Psychiatry,* **64**: 1032–9.

Morrison JR, Stewart MA (1973) The psychiatric status of the legal families of adopted hyperactive children. *Archives of General Psychiatry,* **28**: 888–91.

Morrow DF (2004) Social work practice with gay, lesbian, and bisexual and transgender adolescents. *Families in Society,* **85**: 91–9.

Moulson M, Fox NA, Zeanah CH, Nelson CA (2009) Early adverse experiences and the neurobiology of facial emotion processing. *Developmental Psychology,* **45**: 17–30.

Mrazek DA (2002) Psychiatric aspects of somatic diseases and disorders. In: Rutter M, Taylor E (eds). *Child and Adolescent Psychiatry,* 4th edn. Oxford: Blackwell Publishing, 810–27.

MTA Co-operative Group (1999) A 14 month randomised clinical trial of treatment strategies for ADHD. *Archives of General Psychiatry,* **56**: 1073–86.

Muhle R, Trentacoste SV, Rapin I (2004) The genetics of autism. *Pediatrics,* **113**: 472–86.

My Asperger Child (Accessed March 28 2011). Available from: www.MyAspergerChild.com/Help for parents with Asperger children developing social skills at home and school.

**N**

Nadder TS, Silberg JL, Eaves LJ et al. (1998) Genetic effects on ADHD symptomatology in 7- to 13-year-old twins: results from a telephone survey. *Behavior Genetics,* **28**: 83–99.

National Autistic Society – booklets and leaflets, as well as conferences and local support groups. Available from: www.nas.org.uk

National Black Carers and Carers Workers Network (2008) *Beyond We Care Too: Putting Black Carers in the Picture.* London: NBCCWN and The Afiya Trust.

National Black Carers and Carers Workers Network (2002): *We Care Too: A Good Practice Guide for People working with Black Carers.* London: NBCCWN and The Afiya Trust.

National CAMHS Review (2008).

National Committee for Primary Mental Health Workers in CAMHS and National CAMHS Support Service (2004) The role of the child primary mental health worker, Department of Health, www.camhs.org.

National Institute for Clinical Excellence (2006) *NICE Guideline CG38: The Management of Bipolar Disorder in Adults, Children and Adolescents, in Primary and Secondary Care.* London: National Institute for Health and Clinical Excellence.

National Institute for Clinical Excellence (2004a) *Self-Harm: The Short-term Physical and Psychological Management and Secondary Prevention of Self-harm in Primary and Secondary Care.* CG16. London: National Institute for Health and Clinical Excellence.

National Institute for Clinical Excellence (2004b) *Eating Disorders: Core Interventions in the Treatment and Management of Anorexia Nervosa, Bulimia Nervosa and Related Eating Disorders.* London: National Collaborating Centre for Mental Health.

National Institute for Health and Clinical Excellence (2010a) *Constipation in Children and Young People.* London: NICE.

National Institute for Clinical Health and Excellence (2010b) *Revised Equality Scheme and Action Plan: 2010–2013.* London: NICE.

National Institute for Health and Clinical Excellence (2008) *Clinical guidance CG72. Attention Deficit Hyperactivity Disorder: Diagnosis and Management in ADHD in Children, Young People and Adults.* London: NICE. Available from: www.nice.org.uk/nicemedia/pdf/CG072NiceGuildelinesV2.pdf (last accessed 25/11/2010).

National Institute for Health and Clinical Excellence (2007) *Chronic fatigue syndrome/Myalgic encephalomyelitis (or encephalopathy); diagnosis and management.* CG53. London: National Institute for Health and Clinical Excellence.

National Institute for Health and Clinical Excellence (2005a) *Obsessive Compulsive Disorder: Core Interventions in the Treatment of Obsessive-compulsive Disorder and Body Dysmorphic Disorder (Clinical guideline 31).* London: NICE.

National Institute for Health and Clinical Excellence (2005b) *Depression in Children and Young People: Identification and Management in Primary, Community and Secondary Care.* London: NICE.

National Institute for Mental Health in England (2009) *The Legal Aspects of the Care and Treatment of Children and Young People with Mental Disorder: A Guide for Professionals.* Department of Health Publication, Gateway ref: 10944.

National Portage Association: a charity offering support and information to parents and professionals involved in Portage.

National Prescribing Centre (2003) *Maintaining Competencies in Prescribing. An Outline Framework to Help Nurse Supplementary Prescribers.* Liverpool: NPC.

National Prescribing Centre (1999) Prescribing nurse bulletin. *Prescribing Nurse Bulletin,* **1**:

Neale BM, Lasky-Su J, Anney R et al. (2008) Genome-wide association scan of attention deficit hyperactivity disorder. *American Journal of Medical Genetics. Part B, Neuropsychiatric Genetics,* **147B**: 1337–44.

Nelson RJ, Trainor BC (2007) Neural mechanisms of aggression. *Nature Reviews. Neuroscience,* **8**: 536–46.

Network National Committee PMHWs. Available from: www.egroups.com/group/pmhw

NHS Health Advisory Service (1995) *A Thematic review of child and adolescent mental health services.* London: HMSO.

NHS Health Advisory Service, Mental Health Act Commission and the Department of Health Society Services Inspectorate (1994) *A Review of the Adolescent Forensic Psychiatry Service Based on the Gardener Unit, Prestwich Hospital, Salford, Manchester.* London: Department of Health.

NICE guidelines on Primary Nocturnal Enuresis (2010). Available from: www.NICE.co.uk

Nigg JT (2006) Temperament and developmental psychopathology. *Journal of Child Psychology and Psychiatry,* **47**: 395–422.

Nishida M, Makris N, Kennedy DN et al. (2006) Detailed semiautomated MRI based morphometry of the neonatal brain: Preliminary results. *Neuroimage,* **32**: 1041–9.

Noll RB, LeRoy SS, Bukowski WM et al. (1991) Peer relationships and adjustment of children with cancer. *Journal of Pediatric Psychology,* **16**: 307–26.

Norvilitis JM, Casey RJ, Brooklier KM, Bonello PJ (2000). Emotion appraisal in children with Attention-Deficit/Hyperactivity Disorder and their parents. *Journal of Attention Disorders,* **4**: 15–26.

Nursing and Midwifery Council (2002) *Code of Professional Conduct.* London: NMC Publications.

Nursing and Midwifery Council (2008) *Standards of Conduct, Performance and Ethics for Nurses and Midwives.* London: NMC.

Nyhan WL (1972) Behavioural Phenotypes in Organic Brain Disease. Presidential address to the Society for Pediatric Research, May 1, 1971. Paediatric Research 6. In: O'Brien G, Yule W (eds). *Behavioural Phenotypes (Clinics in Developmental Medicine No. 138)*. London: Cambridge University Press, 1–9.


**O**

O'Connell B, Palmer S (eds) (2003) *Handbook of Solution-Focused Therapy*. London: Sage Publications.

O'Donovan MC, Craddock N, Norton N et al. (2008) Identification of loci associated with schizophrenia by genome-wide association and follow-up. *Nature Genetics*, **40**: 1053–5.

O'Donovan MC, Williams NM, Owen MJ (2003) Recent advances in the genetics of schizophrenia. *Human Molecular Genetics*, **12**: R125–33.

O'Hanlon WH, Weiner-Davis M (2003) *In Search of Solutions: A New Direction in Psychotherapy*, revised edition. New York: W.W. Morton.

O'Herlihy A, Worrall A, Banerjee S et al. (2001) *National Inpatient Child and Adolescent Psychiatry Study*. London: College Research Unit of the Royal College of Psychiatrists and the Department of Health.

Odell-Miller H, Learmonth M, Pembrooke C (2003) *The Arts and Arts Therapists*. Scoping Paper Commissioned by Nuffield Foundation.

Office for National Statistics (2002) *Social Trends No 32*. London: ONS.

Olds DL (2006) The Nurse–Family Partnership: an evidence-based preventative intervention. *Infant Mental Health Journal*, **27**: 5–25.

Ollendick TH, Vasey MW, King NJ et al. (2001) Operant conditioning influences in childhood anxiety. In: Vasey MW, Dadds MR (eds). *The Developmental Psychopathology of Anxiety*. New York: Oxford University Press, 231–52.

Olsen D (2000) Circumplex model of marital and family systems. *Journal of Family Therapy*, **22**: 144–67.

Olsen J, Forbes C, Belzer M (2011) Management of the transgender adolescent. *Archives of Pediatrics and Adolescent Medicine*, **165**: 171–6.

Olweus D (1993) *Bullying at School*. Oxford: Blackwell.

O'Rourke JA, Scharf JM, Yu D, Pauls DL (2009) The genetics of Tourette syndrome: A review. *Journal of Psychosomatic Research*, **67**: 533–45.

Ougtin D, Zundelt NGA (2010) *Self Harm in Young People, A Therapeutic Assessment Manual*. London: Hodder Arnold.


**P**

Paavonen EJ, Porkka-Heiskanen T, Lahikainen AR (2009) Sleep quality, duration and behavioral symptoms among 5-6-year-old children. *European Child and Adolescent Psychiatry*, **18**: 747–54.

Panksepp J (2004) *Affective Neuroscience: The Foundations of Humane and Animal Emotions*. Oxford: Oxford University Press.

Papadopoulos I (2006) The Papadopoulos, Tilki and Taylor model of developing cultural competence. In: Papadopoulos I (ed.). *Transcultural Health and Social Care: Developing Culturally Competent Practitioners*. Oxford: Elsevier.

Papadopoulos I, Tiki M, Lees S (2008) Promoting Cultural Competence in Health Care through a research based intervention in the UK. *Contemporary Nurse*, **38**: 129–40.

Papadopoulos I, Tilki M, Ayling S, Taylor G (2008) *Cultural Competence Assessment Tool (CCA Tool) for Children and Adolescent Mental Health Services, Transcultural Studies in Health*. University of Middlesex and National CAMHS support services.

Papadopoulos I, Tilki M, Taylor G (1998) *Transcultural Care: A guide for Health Care Professionals*. Wiltshire: Quay Books.

Parker SW, Nelson CA and the Bucharest Early Intervention Project Core Group (2005) The impact of early institutional rearing on the ability to discriminate facial expressions of emotion: An event-related potential study. *Child Development*, **76**: 54–72.

Parkes CM (2010) *Bereavement: Studies of Grief in Adult Life*, 4th edn. London: Penguin.

Passamonti L, Fairchild G, Goodyer IM et al. (2010) Neural abnormalities in early-onset and adolescence-onset conduct disorder. *Archives of General Psychiatry*, **67**: 729–38.

Patterson GR (1982) *Coercive Family Process*. Eugene, OR: Castalia Publications.

Payton A, Holmes J, Barrett JH et al. (2001) Examining for association between candidate gene polymorphisms in the dopamine pathway and attention-deficit hyperactivity disorder: a family-based study. *American Journal of Medical Genetics*, **105**: 464–70.

Pederson P, Marshall A (1982) The ethical crisis for cross cultural counselling and therapy. *Professional Psychology*, **13**: 492–500.

Pentecost D (2000) *Parenting the ADD Child*. London: Jessica Kingsley Publishers.

Perrin S, Last CG (1996) Relationship between ADHD and anxiety in boys: results from a family study. *Journal of the American Academy of Child and Adolescent Psychiatry*, **35**: 988–96.

Phillips KA (1998) *The Broken Mirror*. Oxford: Oxford University Press.

Phillips KA, Pinto A, Jain S (2004) Self-esteem in body dysmorpic disorder. *Body Image*, **1**: 385–90.

Phillips KA, Didie ER, Menard W et al. (2006) Clinical features of body dysmorphic disorder in adolescents and adults. *Psychiatry Research*, **141**: 305–14.

Phillips KA, Atala KD, Albertini RS (1995) Case study: body dysmorphic disorder in adolescents. *Journal of the American Academy of Child and Adolescent Psychiatry*, **34**: 1216–20.

Piaget J, Inhelder B (1962) *The Psychology of the Child*. New York: Basic Books.

Pine DS, Monk CS (2009) The development and cognitive neuroscience of anxiety. In: Nelson CA, Luciana M (eds). *Handbook of Developmental Cognitive Neuroscience*. Cambridge, MA: The MIT Press, 755–70.

Pinker S (1994) *The Language Instinct*. New York: Harper.

Pittet I, Berchtold A, Akre C et al. (2010) Are adolescents with chronic conditions particularly at risk for bullying ? *Archives of Disease in Childhood*, **95**: 711–16.

Pliszka SR, Rogeness GA, Medrano MA (1988) DBH, MHPG, and MAO in children with depressive, anxiety, and conduct disorders: relationship to diagnosis and symptom ratings. *Psychiatry Research*, **24**: 35–44.

Plomin R, Owen MJ, McGuffin P (1994) The genetic basis of complex human behaviors. *Science*, **264**: 1733–9.

Pollak SD, Tolley-Schell SA (2003) Selective attention to facial emotion in physically abused children. *Journal of Abnormal Psychology*, **112**: 323–38.

Pollak SD, Messner M, Kistler DJ, Cohn JF (2009a) Development of perceptual expertise in emotion recognition. *Cognition*, **110**: 242–7.

Pollak Y, Benarroch F, Kanengisser L et al. (2009b) Tourette syndrome-associated psychopathology: roles of comorbid attention-deficit hyperactivity disorder and obsessive-compulsive disorder. *Journal of Developmental and Behavioral Pediatrics*, **30**: 413–19.

Pollock JI (1994) Night-waking at five years of age: predictors and prognosis. *Journal of Child Psychology and Psychiatry*, **35**: 699–708.

Posner MI (1980) Orienting of attention. *The Quarterly Journal of Experimental Psychology*, **32**: 3–25.

Prochaska J, DiClemente C (1986) Towards a comprehensive model of change. In: Miller W, Heather N (eds). *Treating Addictive Behaviours: Processes of Change*. New York : Plenum.

Puckering C (2004) Mellow Parenting, an intensive intervention to change relationships. *Bulletin of the World Association for Infant Mental Health*, **12**: 1–5.

Purper-Ouakil D, Wohl M, Mouren MC et al. (2005) Meta-analysis of family-based association studies between the dopamine transporter gene and attention deficit hyperactivity disorder. *Psychiatric Genetics*, **15**: 53–9.

## Q

Quick guide Guidance from the National Institute for Health and Clinical Excellence. Workforce implications for child and adolescent mental health services 2008. Available from: www.camhsnetwork.co.uk

## R

Rangel L, Rapp S, Levin E, Garralda ME (1999) Chronic Fatigue Syndrome: updates on paediatric and psychological management. *Current Paediatrics*, **9**: 188–93.

Rapee RM, Abbott MJ, Lyneham HJ (2006) Bibliotherapy for children with anxiety disorders using written materials for parents: A randomized controlled trial. *Journal of Consulting and Clinical Psychology*, **74**: 436–44.

*Recent Advances in Child and Adolescent Psychiatry*, 3rd edn. Oxford: Blackwell Scientific.

Reich D (1990) Children of the nightmare. *Adoption and Fostering*, **14**: 9–15.

Rhee SH, Waldman ID (2002) Genetic and environmental influences on antisocial behavior: a meta-analysis of twin and adoption studies. *Psychological Bulletin*, **128**: 490–529.

Richman N (1977) Is a behaviour check list for preschool children useful? In: Graham PJ (ed.). *Epidemiological Approaches to Child Psychiatry*. London: Academic Press, 125–36.

Richman N, Douglas J (1988) *My Child Won't Sleep*. London: Penguin.

Richman N, Stevenson J, Graham P (1982) *Preschool to School: A behaviour Study*. London: Academic Press.

Richman N (1977) Is a behaviour check list for preschool children useful? In: Graham PJ (ed.). *Epidemiological Approaches to Child Psychiatry.* London: Academic Press, 125–36.

Rietveld MJH, Hudziak JJ, Bartels M et al. (2004) Heritability of attention problems in children: longitudinal results from a study of twins, age 3 to 12. *Journal of Child Psychology and Psychiatry and Allied Disciplines,* **45**: 577–88.

Rivett M, Street E (2009) *Family Therapy 100 Key Points and Techniques.* London: Routledge.

Robin AL, Siegel PT, Moye AW et al. (1999) A controlled comparison of family versus individual therapy for adolescents with anorexia nervosa. *American Academy of Child and Adolescent Psychiatry,* **38**: 1482–9.

Robins D, Fein D, Barton M, Green J (2001) The Modified Checklist for Autism in Toddlers (M-CHAT): An initial investigation in the early detection of autism and pervasive developmental disorders. *Journal of Autism and Developmental Disorders,* **31**: 131–44.

Rogers C (1976) *Client Centred Therapy.* London: Constable and Robinson.

Rogers C (1961) *On Becoming a Person: A Therapist's View of Psychotherapy.* London: Constable

Rogers C (1951) *Client Centred Therapy.* London, UK: Constable.

Roizen NJ, Blondis TA, Irwin M et al. (1996) Psychiatric and developmental disorders in families of children with attention-deficit hyperactivity disorder. *Archives of Pediatrics and Adolescent Medicine,* **150**: 203–8.

Ronald A, Happé F, Bolton P et al. (2006) Genetic heterogeneity between the three components of the autism spectrum: a twin study. *Journal of the American Academy of Child and Adolescent Psychiatry,* **45**: 691–9.

Rothman AD, Nowicki S Jr (2004) A measure of the ability to identify emotion in children's tone of voice. *Journal of Non Verbal Behaviour,* **28**: 67–92.

Routh CP, Hill JW, Steele H et al. (1995) Maternal attachment status, psychosocial stressors and problem behaviour: Follow up after parent training courses for conduct disorder. *Journal of Child Psychology and Psychiatry,* **36**: 1179–98.

Routh D (1978) Hyperactivity. In: Magreb P (ed.). *Psychological Management of paediatric Problems.* Baltimore, MD: University Press.

Royal College of Psychiatrists (2005) *Building and Sustaining Specialist CAMHS: Workforce, Capacity and Functions of Tiers 2, 3 and 4 Specialist CAMHS.* London: Royal College of Psychiatrists.

Royal College of Psychiatrists (2004) *Mental Health and growing up: Fact Sheet 16.* London: Royal College of Psychiatrists.

Royal College of Psychiatrists (1998) *Managing Deliberate Self-Harm in Young People. Council Report (CR 64).* London: Royal College of Psychiatrists.

Rubin M, Safdieh J (2007) *Netter's Concise Neuroanatomy.* Philadelphia: Saunders.

Russell GFM, Szmukler GI, Dare C, Eisler I (1987) An evaluation of family therapy in anorexia nervosa. *Archives of General Psychiatry,* **44**: 1047–56.

Rust J, Smith A (2006) How should the effectiveness of Social Stories to modify the behaviour of children on the autistic spectrum be tested? Lessons from the literature. *Autism,* **10**: 125–38.

Rutter M (2007) Proceeding from observed correlation to causal inference: The use of natural experiments. *Perspectives on Psychological Science,* **2**: 377–95.

Rutter M (in press). 'Natural experiments' as a means of testing causal inferences. In: Dawid P, Berzuini C, Bernardelli L (eds). *Causal Inference: The State of the Art.*

Rutter M, O'Connor TG (2004) Are there biological programming effects for psychological development? Findings from a study of Romanian adoptees. *Developmental Psychology,* **40**: 81–94.

Rutter M and the English and Romanian Adoptees Study Team (1998) Developmental catch-up, and deficit, following adoption after severe global early deprivation. *Journal of Child Psychology and Psychiatry,* **39**: 465–76.

Rutter M, Taylor E (eds). (2002) *Child and Adolescent Psychiatry,* 4th edn. London: Blackwell.

Rutter M, Sonuga-Barke EJ, Beckett C et al. (2010) Deprivation-specific psychological patterns: Effects of institutional deprivation. *Monographs of the Society for Research in Child Development,* **75**: 232–47.

Rutter M, Beckett C, Castle J et al. (2007) Effects of profound early institutional deprivation: An overview of findings from a UK longitudinal study of Romanian adoptees. *European Journal of Developmental Psychology,* **4**: 332–50.

Rutter M, Kreppner JM, O'Connor TG (2001) Specificity and heterogeneity in children's responses to profound early institutional privation. *British Journal of Psychiatry,* **179**, 97–103.

Rutter M, Tizard J, Yule W et al. (1976) Research Report: Isle of Wight Studies 1964–1974. *Psychological Medicine,* **6**: 313–32.

Rutter M, Cox A, Tupling C et al. (1975) Attainment and adjustment in two geographical areas 1. The prevalence of psychiatric disorder. *British Journal of Psychiatry,* **125**: 493–509.

Rutter M, Tizzard J, Whitmore K (1970) *Education, Health and Behaviour.* London: Longmans.

Rutter M, Bailey A, Lord C (2003) *Social Communication Questionnaire-WPS (SCQ-WPS).* Los Angeles, CA: Western Psychological Services.

Ryan C, Epstein N, Keitner G et al. (2005) *Evaluating and Treating Families.* Hove: Routledge.

Ryan C, Russell ST, Huebner R et al. (2010) Family acceptance in adolescence and the health of LGBT young adults. *Journal of Child and Adolescent Psychiatric Nursing,* **23**: 205–13.

Ryan N (2010) Nurse prescribing: the need to act in a concordant way. *ADHD in Practice,* **2**: 22–3.

Ryan N (2007) Nurse prescribing in child and adolescent mental health services. *Mental Health Practice,* **10**: 35–7.

## S

Saarni C (1999) *The Development of Emotional Competence.* New York: Guilford Press.

Sanchez MM, Hearn EF, Do D et al. (1998) Differential rearing affects corpus callosum size and cognitive function of rhesus monkeys. *Brain Research,* **812**: 38–49.

Sandberg S, Paton JY, Ahola S et al. (2000) The role of acute and chronic stress in asthma attacks in children. *Lancet,* **356**: 982–7.

Sansbury L, Wahler R (1992) Pathways to maladaptive parenting with mothers and their conduct disordered. *Behaviour Modification,* **16**: 574–92.

Saudino KJ (2005) Behavioral genetics and child temperament. *Journal of Developmental and Behavioral Pediatrics,* **26**: 214–23.

Saudino KJ, Plomin R, DeFries JC (1996) Tester-rated temperament at 14, 20, and 24 months: Environmental change and genetic continuity. *British Journal of Developmental Psychology,* 1996; **14**: 129–44.

Saunders K, Goodwin G. (2010) The course of bipolar disorder. *Advances in Psychiatric Treatment,* **16**: 318–28.

Schab DW, Trinh NT (2004) Do artificial food colours promote hyperactivity in children with hyperactive syndromes? A meta-analysis of double-blind placebo-controlled trials. *Journal of Developmental and Behavioral Pediatrics,* **25**: 423–34.

Schachar R (1991) Childhood hyperactivity. *Journal of Child Psychology and Psychiatry,* **32**: 155–91.

Schachar R, Tannock R (1993) Childhood hyperactivity and psychostimulants: a review of extended treatment studies. *Journal of Child and Adolescent Psychopharmacology,* **3**: 81–97.

Scheres A, Milham MP, Knutson B, Castellanos FX (2007) Ventral striatal hyporesponsiveness during reward anticipation in attention-deficit/hyperactivity disorder. *Biological Psychiatry,* **61**: 720–4.

Schnoll R, Burshteyn D, Cea-Aravena J (2003) Nutrition in the treatment of Attention-Deficit Hyperactivity Disorder: A neglected but important aspect. *Applied Psychophysiology and Biofeedback,* **28**: 63–75.

Schreier A, Wittchen HU, Höfler M et al. (2008) Anxiety disorders in mothers and their children: prospective longitudinal community study. *British Journal of Psychiatry,* **129**: 308–9.

Schultz D, Izard CE, Bear G (2004) Children's emotion processing: Relations to emotionality and aggression. *Development and Psychopathology,* **16**: 371–87.

Schwartz S, Vuilleumier P, Hutton C et al. (2005) Attentional load and sensory competition in human vision: modulation of fMRI responses by load at fixation during task-irrelevant stimulation in the peripheral visual field. *Cerebral Cortex,* **15**: 770–86.

Scottish Executive Education Department (SEED) (2002) *Review of Provision of Educational Psychology Services in Scotland.* Edinburgh: SEED.

Segurado R, Detera-Wadleigh SD, Levinson DF et al. (2003) Genome Scan Meta-Analysis of Schizophrenia and Bipolar Disorder, Part III: Bipolar Disorder. *American Journal of Human Genetics,* **73**: 49–62.

Semiz U, Basoglu C, Cetin M et al. (2008) Body dysmorphic disorder in patients with borderline personality disorder: prevalence, clinical characteristics, and role of childhood trauma. *Acta Neuropsychiatrica,* **20**: 33–40.

Sensory Integration (Accessed April 2 2011) Available from: www.autism.com/fam_page.asp?PID=372

Serretti A, Mandelli L (2008) The genetics of bipolar disorder: genome 'hot regions,' genes, new potential candidates and future directions. *Molecular Psychiatry,* **13**: 742–71.

Shaffer D, Gould MS, Bird H et al. (1983). Adaptation of the Adult Global Assessment Scale (Robert L. Spitzer, M.D, Nathan Gibbon, M.S.W, Jean Endicott, Ph.D.)

Shah PE, Fonagy P Stratheart L (2010) Is attachment transmitted across generations? The plot thickens. *Clinical Child Psychology and Psychiatry,* **15**: 329–45.

Sharpley MS, Hutchinson G, Murray RM, McKenzie K (2001) Understanding the excess of psychosis among the African-Caribbean population in England: Review of current hypotheses. *British Journal of Psychiatry,* **178**: s60–s68.

Shields J, Gottesman II (1972) Cross-national diagnosis of schizophrenia in twins. The heritability and specificity of schizophrenia. *Archives of General Psychiatry*, **27**: 725–30.

Shields J, Slater E (1975) Genetic aspects of schizophrenia. *British Journal of Psychiatry*, **9**: 32–40.

Shouldice A, Stevenson-Hinde J (1992) Coping with Security Distress: the Separation Anxiety Test and Attachment Classification at 4.5 years. *Journal of Child Psychology and Psychiatry*, **33**:331–48.

Silva P, Stanton W (1996) *From Child to Adult: The Dunedin Multidisciplinary Health and Development Study.* Oxford: Oxford University Press.

Simpson GA, Bloom B, Cohen RA et al. (2005) U.S. children with emotional and behavioral difficulties: data from the 2001, 2002, and 2003 National Health Interview Surveys. *Advance Data*, **360**: 1–13.

Sinason V (1992) *Mental Handicap and the Human Condition.* London: Free Association Books.

Singh AA, Hays DG, Watson LS (2011) Strength in the face of adversity: resilience strategies of transgender individuals. *Journal of Counselling and Development*, **89**: 20–27.

Singh MK, DelBello MP, Kowatch RA, Strakowski SM (2006) Co-occurrence of bipolar and attention-deficit hyperactivity disorders in children. *Bipolar Disorders*, **8**: 710–20.

Singh R, Dutta S (2010) *Race and Culture. Tools, Techniques and Training.* London: Karnac.

Skinner BF (1969) *Contingencies of Reinforcement.* New York: Appleton-Century-Croft.

Skuse D, Warrington R, Bishop D et al. (2004) The developmental, dimensional and diagnostic interview (3di): a novel computerized assessment for autism spectrum disorders. *Journal of the American Academy of Child and Adolescent Psychiatry*, **43**: 548–58.

Smedje H, Broman JE, Hetta J (2001) Associations between disturbed sleep and behavioural difficulties in 635 children aged six to eight years: a study based on parents' perceptions. *European Child and Adolescent Psychiatry*, **10**; 1–9.

Smith A, Taylor E, Rogers JW et al. (2002) Evidence for a pure time perception deficit in children with ADHD. *Journal of Child Psychology and Psychiatry*, **43**: 529–42.

Smith C (2003) *Writing and Developing Social Stories: Practical Interventions in Autism.* Milton Keynes: Speechmark Publishing Ltd.

Smith K, Leon L (2001) *Turned Upside Down: Developing Community-based Crisis Services for 16–25 year olds Experiencing a Mental Health Crisis.* London: Mental Health Foundation.

Smoller JW, Finn CT (2003) Family, twin, and adoption studies of bipolar disorder. *American Journal of Medical Genetics. Part C, Seminars in Medical Genetics*, **123C**: 48–58.

Sobanski E, Banaschewski T, Asherson P et al. (2010). Emotional liability in children and adolescents with Attention Deficit/Hyperactivity Disorder (ADHD): Clinical correlates and family prevalence. *Journal of Child Psychology and Psychiatry*, **51**: 915–23.

Social Care Institute for Excellence (2009) *Think Child, Think Parent, Think Family: A Guide to Parental Mental Health and Child Welfare.* London: SCIE.

Social Care Institute for Excellence (2005) Adult Services: Practice Guide 5: Implementing the Carers (Equal Opportunities) Act 2004. Available from: www.scie.org.uk, page 19.

Society for the Study of Behavioural Phenotypes. Available from: www.ssbp.org.uk.

Solanto M, Abikoff H, Sonuga-Barke EJS et al. (2001) The ecological validity of delay aversion and response inhibition as measures of impulsivity in AD/HD: A supplement to the NIMH Multimodal Treatment Study of AD/HD. *Journal of Abnormal Child Psychology*, **29**: 215–28.

Sonuga-Barke EJS (2002) Psychological heterogeneity in AD/HD – a dual pathway model of behaviour and cognition. *Behaviour Brain Research*, **130**: 29–36.

Sonuga-Barke EJS, Schlotz W, Rutter M (2010) Physical growth and maturation following early severe institutional deprivation: Do they mediate specific psychopathological effects? *Monographs of the Society for Research in Child Development*, **75**: 143–66.

Sonuga-Barke EJS, Beckett C, Kreppner J et al. (2008) Is subnutrition necessary for a poor outcome following early institutional deprivation? *Developmental Medicine and Child Neurology*, **50**: 664–71.

Sonuga-Barke EJS, Campbell S, Auerbach J et al. (2005) Varieties of pre-school hyperactivity; Pathways from risk to disorder. *Developmental Science*, **8**: 141–50.

Sonuga-Barke EJS, Dalen L, Remmington B (2003) Do executive deficits and delay aversion make independent contributions to preschool attention-deficit/hyperactivity disorder? *Journal of the American Academy of Child and Adolescent Psychiatry*, **42**: 1335–42.

Sonuga-Barke EJS, Daley D, Thompson M (2002) Does maternal AD/HD reduce the effectiveness of parent training for pre-school children's AD/HD? *Journal of the American Academy of Child and Adolescent Psychiatry*, **41**: 696–702.

Sonuga-Barke EJS, Daley D, Thompson M et al. (2001) Parent based therapies for pre-school Attention/ Hyperactivity Disorder: a randomized controlled trial with a community sample. *American Academy of Child and Adolescent Psychiatry*, **40**: 402–8.

Sonuga-Barke EJS, Thompson M, Stevenson J, Viney D (1997) Patterns of behaviour problems among pre-school children. *Psychology Medicine*, **27**: 909–18.

Sood B, Delaney-Black V, Covington C et al. (2001). Prenatal alcohol exposure and childhood behaviour at age 6 and 7: I. Dose-response effect. *Pediatrics*, **108**: e34.

Spence SH (1994) Spence Children's Anxiety Scale. In: Yule W (ed.). *Child Psychology Portfolio: Anxiety, Depression and Post-Traumatic Stress Disorder in Childhood*. UK: Nfer-Nelson.

Spencer T, Biederman J, Mick E (2007) Attention Deficit/Hyperactivity Disorder: Diagnosis, life span, co morbidities, and neurobiology. *Journal of Ambulatory Paediatrics*, **7**: 73.

Staikova E, Marks D, Miller C et al. (2009) Childhood stimulant treatment and teen depression: Is there a relationship? *Journal of Child and Adolescent Psychopharmacology*, **20**: 387–93.

Stallard P (1995) Parental satisfaction with intervention: differences between respondents and non-respondents to a postal questionnaire. *Journal of Child Psychology and Psychiatry*, **34**: 397–405.

Stallard P (1993) The behaviour of 3-year-old children: Prevalence and parental perception of problem behaviour: a research note. *Journal of Child Psychology and Psychiatry*, **34**: 413–21.

Steen S, Bemak F (2008) Group work with high school students at risk of school failure: a pilot study. *Journal For Specialists In Group Work*, **33**: 335–50.

Stein MB, Kerry L, Jang KL, Livesley WJ (1999) Heritability of anxiety sensitivity: a twin study. *American Journal of Psychiatry*, **156**: 246–51.

Steiner C (1984) Emotional literacy. *Transactional Analysis Journal*, **14**: 162–73.

Steinhausen H (2002) The outcome of anorexia nervosa in the 20th century. *American Journal of Psychiatry*, **159**: 1284–93.

Stephens J (2002) *The Mental Health Needs of Homeless Young People. Bright Futures: Working with Vulnerable Young People*. London: The Mental Health Foundation.

Sterzer P, Stadler C, Poustka F, Kleinschmidt A (2007) A structural neural deficit in adolescents with conduct disorder and its association with lack of empathy. *NeuroImage*, **37**: 335–42.

Stevens S, Kumsta R, Kreppner J et al. (2009) Dopamine transporter gene polymorphism moderates the effects of severe deprivation on ADHD symptoms: Developmental continuities in gene–environment inter-play. *American Journal of Medical Genetics Part B: Neuropsychiatric Genetics*, **150B**: 753–61.

Stevenson J (ed.) (1990) *Health visitor based services for pre-school children with behaviour problems. Occasional Papers No 2*. London: Association of Child Psychologists and Psychiatrists.

Stevenson J, Fielding J (1985) Ratings of temperament in families of young twins. *British Journal of Developmental Psychology*, **3**: 143–52.

Stevenson J, Sonuga-Barke E, McCann D et al. (2010) The role of histamine degradation gene polymorphisms in moderating the effects of food additives on children's ADHD symptoms. *American Journal of Psychiatry*, **167**: 1108–15.

Stiles J, Jernigan TL (2010) The basics of brain development. *Neuropsychological Review*, **20**: 327–48.

St James-Roberts I (1989) Persistent crying in infancy. *Journal of Child Psychology and Psychiatry*, **30**: 189–95.

Stoch MB, Smythe PM, Moodie AD, Bradshaw D (1982) Psychosocial outcome and CT findings after gross undernourishment during infancy: A 20-year developmental study. *Developmental Medicine and Child Neurology*, **24**: 419–36.

Stonewall (2010) Average coming out age has fallen by over 20 years. Under 18 now come out at 15 on average. Available from: www.stonewall.org.uk/media/current_release/4867

Strawbridge S, Woolfe R (2003) Counselling psychology in context. In: Woolfe R, Dryden W, Strawbridge S (eds). *Handbook of Counselling Psychology*, 2nd edn. London: SAGE Publications, 1–21.

Stringaris A, Cohen P, Pine DS, Leibenluft E (2009) Adult outcomes of youth irritability:a 20-year prospective community-based study. *American Journal of Psychiatry*, 2009; **166**: 1048–54.

Stringer H, Lozano S, Dodd B (2003) *The Link between Language Disorders and Behavioural Difficulties in Adolescents*. AFASIC Newsletter.

Suomi SJ (1997) Long-term effects of different early rearing experiences on social, emotional, and physiological development in non-human primates. In: Keshevan MS, Murray RM (eds). *Neurodevelopment and Adult Psychopathology (Peer Problems)*. Cambridge: Cambridge University Press, 104–16.

Suris J-C, Michaud P-A, Akre C, Sawyer SM (2008) Health risk behaviours in adolescents with chronic conditions. *Pediatrics*, **122**; 1113–18.

Suris J-C, Michaud P-A, Viner R (2004) The adolescent with a chronic condition. Part 1: Developmental issues. *Archives of Diseases in Childhood*, **89**: 938–42.

Suris J-C, Michaud P-A, Viner R (2004) The adolescent with a chronic condition. Part 2: Healthcare provision. *Archives of Disease of Childhood*, **89**: 943–9.

Sutter J, Eyberg S (1984) Sutter-Eyberg Student Behavior Inventory. Available from: Sheila Eyberg, Department of Clinical and Health Psychology, Box J-165, HSC, University of Florida, Gainesville, FL 32610.

Szatmari P, Saigal S, Rosenbaum P et al. (1990) Psychiatric disorders at five years among children with birth weights <1000g. *Developmental Medicine and Child Neurology*, **32**: 954–62.

Szatmari P, Offord DR, Boyle MH (1989) Ontario child Health study: prevalence of Attention deficit disorder with hyperactivity. *Journal of Child Psychology and Psychiatry*, **30**: 219–30.


**T**

Tackett JL, Krueger RF, Iacono WG, McGue M (2005) Symptom-based subfactors of DSM-defined conduct disorder: evidence for etiologic distinctions. *Journal of Abnormal Psychology*, **114**: 483–7.

Taneli C, Ertan P, Taneli F et al. (2004) Effect of alarm treatment on bladder storage capacities in monosymptomatic nocturnal enuresis. *Scandinavian Journal of Urology and Nephrology*, **38**: 207–43.

Taylor E, Rutter M (2008) Classification. In: Rutter M, Bishop DVM, Pine DS et al. (eds). *Rutter's Child and Adolescent Psychiatry*, 5th edn. Oxford: Blackwell Publishing, 18–31.

Taylor E, Dopfner M, Sergeant J et al. (2004) European Guidelines for hyperkinetic disorder-first upgrade. *European Child and Adolescent Psychiatry*, **13**: 7–30.

Taylor E, Sandberg S, Thorley G, Giles S (1991) *The Epidemiology of Childhood Hyperactivity*. New York: Oxford University Press.

Teicher MH, Andersen SL, Polcari A et al. (2003) The neurobiological consequences of early stress and childhood maltreatment. *Neuroscience and Biobehavioral Reviews*, **27**: 33–44.

Thapar A, Fowler T, Rice F et al. (2003) Maternal smoking during pregnancy and attention deficit hyperactivity disorder symptoms in offspring. *American Journal of Psychiatry*, **160**: 1985–89.

Thapar A, Harrington R, McGuffin P (2001) Examining the comorbidity of ADHD-related behaviours and conduct problems using a twin study design. *British Journal of Psychiatry*, **179**: 224–9.

The Children's Society (2010) *The Princess Royal Trust for Carers Current Guidance on Young Carers for Schools (England and Wales)*. London: The Children's Society.

The Children's Society (2008) *Include Project Information for Professionals: Supporting Children who have a Parent with a Mental Illness*. London: The Children's Society.

The Children's Society (2006) *Emotional Support for Young Carers: A Report Prepared for the Royal College of Psychiatrists by the Children's Society Young Carers Initiative*. London: The Children's Society and Royal College of Psychiatrists.

The Huntington's Disease Collaborative Research Group (1993) A novel gene containing a trinucleotide repeat that is unstable on Huntington's disease chromosomes. *Cell*, **26**: 971–83.

The Joint Formulary Committee (2010) *4.2.1 Antipsychotic drugs. The BNF for children (2010–2011)*. London: The BMJ Publishing Group and the Pharmaceutical Society of Great Britain, 219.

The National Service Framework (2004) Outlined standards and milestones for CAMHS and the CAMHS grant guidance (2003/4).

The Social Baby Understanding Babies' Communication from Birth (2004) The Children's Project London TW10 7FL. Available from: www.socialbaby.com

Thomas A, Chess S, Birch HG (1968) *Temperament and Behavior Disorders in Children*. New York: New York University Press.

Thompson M (2003) Working with Primary care. In: Garralda E, Hyde C (eds). *Managing Children with Psychiatric Problems*, 2nd edn. London: BMJ Publishing.

Thompson M, Laver-Bradbury C, Chen W, Sonuga-Barke EJS (eds) (2009) Directed by Phillips, P. and O'Riordan, T. Southampton City PCT Living with ADHD DVD.

Thompson M, Laver-Bradbury C, Weeks A (2009) *Living with ADHD a DVD for Parents and Professionals*. Southampton: University of Southampton Media Services.

Thompson M, Stevenson J, Sonuga-Barke EJS et al. (1996) The mental health of preschool children and their mothers in a mixed urban/rural population 1. Prevalence and ecological factors. *British Journal of Psychiatry*, **168**: 16–20.

Thompson MJJ (2001) *The Development of Community Service for Young Children in the New Forest: Joint work by a Child Guidance Clinic with Health Visitors*. University of Glasgow: unpublished MD thesis.

Thompson MJJ, Laver-Bradbury C, Ayres M et al. (2009) A small-scale randomised controlled trial of the revised New Forest Programme for Pre-schoolers with Attention Deficit Hyperactivity Disorder. *European Child and Adolescent Psychiatry,* **10**: 605–16.

Thompson MJJ, Laver-Bradbury C, Weeks A (2007) *Information Manual for Professionals Working with Families with a Child who has Attention Deficit Hyperactive Disorder.* Southampton: Southampton City Primary Care Trust.

Thompson MJJ, Coll X, Wilkinson S, Utenbroek D (2003) The development of an effective mental health service for young children. *Child and Adolescent Mental Health Review,* **8**: 68–78.

Thompson MJJ (2001) The Development of Community Service for Young Children in the New Forest: Joint work by a Child Guidance Clinic with Health Visitors. Unpublished MD thesis, University of Glasgow.

Thompson M, Stevenson J, Sonuga-Barke EJS et al. (2005) In: Cooper M, Hooper C, Thompson M (eds). *Child and Adolescent Mental Health: Theory and Practice.* London: Hodder Arnold.

Tiffin PA (2007) Managing psychotic illness in young people: a practical overview. *Child and Adolescent Mental Health,* **12**: 173–86.

Tittle CR, Meier RF (1990) Specifying the ses delinquency relationship. *Criminology,* **28**: 271–99.

Todd RD, Huang H, Smalley SL et al. (2005) Collaborative analysis of DRD4 and DAT genotypes in population-defined ADHD subtypes. *Journal of Child Psychology and Psychiatry,* **46**: 1067–73.

Tottenham N, Hare TA, Millner A et al. (2011) Elevated amygdala response to faces following early deprivation. *Developmental Science,* **14**: 190–204.

Tottenham N, Hare TA, Quinn BT et al. (2010) Prolonged institutional rearing is associated with atypically large amygdala volume and emotion regulation difficulties. *Developmental Science,* **13**: 46–61.

Touchette E, Petit D, Paquet J et al. (2005) Factors associated with fragmented sleep at night across early childhood. *Archives of Pediatric and Adolescent Medicine,* **159**: 242–9.

Treasure J, Ward A (1997) A practical guide to motivational interviewing in anorexia. *European Eating Disorder Review,* **5**: 102–14.

Treisman A (1986) Features and objects in visual processing. *Scientific American,* **255**: 114B–125.

Trentacosta CJ, Fine SE (2010) Emotion knowledge, social competence, and behavior problems in childhood and adolescence: a meta-analytic review. *Social Development,* **19**: 1–29.

Troiden R (1987) Homosexual identity development. *Journal of Adolescent Health Care,* **9**: 105–13.

Tschann JM, Kaiser P, Chesney MA et al. (1996) Resilience and vulnerability among preschool children: family functioning, temperament, and behaviour problems. *Journal for the American Academy of Child and Adolescent Psychiatry,* **35**: 184–92.

Tunnard J (2008) In: Jackson C, Hill K, Lavis P (eds). *Child and Adolescent Mental Health Today: A Handbook.* London: Pavillion, 150.

Turic D, Langley K, Williams H et al. (2005) A family based study implicates solute carrier family 1-member 3 (SLC1A3) gene in attention-deficit/hyperactivity disorder. *Biological Psychiatry,* **57**: 1461–6.

U

Underwood G (1977) Contextual facilitation from attended and unattended messages. *Journal of Verbal Learning and Verbal Behavior,* **16**: 99–106.

UNICEF (2007) Child Poverty in Perspective: An overview of child well-being in rich countries (Innocenti Report Card 7). Florence: UNICEF Innocenti Research Centre. Available from: www.unicef-irc.org/publications/pdf/rc7_eng.pdf

V

Van der Berg MM, Benninga MA, Di Lorenzo C. (2006) Epidemiology of childhood constipation: a systematic review. *American Journal of Gastroenterology,* **101**: 2401–9.

Van der Kolk B, McFarlane A, Weisaeth L (1999) *Traumatic Stress.* New York: Guilford Press.

Van der Lee J, Mokkink LB, Grootenhuis MA, et al.(2007) Definitions and measurement of chronic health conditions in childhood. A systematic review. *Journal of the American Medical Association,* **297**: 2741–51.

Van der Valk J, van den Oord E, Verhulst F, Boomsma D ( 2003) Using shared and unique parental views to study the etiology of 7-year-old twins' internalizing and externalizing problems. *Behavior Genetics,* **33**: 409–20.

Van Fleet R, Guerney L (2003) *Casebook of Filial Therapy.* Crowborough, UK: Play Therapy Press.

Van Tol HH, Wu CM, Guan HC et al. (1992) Multiple dopamine D4 receptor variants in the human population. *Nature,* **358**: 149–52.

Vaughan PJ (2002) *Secure Care and Treatment Needs of Mentally Disordered Adolescents. Report to the National Specialist Commissioning Advisory Group of the Department of Health.* London: Department of Health.

Veale D (2004) Body dysmorphic disorder. *Postgraduate Medical Journal,* **80**: 67–71.

Veale D (2002) Shame in body dysmorphic disorder. In: Gilbert P, Miles J (eds). *Body Shame: Conceptualisation, Research and Treatment.* Hove and New York: Brunner-Routledge, 267–28.

Veale D (2001) Cognitive-behavioural therapy for body dysmorphic disorder. *Advances in Psychiatric Treatment,* **7**: 125–32.

Verhulst F, Van der Ende J (2005) Rating Scales. In: Rutter M, Taylor E (eds). *Child and Adolescent Psychiatry,* 4th edn. Oxford: Blackwell Publishing.

Viding E, Blair RJ, Moffitt TE, Plomin R (2005) Evidence for substantial genetic risk for psychopathy in 7-year-olds. *Journal of Child Psychology and Psychiatry, and Allied Disciplines,* **46**: 592–7.

Von Gontard A, Schaumburg H, Hollmann E et al. *(2001) The genetics of enuresis: a review. Journal of Urology,* **166**: 2438–43.

Vostanis P (2002) Mental health of homeless children and their families. *Advances in Psychiatric Treatment,* **8**: 463–9.

Vostanis P, Grattan E, Cumella S (1998) Mental health problems of homeless children and families: longitudinal study. *British Medical Journal,* **316**: 899–902.

## W

Wallander JL, Varni JW (1998) Effects of pediatric chronic physical disorders on child and family adjustment. *Journal of Child Psychology and Psychiatry,* **39**: 29–46.

Walsh Y, Frankland A (eds). (2006) *Counselling Psychology Review,* 21(1). Special Edition: The First 10 Years. London: The British Psychological Society.

Wang K, Zhang H, Ma D et al. (2009) Common genetic variants on 5p14.1 associate with autism spectrum disorders. *Nature,* **459**: 528–33.

Weare K, Gray G (2003) *What Works in Developing Children's Emotional and Social Competence and Wellbeing?* London: Department for Education and Skills.

Weaver ICG, Cervoni N, Champagne FA et al. (2004) Epigenetic programming by maternal behavior. *Nature Neuroscience,* **7**: 847–54.

Webster-Stratton C (1991) Annotation: Strategies for helping families with conduct disordered children. *Journal of Child Psychology and Psychiatry Newsletter,* **32**: 1047–62.

Webster-Stratton C (1985) Predictors of treatment outcome in parent training for conduct disordered children. *Behaviour Therapy,* **16**: 223–43.

Wechsler D (2003) *The Wechsler Intelligence Scales for Children,* 4th edn (WISC-IV UK). UK: Pearson Assessment.

Wechsler D (2002) *The Wechsler Preschool and Primary Scales of Intelligence,* 3rd edn (WPPSI-III UK). UK: Pearson Assessment.

Weeks A, Laver-Bradbury C, Thompson M (1999) *Manual for Professionals working with Hyperactive Children.* Southampton: Southampton Community Health Services Trust.

Weingarten K (1998) The small and the ordinary: the daily practice of a post-modern narrative therapy. *Family Process,* **37**: 3–15.

Werker JF, Tees RC (2005) Speech perception as a window for understanding plasticity and commitment in language systems of the brain. *Developmental Psychobiology,* **46**: 233–51.

Werker JF, Desjardins RN (1995) Listening to speech in the first year of life: Experiential influences on phoneme perception. *Current Directions in Psychological Science,* **4**: 76–81.

Werner EE (1985) Stress and protective factors in children's lives. In: Nicol AR (ed.). *Longitudinal Studies in Child Psychology and Psychiatry.* Chichester: John Wiley and Sons Ltd, 335–55.

Werner EE (1971) *The Children of Kauai: A Longitudinal Study from the Prenatal Period to Age Ten.* Honolulu: University of Hawaii Press.

West J (1996) *Child Centred Play Therapy,* 2nd edn. London: Edward Arnold.

Wever C, Phillips N (1996) *The Secret Problem.* Australia: Shrink-Rap Press. (Cartoon based book about OCD for young people).

Whitaker DS (1987) *Using Groups to Help People.* New York and Hove: Routledge (reprinted 1992).

White M, Epston D (1990) *Narrative Means to Therapeutic Ends.* London and New York: WW. Norton and Company.

Wierzbicki M (1987) Similarity of monozygotic and dizygotic child twins in level and lability of subclinically depressed mood. *American Journal of Orthopsychiatry,* **57**: 33–40.

Wigal T, Greenhill L, Chuang MS et al. (2006)Safety and tolerability of methylphenidate in preschool children with ADHD. *Journal of the American Academy of Child and Adolescent Psychiatry*, **45**: 1294–303.

Wiggs L (2009) Behavioural aspects of children's sleep. *Archives of Disease in Childhood*, **94**: 59–62.

Wilens TE, Hahesy AL, Biederman J et al. (2005) Influence of parental SUD and ADHD on ADHD in their offspring: preliminary results from a pilot-controlled family study. *American Journal on Addictions*, **14**: 179–87.

Wilens T, Biederman J, Kwon A et al. (2004) Risk of substance use disorders in adolescents with bipolar disorder. *Journal of the American Academy of Child and Adolescent Psychiatry*, **43**: 1380–6.

Williams BF, Williams RL (2011) *Effective Programs for Treating Autistic Spectrum Disorders: Applied Behavior Analysis Models*. New York: Routledge.

Williams R, Kerfoot M (eds). (2005) Chapter 1, Setting the scene: perspectives on the history of and policy for child and adolescent mental health services in the UK. *Child and Adolescent Mental Health Services: Strategy, Planning, Delivery, and Evaluation*. Oxford: Oxford Press.

Wilson K, Ryan V (2005) *A Non-directive Approach for Children and Adolescents*. London: Bailliere Tindall.

Wing L (2003) *The Autistic Spectrum: a Guide for Parents and Professionals*. London: Robinson Publishing.

Wing L (1993) The definition and prevalence of autism: A review. *European Child and Adolescent Psychiatry*, **2**: 61–74.

Winnicott DW (1971) *Playing and Reality*. London: Penguin.

Wismer Fries AB, Ziegler TE, Kurian JR et al. (2005) Early experience in humans is associated with changes in neuropeptides critical for regulating social behavior. *Proceedings of the National Academy of Sciences*, **47**: 17 237–40.

Wittchen HU, Nelson CB, Lachner G (1998) Prevalence of mental disorders and psychosocial impairments in adolescents and young adults. *Psychological Medicine*, **28**: 109–26.

Wolpert M, Thompson M, Tringay K (2005) Data collection, clinical audit, and measuring outcomes. In: Williams R, Kerfoot M (eds). *Child and Adolescent Mental Health Services: Strategy, Planning, Delivery, and Evaluation*. Oxford: Oxford Press.

Wolraich ML, Lindgren S, Stromquist A et al. (1990) Stimulant medication use by primary care physicians in the treatment of attention deficit hyperactivity disorder. *Pediatrics*, **86**: 95–101.

Wonderlich SA (1992) Relationship of family and personality factors in bulimia. In: Crowther JH, Tennenbaum DL, Hobfell SE, Stephens MAP (eds). *The Etiology of Bulimia Nervosa: The Individual and Family Context*. Ohio, USA: Hemisphere Publishing.

Woodbridge K, Fulford KWM (2004) *Whose Values? A Workbook for Values-based Practice in Mental Health Care*. London: The Sainsbury Centre for Mental Health.

Woodhead D (2000) *The Health and Well-being of Asylum Seekers and Refugees*. London: King's Fund.

Woodward L, Taylor E, Dowdney L (1998) The parenting and family functioning of children with hyperactivity. *Journal of Child Psychology and Psychiatry*, **39**: 161–9.

Wordsworth S. (2008) *Young Carers Report, Children's Commissioning*. Birmingham, Birmingham City Council.

World Health Organization (1996) *Multiaxial Classification of Child and Adolescent Psychiatric Disorders: the ICD-10 Classification of Mental and Behavioural Disorders in Children and Adolescents*. Cambridge, UK: Cambridge University Press.

World Health Organization (1993) *The ICD 10 Classification of Mental and Behavioural Disorders: Clinical Descriptions and Diagnostic Guidelines*. Geneva: World Health Organisation.

World Health Organization (1992) *The ICD-10 Classification of Mental and Behavioural Disorders: Clinical Descriptions and Diagnostic Guidelines*. Geneva: World Health Organisation.

World Health Organization (2008) The World Health Report 2008 – Primary Health Care: now more than ever. Available from: *www.who.int/whr/2008/en/index.html*.

Wu E, Martinez M (2006) *Taking Cultural Competency from Theory to Action. The Commonwealth Fund*.

www.acp-uk.eu

www.aft.org.uk/ Association of Family Therapists

www.anxietyuk.org.uk/ General information on anxieties.

www.bacp.co.uk/ The British Association for Counselling and Psychotherapy

www.bapt.info/ British Association of play therapists

www.basw.co.uk/ The College of Social Work

www.camhsnetwork.co.uk

www.childanxiety.net/ The Child Anxiety Network.

www.childhoodconstipation.com. Internet site for parents and children (sponsored by pharmaceutical company).

www.corc.uk.net/

www.cot.co.uk/Homepage/ British Association of Occupational Therapists

www.dur.ac.uk/camhs.mapping/

www.education.gov.uk – ref: DfES 0672 2003

www.egroups.com/group/pmhw

www.epilepsy.org.uk

www.gmc-uk.org/ General Medical Council

www.ican.org.uk

www.kidshealth.org/teen/your_mind/mental_health/phobias.html Information on anxiety and phobias aimed at teenagers.

www.legislation.gov.uk

www.mermaidsuk.org.uk/index.html - For families of those with children and young people who have gender identity issues.

www.moodjuice.scot.nhs.uk/phobias.asp A self-help guide for phobias.

www.nmc-uk.org/Nurses-and-midwives/The-code/The-code-in-full 2008 accessed 29/11/2009

www.psychotherapy.org.uk/ UK Council for Psychotherapy

www.queeryouth.org.uk/community/ - An internet community and support site for young LGBT identified people and those questioning.

www.rcpsych.ac.uk/pdf/Sheet13.pdf Information leaflet from the Royal College of Psychiatrists on helping children to cope with anxieties.

www.stonewall.org.uk - A charity that campaigns on behalf of LGB people. It has excellent guidance on working with young people who identify as LGB.

www.thegraycentre.org

www.youthaccess.org.uk


**Y**

Yang B, Chan RC, Jing J et al. (2007) A meta-analysis of association studies between the 10-repeat allele of a VNTR polymorphism in the 3'-UTR of dopamine transporter gene and attention deficit hyperactivity disorder. *American Journal of Medical Genetics. Part B, Neuropsychiatric Genetics*, **144B**: 541–50.

Yeung CK, Sreedhar B, Sihoe JD et al. (2006) Differences in characteristics of nocturnal enuresis between children and adolescents: a critical appraisal from a large epidemiological study. *BJU International*, **97**: 1069–73.

York A, Kingsbury S (2009) *The Choice And Partnership Approach A Guide To CAPA*. CAMHS Network.

York A, Lamb C (eds) (2005). *Building and Sustaining Specialist CAMHS Workforce, Capacity and Functions of Tiers 2, 3 and 4 Specialist Child and Adolescent Mental Health Services across England, Ireland, Northern Ireland, Scotland and Wales*. Child and Adolescent Faculty, Royal College of Psychiatrists.

Young S (2008) The offender with attention-deficit/ hyperactivity disorder. In: Fitzgerald M, Bellgrove M, Gill M (eds). *Handbook of Attention Deficit Hyperactive Disorder*. Chichester: John Wiley.


**Z**

Zahn-Waxler C, Cole PM, Welsh JD, Fox NA (1995) Psychophysiological correlates of empathy and prosocial behaviors in preschool children with behavior problems. *Development and Psychopathology*, **7**: 27–48.

Zhou K, Dempfle A, Arcos-Burgos M et al. (2008) Meta-analysis of genome-wide linkage scans of attention deficit hyperactivity disorder. *American Journal of Medical Genetics. Part B, Neuropsychiatric Genetics*, **147B**: 1392–8.

Zucker K (2002) Gender identity disorder. In: Rutter MW, Taylor EA (eds). *Child and Adolescent Psychiatry*, 4th edn. Oxford: Wiley-Blackwell, 2002.

Zylke JW, DeAngelis CD (2007) Paediatric chronic diseases-stealing childhood. *Journal of the American Medical Association*, **297**: 2765–6.

# Index